The Lancashire Working Classes c.1880–1930

TREVOR GRIFFITHS

CLARENDON PRESS · OXFORD

OXFORD
UNIVERSITY PRESS

Great Clarendon Street, Oxford OX2 6DP

Oxford University Press is a department of the University of Oxford.
It furthers the University's objective of excellence in research, scholarship,
and education by publishing worldwide in

Oxford New York

Athens Auckland Bangkok Bogotá Buenos Aires Cape Town
Chennai Dar es Salaam Delhi Florence Hong Kong Istanbul Karachi
Kolkata Kuala Lumpur Madrid Melbourne Mexico City Mumbai Nairobi
Paris São Paulo Shanghai Singapore Taipei Tokyo Toronto Warsaw
with associated companies in Berlin Ibadan

Oxford is a registered trade mark of Oxford University Press
in the UK and in certain other countries

Published in the United States
by Oxford University Press Inc., New York

British Library Cataloguing in Publication Data
Data available

Library of Congress Cataloging in Publication Data
Griffiths, Trevor.
The Lancashire working classes: c.1880–1930/Trevor Griffiths
p. cm—(Oxford historical monographs)
Includes bibliographical references and index.
1. Working class—England—Lancashire—History—19th century.
2. Working class—England—Lancashire—History—20th century.
3. Lancashire (England)—Economic conditions. 4. Industries—
England—Lancashire—History. I. Title. II. Series.
HD8399.L36.G75 2001 305.5'62'094276—dc21 2001021694
ISBN 0-19-924738-2

1 3 5 7 9 10 8 6 4 2

Typeset in Ehrhardt by
J&L Composition Ltd, Filey, North Yorkshire
Printed in Great Britain
on acid-free paper by
T.J. International Ltd
Padstow, Cornwall

In memory of my father
HUGH GRIFFITHS (1921–98)
and to my mother
MARY GRIFFITHS (born 1925)

ACKNOWLEDGEMENTS

In the normal course of writing a book, numerous debts are incurred: academic, personal, and, more often than not, financial. When the length of time required to complete the finished product threatens to break all known records, as is the case here, the list of obligations grows to a tedious and embarrassing length. It would be impossible to list all who have provided intellectual and personal support over the years, so that omission from the following should not be taken as evidence either of ingratitude or of forgetfulness.

Initial funding for this research was provided by the British Academy. To that body I extend my most sincere thanks. I am deeply grateful for the services provided, often in the face of declining levels of funding, by the staff at the local and national repositories cited in the bibliography. Without their help, research would have been an altogether more difficult and less pleasurable task.

On a personal level, thanks should first of all go to Philip Waller, an endlessly patient and consistently encouraging supervisor, whose quest for the three-word sentence is not to be realized in the pages that follow. The examiners of the original thesis on which this book is based, Ross McKibbin and John Walton, were assiduous in pointing up areas where the argument could be strengthened or clarified. Any improvement that the published version represents over the original is due to them. More recently, Ross has proved a meticulous editor, urging me to be less reticent and more explicit in my conclusions. What problems remain reflect my failure fully to follow his advice.

Over the years, I have inflicted aspects of this work on several seminar groups and individuals. I am grateful to the following for commenting on particular sections: Professor D. A. Farnie, Professor P. K. O'Brien, Dr Andrzej Olechniwicz, and Philip Hunt. Mention should also be made of those who first excited in me an intellectual interest in history, among whom the principal culprits are David Clayton and Paul Cowell, my teachers at the institution formerly known as Burnley Grammar School.

The personal and intellectual support of friends has kept me sane over the long years of research. If I have not always been able to repay them in kind, thanks should still go to: in Burnley, Jonathan Howarth, and Jason Hunter; in Oxford, Dr I. W. Archer, Dr Robert Cook, Anne Bennett, and

Jan Martin; and in Dundee, Ian and Eleanor Mackie. Since 1994, the Department of Economic and Social History has provided a congenial yet stimulating setting to pursue the work required to transform thesis into book. Here, particular thanks are due to Martin and Hatty Chick, Adam and Carolyn Fox, Graeme, Angela, Sam, and Evie Morton. I write this in the hope that Evie's experiments with rubber frogs and the human ear will one day bear fruit.

An unexpected but altogether delightful bonus from living in Edinburgh has been meeting Elaine. Her love and support, not to mention her decorating skills, have transformed my life in recent years, immeasurably for the better. Her companionship has considerably enriched the latter stages of producing this book. I thank her from the bottom of my heart. My deepest debt remains to those members of my family who have lived with this work since its inception. My sister Janet, her husband Kelvin, and their beloved cat Ben have put up with my presence in their house on numerous occasions and have almost managed to persuade even a hard-bitten Lancastrian like myself that there is something to be said for living in Yorkshire. Above all, however, I have received more support and encouragement from my parents over the years than I had any right to expect. That my father should not have lived to see this book published will forever be a source of regret to me. In truth, this is a meagre return for all the help he and my mother have provided, but it is dedicated to them both with the deepest gratitude and love.

CONTENTS

LIST OF TABLES

ABBREVIATIONS

BA	Bolton Library, Archives and Local Studies Dept.	LCMF	Lancashire and Cheshire Miners' Federation
BCB	Bolton County Borough Council	LCPRS	Lancashire and Cheshire Permanent Relief Society
BEN	*Bolton Evening News*		
BJG	*Bolton Journal and Guardian*	*LG*	*The Labour Gazette*
		LRO	Lancashire Record Office, Preston
BMCSA	Bolton Master Cotton Spinners' Association	MFGB	Miners' Federation of Great Britain
BOCA	Bolton and District Card and Ring Room Provincial Association	MRL	Manchester Central Reference Library, Archives Dept.
BOHP	Bolton Oral History Project	PRO	Public Record Office, Kew
BSA	Bolton and District Operative Spinners' Provincial Association	RC	Royal Commission
		SMA	Standish District Miners' Association
C&W Consolidated	Crosses and Winkworth Consolidated Mills, Ltd	*THSLC*	*Transactions of the Historic Society of Lancashire and Cheshire*
CFT	*Cotton Factory Times*		
EHR	*English Historical Review*		
FMCSA	Federation of Master Cotton Spinners' Association Ltd	*TW*	*Textile Weekly*
		UTFWA	United Textile Factory Workers' Association
FWJ	*Farnworth Weekly Journal*	WA	Wigan Heritage Services, Archives
HRF	Hulton Colliery Explosion (1910) Relief Fund	*WE*	*Wigan Examiner*
		WHS	Wigan Heritage Services, History Shop
JRL	John Rylands Library, Deansgate, Manchester	*WO*	*Wigan Observer*
		WWA	Wigan and District Weavers' Association
JRUL	John Rylands University Library, Manchester		

I
Introduction

In the history of the British working class, the half-century from 1880 has acquired a particular significance. Within that period, it is argued, internal points of difference, bequeathed by the slow and uneven pace and incidence of economic change, became progressively less important as changes in material circumstances encouraged a growing recognition of interests and values held in common by people of similar economic standing. If the precise chronology of change remains open to debate, its outcome is less contested: a consciousness of a 'class in itself'.[1] Various factors have been identified as contributing to this development. First, and in many accounts foremost, were changes in the world of work. The status of skilled labour came under sustained challenge from employers struggling with depressed profits and the growing problem of foreign competition. The most immediate threat was posed by technological innovation, which had the aim of reducing both the quantity and quality of labour inputs. Less obvious, but, in the view of many, of greater long-term significance, were changes in recruitment procedures which removed the supervisory role of skilled hands and transferred authority to management personnel.[2] Reflecting greater uniformity in the work experience, trade-union organization, formerly the bedrock of craft privilege, expanded to encapsulate large sections of the industrial workforce.

Yet class was not simply formed at the point of production. Experiences beyond work, it is argued, also served to point up a common consciousness. One account emphasizes how British workers increasingly resided in stable urban neighbourhoods, in which middle-class influences were largely peripheral. Within what Miles and Savage have termed 'the working-class city', a distinctive culture was nurtured, structured in part around

---

[1] For E. J. Hobsbawm, the process was substantially complete by 1914, 'The Formation of British Working-Class Culture' and 'The Making of the Working Class, 1870–1914', in id., *Worlds of Labour* (1984), 176–213. Others see change as a product of the war years, B. Waites, *A Class Society at War: England, 1914–18* (Leamington Spa, 1987).

[2] A. J. Reid, *Social Classes and Social Relations in Britain, 1850–1914* (Basingstoke and London, 1992), ch.3; M. Savage and A. Miles, *The Remaking of the British Working Class, 1840–1940* (1994), 48–55.

collective organizations, such as Co-operative and friendly societies.[3] Through such agencies, class identity was given institutional expression. The economic context encouraged their growth. The secular fall in retail prices over the last quarter of the nineteenth century meant that, for the first time, most working-class families could anticipate periods during which incomes would exceed immediate needs. Patterns of saving and consumption hitherto restricted to privileged minorities became more widely accessible. A common culture thus grew up around the pub, the music hall, the sporting weekend, and the annual seaside holiday.[4] At various points in their lives, whether as producers, consumers, or savers, workers and their families were made increasingly aware of experiences shared with others of similar status, justifying Richard Johnson's contention that 'It is probable that working-class culture from the 1880s to the 1930s was more homogeneous and distinct than in any period before or after'.[5]

However, the position is not as clear-cut as this would suggest. Of late, increasing doubts as to the significance of class as a focus for identity have been expressed, encouraging many to examine critically the several factors which were thought to have consolidated a common consciousness. In work, it is emphasized, employers continued to rely on the wage mechanism rather than the imposition of direct managerial controls to ensure regularity of output. Far from being displaced by technical change, skilled hands retained and, in certain cases, strengthened their role within the manufacturing process. Wage and skill differentials continued to characterize the industrial workforce in the period to 1930, so that the unifying impact of work cannot be readily assumed.[6] Nor was life in urban neighbourhoods necessarily productive of that shared

---

[3] Savage and Miles, *Remaking*, 59–65.

[4] *Parl. Papers 1903*, lxvii. (1761), Memoranda, Statistical Tables, and Charts Bearing on British and Foreign Trade and Industrial Conditions, 233, 260; M. Mackinnon, 'Living Standards, 1870–1914', in R. Floud and D. McCloskey (eds.), *The Economic History of Britain since 1700*, 2nd ed., ii. *1860–1939* (Cambridge, 1994), 265–90; G. Stedman Jones, 'Working-Class Culture and Working-Class Politics in London, 1870–1900: Notes on the Remaking of a Working Class', in id., *Languages of Class: Studies in English Working Class History* (Cambridge, 1983), 179–238.

[5] R. Johnson, 'Three Problematics: Elements of a Theory of Working-Class Culture', in J. Clarke, C. Critcher, and R. Johnson (eds.), *Working-Class Culture: Studies in History and Theory* (1979), 235.

[6] W. Lazonick, 'Employment Relations in Manufacturing and International Competition', in Floud and McCloskey, *Economic History*, 90–116; P. Joyce, 'Work', in F. M. L. Thompson (ed.), *The Cambridge Social History of Britain, 1750–1950*, ii. *People and their Environment* (Cambridge, 1990), 131–94; C. More, *Skill and the English Working Class* (1980), 28–36, 184–8; J. Zeitlin, 'From Labour History to the History of Industrial Relations', *Econ. Hist. Rev.*, 2nd ser. 40 (1987), 173–4.

commitment to a common set of values which inform notions of working-class community. For Joanna Bourke, among others, the interdependence of neighbours was less a straightforward expression of a collective, communitarian culture than the product of material necessity, enforced by recurrent periods of poverty.[7] At such times, opportunities for consumption and for participation in wider cultural pursuits, including holidays and organized sport, would be severely restricted. Important points of difference continued to mark the class experience in the years from 1880.

The literature on the making of the working class in this period has also been subject to methodological criticism. Too often, it is argued, attitudes and identities are read off from the structural context: the precise mechanism by which shared experiences at home, work, or play translated into a consciousness of class remains obscure. In seeking to bridge this gap, great stress has been laid on the agency of language. Perceptions of the social order were articulated through and shaped by the words employed to describe it. This approach, while it does not deny the salience of class, gives prominence to other identities, drawing on alternative sources of allegiance common to all social groups. In the industrial north of England, economic development is seen to have generated a strong sense of local and regional attachment, given expression through the language of 'the people'. This was an inclusive idea, comprehending a commitment, shared by all classes, to honesty, hard work, and fair dealing. Points of unity were thereby emphasized, while the language of 'class' was employed to identify divisive forces at the cultural margin. In pointing up alternative ways in which the social order could be understood and by questioning the link between economic experience and social attitudes, such arguments are of undoubted value. Yet the possibility of reconstructing identities through the study of language alone remains open to question. In the case of the working class, in particular, the terms of discourse were rarely those of the workers themselves. The records of labour and related institutions provide an obvious exception to this rule, but even here the values articulated tend to be those of skilled, predominantly male minorities. Alternative insights have been sought in the popular literature of the period. Yet, even if the question of readership could be satisfactorily resolved, analysis of readers' response to what is read remains problematic. That response, it might be suggested, would be determined by the

---

[7] J. Bourke, *Working-Class Cultures in Britain, 1890–1960: Gender, Class and Ethnicity* (1994), 148–9; A. Davies, *Leisure, Gender and Poverty: Working-Class Culture in Salford and Manchester, 1900–1939* (Buckingham, and Bristol, Pa., 1992), ch. 2.

individual's broader social experience. 'Language' was thus formulated and interpreted in the light of the structural and ideological forces shaping working-class life. Even studies which make great play with the linguistic turn acknowledge this point. So, although Patrick Joyce in his suggestive and challenging examination of social identities in nineteenth-century England points to the influence of the language of 'populism', he also recognizes the existence through the period of a family of 'populisms', liberal, conservative, and labourist. The forces which would determine which family member would prevail at any one time and in a particular area remains unexplained in Joyce's work.[8] In answering that question, recourse must be had to established techniques of historical inquiry. By contrast, the contribution of language, narrowly defined, must be judged to be marginal.

Nevertheless, the contribution of 'language' need not be discarded, if a broader definition is adopted to comprehend, in addition to the spoken and written word, outward modes of behaviour. At this point, 'language', as a fusion of structural and intellectual influences, becomes virtually interchangeable with the more familiar category of 'culture'. This study is concerned to examine the nature of that culture and the forces which helped to shape it. Its primary focus is local, centring on the industrial area of south–central Lancashire and on the towns of Wigan and Bolton, in particular. The choice of towns throws up important points of similarity and contrast. Although geographically close, being separated by barely 10 miles, and drawing on an industrial base founded substantially on coal and cotton, they exhibited extremes of economic and political development in this period. In Wigan, both major staples were leading employers. In 1921, local pits employed 42 per cent of occupied males, while the town's mills provided work for 43 per cent of wage-earning women.[9] In common with most of the Lancashire coalfield, Wigan experienced sustained decline from the late nineteenth century. At first, regression was merely comparative. The fourth most important field in terms of output in the middle of the century, the county had gradually ceded ground to faster growing areas: Scotland in the 1860s; Yorkshire in the 1890s; and the East Midlands after 1900. From 1907, however, decline became absolute. Annual output halved over the following quarter-century, a trend followed by employment levels from 1920. A workforce of 115,475

---

[8] Savage and Miles, *Remaking*, 17–18; P. Joyce, *Visions of the People: Industrial England and the question of Class, 1848–1914* (Cambridge, 1991), *passim*.

[9] *Census of England and Wales, 1921: County of Lancaster* (HMSO, 1923), table 16, pp. 137, 139.

in the latter year had shrunk to one of 66,264 by 1932.[10] Located at the geographic centre of the field, with reserves increasingly subject to physical exhaustion, Wigan faithfully reflected broader developments. Within ten years, between 1921 and 1931, the number of males employed in coalmining fell from 12,144 to 9,241.[11] Local cotton production fared little better. The period from 1918 witnessed a serious erosion in the county's 'bread and butter' trade in coarse-to-medium cloths manufactured from short-staple American cotton. Lancastrian confidence was, as a result, fatally undermined. Those who, in 1920, had pondered the question, 'Is Lancashire a Modern El Dorado?' were, by 1929, left to wonder 'Is Lancashire Finished?'[12] By the early 1930s, yarn and cloth exports were only 65 per cent and 30 per cent of their respective pre-war levels.[13] Wigan's mills, substantially dependent on the coarse-cotton trade, were exposed to the full force of market change. Many leading firms had, by 1932, ceased trading or had been acquired by the Lancashire Cotton Corporation, as part of the rationalization programme for the American-cotton sector.[14] Local population trends reflected economic difficulties in full. During the 1920s, the town lost the equivalent of 11 per cent of its 1931 population through out-migration, a rate of loss unequalled among Lancastrian county boroughs.[15] In Bolton, by contrast, reliance on fine-cotton production sustained prosperity for longer, enabling local mills to work at virtually full capacity up to the early months of 1929. The onset of global economic depression later that year signalled the start of more difficult times for the town.[16]

[10] R. A. Church, *The History of the British Coal Industry.* iii. *1830–1913: Victorian Pre-eminence* (Oxford, 1986), 3. Output and employment figures calculated from annual Mines Inspectors' Reports.

[11] *Census of England and Wales, 1921: County of Lancaster* (HMSO, 1932), table 16, p. 123; *Census of England and Wales, 1931: Occupation Tables* (HMSO, 1934), table 16, p. 250. Both figures exclude owners, agents, managers, and subordinate superintending staff.

[12] C. W. Macara, 'The Great Cotton Boom: Is Lancashire a Modern El Dorado?', in Macara, *Social and Industrial Reform* (Manchester, 1920), 319–26; 'Is Lancashire Finished?', series of articles by Councillor George Burke, President of Blackburn Chamber of Commerce, in *Textile Weekly* (*TW*), 2 (1–22 Feb. 1929), 627–8,657–8,690–1,717.

[13] J. H. Porter, 'Cotton and Wool Textiles', in N. K. Buxton and D. H. Aldcroft (eds.), *British Industry between the Wars* (1979), 29.

[14] *Worrall's Cotton Spinners' and Manufacturers' Directory* (Oldham, 1933 edn.); H. Clay, *Report on the Position of the English Cotton Industry* (Securities Management Trust, Ltd, 1931), 10; L. Hannah, *The Rise of the Corporate Economy* (1983), 104–5.

[15] *Census of England and Wales, 1931: County of Lancaster (Part II)* (HMSO, 1932), table 2, pp. 2–3.

[16] Cotton was the largest single employer of both men and women in Bolton, accounting in 1921 for 22% and 59% of the respective occupied totals. Coal-miners comprised the fifth

Political differences were also sharply etched across the district. Labour, the principal progressive force within Wigan from 1906, achieved majority status in the immediate post-war years, a position it consolidated during the remainder of the period. In Bolton, however, the party enjoyed only fitful success at parliamentary level, while it remained a minority force in the council chamber, its brief period of control from 1929 being dependent on Liberal support. Whereas, in 1930, Labour claimed forty out of Wigan's fifty-six municipal representatives, both elective and aldermanic, the party's share in Bolton was a mere thirty out of ninety-four.[17] The clear link suggested here between industrial structures, economic fortune and political outcomes provides the starting-point for this study. However, before proceeding to outline the precise approach to be adopted here, a further word of justification might be deemed appropriate.

A local study, it might legitimately be objected, is concerned to analyse a particular combination of circumstances from which ready generalization could be problematic. Against that, focusing on a precisely defined locality facilitates a more detailed and, it is to be hoped, nuanced consideration of the forces shaping the social experience and the ways in which they came together to influence working-class identities. Sensitivity towards the particular need not preclude the broader relevance of any findings. Nevertheless, the appearance of another work on a much-studied region may seem hard to justify. In mitigation, it might, with legitimacy, be argued that Lancastrian evidence has provided the basis for many accounts of social and political change in this period. By concentrating on that county, a direct evaluation of much existing thinking on such issues may be offered. Furthermore, while Lancashire is justly recognized as the 'first industrial society', it also displayed many of the features of the mature urban civilization which Britain had become by the early twentieth century. Lancastrian towns were far removed from the single-industry settlements and company towns of early industrialization. Across the county, a succession of sizeable population centres sustained a diverse industrial base. Even coal-mining was a predominantly urban occupation. In 1923, three-quarters of the insured mining workforce lived in an area of south–central Lancashire defined by the towns of Bolton, Wigan, and Leigh. Unlike their colleagues elsewhere, the county's colliers

largest category of male workers, representing 6% of the whole. *Census of England and Wales, 1921: County of Lancaster* (HMSO, 1923), table 16, pp. 121, 123.

[17] *Bolton Journal and Guardian* (*BJG*) (7 Nov. 1930), 6; *Wigan Observer* (*WO*) (4 Nov. 1930), 2.

were integrated into the greater industrial workforce. In 1911, only 30 per cent of Lancashire's miners were living in administrative districts in which 50 per cent or more of male jobs were provided by the pit. By contrast, in the two largest fields, as measured by output, in this period, south Wales and north-east England, over 80 per cent of colliers were so situated.[18] The pattern carried over into individual neighbourhoods: the street corners of Bill Naughton's Bolton childhood were populated by miners, cotton operatives, and foundry workers.[19] An examination of social identities in such a setting may, therefore, have relevance beyond the immediate area. Certainly contemporaries needed no persuading as to Lancashire's broader importance. Although reconciled, by the end of the period, to a diminished industrial and political role, the county had been in the van of developments in both areas over the preceding half-century. Thus, in 1903, the Lancashire and Cheshire Miners' Federation was the first mining union to affiliate to the Labour Representation Committee, providing an early indication of the growing identification of coal-mining with a politicized class consciousness.[20] In understanding social, economic, and political developments in this period, an appreciation of the Lancastrian experience is crucial.

In the discussion which follows, the forces which helped to shape working-class identities are examined at several points. Reflecting the analytical weight given to developments at the point of production, the early chapters concentrate primarily on the world of work. If employers' readiness to delegate responsibility for workplace operations to selected groups of skilled workers was apparent in both industries through the nineteenth century, its implications for labour unity varied markedly. Divisions appeared most pronounced in the cotton trade, more especially in preparatory and spinning departments, where a relatively small number of adult males exercised authority within a predominantly female and juvenile workforce. The privileges extended to such groups have been seen as an important factor underlying the apparently consensual

[18] Board of Trade, *An Industrial Survey of the Lancashire Area* (HMSO, 1932), 164; *Parl. Papers 1913*, lxxviii (7018), Census of England and Wales, 1911. X. Occupations and Industries. Pt. I, table 15.
[19] Bill Naughton, *On the Pig's Back: An Autobiographical Excursion* (Oxford, 1987), 130; Naughton, *Saintly Billy: A Catholic Boyhood* (Oxford, 1988), 1.
[20] F. Bealey and H. Pelling, *Labour and Politics, 1900–1906: A History of the Labour Representation Committee* (1958), 215; I. F. Scott, 'The Lancashire and Cheshire Miners' Federation, 1900–14' (York University D.Phil. thesis, 1977), 131; D. Lockwood, 'Sources of Variation in Working-Class Images of Society', in M. Bulmer (ed.), *Working-Class Images of Society* (1975), 17–18.

industrial politics of the cotton towns.[21] Internal differences were, by contrast, less prominent underground. Income and skill hierarchies existed,
but lacked wider significance, denoting as they did stages in a uniform
career pattern. The work experience thus confirmed the broader solidarities of colliery societies. An alternative view plays down the implications
of divisions within the cotton workforce, stressing instead the dependent
status of all mill operatives. By this argument, employer authority over all
processes involved in the manufacture of textiles was consolidated by the
successful application of mechanical production techniques by the middle
of the nineteenth century.[22] Yet the scope for innovation was not
exhausted. Indeed, both industries were subject to important technological changes in the half-century from 1880. The practical consequences of
such change and responses to it on the part of both employers and
employed help to clarify the ways in which the work experience helped to
mould class identities. Particular importance attaches to the extent to
which new technology served to undermine or to confirm the status of
skilled labour. The implications of the attitudes thus disclosed are then
traced through the industrial politics of the period, to test notions of
conflict and consensus as reflected in the record of each industry.

To this point, the questions posed and the methods adopted in dealing
with them are relatively unproblematic. Institutional records offer the
most sustained insights into the work experience and the tenor of industrial relations. Yet in addressing the broader question of the relationship
between work and class identities, the perspective they offer has obvious
limitations. In both industries, trade unions articulated the views of
minorities. Skilled male élites shaped policy in both carding and cotton
spinning. Women and children exercised little if any influence over official deliberations. Equally, few colliers participated actively in union
affairs. Labour organizations must thus be judged, at best, a marginal factor in the moulding of popular attitudes. An alternative approach is
essayed here, shifting the focus of analysis from the labour process to the
labour market. Throughout the period, recruitment proceeded substantially through personal, informal contacts.[23] Across the region, industrial
diversity allowed scope for discretion to be exercised over both the timing

---

[21] J. Foster, *Class Struggle and the Industrial Revolution* (1974), 229–34; J. L. White, *The
Limits of Trade Union Militancy* (Westport, Conn., and London, 1978), 34–7; K. Burgess,
The Origins of British Industrial Relations (1975), 245–7.
[22] P. Joyce, *Work, Society and Politics: The Culture of the Factory in Later Victorian England*
(Brighton, 1980), chs. 2 and 3.
[23] R. McKibbin, *Classes and Cultures: England, 1918–1951* (Oxford, 1998), 119–27.

and direction of entry to work. Each decision was the outcome of various influences, from the economic circumstances of the time to calculations which balanced short-term material needs against longer term career prospects. The latter would be determined by earnings potential, opportunities for advancement, and the likely security of any position, the precise weight given to each factor varying significantly over time. This interplay of structural influence and cultural preference has also been described, by Tamara Hareven, in terms of interlocking notions of time: individual, family, industrial, and historical.[24] It may, therefore, be suggested that the study of the factors influencing job choice over the period provides some means of integrating disparate aspects of working-class life, relating more effectively the internal arrangements of mill and mine to the experience of the workforce as a whole.

An alternative perspective on attitudes to work is sought in a related chapter which examines the role of industrial élites in shaping social relationships. At first sight, the evidence from coal and cotton Lancashire would appear to endorse the view which argues for the progressive withdrawal of the wealthier middle classes from the governance of urban areas.[25] The period certainly witnessed profound changes in the structure and personnel of industrial leadership, coincident with a shift from proprietary to joint-stock forms of capital. For many, such developments, entailing as they did the departure of individuals long associated with the region, many of whom were credited with maintaining close personal ties with their workers, signalled an end to a pattern of paternalist leadership which had long characterized the cotton trade in particular. In one respect, at least, empirical inquiry confirms that the practice of industrial leadership underwent a significant change. Paternalism assumed a new, more structured form through the emergence of corporate welfare schemes. Such initiatives have been variously interpreted, but their prime aim appears to have been to construct an alternative work culture, by which a closer identification would be encouraged between the individual worker and the company for which he or she worked. A related concern was to boost recruitment across the cotton trade. The study of labour-market trends provides a means of evaluating the effects of élite strategies and their capacity to influence attitudes more generally. It also serves to identify the precise importance of work in moulding the class experience.

[24] T. K. Hareven, *Family Time and Industrial Time: The Relationship between the Family and Work in a New England Industrial Community* (Cambridge, 1982), 1–8.
[25] Savage and Miles, *Remaking*, ch. 4; G. Crossick and H.-G. Haupt, *The Petite Bourgeoisie in Europe, 1780–1914: Enterprise, Family and Independence* (1995), esp. ch. 6.

It is apparent that, in order to comprehend fully the institutions and values at the centre of working-class culture in this period, the perspective must extend beyond the workplace. Material and moral influences combined most clearly in the manner in which households sought to manage their limited and fluctuating resources. For most families, thrift served a dual purpose, providing a means of alleviating future distress and of funding consumption.[26] As well as reflecting the budgetary disciplines imposed by financial necessity, it also gave expression to working-class aspirations. In both coal and cotton industries, forms of saving emerged which were thought to embody specific patterns of class attitudes and relationships. In cotton, the wide diffusion of share-ownership, extending to the workforce, appeared to provide a basis for lasting social accord. Co-operation was more explicitly manifested in the management of colliery accident relief funds by both miners and coal-owners. Yet, in their modes of operation, these funds throw light on broader social forces. The effective administration of relief required that some check be maintained on all recipients. The most productive, if not necessarily the most reliable, source of information on individual behaviour proved to be the immediate localities within which the funds operated. The work of these institutions thus helps to illuminate many of the processes and the values underlying life in densely populated working-class districts. Particular forms of thrift formed a small part of a complex network of savings organizations, whose operations impinged on other aspects of the class experience, from leisure to religion.

Yet the insights provided by the institutional record remain, at best, extremely partial. Identities were also shaped by other, less tangible influences, which worked either to consolidate or to undermine the impact of shared economic experiences. Among the most frequently cited of these are ties of geography, gender, religion, and kinship, many of which are seen to have cut across occupational solidarities.[27] Each contributed to that broad range of experience comprehended within the concept of 'community'. This attractive, if somewhat slippery, idea is often presented as the converse of class, emphasizing as it does points of similarity

---

[26] P. Johnson, *Saving and Spending: The Working-Class Economy in Britain, 1870–1939* (Oxford, 1985); Johnson, 'Conspicuous Consumption and Working-Class Culture in Late-Victorian and Edwardian Britain', *Transactions of the Royal Historical Society*, 5th ser. 38 (1988), 27–42.

[27] A. Davies, S. Fielding and T. Wyke, 'Introduction', in A. Davies and S. Fielding (eds.), *Workers' Worlds: Cultures and Communities in Manchester and Salford, 1880–1939* (Manchester, 1992), 1–22; Davies, *Leisure, Gender and Poverty*, ch. 1; R. Hoggart, *A Local Habitation (Life and Times, i: 1918–40)* (Oxford, 1988), 126.

and agreement within society. More accurately, it might be seen as complementary, enhancing our appreciation of the complexity and richness of class identities. Yet for the concept to have real analytical value, thus avoiding the very real danger of idealization, it is important that some attempt be made to recapture the quality of the particular networks and linkages which give shape to ideas of community.[28] Joanna Bourke's work, drawing on oral testimony and working-class autobiography, has called into question the precise nature and function of neighbourhood ties, suggesting that they were essentially instrumental, rather than expressive of deeper attachments.[29] Here, such themes are addressed through a more focused body of records, relating to the colliery disaster relief fund set up in the wake of the explosion at the Hulton Colliery Co. Ltd's No. 3 Bank, or Pretoria Pit, in December 1910. The fund offered assistance to almost 300 households, a group that was both occupationally and geographically specific. In so doing, it exercised a close surveillance over dependants for a period exceeding sixty years, before the fund was finally wound up in 1975.[30] This involved an often detailed investigation into family circumstances, the role of kin, and the attitudes of neighbours, along with the nature of marital relationships. The density of documentation enables us to reconstruct less formal aspects of the class experience in unusual depth.

This provides the context for assessing the impact of political change through the period. The dominant feature of the half-century from 1880, the rise of a political party structured around the interests of labour, has often been explained in terms of broader developments in the working-class experience. By this argument, political loyalties were shaped by an inclusive cultural outlook that was essentially non-ideological, defensive, and introverted in character.[31] An alternative view has been advanced which relates political allegiances to a particular set of 'interests'. For wage-earners, the fundamental imperative remained to minimize economic uncertainty in a period in which living standards were subject to marked fluctuations. By the early twentieth century, that need appeared to be best served by political organization. The growth of Labour is thus

[28] A. Macfarlane, 'History, Anthropology and the Study of Communities', *Social History*, 1–2 (1976–7), 631–52.
[29] Bourke, *Working-Class Cultures*, 159.
[30] Bolton Library, Archives and Local Studies Dept. (BA), ABHC/1/9 Hulton Colliery Explosion (1910) Relief Fund (HRF), correspondence and minutes re winding up of Fund, General Committee minutes, 1 Aug. 1975.
[31] Hobsbawm, 'Making of the Working Class'; R. McKibbin, 'Why was there No Marxism in Great Britain?', in id., *The Ideologies of Class* (Oxford, 1990), 1–41.

linked to its capacity, in contrast to existing parties, to satisfy the economic aspirations of the working class.[32] Yet this is to take an unduly narrow view of the factors shaping political identities. Labour's ability to construct a majority position in Lancashire was constrained by extra-economic factors, in particular religious and ethnic pluralism. Unlike other areas, where Labour developed within the prevailing culture, building on established loyalties, electoral progress in societies such as Lancashire required a wholesale restructuring of allegiances. This involved a fundamental reworking of the language of political 'interests' to comprehend labour and related issues. That process had still to be completed by the end of the period considered here. Far from consolidating Labour's position, the nature of the working class, as reflected through the institutions and values which shaped it, operated to hinder the party's electoral effectiveness. The problems encountered can be traced to the process which many have seen to form the very fount of class consciousness, the experience of work itself.

---

[32] M. Savage, *The Dynamics of Working-Class Politics: The Labour Movement in Preston, 1880–1940* (Cambridge, 1987), ch. 2.

2
The Work Experience

The production process provides the starting-point for many studies of class formation. The material and ideological forces shaping wider social processes were most apparent, it is argued, in the workplace, in particular in the conflict between employers and employed over control of the means of production. From this perspective, the logic of industrial development lay in the extension and consolidation of managerial influence over the pace of production, the preferred outcome being to limit the discretion exercised by elements within the workforce, thus securing the dependent and subordinate status of labour. The history of textiles in general and cotton in particular has provided the principal empirical foundation for such an interpretation. Here, the early shift from hand to machine technology appeared driven by a desire to strengthen labour disciplines, subduing recalcitrant groups of skilled workers, from woolcombers to mule-spinners.[1] By the 1850s, that process appeared substantially complete, as the application of power extended to all of the principal manufacturing processes.[2] It has long been acknowledged that, beyond cotton, the progress of industrialization was sufficiently slow and partial to ensure the survival of more 'traditional' techniques, so that considerable responsibility continued to devolve on to labour for maintaining output at an acceptable level and quality.[3] As a result, disciplinary problems exercised employers in many trades into the later nineteenth century. The lock-out enforced by the Engineering Employers' Federation in 1897 had the explicit aim of asserting the 'right to manage'. At the same time, in evidence to official inquiries, colliery owners repeatedly bemoaned

[1] K. Marx, *Capital* i. *Der Produktionsprozess des Kapitals* (Everyman edn., 1974), 419–52; A. Ure, *The Cotton Manufacture of Great Britain*, ii (1836), 195–9; id., *The Philosophy of Manufactures* (1861 edn.), 366–7; E. Baines, jun., *History of the Cotton Manufacture in Great Britain* (1835), 208; T. Bruland, 'Industrial Conflict as a Source of Technical Innovation', *Economy and Society*, 11 (1982), 91–121.

[2] P. Joyce, *Work, Society and Politics* (Brighton, 1980), ch. 2; G. Timmins, *The Last Shift: The Decline of Handloom Weaving in Nineteenth-Century Lancashire* (Manchester, 1993), ch. 1.

[3] R. Samuel, 'Workshop of the World: Steam Power and Hand Technology in Mid-Victorian Britain', *History Workshop*, 3 (Spring 1977), 6–72; R. Floud, *The People and the British Economy, 1830–1914* (Oxford, 1997), ch. 7.

their inability to regulate effort effectively at the coal face.[4] The broader consolidation of employer control awaited a further wave of technological innovations and the application of 'modern' management techniques.

Presented thus, industrial development appears essentially unilinear in character, the tendency to subcontract responsibility to strategic groups of workers constituting a transitional phase in the process. Yet comparative analyses suggest that this approach has serious limitations. The work of Sabel and Zeitlin, in particular, indicates enduring differences in industrial practices, the roots of which are to be traced not only in straightforward economic influences, such as relative factor endowments and varying market expectations, but also in broader social and political circumstances.[5] In the light of this and similar research, interpretations of the British experience of industrialization have been amended to stress continuities in workplace practices in the period from 1880. Technological innovation was rarely accompanied by organizational change, enabling skilled minorities within the labour force to retain an influence over the production process. Nevertheless, it remains an open question how far this was the result of a determined defence of craft privilege, resisting attempts to extend employer control, and how far the deliberate outcome of managerial policies which emphasized the peculiar utility attached to skill.[6]

Both the coal and the cotton trades were subject to important technological changes in this period. The implications such innovations had for work practices have much to tell us about the attitudes and expectations which prevailed on both sides of industry and provide some insight into

---

[4] A. J. McIvor, *Organised Capital: Employers' Associations and Industrial Relations in Northern England, 1880–1939* (Cambridge, 1996), 65; W. Lazonick, 'Employment Relations in Manufacturing and International Competition', in R. Floud and D. McCloskey (eds.), *The Economic History of Britain since 1700*, ii (Cambridge, 1994), 111; for the miners' independence at work, D. Douglass, 'The Durham Pitman', in R. Samuel (ed.), *Miners, Quarrymen and Saltworkers* (1977), 215.

[5] H. Braverman, *Labor and Monopoly Capital: The Degradation of Work in the Twentieth Century* (New York, 1974), 63, 90–116; C. Sabel and J. Zeitlin, 'Historical Alternatives to Mass Production: Politics, Markets and Technology in Nineteenth-Century Industrialization', *Past and Present*, 108 (Aug. 1985), 133–76; J. Turner, 'Man and Braverman: British Industrial Relations', *History*, 70 (1985), 238–9.

[6] The point has been debated most forcefully in the context of the motor vehicle manufacturing industry in the 20th cent., see W. Lewchuk, 'The Motor Vehicle Industry', in B. Elbaum and W. Lazonick, (eds.), *The Decline of the British Economy* (Oxford, 1986), 135–61; S. Tolliday, 'Management and Labour in Britain, 1896–1939', in S. Tolliday and J. Zeitlin (eds.), *The Automobile Industry and its Workers: Between Fordism and Flexibility* (Cambridge, 1986), 29–56.

the relationship between the work experience and class identities. In the process, a broader debate is touched upon. The decline of Britain's established export industries in the early twentieth century has been traced to technological conservatism and the survival of organizational structures inappropriate to altered competitive conditions. Of late, however, a sturdy defence of British entrepreneurship has been mounted. Technical and organizational choices represented, it is argued, the most rational and profitable course in prevailing market circumstances.[7] Extended consideration of such points is not intended here, except as they help to elucidate the role accorded labour in the leading industries of south–central Lancashire.

I

Important points of difference, extending from the organization of production to the techniques employed and the structure of the workforce, distinguished Britain from other leading centres of the cotton manufacture in the early twentieth century. Whereas the industry in New England was dominated by combined firms, in which all operations (spinning, weaving, etc.) were integrated, within Lancashire, a trend towards vertical disintegration had set in around the middle of the nineteenth century, resulting in a clear separation of production functions. Weaving came increasingly to centre on the belt of towns across the north-east of the county, from Blackburn in the west to Colne in the east, while spinning became concentrated in a crescent 'about ten miles from north to south by twelve from east to west' in extent, north and west of Manchester.[8] Combined firms, although not unknown, became exceptional. By 1905, they accounted for a mere 7 per cent of Bolton's spindleage, the remainder being controlled by fifty-one specialist concerns.[9] In terms of

---

[7] S. Pollard, 'Entrepreneurship, 1870–1914', in Floud and McCloskey, *Economic History of Britain*, ii, 62–89; D. N. McCloskey and L. G. Sandberg, 'From Damnation to Redemption: Judgments on the Late Victorian Entrepreneur', in D. N. McCloskey, *Enterprise and Trade in Victorian Britain* (1981), 55–72.

[8] A. J. Taylor, 'Concentration and Specialization in the Lancashire Cotton Industry, 1825–50', *Econ.Hist.Rev.*, 2nd ser. i (1948–9), 119–22; S. Kenny, 'Sub-Regional Specialization in the Lancashire Cotton Industry, 1884–1914', *Journal of Historical Geography*, 8 (1982), 42–59; D. A. Farnie, *The English Cotton Industry and the World Market, 1815–96* (Oxford, 1979), 301–3; *Census of England and Wales, 1921: County of Lancaster*, p. xxxviii; the contrast with New England is explored in W. Lazonick, 'Industrial Organization and Technological Change: The Decline of the British Cotton Industry', *Business History Review*, 57 (1983), 205–10.

[9] *Worrall's Cotton Spinners' and Manufacturers' Directory* (Oldham, 1905 edn.).

technology, Lancashire was unusual for its continued reliance on the mule for spinning. Elsewhere, the ring frame had secured general acceptance. In 1924, 85 per cent of Indian and 95 per cent of Japanese spindles were on rings, the former figure rising to 90 per cent by 1930. In Britain, by contrast, despite attempts to rationalize production by the scrapping of redundant plant, mules continued to account for over 70 per cent of total spindleage by 1939.[10]

Such points of contrast had clear implications for Lancastrian labour deployments. Unlike emergent Asian industries, which relied on unskilled, often transitory labour, British mills placed particular value on the experience gathered through prolonged careers. A delegation of the Bolton and District Managers' and Overlookers' Association to the United States in 1919, although impressed by the sophistication of American techniques, remained convinced that Lancashire's particular advantage continued to reside in having 'the best-trained and most skilled workpeople in the world'.[11] So, although women and children made up a

Table 1. *Cotton mill workforce, 1911*

Mill Department	Number of Operatives Employed	
	male	*female*
Card room	9	46
Frame rooms	—	38
Blowing and mixing rooms	2	—
Spinning rooms	127	—
Overlookers	2	—
Watch house	—	3
Warehouse	8	1
Mechanics' shop	3	—
Engineers and firemen	2	—
Odd hands	7	—
Cleaners	—	2

Source: LRO, Preston Barber-Lomax Collection DDBx 10/14 Cannon Bros, Ltd, Managing Director's Note-Book, 1906–26, workpeople employed, February 1911. A similar pattern applied more generally, see *Handbooks on Trades in Lancashire and Cheshire: Textile Trades* (HMSO, 1915), 6.

[10] H. Clay, *Report on the English Cotton Industry* (1931), 4A, 4B; *Parl. Papers 1939–40*, iv (6157), Spindles Board, 3rd Annual Report, 6. Ring spindles were 50% more productive than their mule equivalents, so that in terms of output, the share, in 1939, was 61:39 in the mule's favour.

[11] *BJG* (17 Oct. 1919), 8. For comparisons with Asia, see *TW* 5 (1 Aug. 1930), 470; 7 (17 April 1931), 208–9.

majority of the cotton labour force, men aged over 20 accounted for almost 30 per cent of workers in spinning districts, a proportion which rose to exceed 40 per cent in weaving areas.[12] What is more, they tended to be concentrated at particular points in the production process. Spinning departments across Bolton recorded a slight preponderance of men in 1911, whereas a balance of six-to-one in favour of women obtained in local weaving sheds.[13] The existence of 'separate spheres' becomes even more apparent if analysis is extended to individual mills. At Cannon Bros, Ltd, of Bolton, male and female jobs were clearly demarcated in 1911.

The presence of strategically significant groups of adult male workers raises questions about the importance which attached to established notions of skill in cotton production during this period. An examination of their role helps to clarify not only the balance of authority between employers and employed within the industry, but also the nature of relationships within a workforce distinguished by marked differentials in income and status. Such points are brought into sharp focus by a consideration of work and workforce structures in carding departments. Here, the raw cotton was prepared for spinning by arranging the fibres parallel to each other and then consolidating them into a loose rope or 'roving'. The latter process was overseen by women, who, in 1920, made up over 90 per cent of card-room employees across the fine-spinning province centred on Bolton.[14] By tradition, tending the frames on which carding took place or frame-tenting was work of low status, a fact exemplified by James Haslam's fictional character, 'Mangy Lucy', a virago, who, when roused, was capable of 'a string of invectives that would have shocked a curate out of recognition'.[15] Low wages provided material confirmation of the impression conveyed by Lucy's linguistic facility. Paid by the piece, frame-tenters' earnings rarely matched those of four-loom weavers. Across Lancashire in 1906, they averaged between 19s. 3d. and 20s. 7d. a week, compared to 23s. 6d. available at the loom. The following year, female card-room wages became subject to the same collective agreements which governed the pay of most other cotton workers. Yet the wage list,

[12] *Parl. Papers 1909*, lxxx (4545), Report of an Enquiry into the Earnings and Hours of Labour. I. Textile Trades in 1906, 35–6, 46–7; *Parl. Papers 1929–30*, xvii (3508), A Study of the Factors Operating to Determine the Distribution of Women in Industry, 6–7.

[13] *Parl. Papers 1913*, lxxix (7019), Census of England and Wales, 1911. X. Occupations and Industries. Part II, table 13, p. 217.

[14] BA, FT/7/1/6 Bolton and District Card and Ring Room Provincial Association (BOCA), Executive Council Minutes, Special EC, 14 Jan. 1920.

[15] *The Woman Worker* (9 Oct. 1908), 484.

as agreed in 1907, merely served to emphasize their lowly status, with standard rates fixed at between 18*s*. and 22*s*. 9*d*. a week.[16]

It should be noted, however, that such figures assume full-time working, a rarity for frame-tenters for much of this period. Reduced hours frequently depressed female pay, as employers responded to market changes by varying the quality of output from the mule without altering preparatory operations. So, while spinning rooms often worked to capacity, frame-tenters were obliged to work short-time. Perhaps unsurprisingly, female card-room careers tended to be brief, terminating on marriage, a pattern common to most women mill workers. In 1911, two out of every three females employed in Bolton card-rooms were aged 25 or under.[17]

Problems of low status had, for much of the nineteenth century, extended to the small number of males employed in preparatory processes. The work of these strippers and grinders largely comprised setting and cleaning the cards, or metal brushes, on which fibres were regularized and laid parallel. High rates of turnover had worked to frustrate earlier attempts at unionization, such as the Card Grinders' and Strippers' Association of the 1860s. Persistent low wages had further limited the job's appeal. The 1886 Wage Census placed average grinders' earnings at 20*s*. 2*d*. a week, compared with 30*s*. 8*d*. to 35*s*. 6*d*. for mule spinners.[18] From that point, however, the status of male card-room workers was to be transformed. Change was, in part, a consequence of technological innovation. The introduction of the revolving flat card, a movable brushing surface placed above the loose blanket or 'lap' of fibres, significantly reduced manpower needs. The secretary of the Bolton Operative Spinners' Association, J. T. Fielding, observed of this period that 'a mill containing 50,000 spindles does not require the services of

---

[16] *Parl. Papers 1909*, lxxx (4545), Earnings and Hours of Labour, 26–7; *Parl. Papers 1910*, xx (5366), Board of Trade (Labour Dept). Report on Collective Agreements between Employers and Workpeople, 166–7.

[17] *Parl. Papers 1913*, lxxix (7019), Census of England and Wales, 1911. X. Occupations and Industries. Pt. II, 217; BA, FT/7/6/63 BOCA, quarterly reports, 31 Aug. 1909, 2–3; FT/7/2/2 BOCA, Bolton Branch Committee Minutes, quarterly meeting, 22 May 1928; John Rylands Library, Deansgate, Manchester (JRL), Ashton Employers' Association Collection, Federation of Master Cotton Spinners' Associations Ltd (FMCSA), annual report, year ending 30 June 1920 (Manchester, 1920), 43–4.

[18] A. Bullen and A. Fowler, *The Cardroom Workers Union: A Centenary History of The Amalgamated Association of Card and Blowing Room Operatives* (Manchester, 1986), 4–6; *Cotton Factory Times* (*CFT*) (14 Nov. 1924), 4; S. J. Chapman, *The Lancashire Cotton Industry* (Manchester, 1904), 232; *Parl. Papers 1909*, lxxx (4545), Earnings and Hours of Labour, p. xxvi.

more than five of this class of operatives'.[19] This diminished grinders' community provided the basis for more effective unionization. Career prospects were, as a consequence, enhanced.

Wage figures encapsulate the change. Under clause 4 of the Brooklands Agreement of 1893, which regulated wage movements in the spinning trade across south-east Lancashire, grinders were exempted from the maximum adjustment of 5 per cent in list rates. So, whereas spinners' average full-time earnings increased by 30–2 per cent between 1886 and 1906, those for grinders rose by 45 per cent. Subsequent collective agreements continued to discriminate in the latter's favour. In 1920, they gained a further 10 per cent over and above the agreed increase in list rates of 70 per cent.[20] Over time, formal wage lists came to determine rates of pay across the industry, that which governed conditions in the American-cotton-spinning district around Oldham being concluded in 1903, while a separate agreement covered the fine-spinning area from 1919. Taken together, such developments ensured a comparative improvement in the grinders' standing, albeit one which fell short of the avowed intention 'to put their calling on a level with their fellows in the spinning trade'.[21] By 1932, estimated average weekly earnings for grinders stood at 60s. 4d., compared with the spinners' 75s. 8d.[22] As a proportion of earnings on the mule, grinders' pay had increased from below two-thirds to approaching 80 per cent in the decades from 1886.

This, however, tends to understate the gains made. In terms of authority in work, achievement outstripped ambition. Unlike most mill operatives, grinders were paid by the hour. This not only provided employers with some guarantee that output quality would be maintained, it also served to secure grinders against any pressure to speed up work. Their duties and responsibilities were clearly defined by the 1903 Universal Card List. Stripping or cleaning the cards was to take place four times

---

[19] BA, FT/14/81 Bolton and District Operative Spinners' Provincial Association (BSA), Cuttings, Circulars, and Handbills, letter dated 15 May, 1883; the revolving flat card is described in Chapman, *Lancashire Cotton Industry*, 72.

[20] *Parl. Papers 1909*, lxxx (4545), Earnings and Hours of Labour, p. xxvi; *BJG* (23 Mar. 1893), 7; *Parl. Papers 1894*, lxxxi, pt. II (7567–I), Board of Trade (Labour Dept). Report on Wages and Hours of Labour. Part II, Standard Piece Rates, 11; *The Labour Gazette* (*LG*), 28 (1920), 318.

[21] *BJG* (20 July 1923), 5; *Parl. Papers 1910*, xx (5366), Collective Agreements between Employers and Workpeople, 164–6; BA, FT/7/1/6 BOCA, Executive Council Minutes, Agreement over Conditions of Work and Schedule of Wages for Strippers and Grinders, 5 Aug. 1919.   [22] *BJG* (28 Oct. 1932), 8.

each day, while grinding, resetting the teeth on the cards, would be undertaken three times every four weeks. Grinders were also responsible for
maintaining the cards and the bands which powered them.[23] As the period
progressed, the scope of grinders' authority extended to cover recruitment and promotion, a development confirmed in formal apprenticeship
agreements. By 1914, minimum ages for promotion to grinding had been
fixed at 20 and 19 in the American- and Egyptian-cotton spinning sectors,
respectively. Qualification in the Bolton district was also dependent on
two years' prior experience of working on the cards.[24] Later in the decade,
regulations were further tightened in coarse-spinning mills. Although 20
remained the age for final promotion, admission to apprenticeships was
limited to youths over the age of 16. Furthermore, remuneration was to
commence at 19s. a week, rising by 1s. each year, while a ratio of one
apprentice for every three grinders was stipulated, thus guarding against
any over-supply of labour. Separate agreements continued to operate in
the Bolton province. Here, apprentices were offered a broad training in
card-room processes, in order to promote the deeper technical understanding considered essential for such a skilled and responsible position.
More importantly, training was to be overseen by the grinders themselves,
in contrast to the position further east, where employers continued to
control the allocation of apprentices. In case of dispute, provision existed
for the settlement of differences by joint discussion, the cotton trade's
customary prophylactic.[25]

The value of such regulations to the grinders was confirmed during the
1920s. At a time when most mill departments were struggling to recruit
sufficient manpower, carding departments faced the contrasting problem
of a surplus of potential recruits, refuting fears expressed by the employers' federation that controls on entry would discourage applicants.[26] To
avert the threat of a labour surplus, moves were made further to restrict
entry. While the federation (American-cotton) scheme was amended to

[23] *LG* 11 (1903), 95; *Parl. Papers 1910*, xx (5366), Collective Agreements between
Employers and Workpeople, 164–6.
[24] JRL, Ashton Employers' Collection, FMCSA, annual report for year ending 30 June
1917 (Manchester, 1917), 89–90; *BJG* (18 Jan. 1918), 3.
[25] JRL, Ashton Employers' Collection, FMCSA, annual report for year ending 30 June
1918 (Manchester, 1918), 76–9; year ending 30 June 1920 (Manchester, 1920), 36–9; BA,
FT/7/1/6 BOCA, Executive Council Minutes, quarterly meeting, 1 June 1920; *BJG* (3
Sept. 1926), 8.
[26] BA, FT/7/2/1 BOCA, Bolton Branch Committee Minutes, quarterly meeting, 24
Feb. 1925; JRL, Ashton Employers' Collection, FMCSA, annual report, year ending 31
Dec. 1926 (Manchester, 1927), 27.

raise the starting age to 18, alternative steps were debated in Bolton. Proposals strongly favoured by the grinders included raising the minimum age for promotion from 19 to 21, introducing a more restrictive employment ratio of one apprentice for every four grinders, and requiring applications for admission to be made within six months of leaving school. The latter was seen to have the additional advantage of minimizing mobility between mill departments, thus closing off a further potential source of recruits.[27] In practice, rather than instituting such formal controls, union branch committees were left to oversee admissions procedures, being guided in their decisions by a census of male card-room hands compiled by the local Card-Room Association. To that extent, the grinders became trustees of their own status. Entry could be refused where figures revealed an existing manpower surplus. Alternatively, an applicant's age could count against him. Individual cases reflect the narrowing of promotional avenues which resulted. Harry Pye entered the card-room from the mill warehouse at the age of 15 in 1920, whereas a similar route was denied 15-year-old Charles Gardner nine years later.[28]

As further confirmation of their enhanced sense of status, grinders were relatively free of supervisory intervention in the performance of their duties. Female frame-tenters were more likely to be subject to supervisory authority. For example, in 1911, Cissie Chadwick, employed on roving frames at Haslam Bros' Burnley mill, was dismissed for being absent from work without permission, having been previously warned about leaving her frames to talk to fellow operatives. In appealing against this decision, she claimed that the carder (card-room supervisor) had struck her 'on the neck, which caused her to fall into a skip'.[29] Grinders, by contrast, enjoyed a much closer, more cordial relationship with carders, to the extent that grinders who secured promotion to supervisory status were allowed to retain their union membership and could, providing that subscriptions continued to be paid in full, return to grinding later in their careers. Card-room traditions thus provided further corroboration for the view, expressed by G. H. Wood that, over time 'an additional

[27] JRL, Ashton Employers' Collection, FMCSA, annual report, year ending 31 Dec. 1926, 136–9; BA, FT/7/2/1 BOCA, Bolton Committee Minutes, mass meeting, 17 Sept. 1924; FT/7/9/1 BOCA, Rules, 1926, par. 10.
[28] BA, FT/7/2/1 BOCA, Bolton Committee Minutes, quarterly meeting, 24 Feb. 1925; Committee meetings, 23, 24 Oct., 3 Nov. 1924 (for Pye); FT/7/2/2 BOCA, Bolton Committee Minutes, 21 Jan. 1929 (for Gardner); see also 19 Mar. 1928; 9 Nov. 1931.
[29] Lancashire Record Office, Preston (LRO), North East Lancashire Textile Manufacturers' Association DDX 1145/1/1/3 Burnley Master Cotton Spinners' and Manufacturers' Association, minutes, 15, 25 Aug. 1911.

skilled employment' had replaced 'one hitherto quite or nearly unskilled'.[30] The change also found sartorial expression. As the *Bolton Journal and Guardian* remarked in 1918, 'A cardroom worker never turns up at his trade-union committee meeting nowadays in handkerchief and cord trousers and he has aspirations that carry him further than the first public-house door that invites him to wash down the day's accumulation of dust.'[31] Altered expectations informed the craft identity which union officials were increasingly keen to propagate. In 1923, the Bolton Committee of the Card-Room Operatives' Provincial Association admonished one member for the poor quality of his work. The complaints which this had attracted were felt to derogate from the grinders' standing within the mill hierarchy.[32]

Developments within the card-room thus indicate the continued importance of skilled labour for Lancastrian cotton production. Nevertheless, to describe change is not to explain it. Some have located the grinders' rise in the emergence of stable union organization, which enabled control to be exerted over labour deployments. The chronological coincidence between the two developments is, at the very least, suggestive. However, such an interpretation still leaves unclear the precise means by which organizational unity was translated into workplace control. The direction of causality could, just as plausibly, be reversed, so that union organization could be seen as a consequence rather than as a cause of the grinders' enhanced status. An alternative view has been proposed by Mike Savage, whereby the decisive factor was the grinders' control of recruitment. In particular, the importance of family ties within the hiring process is seen to have allowed grinders to obstruct the wider utilization of unskilled female labour.[33] For various reasons, this argument fails to convince. First, the extent to which personal ties shaped card-room recruitment may be doubted, given the kind of employment ratio of one male grinder to nine female frame-tenters that applied in Bolton in 1906.[34] More importantly, the attitudes of employers to questions of

[30] G. H. Wood, *The History of Wages in the Cotton Trade during the Past Hundred Years* (1910), 48–9; BA, FT/7/2/2 BOCA, Bolton Committee Minutes, committee meeting, 22 Sept. 1930.   [31] *BJG* (18 Jan. 1918), 3.

[32] BA, FT/7/2/1 BOCA, Bolton Committee Minutes, committee meeting, 3 Nov. 1923.

[33] H. A. Turner, *Trade Union Growth, Structure and Policy: A Comparative Study of the Cotton Unions* (1962), 164, 289; Savage, *Dynamics of Working-Class Politics*, 83; id., 'Women and Work in the Lancashire Cotton Industry, 1890–1939', in J. A. Jowitt and A. J. McIvor (eds.), *Employers and Labour in the English Textile Industries, 1850–1939* (1988), 208.

[34] *Parl. Papers 1909*, lxxx (4545), Earnings and Hours of Labour, 35–6.

labour utilization are not addressed, the assumption being that, left to their own devices, owners and managers would seek to maximize the employment of cheaper, less skilled hands. The validity or otherwise of this view may be assessed by considering the policies adopted by employers at times when existing workplace arrangements were called into question.

The first came during the Great War, when manpower losses enforced the wider utilization of female labour. Under local joint agreements concluded in 1915, women were allowed to work on the cards, on condition that the men they replaced retained the right to return to their machines on the cessation of hostilities. Even then, substitution was less than complete. The job's physical demands were such that females were limited to purely ancillary roles, minding cards set by experienced hands. Wage inequalities were, if anything, heightened, the earnings of absent grinders being divided between those who remained and their female assistants. Male wages thus rose to over £4 a week, some 60 per cent above women's rates.[35] If the nature of their work sustained the grinders' position during wartime, a more fundamental threat was posed, in later years, by technological change. The introduction, during the 1920s, of mechanized (vacuum) stripping threatened to remove physical obstacles to female recruitment. For one 'Farnworth Cotton Worker', writing in the *Cotton Factory Times* in 1922, this raised the prospect of 'strippers walking about the street'.[36] Where the process was applied, however, debate centred more on rates of remuneration than on broader issues of labour deployment. Indeed, the agreement reached in January 1926 not only confirmed the existing division of responsibilities, but also accepted that 'the status of the stripper and grinder in the matter of wages shall not be reduced' and that the new method should neither be used to intensify nor to prolong the workload.[37] If the issue of control was easily resolved, agreement covering work details proved more elusive. The capacity of vacuum strippers to clean up to eighty cards in an hour rendered the work clauses of the 1903 List obsolete. Revisions to that agreement were thus sought by

---

[35] JRL, Ashton Employers' Collection, FMCSA, annual report, year ending 30 June 1915 (Manchester, 1915), 56–60; *Parl. Papers 1919*, xxxi (167), Report of the Committee on Women in Industry. Appendices: Summaries of Evidence, &c., 81; (135), Report of the War Cabinet Committee on Women in Industry, 88, 131; Home Office, *Substitution of Women for Men during the War: Reports Showing the Position in Certain Industries at the End of 1918* (HMSO, 1919), 6.

[36] Home Office, *Substitution of Women*, 6; *CFT* (20 Oct. 1922), 3.

[37] JRL, Ashton Employers' Collection, FMCSA, annual report, year ending 31 Dec. 1925 (Manchester, 1926), 16; year ending 31 Dec. 1926, 122–3.

Bolton employers from 1928. Three years of negotiations followed, during which the grinders resolutely defended existing arrangements. Agreement was eventually reached on an experiment, to be mounted at Musgrave's No. 4 Mill, to test the capacity of grinders to undertake duties additional to those outlined in existing lists.[38] Management's principal aim thus remained a modest amendment to work details. A more fundamental restructuring of the employment relationship was not envisaged, despite the opening offered by new technology.

The grinders' sense of craft, based on comparative wage advance and autonomy at work, never faced a concerted challenge in this period. Employers, if they did not actively encourage, at least acquiesced in a process whereby a small group of male operatives acquired and consolidated skilled status. How far this was an outcome actively willed by mill managements, rather than being enforced by a combination of institutional constraints, including strong and durable trade unionism and an established collective bargaining tradition, remains to be established. An examination of developments in neighbouring spinning departments assists in resolving this problem and points up the continued utility of skilled labour in all parts of the production process.

II

The spinning techniques employed in Lancashire's mills in the late nineteenth century were substantially those developed in the period 1760–1830, which had transformed both the nature of the work and the type of labour required to undertake it. The most fundamental change had seen a part-time, largely domestic female occupation replaced by one in which skilled males were employed full-time in factory settings on machinery of increasing complexity. From the late eighteenth century, the predominant form of spinning was the mule. By then, the focus of innovative effort had come to centre on attempts to mechanize the two principal processes involved in producing yarn. 'Spinning', achieved on the mule on the outward run of the carriage, during which the thread was attenuated and twisted, was easily reproduced mechanically. More problematic was 'winding', the rate of which was determined by the speed of the carriage on its inward run. In the absence of complete mechanization,

---

[38] *BJG* (22 Feb. 1924), 11; *TW* 1 (11 May 1928), 264; BA, FT/7/2/2 BOCA, Bolton Committee Minutes, quarterly meetings, 19 May, 24 Nov. 1931; committee meeting, 25 Jan. 1932.

the mule's operations continued to require that combination of physical strength and fine judgement which skilled male labour was thought to provide.[39] The market power which thus accrued to a small group of workers quickened efforts to render the mule fully self-acting. The success of Sharp, Roberts and Co., in their patents of 1825 and 1830, promised to check what Andrew Ure described as the 'cherished pride and . . . refractory spirits' of the spinners, a claim which the inventors themselves were keen to advance. Their publicity emphasized the extent to which manual operations on the self-actor would be confined to piecing broken threads and cleaning the machinery.[40] Under mechanization, mill-owners need no longer be in thrall to labour.

Yet, in practice, the outcome of innovation was less clear-cut. Technical treatises, written in the late nineteenth century described how, on the self-actor, the spinner had become 'a mere ordinary machine himself'.[41] At the same time, the popular writer and socialist activist Allen Clarke enlarged on the alienating effects of a production process governed by machinery around which workers were seen to 'twist and turn like marionettes round a steam organ'.[42] In one of his dialect sketches, Clarke put similar views into the mouth of one of his characters, Ben Roke, who was emphatic that

There's nowt abeaut mindin. Any foo con mind a pair o' wheels. Aw as theau has for't do is for't lie deawn at t' back o' t' wheel-yed, get up every two heaurs an cuss thy piecers, an run a 'shot' on at t' nearest pub; . . . If theau con tak snuff an sup a pint, theau'rt qualified to be a minder.[43]

However, a brief spell in the mule-gate quickly persuades Ben's fellow 'Tum Fowter' Bill Spriggs that the reality is somewhat different: 'Mindin eh? Theau corn't mind nowt else, for it taks thee aw thy time for t' mind thysel, an then theau't lucky if theau gets away beaut a harm or leg missin. No mooar mindin for me.'[44] In this piece, at least, Clarke was concerned to celebrate the native wit and intelligence of factory folk.

[39] M. Berg, *The Age of Manufactures: Industry, Innovation and Work in Britain, 1700–1820* (Oxford, 1985), 255–7; J. Kennedy, *A Brief Memoir of Samuel Crompton: with a description of his machine called the mule and of the subsequent improvement of the machine by others* (Manchester, 1830), 14–27; H. Catling, *The Spinning Mule* (Newton Abbot, 1970), 42–9.

[40] Ure, *Philosophy of Manufactures*, 366–8; H. W. Dickinson, 'Richard Roberts, his Life and Inventions', *Transactions of the Newcomen Society*, 25 (1945–6 and 1946–7), 127–8.

[41] H. E. Walmsley, *Cotton Spinning and Weaving* (Manchester, 1893), 35–6.

[42] C. A. Clarke, *The Effects of the Factory System* (1899), 74.

[43] C. A. Clarke, 'Bill Spriggs as a Minder', in P. Salveson (ed.), *Teddy Ashton's Lancashire Scrapbook* (Farnworth, 1985), 6.   [44] Ibid. 10.

More importantly, this was the view which prevailed. The mule-spinners' skill drew praise from Arthur Shadwell, while a Home Office report of 1919, concerned with the substitution of women for men during wartime, noted the extensive training and particular expertise required in spinning.[45] Wage figures gave substance to this view. In 1906, sixty-five occupations recorded average adult male earnings in excess of those in the cotton trade. However, mule-spinners, whose average pay ranged from 38s. 10d. to 46s. a week, ranked seventh in the national manual-wages index. Within the mill their position was even clearer; their earnings approached and, in certain cases, exceeded those of mule-room supervisors. Across Bolton, in 1906, weekly earnings for overlookers averaged 43s. 1d., compared with 44s. 2d. to 47s. 6d. for spinners. In addition, among the teams which worked the mules, two-thirds of the wage went to the minder, the remainder being divided between two or three assistants or 'piecers'.[46] Responsibility for the mule carried social as well as material rewards. The presence of 'tippler closets' differentiated spinners' households in Bill Naughton's Bolton in 1920. Similarly, the son of one local minder compared his family's circumstances before and after his father's promotion: 'we were about middle class. I should call ourselves middle class. We wasn't poor, not then. We was poor at the beginning like, when I was born, we were very poor, . . . until my dad got a pair of wheels and then we got higher up [the street] and we wasn't as poor then.'[47] However questionable in sociological terms, such comments reflect the widespread perception that spinners, against the expectations of Ure, Sharp, and Roberts, had succeeded in maintaining a privileged status within both the workplace and the world beyond.

The wider implications of this point will be traced in subsequent chapters. Here, our concern is to account for the persistence of income and skill differentials and to examine their consequences for the work experience over this period. The immediate roots of the minders' status lay in the regulations governing wages and working practices across the spinning trade. Wage movements were determined by two lists: that agreed in 1876 at Oldham concerned the coarse-to-medium American-cotton sector, while mills producing finer yarns followed the Bolton list, first agreed

[45] A. Shadwell, *Industrial Efficiency* (1909 edn.), 61; Home Office, *Substitution of Women*, 7.
[46] J. Jewkes and E. M. Gray, *Wages and Labour in the Lancashire Cotton Spinning Industry* (Manchester, 1935), 17; *Parl. Papers 1909*, lxxx (4545), Earnings and Hours of Labour, 29–30.
[47] BA, Bolton Oral History Project (BOHP) 87 (male, born 1902), transcript, 13; Naughton, *Saintly Billy*, 4.

in 1858 and revised in 1887. Differences between these lists reflected conditions in each area. In Oldham, standardized output tied rates directly to machine capacity, as measured by the numbers of spindles and the speed of operation. The division of mule-team wages was also specified, piecers being apportioned between 31 and 48 per cent of the whole.[48] In Bolton, by contrast, wages were more closely tied to the quality of output as measured by 'counts',[49] reflecting the shorter, more varied runs common in fine-yarn production. In 1923, for example, the Great Lever Spinning Co., Ltd produced twenty different counts, ranging from 58s to 145s, on its sixty-five mules.[50] The list made no allowance for increased speeds or longer carriages. Rates remained unchanged on all mules of over 900 spindles, despite the fact that most machines installed after 1885 exceeded that capacity. Of mules supplied by the Bolton engineering firm of Dobson and Barlow between 1910 and 1919, only 14 per cent had carriages shorter than 900 spindles.[51] In such circumstances, productivity gains were weighted in favour of labour. Spinners were the particular beneficiaries of this peculiarity as, unlike the Oldham list, the division of rewards was left to the discretion of individual teams. The result was that, whereas minders' earnings under the Bolton list exceeded the county median (44s. 6d. against 43s. on counts between 40s and 80s in 1906), those for piecers fell below those elsewhere (10s. 6d. to 15s. as against 11s. 6d. to 16s. 6d. for piecers aged under 20).[52]

The problem of piecers' pay was debated within the Bolton Province from the turn of the century, with the result that, from 1908, minimum and maximum rates were fixed for specified carriage lengths. The aim was to ensure uniformity in pay scales, rather than to address the issue of income inequalities. Differentials thus persisted well beyond 1908. A wage census organized by the local Spinners' Association in 1923 showed minders drawing between 61 and 68 per cent of team earnings, shares

[48] *Parl. Papers 1894*, lxxxi, pt. II (7567–I), Wages and Hours of Labour, 2–3; *Parl. Papers 1910*, xx (5366), Collective Agreements between Employers and Workpeople, 141; Wood, *History of Wages*, 53.

[49] 'Counts' measured the number of 'hanks', lengths of 840 yards, making up each lb. of yarn; the higher the count, therefore, the finer the yarn.

[50] BA, FT/8/8/1 BSA, wages returns, Great Lever Spinning Co., Ltd.

[51] LRO, Platt-Saco-Lowell DDPSL/2/25/13 Dobson and Barlow, Ltd, Machine Order Books, Mules, 1910–19; *Parl. Papers 1894*, lxxxi, pt. II (7567–I), Wages and Hours of Labour, 5; Jewkes and Gray, *Wages and Labour*, 58–9; Chapman, *Lancashire Cotton Industry*, 268.

[52] *Parl. Papers 1910*, xx (5366), Collective Agreements between Employers and Workpeople, 149; Wood, *History of Wages*, 62; *Parl. Papers 1909*, lxxx (4545), Earnings and Hours of Labour, 29–30; *BJG* (20 Oct. 1911), 9, letter by James Haslam.

The Work Experience

similar to the averages recorded in 1906 (62–4 per cent).[53] The position remained little altered at the end of the period. In 1932, while Oldham minders claimed 52 per cent of each team's wages, their counterparts in Bolton commanded a 65 per cent share.[54]

Wage arrangements reflected the authority which spinners exercised within the mule-gate (the passage between carriages in which work was carried out). Piecers were employed by their minders, rather than by the mill-owners, so that while the latter oversaw payments in the aggregate, responsibility for the subsequent distribution of wages among team members devolved on to individual spinners. Discipline within the mule-gate was also exercised at the minders' discretion, an arrangement endorsed by the Bolton Employers' Association secretary, Alfred Hill, in 1923: 'it is the duty and privilege of Spinners to engage and control their own piecers, and also to be responsible for their dismissal when necessary'.[55] Furthermore, as in the card-room, workers were charged with ensuring that machinery remained in good working order. Both the Oldham and Bolton lists included clauses covering the repair of bands which supplied the motive power to each mule. Within individual mills, spinners were encouraged to co-operate when any colleague was engaged in more than basic machine maintenance. At Bolton's Clarence Mill, union rules enjoined minders 'to send help when any member is strapping or turning bands, etc.'.[56]

Supervisors barely impinged on the minders' authority. Paid by time rates, and so not materially affected by production levels, foremen were a marginal disciplinary presence in mule-rooms. Their intervention in mule-gate operations was confined to rectifying major mechanical breakdowns and overseeing changes in 'counts', which required adjustments to the mules' gearing.[57] The division of responsibilities differed from that which applied in Scotland, where foremen oversaw all aspects of machine maintenance, limiting the spinners' duties to piecing. In Lancashire, overlookers were more likely to be drawn from engineering backgrounds. For example, Frank Wright, general manager of the Bolton mill combine,

[53] John Rylands University Library, Manchester (JRUL), BCA/1/3/8 BSA, Minutes, Special General Meetings, 27 Feb., 16 Mar. 1908; BA, FT/8/8/1 BSA,Wages returns for the four weeks ending 13 Oct. 1923; *Parl. Papers 1909*, lxxx (4545), Earnings and Hours of Labour, 35–6.   [54] *BJG* (21 Oct. 1932), 8.

[55] JRUL, BCA/12/5/1 BSA, Joint Meeting Negotiations, local joint meeting, 25 July 1923; *BJG* (1 Sept. 1911), 12.

[56] BA, FT/8/2/11 BSA, Rules of the Clarence Mill Shop Club, cl. 11; *Parl. Papers 1894*, lxxxi, pt. II (7567–I), Wages and Hours of Labour, 7, 14–15.

[57] Catling, *Spinning Mule*, 153; BA, BOHP, 161 (male, born 1907), tape.

Crosses and Winkworth, in the 1920s, acquired experience of mules at Platt Bros of Oldham before being appointed overlooker at Rose Hill Mills, Bolton. Over time, distinct promotional avenues developed, so that, by the 1920s, machine fitters were likely to be preferred to mill operatives in appointments to supervisory posts.[58]

In effect, the mule-gate remained the spinners' domain, an arrangement little different from that which had applied on hand mules. In part, such continuity reflected the gradual nature of technological diffusion. For five decades after 1830, the self-actor's limitations and enhanced hand-mule capacities on extended carriages had sustained the commercial viability of established techniques. Only in the 1880s, when Fielding could observe that 'there are not more than 80 pairs of hand mules in the whole country engaged in spinning yarn of a fineness that cannot, and in fact is being equalled upon self-actor mules', did the benefits of innovation become unquestionable.[59] The creeping pace of change facilitated continuity in labour's outlook, a tendency further encouraged by organizational developments. Initially, hand-spinners and self-acting minders belonged to separate associations, giving rise to occasional friction. Any differences were substantially overcome by the amalgamation of the two organizations in the third quarter of the nineteenth century, a process which enabled individuals to move between hand mules and self-actors without hindrance. Working practices came to carry the weight of tradition, so that it appeared, in Harold Catling's words, 'a mere oversight that the hierarchy of mule spinning had not been set down in the First Book of Moses'.[60]

The effect of such continuities was that minders, like hand-spinners before them, developed a particular attitude to and relationship with the machines on which they worked. This became explicit on occasions such as that in 1911, when mules were moved during reorganization at McConnell's of Manchester. In this case, minders claimed the right to remain with their own machines. On similar grounds, management attempts to alter labour deployments in the peculiar conditions of

---

[58] M. Freifeld, 'Technological Change and the 'Self-Acting' Mule: A Study of Skill and the Sexual Division of Labour', *Social History*, 11 (1986), 340–1; *BJG* (21 Mar. 1924), 6; (9 Nov. 1923), 12; BA, 'Bolton Biographical Notes', iii, 126 (Wright, obit.).

[59] BA, FT/14/81 BSA, Circulars, letter of May 1883; *Bolton Weekly Journal* (7 Aug. 1886), 8.

[60] Catling, *Spinning Mule*, 178; J. Mason, 'Spinners and Minders', in A. Fowler and T. Wyke (eds.), *The Barefoot Aristocrats* (Littleborough, 1987), 36–58; *Bolton Weekly Journal* (9 Oct. 1886), 8; *BJG* (18 Mar. 1921), 10; (8 May 1925), 5.

wartime were vigorously resisted.[61] The thinking which informed this outlook was articulated most clearly in a context of economic decline during the 1920s, when mill closures and the resulting sale of plant exposed conflicting notions of authority. Managements' responsibility for recruitment and the spinners' control of the mule-gate were seen to be increasingly incompatible. In 1930, the Fine Cotton Spinners' and Doublers' Association, following its purchase of the Ena Mill in Atherton, proposed staffing it with workers from its factories in Manchester. In response, the local Spinners' Association pressed that the existing workforce be retained and threatened any of its members accepting work at Atherton with expulsion. Financial concerns may have contributed to the strength of feeling expressed: of forty spinners previously employed at the Ena, twenty-five held shares with a nominal value of £3,340 in the mill, along with £122. 10s. in fixed-interest loans.[62] Yet such commitments alone cannot account for the spinners' attitude. Three years earlier, the Bolton firm of Barlow and Jones, Ltd had acquired the Wellington Mill in Turton as a more cost-effective method of expansion than building on to existing plant. The mill, which had been closed for two years, was staffed with piecers drawn from other Barlow and Jones works, an act justified by the local Employers' Association on the grounds that, as the Wellington had been purchased through the Official Receiver, all obligations to the native workforce had ceased. In countering this, William Wood, the Provincial Spinners' secretary restated the established perception of workers' rights: 'when a mill has been stopped, the workpeople look upon their positions as their own, as if they had paid for them'.[63]

Over time, the property of labour, manual skill, had become objectified in the machine. A distinctive notion of ownership resulted which took no account of changes in company structures or management personnel. An independent outlook, drawing on artisanate notions of 'skill', had thus come to flourish in a highly mechanized industry. Defined by areas of

---

[61] JRUL, BCA/1/3/9 BSA, Minutes, Council meeting, 17 July 1911; BCA/1/3/11 BSA, Council meetings, 3 Nov. 1914, 1, 22 June 1915.

[62] JRUL, BCA/1/3/14 BSA, Minutes, joint meeting with Card Room EC, 14 Nov. 1930; Special Districts meeting, 16 Jan.; Council meetings, 14 April, 1 June, 13 July 1931; BCA/12/5/2 BSA, Joint Meeting Negotiations, local joint meetings, 1 Oct. 1930, 16 Feb. 1931; central joint meeting, 2 Mar. 1931.

[63] BA, FT/21/11 BSA, Annual Report for 1927, 9; JRUL, BCA/1/3/13 BSA, Minutes, Council meeting, 25 Oct.; Special Districts Meeting, 11 Nov. 1927; BCA/13/4/44 BSA, Employers' Correspondence, 15 June, Wood to Hill; 15 July 1927, Wood to Boothman (Amalgamation secretary); BCA/12/5/2 BSA, Joint Meeting Negotiations, local joint meeting, 5 Oct. 1927.

responsibility in work and given constitutional force by successive joint agreements, it was an idea which survived the economic changes of the early twentieth century. The resultant sense of status persisted, despite evident limits to the spinners' authority within the mule-gate. Here, unlike the card-room, no formal apprenticeship agreements regulated internal promotional networks. Piecers gained experience on the mule in two distinct phases. The first, as little piecers or 'creelers', involved them in cleaning the carriage, piecing broken threads, and removing, or 'doffing', completed cops of yarn. Such work was carried out under the close supervision of the minder and continued until the age of 16, at which point creelers could anticipate promotion to big- or side-piecing. Although their duties were substantially unchanged, they became less subject to close regulation from this point. Promotion to minding could follow from the age of 20.[64] At all stages, advancement was determined by seniority and mechanical competence. Piecers progressed by filling 'dead men's shoes', having proved their capacity to manage machinery. Evaluation of the individual's fitness for promotion lay wholly within the employer's competence, a point which has been used by both Patrick Joyce and Mike Savage to question the minders' true status within the workplace. Their dependence appeared confirmed by internal promotional procedures which tied workers to particular mills. Attempts at independence through job mobility could fatally undermine opportunities for advancement.[65]

In practice, however, agreed guidelines for promotion worked to limit employers' capacity to exercise discretion. Promotion was thus rarely a cause of grievance in labour relations. Indeed, during the 1920s, the executive of the Bolton Provincial Operative Spinners' Association received only two complaints on this issue on average each year. Minders themselves acknowledged the importance of promoting only the technically competent, recognizing that to do otherwise would jeopardize their craft status. When one little-piecer was passed over for promotion, the protests of his mother met with a stern response from the Association secretary: 'no-one will have your son as a side piecer, . . . he has been discharged a time or two as a little piecer, and . . . until that last week or two has been indifferent about his work . . . If he expects to gain promotion it is up to

---

[64] Catling, *Spinning Mule*, 154–61; BA, BOHP, 58 (male, born 1905), transcript, 3; 161 (male, born 1907), tape; *Parl. Papers 1892*, xxxv (6708–VI), Royal Commission on Labour. Minutes of Evidence taken before Group 'C'. i. Textile, q. 782.

[65] BA, BOHP, 1A (male, born 1901), transcript, 5; 15 (female, born 1906), tape; 58 (male, born 1905), transcript, 6; *Parl. Papers 1892*, xxxv (6708–VI), RC on Labour. Textile, qq. 794–7; Joyce, *Work, Society and Politics*, 97; Savage, *Dynamics of Working-Class Politics*, 86–7.

him to justify it by making every effort to become efficient.'[66] What is more, mobility was controlled rather than being prohibited by the system. In Bolton, at least half of all vacancies were to be filled from within the mill.[67] The latitude available to employers to exploit potential slack in the labour market and so to challenge the minders' privileged position was thus limited. Continuity and quality of output came to demand that a premium be placed on proven competence and skill. The minders' status was thereby confirmed.

If unchanging work structures maintained the status quo for spinners, developments in the period from 1880 had major implications for piecers. The numerical preponderance of assistants under existing arrangements ensured that, at any one time, aspirants for promotion would exceed potential vacancies. As James Mawdsley, general secretary of the Operative Spinners' Amalgamation, admitted in evidence to the Royal Commission on Labour, during the course of an average career in charge of the mule, a spinner could expect to train at least three piecers to take his place.[68] To obviate the threat of promotional bottlenecks, the industry required a regular turnover of juvenile labour and prosperous conditions to encourage investment in new plant, the additional capacity siphoning off any manpower surplus. Neither condition was consistently achieved in this period. Throughout the nineteenth century, mill construction had proceeded sporadically, varying with cyclical fluctuations in trade, so that problems were apparent even at the height of the Edwardian boom. The 1906 survey of earnings and hours found that two-thirds of side-piecers across Lancashire were aged 20 or over, while in the following year, an investigation of seven Bolton mills by the journalist and novelist James Haslam revealed men still awaiting promotion to minding aged 29. Twenty of the side-piecers discovered by Haslam were married, endeavouring to support families on pay scales intended for juveniles.[69] Post-war developments compounded the difficulties of those similarly placed. Opportunities for promotion stagnated or even contracted over the 1920s, a decade in which Lancashire's aggregate spindleage fell by 4 per cent, while growth in the more prosperous fine-cotton sector was

[66] JRUL, BCA/1/3/11–15 BSA, Minutes 1920–32; BCA/13/2/40 BSA, General Correspondence, Wood to Sarah Fishwick, 10 Feb. 1932.
[67] Jewkes and Gray, *Wages and Labour*, 180; S. J. Chapman, 'Some Policies of the Cotton Spinners' Trade Unions', *Economic Journal*, 10 (1900), 473.
[68] *Parl. Papers 1892*, xxxv (6708–VI), RC on Labour. Textiles, qq. 791–2.
[69] *Parl. Papers 1909*, lxxx (4545), Earnings and Hours of Labour, 29–30; J. Haslam, *Cotton and Competition* (1909), 7.

limited to 2.6 per cent. Those whose mill careers commenced in this period thus recalled contemporaries trapped in side-piecing beyond the age of 30. Reflecting this, the study of the cotton-spinning workforce undertaken by Jewkes and Gray in 1934 devoted a chapter to 'The Piecer Problem'. By then, over 50 per cent of Bolton side-piecers were aged over 24 and over a quarter were married.[70]

Escape from the mule-gate was rendered more difficult by developments in other mill departments. Tighter apprenticeship regulations in card-rooms from 1920 were designed in part to prevent them becoming 'a dumping ground for . . . youths who have failed to make their mark in the spinning-room'.[71] At the same time, narrowing opportunities beyond the mill prolonged spinners' careers on the mule. Between 1916 and 1932, the average age at which superannuation benefits, administered by the Bolton Operative Spinners' Association, were first claimed rose from 58 to 63.[72] 'Dead men's shoes' became progressively more difficult to fill, more especially as the gender balance within spinning departments underwent a significant change.

Although spinning was unambiguously a male occupation, women and girls were, for much of the nineteenth century, employed as piecers. In 1886, it was estimated that some 500 females were employed in mule-rooms across the Bolton district; none was allowed to advance beyond piecing. In that year, however, moves were made to prevent women working on the mule in any capacity, by amending union rules to prohibit the employment of female piecers. Although that revision was subsequently reversed, female numbers never recovered their 1886 levels. By 1914, only ten women and girls were reported to be working in Bolton mule-rooms.[73] The result was to swell the number of piecers eligible for promotion and thereby the ranks of surplus labour along the mule carriage. To that extent, the 'piecer problem' was compounded by trade-union action.

The combined effect of changes in the wider economy and internal recruitment patterns was to transform piecing from an informal apprenticeship into something approaching a distinct grade of low-wage labour. Over time, piecers came to resemble, in the words of Jewkes and Gray, 'a

---

[70] Spindleage calculated from *Worrall's Cotton Spinners' Directory* (Oldham, 1921 and 1931 edns.); BA, BOHP, 87 (male, born 1902), transcript, 3; 161 (male, born 1907), tape; Jewkes and Gray, *Wages and Labour*, ch. 12 and p. 178.   [71] *CFT* (15 June 1923), 2.

[72] Calculated from JRUL, BCA/1/19/1 BSA, Bolton branch, superannuation payments, 1916–34.

[73] *Bolton Weekly Journal* (13 Nov. 1886), 7; (1 Jan. 1887), 7; *BJG* (23 Jan. 1914), 12.

submerged class',[74] a product of increasing income and gender differences. In explaining this outcome and the failure of mechanization to remove or even to reduce such inequalities, importance has often attached to the spinners' bargaining position. Their organizational strength and consequent influence within the workplace, it is argued, allowed their priorities to mould working practices, promoting the exploitation of the piecers. As this suggests, trade-union policies had implications for intra-class relations both in work and in the wider world. This broader perspective is pursued in later chapters. For the present, the focus remains the world of work.

If the consequences of trade-union policy appear transparent, the extent to which it alone could determine the development of work practices has still to be established. Its impact could be observed most readily in the exclusion of females from the mule-room. This followed the appointment, in 1886, of three women to mind short-length mules at the firm of T. and J. Heaton of Lostock, to the west of Bolton. The spinners' opposition rested largely on the moral implications of the sexes working in close proximity in a humid atmosphere. It was a theme to which many reverted with relish. Writing thirty years later, James Haslam recalled conditions on hand mules where

Men simply wear a pair of linen drawers and shirt—the legs of the drawers and the sleeves of the shirt being rolled up. The women wear nothing more than skirts and a blouse. Their legs are bare almost to the knees; their arms usually bare to the shoulders. Men and women, as did lads and girls, undressed and dressed in sight of one another.[75]

Although many local mills refused to employ women under such conditions, the Employers' Association opposed any change likely to exclude them, an attitude which led Fielding to enquire of mill-owners whether 'each of them has no objection to appearing before his grown up daughters two or three times a day in his shirt only'.[76] However genuine the spinners' modesty, it was not difficult to detect a further motive behind their campaign. Given that work on the self-actor posed no insurmountable physical obstacle to female employment, any change in work practices raised fears of competition from low-wage labour. The point was stated openly by a correspondent to the *Cotton Factory Times*, following

---

[74] Jewkes and Gray, *Wages and Labour*, 174.
[75] J. Haslam, 'Lancashire Women as Cotton-Piecers', *The Englishwoman*, 22 (Apr.–June 1914), 276–7.
[76] *Bolton Weekly Journal* (8 Jan. 1887), 7; for the employers' view, see (15 Jan. 1887), 7.

the introduction of greater numbers of women to piecing during the First World War: 'We shall have the employers saying that there is nothing in spinning if a girl can learn it, and will pay according [sic]'.[77]

Despite such fears, there was nothing to suggest that employers were anxious to enrol female labour in order to challenge trade-union privileges. In the first two years of the war, 644 women and girls were taken on as piecers and creelers in Bolton, accounting for 15 per cent of all assistants. Across the fine-spinning province as a whole, the proportion was nearer 35 per cent. Yet joint agreement between unions and management stipulated that, on the cessation of hostilities, wartime recruits should make way for returning servicemen.[78] Union exclusivity was thereby upheld. Nor was this unusual. Although females had been banned from spinning rooms in the 1880s, union ballots reversed that decision in 1899. The results, which in Bolton and Farnworth produced majorities of two-to-one in favour of reform, owed much to immediate circumstances. A combination of increases in the minimum school-leaving age and trade depression had worked to discourage recruitment to the cotton trade. Women's reinstatement was thus seen to offer a solution to problems of labour supply. Employers, however, were not persuaded of the benefits of reform. Fears that the employment of loosely attired women close to moving machinery would increase both the potential for accidents and the cost of compensation ensured that female numbers remained low after the 1899 rule change.[79] The only exception to this came in mining districts, where pits absorbed most young male labour. So, whereas only ten girls worked on Bolton mules by 1914, females accounted for half of all little-piecers in neighbouring Atherton.[80]

Subsequent attempts to boost female representation in the mule-room continued to be informed by the need to overcome failure in established recruitment networks. In 1925, for example, the Federation of Master Cotton Spinners' Association's deposition to the Balfour Committee on Industry and Trade referred to the contribution women and girls could make to surmounting the existing shortfall in school-leavers entering the

---

[77] B. Drake, *Women in Trade Unions* (1921), 85; see also *Bolton Weekly Journal* (18 Dec. 1886), 7, letter by 'Chopsticks'.

[78] BA, FT/21/9 BSA, Annual Report for 1916, 213; FT/21/10 BSA, Annual Report for 1919, 31–2.

[79] JRUL, BCA/1/3/7 BSA, Minutes, Special Districts Meeting, 4 Oct. 1899; *BJG* (14 Oct. 1899), 8.

[80] *BJG* (23 Jan. 1914), 12; (30 Jan. 1914), 10.

industry.[81] Across the county, however, managements were more likely to discourage than to invite female recruitment. The requirement that those returning to work after an interruption to their employment recommence at the lowest starter grade was maintained throughout the inter-war period, and proved a sufficient deterrent for many.[82] Employers' attitudes would only change after the Second World War, when a Board of Trade inquiry reported a 42 per cent shortfall in labour across the industry. In such circumstances, no source of manpower could knowingly be over-looked. In the course of Bolton's Textile Recruiting Week in 1946, firms made much of the facilities available to married-women workers. Cannon Bros, Ltd offered grants of up to £5 each to its female staff on marriage, while Barlow and Jones, Ltd promised prospective workers that 'The skill and dexterity once learned will never be lost, and if, say, years after you marry, you want a job again, you can always come back to us'.[83] It had not always been so. Before 1939, female recruitment was only advanced as a solution to specific recruitment problems. Not only would the problem of shortages be addressed, but, with women still barred from proceeding beyond piecing, existing work practices would be maintained. Both unions and employers thus worked to limit female numbers in Lancashire's mule-rooms.

Other attempts to amend mule-room operations in this period were informed by similar concerns, in which priority was given to ameliorating 'the piecer problem' rather than to confronting the issue of status inequalities. The earliest involved a partial restructuring of mule teams, whereby two minders or 'joiners' would supervise one little-piecer. In 1908, proposals were advanced to establish joining on 10 per cent of all mules. The intention was, in part, that 'joiners' would constitute an intermediate grade between side-piecing and minding, thereby providing a more structured and hence more predictable path to promotion.[84]

[81] JRL, FMCSA, annual report, year ending 31 Dec., 1925, 60; see also the remarks by William Howarth, president of the Bolton Master Cotton Spinners' Association, in *Bolton Evening News* (*BEN*) (24 Nov. 1922), 6.

[82] *BJG* (8 Nov. 1929), 5; (19 Feb. 1932), 10; BA, ZFO/6 Alice Foley Collection: A. Foley, 'Married Women Cardroom Workers and Unemployment Benefit', 2–3.

[83] Board of Trade, *Working Party Reports: Cotton* (HMSO, 1946), 54–7; LRO, Pamphlet Box 93 Barber-Lomax Reference Collection 'Welcome to Cannon Bros, Ltd, Stanley Mills, Bolton'; 'Looking for a Job?: some good advice from Barlow and Jones of Bolton', 1.

[84] JRUL, BCA/1/3/8 BSA, Minutes, Special Council Meeting, 9 Mar. 1908. The proposal resurfaced on several occasions in later years, BA, FT/21/9 BSA, Annual Report for 1913, 138; JRUL, BCA/12/5/1–2 BSA, Joint Meeting Negotiations, local joint meetings, 17 Sept. 1924, 23 May 1927; *BEN* (28 Nov. 1922), 4.

A further benefit was anticipated from the redistribution of team wages required under the new arrangement. Additional payments to side-piecers would, as the secretary of the Bolton Master Cotton Spinners' Association argued in 1913, 'help to relieve many cases of hardship caused by side piecers having to wait a long time for the position of minder . . . and consequently would be an inducement to parents to send their sons to the mill as little piecers.'[85] The freeing of promotional bottlenecks took precedence over any more radical progamme of reform. Yet, although no challenge to their status was implied, local minders were largely hostile to the proposed changes, arguing that the promise of higher earnings would encourage older juveniles to remain in the mule-gate, compounding the 'blind-alley' problems associated with the job. Such concerns appeared less pressing elsewhere. With the agreement of the district union, 20 per cent of Oldham's mules were operated by 'joiners' by 1934. In Bolton, by contrast, the system remained untried.[86]

When the issue of joiner-minding was raised again in 1927, it was combined with calls to reorganize work time. Existing agreements set aside a fixed period for cleaning the mule, during which full rates of pay continued to apply. Employers now proposed that these duties be assigned to gangs of three to four side-piecers. Under such an arrangement, interruptions to production would be minimized, while increased productive time would reduce unit labour costs. At the same time, higher mule-team earnings would be used to supplement the wages of gang members, thereby encouraging higher levels of recruitment among school-leavers.[87] Negotiations extended over the next five years before a settlement was concluded in November 1932. Difficulty was encountered over the issues of employment ratios, the status of gangs, and the time to be set aside for cleaning. The question of control, by contrast, was speedily resolved. Cleaners would, it was agreed in 1929, be subject to the authority of the minder on whose mules they were engaged.[88] The observation offered by Robert Tootill, secretary of the Bolton United Trades Council in 1911, thus continued to hold good: 'Mill-owners have permitted and encouraged

[85] JRUL., BCA/13/4/28 BSA, employers' correspondence, Hill to Bullough, 7 Jan. 1912 (sic); see also the debate in *BJG* (23 Jan. 1914), 12; (30 Jan. 1914), 10; (6 Feb. 1914), 9.

[86] JRUL BCA/12/5/2 BSA, Joint Meeting Negotiations, local joint meeting, 4 Feb. 1929; Jewkes and Gray, *Wages and Labour*, 189.

[87] BA, FT/8/2/8 BSA, Rules and Regulations for the Government of Minders Employed at Robin Hood No. 1 Mill, cl. 2; FT/8/2/9 BSA, Barton Bridge Shop Club Rules, cl. 9; FT/21/11 BSA, Annual Report for 1929, 35; *BJG* (25 Nov. 1927), 11.

[88] JRUL, BCA/12/5/2 BSA, Joint Meeting Negotiations, local joint meetings, 11 Feb. 1929, 21 Nov. 1932, *BJG* (2 Dec. 1932), 8.

the practice of minders being made responsible for the conduct and wages of their piecers, at the same time holding the minder entirely responsible for the proper care of his machinery, and for more or less efficient and ample results.'[89] Continuity in this regard owed as much to managerial compliance as it did to the minders' bargaining power.

This finding would appear to call into question the view, propounded most forcefully for the cotton industry by William Lazonick, that technological continuity was primarily a consequence of institutional constraints. By this argument, the trade's nineteenth-century inheritance of vertical specialization and subcontracted authority within the workplace generated a system of labour relations which tied managements in to less productive and increasingly uncompetitive technologies.[90] Yet the reforms sought by employers through the period do not suggest that work practices were seen as an important obstacle to economic success. Rather, they provided a means of addressing a more specific problem: the developing shortage of new recruits to the mill. The absence of more radical initiatives might be taken as evidence of complicity between managements and unions to ensure the continued use of labour-intensive production techniques, a tendency noted in other sectors.[91] Even this, however, overlooks the solid grounding for continued confidence in the mule's commercial viability. At least until 1914, levels of profitability remained as high for firms using mules as for those employing more productive ring frames.[92] Although market conditions were to alter dramatically after 1918, Lancashire's commitment to existing technologies remained undiminished. A meeting of the Oldham Mill Managers' Association in 1924 readily agreed that, in spinning, the county was some fifty years in advance of its competitors.[93] Such confidence was not merely a product of blind faith. It reflected a firm belief that market trends after the war would work decisively in Lancashire's favour, a view endorsed by the report of the Departmental Committee appointed by the Board of Trade to consider the position of the textile trades in the post-war

    [89] *BJG* (6 Oct. 1911), 9.

    [90] Lazonick, 'Industrial Organization and Technological Change', 205–10; id., 'Industrial Relations and Technological Change: The Case of the Self-Acting Mule', *Cambridge Journal of Economics*, 3 (1979), 245–50; id., 'The Cotton Industry', in Elbaum and Lazonick (eds.), *The Decline of the British Economy* (Oxford, 1986), 21–7.

    [91] Lazonick, 'Employment Relations', 90–116.

    [92] J. S. Toms, 'The Financial Performance of the Lancashire Cotton Industry, 1880–1914', in I. Blanchard (ed.), *New Directions in Economic and Social History* (Newlees Farm, Avonbridge, 1995), 29–36.

    [93] *BJG* (22 Feb. 1924), 11; see also, *TW* 3 (21 June 1929), 404.

world. From the perspective of 1918, an erosion of Lancashire's share of the market for staple qualities of cloth was considered inevitable as low-wage Japanese and more especially native Indian production continued to expand. Elsewhere, however, developments would, it was argued, work in Lancashire's favour. A growing demand for fine cloths was anticipated as greater prosperity extended to developing markets, such as Latin America, Africa, and China. The optimal response to such trends lay in a differentiated rather than a standardized product, mobilizing native advantages in 'climate, labour, and machinery'. A vertically specialized industry, structured around the mule and the Lancashire loom, appeared best placed to respond effectively to changing circumstances. Although the need for greater efficiency was emphasized, the committee did not see work practices as a significant barrier to progress. Reference was made to the constraints imposed by apprenticeship agreements in the card-room, but mule spinning was exempted from criticism. The existing pattern of labour relations was seen to heighten rather than to weaken competitiveness.[94]

In many respects, the committee's findings reflected practices across the industry. The process of product diversification was pursued by American-cotton spinners, who tended increasingly to utilize a mixture of fibres, including finer Egyptian cottons. In 1905, 30 per cent of Oldham firms for which detailed entries appeared in *Worrall's Cotton Spinners' and Manufacturers' Directory*, made some use of Egyptian cottons. By 1929, that proportion had risen to 43 per cent of a slightly larger sample. The change in practice required that existing wage lists be revised. In 1907, allowances were incorporated into the Oldham List to compensate for the slower speeds necessitated by working finer fibres.[95]

An insistent threat to the quest for diversity in output was posed by problems of raw material supplies. Over time, increasing levels of consumption in the United States endangered Lancashire's dependence on the American crop. Supply constraints were such that years of peak activity, such as following the revival in trade after 1911, witnessed a proliferation in complaints about inferior cotton. The desire to achieve a higher quality of output from often inferior inputs justified continued use of 'low throughput' technology and ensured that skilled labour in both card- and

---

[94] *Parl. Papers 1918*, xiii (9070), Report of the Departmental Committee Appointed by the Board of Trade to Consider the Position of the Textile Trades After the War, 10–17, 49–61.

[95] *Worrall's Directory* (Oldham, 1905 and 1929 edns.); *BJG* (6 Dec. 1907), 16; LRO, DDBx 13/1 Barber-Lomax Reference Collection, Croal Spinning Co., Ltd, scrapbook, cutting from *Manchester Courier*.

mule-rooms remained the most effective guarantor of product quality, by enabling a greater variety of counts to be manufactured from existing plant.[96]

In practice, political and economic developments after 1918 disappointed hopes of a widening market for fine cottons. For most of the period under review here, however, the world context justified an approach which saw manual skill as an essential component of economic success. Mechanization worked, in the case of the minder, to confirm and, in that of the grinder, to establish the privileged status of labour within the work process. The outcome was less the diminution of differentials than their confirmation and consolidation. If anything, therefore, the work experience within Lancashire spinning mills in the period 1880–1939 became more rather than less diverse. Before turning to address the broader implications of such differences, it remains to establish how far conditions underground resembled or diverged from those described here.

III

Colliery work lacked the inequalities of income and status which figured so prominently in carding and spinning departments. Different grades described stages in a unitary career pattern. Initial experience underground was gained close to the winding shaft, loading and unloading tubs. From that point, progress could be measured by the distance travelled along the haulage roads. Up to the age of 17, boys assisted in haulage operations, before moving on to drawing. Working in an ancillary capacity to hewers (or colliers), drawers helped to fill tubs, acquiring, in the process, direct experience of work at the coal face. Most would complete the transition to hewing between the ages of 22 and 27. An average career of thirty years at the face would follow, before a gradual retreat commenced back along the haulage roads into repair or 'datal' work.[97] It was a pattern replicated, with only minor variations, in most

---

[96] PEP Industries Group, *Report on the British Cotton Industry* (1934), 10; *TW* 2 (28 Sept. 1928), 91; (25 Jan. 1929), 596; the average number of complaints of 'bad spinning' heard by the Bolton Spinners' executive increased from 14 a year in 1908–10 to 39 in each of the following three years, JRUL, BCA/1/3/8–10 BSA, Minutes, 1908–14; Lazonick, 'The Cotton Industry', 22–7.

[97] *Parl. Papers 1907*, xv (3505) Final Report of the Departmental Committee Appointed to Inquire into the Probable Economic Effect of a Limit of Eight Hours to the Working Day of Coal Miners. Part I. Report and Appendices, 45; H. F. Bulman and Sir R. A. S. Redmayne, *Colliery Working and Management* (1923), 113; the career outline presented here reflects the age structure of victims of the explosion at the Hulton Colliery Co., Ltd's

coalfields, and operated without the promotional bottlenecks observed in the cotton trade. Any complaints arising in this period from delayed promotion were sporadic and localized, such as the resolution from union branches in Burnley which, in 1922, made reference to men employed on drawing beyond the age of 30.[98]

Such complaints aside, the haulage road was never, in occupational terms, a 'blind alley'. In part, this reflected the ease of transition from one mining grade to the next. For most of the period, extractive activity was confined to one 'getting' shift. The distribution of labour on this shift can be reconstructed with some precision from the fatalities which arose from the explosion at the Pretoria Pit in December 1910. These comprised all but one of those employed in the Yard Mine ('Mine' in Lancastrian 'pit talk' denoted the individual seam being worked). The victims included thirty-two haulage hands, sixty-three drawers, and 176 colliers.[99] That this was a broadly representative picture is indicated by aggregate Census figures. In 1911, between 66 and 76 per cent of male colliery workers in the county boroughs of Wigan and Bolton were aged 25 or over. The proportion in Bolton spinning rooms, by contrast, was only 40 per cent.[100] Such differences carried over into individual work-team structures. Rather than the predominance of ancillary grades, observed in the mulegate, the coal face was worked by teams comprising two or three hewers to one drawer. As on the mule, employers were responsible for team payments only. Individual shares were apportioned at the colliers' discretion. Drawers received either fixed time rates or, as was increasingly common, a set proportion of the team's piece-rate earnings.[101] Compensation

---

No. 3 Bank Pit, near Westhoughton, in Dec. 1910, for which see *Parl. Papers 1911*, xxxvi (5676–IV), Mines and Quarries. Reports of HM Inspector of Mines for the Manchester and Ireland District (No. 5) for the year 1910, 28–9.

[98] M. J. Daunton, 'Down the Pit: Work in the Great Northern and South Wales Coalfields, 1870–1914', *Econ.Hist.Rev.*, 2nd ser., 34 (1981), 590; Lancashire and Cheshire Miners' Federation (LCMF), monthly conference minutes, 14 Oct. 1922.

[99] *Parl. Papers 1907*, xv (3506), Eight Hours Committee. Final Report. Part II. Minutes of Evidence, qq. 10119, 10186; appendix 36, no. 1, p. 311; *BEN* (23 Dec. 1910), 4; *The Times* (23 Dec. 1910), 7; *Parl. Papers 1911*, xxxvi (5676–IV), Report of Inspector of Mines for Manchester and Ireland District, 28–9.

[100] *Parl. Papers 1913*, lxxix (7019), Census of England and Wales, 1911. X. Occupations and Industries. Part II, table 13, pp. 216–17, 222.

[101] BA, BOHP, 92 (male, born 1903), transcript, 1, 5; 108A (male, born 1917), tape; LCMF, joint committee minutes, 20 Aug. 1923; *Parl. Papers 1907*, xv (3428), Eight Hours Committee. First Report. Pt. III. Minutes of Evidence, qq. 483, 487; C. Forman, *Industrial Town: Self Portrait of St Helens in the 1920s* (St Albans, 1979), 3–4.

returns suggest that, at the Pretoria, this guaranteed drawers between 26 and 36 per cent of the whole. With the remainder divided between two adults, no individual would command the two-thirds' share which accrued to minders. Beyond the haulage, wage differentials were slight. Average weekly earnings at the Pretoria during the three years 1908–10 varied from 10s. 5d. for haulage hands, to 25s. 8d. for drawers, and 29s. for hewers below the age of 25.[102] The drawers' position was further underpinned by the minumum wage scale for boys agreed in 1911. Assuming an average of eleven shifts worked each fortnight, this guaranteed weekly rates of 10s. 1d. at the age of 14, rising to 27s. 6d. at 21.[103]

Trends over time offered a further point of contrast with the mill, the tendency being for differentials to narrow rather than to widen. The introduction of minumum pay scales initiated the process. Furthermore, in 1917 and 1918, flat-rate 'war wage' payments were introduced with the explicit intention of assisting lower paid workers, who were thought to stand 'in equal or greater need of the advance than the coal hewers'.[104] The result was that, by July 1920, surface rates, according to estimates prepared by the Lancashire and Cheshire Miners' Federation, had increased by 181 per cent since 1914, compared with a gain of only 100 per cent for colliers, who were now 'the bottom dog', in the words of one Federation delegate. Wholesale food prices, in the interim, had risen by 166 per cent.[105] In subsequent years, differentials were further squeezed. On the eve of de-control in March 1921, shift rates across the county varied from 13s. 4d. to 15s. 9d. for drawers and from 16s. 5d. to 18s. 1d. for hewers. From that point, a combination of limited profitability and short-time working ensured that a large and growing portion of the mining workforce became subject to statutory minimum rates of pay. Even in 1920, this had applied to 30 per cent of hewers across the county. By the middle of the decade, minimum rates were being paid to a majority of the workforce at certain collieries. Three-quarters of the hewers at the Jubilee Pit, St Helens, received the minimum in 1925.[106]

---

[102] J. Rowe, *Wages in the Coal Industry* (1923), 72–3; Pretoria figures calculated from LRO, Coal Board Records NCHu 9/2 Hulton Colliery Co., Ltd, Transcript of an Adjourned Inquest at Carnegie Hall, Westhoughton, Jan. 1911, qq. 2211, 2491–2, 2848; BA, HRF ABHC/5/1–344 Personal Files, Compensation statements.

[103] LCMF, agreement at joint meeting at Queen's Hotel, Manchester, 17 Oct. 1911.

[104] Sir R. A. S. Redmayne, *The British Coal-Mining Industry during the War* (Oxford, 1923), 181; LCMF, monthly conference minutes, 22 Sept. 1917.

[105] LCMF, special conference minutes, 2 July 1920; A. L. Bowley, *Prices and Wages in the United Kingdom, 1914–20* (Oxford, 1921), 19–21.

[106] LRO, Coal Board Records NCLc 1/10 Lancashire and Cheshire Coal Association, Joint District Wages Board, Correspondence, 2 Nov. 1921; LCMF, statistics on wages and

If greater equality of incomes distinguished pit from mill work, a further point of contrast, at least in the view of colliery owners, lay in the effectiveness of managerial discipline. Successive inquiries through the period heard complaints about the capacity and readiness of miners to flout employers' controls. The position was summarized in a succinct, if exaggerated, manner by the Wigan colliery director, George Caldwell, in evidence to the Royal Commission on Labour: 'we cannot control them, we have no power to control them . . . they are masters of the situation entirely'.[107] Material presented to the Departmental Committee into the Eight Hour Day added substance to this assertion. In contrast, it was claimed, to factory workers, who were tied to the rhythms of the machine, miners enjoyed much greater discretion over the hours and pace at which they worked in often remote places, upwards of 2 miles from the bottom of the shaft. The sanctions available in the mill, where, as one mining engineer expressed it, 'you can go and shout and make everybody go', were lacking underground.[108]

Further evidence of the relative balance of power within Lancashire's collieries was found in unusually high rates of absenteeism, unmatched elsewhere in Britain and more than double those encountered in south Wales. A detailed breakdown of daily attendances in 1924, collated by the Lancashire and Cheshire Coal Association, indicated the extent of the problem. Over the course of the working week, 'avoidable' absenteeism, excluding cases attributable to illness or accidents, varied between 12.3 per cent on Saturdays and 4.8 per cent on Fridays. These figures were liable to increase in periods of full-time working. High levels of activity during 1915 thus raised average absenteeism rates across the county to 17 per cent. Various explanations were offered for the persistence of this problem, including the limited material and cultural expectations which sustained notions of a 'customary wage' and high leisure preference among miners. The latter was also linked to the diversions offered in large urban centres close to many pits.[109] Yet, as many acknowledged, absenteeism reflected more than the wilful pursuit of independence; it also

prices, May 1924; special conference minutes, 2 July 1920; EC minutes, 26 Dec. 1925; *LG* 36 (1928), 352.

[107] *Parl. Papers 1892*, xxxiv (6708–IV), RC on Labour: Minutes of Evidence before Group 'A', i. Mining, q. 6064.

[108] *Parl. Papers 1907*, xv (3428), Eight Hours Committee. First Report. Pt. III. Minutes of Evidence, qq. 5157, 6460; (3506), Eight Hours Committee. Final Report. Pt. II. Minutes of Evidence, q. 13384.

[109] *Parl. Papers 1907*, xv (3506), Eight Hours Committee. Final Report. Pt. II. Minutes of Evidence, q. 16362; (3505), Pt. I. Reports and Appendices, 17; *Parl. Papers 1914–16*, xxviii

pointed up the particular conditions encountered in mining coal across the county.

Three features attracted comment. First, Lancashire's coal was won at unusual depths. Setting aside Pendleton Colliery, west of Manchester, thought to be the deepest pit in the world in 1925, workings at the centre of the field typically extended over 600 yards down to the lower 'cannel' seam. The temperatures encountered at such depths were high, a difficulty compounded by the second distinguishing feature, the sharp inclines and frequent faults on many seams. The third and perhaps most important complication was provided by the intensive nature of mining operations. Fragmented patterns of landholding obliged many companies to maximize returns by working several measures simultaneously. At the Pretoria, for example, five seams were worked at depths ranging from 146 to 434 yards. The geological pressures created by working in such close proximity increased the potential for accidents through falls of ground.[110] The particular combination of heat and difficult and unpredictable strata may have persuaded many miners to take time off work so as to avoid physical exhaustion and so forestall any more extended loss of earnings.

These conditions also helped to determine the precise division of responsibilities underground. Instabilities in both roof and floor meant that repair work could not be left to a separate shift, as was the case in County Durham. Hewers undertook all facets of production, including the 'dead work' essential for the maintenance of each workplace.[111] In effect, owners had no choice but to delegate full responsibility to colliers, who, over time, acquired a close familiarity with the properties of each workplace and so were best placed to judge the extent of cutting, 'spragging' (setting supports under the seam), and repair work required. Nevertheless, the recurrence of falls of ground, which

(8009), Report of the Departmental Committee Appointed to Inquire into the Conditions Prevailing in the Coal Mining Industry due to the War. Pt. II. Minutes of Evidence, q. 2130; LRO, Coal Board Records NCWi 7/3 Wigan Coal and Iron Co., Ltd, Clock Face Colliery, monthly reports, May 1924.

[110] LCMF, monthly conference minutes, 7 Nov. 1925; *WO* (22 Aug. 1908), 9; *Reports of HM Inspectors of Mines for 1923* (HMSO, 1924), 'Lancashire and North Wales Division', 16–17; *Parl. Papers 1907*, xv (3428), Eight Hours Committee. First Report. Pt. III. Minutes of Evidence, q. 6615; *Parl. Papers 1911*, xxii (5692), Home Office: Reports on the Explosion which occurred at the No. 3 Bank Pit, Hulton Colliery, on the 21st December, 1910, 3.

[111] Daunton, 'Down the Pit', 584; *Parl. Papers 1908*, xix (4045–VI), Report of HM Inspector of Mines for Liverpool and North Wales District, 16; *Parl. Papers 1907*, xv (3428), Eight Hours Committee: First Report. Pt. III. Minutes of Evidence, qq. 7270–1.

accounted in 1922 for 60 per cent of all fatal and 70 per cent of reportable non-fatal accidents, suggested to many, including the Mines Inspectorate, that 'Too much is frequently left to the discretion of the collier'.[112]

The supervision necessary to hold such independence in check was exercised by firemen, a group recruited from within the workforce which was responsible for both safety and output levels. The effectiveness of their control was, however, qualified by a combination of physical obstacles, low numbers, and poor labour relations. The size of district overseen by each fireman was sufficient to prevent close supervision of operations at the face. At Altham Colliery, near Accrington, in 1907, eight firemen oversaw a workforce of 500, while at the Pretoria each official supervised an average of fifty-seven miners. The imbalance was such that each place would only be inspected an average of twice in each shift, a practice which became a minimum statutory requirement from 1911.[113] Distrust of firemen further impeded their authority. Among miners, the belief persisted that, in pursuit of the seemingly irreconcilable goals of profitability and safety, priority would always be given to the former. Such was the view expressed by Herbert Smith and Robert Smillie of the Miners' Federation of Great Britain during the first stage of the Sankey Commission's investigations in 1919.[114] As a result, owners encountered difficulty in recruiting new firemen. At the Pretoria, attempts to encourage applications from hewers had failed, forcing management to appoint younger datal hands. These included Isaac Ratcliffe, aged 23, whose background, in the opinion of the general manager, A. J. Tonge, made up for his lack of direct experience of face work. As Tonge explained to the Pretoria disaster inquest, 'I don't think he had ever been a collier, but he was the son of a fireman, he had attended mining classes and he had asked me years before I appointed him if I would allow him to become a fireman.'[115] The recruitment of mining novitiates ensured that disciplinary controls at the coal face were, at

---

[112] *Reports of HM Inspectors of Mines for 1922* (HMSO, 1923), 'Lancashire and North Wales Division', 31; H. S. Jevons, *The British Coal Trade* (1915), 520–1.

[113] *Parl. Papers 1907*, xv (3506), Eight Hours Committee: Final Report. Pt. II. Minutes of Evidence, q. 13598; *Parl. Papers 1911*, xxii (5692), Report on Hulton Colliery Explosion, 13; *Parl. Papers 1914*, xliii (7439–III), Report of HM Inspector of Mines for Manchester and Ireland District, 14.

[114] *Parl. Papers 1919*, xi (359), Coal Industry Commission. I. Interim Reports and Minutes of Evidence, q. 5036.

[115] LRO, Coal Board Records NCHu 9/1 Hulton Colliery, Inquest transcript, q. 1073.

best, permissive. The reluctance of young officials to confront face workers was noted by the Mines Inspectorate in 1930.[116]

In such circumstances, piece-rate payments became the principal
instrument of managerial control. Separate rates were established for
every district within the pit, so as to reflect their geological peculiarities.
The productive potential of each district was assessed as places were
opened out. At this stage, payments were made by the day. The final
tonnage rate emerged from a bargaining process which sought to balance
management's concern to guard against 'ca' canny' tactics with the miners' desire to guarantee an adequate income without undue expenditure
of effort ('a fair day's pay for a fair day's work'). The means by which
negotiations were conducted are suggested by the following report, sub-
mitted in 1925 to employers at the Clock Face Colliery, St Helens, by
officials in the pit's Yard Mine: 'the men do not appear to be as keen to
send coal as they have been. It is probably a "try on" to get a higher tonnage rate. The Miners' Agent asked me to meet a deputation, and asked
the ridiculous price of 5s. 10d. a ton. The men have obtained very good
wages at 3s. 11d.'[117]

Particularly difficult conditions often precluded payment by the piece.
Where this applied, receipt of wages was made conditional on regular and
high levels of attendance. The statutory minimum rates fixed in 1912 thus
stipulated that miners attend 80 per cent of shifts over two consecutive
weeks in order to qualify. Similar conditions attached to subsistence
allowances, introduced from 1922 to supplement low wages and to guarantee minimum shift earnings of 6s. 9d. In the following year, allowances
were denied eighty-seven miners at Ellerbeck Colliery, Coppull, due to
absenteeism.[118] The scope for such action widened over time as a larger
proportion of the workforce became dependent on such supplements.
The wage mechanism thus remained the employers' primary disciplinary
resource.

A further potential sanction lay in the allocation of workplaces. Save
for isolated exceptions, such as at the Cronton Pit, near Prescot, where
dispositions were settled by joint committee, there was no equivalent in

[116] *Reports of HM Inspectors of Mines for 1930* (HMSO, 1931), 'North West Division', 11;
LRO, Coal Board Records NCEv 14/1 Richard Evans and Co., Ltd. Inquiry into the cause
of an Explosion at Lyme Colliery, Haydock, Apr. 1930, qq. 328–30, 678.

[117] LRO, Coal Board Records NCWi 7/4 Wigan Coal and Iron Co., Ltd., Clock Face
Colliery, monthly reports, Jan. 1925; see also Jevons, *British Coal Trade*, 332, 338–46.

[118] *LG* 20 (1912), 217; LCMF, Joint District Board minutes, 12 July 1922; EC minutes, 13
Jan. 1923.

Lancashire of the north-eastern practice of determining places by lot, or 'cavilling'.[119] The scope for managerial action was wide, a fact reflected in sporadic protests to the LCMF executive. In 1913, a dispute at Astley and Tyldesley Collieries concerned 'men being removed from one working place to another', resulting in victimization of, among others, the local branch secretary, while at Nordern Colliery in 1925, seventeen miners were transferred to soft-coal districts at reduced rates of pay.[120] Complaints increased following the end of the 1926 stoppage. Settlement terms, which required that each miner be allowed back to his former workplace, were, on occasion, ignored. Two hewers at Hindley Field, near Wigan, were allotted four different places in quick succession, before being dismissed for poor levels of production. The most concerted exercise of managerial authority occurred at the Abram Coal Co., Ltd, where, as part of a sustained offensive against Federation organization, the branch president and secretary were assigned unproductive places and miners active in LCMF recruitment campaigns were dismissed.[121] In this, however, Abram was exceptional. Federation minutes recorded few instances in which authority was exercised in such an arbitrary fashion. As a disciplinary weapon, workplace allocation remained largely hypothetical.

Managerial reticence on this point reflected, in part, the existence of significant constraints on the effective imposition of controls underground. In particular, the availability of alternative sources of work, either in neighbouring pits or in other local industries, compromised the ability of owners to determine the pace and pattern of colliery development. In 1921, second getting shifts were introduced at a number of pits across the county, in an attempt to boost output as activity resumed following the national stoppage. However, the disruption to routine which this involved, along with an established antipathy to work sharing, ensured that second turns remained short staffed. As a result, the experiment was quickly abandoned.[122] Even on single shifts, it often proved difficult to recruit labour to work in less productive districts. In order to

[119] LCMF, EC minutes, 17 May 1924; Daunton, 'Down the Pit', 585–6; Douglass, 'The Durham Pitman', 229–31.

[120] T. Ashton, *Three Big Strikes in the Coal Industry*, pt. III (Manchester, n.d.), 34; LCMF, EC minutes, 21 Feb. 1925.

[121] LCMF, special conference minutes, 25 Nov. 1926; monthly conference minutes, 7 Nov. 1925; EC minutes, 31 Dec. 1926, 20 Aug., 12 Nov. and 24 Dec. 1927.

[122] LCMF, EC minutes, 16 July 1921, 26 July 1924, 23 Jan. 1926. Hostility to the two-turn system is noted in *Parl. Papers 1907*, xv (3506), Eight Hours Committee: Final Report. Pt. II. Minutes of Evidence, q. 10119.

ensure that such places were filled, therefore, additional payments were offered. Inducements also guarded against the loss of hands to other works nearby. In February 1924, officials at the Wigan Coal and Iron Co., Ltd's Clock Face Colliery, were prepared to pay haulage hands in excess of list rates to ensure that sufficient numbers were retained.[123] Control over pit development was never absolute.

If labour deployments were rarely a prominent facet of discipline underground, they still had important implications for the work experience. Datallers' responsibility for repair work ensured them a peripatetic existence. One widow recalled, in evidence to the Pretoria Inquest, that her husband had 'had to go to any place he was sent, and he never had a place of his own'.[124] Even for colliers, continuity in work could not be guaranteed. Geological difficulties, caused by faults or gas emissions, could interrupt work and, in extreme cases, render places unviable. In 1910, labour was reallocated when gas halted operations in the Pretoria's Top Yard District. Evidence presented to the disaster inquest in January 1911 indicated that many victims had occupied their places for only a few months prior to the explosion. On occasion, enforced mobility led to the break-up of work teams. Samuel and Henry Cowburn, respectively father and son, had worked as part of a team at the Pretoria for two years to 1910, but were separated once their place was exhausted.[125] Over time, such changes were likely to recur. This had two important consequences. First, it compromised a central element in the collier's 'skilled' status, his knowledge of local conditions. Miners repeatedly engaged in a relearning process as they acquired a familiarity with their new surroundings. Second, mobility denied colliers that identification with their workplace which minders and grinders enjoyed in the mill. So, despite exercising a degree of autonomy at the end of lengthy haulage roads, hewers were rarely truly 'independent'. Even their control over the pace of work was compromised at several points. Piece-rate payments were fixed so as to secure continuity of effort, while management also controlled vital ancillary services which helped determine the productive potential of each place. The supply of tubs and the maintenance of tools

[123] LRO, Coal Board Records NCWi 7/3 Wigan Coal and Iron Co., Ltd., Clock Face Colliery, monthly reports, Feb. 1924; see also Oct. 1924, for the need to compensate men for working in wet conditions.

[124] LRO, Coal Board Records NCHu 9/2 Hulton Colliery, Inquest transcript, q. 2878; see also NCHu 9/3, q. 3982.

[125] *Parl. Papers 1911*, xxii (5692), Report on Hulton Colliery Explosion, 14; LRO, Coal Board Records NCHu 9/2 Hulton Colliery, Inquest transcript, qq. 2054, 2141–8, 2283, 2551–2, 2764–5; LCMF, EC minutes, 28 Feb. 1920.

were, in most cases, company responsibilities.[126] The complaints of inadequate discipline which Lancastrian witnesses offered to official inquiries thus presented a heightened version of reality. Potential sources of control existed, but that most frequently employed was also the most indirect. Piece-rate payments allowed colliers to determine, within limits, the pace and intensity of their work. That certain aspects of mining operations remained subject to the colliers' discretion was a point which employers appeared willing to countenance.

Technological change challenged this balance of interests. In the first decade of the twentieth century, over 90 per cent of coal cut in Lancashire was won by hand. Thereafter, if the progress of mechanization was slow, its cumulative effect was marked. By 1930, machinery accounted for over a quarter of district output.[127] A fundamental restructuring of work practices was anticipated from the adoption of mechanical cutting, involving, as David Greasley puts it, 'the introduction of "factory type" production at the coalface . . . the replacement of unspecialized, small scale and largely unsupervised working with concentrated operations characterized by a high division of labour and close supervision'.[128] The rhythm of the working day would also, it was thought, undergo a fundamental transformation. With undercutting and filling being carried out in separate shifts, activity would, as W. J. Charlton, the Mines Inspector for the North Western Division, argued in 1930, no longer centre on the day shift. Instead, the majority of miners would be employed on afternoon or night turns.[129] Yet by the end of this period, expectations of radical change had still to be realized. Mechanization had wrought no fundamental alteration in working practices or in the approaches of employers or miners.

In part, such continuities arose from the gradual and piecemeal adoption of machine technology. Although, in terms of the total output cut by

---

[126] On the 'independent collier', see R. Harrison, 'Introduction', in id. (ed.), *Independent Collier: The Coal Miner as Archetypal Proletarian Reconsidered* (Hassocks, 1978), 4; A. B. Campbell, *The Lanarkshire Miners: A Social History of their Trade Unions, 1775–1874* (Edinburgh, 1979), 26–48; A. J. Taylor, 'The Wigan Coalfield in 1851', *Transactions of the Historic Society of Lancashire and Cheshire* (*THSLC*), 106 (1954), 118–19; *Parl. Papers 1908*, lix (4443), Departmental Committee on the Truck Acts. II. Minutes of Evidence, qq. 7491–7500, 7506, 7934.

[127] *Parl. Papers 1908*, xix (4045–V), Report of HM Inspector of Mines for Manchester and Ireland District, 6–7; (4045–VI), Report for Liverpool and North Wales District, 8; Board of Trade, *An Industrial Survey of the Lancashire Area*, 176.

[128] D. G. Greasley, 'The Diffusion of a Technology: The Case of Machine Coal Cutting in Great Britain, 1900–38' (Liverpool Univ. Ph.D. thesis, 1979), 36–7.

[129] Mines Dept., *Reports of HM Inspectors of Mines for 1930*, W. J. Charlton, 'North Western Division' (HMSO, 1931), 12–13.

machine, Lancashire was in step with national trends, this tends to overstate the extent of innovation across the county. Between 1907 and 1930,
district output almost halved. As a result, the 26 per cent of output that
was machine cut in 1930 represented only 14.7 per cent of 1907 levels.
Equally, in productivity terms, Lancashire failed to match even the modest gains made elsewhere. Whereas, across Britain, the annual average
tonnage cut per machine rose from 7,800 in 1914 to 8,200 in 1927, in
Lancashire, over a slightly longer period, the figure fell from 5,600 to
4,300. In part, this decline reflected the impact of short-time working.
Over the same period, the average number of days worked each week fell
from 5.4 to 4.2.[130] However, the county's modest performance can also be
explained by the fact that most of the additional 800 cutters employed
between 1907 and 1928 were of limited size and capacity. Many were per-
cussive in action and powered by compressed air. Although accounting for
60 per cent of cutters employed in the Lancashire and North Wales
Division in the latter year, such machines were responsible for only 23 per
cent of the tonnage raised.[131]

Even where new techniques were adopted, the impact on work practices was slight. Cutters were rarely utilized as part of a fully mechanized production sequence. While 111 pits in Lancashire and North
Wales had installed machine cutters by 1928, only thirty-five employed
powered conveyors to carry coal to the haulage roads. The tonnage carried on conveyors in that year (2.18 million) was only half that mined by
machinery (4.34 million).[132] Cutters were more likely to be applied in
individual districts within the pit. They operated on two of the seven
faces in the Pretoria's Yard Mine in 1910. At most collieries, therefore,
hand and machine cutting coexisted.[133] Established work structures carried over from the one to the other. Machines were operated by small
work-teams, responsible for their stretch of face. Teams of three worked
cutters at Lyme Colliery, Haydock, in 1930. As on hand-cut faces, super-

---

[130] National output figures calculated from B. Supple, *The History of the British Coal
Industry*. iv. *1913–1946: The Political Economy of Decline* (Oxford, 1987), 380; the Lancashire
figures refer to 1913 and 1928 and are calculated from *Reports of HM Inspectors of Mines* for
the relevant years; *LG* 21–2 (1913–14); 35–6 (1927–8).

[131] Greasley, thesis, table 3.20; Mines Dept., *Reports of HM Inspectors of Mines for 1928*
(HMSO, 1929), A. D. Nicholson, 'Lancashire and North Wales Division', 6–7.

[132] Mines Dept., *Reports of HM Inspectors of Mines for 1928*, 'Lancashire and North Wales
Division', 6–7.

[133] *Parl. Papers 1911*, xxii (5692), Report on Hulton Colliery Explosion, 3, 11; LCMF,
Joint District Board minutes, 10 Jan. 1919; EC minutes, 2 May 1925, noting hand and
machine price lists at Worsley Mesnes Colliery, Wigan.

vision was exercised by firemen, two of whom oversaw operations on the Lyme Pit's afternoon shift.[134] This example has further importance. Lyme Pit had been sunk in 1924. Continuity in work practices thus applied on new as well as on older colliery layouts. The constraints on development posed by established workings were, in this instance, limited. Overall, therefore, contemporary expectations of the intensification of control underground were not borne out in practice.

Limited managerial expectations help to explain this outcome. George Macalpine, proprietor of Altham Colliery, near Accrington, expressed scepticism as to the value of machinery on soft-coal seams, where the coal was liable to fragment into small, unmarketable pieces. Later work has tended to confirm that a significant cost advantage, along with an improved quality of output, was only likely on thin seams of hard coal. Greasley's estimates suggest a 30 per cent saving in such conditions and even that was conditional on the absence of the kind of severe faulting encountered in Lancashire.[135] Employers thus anticipated only marginal gains in efficiency from the application of machine technology at the face. The potential for more significant savings was identified elsewhere. Evidence to official inquiries by, among others, Alfred Hewlett, managing director of the Wigan Coal and Iron Co., Ltd, and George Bramall, who held the equivalent post in the Manchester firm of Andrew Knowles and Son, pointed to deficiencies in haulage and winding capacities.[136] The scale of investment required to effect such improvements presented an enduring constraint on action, more especially in a period of low and declining profitability.

As technological innovation appeared to offer such questionable benefits, managements readily embraced an option which was both less costly and which promised greater certainty of return. Moves to contain competitive pressures through co-operative marketing and production agreements, widely adopted by British industry between the wars, held out

[134] LRO, Coal Board Records NCEv 14/1 Richard Evans and Co., Ltd., Inquiry into the Cause of an Explosion at Lyme Colliery, Haydock, 1930, duplicated transcripts of solicitor's notes, qq. 203–7; NCEv 14/2, qq. 2570–2; *Parl. Papers 1930–1*, xv (3698), Mines Department: Report on the Causes of and Circumstances attending the Explosion which occurred at the Lyme Colliery, Haydock, on the 26th February, 1930, 6.

[135] Greasley, thesis, p. 53; *Parl. Papers 1907*, xv (3506), Eight Hours Committee: Final Report. Pt. II. Minutes of Evidence, qq. 10287–8, 13606; *Parl. Papers 1914–16*, xxviii (8009), Coal Mining Industry in Wartime, Pt. II. Minutes of Evidence, q. 2130.

[136] *Parl. Papers 1907*, xv (3428), Eight Hours Committee. First Report. Pt. III. Minutes of Evidence, qq. 6487, 7298–7301, 7375; (3506), Final Report. Pt. II. Minutes of Evidence, q. 13438.

particular attractions for Lancastrian colliery owners. For many decades, local markets had been subject to incursions by producers in neighbouring fields. National control during the Great War had alleviated the threat of competition and so helped to check Lancashire's comparative decline.[137] The experience of those years encouraged owners to welcome with enthusiasm the Samuel Commission's proposals for rationalization in 1926. By 1930, a series of voluntary amalgamations had produced two combines, Manchester Collieries Ltd and the Wigan Coal Corporation, responsible between them for 37 per cent of district output. At the same time, the position of individual concerns was guaranteed by a system of production quotas operated by the Central Collieries Commercial Association, an arrangement given statutory force by the Coal Mines Act of 1930.[138] Commercial collusion rather than the detailed revision of work practices remained the favoured approach of management for much of this period.

Even where it was adopted, mechanization rarely provoked concerted labour resistance, even though *The Times Engineering Supplement* in 1920 detected widespread distrust of innovation, largely due to the redundancies which were thought likely to ensue.[139] Opposition, where encountered, was motivated by more particular concerns. The installation of electrically powered machinery at the Pretoria gave rise to fears over safety. The view of one miner, expressed before the disaster inquest, gained wider currency: 'they were no fit things to be down yon place and if they happened to spark it would cause an explosion'. Although no evidence could be found linking machinery to the explosion, the conviction remained, given voice in the MFGB's report on the disaster produced in 1911, that safety considerations had been subordinated to the drive for higher levels of output.[140] Significantly, however, such concerns were not

---

[137] See below, Ch. 3, pp. 84–9; on industry more generally, see J. Foreman-Peck, 'Industry and Industrial Organisation in the Inter-War Years', in Floud and McCloskey (eds.), *Economic History of Britain*, ii. 403–8; S. Bowden and D. M. Higgins, 'Short-Time Working and Price Maintenance: Collusive Tendencies in the Cotton-Spinning Industry, 1919–1939', *Econ.Hist.Rev.*, 2nd ser., 51 (1998), 319–43.

[138] *Parl. Papers 1926*, xiv (2600), Report of the Royal Commission on the Coal Industry (1925). I. Report, 60–2; *Parl. Papers 1929–30*, xvi (3454), Mines Department: Mining Industry Act, 1926. Second Report by the Board of Trade under Section 12 on the Working of Part I of the Act, 3–4; *Parl. Papers 1930–1*, xv (3743), Mines Department: Mining Industry Act, 1926. Third Report by the Board of Trade under Section 12 on the Working of Part I of the Act, 3; Board of Trade, *An Industrial Survey*, 161–2; Supple, *History of British Coal Industry*, 211.

[139] *Times Engineering Supplement* (May 1920), 155.

[140] LRO, Coal Board Records NCHu 9/2 Hulton Colliery, Inquest transcript, q. 2832; *The Times* (10 April 1911), 13.

used to block the pace of technological change at the Pretoria. New machinery continued to be installed, albeit powered by compressed air.[141] No general antipathy to mechanization was evident and few instances of outright opposition are encountered in union records. Where innovation occurred, debate centred less on the use of machinery than on 'bread-and-butter questions of pay and hours'.[142] In cases where machine rates were to be decided, union branches pressed that existing scales for drawers and hewers be utilized, to reflect the continuity in work practices which applied. At Lyme Colliery, for example, men at the cutter face remained responsible for timbering and workplace maintenance. The issue of hours was more complex. Machine cutting required greater flexibility, as the need to complete a cut often required that shifts be extended beyond their statutory limit. Yet the demand for extra hours rarely provoked discontent. An inquiry into overtime worked in Lancashire in 1934 found that miners broadly welcomed the chance to augment their earnings.[143]

It is, perhaps, telling that the Federation made no attempt to control the disposition and use of machine cutters in the manner of the grinders on the revolving flat card. Workplace allocations remained a managerial responsibility and continued to be subject to change at short notice. At the Pretoria, a dataller was employed on the cutter on a daily basis, while one collier at Lyme Pit, employed on machinery for three months, had worked with his mates for only three days prior to the explosion in 1930.[144] The owners' prerogative was only likely to be challenged when inexperienced men were allotted machine places or where, as at Blackrod Colliery, near Horwich, in 1923, non-union men were taken on.[145] Otherwise, managerial authority encountered few concerted challenges in this period.

Despite the spread of novel production techniques, payment by the piece remained the principal disciplinary tool underground. Continuity in supervisory structures and payment systems ensured that, for miners, the

---

[141] *BJG* (13 Sept. 1918), 3.   [142] Supple, *History of British Coal Industry*, 439.
[143] *Parl. Papers 1933–4*, xiv (4626), Mines Department. Coal Mines Regulation Act, 1908. Report of a Special Inquiry into the Working of Overtime in Coal Mines in Lancashire, 4–5; LRO, Coal Board Records NCEv 14/2 Richard Evans and Co., Ltd., Lyme Colliery, Inquest transcript, q. 3176; for debates on pay, see LCMF, monthly conference minutes, 16 Dec. 1916; Joint District Board minutes, 22 Oct. 1917; EC minutes, 29 Jan. 1921.
[144] LRO, Coal Board Records NCHu 9/2 Hulton Colliery, Inquest transcript, q. 2828a; NCEv 14/2 Richard Evans and Co., Ltd., Lyme Colliery, Inquest transcript, qq. 2709–10, 2773.
[145] LCMF, EC minutes, 22 June 1918; monthly conference minutes, 24 Mar. 1923.

impact of innovation was slight. To the occasional frustration of management, hewers retained limited discretion over the pace of work. They also possessed the means to challenge the status quo. Yet the form this most commonly assumed, voluntary mobility in search of better conditions, undermined a central aspect of the collier's 'craft', his familiarity with the properties of a particular place. Skill, acquired through accumulated experience of varied working conditions, remained central to the production process. However, high levels of labour turnover prevented this providing the basis for the craft identities developed in neighbouring mule- and card-rooms.

IV

Although both coal and cotton industries were subject to essays in technological innovation through this period, the work practices current in Lancashire's mines and mills in 1930 remained substantially unchanged from those of 1880. In particular, the tendency to delegate responsibility for important facets of production to groups of skilled workers persisted. In neither industry did changes in techniques occasion struggles for control within the workplace. Employers continued to acknowledge constraints to their authority, so that attempts to amend working patterns were rare and were more likely to be motivated by specific concerns over recruitment levels than by a desire to challenge the privileged status of skilled labour. For both mill- and mine-owners, skill remained an unqualified asset, ensuring both continuity and, where appropriate, quality in output. Only in the exceptional conditions of wartime were employers prepared to countenance the utilization of low-wage and low-skill labour. Far from being subdued, workplace hierarchies flourished in the period, more especially in the cotton trade, where a new labour élite emerged, capable of extending its authority from basic machine operations to levels of recruitment and promotional procedures.

A number of observations flow from this. The first and perhaps the most important for our purposes is that the interlinking sequence of social, economic, and political change described at the outset is called into question. The assumption that work became a progressively more homogeneous experience in this period appears mistaken. Differences of income and status, characteristic of British industry for much of the nineteenth century, became, if anything, more pronounced over the early decades of the twentieth. If a diminution in differentials is apparent in some industries from 1914, that trend was far from uniform. The extent to which the work experience could, of itself, provide the basis for a united sense of class may therefore be doubted. A more definitive judgement on this point requires us to adopt a broader perspective, to assess the wider social significance of work inequalities. At root is the relationship between skilled minorities and the remainder of the workforce. In traditional labour historiography, this theme is most often pursued within the institutional framework of trade unionism and formal collective bargaining procedures. It is an approach which still has much to offer those keen to explore the nature of class relationships and identities in this period. It also enables us to pursue a second point to emerge from the foregoing. The finding that work practices were rarely a cause of conflict within industry raises questions about the tenor of industrial relations more generally. In addressing those issues, some insight into the true social and political significance of the work patterns observed here may also be gained.

3
The Temper of the Times: Trade Unionism and Industrial Relations

Over the half-century from 1880, class identities appeared to find their most overt expression in the growth of trade-union organization. Associational ties, for long confined to craft minorities, came to extend to a peak of over eight million workers by 1920.[1] At the same time, a shared sense of interests within and across trades was seen to emerge from a series of large-scale industrial conflicts in the second and third decades of the twentieth century. The necessary basis for the emergence of a collective consciousness of class appeared substantially in place.[2] Against this, it may be urged that the coverage of labour organizations remained patchy, representing, at its height in this period, less than half of the total occupied workforce. Even that figure was sustained only briefly, wartime gains being all but cancelled out over the following decade and a half.[3] Nevertheless, in certain sectors, coal and cotton included, the density of union membership was such that questions concerning the role of labour organizations in promoting or containing class loyalties remain significant.

Here, the issue is pursued in two ways. The first, long a staple of labour history, considers the extent to which the temper of industrial relations gave rise to an unambiguous sense of class unity. It is an approach which appears particularly fruitful in the case of coal-mining. The miners have long enjoyed a reputation for being the most militant, because the most strike-prone, group of workers in British industry. Their standing in this regard gained substance from the succession of national disputes, involving confrontations with both employers and the state, between 1912 and 1926. The prolonged nature of these stoppages testifies to an enduring capacity for collective action, drawing on solidarities generated in the

---

[1] J. Stevenson, *British Society, 1914–45* (Harmondsworth, 1984), 195; S. Pollard, *The Development of the British Economy*, 3rd edn., *1914–1980* (1983), 43.

[2] P. Joyce, *Visions of the People* (Cambridge, 1991), 6–7.

[3] R. McKibbin, *Classes and Cultures* (Oxford, 1998), 142; Pollard, *Development,* 171. Total union membership fell from 8.3 million in 1920 to a post-war low of 4.4 million in 1933.

workplace and expressed in the world beyond the pit.[4] Recent work has encouraged a more nuanced interpretation of mining militancy, stressing the importance of local and regional variations. In the case of Lancashire, the industry's reputation for confrontation appeared well founded, poor working conditions and comparative decline providing enduring points of discord.[5] Mining militancy contrasted strongly with the conciliatory temper of relations within the cotton industry. For contemporaries, including Gerhart von Schulze-Gaevernitz, the highly developed organizations of employers and unions which emerged in the second half of the nineteenth century had worked to extirpate 'that principle of antagonism' from the trade.[6] Where they emerged, differences mostly centred on individual points of detail within complex wage lists, capable of resolution by the application of set arithmetical formulae. Among union officials, numeracy and a clear script came to be valued above rhetorical eloquence. Their administrative competence impressed many, including the Webbs, and was seen to inform a pragmatic approach to difficulty. For William Haslam Mills, chief reporter on the *Manchester Guardian*, their outlook was characterized by the kind of 'unenthusiastic common sense' which rendered them 'hardly distinguishable from a board of directors'.[7] Relations within the cotton industry were thus marked by conciliation and accommodation, rather than confrontation. It was an attitude which appeared to extend to the shopfloor, to workers who, in the words of a recent historian of the region, 'came to accept and internalise the political economy of their employers'.[8]

---

[4] D. Gilbert, 'The Geography of Strikes, 1900–39', in A. Charlesworth, D. Gilbert, A. Randall, H. Southall, and C. Wrigley, *An Atlas of Industrial Protest in Britain, 1750–1990* (Basingstoke and London, 1996), 132; on the miners' militancy more generally, see V. L. Allen, *The Militancy of British Miners* (Shipley, 1981), *passim*; K. Burgess, *The Origins of British Industrial Relations* (1975), 165–7; D. Douglass, '"Worms of the Earth": The Miners' Own Story', in R. Samuel (ed.), *People's History and Socialist Theory* (1981), 61.

[5] I. M. Zweiniger-Bargielowska, 'Miners' Militancy: A Study of Four South Wales Collieries during the Middle of the Twentieth Century', *Welsh Historical Review*, 16 (1992–3), 356–89; R. Church, Q. Outram and D. N. Smith, 'British Coal Mining Strikes, 1893–1940: Dimensions, Distribution and Persistence', *British Journal of Industrial Relations*, 28 (1990), 329–49; R. Challinor, *The Lancashire and Cheshire Miners* (Newcastle, 1972), 235.

[6] G. von Schulze-Gaevernitz, *The Cotton Trade in England and on the Continent* (1895), 142.

[7] W. Haslam Mills, *Sir Charles Macara, Bart.* (Manchester, 1917), 59–60, 77–8; N. Cardus, *Autobiography* (1947), 94–6; H. A. Clegg, A. Fox, and A. F. Thompson, *A History of British Trade Unions since 1889*. i (Oxford, 1964), 468.

[8] J. K. Walton, *Lancashire: A Social History, 1558–1939* (Manchester, 1987), 269; see also, J. L. White, 'Lancashire Cotton Textiles', in C. J. Wrigley (ed.), *A History of British Industrial Relations, 1875–1914* (Brighton, 1982), 217.

Yet the dichotomy thus far advanced proved far less straightforward in practice. In terms of the propensity to strike, as measured by the frequency of disputes, textiles ranked second only to mining in the years to 1914. Furthermore, if, as Richard Price suggests, the definition of militancy is broadened to comprehend 'the vigilant defence of work control and other workplace interests',[9] then this describes the temper of relations within the mill as effectually as it does that down the mine. As the period progressed, points of difference were further obscured. While collective-bargaining procedures developed as a means of containing disputes in mining, problems in the cotton trade proved sufficiently intractable to undermine confidence in established conciliation machinery. The difficulties were such that, by 1932, *The Observer* was offering what it considered a pertinent alternative to a familiar aphorism: 'What Lancashire does today, we hope no part of England will be doing tomorrow'.[10] The industrial relations record of each industry thus needs closer investigation.

The second issue confronted in this chapter is the extent to which the trade-union record accurately reflects the views of the rank and file. This extends beyond the differences between workers created by trade-union policies and practices.[11] Rates of participation in meetings and debates were such that the ability of labour organizations to articulate a collective sense of identity among cotton and coal workers remains open to question. Among the former, trade-union deliberations were guided by the interests of skilled male minorities, while an often weak union presence underground channelled colliers' protests into forms inimical to a united sense of class.

I

In evidence before the Royal Commission on Labour in 1892, cotton-trade representatives were leading advocates of the benefits of agreed bargaining procedures. Collective discipline, a product of high levels of organization, had, they agreed, encouraged a spirit of conciliation within

---

[9] R. Price, '"What's in a Name?": Workplace History and "Rank-and-Filism"', *International Review of Social History*, 34 (1989), 72; R. A. Church, 'Edwardian Labour Unrest and Coalfield Militancy, 1880–1914', *Historical Journal*, 30 (1987), 848; R. A. Church, Q. Outram, and D. N. Smith, 'Towards a History of British Miners' Militancy', *Bulletin of the Society for the Study of Labour History*, 54/1 (Spring 1989), 22.

[10] Cited in *TW* 8 (5 Feb. 1932), 587.

[11] J. Zeitlin, '"Rank-and-Filism" in British Labour History: A Critique', *International Review of Social History*, 34 (1989), 45–6.

the industry. Such views drew on experience of mechanisms for joint negotiations dating back to the middle of the nineteenth century, when mill-owners had combined to promote their collective interests and to check the effects of damaging internal competition. To the same end, operative organizations had also been encouraged.[12] Union co-operation was sought to secure adherence to joint agreements, as in 1915, when master weavers in Burnley supported strike action in the outlying district of Harle Syke to ensure that mills in the area observed locally agreed wage lists.[13] The trend established in the later nineteenth century continued beyond 1900, as levels of organization were further enhanced. In 1905, the Federation of Master Cotton Spinners' Associations, active in the American-cotton sector since 1891, incorporated the fine-spinning district around Bolton. Across the county, by 1914, Federation affiliates controlled 65 per cent of all spindles. In Bolton, the figure stood at 86.3 per cent and, even then, the eight firms which remained outside the Federation adhered to collective agreements.[14] Trade-union organization had progressed to a similar degree. Approximately two-thirds of eligible workers were members of the Operative Spinners' and Card-Room Amalgamations in 1913. In Bolton, representation was all but complete. Among minders, the only non-union shop was Heatons' of Lostock, a legacy of an earlier conflict over the employment of female spinners. Even that gap was closed in 1916.[15] Areas where both employers and employed remained unorganized were brought within the collective-bargaining tradition after 1900. The organization of female ring spinners, neglected by the minders, was taken up by the Card-Room Amalgamation from 1909. An effective union presence was also established on the cotton belt's south-western extremity, in Wigan, through the offices of the Women's Trade Union League. Local card-room

---

[12] *Parl. Papers 1892*, xxxv (6708–VI), RC on Labour: Minutes of Evidence. Textile, q. 46; *Bolton Master Cotton Spinners' Association, Centenary Commemoration* (Bolton, 1961); S. J. Chapman, 'An Historical Sketch of Masters' Associations in the Cotton Industry', *Transactions of the Manchester Statistical Society* (Session 1900–1), 76–7; A. C. Howe, *The Cotton Masters, 1830–1860* (Oxford, 1984), 163–74; A, J. McIvor, *Organised Capital* (Cambridge, 1996), 48–53.

[13] LRO, North East Lancashire Textile Manufacturers' Association DDX 1145/1/1/3 Burnley Master Cotton Spinners' and Manufacturers' Association, minutes, 17 Dec. 1915.

[14] A. J. McIvor, 'Cotton Employers' Organisations and Labour Relations, 1890–1939', in J. A. Jowitt and A. J. McIvor (eds.), *Employers and Labour in the English Textile Industries*, (1988), 4–5; *BJG* (30 Dec. 1904), 5; (3 Oct. 1913), 10.

[15] *Parl. Papers 1914–16*, lxi (7733), Board of Trade (Department of Labour Statistics). Seventeenth Abstract of Labour Statistics, 200–1; BA, FT/7/6/61 BOCA, quarterly report, Apr. 1909, 2; JRUL, BCA/1/3/10 BSA, minutes, Council meeting, 29 Feb. 1916.

membership, which had stood at only 200 in 1900 rose to 3,500 in 1922. The process of incorporation was completed in 1918, when the Wigan Employers' Association affiliated to the Federation.[16]

In the early 1920s, Federation membership, at 80 per cent of machine capacity, was at its peak. However, economic developments over the following decade worked to undermine central authority. Post-war speculation in mill stock encouraged the emergence of groups whose interests ran counter to the thrust of Federation policy. In 1922, a number of firms which had undergone recapitalization formed the Provisional Emergency Cotton Committee to press a change of approach on the industry's leadership.[17] Subsequent attempts to address the trade's difficulties served further to fracture unity. The Cotton Yarn Association was founded in the late 1920s to regulate production and so stabilize prices in the American-cotton sector. Yet the obligation to maintain payments to loanholders, regardless of profitability, forced many companies to ignore such restrictions. The Federation's authority was further weakened with the formation of the Lancashire Cotton Corporation. Concerned to rationalize production among spinners of American cotton, the Corporation did not affiliate to the Federation, so that, by 1931, the latter controlled less than 60 per cent of spindleage in that sector.[18]

Operatives' organizations experienced no comparable decline over this period. Yet aggregate statistics conceal enduring divisions, sectional and local in origin, which ran through union structures. Co-operation between amalgamations was largely confined to parliamentary lobbying, undertaken by the United Textile Factory Workers' Association. Save for the negotiations surrounding the reduction in working hours in 1919, that body was never active in industrial bargaining.[19] Each amalgamation oversaw its own interests. Although proposals to establish a single union for all cotton workers were advanced by the Weavers' Amalgamation in the 1920s, these foundered on questions of administrative detail. Under

[16] BA, FT/7/6/55 BOCA, quarterly report, 31 May 1907; FT/7/6/62, quarterly report, 31 May 1909; Jewkes and Gray, *Wager and Labour*, ch. 9; *Parl. Papers 1902*, cxix (1002), Census of England and Wales, 1901: County of Lancaster, table 35, p. 173; J. Liddington and J. Norris, *One Hand Tied Behind Us: The Rise of the Women's Suffrage Movement* (1978), 97–8; *CFT* (3 Feb. 1922), 1; JRL, Ashton Employers' Collection, Wigan and District Cotton Employers' Association, subcommittee minutes, 26 July, 17 Oct. 1918.

[17] Provisional Emergency Cotton Committee, *The Crisis in the Cotton Industry*, i (Manchester, 1923), 397; JRL, Ashton Employers' Collection, FMCSA, annual report, year to 30 June, 1923 (Manchester, 1923), 99–106.

[18] B. Bowker, *Lancashire under the Hammer* (1928), 82–7; *TW* 6 (20 Feb. 1931), 655.

[19] *BEN* (27 June 1919), 4; S. and B. Webb, *The History of Trade Unionism* (1926 edn.), 435.

the Weavers' scheme, representation on the central executive would be determined by the membership of each association. A similar arrangement already applied on the UTFWA's Legislative Council and ensured the Weavers' and allied bodies twenty-three representatives, against ten for the Spinners' and Card-Room Amalgamations combined. The threat which this seemed to pose to administrative and financial autonomy, both important considerations given the high levels of subscriptions and benefits paid by the Spinners', sufficed to ensure that sectional organizations survived.[20] Nevertheless, less formal arrangements were concluded to cover cases where action in one mill department would affect workers in another. Between 1904 and 1913, the Spinners' and Card-Room Amalgamations agreed to take sympathetic action in disputes involving the other organization. Co-operation was continued thereafter, albeit only on an *ad hoc* basis.[21]

Within amalgamations, local interests were jealously safeguarded. Among the Spinners', although payments in case of dispute were administered through Amalgamation offices, individual districts oversaw a variety of friendly benefits. Consequently, of each minder's weekly subscription, over half was retained at provincial level. Calls to centralize the administration of benefits were resisted by the Bolton Association, which remained reluctant to subsidize less prosperous areas.[22]

The organizational structures in place in this period reflected the realities of operating within a vertically disintegrated industry. Of more immediate moment, the morphology and ideology of cotton trade unionism also drew on identities generated within the workplace, and placed particular stress on the privileged position of skilled minorities. This applied even in the card-room, where union organization was based on an ostensibly 'open' constitution, which embraced 'Any Cotton, Blowing, Card, Ring Room Workers or Reelers, Winders and Doublers'. Reflecting the gender balance in preparatory departments, 90 per cent of amalgamation members were female. Women's support was thus essential for any campaign conducted from the card-room.[23] Yet their participation in

[20] *BJG* (12 Nov. 1920), 6; BA, FT/21/10 BSA, annual report, 1922, 4; JRUL, BCA/1/3/13 BSA, minutes, quarterly districts meeting, 15 Sept. 1928.

[21] JRUL, BCA/1/3/8 BSA, minutes, Special General Representative Meeting, 28 Mar. 1904; BCA/1/3/12, Council meeting, 21 Oct. 1924.

[22] Jewkes and Gray, *Wages and Labour*, 157–62; JRUL, BCA/1/3/9 BSA, minutes, districts' quarterly meetings, 17 Sept. 1910; BCA/1/3/11, 20 Mar. 1920; BCA/1/3/12, 18 Mar. 1922.

[23] BA, FT/7/9/1 BOCA, rules, 2, 7; FT/7/1/6 BOCA, Executive Council minutes, 14 Jan. 1920.

union affairs rarely extended beyond the payment of weekly dues. The collection of subscriptions at the home rather than, as in the case of the minders, in the workplace, confirmed a tendency to passivity. Although women were, on occasion, employed as collectors, executive discussions were dominated by male grinders. The lack of women's influence was noted by Martha Hopper, a German delegate to the UTFWA's annual conference, who expressed disappointment that 'after all she had heard of the Lancashire cotton women workers and the strength of their trade unionism, they were unrepresented by their own sex in what was supposed to be their annual conference.'[24] An examination of the situation in individual districts would merely have served to compound her dismay. The appointment of women to official positions was sufficiently rare to attract comment and was more often the result of individual initiative than of collective effort. Cissy Foley, an official of the Bolton Card-Room Association, drew inspiration from a broad socialist outlook that embraced the Labour Church, the Co-operative movement, and the works of William Morris, enthusiasms shared by few of her fellow workers.[25] In this respect, it may be significant that spinning towns failed to encourage the kind of popular suffrage agitation which developed in weaving towns to the north. Certainly the Bolton Women's Suffrage Association, founded in 1908, appears to have found more fertile recruiting ground in middle-class drawing-rooms than in the card-room.[26]

Indirect evidence of the prevailing power balance in union counsels can be found in the formation, after 1918, of grinders' 'locals'. Although seen by some as vehicles for shopfloor radicalism, 'locals' were essentially defensive reactions to a perceived growth in female activism, arising from the wider employment of women in wartime. By 1922, the *Bolton Journal and Guardian* could remark that 'it is a remarkable meeting of the trade union at which several girls do not make a speech'.[27] The formation of 'locals' enabled grinders to co-ordinate policies in advance of such meetings, enabling them to influence the flow of debate. Yet, by 1923, all 'locals', save those in Chorley and Bolton, had been disbanded.[28] Over

---

[24] *CFT* (2 Aug. 1918), 3; B. L. Hutchins, *Women in Modern Industry* (1915), 103–4; *BJG* (12 July 1929), 8.

[25] A. Foley, *A Bolton Childhood* (Manchester, 1973), 44–7; B. Drake, *Women in Trade Unions* (1921), 99.

[26] Liddington and Norris, *One Hand Tied Behind Us*, 224; BA, FW/2/4 Bolton Women's Suffrage Association, First Annual Report, year ending 30 Apr. 1910, 1.

[27] *BJG* (23 June 1922), 7.

[28] *CFT* (22 Sept.), 1, letter by 'Grinder'; (29 Sept. 1922), 3, letter by 'A Builder Up'; (28 Sept.), 3; (30 Nov. 1923), 3.

time, female indifference rather than female activism came to concern union executives, more especially as a reluctance to attend mill meetings was combined with a disinclination to observe the terms of collective agreements. The willingness of two women reelers to work on Saturday afternoons convinced the Bolton Association of the need to prohibit female overtime working from 1923.[29] As the decade progressed, increasing numbers of women allowed their memberships to lapse. In 1926, some districts in the Bolton Province were reporting that up to 30 per cent of workers were not paying to the union. Recruitment campaigns were thus launched with the specific intention of bolstering female loyalty. Yet grinders were not always assiduous in pressing for full representation on the shopfloor. Indeed, at Heatons' Lostock mill, they tolerated a situation in which only 25 per cent of female employees belonged to the union.[30]

Although institutional records emphasize the passivity of women cotton workers, they proved capable of radical action, albeit often independently of their local union. In 1906, a strike at Tootal Broadhurst Lee's Sunnyside Mill in Bolton resulted from the introduction of warp stop motions on the firm's looms, an innovation designed to render their movements almost fully automatic. The dispute centred on women who were not members of the Bolton Weavers' Association. It lasted over nine months, drawing support from the immediate locality and attracting the interest of outsiders, including the Pankhursts. Hopes that the campaign would alter the women's industrial and political outlook were, however, disappointed. Following the settlement of the strike in September 1906 and the reinstatement of those who had not secured work elsewhere, no attempt was made to establish a lasting union presence at Sunnyside.[31]

Not all female operatives were indifferent to the demands of trade-union organization. In Wigan, the efforts of the Women's Trade Union League, combined with a prevailing gender balance heavily skewed in favour of women, ensured that both the Card-Room and the Weavers' Associations locally were run by predominantly female executives. Even

---

[29] BA, FT/7/2/1 BOCA, Bolton Committee Minutes, quarterly reports, 20 Feb. 1923, 2; 19 Feb. 1924, 1; FT/7/2/2 BOCA, quarterly report, 20 Nov. 1928, 3; *BEN* (21 March 1923).

[30] BA, FT/7/2/2 BOCA, Bolton Committee Minutes, quarterly report, 24 Aug. 1926, 2; JRUL, BCA/1/3/14 BSA, minutes, Council Meeting, 30 Mar. 1931; BA, BOHP, 88A (female, born 1901), transcript, 2–3, 9–10.

[31] *BJG* (7 June 1906), 6; (6 July), 6; (20 July), 6; (10 Aug.), 6; (24 Aug.), 5; (21 Sept.), 6; (28 Sept.), 2, 6; Z. Munby, 'The Sunnyside Women's Strike', *Bolton People's History*, 1 (1984), 8–13; BA, BOHP, 5 (female, born 1917), transcript, 11.

here, however, limits to women's 'legitimate' industrial role remained evident. In both organizations, salaried posts were invariably filled by men. As these officials were responsible for negotiations with employers, often involving detailed calculations from complex price lists, appointments were determined by arithmetical competence, assessed by means of written examinations. In 1920, six candidates sat the examination for the post of assistant secretary of the Wigan Weavers' Association. One woman qualified for the short list, Alice Foley, sister of Cissy, who had previously been employed as a Sick Visitor by the Bolton Association. In the end, the appointee was male. Although numerical competence was clearly important in such appointments, it is possible that other factors determined the choice, including the calculation that men would be more effective in face-to-face negotiations with employers.[32]

Beyond Wigan, female involvement in union affairs was tightly circumscribed. Despite a superficially open structure, card-room unionism was driven by the grinders' governing sense of craft. A similar pattern obtained in the mule-room. Here, the associational culture cut deep, more especially in Bolton, where the mill was the fundamental unit of administration. Here, each shop was run by elected officials, who were answerable to monthly members' meetings. Fines for non-attendance at such gatherings, held in nearby pubs, ensured high levels of participation.[33] The benefits of an active democracy were recognized in Oldham, whose executive recommended adoption of the Bolton system in 1918, in preference to the prevailing arrangement whereby mills were clustered into 'districts'. Doubts were expressed as to the efficacy of increasing the autonomy of officials at plant level at a time of emerging shop-steward radicalism.[34] However, the mule-room was never a likely focus for sustained workplace militancy. Indeed, branch autonomy was as likely to result in co-operation, often in defiance of collective agreements, as it was in conflict. In 1929, shop officials at Parrot St Mills, Bolton, agreed a

[32] *CFT* (19 Dec. 1919), 1; *Census of England and Wales, 1921: County of Lancaster*, table 16, p. 139 (out of 2,496 employed in local weaving sheds, 2,403 were women); Wigan Heritage Services, Archives (WA), D/DS 3 ADD/1 Wigan and District Weavers' Association (WWA), members' meeting minutes, Annual Meeting, 25 Nov. 1915; D/DS 3 ADD/2 WWA Committee minutes, special meetings, 25 Mar.; 5 Apr. 1920; Foley, *Bolton Childhood*, 75–6.

[33] BA, FT/8/2/11 BSA, Rules of Clarence Mill Shop Club; FT/21/9 BSA, annual report, 1917, 13; BA, BOHP, 1A (male, born 1901), transcript, 14; 87 (male, born 1902), transcript, 15–16.

[34] *CFT* (18 Feb. 1918) 3; (30 Aug. 1918), 1; *BEN* (8 July 1919), 3; *The Times* (12 July 1919), 12; A. Fowler, 'War and Labour Unrest', in A. Fowler and T. Wyke (eds.), *The Barefoot Aristocrats* (Littleborough, 1987), 164.

reduction in standard mule speeds and, by extension, earnings, without reference to the local executive. Elsewhere, independent changes to cleaning times were agreed.[35] Yet the gap between official and rank-and-file attitudes was never as profound as this would suggest. Unofficial strike action by minders was rare. Indeed, the stoppage at Bolton's Maco Mill in 1907 was considered 'almost unprecedented'.[36] The strong associational culture which became rooted in individual shops did not, of necessity, imply the existence of a vigorous rank-and-file radicalism.

More importantly, this culture was not all-embracing. It excluded piecers, who were prohibited from attending shop meetings, any decisions taken being communicated by their minders. Similarly, spinners were responsible for the payment of all union subscriptions. As a result, the Bolton Association was able to claim complete representation of local piecers from the 1890s.[37] Nevertheless, piecer participation remained highly circumscribed, being confined to votes on local or general stoppages, occasions on which unity was a prerequisite. To ensure loyal observance of any strike action, piecers received benefits through the nominally independent Bolton Piecers' and Creelers' Association, a body overseen by minders which had as its object the consolidation of 'the good feeling already existing between Spinners, Twiners and their Piecers'.[38]

These arrangements sufficed to frustrate recurrent attempts to establish independent piecers' organizations. The earliest in this period, the Lancashire Piecers' Association, was part of a broader socialist campaign to extend organization to unskilled workers. Branches existed in most spinning towns in the early 1890s. That in Bolton was headed by members of the local branch of the Social Democratic Federation: the shoemaker, Joseph Shufflebotham, acted as president, and the journalist, Allen Clarke, was treasurer.[39] As with many 'new' unions, its existence proved transient. Particular factors compounded its difficulty, as J. R. Clynes described, recalling a public meeting in Oldham, where one piecer's attack on minders for exploiting the bodies of their assistants so as to sustain their own inflated standard of living, drew forth an unanswerable response: '"Ah'll show thee what we do to the bodies o' the

---

[35] JRUL, BCA/1/3/14 BSA, minutes, Council meetings, 10 Dec. 1929, 18 Jan. 1932.

[36] *BJG* (25 Oct. 1907), 8.

[37] Jewkes and Gray, *Wages and Labour*, 167–8; BA, BOHP, 161 (male, born 1907), tape.

[38] *BEN* (2 Nov. 1932), 5; BA, FT/8/2/19 BSA, Rules and Regulations of the Piecers' and Creelers' Association in Connection with the Bolton Operative Spinners' Association, 1.

[39] *Bolton Weekly Journal* (20 Sept. 1890), 7; P. Salveson, *Will Yo Come O Sunday Mornin?* (Bolton, 1982), 11; BA, 'Bolton Biographical Notes', iii, 65.

piecers!" came an angry rumble from among the audience. "Get thee
back home this minute, young Albert, and I'll coom after thee wi' t' old
stra-ap!"[40] Subsequent attempts at organization fared little better. The
United Piecers' Association, which affiliated to the Trades Council in
Farnworth, south-east of Bolton, in 1914, was not recognized by the
Spinners' executive.[41] In later years, the effects of economic decline gave
renewed impetus to such initiatives. The Piecers' Reform Movement,
founded in 1927 with Communist backing, sought increased earnings for
workers whose prospects of promotion appeared increasingly uncertain.
Yet after two years, its membership stood at a mere 250, compared with a
potential constituency of some 12,000 in the Bolton district alone.[42]

Piecers were capable of independent strike action, most often in
defence of promotional procedures which were intended to guarantee
advancement by seniority. The transitional nature of their work, however,
ensured that the defence of mule-gate customs received priority over
attempts to reform them. As a 'Piecer' sagely observed in 1911, 'there
would be something Gilbertian in men of a congenial trade uniting to
wrest advantages from their fellow-workers whose ranks they will ultimately join'.[43] Piecers' movements sought, for the most part, to work
within minders' organizations. In 1915, the general secretary of the
United Piecers' Association addressed the Bolton Spinners' executive in
what he claimed to be a spirit of 'Industrial Unity', while in 1929, officials of the Piecers' Reform Movement rejected calls to break with the
Spinners' Amalgamation.[44] The shifting, mostly transient, constituency
provided an unpromising basis from which to launch independent
collective action. Movements to challenge the control exerted by the
Spinners' Amalgamation remained stillborn. Throughout the period,
therefore, the pace and temper of industrial relations continued to be
regulated by skilled minorities.

[40] J. R. Clynes, *Memoirs.* i. *1869–1924* (1937), 57–8.
[41] *BJG* (3 April 1914), 9; JRUL, BCA/13/2/17 BSA, general correspondence, 1914,
Notice of United Piecers' Association, n.d.
[42] JRUL, BCA/1/3/13 BSA, minutes, Council meeting, 24 May 1927; BCA/13/2/34
BSA, general correspondence, 1929, Caine to Wood, n.d.; CPGB, Manchester District
Committee, circular, n.d.; *BJG* (7 June 1929), 11; (26 July 1929), 5.
[43] *BJG* (1 Sept. 1911), 9; (30 Jan. 1914), 11; *Parl. Papers 1912–13*, xlvii (6472), Board of
Trade (Labour Department): Report on Strikes and Lock-Outs and on Conciliation and
Arbitration Boards in 1911, 106–7; *Parl. Papers 1914*, xlviii (7089), Strikes and Lock-Outs
in 1912, 94–5.
[44] JRUL, BCA/13/2/18 BSA, general correspondence, 1915, P. Eagan to Executive
Council, n.d; *BJG* (26 July 1929), 5.

II

Élites within the cotton workforce are often accorded a crucial role in determining the co-operative temper of labour relations in the mill. Whether seen as classical 'labour aristocrats', mediating proprietorial authority through the workplace or as, in J. L. White's phrase, 'contrived aristocrats', whose control over the production process was 'tenuous and fragile', minders and, by extension, grinders are seen to have exerted a conciliatory influence on industrial politics, a stance determined by their commitment to the status quo.[45] At various points in the half-century from 1880, collaboration between employers and unions was encouraged, most often in response to external threats to local prosperity. In 1895, the industry united in opposition to a 5 per cent import duty on cotton cloths imposed by the Indian government. The campaign, informed by the perceived threat to Lancashire's largest export market, secured concessions from the incoming Unionist administration in London.[46] Thereafter, concern came to centre on the county's raw material supply. By the 1890s, over 85 per cent of Lancashire's cotton needs were being met from the southern United States. Over time, that source was threatened from two directions. Southern cultivation had increased in response to growing demand from continental European and north American as well as Lancastrian producers, to the extent that the area of land under cotton began to approach its physical limits. Out of a possible thirty-five million acres, some thirty million were under cultivation by 1906.[47] In addition to the uncertainties created by such trends, the crop was also subject to speculation designed to enhance its price. In 1904, consortia on the New York exchange, headed by one Daniel J. Sully, 'cornered' three million bales of raw cotton, equivalent to Lancashire's purchases for one year. In response, mill-owners across the Oldham Province endeavoured to limit consumption by agreeing a maximum working week of forty hours. This arrangement, supported by both sides of industry and sustained over eight months, provided, in the words of C. W. Macara, president of the employers' federation, 'an example to the world of a whole industrial community acting with one motive and upon one plan with

---

[45] J. White, *The Limits of Trade Union Militancy* (Westport, Conn., and London, 1978), 37; id., 'Lancashire Cotton Textiles', 217; M. Holbrook-Jones, *The Supremacy and Subordination of Labour* (1982), 177–85.

[46] P. Harnetty, 'The Indian Cotton Duties Controversy, 1894–6', *EHR* 77 (1962), 684–702.

[47] Cotton Trade Tariff Reform Association, *Report of the Council* (Manchester, 1910), 5; JRUL, BCA/13/2/9 BSA, general correspondence, Circular, Mar. 1906.

incalculable benefit to industry as a whole'.[48] Sully's eventual bankruptcy was celebrated across Lancashire, David Shackleton, the Darwen Weavers' secretary, interpreting it as a victory for virtue over an 'un-Christian like and commercially immoral' force.[49]

The New York 'corner' had exposed Lancashire's vulnerability to commodity speculation. Lasting security against this was sought in the development of alternative sources of raw cotton. In 1904, the British Cotton Growing Association, a scheme first floated three years earlier by the Oldham Chamber of Commerce, was reconstituted under a Royal Charter. It aimed to promote cotton cultivation in appropriate parts of the Empire. Given the benefits that were intended to accrue from such work, bipartisan support was encouraged and, at official level, achieved: representatives of employers' organizations and operative amalgamations sat side by side on the Association's governing council.[50] Union assistance was also financial, the Bolton Spinners' Association subscribing £1,500, a sum later converted into share capital, while the local Card-Room Association acquired 200 shares. Direct operative support was encouraged through the organization of workplace collections. In 1910, the Bolton Spinners' Council recommended that each mule-team subscribe 3s. 9d. to the Cotton Growing Association. The response was, however, muted. By February 1911, only £158. 8s. 3d. had been raised from over 5,000 teams.[51] Despite this, union officials readily acknowledged that an augmented cotton crop would be of benefit to the industry as a whole. Speaking at a banquet held in 1905 in Manchester to promote the Cotton Growing Association, the Bolton Spinners' secretary, A. H. Gill, gave expression to this shared outlook: 'They looked upon it that what was of interest to the employer was also the interest of the operative in this case, because if the movement was successful it would certainly find employment for the operatives at the same time that it made profit for the employers.'[52] Similar perceptions coloured

---

[48] C. W. Macara, *Recollections* (1921), 37; *BJG* (8 Jan. 1904), 6; (5 Feb.), 6; (12 Feb.), 9.

[49] *BJG* (25 March 1904), 6.

[50] W. F. Tewson, *The British Cotton Growing Association, 1904–54* (Manchester, 1954), 15–17; JRUL, BCA/13/2/9 BSA, general correspondence, circular on the Association, Mar. 1906.

[51] JRUL, BCA/1/3/7–9 BSA, minutes, Council meetings, 26 May 1903, 29 Mar. 1910; districts' quarterly meeting, 16 June 1906; general representative meeting circular, 8 Feb. 1911; BA, FT/7/6/48 BOCA, quarterly report, 1 Sept. 1905, 5.

[52] *Bolton Chronicle* (16 Dec. 1905), 7; see also JRUL, BCA/1/3/9 BSA, minutes, circular, 5 Apr. 1910; BCA/13/2/9 BSA, general correspondence, Amalgamation officials to Gill, 28 Apr. 1906.

the UTFWA's deposition to the Committee on Industry and Trade in 1925.[53]

Despite the work of the Association, augmented after 1918 by the semi-official Empire Cotton Growing Corporation, American cotton continued to account for 70 per cent of non-Egyptian purchases by the late 1920s. Utilization of short-staple Indian and African fibres remained constrained by the weight given in the post-war period to output quality and by abiding memories of the problems encountered in working 'Surat' cotton during the Famine of the 1860s. So, although the Economic Advisory Council recommended the adoption of alternative sources of supply, over 90 per cent of the Ugandan crop of 1931 was destined for India and Japan.[54] The practical impact of the various cotton-growing initiatives was thus modest. Nevertheless, this should not be allowed to obscure the genuine unity of purpose demonstrated by both sides of industry over this question.

Co-operation was also encouraged by the controversies surrounding the introduction of Safeguarding legislation after 1918. Those industries seeking support from government had flourished under the protective regime inaugurated during the First World War. One such, the East Midlands fabric glove trade, had experienced a sixfold increase in output over the four years from 1914, enabling it to secure a domestic market formerly supplied from Saxony with gloves made from Lancastrian cotton yarn. Saxon demand had accounted for 40 per cent of British yarn exports to Germany before the war, a volume sufficient, according to the president of the Bolton Chamber of Commerce, to employ 3,000 workers locally. The application by native glove manufacturers in November 1921 for a 33.3 per cent impost on imported goods provoked disquiet across Lancashire. The fear was that, faced with a move to protection in Britain, foreign producers would look elsewhere for their fine yarns.[55]

Concern united unions, Chambers of Commerce, and firms directly involved in the Saxony trade. Employers' organizations, by contrast, were

---

[53] JRUL, BCA/13/2/28 BSA, general correspondence, UTFWA memorandum, 5 Feb. 1925.

[54] BA, FT/7/6/65 BOCA, quarterly report, 28 Feb. 1910, 3; *TW* 2 (25 Jan. 1929), 597; 5 (18 July), 424; (15 Aug. 1930), 508; 7 (6 Mar.), 11; (22 May 1931), 370; *Parl. Papers 1929–30*, xii (3615), Economic Advisory Council: Committee on the Cotton Industry. Report, pars 39–42.

[55] R. K. Snyder, *The Tariff Problem in Great Britain* (Stanford, Calif.,1944), 98, 101; *BJG* (23 Dec. 1921), 9; (23 June 1922), 9; JRUL, BCA/13/4/37 BSA, employers' correspondence, James Fishwick to Captain W. Edge, MP, 11 Jan.; statement re fabric gloves, 22 June 1922; evidence before Board of Trade Committee, n.d.

at first reluctant to become embroiled in political controversy. Lancashire's argument that, should protection be afforded English fabric glove manufacturers, the future of an important export trade would be sacrificed to sustain 'an incompetent industry of about 18 concerns', producing goods inferior to those previously imported, failed to carry the day. The Safeguarding Sub-Committee, reporting in January 1922, recommended that East Midlands producers should benefit from the tariff, although it was made clear that the implications of any decision for the cotton industry lay outside its terms of reference.[56] Lancastrians, convinced that their concerns had been treated 'as not worthy of consideration', pressed that the Sub-Committee reconsider its verdict and that its remit be extended to take in the broader implications of any decision. On this occasion, employers' representatives were active in promoting the industry's cause. Submissions to government were offered jointly by the Federation of Master Cotton Spinners' Associations and the UTFWA. Political lobbying complemented written depositions. Particularly active in the industry's case was Captain William Edge, Coalition Liberal member for Bolton and a junior government whip, whose efforts culminated in his resignation to vote against the Safeguarding Order in July 1922. In response, the local Spinners' and Card Room Amalgamations paid tribute to the 'valuable time and energy' expended by Edge 'in the interests of his constituents in particular and Lancashire in general'.[57] A more direct approach to Downing Street was attempted through the 'King of Lancashire', Lord Derby. The outcome, however, revealed the Stanley connection's declining influence in national Unionist counsels. Baldwin, the President of the Board of Trade, was determined to uphold a central tenet of party policy and to secure subsequent safeguarding initiatives. The Safeguarding Order was thus confirmed, resulting in the loss of an important export market.[58]

Lancashire's waning political influence had already been exposed the previous year, when a joint deputation to the Secretary of State for India had failed to secure equality in Indian import and excise duties. Thereafter, constitutional changes within the Empire and an unfavourable

[56] JRUL, BCA/1/3/12 BSA, minutes, Council meeting, 20 Dec. 1921; BCA/13/3/7 BSA, outward correspondence, circular, 20 Jan. 1922; *BJG* (16 Dec. 1921), 9.

[57] JRUL, BCA/13/2/26 BSA, general correspondence, letter, reproduced in *Bolton Liberal Searchlight* (Aug. 1922); *BJG* (14 July 1922), 9; K. O. Morgan, *Consensus and Disunity: The Lloyd George Coalition Government, 1918–1922* (Oxford, 1979), 334.

[58] K. Middlemas and J. Barnes, *Baldwin: A Biography* (1969), 88–91; Snyder, *Tariff Problem*, 103; *TW* 10 (9 Sept. 1932), 32.

exchange-rate policy at home combined to consolidate an embattled regional identity.[59] That Lancashire's salvation was seen to lie in its own hands was confirmed by the formation of the Joint Committee of Cotton Trade Organizations, an association of master spinners, manufacturers, finishers, merchants, and, from 1928, trade unions, which attempted to ensure that the industry spoke with a single voice on the political decisions which affected it.[60] Although this putative 'Cotton Parliament' failed significantly to amplify the county's voice, conventional wisdom continued to emphasize the need for vigilance against external influences, a point reiterated by the, presumably apocryphal, story of the mule minder who enrolled for military service only to find himself assigned to the Veterinary Corps.[61]

If unity between operatives and employers was encouraged by a series of external challenges, it also appeared to be promoted by developments within the industry. The elaborate conciliation machinery which governed relations in the trade from the later nineteenth century depended on the work of full-time officials and their capacity to master the details of complex price lists. The technical expertise thus acquired fitted many for wider administrative roles. A number progressed to work with employers' organizations or within the burgeoning state apparatus. A shared culture was seen to develop, integrating the interests of unions, management, and government, to the extent that James Crinion was considered unusual in that, on retiring as president of the Oldham Card Room Association in 1930, he declined a post with the local employers' association and 'decided to stick to the rank and file'.[62] More typical was Peter Bullough, secretary of the Bolton Operative Spinners', who was appointed fencing inspector for the Federation in 1920.[63] In the decade which followed, employer opinion in the town was articulated by two former union officials: Alfred Hill and William Howarth, respectively the secretary and president of the local Master Spinners' Association. Howarth, a former general secretary of the

---

[59] JRL, Ashton Employers' Collection, FMCSA, annual report, year to 30 June 1921 (Manchester, 1921), 14; J. D. Tomlinson, 'The First World War and British Cotton Piece Exports to India', *Econ.Hist.Rev.*, 2nd ser., 32 (1979), 502–3; M. Dupree, 'Foreign Competition and the Interwar Period', in M. B. Rose (ed.), *The Lancashire Cotton Industry* (Preston, 1996), 270–2; *TW* 6 (10 Oct. 1930), 114.

[60] *BJG* (24 April 1925), 8; *TW* I (22 June 1928), 435; 8 (20 Nov. 1931), 298; 9 (1 July 1932), 401.   [61] *TW* 3 (16 Aug. 1929), 606.

[62] *TW* 6 (17 Oct. 1930), 122; S. and B. Webb, *Industrial Democracy* (1926 edn.), 16, 236.

[63] JRUL, BCA/1/3/11 BSA, minutes, special districts' representative meeting, 24 Jan. 1920; *BJG* (11 May 1923), 8.

Operative Spinners' Amalgamation, had taken up a managerial post with
the Fine Cotton Spinners' and Doublers' Association in 1904, becoming
managing director of the combine in 1922. On his death in 1933, the
Cotton Factory Times felt bound to observe that his career 'reflected credit
on the class from which he sprang'.[64]

Yet, as the language in which this tribute was couched suggests, co-
operation had its limits. Not all transfers involved a shift in allegiances.
Thomas Birtwistle was appointed to the Factory Inspectorate in 1892
to check cases of time cribbing (working outside agreed hours), while
Bullough's responsibility for machine safety allowed him to retain his
union links. He continued to represent the Operative Spinners' Association
on the Bolton Infirmary and Hospital Saturday Committees through the
1920s.[65] What is more, the outward appearance of industrial unity often concealed markedly differing perspectives on individual issues. The unions'
stance on Indian fiscal affairs obscured growing support for constitutional
change across the subcontinent. In 1924, the Bolton Operative Spinners'
Association supported resolutions calling for the concession of Indian self-
government. Furthermore, India's adoption of tariffs was criticized from a
distinctively labourist perspective. Protection was viewed as a class measure,
operating in the interests of Bombay capitalists, against those of consumers
who were obliged to purchase goods that were both more expensive and of
inferior quality. India's problems were seen to lie in under-consumption,
a remedy for which was to be found in increased wages.[66]

Issues more directly concerned with work confirm the survival of a distinctive operative outlook. In 1910, a stoppage was precipitated throughout the spinning trade by the refusal of George Howe, a grinder at Fern
Mill in Shaw, near Oldham, to undertake duties outside the terms of the
Universal Card list. While grinders saw the list as the guarantor of their
privileges, employers interpreted Howe's stance as a challenge to their
prerogative. A settlement was eventually reached whereby the list
remained unchanged, but Howe was transferred to another mill. The dispute pointed up the potential for fundamental disagreement over work
details, leading William Mullin of the Card Room Amalgamation to draw
the lesson that 'it is only by our strong combination that we are enabled

---

[64] BA, 'Bolton Biographical Notes', iv, 108 (Hill); *BJG* (20 Jan. 1933), 11; *Textile Mercury*, 88 (20 Jan. 1933), 50; *CFT* (20 Jan. 1933), 1 (Howarth).

[65] For Birtwistle, see Webb and Webb, *History of Trade Unionism*, 308–9; for Bullough, see n. 63.

[66] JRUL, BCA/1/3/12–14 BSA, minutes, Council meeting, 3 June 1924; quarterly districts' meetings, 11 Dec. 1926, 18 June 1931.

to combat this threatened terror'.[67] In fact, workplace practices occasioned few differences in the years that followed, although in the 1920s discussion centred for a time on unofficial extensions to the dinner hour, which allowed piecers to bring meals prepared at home.[68] The prerogatives of skilled labour were not subject to sustained challenge. However, increasing difficulty was encountered in negotiating levels of pay within the industry.

Conciliation procedures had developed across the cotton trade in the second half of the nineteenth century and assumed their most complete form in the agreement reached between the employers' Federation and the Operative Spinners' Amalgamation at the Brooklands Hotel, near Sale in Cheshire, in March 1893. The later writings of Sir Charles Macara and Sidney and Beatrice Webb enshrined the elaborate consultative procedures put in place at Brooklands as the 'Magna Charta of the Cotton Trade'.[69] In its detailed provisions, Brooklands incorporated features of existing agreements, combining the Bolton Province's system of local joint discussions with the central negotiations allowed for in the weaving sector, to produce a three-tier bargaining structure. Before any stoppage could be sanctioned, the point at dispute had to be considered at mill, district, and county levels. A twin gain was envisaged: extended deliberation would preclude precipitate action, while a strict timetable for negotiations, which allowed a maximum of seven days between meetings, would check any tendency to prevarication.[70] Wage adjustments were limited to 5 per cent changes to list rates and were to last for a minimum of twelve months. Any movement was dependent on levels of profitability within the industry, determined by the 'margin' between raw- and finished-cotton prices. By limiting the extent and frequency of such adjustments, a stable cost structure would, it was thought, be created. In 1893, therefore, the expectation was that Brooklands would provide the basis for 'steady and unbroken co-operation for a long time to come'.[71] Its proponents accorded the agreement a central place in the 'reign of

---

[67] *LG* 18 (1910), 331; *BJG* (16 Sept. 1910), 14; (23 Sept.), 5; (7 Oct.), 5; (14 Oct.), 14.

[68] JRUL, BCA/1/3/12–15 BSA, minutes, Council meetings, 27 Apr. 1925, 29 Jan. 1929, 21 Nov. 1932.

[69] Webb and Webb, *Industrial Democracy*, 203; Macara, *Recollections*, 17–26.

[70] *Parl. Papers 1892*, xxxv (6708–VI), RC on Labour: Minutes of Evidence. Textile, qq. 2478–80; *Parl. Papers 1894*, lxxxi, pt. II (7567–I), Wages and Hours of Labour, 9–11; *BJG* (11 Apr. 1924), 9.

[71] *BJG* (23 Mar. 1893), 5, editorial; *Parl. Papers 1910*, xx (5366), Collective Agreements between Employers and Workpeople, 136.

reason' which was seen to apply across the cotton trade in the decades which followed.

Yet Brooklands' role, in this regard, was far from straightforward. Certainly, its clearly defined procedures recommended its wider adoption. Initially, it covered the Oldham district only, but, in 1906, it came to govern negotiations in fine-spinning areas also. What is more, despite, or perhaps because of, the provision for further stages of joint consultation, most disputes were settled at the initial, mill stage. Of almost 4,000 complaints between 1906 and 1913, only 288 (7 per cent) were referred to central negotiations in Manchester.[72] At times, however, the Brooklands mechanism proved more of a hindrance than an aid to agreement. The limitations of an inflexible negotiating timetable were exposed during bad-spinning disputes, when spinners could be left to work for some weeks with inferior material. Workers thus pressed for more prompt treatment of such complaints. Amendments were introduced, so that, in 1900, a three-day time limit for mill inspections was set and, six years later, an abbreviated schedule was agreed where problems recurred. The persistence of bad-spinning disputes encouraged calls to withdraw from Brooklands. Although a depression in trade from 1908 worked to subdue such cases, they revived as industrial activity recovered, a trend which culminated in the Spinners' secession from the agreement in February 1913.[73]

If bad-spinning complaints were the immediate cause of Brooklands' collapse, earlier problems over wage bargaining had already worked to erode confidence in the central principles of the agreement. Co-operation over list-rate adjustments had proved increasingly elusive in the years from 1900, as a period of secular advance in real and money incomes had come to an end. Between 1886 and 1906, a 15 per cent increase in the Bolton Spinning List had produced, through productivity gains, an advance of 30 per cent in average earnings. A sustained fall in basic commodity prices made the gain even greater, in real terms.[74] From that point, until the outbreak of war, list rates tended to fluctuate around their existing levels. Earnings growth was maintained, especially in the fine-

[72] JRUL, BCA/1/3/8 BSA, minutes, Districts' Special Meeting Circular, 20 Dec. 1906; figures calculated from annual Reports on Strikes and Lockouts, 1906 to 1913.

[73] *Parl. Papers 1910*, xx (5366), Collective Agreements between Employers and Workpeople, 136–7; *BJG* (30 Mar. 1906), 2; (4 Oct. 1907), 14; *BEN* (1 Feb. 1913), 3; BA, FT/21/9 BSA, annual report, 1913, 3–4.

[74] Wood, *History of Wages*, 133; *Parl. Papers 1909*, lxxx (4545), Earnings and Hours of Labour, p. xxvi.

spinning sector. In the six years following the Wage Census of September 1906, cotton workers in Bolton and Leigh enjoyed a 14.7 per cent rise in average incomes. Further east, in Oldham, the gain was a much more marginal 0.16 per cent. More significantly, in real terms, take-home pay declined across the county. The Board of Trade index of rents and retail prices recorded increases of 18 and 11 per cent in Bolton and Oldham respectively between 1905 and 1912.[75] The context for wage negotiations appeared increasingly unpromising. Developments in workplace politics confirmed the trend towards wage rigidities. As a result of the grinders' exemption from the 5 per cent limit on list changes agreed at Brooklands, earnings differentials between card- and mule-rooms had been eroded. Anxious to defend their enhanced status, grinders rejected calls for a 5 per cent cut in rates in 1908, the first in the Bolton Province since 1885. Their opposition over-rode the Spinners' vote for acceptance, precipitating a six-week stoppage across the spinning trade.[76]

As the period progressed, therefore, the 'spirit of mutual forbearance and goodwill' to which Brooklands had appeared to give expression came under increasing strain. Wage rates were the subject of negotiations in each year between 1905 and 1908. On two of these occasions, conciliation procedures were exhausted without agreement being reached and settlements were only achieved through the mediation of local municipal leaders.[77] In a period of greater trade and financial instability, wage negotiations became an annual process, giving rise to a sense of recurrent crisis. When, twelve months after the delayed implementation of the 1908 cut, the Federation sought a further 5 per cent reduction in rates, both sides responded with weary cynicism. For A. H. Gill of the Bolton Operative Spinners', Brooklands, by transforming conflict into an annual ritual, had made Lancashire 'the laughing-stock of the rest of the country'. For employers, faced with renewed opposition to the downward mobility of wages, the agreement had become little 'more than an instrument for regulating advances to the operatives'.[78] As a solution to the repeated threat of breakdown, it was agreed that rates be

---

[75] Earnings figures calculated from *LG* 15–20 (1907–12), returns for Sept. of each year; *Parl. Papers 1913*, lxvi (6955), Report of an Enquiry by the Board of Trade into Working-Class Rents and Retail Prices in 1912, 22–3.

[76] *BJG* (25 May 1899), 5; (25 Sept. 1908), 16; *LG* 16 (1908), 335; *The Woman Worker* (4 Sept. 1908), 349.

[77] JRUL, BCA/13/2/8 BSA, general correspondence, Lord Mayor of Manchester's address at Cotton Trade Conference, n.d. (Aug. 1905); *BJG* (6 Nov. 1908), 5; (13 Nov.), 16.

[78] *BJG* (6 May 1910), 8, 16.

frozen for five years from 1910 and that the minimum duration of future adjustments be increased to two years.[79]

The collapse of Brooklands in 1913 did not signal an abandonment of collective-bargaining procedures. A simplified arrangement emerged by which both sides were committed to local and central negotiations before a stoppage could be endorsed. Although lacking Brooklands' procedural complexities, the agreement survived into the 1920s with the backing of both sides of industry. The UTFWA felt able to commend it to the Balfour Committee as 'fully effective and efficient'.[80] As before, local negotiations sufficed to resolve most points of dispute. Out of 630 complaints at Bolton mills between 1921 and 1931, only sixteen (2.5 per cent) proceeded to county level.[81] However, wage negotiations continued to pose problems. From 1915, an industry which, in the words of the government's Chief Industrial Commissioner, G. R. Askwith, 'had always prided itself on settling its own differences', had repeated recourse to external arbitration.[82] Established procedures proved incapable of accommodating wage demands based on inflated living costs, rather than movements in the 'margin', so that, in each of the three years from 1915, changes to list rates were only agreed as the result of arbitration by the Committee of Production.[83] The agencies of the state were again employed after the war. Mediation by the Ministry of Labour facilitated agreement on list-rate adjustments in 1920 and 1921, while the employers' call for a 25 per cent cut in rates, in 1929, was referred to arbitration by the former Recorder of Wigan, Mr Justice Rigby Swift.[84] As a means of maximizing scope for the internal settlement of differences, government officials proposed the formation of a joint Consultative Committee, with an executive as well as a conciliatory role. Consideration of any such reform was delayed until 1932, by which time, wage inflexibility had once more produced a breakdown in the spinning trade. Along with a 14 per cent reduction in rates, the settle-

[79] *BJG* (22 July 1910), 5, 8.

[80] JRUL, BCA/13/2/28 BSA, general correspondence, UTFWA memorandum, 5 Feb. 1925; *BJG* (1 Jan. 1915), 8; *Parl. Papers 1919*, xiii (185), Twelfth Report of Proceedings under the Conciliation Act, 1896, and Report on Arbitration under the Munitions of War Acts. General Report. 1914–18, pt. III, appendix v. 70.

[81] Calculated from JRUL, BCA/1/3/11–15 BSA, minutes; BCA/12/5/1–2 BSA, joint meeting negotiations.

[82] G. R. Askwith, *Industrial Problems and Disputes* (Brighton, 1974 repr.), 137–8.

[83] JRL, Ashton Employers' Collection FMCSA, annual reports, year to 30 June 1915 (Manchester, 1915), 55; year to 30 June 1916 (Manchester, 1916), 24–34; *LG* 25 (1917), 82.

[84] *BEN* (22 Apr. 1920), 3; (28 Apr. 1920), 3; (23 Aug. 1929), 5; *BJG* (10 June 1921), 6; (28 June 1929), 8; (16 Aug. 1929), 8; *TW* 3 (23 Aug. 1929), 630.

ment concluded in November 1932 included an overhaul of bargaining procedures. Under the arrangements agreed at the Midland Hotel, Manchester, once all stages of joint negotiation had been exhausted, the dispute would be referred to an advisory Conciliation Committee, under an independent chairman. Author of cotton's latest 'Magna Charta' was F. W. Leggett, principal assistant secretary at the Ministry of Labour.[85] The consistent involvement of state officials in industrial bargaining over the better part of two decades testifies to the continued failure of the cotton trade's representatives to resolve internal differences.

In the light of such problems, what had become conventional wisdom in the trade was subject to re-evaluation. By 1918, C. W. Macara, for long a proponent of collective-bargaining machinery, felt

> bound to admit that our organized strength, both on the part of the employers and of the employed, has been our weakness. Disputes which ought to have been settled in a day have been allowed to drag on for weeks, simply because neither side was concerned so much with the reasonableness of the claims, . . . This was our method of dealing with many disputes in the cotton trade, and the loss to both sides has been very serious.[86]

The accumulated evidence of irreconcilable differences between employers and employed had sapped the optimism of at least one prominent figure in the trade. Nevertheless, Macara's views were not wholly representative. More generally, belief in the utility of collective bargaining survived, albeit only due to the lack of any credible alternative. The one most favoured, and discussed intermittently between 1899 and 1909, involved a sliding scale, which would allow wage rates to move automatically, in line with changes in profitability. In proposals advanced by the Federation in 1906, a movement of 2 per cent in the latter would result in an alteration of 2.5 per cent in list rates.[87] Practical difficulties blocked the adoption of such a scheme. Discussions in 1901 and 1909 foundered on the question of the standard from which changes would be measured. Union representatives argued that existing rates should be taken as standard, while employers pressed that they should be 5 per cent above standard. On such differences depended the magnitude of subsequent

[85] *TW* 3 (23 Aug. 1929), 629; 10 (11 Nov. 1932), 281; *BJG* (20 May 1932), 8; (11 Nov. 1932), 8; R. Lowe, *Adjusting to Democracy: The Role of the Ministry of Labour in British Politics, 1916–1939* (Oxford, 1986), 69–70.
[86] C. W. Macara, *Social and Industrial Reform* (Manchester, 1920), 81.
[87] *BJG* (20 April 1906), 14.

fluctuations in wages.[88] Reform was further impeded by the grinders' desire to limit wage flexibility. The Card Room Amalgamation argued that wage minima be specified in any agreement and refused to countenance, as James Crinion succinctly if ungrammatically expressed it, 'a scale that slided down'.[89]

However, such points of detail obscured a more fundamental source of division. The linking of wages to profitability required an accurate knowledge of working costs. In 1901, it was proposed that this could be gained from the returns of twelve representative firms. This necessitated the inclusion of concerns operating on joint-stock lines, which, in 1910, accounted for over three-quarters of firms in the Oldham district and almost 25 per cent of Bolton's spinning capacity.[90] Union officials placed little trust in the accounting methods of such companies, many of which had, they felt, been floated on insubstantial share capital. For them, the 'margin' was preferred as a more objective measure of trading conditions.[91] A further concern, voiced by the secretary of the Bolton Card Room Association, Joseph Edge, in 1908, was that firms organized along limited-liability lines were overly sensitive to the needs of shareholders. The suspicion remained that the money saved through list-rate reductions would be used to bolster company dividends and directorial salaries. Recent work on the investment strategies pursued by Edwardian cotton firms suggests that such fears may not have been without foundation.[92]

Union opposition rested on more than the practicalities of the sliding scale. Joint-stock finance worked to reduce the threshold of entry to the industry, enabling, it was argued, 'a few men—an architect, a builder, and two or three commission hunters—[to] run up a mill and then slide out of it'.[93] Speculative company flotations, at their height in periods of buoyant trade, exaggerated cyclical fluctuations in activity. For some, therefore,

---

[88] *Conciliation in the Cotton Trade* (Manchester, 1901), 22, 37; J. H. Porter, 'Industrial Peace in the Cotton Trade, 1875–1913', *Yorkshire Bulletin of Economic and Social Research*, 19 (1967), 54, 56.   [89] *BJG* (19 Mar. 1909), 14.

[90] S. J. Chapman and T. S. Ashton, 'The Sizes of Businesses, Mainly in the Textile Industries', *Journal of the Royal Statistical Society*, 77 (1913–14), 476; E. L. Thorpe, 'Industrial Relations and Social Structure: A Case Study of Bolton Cotton Mule Spinners, 1884–1910' (Salford Univ. M.Sc. thesis, 1969), ii, statistical appendix, 19.

[91] C. W. Macara, *Modern Industrial Tendencies* (Manchester, 1927), 4; L. L. Price, 'Conciliation in the Cotton Trade', *Economic Journal*, 11 (1901), 240; *Conciliation in the Cotton Trade*, 36, 50; *BJG* (25 May 1899), 5.

[92] *BJG* (21 Aug. 1908), 16; J. S. Toms, 'Financial Constraints on Economic Growth: Profits, Capital Accumulation and the Development of the Lancashire Cotton-Spinning Industry, 1885–1914', *Accounting, Business and Financial History*, 4 (1994), 374–7.

[93] *BJG* (27 Aug. 1909), 2.

the industry's lapse into short-time working in 1908 could be traced to the most recent wave of mill-building between 1905 and 1907. By failing to observe established notions of respectability, which emphasized preventive thrift in anticipation of future need, 'company-mongers' became liable to the kind of moral censure previously reserved for 'the cotton cornerers of New York'.[94] Craft perspectives also coloured union thinking. Whereas, for piecers, increased productive capacity enhanced opportunities for promotion, minders placed a higher value on the security brought by economic stability. The importance attached to regularity of employment was reflected in union calls for a reduction in working hours to eight per day from 1909. In support of this demand, the secretary of the UTFWA pointed out that, in the five years from 1904, the average number of hours worked each week had not exceeded forty-eight. Significantly, the motion from the Card Room Amalgamation which initiated this campaign linked the issue of hours to that of limited-liability capital. Along with the cut in working hours, changes to company law were proposed as a means of checking speculative expansion. Under the scheme advanced by the Amalgamation, mill-building could only commence once 75 per cent of shares had been allotted and 20 per cent of the capital paid up.[95] Although the proposals were not pressed further, a commitment to reform was maintained. Unions were therefore prominent in support of the Cotton Spinning Companies Bill of 1912, introduced by the Bolton Liberal MP, George Harwood, which also outlined more stringent conditions for company flotations.[96]

Mill finances remained central to union thinking on the problems of the cotton trade into the 1920s. The industry's difficulties during that decade were traced to the 'reckless over-capitalisation' encouraged by speculative investment in the immediate post-war years.[97] By contrast, proposals advanced by employers to lift the threat of recession, from list-rate reductions to organized short-time working, were rejected as mere palliatives. The scheme favoured by the Provisional Emergency Cotton Committee in 1922, for a co-ordinated limitation of output and a system

---

[94] LRO, Barber-Lomax Reference Collection, DDBx 13/1 Croal Spinning Co., Ltd., scrapbook, cutting from *BEN* (28 June 1907); *BJG* (9 Oct. 1908), 16; (11 Dec. 1908), 8, 'Notes on Labour'.

[95] *BJG* (23 July 1909), 2; (12 Nov. 1909), 16; JRUL, BCA/1/3/9 BSA, minutes, circular on the eight-hours ballot, 20 Oct. 1909; the earlier campaign for shorter hours, in 1894, had also coincided with a slump in trade, Council meeting, 27 Oct. 1909.

[96] *Parl. Debates, House of Commons*, 5th ser., xxxix, cols. 1678–80.

[97] BA, FT/21/10 BSA, annual report, 1919, 8; *BJG* (12 July 1929), 8; *TW* 9 (26 Aug. 1932), 593.

of benefit payments, funded from levies on the industry, to sustain earnings levels, was further tainted by associations with limited-liability capital. The Bolton Operative Spinners' Council was quick to dismiss
proposals emanating from an 'employers' shop-steward movement', dominated by re-capitalized concerns, seeking financial viability through a
system of price-maintenance.[98] Rather than throwing a line to firms in
straitened circumstances, organized labour pressed, from the mid-1920s,
for their liquidation. The Bolton Card Room Association was clear that it
was 'useless to subsidise inefficiency'.[99] Similarly, in 1930, Albert Law,
Labour MP for Bolton and a former Operative Spinners' president, criticized the Economic Advisory Council's conviction that recovery necessitated re-equipment with new machinery. For Law, as for other labour
spokesmen, effective reconstruction was predicated on the need for widespread bankruptcies.[100] Nevertheless, it was clear that these should be
achieved in an organized fashion and not as a result of random market
forces. Many of the county's most technologically advanced mills had
undergone recapitalization after 1918; these would be lost in an uncon-
trolled programme of redundancies. For the Burnley employer, J. H.
Grey, the implications of such an approach went wider: under evolution-
ary systems left unchecked, 'the prize fighter . . . might have survived
while Shelley died'.[101] For most workers, the promise of wage security
was a more persuasive argument. Their priorities were succinctly summarized by the Card Room Amalgamation in 1923: 'a trade which can not
keep the operatives necessary to its existence in a state above distress
ought to be scrapped'.[102] Stable and adequate rewards were most likely to
be achieved in an industry shorn of its 'boom canker'.[103]

In addition to seeking a more efficient and compact sector, the cotton
unions continued to press for a cut in hours in order to maximize
employment opportunities. In 1922, the UTFWA proposed a staggered
reduction in hours to forty a week, a call renewed from 1931.[104] At all
times, however, change was pursued within existing work patterns. A pro-

---

[98] *The Crisis in the Cotton Industry*, i, 26–7, 80–2; *BJG* (22 Sept. 1922), 9; BA, FT/21/10
BSA, annual report, 1922, 8.
  [99] BA, FT/7/2/2 BOCA, Bolton Committee minutes, quarterly report, 8 May 1926, 1.
  [100] *BJG* (11 July 1930), 11; BA, FT/21/11 BSA, annual report, 1926, 5; FT/21/11 BSA,
annual report, 1929, 4–5; FT/7/2/2 BOCA, Bolton Committee minutes, quarterly report,
18 Nov. 1930, 1.
  [101] *TW* 8 (8 Jan. 1932), 479.   [102] *BJG* (7 Sept. 1923), 8.
  [103] *TW* 2 (14 Dec. 1928), 425, for the term 'boom canker'.
  [104] *BJG* (22 Sept. 1922), 9; JRUL, BCA/1/3/11–14 BSA, minutes, Council meetings, 10
Feb., 8 Nov. 1920, 7 May 1923, 22 Dec. 1931; quarterly districts meeting circular, 19 Sept.
1931.

posal to move to two-shift working, spreading fixed costs by extending machine hours at the same time that those of manual labour were reduced, was vigorously resisted. As outlined by W. H. Lever, when Mayor of Bolton in 1918, the scheme involved a working week of 37.5 hours, with morning shifts commencing at 6 a.m. and second turns terminating at 9 p.m. The local Operative Spinners' Association saw no merit in the plan. Not only would established domestic and leisure routines be disrupted and attendance at shop meetings be hindered, but the existing distribution of authority within the mule-room would also be challenged. As Peter Bullough argued, 'Responsibility for the mules would be divided, with a constant loss of efficiency. Work would be left, which the other man would think was deliberately pushed on him.'[105]

Similar concerns had given rise to differences in the latter months of the Great War. From June 1917, the industry operated a system of short-time working, administered by the Cotton Control Board. Established with government support, its remit was to maintain Lancashire's 'tranquillity and morale' at a time when wartime shipping priorities reduced the capacity available for raw cotton and so necessitated some contraction in activity. To achieve this, without compromising the primary aim of upholding social and political stability, the Board, comprising employer, union, and mercantile interests, rationed cotton supplies and set limits to the proportion of machinery each mill was allowed to operate.[106] The limit could be exceeded on payment of a levy, which would be used to support those workers affected by the restrictions. To avoid the widespread discharge of labour, workers were 'played off' in rotation for one week at a time. Only grinders were exempted from such regulations, being guaranteed full-time working.[107] By maintaining living standards while ensuring against victimization in the allocation of work, the scheme quickly gained widespread acceptance. Reviewing the first twelve months of the Board's operations, the *Cotton Factory Times* was of the opinion that 'For once the organisation of the trade . . . has been perfect'.[108]

[105] *BJG* (8 Feb. 1918), 2; (1 Mar. 1918), 3; see also BA, Alice Foley Collection ZFO/5, A. Foley, 'Shift Working in Cotton Mills: A Woman's Point of View'.

[106] H. D. Henderson, *The Cotton Control Board* (Oxford, 1922), 1–8; JRUL, BCA/13/2/20 BSA, general correspondence, Notice of Cotton Control Board instructions; *BEN* (28 June 1917), 3.

[107] BA, FT/7/6/75 BOCA, quarterly report, 1 June, 1918, 1; JRUL, BCA/1/3/10 BSA, minutes, Council meeting, 6 Sept. 1917; LRO, NE Lancs Textile Manufacturers' Association, DDX 1145/1/1/3 Burnley Master Cotton Spinners' and Manufacturers' Association, minutes, Local Joint Committee for Spinners, 13 Sept. 1917.

[108] *CFT* (12 July 1918), 1; LRO, DDX 1274/6/2 Burnley and District Weavers' Association, quarterly report, 30 Jan. 1918.

Employers were less convinced. Over time, benefit payments worked to limit labour mobility. While workers at one mill were played off, neighbouring cotton and munitions plant experienced a shortage of hands. To overcome this, the Board sought, in May 1918, to abolish rotation. Union officials were hostile, interpreting the move as a shift towards industrial conscription. By extending managerial control over deployments, Control would become 'a potent instrument of victimisation'.[109] In August, spinners voted decisively to retain the rota week. A one-week stoppage resulted, settled only by Lloyd George's mediation and the appointment of a government tribunal to investigate all grievances.[110] The experience of control indicated that 'tranquillity and morale' could only be assured so long as existing work practices were maintained. The thinking underlying the rotation principle carried over into the 1920s, when the Spinners' Amalgamation was insistent that short-time working should be apportioned equally within each shop.[111] Management's capacity to determine work allocations was thereby checked.

Workplace control thus remained a central preoccupation of spinning and card-room trade unionism. Notions of industrial accommodation, encouraged by Victorian confidence in the efficacy of collective-bargaining procedures, were most sharply qualified at this point. The privileged status accorded small groups of operatives sustained an independent outlook, the antithesis of the deference which some have argued characterized the work relationship in nineteenth-century factories.[112] Yet if industrial agreement proved elusive in this period, relations rarely degenerated into outright conflict. A sense of difference was seen by contemporaries as inevitable in a technologically complex industry. Nevertheless, representatives on both sides stressed the degree to which separate interests were tolerated.[113] The regulations governing collective agreements marked the boundaries of 'acceptable' behaviour. So long as rules were observed, a fundamental breakdown was unlikely. Experience

[109] Henderson, *Cotton Control Board*, 31–2; JRUL, BCA/13/2/22 BSA, general correspondence, Control Board regulations, 8 July 1918; *CFT* (12 July 1918), 3.

[110] Henderson, *Cotton Control Board*, 57–8; *CFT* (23 Aug. 1918), 1; *BEN* (17 Sept. 1918), 2; *LG* 26 (1918), 408.

[111] JRUL, BCA/12/5/2 BSA, joint meeting negotiations, central joint meeting, 12 Aug. 1926; BCA/1/3/14 BSA, minutes, Council meeting, 17 Mar. 1930; JRL, Ashton Employers' Collection, FMCSA, annual report, year to 30 June 1919 (Manchester, 1919), 80–1.

[112] P. Joyce, *Work, Society and Politics* (Brighton, 1980), ch. 3.

[113] BA, FT/21/8 BSA, annual report, 1911, 4; the point was given prominence in William Howarth's speeches to annual meetings of the Bolton Master Cotton Spinners' Association, *BJG* (4 Mar. 1921), 10; (28 March 1924), 9.

worked to temper but not fundamentally to weaken faith in conciliation procedures. To that extent, A. J. McIvor's contention that the employers' decision to revoke joint agreements in 1932 constituted 'a mid-nineteenth century style experiment in unregulated class warfare' manages to be both melodramatic and misleading.[114] Over time, however, state officials had become regular, if reluctant, participants in the industrial politics of the cotton trade. The progressive decline in internal cohesion among employers' organizations, which contrasted sharply with trade-union craft disciplines, rendered government agencies the most effective guarantors of collective agreement. Cotton's ability to shape its own future, as celebrated by Askwith, had been fatally compromised. Although the industry was capable of speaking with one voice when faced with external challenges, this obscured underlying differences in inflection. Over a range of issues, from wages to company administration, the union outlook was informed by craft concerns. The interests of the female and juvenile majorities in both mule- and card-rooms found no effective outlet. Throughout, trade unionism in the spinning trade acted as a vehicle for sectional interests. Its capacity to express a broader identity remained limited.

III

No such ambiguities appeared to mark the industrial politics of coal. Over the period as a whole, the miners displayed an unparalleled propensity for militancy, a tendency which many have explained in terms of a highly developed occupational and social solidarity. In the context of isolated, single-industry settlements, the loyalties of work appeared to translate readily into those of class, finding their most powerful expression through local union lodges.[115] Recent work has tended to cast doubt on generalized explanations of mining militancy, based on concepts of an 'isolated mass' or 'occupational community'. Rather, prominence has been given to marked local and regional variations in the frequency and intensity of strike action. The roots of such differences are sought in

[114] A. J. McIvor, 'Employers' Associations and Industrial Relations in Lancashire, 1890–1939' (Manchester Univ. Ph.D. thesis, 1983), 424–5; the published version of this work adopts a more measured tone, id., *Organised Capital*, 200–1.
[115] J. Saville, 'Notes on Ideology and the Miners before World War One', *Bulletin of the Society for the Study of Labour History*, 23 (Autumn 1971), 25; Allen, *Militancy*, 62; Hobsbawm, *Worlds of Labour*, 191; M. Bulmer, 'Social Structure and Social Change in the Twentieth Century', in id. (ed.), *Mining and Social Change* (1978), 23–8.

particular circumstances, among which the most potent were poor working conditions and low levels of profitability.[116] Both applied with particular force to Lancashire, justifying contemporary perceptions of a
coalfield marked by strained industrial relations and high levels of labour
militancy. Such at least was the view of the *Daily News*, which, in 1912,
commented on an industrial history of 'miserable strikes following miserable strikes in weary and often futile repetition', resulting in 'an estrange-
ment between masters and men such as exists nowhere else except in
South Wales'.[117] The tenor of debate within the MFGB, particularly during the 1920s, confirmed this identification. Lancashire often found its
most consistent supporters in national mining counsels among the south
Wales delegations. Yet this was an alignment that owed more to local circumstances than to any broader commitment to the cause of industrial
radicalism. An examination of labour relations within Lancashire casts
doubt on the county's supposed militancy and, more importantly, calls
into question the ability of trade unionism to act as the focus for collective loyalties.

Collective-bargaining procedures were slow to develop within the
Lancashire coalfield. In the 1890s, at the time that the Brooklands
Agreement consummated the cotton trade's reputation for conciliation,
no formal machinery governed relations in mining. As the Royal
Commission on Labour discovered, employers lacked any central agency
for negotiating purposes, being divided into three districts centred on
Manchester, North, and West Lancashire. Formal organization was even
lacking at district level. Owners in the North tended to follow the terms
of agreements concluded further south, while in the West, around Wigan
and St Helens, although *ad hoc* meetings adjudicated on wage adjustments, disputes over working conditions were left to individual collieries.
The employers' one county forum, the South Lancashire Coal Association,
established in 1843, was concerned specifically with parliamentary matters. Calls to extend its remit to cover labour relations within the county,
advanced in 1903 by the LCMF secretary Thomas Ashton, were

---

[116] D. Gilbert, *Class, Community and Collective Action: Social Change in Two British Coalfields, 1850–1926* (Oxford, 1992), ch. 2; G. Salaman, 'Occupations, Community and Consciousness', in M. Bulmer (ed.), *Working-Class Images of Society* (1975), 219–20; Zweiniger-Bargielowska, 'Miners' Militancy'; Church, Outram, and Smith, 'British Coal Mining Strikes'.

[117] Cited in R. Gregory, *The Miners and British Politics, 1906–1914* (Oxford, 1969), 57; Challinor, *Lancashire and Cheshire Miners*, 235.

opposed.[118] In part, decentralized bargaining practices reflected important variations in geological conditions. The Wigan Coal and Iron Co.,
Ltd, the largest concern within the county, operated separate wage lists at
each of its twenty-five Lancashire pits.[119]

Nevertheless, by 1914, a comprehensive bargaining structure, allowing
for joint consultations over wages and working conditions, was in place.
Change was the result of developments within and beyond the county.
Among internal factors, the consolidation of trade unionism was central.
Effective labour organization across the county dated from 1881 and
quickly expanded to take in areas where a union presence had hitherto
been unknown, including the north-eastern fringe around Burnley.[120]
Coal-owners acquiesced in the Federation's growth. Most shared George
Watson Macalpine's preference, expressed before the Royal Commission
on Labour, for negotiations with accredited labour representatives. At
Norley and Orrell Collieries, to the west of Wigan, employers agreed in
1913 to assist efforts to encourage non-unionists to join the Federation.
Not all firms were as accommodating, although outright obstruction was
rare. Management at Garswood Hall, Ashton-in-Makerfield, was unusual
in refusing recognition to branch or Federation officials.[121] Breakaway
'blue button' unions, set up in opposition to the LCMF, thus received
minimal support from local owners. The example of Abram in the 1920s,
where a determined management was able to support and sustain a company union, indicates the extent to which surrogate organizations were
able to thrive with proprietorial backing. In its absence, both the Ashton-
in-Makerfield Conservative Miners' Association, founded in 1910, and
the United Miners' Federation, active around Leigh in 1912, failed to
make significant headway. At its height, the latter represented a mere 500
miners, a figure which soon fell to forty.[122]

Yet, if the disciplined observance of agreements encouraged union
recognition at individual pits, employers still fought shy of a county

---

[118] *Parl. Papers 1892*, xxxiv (6708–IV), RC on Labour: Minutes of Evidence. Mining, qq.
5809, 5818–19, 6124–8; LCMF, monthly conference minutes, 19 Sept. 1903; Scott,
'Lancashire and Cheshire Miners' Federation', 50.

[119] *Lancashire: Its History, Growth and Importance*, i (n.d.), 177; *Wigan Coal and Iron Co.,
Ltd* (Altrincham, 1908), 25–7; LCMF, monthly conference minutes, 3 Jan., 28 Mar., 25
April, 23 May 1903.

[120] T. R. Threlfall (ed.), *Lancashire Miners' Federation: Official Programme of the Second
Annual Miners' Demonstration* (Southport, 1890), 5, 13–15.

[121] *Parl. Papers 1892*, xxxiv (6708–IV), RC on Labour: Minutes of Evidence. Mining, qq.
6182–3; *WO* (7 June 1913), 7; LCMF, monthly conference minutes, 16 Apr. 1910.

[122] *LG* 18 (1910), 217; 20 (1912), 487; Scott, 'Lancashire and Cheshire Miners' Federation',
336–8.

conciliation scheme. External factors were a crucial constraint here. Lancashire's pits were often unable to satisfy the demands of local industrial and domestic users. As a result, the county was a consistent net importer of fuel. The volumes involved varied with economic circumstances and increased when neighbouring fields were denied alternative outlets. In 1908, for example, Richard Brancker, managing director of the Hulton Colliery Co., Ltd, complained of the loss of the Liverpool bunkering trade to pits in Barnsley and the Dearne Valley, which had responded to recession by boosting sales to Lancashire. Similarly, following the outbreak of war in 1914, local owners opposed moves to restrict coal exports, fearing renewed dumping from Yorkshire.[123] Awareness of Lancashire's competitive disadvantage remained current throughout the period and could only be heightened by advertising campaigns, such as that launched by a local Co-operative Society, which invited its coal customers to 'Try our Selected Yorkshire Best, it will certainly please you'.[124] Over time, the contrast with conditions east of the Pennines became progressively more stark. One correspondent may have been guilty of exaggeration in describing Yorkshire in 1926 as an area where 'No one is on the dole, no one looks miserable; they are prosperous and undesirous of change'.[125] Nevertheless, such remarks encapsulated popular perceptions—as further confirmation of which, it was rumoured that the first £5 note seen in Wigan had been earned in a Yorkshire wage packet.[126]

Repeated indications of comparative decline coloured attitudes on both sides of the industry to the question of conciliation. Employers opposed any agreement likely to weaken further an already tenuous hold on local markets. Any movement on collective bargaining had to be made in step with developments in other districts.[127] The county was thus first constituted as an undivided unit for conciliation purposes on the Federated Districts Board, established in 1888, which regulated wage movements across Yorkshire and the English Midlands as well as in Lancashire. Inter-district competition was, to some degree, contained, although disputes over working conditions remained subject to local negotiations.[128] Here again, national developments assisted in the formula-

    [123] W. Prest, 'The Problem of the Lancashire Coal Industry', *Economic Journal*, 47 (1937), 288–9; *BJG* (31 July 1908), 15; *Parl. Papers 1914–16*, xxviii (8009), Coal Mining in Wartime: Minutes of Evidence, qq. 2258–63, 2270–1, 2277, 2359–60.
    [124] LCMF, monthly conference minutes, 23 Dec. 1911.
    [125] *BJG* (30 April 1926), 11, reporting the observations of Ernest Polden of Farnworth.
    [126] J. Seabrook, *Unemployment* (1983), 155.   [127] *BJG* (30 May 1924), 11.
    [128] Rowe, *Wages in the Coal Industry*, 39; Jevons, *British Coal Trade*, 505–13; *Parl. Papers 1910*, lviii (5325), Strikes and Lock-Outs in 1909, 95–6.

tion of agreed procedures. A mechanism for the resolution of individual points of dispute had been devised as a means of settling the twenty-three-week stoppage at Douglas Bank Colliery, Wigan, in 1911. This allowed for a system of joint inspections in cases of geologically difficult ('abnormal') workplaces. The LCMF pressed that the settlement form the basis of a county conciliation scheme. However, the Lancashire and Cheshire Coal Association declined to negotiate in the absence of a national agreement. Once this was in place, following the Minimum Wage strike of 1912, the Douglas Bank formula was promptly adopted. Indeed, Lancashire was alone among major fields in agreeing terms without reference to an independent chairman. Disputes over working conditions would, in future, be discussed by Pit and Local District Committees.[129] Change within Lancashire continued to be dependent on developments elsewhere. So, while owners accepted the principle of a separate wage list for surface workers in 1913, any agreement was made conditional on national trends.[130]

Federation officials were also keen advocates of inter-district co-operation. Failure to staunch the flow of coal into Lancashire had blunted the impact of strike action in 1881.[131] LCMF spokesmen thus became convinced advocates of national organization, with the result that the Miners' Federation of Great Britain (MFGB), formed in 1888 to co-ordinate action across the English north and Midlands, carried an indelible Lancastrian imprint. Thomas Ashton, first general secretary of the LCMF, filled the equivalent post within the MFGB. What is more, until national offices were transferred to London in 1918, in response to government involvement in the management of the industry, executive functions centred on Manchester. National organization remained a central plank of LCMF policy, uniting a politically disparate executive, comprising, in 1903, the Conservative Ashton, the Lib-Labism of the president, Sam Woods, and the ILPer Thomas Greenall.[132] It also over-rode recurrent problems over wage negotiations. Under the

---

[129] *Wigan Examiner (WE)* (26 Oct. 1911), 2; LCMF, monthly conference minutes, 23 Dec. 1911; *LG* 20 (1912), 216–18; Scott 'Lancashire and Cheshire Miners' Federation', 188, 305–10.   [130] Ibid. 320–1.

[131] Challinor, *Lancashire and Cheshire Miners*, 169–88; *Parl. Papers 1892*, xxxiv (6708–IV), RC on Labour: Minutes of Evidence. Mining, qq. 5829, 5953.

[132] J. Saville, 'Thomas Ashton (1844–1927): Miners' Leader'; J. Bellamy, 'Samuel Woods (1846–1915): Miners' Leader and Lib-Lab M.P.', both in J. M. Bellamy and J. Saville (eds.), *Dictionary of Labour Biography*, i (1972), 30–2, 351–3; J. Hill, 'The Lancashire Miners, Thomas Greenall and the Labour Party, 1900–6', *THSLC*, 130 (1981), 116–17; LCMF, special conference minutes, 10 Aug. 1918.

Federated Districts Board, Lancastrian rates were tied to those in more prosperous and productive fields. The conviction that earnings were, as a result, artificially depressed stimulated calls, such as those by Hindley and Sutton Heath (St Helens) branches in 1904 and 1906 respectively to secede from the Board. Yet all were defeated, as the LCMF remained reluctant to undermine an effective example of inter-district co-operation.[133]

This shared belief in the benefits of national organization provided the basis for the broader regional consensus which emerged during the Great War. In October 1915, it was agreed that differences left unresolved by joint discussions would be referred to independent binding arbitration. Federation officials justified this unprecedented abandonment of the strike weapon by arguing that such a procedure would oblige employers to co-operate on the issue of non-membership.[134] However, this question remained a source of friction throughout the war, as employers, although they agreed to afford the LCMF organizing facilities, declined to make union membership a condition of employment. Obstructions encountered at particular collieries persuaded Federation officials to apply to the Coal Controller, Guy Calthrop, in July 1917. He pressed owners to concede the closed shop. Most agreed to comply for the duration of the war. Exceptions, nevertheless, persisted. An estimated 400 non-unionists were employed at Garswood Hall late in 1917.[135] Otherwise, industrial accord was barely threatened in the four years of war. Only one dispute was sufficiently serious to merit inclusion in the detailed returns on strikes and lock-outs prepared by *The Labour Gazette*. In January 1918, Burnley pits were closed for two working days following complaints over the administration of food control.[136] The prevailing mood was such that third-party arbitration, as provided for under the 1915 agreement, was never required. When the Joint District Board reconvened in January 1919 under the chairmanship of Judge Francis H. Mellor, KC, CC, the industry's representatives felt obliged to apologise for their apparent neglect of his services. As Lionel Pilkington, chairman of Richard Evans and Co.,

---

[133] LCMF, supplementary conference programme, 2 Jan. 1904; monthly conference minutes, 8 Sept. 1906.

[134] *Parl. Papers 1914–16*, xxviii (8147), Coal Mining in Wartime: Second General Report, appendix C, 33; LCMF, monthly conference minutes, 23 Oct. 1915.

[135] LCMF, monthly conference minutes, 18 Nov. 1916, 22 Sept. 1917; Joint District Board minutes, 14 Aug. 1917.   [136] *LG* 26 (1918), 68.

Ltd of St Helens, explained, 'We have managed to agree pretty well, and that is why we have not troubled you'.[137]

The basis for local accommodation lay less in the terms of the 1915 agreement than in the economic and administrative conditions of wartime. The demand for coal maintained activity at high levels for the duration of the conflict. The average number of days worked each week increased from 5.2 in the four years to the outbreak of war, a period of prosperity within the trade, to 5.8 in the quadrennium from January 1915. Moreover, monthly fluctuations in activity narrowed considerably. In 1911, minimum and maximum figures for days worked each week varied between 3.8 and 5.6. The comparable figures for 1917 were 5.4 and 5.9. More significantly, the war provided relief from long-term comparative decline, as the pooling of 'surplus' profits under national control provided inoculation against the effects of inter-regional competition.[138] Looking back from the 1920s, Lancastrians, with pardonable exaggeration, viewed the period from 1914 to 1921 as 'an Augustan peace', during which the industry had operated with 'complete smoothness and freedom from disputes'.[139] If this tended to overstate matters, it was still an experience which contrasted sharply with the cotton trade's repeated recourse to state arbitration and the moves towards political radicalization detected in other coalfields. While the Commission of Inquiry into Industrial Unrest encountered evidence of fundamental alienation along the south Welsh valleys, the report for the North-Western Area made no reference to Lancashire's colliers.[140]

As national control had been vital to the maintenance of local equilibrium, so moves to de-control from 1921 gave rise to unease across Lancashire. With collieries operating at losses averaging 8s. 11d. a ton, W. H. Hewlett of the Wigan Coal and Iron Co., Ltd warned that the ending of subsidies would result in closures. In January, therefore, the county's Joint Committee registered an 'emphatic protest' against decontrol. Nationally, however, the interests of exporting fields prevailed. For Evan Williams, president of the Mining Association of Great Britain, the pooling of profits had done little more than offer succour

---

[137] LCMF, Joint District Board minutes, 10 Jan. 1919; *Who's Who 1918: An Annual Biographical Dictionary with which is Incorporated 'Men and Women of the Time'. Seventieth Year of Issue* (n.d.), 1645.

[138] *LG* 18–27 (1910–19); Redmayne, *The British Coal-Mining Industry during the War*, 95.

[139] LCMF, Joint Committee minutes, 17 Dec. 1923.

[140] *Parl. Papers 1917–18*, xv (8668), Commission of Enquiry into Industrial Unrest. No. 7 Division. Report of the Commissioners for Wales, including Monmouthshire, par. 22; (8663), Industrial Unrest. No. 2 Division. Report for the North-Western Area, *passim*.

to 'inefficiency and indifference'.[141] In Lancashire, the consequences of any reversion to district settlements were clear. Addressing a gathering of Bolton colliers during the 1921 dispute, Henry Twist, Federation agent for the Ashton-in-Makerfield district, predicted that under such conditions, 'Yorkshire, well blessed by nature with good seams, would be offering coal to Lancashire at less than they could serve it at even after reducing their wages. Then Lancashire men, with their impoverished coalfield, would be idle.'[142] Within the MFGB, Lancashire alone stood out against any decentralization of bargaining arrangements right to the end of the 1921 strike.[143]

Yet the imposition of district settlements did not eliminate the possibility of industrial co-operation. As limited profitability worked to reduce wage rates from the second half of 1921, employers and unions combined in an attempt to ameliorate the impact of changes in pay levels. They proposed utilizing the welfare fund established following the recommendations of the Sankey Commission. Based on a 1*d.* per ton levy on coal sales, the fund was intended to finance improvements to housing and social amenities across colliery districts. In December 1921, the Lancashire Joint Committee resolved to employ the £60,000 available within the county to boost the wages of low-paid workers. The proposal came to nothing, the Central Welfare Committee judging it an inappropriate use of the fund.[144] Instead, from August 1922, minimum shift payments or 'subsistence allowances' were introduced for all miners on day rates.[145] Within the LCMF, the suspicion remained that owners were camouflaging profits by boosting reserves and concealing receipts from by-product plant, in order to keep wages at the minimum of 32 per cent above the 1911 standard. County officials were, however, sceptical whether the effects of such creative accountancy would be anything other than cosmetic. For Thomas Greenall, Federation president in 1924, only a national agreement could ensure a sustained and significant rise in earnings.[146] Lancashire's stand against the settlements of 1921 and 1926, although they aligned the county with south Wales, was informed more by particular, regional concerns than by any underlying 'militancy'.

---

[141] LCMF, Joint Committee minutes, 10 Jan.; monthly conference minutes, 5 Mar. 1921.

[142] *BJG* (6 May 1921), 6; see also LCMF, Joint Committee minutes, 7 Mar. 1921.

[143] *BJG* (1 July 1921), 6.

[144] *Parl. Papers 1919*, xi (359), Coal Industry Commission: Interim Reports, p. ix; LCMF, monthly conference minutes, 10 Dec. 1921; Joint Committee minutes, 12 Dec. 1921, 13 Mar. 1922.

[145] *LG* 30 (1922), 377; LCMF, EC minutes, 12 Aug. 1922.

[146] LCMF, annual conference minutes, 5 Jan. 1924; adjourned annual conference minutes, 2 Feb. 1924; special conference minutes, 14 Feb. 1925.

Confirming the pattern thus far presented, pit stoppages were rare throughout the period. Douglas Bank aside, only two disputes seriously disrupted production before 1914: the first followed the introduction of pit ponies at Pemberton Colliery, Wigan, in 1905 (129 days lost); and the other, in the Burnley area in 1910, concerned payments for the removal of timber supports (88 days). Comparative figures, compiled by Church, lend statistical weight to this observation. Between 1894 and 1913, Lancashire and Cheshire pits, although employing 11 per cent of the national mining workforce, accounted for only 7 per cent of days lost through disputes in the industry, a distribution which identifies the region with the East Midlands, an area of impeccable Lib-Lab moderation.[147] Confrontation was no more apparent in later years. *The Labour Gazette* recorded only nine minor disputes in Lancashire pits between 1918 and 1932. After 1927, figures showing the ten most strike-prone collieries across Britain did not include one from Lancashire.[148]

Particular features of work underground continued to provide potential sources of friction. Complaints persisted, for much of this period, over deductions from wages for the supply of tools and lights by management. The extent of the problem is suggested by the fact that the LCMF was alone among unions affiliated to the MFGB in presenting evidence on this point to the Departmental Committee on the Truck Acts in 1908.[149] Increases in the amounts charged, estimated at 300 per cent during the Great War, led to renewed protests, which continued into the postwar period.[150] Yet, at the same time, machinery developed which was designed to blunt the force of such points of grievance. Monthly joint committee meetings provided the industry with an effective system of conciliation through the 1920s. These deliberations revealed a collective discipline which had been lacking before 1912. Thus, the refusal, in 1927, of George Hargreaves and Co. of Accrington to adjust meal breaks for surface workers in line with terms jointly agreed elsewhere was thought

[147] *LG* 14 (1906), 92; 19 (1911), 108; D. Anderson, 'Blundell's Collieries: Wages, Disputes and Conditions of Work', *THSLC*, 117 (1965), 129; Church, 'Edwardian Labour Unrest', 856.

[148] *LG* 27–40 (1919–32), *passim*; Church, Outram, and Smith, 'British Coal Mining Strikes', 343.

[149] *Parl. Papers 1908*, lix (4443), Departmental Committee on the Truck Acts. II. Minutes of Evidence, qq. 7506, 7920–34; deductions also implied an extension of managerial control, Wigan Heritage Services, History Shop (WHS), WTN 419 S7 Standish District Miners' Association (SMA), monthly council minutes, 2 June 1894.

[150] LCMF, monthly conference minutes, 6 Apr., 19 Oct. 1918, 12 Nov. 1921; Joint Committee minutes, 12 Dec. 1921, 14 May 1923.

to be without precedent.[151] With the exception of Abram Colliery, the coal industry experienced a consolidation of central authority in the inter-war period, in sharp contrast to events in the cotton trade.

Institutional sources significantly amend the emphasis which second-ary authorities have given to the bitterness and militancy of Lancashire's mining politics. Moves towards formal accommodation were quickened by awareness of comparative decline and confirmed by the county's ex-perience in wartime. A conciliatory tradition was established which would be cemented through the years of depression that followed. Such, at least, is the conclusion suggested by official perspectives. How representative these were of feeling at pit level remains to be established. The central position of trade unionism in most mining districts has virtually elimi-nated any scope for doubt on this point. The finding of the Industrial Unrest Commissioners in 1917, that union lodges across south Wales were 'centres of social and political activity more potent perhaps than any other . . . in the community', has come to inform many subsequent stud-ies of colliery societies.[152] Its applicability to Lancashire, however, is open to doubt. At various points, the LCMF's authority was fundamentally compromised.

Problems were not founded primarily on the work experience. The absence of craft distinctions underground enabled the Federation to adopt an almost fully 'open' structure. Although initially confined largely to piece-rate hewers, membership had, by 1914, spread to day-wage and surface hands, for whom separate wage lists were agreed in 1911 and 1914 respectively.[153] The most significant group still to be excluded comprised the almost 3,000 women employed in moving and sorting coal on pit banks. Rule 2 of the LCMF's constitution, confirmed by a vote of branch delegates in January 1912, limited membership to male workers in and around the pit. Attempts to organize female colliery workers were thus left to other bodies, such as the Trades Council in Westhoughton, near Bolton, which, in 1913, sought to establish a branch of the National Federation of Women Workers on the pit brow.[154] The outbreak of war

   [151] LCMF, monthly conference minutes, 26 Mar. 1927.

   [152] *Parl. Papers 1917–18*, xv (8668), Industrial Unrest: Wales, par. 17; see e.g. K. Brown, 'The Lodges of the Durham Miners' Association, 1869–1926', *Northern History*, 23 (1987), 148–52.

   [153] *WO* (26 July 1905), 3; LCMF, joint meeting at Midland Hotel, Manchester, 17 Oct. 1911; Scott, 'Lancashire and Cheshire Miners' Federation', 322.

   [154] *Parl. Papers 1914–16*, xxviii (8023–III), Report of HM Inspector of Mines for Lancashire, North Wales and Ireland Division, 7; LCMF, annual conference minutes, 20 Jan. 1912; *BJG* (21 Nov. 1913), 11; (12 Dec. 1913), 11.

checked this initiative and heralded a reversal in LCMF policy. Female numbers had grown to 3,500 by 1918, the year in which Federation delegates voted to rescind Rule 2. If their intention was to introduce a minimum pay scale for women workers, thereby eliminating the potential for wage competition on the pit surface, the immediate effect was to open Federation membership to all save supervisory staff.[155]

The progressive expansion in the LCMF's constituency concealed, however, significant short-term variations in membership levels. In 1908, 76 per cent of eligible miners subscribed to the Federation. Within two years, this figure had fallen to 55.6 per cent (57,500).[156] Union organization prospered in wartime, assisted by full-time working and employer cooperation over non-members. In his 1921 presidential address to the Federation's annual conference, Greenall could boast of almost complete representation: LCMF members made up 102,100 out of a workforce of 105,600.[157] That position was rapidly undermined with the onset of decontrol and economic depression. In two years, during which employment levels remained substantially unchanged, Federation membership fell by 40 per cent to 60,700. Thereafter, the LCMF was rarely able to claim more than 75 per cent of its potential constituency.[158]

If trade-cycle fluctuations provide the most obvious explanation for the volatility of union support, the impact of organizational weaknesses should not be discounted. Mining unionism in Lancashire had developed around associations centred on often loosely defined geographical districts. The most extreme example of this, the Ashton and Haydock Miners' Association, organized pits to the west of Wigan, along with branches on the eastern edge of the coalfield, from Burnley in the north to Pendlebury in the south. Although most associations were more compact, administrative boundaries were not always clearly defined. Overlapping areas of responsibility thus resulted, more especially at the centre of the field, around Wigan. For example, the local Miners' Provident

[155] LCMF, annual conference minutes, 12 Jan. 1918; Joint Committee minutes, 13 Oct., 10 Nov. 1919.

[156] Scott, 'Lancashire and Cheshire Miners' Federation', table S14, 458; *Parl. Papers 1909*, xxxiii (4672–V), Report of HM Inspector of Mines for Manchester and Ireland District, 5; (4672–VI), Liverpool and North Wales District, 7; *Parl. Papers 1911*, xxxvi (5676–IV), Report of HM Inspector of Mines for Manchester and Ireland District, 4; (5676–V), Liverpool and North Wales District, 6.

[157] LCMF, annual conference minutes and membership returns, 8 Jan. 1921; Mines Dept., *Reports of HM Inspectors of Mines for 1921* (HMSO, 1922), A. D. Nicholson, 'Lancashire, North Wales and Ireland Division', 4.

[158] LCMF, membership returns, 6 Jan. 1923; Mines Dept., *Reports of HM Inspectors of Mines for 1923* (HMSO, 1924), A. D. Nicholson, 'Lancashire and North Wales Division', 6.

Benefit Society, founded in 1862, included branches 10 miles to the north in Chorley and Adlington, but not in the contiguous townships of Standish and Pemberton, each of which maintained autonomous associations.[159] Employment patterns compounded the difficulties thereby created, a fact which became especially apparent when new pits were sunk. The opening of Victoria Colliery in 1900 gave rise to friction between organizations in Wigan and Standish, as each claimed the right to represent the workforce. The problem was that, whereas the Victoria was located within Standish's boundaries, most of the miners it employed lived in Wigan. The latter point was of importance, given that membership of the forty-nine lodges which comprised the Wigan Society was determined by ties of residence, with meetings held in local pubs, rather than of work.[160] It was a structure which local officials were determined to maintain. They thus opposed reforms proposed by the county Federation, involving a move to pit-lodge branches. The strength of feeling on this point was such that the formation of a breakaway Federation was contemplated in 1906.[161]

Opponents of reform stressed the utility of existing arrangements. First, it was argued, they enabled miners living some distance from their place of work to attend branch meetings. Home and work were more sharply differentiated in Lancashire than most other coalfields, a fact attributable to the clustering of large urban centres across south–central Lancashire and the existence of a well-developed transport network. In evidence to the Eight Hours Committee, Henry Hall, Government Inspector for the Liverpool and North Wales Division, explained that many miners opted to 'travel to their work in wagonnettes where there are no tramways, but now a good many of them come in trams and others by train from one station to another.' [162] The average distance covered in journeying to work was put at 2.5 miles. In 1922, the LCMF launched an inquiry into the cost of railway travel for its members. In the process, it drew evidence from a quarter of all branches. Physical constraints limited the ability of trade unionism to draw on conventional solidarities, a point emphasized by Greenall in 1923. Responding to criticism from national

[159] Threlfall (ed.), *Lancashire Miners' Federation*, 1–3, 13–15, 17–18.

[160] LCMF, monthly conference minutes, 7 Oct. 1905; WHS, WTN 419 L2 SMA, monthly council minutes, 23 Sept. 1905; *WE* (27 Oct. 1900), 6; (17 Oct. 1903), 5. A ballot of Victoria colliers resolved the dispute in favour of Wigan, LCMF, monthly conference minutes, 4 Nov. 1905.

[161] LCMF, monthly conference minutes, 21 Apr., 8 Sept. 1906.

[162] *Parl. Papers 1907*, xv (3506), Eight Hours Committee: Final Report. Pt. II. Minutes of Evidence, q. 16217.

officials, who contrasted Lancashire's aggressive stance against existing wage agreements with declining membership levels within the county, he pointed to the particular obstacles encountered in seeking to build an effective organization: 'in Northumberland and Durham the men live in villages, purely mining villages, and if a man does not pay, every man, woman and child knows about it, and he does not get any peace. In Lancashire, a man may live miles away from the place where he works.'[163] For many within the LCMF, a residential focus for branch organization was more in keeping with local realities.

Financial calculations also informed opposition to reform in 1906. Federation finances were decentralized, with members' subscriptions divided equally between county and branch offices. While central support was limited to strike and victimization cases, some district associations administered a range of friendly benefits, including funeral and accident relief. More often, however, district resources did not suffice to sustain additional payments. The Standish Association was obliged to end out-of-work payments in the 1890s. Many branches thus opted to divide funds on an annual basis, a practice initially designed to enable members to attend the Federation's annual demonstration, but which survived the decision to discontinue such gatherings from 1903.[164] If anything, the tendency to divide funds increased over time. The spread of pit-lodge organization, encouraged by the county leadership, fragmented district finances, thus reducing the scope for friendly benefits. On the dissolution of the Standish Association in 1907, its assets were divided among members in proportion to the number of contributions paid by each. The Wigan Society voted to disband the following year. From that point, the relevant branches chose to divide their funds.[165] The continued decentralization of finances limited the LCMF's resources, so that concerted strike action, as in 1921, rapidly depleted available reserves. After four weeks, a mere £500 remained in Federation coffers. Rank-and-file opinion rejected attempts to bolster union finances, dismissing proposals likely to turn the Federation into 'a kind of Savings Club'. Rather, savings were entrusted to a range of alternative bodies, including funds run jointly

---

[163] LCMF, monthly conference minutes, 10 Nov. 1923, 4 Feb. 1922; see also EC minutes, 8 Sept. 1923, for complaints over the cost of travel.

[164] J. Benson, 'English Coal-Miners' Trade-Union Accident Funds, 1850–1900', *Econ.Hist.Rev.*, 2nd ser. 28 (1975), 406–7; WHS, WTN 419 S7 SMA, monthly council minutes, 2 Nov. 1895; LCMF, monthly conference minutes, 23 Apr. 1904.

[165] WHS, WTN 419 L2 SMA, monthly council minutes, 12 Jan. 1907; LCMF, monthly conference minutes, 19 Sept. 1903, 29 Aug. 1908, 16 Aug. 1924.

with management representatives. In other coalfields, the administration of benefits placed union officials at the centre of social life.
Financial weaknesses denied comparable importance to their Lancastrian
counterparts.[166]

Organizational difficulties were compounded by indifference to union
affairs. Participation in branch meetings was often thin, even though
points of importance were being debated. A move to press union recognition at Garswood Hall in April 1910 drew only forty to fifty miners out
of a workforce of 1,200. Proprietorial hostility may have complicated matters for the Federation here. However, other comments suggest that this
experience was not untypical. In October 1924, the Worsley Mesnes
(Wigan) delegate attempted to warn the Federation conference that
monthly meetings were attracting a small minority of members only. A
clerical error distorted his estimate of the extent of the problem, however,
necessitating an amendment of the original claim that 'not twenty-five per
cent' of members attended meetings to what was considered the more
realistic figure of 'not five per cent'.[167] The union culture underlying the
sense of craft shared by minders and grinders was not manifested among
the county's colliers.

The LCMF's inability to articulate wider solidarities was fully exposed
at times of dispute. In the absence of support from union funds during
prolonged stoppages, families were thrown back on to their own
resources. The miners themselves looked to alternative sources of work in
labouring trades or winning coal from shallow outcrop workings close to
the surface, which would then be sold locally. Federation officials vigorously opposed outcropping, seeing it as tantamount to strike-breaking.
However, attempts to suppress it enjoyed only fitful success. The
LCMF's claims to have eliminated the practice during the 1926 stoppage
appeared somewhat optimistic in the light of reports that over 1,000
Lancashire miners were working coal in the hills of West Yorkshire.[168]
The persistence of outcropping raises questions about the capacity of
unions to influence their members, even at the height of major disputes
and suggests that rank-and-file behaviour often assumed forms which
were antithetical to the drive for collective unity. The point is confirmed

---

[166] LCMF, monthly conference minutes, 30 Apr. 1921, 19 July 1924; N. Dennis, F.
Henriques, and C. Slaughter, *Coal is our Life: An Analysis of a Yorkshire Mining Community*
(1956), 117; the institutions referred to here are discussed at greater length in Ch. 6.
[167] LCMF, monthly conference minutes, 19 Apr. 1910, 8 Nov. 1924.
[168] Miners' Federation of Great Britain (MFGB), special conference minutes, 29 Sept.
1926; *BJG* (2 July 1926), 8; BA, BOHP, 92 (male, born 1903), transcript, 9.

if we turn to examine modes of protest in disputes at pit level. These most often turned on questions of pay and working conditions. Significantly, the sanction most often applied by miners in such cases was not the strike, but mobility. Conditions in Lancashire, as George Caldwell observed in evidence to the Royal Commission on Labour, peculiarly suited such a response. Where colliery settlements were remote, miners remained dependent on their local pit for work. By contrast, 'in West Lancashire, where there are plenty of houses . . . they ship about from one house to another and from one colliery to another, there being so many collieries in the same neighbourhood, they change about as often as two or three times sometimes in a week.' [169] In all probability, this exaggerates the frequency of mobility. Nevertheless, evidence presented elsewhere by managerial witnesses suggests that Caldwell's observation was not entirely without foundation. Speaking before the Eight Hours Committee, Alfred Hollingsworth of Oldham noted a tendency for miners to seek the most 'comfortable' places, often in response to monetary inducements. [170] The residential propinquity of men employed at different pits facilitated a ready exchange of information on comparative levels of reward, so that any deterioration in conditions was likely to stimulate the search for alternative work. Applications for jobs at neighbouring pits followed the introduction of short-time working at Eccleston Hall Colliery, near Chorley, in 1904. Similarly, the use of electrical machinery in the Pretoria Pit gave rise to acute disquiet. The disaster inquest heard evidence that many of the deceased had 'played' days prior to the explosion to inquire into openings at other firms. Some planned to leave the trade altogether. William Calderbank (aged 21) had hopes of joining the police. [171]

Movement within the county had supplied the Pretoria with its initial workforce as it was opened out between 1900 and 1904. Recruitment was mostly from pits around Wigan. [172] Twenty years later, as the geographical centre of the field experienced incipient exhaustion, areas to the south and west, around St Helens and Leigh, provided growing employment

[169] *Parl. Papers 1892*, xxxiv (6708–IV), RC on Labour: Minutes of Evidence. Mining, q. 6105; see also qq. 5867–9.

[170] *Parl. Papers 1907*, xv (3428), Eight Hours Committee: First Report. Pt. III. Minutes of Evidence, qq. 5182, 5287.

[171] Forman, *Industrial Town*, 58; LCMF, monthly conference minutes, 18 June 1904; LRO, Coal Board Records NCHu 9/2 Hulton Colliery Co., Ltd., Transcript of Adjourned Inquest, qq. 2424–9, 2869; BA, HRF ABHC/5/40 Personal Files, 2 Mar. 1911, Revd Lord to Cooper.

[172] BA, BOHP, 108A (male, born 1917), transcript, 2.

opportunities as new measures were exploited. For example, Sutton Manor Colliery, St Helens, drew labour from Pemberton, near Wigan. Mobility thus continued within the superficially stable parameters of a declining coalfield and remained especially marked in districts undergoing expansion. Addressing the LCMF's monthly conference in November 1923, the Havannah branch delegate raised the issue of high levels of turnover: 'Take Sutton Manor for instance, there were forty-one sets of men left that particular colliery and went to another colliery; and other men went to their places, and they are continually crossing from one colliery to another.' [173] As before, precise quantification of such movement is impracticable. Nevertheless, the fact that it aroused concern among both union and management representatives suggests its significance. Access to company books gave Federation officials a partial insight into its extent at one branch, Westleigh. In the first six months of 1924, 1,098 had applied for work, of whom only 300 had gone on to jobs underground. [174]

Recourse to managerial records by the LCMF reflected the absence of a reliable mechanism for measuring mobility. In theory, whenever union members moved pits, they took with them documents ('clearances'), which recorded all contributions paid to the Federation. The use of clearances ensured that rights to benefit would not be interrupted. However, the practice of dividing funds rendered such arrangements supererogatory. Movement often resulted, therefore, in a recrudescence of non-membership, as miners saw no necessity to make use of clearances. In 1918, of forty Federation members at Garswood Hall who moved to pits near Wigan, only half had the relevant documentation. The problem was even more acute in areas of high labour turnover. In 1922, under half the workforce at Sutton Manor paid to the Federation. [175] Attempts to plug such gaps by enlisting the co-operation of employers foundered. During the war, owners had agreed to refer all applicants lacking documentation to branch officials. However, they refused to allow clearances to be administered through company offices, fearing that this would imply acceptance of union membership as a condition of employment. [176] In the absence of agreement, the Federation mounted organizational campaigns at selected

---

[173] LCMF, monthly conference minutes, 10 Nov. 1923, 11 Dec. 1920; *BJG* (13 Sept. 1918), 3.

[174] LCMF, monthly conference minutes, 31 Jan. 1925.

[175] LCMF, monthly conference minutes, 16 May 1908, Hewlett No. 2 (Westhoughton) resolution; 9 Feb. 1918, 1 Apr. 1922.

[176] LCMF, monthly conference minutes, 16 Dec. 1916; Joint Committee minutes, 12 Nov. 1923, 14 Jan. 1924.

collieries, exposing, in the process, the limited adherence of large numbers of miners to the county union. Activity at seven branches in Leigh and St Helens between 1924 and 1926 boosted membership by 645. All but nineteen had previously belonged to the Federation. Yet, of these, only 200 (or 31 per cent) were able to provide clearances.[177]

The Lancastrian experience thus offers alternative perspectives on the nature of mining militancy. Throughout the period, the propensity to strike remained low, as both miners and owners manifested a commitment to collective-bargaining procedures, secured by a framework of national agreement. Conciliation machinery was put in place in the two decades to 1914, which proved sufficiently robust to contain areas of conflict, particularly in the period from 1921, when Lancashire's national safety net was withdrawn. To that extent, the county's miners could be depicted, with justification, as industrial moderates. However, if militancy is defined more broadly, to encompass all forms of resistance to management prerogatives, then the picture is altered. Lancashire's colliers were vigorous in defence of their own interests, but their actions more often assumed an individual than a collective character. The LCMF remained only one of the media through which grievances were expressed. Structural weaknesses prevented the Federation from becoming a focus for allegiance among more than a minority of members. The social and political influence ascribed to pit lodges in areas such as south Wales consistently eluded branches of the LCMF. As with cotton operatives, attempts to reconstruct the outlook of Lancastrian miners must look beyond the institutional record.

IV

A comparative study of the industrial politics of Lancashire's coal and cotton trades in the half-century from 1880 invalidates any straightforward contrast between accommodative and confrontational labour relations. Over time, workers in both industries displayed varying degrees and forms of militancy. From 1900, wage adjustments provided a recurrent source of friction in the cotton trade. Although existing collective-bargaining machinery proved incapable of reconciling differences, attempts to develop alternative forms of conciliation were consistently

---

[177] LCMF, monthly conference minutes, 31 Dec. 1927; figures calculated from EC minutes, 13 Sept. 1924 to 27 Mar. 1926 (the branches involved were Westleigh, Bold, Lyme, Sutton Manor, Plank Lane, Wood Pit, and Parsonage).

blocked by union suspicions of company accounting procedures. Under-lying points of difference, confirmed by the vigilant defence of workplace privileges by skilled male élites in mule- and card-rooms, defined the lim-its of accommodation within the mill. The miners' reputation for mili-tancy rested substantially on their involvement in large-scale national disputes in the period to 1926. In Lancashire, awareness of comparative disadvantage, although it had the potential to embitter relations at pit level, provided the basis for lasting accord. In neither trade can an unam-biguous shift towards radicalization be discerned in the period. The lim-its of compromise were clear to cotton workers well before 1914, as the inability of Brooklands and related agreements to promote ordered rela-tions became apparent. In coal, by contrast, the gradual consolidation of collective-bargaining traditions progressively limited the scope for out-right confrontation. Recourse to strike action was infrequent in both industries and rarely resulted in a breakdown in relations.

Of greater moment than the extent of cotton or coal-mining militancy was its nature. Although a high level of collective organization character-ized both industries, in neither did trade unionism and industrial activism act as unifying forces. Craft interests directed union policy in the mule- and the card-room, so that the views of the female and juvenile majority were rarely, if ever, represented. In mining, labour protest often assumed forms inimical to union interests. Mobility, encouraged by the social and economic context within which mining operated in Lancashire, exposed fundamental structural weaknesses in the organization of labour. In nei-ther case, therefore, could militancy work to mobilize broader class inter-ests. Rather, it worked to underscore significant divisions within each workforce. The wider implications of these differences would be deter-mined by the precise relationship between particular groups of workers, including minders and their piecers, grinders and their apprentices, and the teams of hewers and drawers responsible for working the coal face. It is to that issue that the next chapter will turn, extending the focus, in the process, from the experience and outlook of active minorities in each industry to those of the workforce as a whole.

4

Keeping it in the Family? The Search for Work in Coal and Cotton Lancashire

The role of work in promoting or retarding a united sense of class among British workers has provided a recurrent topic for debate. Although class was long seen as the inevitable product of the antagonism inherent in the employer–employee relationship, greater emphasis has recently been placed on work's capacity to divide the labour force. The readiness of managements to delegate authority to selected groups of workers encouraged the emergence of marked differentials in skill and income levels. Control of promotional procedures, the 'internal' labour market, consolidated the position of this privileged stratum.[1] If this argument comprehends the position in spinning mills, it also helps to point up the absence of comparable divisions in coal-mining. The diversity of the work experience, which, as earlier chapters indicated, endured throughout the period, is effectively caught. However, the capacity of such arguments to explain broader developments in working-class life, in particular the failure of industrialization to generate a united consciousness of class, remains open to doubt. Two objections may be noted here: first, the significance attached to internal work hierarchies fails to clarify the relationship between groups of workers; and second, the precise means by which the work experience contributed to the construction of class identities tends to be implied rather than being fully addressed. This chapter pursues both these points through an examination of the process of recruitment, the factors determining the timing and the direction of the individual's entry to work.

Throughout the period, despite the increasing intervention of state agencies, entry to work was mostly determined by personal connections.[2]

---

[1] C. R. Littler, 'A Comparative Analysis of Managerial Structures and Strategies', in H. F. Gospel and C. R. Littler (eds.), *Managerial Strategies and Industrial Relations* (1983), 175–8; M. Huberman, 'Invisible Handshakes in Lancashire: Cotton Spinning in the First Half of the Nineteenth Century', *Journal of Economic History*, 46 (1986), 987–8.

[2] The problems created by an unstructured, casualized labour market exercised the official mind before 1914, J. Harris, *Unemployment and Politics: A Study in English Social*

Responsibility for recruitment continued to devolve on to the workforce itself. In such circumstances, it is argued, family linkages were readily utilized, so that sons tended to follow their fathers into the same trade, often finding themselves employed alongside them on the same machine or section of coal face. Yet the importance which has been attached to the hereditary principle calls into question the broader cultural implications of internal work hierarchies. Such points of division were likely to be of limited significance in settings where different grades comprehended members of the same family.[3] The kinship tie has figured prominently in studies of both coal and cotton society. It is central to the identification of the factory with the wider neighbourhood which informs Patrick Joyce's interpretation of Lancastrian politics and society in the later nineteenth century. Relationships forged at the point of production came, by this process, to resonate through the surrounding locality. In mining, by contrast, family interests were seen to underpin more class-specific occupational solidarities.[4] As this diversity of interpretation suggests, despite the explanatory weight which has been placed on the family's presence in work, the extent to which kinship ties were reproduced in the workplace remains thinly documented. This is significant for the industries being studied here, for, if the assimilation of domestic and industrial life can be readily assumed for single-industry settlements dominated by one major source of employment, its applicability to the more complex economy of south–central Lancashire is more doubtful. Here, the presence of several industries afforded workers greater discretion in their search for work. Choice could be exercised over both the timing and the direction of entry to paid employment, throwing important light in the process on the family's role in work and thus on the precise significance of internal work hierarchies. What is more, the criteria guiding such decisions were subject to important changes in the light both of altered family circumstances and broader economic developments in the half-century from 1880. In tracing these changes, a more accurate evaluation may be offered of

Policy, 1886–1914 (Oxford, 1972), 7–33; G. Stedman Jones, *Outcast London: A Study in the Relationship between Classes in Victorian Society* (Harmondsworth edn., 1984), ch. 18; for the position in subsequent decades, R. I. McKibbin, *Classes and Cultures* (Oxford, 1998), 119–27.

[3] R. Gray, *The Aristocracy of Labour in Nineteenth-Century Britain, c.1850–1900* (London and Basingstoke, 1981), 63; P. Joyce, *Work, Society and Politics* (Brighton, 1980), 50–64.
[4] Ibid., pp. xxi, 117–18; the importance of the kinship tie in mining is set out in H. S. Jevons, *The British Coal Trade* (1915), 621; M. J. Daunton, 'Down the Pit', *Econ.Hist.Rev.*, 2nd ser. 34 (1981), 590.

contemporary attitudes to work and the ways in which this experience helped to shape the social outlook and the evolution of class identities.

I

For most of those commencing work in late nineteenth- and early twentieth-century Lancashire, personal contacts provided the principal medium through which jobs were secured. The importance of informal recruitment networks was noted by a Board of Education report, published in 1904, into employment among the county's school-leavers. The result was, it was argued, to encourage acceptance of the first available job opportunities, regardless of prospects in the longer term.[5] In the decade which followed, agencies were established to rationalize the search for work, taking the place, as the chairman of one such body, the Bolton Juvenile Employment Advisory Committee, expressed it, of 'friends and influence'.[6] In practice, however, their impact was minimal. In 1922, a Bolton headmaster could claim that 99 per cent of children leaving his school had sought work without reference to the local advisory committee. Subsequent investigations revealed such figures to be broadly representative of the whole. A report by the borough's Primary Education Sub-Committee, prepared in 1928, found that of 2,171 school-leavers that year, only 122, or 5.6 per cent, had received institutional assistance in finding work. Ten years later, the Jewkeses' survey of juvenile employment in six Lancashire towns reported little change: fewer than one-third of all placements were made through advisory bodies or labour exchanges. For most, recruitment proceeded through 'Family, trade or social connections', or by means of personal applications at individual workplaces.[7]

In the light of such evidence, the importance which historians have attached to the kinship tie in shaping the work experience seems eminently justifiable. The persistence of labour-intensive production methods in a wide range of industries and the greater stability of households in an urban setting appeared to ensure that the family tie became central

[5] *Parl. Papers 1904*, xix (1867), Board of Education: Report on the School Training and Early Employment of Lancashire Children, 19.

[6] *BJG* (12 Dec. 1919), 7, article by J. T. Cooper, 'When Schooldays End'.

[7] *BJG* (7 July 1922), 7; (24 Feb. 1928), 6; J. and S. Jewkes, *The Juvenile Labour Market* (1938), 33–5: the towns covered were Ashton-under-Lyne, Atherton, Burnley, St Helens, Tyldesley, and Warrington.

to employment structures.[8] By this argument, work's capacity to unite outstripped its potential to divide, as labour hierarchies merely mirrored the balance of power within the home.[9] Yet the family's importance in this regard, although crucial to assessments of work's wider significance, is more often inferred than directly addressed. The availability of evidence presents a problem here. Although wage books provide the most tangible measure of the presence of kin, their survival is patchy. What is more, existing examples are less than representative, often comprising firms in small or peripheral settlements, where the absence of alternative forms of work would predetermine the family's role as the primary avenue of recruitment.[10] A prolonged trawl through company records might produce a larger and more valid data set. Even then, however, it would remain to determine the precise meaning to be assigned to any figures that resulted. An alternative, less statistical but perhaps more productive, approach would be to examine the attitudes of workers themselves to family employment as revealed through the policies of the cotton unions.

Bolton grinders' control over the recruitment and placing of apprentices aside, work practices in mule- and card-rooms offered little scope for the exercise of hereditary influence. Employers oversaw the disposition of the majority of card-room hands, while on the mule, promotion was determined by agreed procedures which emphasized seniority and proven competence. Despite mounting evidence of the increasingly 'blind-alley' nature of work in the mule-gate, operative spinners gave priority to the maintenance of existing practices. Reforms designed to ease promotional bottlenecks were thus consistently resisted.[11] Problems affecting particular firms elicited a similar response. In 1937, the North End Spinning Co., Ltd in Bolton reported a 50 per cent shortfall in little-piecers. The workforce accepted management proposals that unemployed side-piecers be

---

[8] The debate on family employment as it relates to cotton textiles is set out in N. J. Smelser, *Social Change and the Industrial Revolution: An Application of Theory to the British Cotton Industry* (Chicago, 1959), 180–224; M. M. Edwards and R. Lloyd-Jones, 'N. J. Smelser and the Cotton Family: A Reassessment', in N. B. Harte and K. G. Ponting (eds.), *Textile History and Economic History: Essays in Honour of Miss Julia de Lacy Mann* (Manchester, 1973), 304–19; M. Anderson, 'Sociological History and the Working-Class Family: Smelser Re-visited', *Social History*, 1–2 (1976–7), 317–34.

[9] Joyce, *Work, Society and Politics*, 56.

[10] Ibid., 129–30, cites the example of a mill in Barrowford, on Lancashire's north-eastern fringe. Cotton was, however, an unusually large employer in the township, accounting for 73% of an occupied workforce of 3,168 in 1911, *Parl. Papers 1913*, lxxviii (7018), Census of England and Wales, 1911. X. Occupations and Industries. Pt. I, tables 15A and 15B, 398–9, 436–7.

[11] See above, Ch. 2, pp. 36–8.

taken on to make good this deficit, but only on condition that new hands would 'not rank as piecers for minding'.[12] The principle of promotion by seniority was thereby upheld. Changes to wage lists offered an alternative solution to the trade's 'blind-alley' problems. In 1911, employers proposed that payments to older side-piecers be augmented by replacing fixed time-rate payments with a scale graduated according to age. In this case, opposition centred on the suggestion that any increases should be funded out of a reallocation of mule-team shares. Spinners were adamant that any improvement in the piecers' standing should not be achieved at their expense.[13] A clear conflict of interests was perceived to exist between different grades within the mule-room, sufficient to cast significant doubt on the unifying role of the family. Problems of funding which blocked the 1911 scheme resurfaced to scupper a further attempt at reform in 1927. On this occasion, proposals for a sliding scale for side-piecers over the age of 21 originated with the Operative Spinners' Association. However, while minders continued to insist that employers should bear any additional costs, mill-owners reiterated that their reponsibility did not extend beyond payments to work-teams as a whole and that the distribution of those rewards lay wholly within the spinners' competence.[14] No change of substance resulted. Although a subvention of 2s. a week to all side-piecers, to be paid by employers, was agreed in 1932, this was primarily intended to mitigate the effects of the agreed 14.5 per cent cut in rates and so represented no significant improvement in either the pay or the prospects of mule-room assistants.[15]

Union officials were not indifferent to the piecers' plight. Nevertheless, any attempt to ameliorate the 'blind-alley' nature of work in the mule-gate had, in order to gain support, to be consistent with existing practices. An alternative means of increasing promotional opportunities lay in encouraging early retirement among minders. Under a superannuation scheme launched in 1893 by the Bolton Operative Spinners' Association, benefit payments of 5s. a week were offered from the age of 50.[16] Further

[12] BA, FE/1/3/50 Bolton Master Cotton Spinners' Association (BMCSA), correspondence files, 8, 23, 24 Mar. 1937.

[13] *BJG* (1 Sept. 1911), 9; (29 Sept. 1911), 9.

[14] JRUL, BCA/12/5/2 BSA, joint meeting negotiations, letter, 12 Apr. 1927; BCA/13/2/33 BSA, general correspondence, Report of conference between representatives of the Bolton Employers' Association, Operative Spinners', and the Special Enquiry Sub-Committee of the Bolton Juvenile Advisory Committee, 19 July 1928.

[15] *BJG* (11 Nov. 1932), 8; BA, FT/21/12 BSA, Annual Report for 1933, 54–5.

[16] *CFT* (17 Nov. 1893), 6; JRUL, BCA/1/3/8 BSA, minutes, quarterly districts meeting, 16 Sept. 1905.

inducements were available in the form of a lump–sum Changing Business benefit, the amounts payable varying between the equivalent of six weeks' out-of-work benefit and a maximum of £15. From 1913, this could be supplemented by a refund of 75 per cent of superannuation contributions, conditional on the commutation of all claims to benefit.[17] The Association effectively subsidized the search for alternative forms of work, enabling one minder from Astley Bridge to the north of Bolton, who left the mill at the age of 59, to purchase a five-seater Ford, with which he ran a bus service for the outlying district of Harwood.[18] However, opportunities beyond the mill were to narrow with the onset of economic depression from 1920–1. As a result, careers in the mule-gate became more highly valued. In the following decade, the average age at which superannuation benefit was first claimed rose markedly, while many who had received Changing Business benefit sought to return to the mill. Reinstatement was made conditional on reversionary payments which, by the mid-1920s, ranged from 5s. to 20s. a week, in addition to standard union contributions.[19] The readiness with which such obligations were accepted indicates the importance which attached to the defence of adult earnings. What is more, the fact that prolonged careers at the mule served further to restrict promotional opportunities suggests that strategies designed to maximize the employment of family members were not uppermost in the minders' thinking.

Attitudes to women's work corroborate this impression. Across the spinning trade, male custody of the 'family wage' was seen as the ideal. Addressing a Labour Party election rally in 1905, the Bolton Operative Spinners' president advanced such an arrangement as the foundation of domestic stability and respectability: with wives no longer obliged to seek paid employment, 'homes would be better kept and men would spend their leisure time at home'.[20] Card-room officials, despite the Amalgamation's predominantly female membership, concurred. In evidence to the Royal Commission on Labour, William Mullin commended the payment of wages to men which would enable them to support and

---

[17] JRUL, BCA/1/3/9–11 BSA, minutes, Council meeting, 20 Apr. 1909; quarterly districts meeting circular, 20 Sept. 1913; quarterly districts meeting, 21 June 1919.

[18] *BJG* (23 Mar. 1934), 6.

[19] Ages of superannuation claimants calculated from JRUL, BCA/1/19/1 BSA, Bolton branch, Superannuation Payments, 1916–34; BCA/1/3/12–13 BSA, minutes, Council meetings, 25 July 1922, 3 Jan. 1923, 26 Oct. 1925, for repayments of Changing Business benefit.

[20] *BEN* (28 Oct. 1905), 4.

maintain their families. The role of women's work was seen to be essentially secondary, supplementing otherwise inadequate earnings.[21] Individual career profiles suggest that this view was not confined to union élites. For most women, work in the mill ceased at or shortly after marriage, the precise timing varying according to family means. One Bolton reeler continued to work beyond marriage as her wage exceeded her husband's earnings from side-piecing. However, within three years of his promotion to minding, she had left the mill. Even women who expressed enthusiasm about their work, including a weaver at Tootal Broadhurst Lee's Sunnyside Mill, who claimed to feel more relaxed at the loom than she did at home, were no more likely to prolong their careers. Most observed the maxim advanced by a female bleacher: 'you didn't work on if you were being married. That was the main thing, to be at home.'[22] Fewer than 10 per cent of married women in Wigan were in paid employment in 1911. Further east, in Bolton, the figure was little higher at 15 per cent. Significantly higher participation rates were recorded in weaving districts to the north, where the near equality of men's and women's wages ensured that families could not subsist on male earnings alone.[23]

Employment patterns suggest that, in large measure, married women's work outside the home was an inverse function of male earning power. It was thus considered unlikely that the wives of highly paid cotton operatives would be drawn to the mill. George Silk, president of the Card Room Amalgamation, argued before the Royal Commission on Labour that the majority of female tenters were the wives of labourers. May Abraham of the Women's Factory Inspectorate agreed: 'The wife of the cotton operative has . . . less necessity to work than the wife of the woollen operative, and about half the number of married women working in the Lancashire mills are wives of colliers and other workmen'. [24] The defence of married women's jobs thus ranked low in union priorities. Temporary stoppage benefit was often denied those laid off from work in

[21] *Parl. Papers 1892*, xxxv (6708–VI), RC on Labour: Minutes of Evidence. Textiles, qq. 318–22, 345, 382; later debate over the redeployment of labour indicated that the Weavers' Amalgamation held to a broadly similar view, *BJG* (8 April 1932), 10; *TW* 6 (12 Dec. 1930), 351.

[22] BA, BOHP, 74 (female, born 1899), transcript, 17; 5 (female, born 1917), transcript, 4, 6–7; 1A (male, born 1901), transcript, 13.

[23] *Parl. Papers 1913*, lxxix (7019), Census of England and Wales, 1911. X. Occupations and Industries. Pt. II, table 13, 215–17, 221–3, 254–6.

[24] *Parl. Papers 1893–4*, xxxvii, pt. I (6894–XXIII), RC on Labour: The Employment of Women: Report by Miss May E. Abraham (Lady Assistant Commissioner) on the Conditions of Work in the Cotton Industry of Lancashire and Cheshire, 118; *Parl. Papers 1892*, xxxv (6708–VI), RC on Labour: Minutes of Evidence. Textiles, qq. 594–606.

the card-room.[25] As has been seen, women had, for a time, been prohibited from working in the mule-gate. Their reinstatement at the end of the nineteenth century had resulted in only small numbers being taken on. Nevertheless, the increased use of female labour was advocated, from 1900, as a means of relieving pressure in the 'blind-alley'. Significantly, a further gain was also anticipated. As the *Bolton Journal and Guardian* remarked in 1914, 'the re-establishment of female labour in the spinning room would probably mean that whole families, father, sons, and daughters would be working in the same room'.[26] The family's presence in the workplace, far from being established fact, appeared the solution to particular problems of recruitment and promotion. It was also a development which required a fundamental shift in trade-union and rank-and-file attitudes, which continued to give precedence to defence of the male breadwinner wage.

This attitude may be better understood by being placed in the context of long-term industrial development. The cotton trade's dependence on export markets for 85 per cent of its business by volume towards the end of the nineteenth century rendered it vulnerable to severe fluctuations in levels of activity.[27] During upswings in the trade cycle, new capacity was put down, a trend encouraged by the absence of restrictions on company formation. Towns across the region thus experienced concentrated waves of mill-building. In the quarter-century to the outbreak of the First World War, Bolton's cotton industry experienced two distinct phases of development. In the 1890s, reflecting wider difficulties within the trade, only nine additions to the town's productive capacity, including both new building and additions to existing plant, were recorded. By contrast, in the years from 1900, twenty-five such additions were made.[28] Fluctuations in building activity were also reflected in employment trends. Male recruitment proved a particularly sensitive indicator of change. Taking each of the three decades from 1880, numbers working in mill departments across the county grew by 18 per cent between 1881 and 1891, fell by 9 per cent in the ten years that followed, before rising by over 19 per cent from 1901. Variations in female employment were only

[25] BA, FT/7/2/2 BOCA, Bolton Committee minutes, 27 July 1931, 22 Feb. 1932.

[26] See above, pp. 34–6; *BJG* (24 July 1914), 12.

[27] T. Myers, *Real Facts about the Cotton Trade* (ILP Publications Dept., 1929), 3–4.

[28] BA, B677/B/BOL 'Spinning Mills: Dates of Erection and Spindleage' (unpublished TS); J. H. Longworth, *The Cotton Mills of Bolton, 1780–1985: A Historical Directory* (Bolton, 1987), 137–83. The figures cited cover spinning mills, weaving sheds, and bleaching plant.

marginally less marked: 13 per cent growth in the decades 1881–91 and 1901–11 contrasting with a fall of 2.6 per cent in the intervening ten years.[29] Even then, aggregate figures tend to understate local and sectoral changes. In Bolton, for example, male employment in cotton-manufacturing processes increased by over 29 per cent between 1901 and 1911 (11,625 to 15,003). In local mule-rooms over the same period, growth exceeded 46 per cent (7,059 to 10,326).[30] This contrasted with a slowdown in the rate of overall population growth. The increase of 7.5 per cent in the town in the ten years to 1911 was barely half that for the preceding decade.[31]

Recruitment trends thus operated regardless of the broader demographic context. Mills were required to look beyond established familial networks for their staff. Most additional hands, it may be assumed, would be drawn from households not primarily dependent on the cotton trade. The pull exerted on adolescent labour was reflected in Chapman and Abbott's survey of employment patterns among youths attending continuation classes in Lancashire in 1912. In many cases, a greater number secured work in the mill than in their fathers' occupations. Yet, if anything, the sample may have overstated the extent of familial connections.

Table 2. *Family patterns of employment in Lancashire, 1912*

Fathers' Occupations	Children's Occupations (%)	
	textiles	*as fathers' occupation*
Textiles (mainly cotton)	61.7	61.7
Metal	33.3	33.3
Building	33.5	24.2
Mining	33.2	36.0
Tradesmen	22.5	27.4
Clerical	17.5	49.1
Unskilled	48.0	10.9

Source: S. J. Chapman and W. Abbott, 'The Tendency of Children to Enter their Fathers' Trade', *Journal of the Royal Statistical Society*, 76 (1912–13), 600. The returns covered male scholars in evening continuation classes in Oldham, Bolton, Blackburn, Burnley, and Rochdale.

[29] Board of Trade, *An Industrial Survey of the Lancashire Area* (HMSO, 1932), 58–9.

[30] *Parl. Papers 1902*, cxix (1002), Census of England and Wales, 1901: County of Lancaster, table 35, 149; *Parl. Papers 1913*, lxxix (7019), Census of England and Wales, 1911. X. Occupations and Industries. Pt. II, table 13, 217.

[31] *Parl. Papers 1912–13*, cxi (6258), Census of England and Wales, 1911. I. Administrative Areas, table 3, 3–7, across the cotton districts only Oldham and Rochdale experienced an acceleration in population growth after 1901.

Attendance at continuation classes was often seen as a preliminary to undertaking a position of responsibility within the relevant trade. Many of those seeking promotion were themselves the sons of supervisory workers, as was the Pretoria fireman, Isaac Ratcliffe.[32] Patrimonial influence functioned most effectively in such cases. As a later survey of juvenile recruitment in Warrington concluded, 'the capacity of the father to place his son in the same firm where he works diminishes with his fall of status in industry'.[33] Chapman and Abbott's findings corroborate this view. Of more immediate significance, they also suggest that the mill's influence was felt considerably beyond the families of cotton operatives.

Two-thirds of Bolton children aged 10 to 15 and in paid employment in 1901 worked in the mill. Few did so on the basis of direct kinship ties. Indeed, the factory inspector's report for the Bolton district in 1898 found that only 14 per cent of children entering the industry had parents who were cotton workers. In one-third of cases, coal-mining provided the household's principal support, while the fathers of a further 44 per cent 'worked at miscellaneous trades, the majority being labourers in iron foundries'.[34] The figures are not, in themselves, definitive. The inspectorate district included Wigan and a number of neighbouring colliery townships in which cotton was a marginal employer of male labour. In such areas, the scope for familial employment would be, of necessity, limited. More specific evidence, drawing on labour certificates for workers at the Bolton waste-spinning firm of Robert Walker, Ltd, between 1889 and 1936, suggests however that the overall impression conveyed by the inspector's report was not inaccurate. Eighteen of the twenty-three certificates recorded the fathers' occupations. The largest single group comprised labourers, most of whom were employed at a nearby iron works.[35] The observations of a Bolton mill director in 1921 suggest the broader relevance of such figures: 'the majority of children who are employed as piecers, are not the sons of cotton operatives. Mainly are they drawn from the unskilled and labouring classes.'[36]

Internal work structures also ensured that mule-teams were rarely bound by family ties. In the course of an average career in charge of the

---

[32] See above, p. 45.

[33] C. Bottomley, 'The Recruitment of Juvenile Labour in Warrington', *Transactions of the Manchester Statistical Society* (Session 1930–1), 141.

[34] *Parl. Papers 1902*, cxix (1002), Census of England and Wales, 1901: County of Lancaster, table 35, 148–9; *Parl. Papers 1900*, xi (27), Annual Report of the Chief Inspector of Factories and Workshops for the Year 1898. Pt. II, 70–1.

[35] BA, ZWA/23/1–4 Robert Walker, Ltd, employment of children and young persons.

[36] *BJG* (2 Sept. 1921), 5.

headstock (or mule mechanism), extending over some twenty-five years, a single minder would help to train up several piecers. Estimates of the numbers involved varied. James Mawdsley, in his submission to the Royal Commission on Labour, argued that three was the likely figure, while a later survey put the average at between four and ten.[37] Such an imbalance required that, in prosperous times, the recruitment net be spread as wide as possible. When trade turned down, by contrast, narrowing opportunities could frustrate attempts to follow the parental path into work. One boy, although able to secure a position at the same Bolton firm as his father, John Ashworth's of Astley Bridge, was not engaged on the same carriage. Others failed altogether: a minder at Stanley Mill, Bolton, was unable to find his son a job with the firm in 1924 as no vacancies then existed.[38] The contingent nature of parental influence, which remained heavily dependent on the immediate economic context, assists in explaining the determination of most cotton workers to defend the male bread-winner wage. It was an approach which offered a more effective safeguard against domestic difficulty than did fitfully successful attempts to maximize familial employment.

If the timing of mill-building played a significant part in operative calculations, so did its location. The development of early industrial towns has often been presented as a process of cellular growth, whereby factory and residential building proceeded substantially in step, so that each plant could draw labour from its immediate hinterland. By this argument, individual works came to define distinctive areas within towns, providing urban echoes of the rural factory settlements of early industrialization.[39] Yet locational decisions were subject to a variety of constraints. The importance of water, both as an element in the production process and as a means of transport, encouraged productive capacity to emerge in clusters. Bleaching plant was dispersed along river valleys, while mills in Burnley, Blackburn, and Wigan congregated along stretches of the Leeds–Liverpool Canal.[40] In Bolton, clustering was

---

[37] *Parl. Papers 1892*, xxxv (6708–VI), RC on Labour: Minutes of Evidence. Textiles, qq. 791–2; Board of Trade, *Handbooks on Trades in Lancashire and Cheshire: Textile Trades. Prepared on Behalf of the Board of Trade for the Use of Advisory Committees for Juvenile Employment* (HMSO, 1915), 11–12.

[38] BA, BOHP, 161 (male, born 1907), tape; JRUL, BCA/12/5/1 BSA, joint meeting negotiations, local joint meeting, 19 Nov. 1924.

[39] Joyce, *Work, Society and Politics*, 103–10; J. Marshall, 'Colonisation as a Factor in the Planting of Towns in North-West England', in H. J. Dyos (ed.), *The Study of Urban History* (1968), 215–30.

[40] G. Trodd, 'Political Change and the Working Class in Blackburn and Burnley,

evident along the London Midland Scottish railway line running south-east to Manchester and along the principal arterial roads running north, west, and south-west out of the borough.[41] Waves of mill-building did little to alter this distribution. Until 1900, expansion centred on Bolton's seven inner wards. Of the nine additions to the town's cotton-producing capacity in the 1890s, six were located in inner Bolton. Thereafter, the focus of growth shifted to outer areas, comprising satellite townships absorbed between 1872 and 1898. Sixteen of the twenty-five building projects completed between 1900 and 1914 centred on six of Bolton's eight outer wards. Significantly, however, new plant continued to fringe the inner area.[42] Rather than opening out new centres of activity, locational decisions committed employers to exploiting existing transport and recruitment networks. As a result, firms often found themselves competing for the same pool of labour. Employment boundaries, far from being distinct, overlapped, to produce an often confused pattern of recruitment.

In such circumstances, dependence on personal, informal contacts in the search for work, rather than working to consolidate family ties, could have the effect of dispersing members of the same household across different firms. One youth, whose father was a minder at the Bolton Union Spinning Co., Ltd, started work at the Falcon Mill in Bolton through the good offices of a neighbour. The father's absence on military service complicated the search for work in this case. Nevertheless, other evidence suggests that this experience was not unusual. An engine tenter at Firwood Bleach Works had two daughters employed in a local weaving shed, while another worked at various bleaching firms across Bolton.[43] Firms were often obliged to recruit from well beyond the immediate area, attenuating the tie between home and work that lies at the centre of cellular models of urban development. Thus, William Heaton and Sons, a dominant presence in the township of Lostock, looked to Westhoughton

1880–1914' (Lancaster Univ. Ph.D. thesis, 1978), 20, 26–7; J. Jackson, 'Housing and Social Structure in Mid-Victorian Wigan and St Helens' (Liverpool Univ. Ph.D. thesis, 1977), 39.

[41] K. Winward, 'The Economic and Urban Geography of Bolton in the Twentieth Century' (Manchester Univ. MA thesis, 1956), 28–30.

[42] Ibid., 16–20; BA, Bolton County Borough Council (BCB) ABCF/21/1 Housing and Town Planning Committee, Housing of the Working Class, Report (8 June 1918), 1; B677/B/BOL 'Spinning Mills: Dates of Erection and Spindleage'; Longworth, *Cotton Mills of Bolton*, 137–83; locations of industrial plant traced through *Ordnance Survey*, 25 ins to 1 mile (1:2500), edns. of 1908–10 and 1929.

[43] BA, BOHP, 58 (male, born 1905), transcript, 3–14; 74 (female, born 1899), transcript, 4–7.

and Bolton to supply its male workforce. By 1916, almost 45 per cent of men employed at Heaton's lived outside Lostock. The net for female recruitment was spread even wider. Most of the women employed on the firm's carding frames travelled over 10 miles to work each day, from towns such as Wigan and Ashton-in-Makerfield.[44] As with the county's miners, many mill workers faced lengthy journeys to their places of employment, so that the issue of concessionary rail fares became significant in the early 1920s.[45] One boy from the colliery township of Blackrod, to the north of Wigan, commenced work in 1915 at a mill 4 miles away, while a piecer at Bolton's Falcon Mill travelled a comparable distance from his home in Horwich. J. R. Clynes recalled walking 2 miles each day to work in an Oldham mill, a job secured through his father, a Corporation labourer.[46]

Clynes' experience points up the fact that, despite informal methods of recruitment, kinship ties were, more often than not, absent from the employment relationship. The long-run development of the cotton industry, based around a chronological and geographical clustering in activity, sufficed to ensure that direct familial employment was limited to a small and decreasing minority. Once this is recognized, then the exclusivity pursued by skilled minorities in the mill becomes explicable. Such policies rarely penalized offspring and helped to maximize household incomes in the short term. Furthermore, the finding that home and workplace were often clearly separate spheres gives rise to a broader observation. The notion that work provided a primary point of focus for factory operatives and was crucial in shaping their perception of the social order more generally appears open to question. This becomes clear if we turn to examine popular attitudes to work, which, before 1920, were reflected most clearly through the workings of the half-time system.

II

As established in 1844, the half-time system served a dual purpose. It was intended both to ensure observation of legislation limiting working hours and to guarantee children working in textile factories access to formal education. Under the system as it was to develop, children were to be

---

[44] BA, BOHP, 121A (male, born 1899), tape; 88A (female, born 1901), transcript, 3; ZZ/316/1 William Heaton and Sons, Ltd., register of male employees over the age of 16, 20 Apr. 1916.
[45] BA, FT/21/10 BSA, Annual Report for 1923, 6–7.
[46] BA, BOHP, 92 (male, born 1903), transcript, 3; 58 (male, born 1905), transcript, 9, 12; Clynes, *Memoirs*, i, 27–9.

employed for part of the day only, the remaining time to be spent at school.[47] Although half-timers were present in a variety of trades, textiles provided the largest single source of employment. Of an estimated 47,360 employed nationally in 1906–7, 30,800 (65 per cent) were to be found in Lancashire and Yorkshire. Locally, the position was even more striking. Over 70 per cent of half-timers in Bolton in 1908 found work in the cotton industry.[48] Despite its widespread use, the system attracted increasing criticism from the late nineteenth century onwards. Many sought to question the value of any schooling which half-timers received. Involvement in paid work, it was argued, impaired their ability to concentrate on lessons and rendered them fractious and ill-disciplined.[49] In a period of growing anxiety over comparative economic decline and racial degeneration, such arguments carried particular force. An explicit link between the half-time system and Britain's international position was made in a tribute to the retiring president of the National Union of Teachers, Richard Waddington of Bolton, in 1899. Whereas, it was lamented, children in Germany received compulsory education to the age of 16,

> . . . here, if lads an' wenches just scrap through,
> Say Stonnard Four, fowk think they'n larnt anno,
> An' then they gape an' wonder when they see
> On things by th' thousand: 'Made in Germany'. [50]

Across Lancashire, the minimum educational requirement for partial exemption varied between Standard III, where pupils were tested on arithmetical problems involving numbers up to 100, and Standard VI. However, exemption was also allowed on the basis of a minimum of 300 attendances in five previous years. One estimate had it that for every one child qualifying by means of examination, thirty did so through their attendance record. Speaking at a meeting of the Bolton Education Society in 1917, the Master of Balliol College, A. L. Smith, was forthright

---

[47] B. L. Hutchins and A. Harrison, *A History of Factory Legislation* (1911), 72–85; E. H. Hunt, *British Labour History, 1815–1914* (1981), 9–11; P. Horn, *Children's Work and Welfare, 1780–1880s* (Basingstoke and London, 1994), 54–5; H. Challand and M. Walker, '"No School, No Mill; No Mill, No Money": The Half-Time Textile Worker', in M. Winstanley (ed.), *Working Children in Nineteenth-Century Lancashire* (Preston, 1995), 49.

[48] *Parl. Papers 1900*, xi (27), Chief Inspector of Factories. Report for 1898, 71, for the diversity of half-time jobs in Wigan; 'The Development of the Textile Industry: The Half-Time Question', *Journal of the Royal Society of Arts*, 60 (1911–12), 604–5; *BJG* (26 Feb. 1909), 2; (13 Aug. 1909), 8.

[49] Challand and Walker, 'No School, No Mill', 65–6.

[50] BA, 'Bolton Biographical Notes', ii, 39; Webb and Webb, *Industrial Democracy*, 768–9.

in declaring that the half-time system allowed 'the factory and the street to undo what the school was trying to do'.[51]

The shift in opinion was reflected in legislation which progressively narrowed the scope for partial exemptions. The minimum age for half-time work was increased to 10 in 1874, 11 in 1893, and 12 in 1899, before the system was finally abolished by the Fisher Education Act of 1918.[52] While much of the literature on half-time has focused on the progress of reform, the system's persistence into the twentieth century and the attitudes which sustained it have rarely received detailed examination.[53] This omission is of particular significance, given that workers themselves were half-time's most consistent supporters. An examination of their outlook and the role which the half-time system played in their lives may go some way towards clarifying the importance of work in Lancastrian working-class culture.

Opinion within the cotton trade was far from united in favour of partial exemptions. Managements at several mills across Lancashire refused to countenance the recruitment of half-timers.[54] The variety of attitudes among employers was revealed in the course of debates over specific reform proposals. So, while the abolition of partial exemptions, as outlined in Fisher's original 1917 bill, was supported by manufacturers in Burnley, along with master spinners in Bolton and Stockport, the Wigan Employers' Association expressed 'strong disapproval' of a change which would 'seriously jeopardize the Cotton Industry'.[55] The Bolton Chamber of Commerce also opposed abolition, albeit only on the chairman's casting vote. Overall, the Federation of Master Cotton Spinners' Associations divided 60:40 against change, a vote which reflected unease over other aspects of the bill, including the proposed introduction of part-time

---

[51] *Parl. Debates, House of Commons*, 4th ser. lxvii, col. 925; *Parl. Papers 1909*, xvii (4791), Report of the Inter-departmental Committee on Partial Exemption from School Attendance. I. Report, par. 9; *BJG* (17 June 1899), 6; (6 July 1917), 3; (26 Oct. 1917), 4.

[52] E. and R. Frow, *The Half-Time System in Education* (Manchester, 1970), 23–4; Challand and Walker, 'No School, No Mill', 50.

[53] Frow and Frow, *Half-Time System*, 33–83; M. Cruickshank, *Children and Industry* (Manchester, 1981), 93–101.

[54] *Parl. Papers 1901*, x (668), Chief Inspector of Factories: Annual Report. 1900, 312; *BJG* (13 Aug. 1909), 8; see also P. Bolin-Hort, *Work, Family and the State: Child Labour and the Organization of Production in the British Cotton Industry, 1780–1920* (Lund, 1989), 210–11.

[55] JRL, Ashton Employers' Collection Wigan and District Cotton Employers' Association, quarterly committee meeting, 14 Jan. 1918; LRO, NE Lancs Textile Manufacturers' Association DDX 1145/1/1/3 Burnley Master Cotton Spinners' and Manufacturers' Association, minutes, general meeting, 26 Apr. 1918.

continuing education to the age of 18.[56] One Federation circular estimated that the reforms outlined by Fisher would necessitate a 21 per cent
increase in adult recruitment to make good the loss of child labour, adding
£867,000 to the annual wage bill, equivalent to a 3⅛ per cent dividend.[57]
Despite such alarmist figures, employers displayed no fundamental commitment to the half-time system. For the most part, their attitudes varied
between indifference and outright hostility.

Cotton unions had long supported partial exemptions, a stance which
left them isolated in debates on education reform at the TUC in 1897 and
1901.[58] Many officials were outspoken in defence of half-time, none more
so than William Mullin, 'the burly secretary of the cardroom workers'.
Addressing a Manchester conference on the question in 1899, involving
workers' and employers' representatives, along with teachers and local
MPs, Mullin sought to counter claims that factory work undermined
physical health by comparing 'the representatives of the operatives present, all of whom had been half-timers, and the school teachers, and he
more than hinted that if it came to a "scrap" man for man, the chances
were that the teachers would come off second best'. [59] A weight advantage
of 4 stone a head lent his claim undeniable substance. Over time, however,
official attitudes changed. By 1908, the UTFWA had turned to support
an increase in the minimum age for partial exemption.[60] Equally, in the
debate over Fisher's bill, union concern centred on the proposals for continuing education. The abolition of the half-time system produced few
expressions of unease.[61]

This shift in outlook was not provoked by a change in rank-and-file
attitudes. In 1899, weavers voted against raising the minimum age for
half-time work to 12 by majorities of between 5:1 in Bolton and 11:1 in
Blackburn. Ballots in 1908 and 1911 produced votes of 76.7 and 79.6 per
cent against further change. Indeed, so certain was the Burnley Weavers'

[56] Bolton Chamber of Commerce and Industry, Bolton Chamber of Trade and
Commerce, Council meeting minutes, 26 July 1916; JRL, Ashton Employers' Collection
FMCSA, annual report, year ending 30 June 1918 (Manchester, 1918), 33; *BJG* (6 July
1917), 3; (7 Sept. 1917), 4; B. L. Simon, *Education and the Labour Movement* (1965), 351.

[57] JRL, Ashton Employers' Collection FMCSA, annual report, year ending 30 June 1918,
40–1, circular dated 23 Jan. 1918.

[58] Frow and Frow, *Half-Time System*, 42, 58; J. L. White, *The Limits of Trade Union
Militancy* (Westport, Conn., and London, 1978), 59.

[59] *BJG* (11 Feb. 1899), 8, which also includes the description of Mullin.

[60] White, *Limits of Militancy*, 60–1; *BJG* (13 Aug. 1909), 8; *Parl. Papers 1909*, xvii (4887),
Inter-departmental Committee on Partial Exemption. II. Minutes of Evidence, q. 1577.

[61] BA, FT/7/6/74 BOCA, quarterly report, 1 March 1918, 2; FT/21/10 BSA, Annual
Report for 1922, 5; *BJG* (22 Feb. 1918), 5; (31 May 1918), 3.

Association of the outcome in the latter year that the wisdom of holding a ballot at all was debated.[62] Even in 1918, operatives remained fixed in their opposition to reform. A doorstep canvass of his constituents quickly convinced Captain Albert Smith, Labour MP for Clitheroe, of the strength of feeling on this issue, while Sir Henry Hibbert, Unionist member for Chorley, warned that abolition would result in the loss of 'dozens of seats' by the government.[63]

Various explanations were offered for operatives' continued attachment to the half-time system. For some, it expressed an underlying cultural conservatism, reflected in the stoicism with which, in Allen Clarke's novel *Lancashire Lasses and Lads*, the mill-workers of 'Spindleton' responded to the death of the half-timer Florrie Heyes: 'the town went on with its work and business; and the children went about their toils in the mills; . . . and death had marked most of them for the early taking; but nobody thought anything about it; it had always been so, and always would be so'. [64] Equally, Fisher traced opposition to his bill to 'Hard-bitten old half-timers', who fostered 'a secret liking for the system under which they had been schooled for success'.[65] Apparent endorsement of such a view could be found in a survey of attitudes in the mule-gate undertaken by the Bolton Factory Inspector in 1898. Of 113 adult males in one spinning mill who had commenced work as half-timers, 110 had voted against any increase in the minimum age for partial exemptions during the 1890s.[66] Yet however suggestive such evidence is of the force of cultural continuity, it does not, of itself, suffice to explain the survival of the half-time system into the early twentieth century. Crucially, it overlooks the way in which utilization of partial exemptions varied with changing economic circumstances.

In opposing the abolition of half-time work, Allen Clarke's fictional mill-owning parliamentarian, Timothy Bunkholme, the member for 'Slopborough', gave voice to a commonly held view: change would 'rob . . . parents of a certain portion of income they can ill spare'.[67] Correspondents to the *Cotton Factory Times* saw in the result of the

---

[62] *BJG* (18 Feb. 1899), 6; *CFT* (19 Jan. 1912), 5; (26 Jan. 1912), 8; Bolin-Hort, *Work, Family and the State*, 231–3.

[63] *Parl. Debates, House of Commons*, 5th ser. 104, cols. 371, 378–9; 106, cols. 853–4, 1064–5, 1068.

[64] C. A. Clarke, *Lancashire Lasses and Lads* (Manchester, 1906), 215.

[65] H. A. L. Fisher, *An Unfinished Autobiography* (Oxford, 1940), 110.

[66] *Parl. Papers 1900*, xi (27), Chief Inspector of Factories. Annual Report. 1898. Pt. II, 71.

[67] C. A. Clarke, 'Killed by Kindness', in id., *Tales that Ought to be Told* (Manchester, n.d.), 3.

1911 ballot evidence of widespread financial need, an interpretation which also served to temper Albert Smith's exasperation at his constituents' continued opposition to reform.[68] Particular examples confirm that, for some families, half-time earnings helped to supplement inadequate incomes. George Tomlinson, a future Minister of Education, recalled how his wage of 2s. 3d. a week assisted in supporting a family of seven. Similarly, the earnings of one girl, when she commenced work at the age of 12 in 1918, reduced her family's dependence on relief from the Bolton Guild of Help.[69] Yet not all applications for partial exemption fit this picture. Contemporary surveys revealed a marked diversity in means among households with half-timers. Of 13,000 cases examined by the Inter-departmental Committee on Partial Exemption in 1909, fewer than 10 per cent belonged to families headed by widows. Returns covering 200 mills across the Bolton province in 1899 revealed a comparable picture: 62 of the 715 children surveyed (8.7 per cent) were so placed. In other cases, the search for half-time work may have been quickened by low parental earnings. The fathers of 114 of the Bolton half-timers worked as labourers or carters. In almost a quarter of households, therefore, half-time earnings would contribute to lifting the family out of Rowntree's state of 'primary poverty', where incomes did not suffice to meet basic physical needs. In the majority of cases, however, the imperative of financial necessity was absent. Within the Bolton sample, 291 families were headed by colliers or mule-spinners.[70] Nor was this pattern unusual. A report to the Half-Time Council for Lancashire and neighbouring counties in 1907 indicated that the children working in Bradford's worsted mills were mostly drawn from 'families who were making big incomes by it'.[71]

The apparent readiness of comparatively affluent families to commit their offspring to work at the earliest opportunity attracted much contemporary criticism. For Allen Clarke, this merely served to confirm his view that 'Money seems to be the first consideration with most cotton operatives; the health and happiness and even lives of their children,

---

[68] *CFT* (12 Jan. 1912), 5; (19 Jan. 1912), 5; *Parl. Debates, House of Commons*, 5th ser. 114, cols. 379–80.

[69] Frow and Frow, *Half-Time System*, 31–2; F. Blackburn, *George Tomlinson* (1954), 15–17; BA, BOHP, 15A (female, born 1906), tape.

[70] *Parl. Papers 1909*, xvii (4791), Inter-departmental Committee on Partial Exemption. Report, par. 63; *BJG* (13 Aug. 1909), 8; (18 Feb. 1899), 6; B. S. Rowntree, *Poverty: A Study of Town Life* (1902 edn.), 110–11, 118, 122.

[71] *BJG* (5 July 1907), 6; see also H. A. L. Fisher, *Educational Reform: Speeches* (Oxford, 1918), 83.

are but of minor importance'.[72] Richard Waddington, dubbed 'The Wilberforce of the white slaves of England' for his opposition to half-time work, agreed that material considerations figured largely in parental calculations. Outward indications of prosperity and respectability, from seaside holidays to home ownership, were substantially owing, he argued, to the level of juvenile earnings.[73] However, patterns of recruitment over time suggest an alternative interpretation. Numbers of half-timers had declined as the minimum age for partial exemption was raised through the 1890s, encouraging a belief that the system would lapse into desuetude. Yet, contradicting such expectations, recruitment levels increased as trade revived early in the twentieth century. Figures collated by the press secretary of the NUT indicated that, in the eight years to 1908, the number of half-timers in Bolton had risen by 57 per cent (1,068 to 1,681), a magnitude of increase only exceeded in Rochdale (68 per cent).[74] The very fact that rates of entry increased in step with an improvement in trade confirms that poverty was not a prime motivation for seeking half-time work. Of greater moment, expansion was checked as activity slackened from April 1908, but revived as recovery set in in 1910. The search for substitute labour sustained half-time numbers through the Great War, while buoyant trade in the immediate post-war period meant that even impending abolition did not discourage recruitment. Indeed, the proportion of 12-year-olds entering Oldham mills (68 per cent) was higher than four years previously (59 per cent). What is more, the 1919 Bolton enrolment (1,980) comfortably exceeded figures at the peak of Edwardian prosperity.[75] Rather than being constrained by cultural inertia, parents' decisions over placing their children in work were informed by an assessment of likely career prospects. As promotion within the mill was dependent on seniority, a preference for early employment at times of maximum promotional opportunities appeared wholly rational. Such thinking guided the efforts of one Westhoughton widow to place her daughter in the mill at the age of 12 in 1920, the last year of partial

---

[72] C. A. Clarke, *The Effects of the Factory System* (1899; repr. Littleborough, 1985), 101.

[73] *BJG* (31 May 1912), 10; BA, 'Bolton Biographical Notes', vii, 287; *Parl. Papers 1892*, xxxv (6708–VI), RC on Labour: Minutes of Evidence. Textiles, q. 3724.

[74] *The Times: Textile Numbers* (1914), 27; *Parl. Papers 1901*, x (668), Chief Inspector of Factories: Annual Report. 1900, 312–13; *Parl. Papers 1907*, x (3586), Chief Inspector of Factories: Annual Report. 1906, 136; *BJG* (17 July 1908), 2; in aggregate terms, the number of half-timers increased from 74,468 to 84,298, *Parl. Papers 1909*, xvii (4791), Interdepartmental Committee on Partial Exemption. Report, par. 20.

[75] *BJG* (24 July 1908), 4; (6 July 1917), 3; *Times Educational Supplement* (23 Oct. 1919), 538; (6 Nov. 1919), 565.

exemptions: 'the Mother's hope [was] that by the time the girl was 14 years of age she would be ready for a regular place at the Mill: Girls have sometimes so long to wait for these regular situations that Mothers try to get their girls into training as early as possible'. [76]

Wage structures accommodated such an approach. Working full-time, little-piecers earned between 10s. 7d. and 16s. 6d. a week in 1906, rates well in excess of those available in other trades. Apprenticeships commenced at 5s. a week, while colliery wage lists, agreed in 1911, fixed starting rates for boys commencing underground work at the age of 14 at 10s. 1d.[77] Earnings differentials influenced many in their search for work. As a 'Humble Piecer' explained to the *Bolton Journal and Guardian* in 1911, 'it was only because the wages were so big to start with that I was put in the factory and it is the same with hundreds of others'.[78] Similarly, the son of a Westhoughton miner was forced to accept a position in a local mill, his plan to take up a joinery apprenticeship being sacrificed to the family's need for an immediate financial return.[79] The fact that the size of the wage packet appeared to figure so prominently in parental calculations served to confirm contemporary perceptions of a working-class mentality bounded by the short term. C. E. B. Russell noted that youths in Edwardian Manchester appeared disinclined to pursue a trade, preferring instead to take jobs offering high starting wages.[80]

Yet not all new entrants anticipated a prolonged career in the mill. For many, cotton offered an interim source of employment, enabling earnings to be maximized over a brief period before work was sought elsewhere. The flexible way in which the half-time system could be utilized was outlined in a letter to the Bolton press: 'I have known many children sent by their parents until they attained the age of 14, and have been transferred to learn the same trade as the father'.[81] Several examples of career mobility can be cited. Robert Demaine, later president of the Bolton branch of the Friendly Society of Ironfounders, worked for three years as a loom-tenter at Barlow and Jones, Ltd, before being apprenticed at the age of 14

---

[76] BA, HRF, ABHC/5/239 Personal Files, Shaw to Hon. Sec., 15 Dec. 1922,

[77] *Parl. Papers 1909*, lxxx (4545), Earnings and Hours of Labour, 34, 35, the figures for piecers' earnings refer to Oldham and Bolton; LCMF, agreement at joint meeting held at the Queen's Hotel, Manchester, 17 Oct. 1911; C. More, *Skill and the English Working Class* (1980), 74–5.

[78] *BJG* (8 Sept. 1911), 9   [79] BA, BOHP, 108A (male, born 1917), tape.

[80] R. I. McKibbin, 'Class and Poverty in Edwardian England', in id., *The Ideologies of Class* (Oxford, 1990), 175–8; C. E. B. Russell, *Manchester Boys: Sketches of Manchester Lads at Work and Play* (Swinton, 1984 repr.), 5; *Parl. Papers 1904*, xix (1867), School Training and Early Employment of Lancashire Children, 36.   [81] *BJG* (13 Aug. 1909), 8.

to the textile engineers Dobson and Barlow. Similarly, Thomas Halstead, who would later become secretary of the Federation of Colliery Officials of Great Britain and leader of the Labour group on Bolton Borough Council, started work in a mill before moving, aged 15, to Scowcroft's Colliery. In both cases, earlier entry to their intended career was precluded, by apprenticeship restrictions on the one hand and by parliamentary statute, which from 1887 prohibited half-time employment underground, on the other.[82]

The evidence suggests, however, that not all careers followed such an ordered progression. Receding promotional opportunities in the mill's blind alleys obliged many to quit the cotton trade in early adulthood. James Alfred Russell, a future Mayor of Bolton, left the Darcy Lever firm of William Gray and Sons after eight years to become a porter at a local railway station. Similarly, James Mawdsley's two brothers worked in the mill through adolescence, before taking up jobs at an Oldham coal depot.[83] Aggregate figures suggest that such cases were not infrequent. Comparing the age structure of Bolton's male cotton workforce as revealed in the Census reports of 1901 and 1911 suggests a decennial wastage rate of 33 per cent among the group aged 15 to 25 at the earlier date (4,057 reduced to 2,719).[84] As productive capacity increased over this same decade, with the result that promotional opportunities expanded, this can be assumed to represent a lower than average rate of loss. Statistics on other industrial sectors suggest that, on departing the mill, workers were dispersed across a broad range of local industries. If the proportion of adult males (aged 25 and over) is compared with the share of the male labour force as a whole, most sectors showed modest gains.[85] James Haslam, who himself abandoned the mill while still a big-piecer aged 23, was drawn to conclude that the cotton industry in general and its spinning branch in particular constituted 'the biggest recruiting ground we have for the form of unskilled labour arising out of blind-alley occupations; it creates not only

[82] BA, 'Bolton Biographical Notes', iii, 216; iv, 66; *BJG* (23 Sept. 1899), 8.
[83] BA, 'Bolton Biographical Notes', iii, 96; *Parl. Papers 1892*, xxxv (6708–VI), RC on Labour: Minutes of Evidence. Textiles, q. 797.
[84] *Parl. Papers 1902*, cxix (1002), Census of England and Wales, 1901: County of Lancaster, table 35, 149; *Parl. Papers 1913*, lxxix (7019), Census of England and Wales, 1911. X. Occupations and Industries. Pt. II, table 13, 217.
[85] *Parl. Papers 1913*, lxxix (7019), Census of England and Wales, 1911. X. Occupations and Industries. Pt. II, table 13, 215–17, Road and Rail Transport increased its share from 6.4% of the total to 7.7% of adult males, while the growth in Building and Works of Construction was from 7.2% to 8.7%. Cotton spinning, by contrast, registered a decline from 17.3% to 10.3%.

workers for the unskilled market, but leads many young men into the sordid realm of the infirm and the unemployables'. [86] The examples already cited cast doubt on such a bald generalization. Nevertheless, it is clear that continuity in work between leaving school and the attainment of adulthood was experienced by a minority of mill workers, and that the half-time system was integral to such occupational flexibility.

As wage lists encouraged early recruitment to cotton, so they also contributed to labour turnover in later years. As their ages advanced, the piecers' earnings advantage was eroded. Colliery wage scales stipulated payments in excess of piecers' rates from the age of 19. At the same time, cotton unions opposed list reforms likely to discourage wastage. Piecers should not, it was argued, be encouraged to remain in the mill in anticipation of higher earnings in the future. Rather, a clear demarcation between juvenile and adult responsibilities and rates of pay should be maintained.[87] In the absence of reform, wastage continued unchecked, ensuring that demand for child labour remained relatively constant, regardless of the economic context. The mill thus came to offer security of employment at times of wider uncertainty. A tendency to use cotton as a 'fall-back' source of work is apparent in a number of careers. Edward Faulkner, later Bolton branch secretary of the TGWU, started work as a half-timer in a local weaving shed. Although he became an errand boy on leaving school at 14, within a year he had returned to textiles, taking a job in a local bleach works. After a brief spell in the army, he became a van driver for a firm of wholesale bakers.[88] Given that career choices for girls were more circumscribed, the mill figured even more prominently in their calculations. Alice Foley was discouraged by her elder sister from following her into the industry. However, alternative work was in short supply, so that 'After weeks of aimless searching mother stoically suggested "Well tha'd better put thi clogs on an' ger' a job in t' mill" '.[89]

Motives for placing children in the cotton trade thus varied with family circumstances and the immediate economic context. Many sought to

---

[86] Haslam, 'Lancashire Women as Cotton-Piecers', 273–4; J. Bellamy and H. F. Bing, 'James Haslam (1869–1937): Co-operative Author and Journalist', in Bellamy and Saville (eds.), *Dictionary of Labour Biography*, i. (1972), 155–6.

[87] LCMF, agreement at joint meeting held at the Queen's Hotel, Manchester, 17 Oct. 1911; *Parl. Papers 1909*, lxxx (4545), Earnings and Hours of Labour, 29; *BJG* (6 Oct. 1911), 9, letter by 'Not Guilty'.

[88] BA, 'Bolton Biographical Notes', iii, 176.

[89] Foley, *A Bolton Childhood*, 50; J. Jewkes and A. Winterbottom, *Juvenile Unemployment* (1933), 31, 146–7; J. Jewkes and E. M. Gray, *Wages and Labour in the Lancashire Cotton Spinning Industry* (Manchester, 1935), 180.

take advantage of periods when promotional prospects appeared most promising. For others, high initial earnings were decisive, ensuring as they did a brief if profitable interlude before permanent work was sought elsewhere. Should alternative avenues disappoint, the mill offered some security of employment. Whatever the motivation, the result was that careers in cotton were often fragmented, a fact which prevented the workplace from forming a primary focus for working-class loyalties. Rather, attitudes to work appear to have been predominantly functional, a point further reflected in the recurrent manpower problems which afflicted the industry over the period.

Although demand for ancillary staff remained relatively constant, the supply of labour was subject to marked fluctuations in the short term. During the 1890s, poor trade combined with increases in the minimum age for partial exemptions to reduce the flow of school-leavers into the mill. In Bolton, vacancies for 140 little-piecers remained unfilled in 1899, a shortfall sufficient, as has been seen, to force a revision of union rules on female recruitment.[90] The subsequent trade recovery boosted half-time numbers and so ameliorated the immediate shortage. However, growth in capacity ensured that demand progressively outstripped the available supply of labour. By January 1914, Bolton mule-rooms were reported to be some 500 short of full complements.[91] The drain of manpower in wartime rendered staffing difficulties even more acute and, although demobilization made good shortages among older piecers, the deficiency among school-leavers remained.[92]

From 1918, the problem of child recruitment underwent a qualitative change; no longer subject to cyclical variation, it became an immutable feature of the cotton industry between the wars. An employers' census of 129 firms across the Bolton Province in October 1922 revealed a full hand of side- and cross-piecers, alongside rates of undermanning among creelers of between 0.67 per cent in Leigh and 21.7 per cent in Bolton.[93] Such problems were less apparent in the American-cotton sector, where short-time working concealed potential labour shortages. Nevertheless, aggregate recruitment figures suggest that the industry's difficulties, although

[90] See above, p. 35; JRUL, BCA/1/3/7 BSA, minutes, districts special meeting, 4 Oct. 1899.
[91] *BJG* (23 Jan. 1914), 12; BA, FT/21/9 BSA, Annual Report for 1913, 3, 15.
[92] BA, FT/21/9 BSA, Annual Report for 1915, 7; Annual Report for 1916, 5; *BJG* (21 Nov. 1919), 8.
[93] BA, FE/1/3/53 BMCSA, correspondence files, Summary of Return re Scarcity of Piecers, 27 Oct. 1922.

obscured, were real. Whereas, in 1920, 58 per cent of male school-leavers in Oldham sought work in the cotton trade, that share had fallen to 36 per cent eight years later and to below 30 per cent in the wake of deepening recession after 1929. The managers' journal was doubtful whether the trend could be reversed and went on to argue that 'if there came a boom in trade some mills would find a difficulty in getting fully staffed. Especially would there be a shortage of juvenile labour'.[94] Full-time working in the Bolton district for much of this period rendered the problem there more explicit. Although all mules were reported to be fully staffed by 1928, this was largely achieved through the expedient of importing labour. Some 42 per cent of the little-piecers employed in Bolton mills in that year came from neighbouring districts, such as Salford and Pendlebury.[95]

In part, problems of child recruitment could be traced to the abolition of half-time work, which had, according to a report by the British Cotton Industry Research Association, deprived the industry of some 21,000 workers between the ages of 12 and 14. Although many would simply enter the mill at a later age, abolition had resulted in the permanent loss of those transient hands who had gained their earliest work experience during a brief stop in the mule-gate. As the Bolton Operative Spinners' executive remarked in 1923, 'Under the old system a large number of piecers were brought into the mills at an early age and worked for several years, after which a fair percentage left to follow other occupations, and in those days the mills were kept almost fully staffed.'[96] If, for some, this was a sufficient explanation of the industry's post-war difficulties, the problems encountered in seeking to augment recruitment levels suggests that parental priorities had also undergone a fundamental change.[97] Official agencies detected an increasing antipathy to the mill as a place of work. Approached by Tootal's to supply recruits for weaving in 1922, the Bolton Juvenile Employment Advisory Committee was unable to oblige. Although it had 200 girls on its books, none was 'willing to learn to weave

[94] *TW* 2 (27 Dec. 1928), 423; Jewkes and Gray, *Wages and Labour*, 179; JRUL, BCA/12/5/1 BSA, joint meeting negotiations, joint meeting with Wigan Employers' Association, 14 Jan. 1925.

[95] *BJG* (2 May 1924), 9; JRUL, BCA/13/2/33 BSA, general correspondence, report of conference between representatives of Bolton Employers' Association, the Operative Spinners' and the Special Enquiry Sub-Committee of the Bolton Juvenile Advisory Committee, 19 July 1928.

[96] BA, FT/21/10 BSA, Annual Report for 1923, 6; JRL, Ashton Employers' Collection, FMCSA, annual report for 1926 (Manchester, 1927), 66.

[97] For the view that half-time abolition alone explained things, see the report on juvenile employment by the Primary Education Sub-Committee of Bolton Borough Council, *BJG* (24 Feb. 1928), 6.

or [to undertake] any other monetary job in a factory'.[98] It was a feeling shared by many of those already employed in the trade. Parental concern to seek alternative work for their children often overcame any lingering hereditary instincts. The Bolton weaver who declared a decided preference for mill work for herself was reluctant to commit her daughter to the loom. By 1928, this attitude appeared to have hardened into local tradition. It was, the mill director Thomas Higham remarked, 'customary for parents to choose an occupation different from their own for their children'.[99]

Cotton's increasing unpopularity among school-leavers was most frequently ascribed to the declining status of mill work. The Weavers' Amalgamation pointed to the alienating effect of poor working conditions, while others emphasized the uncertain prospects open to new entrants. Attempts to reform work practices through the 1920s identified the 'blind alley' as the principal deterrent to recruitment.[100] Alternative forms of work compounded the industry's problems. Engineering jobs had siphoned off male school-leavers in the 1890s, but, by 1909, a more insistent threat was seen to exist in the expanding clerical sector. Lancastrian families, it was lamented, appeared increasingly to hold to the view that their children 'should work in an office, or be a teacher, or some class of work in which they will not have to doff their jackets'.[101]

Developments between the wars merely served to strengthen this conviction. By 1924, William Howarth had come to regard the training of short-hand typists as inimical to the national interest.[102] For Howarth, as for others, the industry's problems were exacerbated by a monetary regime which burdened export trades with an unfavourable exchange rate and high levels of taxation, at the same time that 'sheltered' public-sector occupations were supported out of local and central government revenues. The mill-managers' journal was drawn to speculate 'how long the weaver or the miner will be content to hand his [sic] tram-fare to a conductor whose relatively munificent wage is made possible by the rates wrung from the stricken staple industries'.[103] The opportunities formerly

---

[98] *BJG* (24 Nov. 1922), 7; (2 May 1924), 9.

[99] JRUL, BCA/13/2/33 BSA, general correspondence, report of conference, 19 July 1928; BA, BOHP, 5 (female, born 1917), transcript, 7; *CFT* (17 July 1914), 5; *BJG* (23 Jan. 1914), 12.

[100] *TW* 3 (30 Aug. 1929), 661; BA, FE/1/3/53 BMCSA, correspondence files, newspaper cuttings; see above, pp. 36–7.

[101] *BJG* (30 Jan. 1914), 10; (15 Jan. 1909), 8; see also Russell, *Manchester Boys*, 12–13.

[102] *BJG* (28 Mar. 1924), 9.

[103] *TW* 5 (20 June 1930), 337; also 6 (24 Oct. 1930), 150; 7 (24 Apr. 1931), 245; JRL, Ashton Employers' Collection, FMCSA, annual report for 1926, 69.

sought in the mill were increasingly found elsewhere. The cultural shift against 'traditional' occupations is documented through the records of the Hulton Colliery Disaster Relief Fund, which maintained a close supervision over the victims' children to the point at which they drew their first wage packet. Particular interest centred on their choice of occupations. Given that, in many cases, the death of a father deprived children of paternal assistance in their search for work, the experience of fund dependants cannot be taken as representative. Nevertheless, as decisions were largely unconstrained by hereditary ties, they were acutely sensitive to changes in occupational preferences. The use of such records in reconstructing attitudes to work is not, therefore, to be discounted.

For daughters, clerical work was increasingly preferred to mill employment, as it was seen to offer more marketable skills than the basic dexterity required to operate textile machinery. In 1914, the widow Annie Greenall approached the fund for financial assistance to allow her elder daughter to attend a training course at Bolton's Commercial Institute. At the same time, Elizabeth Cowburn was anxious that her daughter Ada, employed for two years as a cop-packer at W. H. Brown's mill at Daubhill, Bolton, receive support to enable her to learn 'Shorthand, Typewriting and general work'.[104] For a time, officials appeared prepared to indulge such requests. From 1918, however, the haemorrhage of labour from staple trades resulted in assistance being rendered on a more selective basis. In 1924, Edith Foster's appeal for an allowance to fund her daughter's training as a shorthand typist was rejected, as were further approaches from the Greenall and Cowburn households. Maggie Cowburn's desire to quit the cotton trade at the age of 18 after attending commercial classes was criticized; officials were convinced that 'in this case as in so many others the girl is now and would be in future much better off in her present situation in the mill'.[105] Similarly, Kathleen Greenall was advised against attempting a secretarial career, given that 'Girl clerks are a drug on the market'.[106] Such warnings had little effect. Throughout the 1920s, the Juvenile Employment Advisory Committee reported a surplus of applicants for clerical vacancies.[107] Yet, despite the

---

[104] BA, HRF, ABHC/5/112 Personal Files, Shaw to Hon. Sec., 3 Nov. 1914; Hon. Sec. to Shaw, 17 Nov. 1914; ABHC/5/57 Personal Files, Shaw to Hon. Sec., 4 May 1916.

[105] BA, HRF, ABHC/5/57 Personal Files, Shaw to Hon. Sec., 22 Mar. 1918; Hon. Sec. to Shaw, 15 Apr. 1918; ABHC/5/96 Personal Files, Shaw to Hon. Sec., 21 Jan. 1924; Hon. Sec. to Shaw, 23 Jan. 1924; 5 Mar. 1924.

[106] BA, HRF, ABHC/5/112 Personal Files, Shaw to Hon. Sec., 21 Oct. 1919.

[107] *BJG* (5 Oct. 1923), 7; (29 May 1925), 5.

shift in parental priorities, cotton remained the largest local employer of female labour. Even in the early 1930s, over 60 per cent of girls leaving school in the Bolton area were destined for the mill.[108]

A wider range of career choices was open to boys, a fact reflected in the ambitions which one Hulton widow held out for her son, James. Concerned that his talents were being wasted at the Westhoughton weaving firm of Taylor and Hartley, Ltd, she wrote to the fund in 1925, seeking its assistance in enabling James to realize his potential. In support of her appeal, she cited the opinion of 'the man in charge of the Employment Exchange', who had advised that James would 'make a good Accountant, or he would do well in Commercial Law, or as a shorthand Typist or Architect'.[109] A subsequent investigation revealed that this evaluation owed less to official percipience and more to James' cranial peculiarities: its source was a Blackpool phrenologist. Nevertheless, the mother's creativity was eventually rewarded when the fund agreed to finance an electrical engineering course at Wigan Mining College, which enabled James to secure work with the Westhoughton Coal and Cannel Co., Ltd.[110]

In practice, the security promised by alternative careers outside the mill often proved illusory. Many boys placed on apprenticeships faced dismissal on completing their terms, as employers endeavoured to limit costs by encouraging a regular turnover of low-wage juvenile labour. Harry Hardcastle, hero of Walter Greenwood's novel of inter-war Salford, *Love on the Dole*, was not alone in pondering his fate as 'Every year new generations of school boys were appearing, each generation pushing him and his a little nearer to that incredible abyss of manhood and the dole.'[111] In the later 1920s, with over one in five males unemployed in the age group 18 to 24, that prospect appeared even more immediate. A former Hulton dependant, Albert Holt, was laid off by the textile machinists Dobson and Barlow at the age of 19 in 1930. To that point, his career had encapsulated contemporary attitudes, as his grandparents had been determined that Albert should leave his first job in a Bolton weaving shed. With the fund's assistance, work was found at Dobson's and the Hulton Colliery Co., Ltd. Neither job proved secure, and periods of unemployment followed, brought about by trade depression in one case and plant closure in the other. On each occasion, the Holts pressed that Albert be

---

[108] Jewkes and Winterbottom, *Juvenile Unemployment*, 146–7.
[109] BA, HRF, ABHC/5/181 Personal Files, Clara Leigh to Shaw, 4 Aug. 1925.
[110] Ibid., Shaw to Hon. Sec., 2 Sept. 1925; Hon. Sec. to Shaw, 4, 15 Sept. 1925; Shaw to Hon. Sec., 5 Mar. 1926, 26 Sept. 1928; Hon. Sec. to Shaw, 29 Sept. 1928.
[111] W. Greenwood, *Love on the Dole* (Harmondsworth edn., 1969), 92.

found work with Bolton Borough Council, either in the Parks or the Passenger Transport Departments.[112] Although in this case, as in others, help was denied, the stability promised by public-sector employment continued to influence parental thinking. A particular value came to attach to jobs which offered security against cyclical fluctuations in activity, an ordered career structure, and held out the prospect of a pension on retirement. In such circumstances, even outwardly unpromising positions, such as that of municipal lavatory attendant in Bethnal Green in the 1930s, became much prized.[113]

Over time, therefore, 'traditional' skills were progressively devalued. In 1928, at a time when Bolton's spinning rooms were increasingly dependent on imported labour, a motor engineering course at the town's Technical School received applications from 'about fifty "little piecers"'.[114] The mule-room's decline was not shared by all mill departments. The card-room reported a surplus of male applicants through the 1920s, many of whom were side-piecers.[115] This drift of labour into carding departments attracted much criticism. Speaking in 1928, an official on Bolton's Juvenile Advisory Committee 'deplored the present attitude of parents in giving cardroom work a higher status than spinning, although wages in the spinning room were better than in the cardroom'.[116] Pay differentials were no longer central to parental calculations. Rather, they were outweighed by certainty of advancement, guaranteed, in the case of the card-room, by the grinders' apprenticeship system. Carding thus promised the long-term security absent from most staple occupations between the wars.

Economic change from 1918 effectively redefined the spinning trade's role. It no longer provided a brief introduction to work for those intending to pursue careers elsewhere, while its attraction as a lasting source of employment was diminished. Nevertheless, it retained a particular utility, especially as restricted opportunities beyond the mill worked both to

---

[112] Board of Trade, *Industrial Survey*, table XIII, 114; BA, HRF, ABHC/5/150 Personal Files, Shaw to Hon. Sec., 22 Oct. 1925, 14 Dec. 1926, 31 July 1928, 20 Jan. 1930, 8 Oct. 1931, 5 Oct. 1936; Hon. Sec. to Shaw, 17 Oct. 1936; ABHC/5/132 Personal Files, Shaw to Hon. Sec., 4 Aug. 1927; ABHC/5/248 Personal Files, Shaw to Hon. Sec., 15 May 1931.

[113] M. Young and P. Wilmott, *Family and Kinship in East London* (Harmondsworth edn., 1962), 96.

[114] BA, HRF, ABHC/5/150 Personal Files, Shaw to Hon. Sec., 1 Oct. 1928.

[115] Such transfers were usually blocked by the union branch committees which oversaw recruitment to the card-room, BA, FT/7/2/2 BOCA Bolton Committee minutes, committee meetings, 15 Aug. 1927, 30 July 1928, 26 Aug. 1929; FT/7/9/1 BOCA Rules, cl. 10.

[116] JRUL., BCA/13/2/33 BSA general correspondence, report of conference, 19 July 1928.

detain minders in the mule-gate and to draw former piecers back to the industry. A further attraction lay in the manner in which short-time work was organized, allowing workers to maintain insurance payments and so retain their eligibility to benefit under continuity regulations. Cotton continued to offer stable, if not substantial incomes through the 1920s, so that, in 1933, the Bolton Operative Spinners' secretary could observe the behaviour of workers 'who spent one or two years as little piecers and gone [sic] to the pit for several years became unemployed and returned to the mill to qualify for unemployment benefit'.[117] For men such as these, the cotton trade increasingly acted as the employer of last resort.

Aggregate shifts in recruitment provide evidence of a flexible response to fluctuations in the demand for labour. The readiness to consider alternative career avenues was characteristic of a workforce which was not culturally bound to one industry or place of work by ties of family. This point becomes clear if the analysis is extended to consider developments at the level of the individual firm. At times of labour shortage, mills were drawn to compete for hands, so that it was not unknown for spinners to be pressed to offer monetary inducements to encourage piecers to move between firms.[118] As the shortfall became more acute in time of war, competition intensified. This worked to the advantage of firms operating modern plant, as they were able to offer higher wages. Most remained fully staffed at a time when older less efficient mills had up to 70 per cent of their machines idle. Employers advanced various expedients to stem the loss of manpower, including accelerated promotion to minding. To prevent the dilution in skilled status which this and similar measures implied, the Operative Spinners' Association proposed the formal supervision of all transfers. From February 1916, movement between mills was made subject to official sanction by union branch committees.[119] Problems caused by competition for labour continued beyond 1918. To contain such pressures, employers' and operatives' representatives issued a joint statement in 1924, which emphasized that creelers who had completed

---

[117] JRUL, BCA/13/4/48 BSA employers' correspondence, Wood to Boothman, 15 Nov. 1933; see also BCA/12/5/2 BSA joint meeting negotiations, local joint meeting, 22 Dec. 1933; Board of Trade, *Industrial Survey*, 104.

[118] *BJG* (7 Oct. 1899), 8; (24 July 1914), 12; JRUL, BCA/1/3/7 BSA minutes, delegate meeting, 11 Oct. 1899; Council meeting, 30 Apr. 1901; BA, FT/21/9 BSA Annual Report for 1914, 9.

[119] JRUL, BCA/13/2/19 BSA general correspondence, Lewitt and Gerrey, hon. secs of the Bolton and District Advisory Committee, to Bullough, 9 Aug. 1916; BCA/13/4/32 BSA employers' correspondence, Hill to Bullough, 24 Oct. 1917; BCA/1/3/10 BSA minutes, Council meeting, 29 Feb. 1916.

their training had a 'moral obligation to remain in the employment of the firm for a considerable period after becoming efficient'.[120] The absence of any other sanction to ensure loyalty to a particular firm indicates the conditional relationship which prevailed between the individual worker and his/her employer.

The absence of any close sense of attachment is further suggested by the results of manpower surveys undertaken over the period. Returns to the Bolton Master Cotton Spinners' Association from mills across the province in 1924 confirmed that estimates of labour shortages for the area as a whole concealed significant variations between individual firms. So, while twenty of the seventy-five factories surveyed were fully staffed, eleven reported creeler shortages in excess of 50 per cent. In explaining such differences, location appeared to count for little. Neighbouring mills experienced sharply varying fortunes. Although all of the Dart Mill's fifty-two mules were fully manned, one mill run by the Mill Hill Spinning Co., Ltd had no little-piecers. The close territorial bond between the factory and the surrounding locality, which figures prominently in interpretations of nineteenth-century industrial society, appears to have diminished significantly by the early twentieth century. Equally, management structures appear to have exerted little influence over recruitment decisions. Firms under family ownership were no more secure against shortages than were newer public-limited companies. If anything, the reverse applied: at six Bolton mills constructed after 1900, only 4.3 per cent of mules were short-staffed.[121] Here, the higher rewards available on longer carriages appear to have been decisive in determining the precise distribution of manpower. Comparing the 1924 returns with the Bolton Operative Spinners' Association wage census of the previous year suggests a definite, albeit modest, correlation between recruitment and earnings levels. In mills reporting no shortages, creelers' incomes averaged 17s. 10d. a week, compared with 16s. 9½d. in plant where the average shortfall for the district as a whole was exceeded.[122]

The involvement of long-established industrial dynasties, by contrast, had little effect on recruitment patterns. For example, the Hesketh family had long exerted social and economic influence in the township of

---

[120] *BJG* (28 Nov. 1924), 11; see also JRUL, BCA/12/5/1 BSA joint meeting negotiations, local joint meetings, 23 April 1923, 17 Sept. 1924.

[121] BA, FE/1/3/53 BMCSA correspondence files, summary of returns re scarcity of piecers and creelers, Oct. 1924; the post-1900 concerns comprised the Croal, Dart, and Dove mills, along with the three factories owned by the Swan Lane Spinning Co., Ltd.

[122] BA, FE/1/3/53 BMCSA correspondence files, 1924 returns; FT/8/8/1 BSA wages returns from mills in the Bolton area for the four weeks ending 13 Oct. 1923.

Astley Bridge. The Heskeths owned four mills locally and also chaired meetings of the District Board. The extent of their involvement is suggested by the career of Colonel George Hesketh, JP (1852–1930), who supported local causes including the church, schools, charities and the Volunteer Corps. The scope of his patronage, which the *Bolton Journal and Guardian* considered had 'not been excelled in local annals', marked him out as a model paternalist.[123] The result, according to the local press, was a society which continued to bind 'in an almost ideal way the middle classes and artisans of the district'.[124] Despite this, the Heskeths' mills were not immune from labour-supply problems. In 1924, they recorded creeler shortages varying between 8 and 66 per cent.[125] Competition for labour within the township was provided by two other companies: John Ashworth (1902), Ltd, acquired in 1918 by the London-based combine the Amalgamated Cotton Mills Trust; and Sir John Holden & Sons, Ltd, whose electrically powered mill was completed in 1927.[126] The impact on recruitment decisions is reflected in a later (undated) employers' census: while Holden's was fully staffed, Ashworth's showed a 32 per cent shortfall in little-piecers, and the average across the Heskeths' four mills stood at 45 per cent.[127] The implication is clear that the higher wages on offer at firms operating new plant figured more prominently in contemporary calculations than did any lingering sense of attachment to established social leaders.

Nevertheless, wage levels alone were no guarantee against recruitment difficulties. A firm's trading performance, along with the career prospects held out at individual mills, also influenced the search for work. Where circumstances appeared particularly propitious, the labour problem could be transformed from one of shortage into one of surplus. Tootal Broadhurst Lee, Co., Ltd was obliged to operate a waiting list for recruits to its Sunnyside Mill in Bolton. Not only had the firm achieved, through vertical integration, a secure place in the prosperous home market, it also offered, in the form of 'trainingships', a more formal and structured

[123] BA, 'Bolton Biographical Notes', ii, 138–9; E. L. Thorpe, 'Industrial Relations and Social Structure' (Salford Univ. M.Sc. thesis, 1969), ii, appendix, 'Old Bolton Families', 14–15.

[124] *BJG* (19 Dec. 1919), 7.

[125] BA, FE/1/3/53 BMCSA correspondence files, 1924 returns.

[126] Amalgamated Cotton Mills Trust, Ltd, *Concerning Cotton* (1920); *BJG* (4 Oct. 1918), 3; (11 Oct. 1918), 3; (9 Apr. 1920), 10.

[127] BA, FE/1/3/53 BMCSA correspondence files, shortage of piecers; although the census is undated, references to piecers' wage allowances, introduced by joint agreement in May 1933, suggests a date in the mid-1930s at the earliest, FT/21/12 BSA Annual Report for 1933, 54–5.

induction into work, thereby reducing the threat of promotional bottle-necks. As one weaver observed of Tootal's, 'You had to go out and get your name down and if you got in there, you were made for life. That was *the* firm' (emphasis in original).[128] A capacity to distinguish between the employment prospects offered by different firms and a readiness to adjust recruitment decisions accordingly characterized a labour force whose behaviour remained largely unconstrained by ties of consanguinity.

An independent outlook, articulated most powerfully through craft organizations, thus extended to the bulk of the cotton workforce and was expressed primarily through a highly flexible approach to the search for work. The discretion thereby exercised extended from the place of work to the job itself and was guided by a rational evaluation of employment prospects. All were subject to change over time, as the experience of the cotton trade indicates. Its precise function varied according to the economic and legislative context. After 1920, prolonged trade depression and the abolition of the half-time system meant that it no longer provided a focus for parental ambition, nor did it offer a short-term introduction to the world of work for school-leavers. Increasingly, families sought to explore alternative employment avenues, resulting in a secular shortage of manpower. For those who remained, the mill increasingly assumed the role of employer of the last resort, as many reverted to the mule-gate when seeking insurance against wider economic uncertainties.

Such trends were not unique to Lancashire. A comparable flexibility was shown by the cotton operatives of Manchester, New Hampshire, studied by Tamara Hareven. Here, although one source of work, the Amoskeag mill complex, predominated, workers rarely experienced stable or predictable careers. Many sought alternative forms of work, confident in the knowledge that the Amoskeag's consistent need for labour offered some security against failure. In one respect, however, the comparison with New Hampshire reveals an important point of difference. Hareven concludes that Manchester workers shared a deep sense of attachment to the mill, as, in the shade of the Amoskeag, work came to assume an 'all-encompassing character'.[129] Central to this feeling was the way in which neighbourhood and family relations crossed the threshold on to the shopfloor. In Lancashire, by contrast, the evidence suggests that these ties remained distinct. Dependence on the mill was only manifested when

---

[128] BA, BOHP 5 (female, born 1917), transcript, 2, 3, 11; FE/1/3/53 BMCSA correspondence files, 1924 returns; *BJG* (12 Aug. 1927), 6.

[129] T. K. Hareven, *Family Time and Industrial Time* (Cambridge, 1982), 228–58.

parental ambitions were frustrated. An instrumental attitude, which stripped work of much of its broader cultural significance, appeared to pervade the cotton workforce for much of this period. The role of work in shaping class identities would thus appear open to fundamental question.

III

In most mining areas, the family appeared to be central to the recruitment process. Across much of Britain, activity centred on geographically distinct settlements, marked by occupational homogeneity and low levels of labour turnover, conditions encapsulated in the 'family' pit model described by Christopher Storm-Clark. Here, 'family' not only acts as a metaphor for underlying social unity, it also emphasizes the central role which kin played in the entry to work.[130] Although expressed in heightened form, Storm-Clark's model has some basis in fact. In 1911, over 80 per cent of miners in Glamorgan and County Durham lived in administrative districts in which collieries employed a majority of occupied males and in which job opportunities for women were severely restricted.[131] Equally, studies of both areas have suggested that the introduction to and initial training on the job were often effected by family members.[132]

Lancastrian evidence, however, suggests that such a pattern was far from uniform. Although a mature coalfield, dependent to a large extent on local reserves of manpower, the county displayed few of the characteristics of 'family' pit society. A little over 30 per cent of the county's miners lived in districts in which a majority of adult males worked down the pit, while areas in which mining accounted for less than one-third of male employment contained 40 per cent of the workforce. What is more, participation rates for females in paid employment beyond the home were more than double those recorded in Glamorgan and County Durham.[133] High rates of labour mobility within this more variegated employment pattern produced a society in which the solidarities of work

---

[130] C. Storm-Clark, 'The Miners, 1870–1970: A Test-Case for Oral History', *Victorian Studies*, 15 (1971–2), 49–74.

[131] *Parl. Papers 1913*, lxxviii (7018), Census of England and Wales, 1911. X. Occupations and Industries. Pt. I, table 15; for the development of one such settlement, see D. Pocock, *A Mining World: The Story of Bearpark, County Durham* (Durham, 1985), 8–26.

[132] R. A. Church, *The History of the British Coal Industry* (Oxford, 1986), 231–3; Daunton, 'Down the Pit', 590.

[133] *Parl. Papers 1913*, lxxviii (7018), Census of England and Wales, 1911. X. Occupations and Industries. Pt. I, table 15.

had more limited relevance. The occupational and cultural homogeneity characteristic of 'traditional' mining settlements was substantially lacking in Lancashire.

   The urban setting of much mining activity within the county provides the most immediate contrast with conditions elsewhere. The *Bolton Journal and Guardian* noted how, across central Lancashire in particular, 'Miners intermingle with the rest of the industrial population. Enquiries made by the writer at a typical group of mines under one ownership and within two miles of the coalfield centre, revealed that the 2,000 miners are distributed over half-a-dozen neighbouring villages alongside textile operatives'. [134] Pit settlements, demarcated by their occupational structures, were not unknown in Lancashire. However, few, if any, were self-sufficient. Through the period, miners living in Blackrod, between Wigan and Chorley, could be found working in the adjacent townships of Aspull, Coppull, and Haigh. [135] Of Abram's occupied male workforce of 2,438 in 1911, 75 per cent were employed in coal-mining. Despite this, labour was drawn from beyond the township, as the residential distribution of victims of the Maypole Colliery disaster in August 1908 indicates. Thirty-three of the seventy-five who were killed lived in Abram. The remainder travelled to work from districts extending over a radius of 8 miles, from Wigan in the north (twenty-two victims), to Leigh in the east (five), and Golborne in the south (eleven). The disaster occurred during the pit's afternoon shift. Yet the evidence suggests that the men making up the

Table 3. *Places of residence. Pretoria pit disaster victims, December 1910*

Residence	No. of Victims	Residence	No. of Victims
Westhoughton	161	Bolton	72
Chequerbent	33	Daisy Hill	23
Atherton	23	Wingates	22
Tyldesley	2	Over Hulton	1
Hindley	1	Little Hulton	1
Westleigh	1	Hindley Green	1
Walkden	1	Middle Hulton	1
not specified	1		

Source: BA, HRF, ABHC/5/1–344 Personal Files.

[134] *BJG* (21 Mar. 1919), 8.
[135] *Parl. Papers 1912–13*, cxi (6258), Census of England and Wales, 1911. I. Administrative Areas, table 8; BA, BOHP 92 (male, born 1903), transcript, 1, 4; BA, R. J. Davies, MP, 'The Industrial Depression in the Urban Districts of Aspull, Blackrod, Hindley, Horwich and Westhoughton' (unpublished memorandum, 1936), 3.

main day shift were similarly dispersed: many of the Maypole's hewers lived in Wigan and Ince.[136] The practice of working at some distance from home was not peculiar to the Maypole. The 344 miners killed in the Pretoria Pit explosion in December 1910 were drawn from fourteen separate townships, all within 5 miles of the pit head.

Recruitment networks were thus rarely geographically distinct, a complexity compounded by ownership structures. Mining operations across Lancashire ranged from small outcrop workings to huge multi-pit combines. Of 133 firms recorded by the *Colliery Yearbook and Coal Trades' Directory* in the mid-1920s, 41 per cent had workforces numbering fifty or fewer, while, at the other extreme, 36 per cent recorded staffing levels in excess of 500.[137] Eclipsing all others, the Wigan Coal and Iron Co., Ltd employed 10,000 miners at twenty-four pits through Lancashire. In addition to the 2.5 million tons of coal raised each year, the company produced, around 1908, an average of six million bricks a year, 3,500 tons of coke a week, and 1,300 tons of basic steel each week from five blast furnaces. Furthermore, with pits located in Wigan, Leigh, Westhoughton, and St Helens, the combine was a substantial ratepayer in fourteen boroughs and urban districts.[138] In such circumstances, each company's catchment area for labour was unlikely to be discrete. Rather, recruitment networks overlapped, producing a complex pattern of employment.

The point is clarified if attention is focused on a particular area. Located close to the geographical centre of the coalfield, the urban district of Westhoughton resembled, in occupational terms, a 'traditional' mining settlement: its colliery workforce of 2,573 in 1911 represented 53 per cent of all occupied males. The pattern of employment suggests, however, that the resemblance to familiar paradigms extended no further than this. In 1913, three concerns operated ten collieries in the immediate vicinity of Westhoughton: the ubiquitous Wigan Coal and Iron Co., Ltd employed 988 at its Eatock and Hewlett pits; three collieries owned by the Westhoughton Coal and Cannel Co., Ltd provided employment for 821; while 1,920 worked at the Hulton Colliery Co., Ltd's three pits. In addition,

---

[136] *Parl. Papers 1913*, lxxviii (7018), Census of England and Wales, 1911. X. Occupations and Industries. Pt. I, table 15A, 398; WA, PC 4/B8 Maypole Colliery Explosion (1908) Relief Fund, Declaration of Trusts, 1927; *WO* (22 Aug. 1908), 12; (25 Aug. 1908), 3.

[137] *Colliery Yearbook and Coal Trades' Directory* (1924 edn.); the pattern had barely altered by the early 1930s, Board of Trade, *Industrial Survey*, 162.

[138] H. T. Folkard, R. Betley, and C. M. Percy, *The Industries of Wigan* (Wigan, 1889), 35–6; *Lancashire: Its History, Growth and Importance* (n.d.), i, 177; D. H. Turner, 'The Wigan Coal and Iron Company (1865–1885)' (Strathclyde Univ. MA thesis, 1968), 1–2; *Wigan Coal and Iron Co., Ltd*, 6–27.

the four-colliery complex of Fletcher, Burrows and Co., Ltd at nearby
Atherton offered openings for a further 2,650.[139] With firms competing
for labour in such close proximity, a straightforward reproduction of family relationships within the workplace could not be assumed.

The records of the Hulton Colliery Disaster Relief Fund assist in
establishing the precise importance of the kinship tie. Employment patterns were reconstructed from returns covering dependants' entitlement
to relief under the Workmen's Compensation Act of 1897, which, in
many cases, itemize the earnings and place of work of co-resident family
members. Thus, of thirty-two haulage hands killed in the explosion,
information on employment patterns was available for twenty-six. In
nineteen cases, a father was currently or had formerly been employed in
mining; eight were working at the Pretoria, while five were at pits owned
by other companies. Of those who had been miners, one had worked at
the Pretoria, while another had been employed at Bridgewater Collieries.
It was not possible to locate the place of work for the remainder. Among
the fifty unmarried drawers, twenty-three had fathers active in the coal
trade, of whom fourteen were at the Pretoria. At least eight had fathers or
other kin employed at pits elsewhere. In all, therefore, a direct paternal
link could be established in only twenty-three out of seventy-six cases for
which full information was available.[140]

So in many cases households drew their incomes from a variety of
sources. The father of James Edward Hogan, a haulage hand at the
Pretoria, worked at Ramsden's Collieries in Tyldesley, while a brother
worked at Fletcher, Burrows and Co., Ltd, in Atherton. As well as the
Pretoria, members of the Tonge family of Westhoughton found employment with the Westhoughton Coal and Cannel Co., Ltd, and at the Wigan
Coal and Iron Co., Ltd's Eatock Pit. In this case, the family wage was further boosted by the earnings of a daughter who worked at Taylor and
Hartley's mill in Westhoughton.[141] Equally, employment patterns within
individual pits indicate the family's attenuated presence. A number of
Pretoria work-teams were structured around ties of kinship. For example,

[139] *Parl. Papers 1913*, lxxviii (7018), Census of England and Wales, 1911. X. Occupations
and Industries. Pt. I, table 15A, 400; Home Office, *List of Mines in Operation in Great Britain
and Ireland in 1913* (HMSO, 1914), 175–6, 177–8, 181–2.

[140] Calculated from BA, HRF, ABHC/5/1–344 Personal Files, Compensation
statements; occupational details were derived from the official list of fatalities contained in
Parl. Papers 1911, xxxvi (5676–IV), Report of HM Inspector of Mines for Manchester
and Ireland District, 28–9.

[141] BA, HRF, ABHC/5/145 Personal Files, report, 20 Mar. 1911; ABHC/5/302
Compensation statement.

the Seddon family from the Daubhill area of Bolton, a father and two sons, worked together in the pit's Top Yard District, while the Goulding brothers from Westhoughton shared a place in the Yard Mine's Downbrow District. Nevertheless, evidence presented to the disaster inquest suggests that this pattern was not invariable. Many teams comprised members from diverse backgrounds. William Lees Ashcroft from Chequerbent worked as a haulage hand with three colliers who lived in Westhoughton, Daubhill, and central Bolton. Similarly, Fred Radcliffe of Westhoughton drew for two Daubhill hewers.[142] In such circumstances, it cannot be assumed that relationships which developed undergound would carry over into the world beyond the pit. The structural underpinnings for the kind of occupational solidarities which are held to distinguish mining communities appear to have been less prominent in Lancashire.

The dynamics of colliery development also worked to weaken any sense of collective unity around the pit. Variable working conditions underground often necessitated the redisposition of teams. In the absence of 'cavilling' traditions, miners lacked the capacity to ensure the continuance of family ties.[143] Over time, as geological uncertainty exposed the transient nature of mining operations, the effects were felt more widely. The closures which followed the exhaustion of more accessible measures resulted in sizeable reallocations of labour. When operations at the Darcy Lever Coal Co.'s Croftside and Victoria Collieries, near Bolton, ceased in 1901, the workforce was obliged to seek work over a wide area. Some secured jobs locally, others moved west to Wigan, while it was further reported that 'Those who lived at Farnworth have found employment at Walkden, Great Lever, and Clifton, and the larger number seem to have secured places at the Wet Earth Collieries of the Clifton and Kersley Coal Co., Ltd.'[144] The impact of such changes could be mitigated by redeployment to pits owned by the same company. However, this prospect was only open to a few. Of 260 miners affected by the closure of Ellesmere Colliery, Walkden, in 1923, barely 100 were found alternative work by Bridgewater Collieries, Ltd. Similarly, when the Pretoria Pit closed in 1934, the migration which had marked its opening three decades earlier was resumed. In 1900, a large proportion of the workforce had been drawn from the declining part of the field around Wigan. Few of those laid off in 1934 could be taken on at the Hulton Colliery Co., Ltd's

---

[142] LRO, NCHu 9/2 Hulton Colliery Co., Ltd, Inquest transcript, qq. 2491–2, 2848, 3000; NCHu 9/3, qq. 3891–6.
[143] See above, pp. 46–8; see also LCMF, EC minutes, 28 Feb. 1920.
[144] *BJG* (17 Jan. 1902), 7; (2 Feb. 1901), 7.

remaining pit at Huyton. The majority were obliged to seek work elsewhere. As a result, many work-teams were broken up, including one made
up of a father and his son. Although the latter found work at Bolton's
Brackley Pit, his father remained unemployed.[145]

There is little in any of this to suggest an inevitable evolution towards
a stable 'family' pit society. Rather, continued high levels of labour
turnover rendered employment patterns peculiarly volatile. Whether col-
lectively, as a consequence of changes in mining activity, or individually,
the Lancashire colliery workforce remained unusually peripatetic. What
is more, movement proceeded unhindered by institutional or familial
constraints as, in a labour market in which hereditary influences appeared
far from preponderant, the domestic implications of a change in the place
or type of work were likely to be slight. Conditions within the trade call
into question the strength of 'traditional' solidarities based around shared
work experiences. The point is confirmed if we consider the profile of a
'typical' mining career in this period. Most Lancashire miners gained
their first experience of paid work outside the pit. Although half-time
work underground was outlawed from 1887, opportunities remained
available on the pit surface. These were rarely utilized, however, the practice being to reserve such work for elderly or disabled ex-colliers. Thus,
of 19,179 male hands employed on pit banks across the county in 1911,
only 528 (2.7 per cent) were aged under 14. The pattern applied regardless of local circumstances. So, half-timers were a marginal element in pit
workforces in both Bolton and St Helens, accounting for 1.3 and 2.1 per
cent respectively of male surface workers. Yet overall rates of child
employment differed significantly between the two towns. Whereas
almost three-quarters of Bolton children below the age of 14 were in paid
work, that was the case with only 22 per cent of those in St Helens.[146]

The cotton trade was the critical variable here. The earnings opportunities available to half-timers in the industry persuaded many mining
families to place their sons in the mill at the earliest permissible age.
In the east of the county, this practice gave rise to concern. In evidence before the Royal Commission on Labour, the Accrington colliery

---

[145] *BJG* (9 Mar. 1923), 9; Westhoughton Public Library, Pretoria Pit Disaster Pamphlet
Box, *Horwich and Westhoughton Journal and Guardian* (9 Mar. 1934); BA, BOHP 108B (male,
born 1917), transcript, 2–3.
[146] BA, BOHP 111 (male, born 1905), transcript, 2; LCMF, EC minutes, 27 June 1925;
Parl. Papers 1912–13, xli (6237–IV), Report of HM Inspector of Mines: Manchester and
Ireland District, 4; (6237–V), Liverpool and North Wales District, 6; *Parl. Papers 1913*, lxxix
(7019), Census of England and Wales, 1911. X. Occupations and Industries. Pt. II, table 13,
216, 243; lxxviii (7018), Pt. I, 462–3.

proprietor George Macalpine argued that boys who entered weaving sheds at the age of 10 represented a permanent loss to the coal trade.[147] For the most part, however, mill employment constituted a brief and remunerative prelude to an underground career. Thus, having worked half-time in the mule-room, the son of a Blackrod collier left the mill at the age of 14 to join his father down the pit.[148] Recruitment patterns more generally suggest that his experience was not unusual. In the absence of precise recruitment figures, Table 4 depicts hypothetical rather than actual changes in numbers. Annual movements between age groups were calculated using the age structure of the county's population as recorded by the 1911 Census. Thus, it was assumed that, in each year, 53.2 per cent of miners aged 14 and under, and 62.6 per cent of those aged 15 and 16, would move to the higher age group. The difference between this predicted number and actual numbers recorded in the annual Mines' Inspectors' reports gave some indication of net movements in or out of the industry. The calculations could not be taken beyond 1911 as, from that date, all miners aged 16 and under were subsumed within one age division. Nevertheless, it is clear that the tendency for recruitment to continue into later teenage years persisted. As late as 1930, the North Western Divisional Inspector could observe that 'The average age of

Table 4. *Net recruitment to Lancashire collieries, 1908–1911*

Year	Ages (years)		
	14 and under	*15–16*	*over 16*
1908	+588	+1,597	+2,671
1909	+706	+1,532	+1,201
1910	+771	+1,578	−1,541
1911	+744	+1,710	−3,113

Sources: Parl. Papers 1908, xix (4045–V), Report of HM Inspector of Mines. Manchester and Ireland District, 6; (4045–VI), Liverpool and North Wales District, 7–8; *Parl. Papers 1909*, xxxiii (4672–V), Manchester and Ireland District, 5; (4672–VI), Liverpool and North Wales District, 7–8; *Parl. Papers 1910*, xliii (5177–V), Manchester and Ireland District, 4; (5177–VI), Liverpool and North Wales District, 7–8; *Parl. Papers 1911*, xxxvi (5676–IV), Manchester and Ireland District, 4; (5676–V), Liverpool and North Wales District, 6; *Parl. Papers 1912–13*, xli (6237–IV), Manchester and Ireland District, 4; (6237–V), Liverpool and North Wales District, 6.

[147] *Parl. Papers 1892*, xxxiv (6708–IV), RC on Labour: Minutes of Evidence. Mining, qq. 6192–4.
[148] BA, BOHP 92 (male, born 1903), transcript, 3; see also 108A (male, born 1917), tape.

entry into the coal mining industry . . . is later than in most of the other Divisions.'[149]

The industry's limited dependence on child labour coloured attitudes to educational reform. In contrast to opinion within the cotton trade, the LCMF was expected to support an increase in the minimum age for partial exemption in 1899. Twelve years later, proposals in the Coal Mines Amendment Bill further to restrict child labour occasioned less debate than did clauses abolishing female surface work.[150] Equally, the county Federation endorsed Labour Party policy in 1918, which included raising the age of compulsory attendance to 15, with a local option to raise that further to 16. Nevertheless, the narrow vote in favour (65 to 64) indicated the benefits which mining families continued to derive from early entry to the mill.[151]

To a large extent, therefore, the manpower needs of the coal and cotton trades complemented each other: the initial experience of work provided by the mill boosting household incomes at the same time that children were exposed to work disciplines, while later entry to the pit helped to siphon off surplus labour from local mule-rooms. Comparative rates of pay assisted this process, as the earnings differential which attracted school-leavers to the mill tipped inexorably in favour of coal. Under wage lists for juvenile hands, agreed in 1911, colliery earnings would outstrip those available from piecing from the age of 19. Actual earnings figures suggest that the differential may, in practice, have been even greater. Returns on victims of the Hulton Colliery disaster recorded average incomes for drawers aged 16 to 18 of between 21s. and 25s. 7d. a week. The equivalent figure for big-piecers was only 18s. 4d.[152] This differential became a powerful factor in colliery recruitment, more especially at times when opportunities for promotion within the mill were limited. Substantial numbers of side-piecers were reported to be seeking transfers to local pits in the 1890s, a decade in which the consolidation of mining unionism raised wages across most inland fields, and in 1914, when concern was again being voiced over the 'blind-alley' nature of mill work.[153]

---

[149] Mines Dept., *Reports of HM Inspectors of Mines for 1929* (HMSO, 1930), W. J. Charlton, 'North Western Division', 40.

[150] *BJG* (23 Sept. 1899), 8; A. V. John, *By the Sweat of their Brow: Women Workers at Victorian Coal Mines* (1984), 225; *WE* (1 Aug. 1911), 3.

[151] LCMF, special conference minutes, 5 Jan. 1918.

[152] LCMF, agreement at joint meeting held at Queen's Hotel, Manchester, 17 Oct. 1911; *Parl. Papers 1909*, lxxx (4545), Earnings and Hours of Labour, 29; BA, HRF ABHC/5/1–344 Personal Files, Compensation statements.

[153] *BJG* (23 Sept. 1899), 8; (6 Feb. 1914), 9.

Patterns of work among older juveniles, aged between 17 and 22, may thus have owed more to market conditions than to the influence of family links. Entry into the pit was eased by the absence of close controls on the hiring and disposition of labour underground.

These conditions also encouraged applications for work from large numbers of adults. LCMF officials repeatedly expressed concern at the presence of 'market men' attracted to the trade by the prospect of high wages during periods of full-time working. Although lack of experience precluded their employment at the coal face, the deployment of new entrants on repair work underground threatened to restrict opportunities for elderly colliers no longer fit for hewing duties. This prospect assumed immediacy with the introduction of legislation limiting working hours, which encouraged owners to concentrate younger, more productive hands at the face.[154] High levels of activity in wartime revived fears of an influx of 'market men'. Although official returns suggest that adult entrants accounted for no more than 8.2 per cent of the county workforce by August 1916, their presence sufficed to render the Federation hostile to government demands for more manpower for the war effort. Officials insisted that recruits new to the pit be 'combed out' before more experienced hands were called up.[155]

Manpower problems altered, but were hardly alleviated, following the Armistice. Within two years, the divisional workforce increased by 20 per cent, from 112,815 to 135,957.[156] Rather than the labour shortages which afflicted the post-war cotton trade, the county's pits faced the problem of consistent surplus from 1920, an imbalance exacerbated by a series of closures. The absence of alternative openings meant that, six months after the Great Lever Colliery, near Bolton, ceased operations in 1922, 130 out

---

[154] *Parl. Papers 1907*, xv (3428), Eight Hours Committee: First Report. Pt. III. Minutes of Evidence, qq. 6485, 7397–7401; *Parl. Papers 1908*, xix (4045–V), Report of HM Inspector of Mines. Manchester and Ireland District, 5; (4045–VI), Liverpool and North Wales District, 7; 'market men' was the term used by LCMF agent and Labour MP, Stephen Walsh, *Parl. Papers 1914–16*, xxviii (8009), Coal Mining in Wartime. Pt. II. Minutes of Evidence, q. 2419.

[155] *Parl. Papers 1914–16*, xxviii (8009), Coal Mining in Wartime. Pt. II. Minutes of Evidence, qq. 474, 2121–6; appendix A, 28; *Parl. Papers 1917–18*, xxxvii (8732), Mines and Quarries: General Report, with Statistics, for 1916, by the Chief Inspector of Mines. Pt. I. Divisional Statistics and Reports, 4, 46; LCMF, monthly conference minutes, 11 Mar. 1916 (White Moss resolution); 31 Mar., 25 Aug. 1917 (Coppull resolution); 6 Apr. 1918; special conference minutes, 29 Jan. 1918; EC minutes, 23 Mar. 1918.

[156] *Parl. Papers 1919*, li (339), General Report by Chief Inspector of Mines for 1919, 4; Mines Dept., *Reports of HM Inspectors of Mines for 1920* (HMSO, 1922), A. D. Nicholson, 'Lancashire, North Wales and Ireland Division', 117.

of 305 Federation members formerly employed at the pit remained out of work. Three years later, over half the workforce of 780 at Ashton Field Colliery were unemployed five months after its closure.[157] In order to maximize opportunities for re-employment, Federation delegates called for restrictions on recruitment from outside the industry. In successive years from 1920, delegate conferences voted to prohibit entry first to those above the age of 18 and then to those over 16 years of age.[158] Change was not forthcoming. Managements opposed restrictions on the pool of available labour, while support within the MFGB was also lacking. In 1924, the national conference rejected Lancashire's calls to place an upper age limit of 18 years on new recruits.[159] Delayed entry appeared a problem particular to one region. It thus remained the case that, across Lancashire, recruitment from other industries regularly exceeded the numbers of school-leavers entering the trade.[160]

If the extent of occupational mobility cannot be precisely quantified, the impression remains that, at some stage in their careers, a majority of Lancashire miners experienced work beyond the pit. For most, this involved a brief period of mill employment at an age when underground work was proscribed. Nevertheless, the prospect of higher than average earnings continued to attract older juveniles and unskilled adults to the pit in large numbers. This suggests that only in a comparatively few cases would recruitment reflect the direct influence of kin. The family interest was more likely to be dispersed over various places and types of work, a pattern which became more pronounced in the changing economic climate of the 1920s.

The contraction in activity over that decade ensured continued growth in the incidence both of short-time working and of outright unemployment. In the summer of 1925, almost 50 per cent of Federation members sought 'waiting period' payments to cover the interval before they became eligible for unemployment insurance under continuity regulations. In the years that followed, organized short-time working was, for many, translated into full unemployment. By June 1928, over 10 per cent of the

---

[157] LCMF, monthly conference minutes, 16 Sept. 1922 (Great Lever resolution); 10 Oct. 1925 (Ashton Field resolution); membership return, 7 Jan. 1922; *Colliery Yearbook and Coal Trades' Directory* (1924 edn.), 73.
[158] LCMF, monthly conference minutes, 11 Dec. 1920 (Atherton resolution); 17 Sept. 1921 (Bold resolution).
[159] LCMF, monthly conference minutes, 11 Oct. 1924.
[160] *Parl. Papers 1926*, xiv (2600), RC on the Coal Industry. Report, appendix 18, table 14, 213.

insured workforce was wholly without work, a proportion which, four years later, had almost doubled. If all temporarily stopped miners are added, the annual average unemployment rate rose from 25.3 to 35.4 per cent over the same period.[161] Wage cuts and short-time working reduced the remainder, in Thomas Greenall's words, to a 'deplorable and an intolerable position'.[162] Perceptions of comparative earnings confirmed the declining attractions of work underground. In 1924, the Federation delegate from Hapton Valley complained that there were 'road sweepers in Burnley getting 80 per cent more than a man in Burnley collieries gets'.[163]

One response to economic difficulty, movement between pits in search of more remunerative places, has already been noted. Others attempted more drastic solutions. Youths across north-east Lancashire were reported to be leaving the pit in 1922, lured away by the higher returns offered in alternative trades. Further west, in St Helens, the glass manufacture exerted a powerful pull on many. The enforced closure of Clock Face Colliery during a ten-day railway stoppage in 1924 led haulage hands to apply for work at the neighbouring Pilkingtons' works.[164] Symptomatic of such trends was the behaviour of the former Hulton dependant, Harold Jolley, who on the closure of his place in 1927 sought to acquire more marketable motor-engineering skills.[165]

Juvenile recruitment offers the most sensitive indicator of this shift in priorities. In two years from 1920, the Mines' Inspectorate reported a 43 per cent fall in the number of boys aged 16 and under employed underground and on the pit surface. Although part of this may be attributed to the effects of the Fisher Act, the fact that the trend was sustained in later years suggests a more fundamental change in attitudes. So, whereas the workforce as a whole contracted by one-third during the 1920s (115,475 to 75,535), the fall in male juvenile hands exceeded 67 per cent (6,304 to 2,043).[166] In many cases, pit work was only pursued when ambitions elsewhere had been frustrated. For example, having been refused a clerical position at Horwich Railway Engineering Works, the Hulton dependant

---

[161] LCMF, special EC minutes, 26 Sept. 1925; unemployment figures calculated from *LG* 36–41 (1928–33).

[162] LCMF, annual conference minutes, 3 Jan. 1925.

[163] LCMF, monthly conference minutes, 24 May 1924.

[164] LCMF, EC minutes, 17 June 1922; LRO, Coal Board Records NCWi 7/3 Wigan Coal and Iron Co., Ltd, Clock Face Colliery, monthly reports, Potato Delf Mine, Dean's Jig, Jan. 1924.

[165] BA, HRF, ABHC/5/173 Personal Files, Shaw to Hon. Sec., 3 June 1927.

[166] *Reports of HM Inspectors of Mines for 1920*, 'Lancashire, North Wales and Ireland Division', 117; *Reports for 1930*, 'North Western Division', 7.

Ralph Shaw began work as a pony driver at Lostock Hall Colliery, near Bolton.[167] If a desire to avoid sending their sons underground was most obvious among families affected by the disaster, recruitment trends more generally indicate that this preference was widely shared after 1920. With few obvious alternative outlets for school-leavers, many had recourse to a familiar source of work: the mill. Addressing a conference on juvenile employment in 1928, the president of the Bolton Operative Spinners' Association observed that, in contrast to cotton operatives, colliers, especially those in the Leigh district, were anxious to place their sons in mule-rooms. The contemporaneous return of former piecers suggests that, for mining families, the mill increasingly provided an alternative, rather than, as under the half-time system, a supplementary source of employment.[168]

Throughout the period, therefore, Lancashire miners consistently displayed a propensity to pursue alternative career paths. Their attachment to the pit remained, at best, conditional. Solidarities founded on work, a key organizing principle of Storm-Clark's 'family' pit society, remained underdeveloped across Lancashire. The problems encountered by mining unionism across the county thus had clear social origins. The network of district associations which combined in 1881 to form the Lancashire and Cheshire Miners' Federation had evolved to accommodate local circumstances. With branches organized around ties of residence rather than of work, uniting miners from different pits, union structures reflected the often diffuse character of family relationships underground. They had a particular utility, enabling a number to resist attempts at reorganization through the period. Tyldesley's miners, for example, continued to combine as a district into the 1920s.[169] Over much of Lancashire, however, the pit became the fundamental unit of mining unionism. Administrative efficiency was the principal gain anticipated from this reform. By removing intermediate layers of authority, change would, it was argued, strengthen the influence of the county executive. Yet, however rational in bureaucratic terms, the organizational implications of this restructuring were less favourable. With members of the same household often employed at different collieries under separate ownerships, pit branches lacked the important socializing influence of the family. If anything, therefore, problems of non-membership and low levels of participation

---

[167] BA, HRF, ABHC/5/282 Personal Files, Shaw to Hon. Sec., 12 Feb. 1923.
[168] JRUL, BCA/13/2/33 BSA, general correspondence, report of conference, 19 July 1928; on the attitude of Hulton families, BA, HRF, ABHC/5/210 Personal Files, Ada Barlow to J. T. Cooper, 3 Feb. 1911.
[169] LCMF, annual conference minutes, 3 Jan. 1925.

were likely to intensify with time. Class identity which, in the unitary set-tlements characteristic of mining activity elsewhere in Britain, was forged by the work experience and articulated through union debate, was, in the case of Lancashire, refracted by a complex pattern of recruitment and employment. In such circumstances, whatever the importance of work in defining the individual experience, its capacity to generate and sustain a sense of collective identity remains open to doubt.

IV

A concentration on the search for work helps to focus the analysis on the interface between structural context and individual choice, the point at which identities and cultures are formed. No longer are we obliged to 'read off' attitudes from the records of labour organizations, distorted as they are both by institutional practices and, particularly in the case of cotton, by sectional preoccupations. Instead, it becomes possible to recon-struct values and patterns of behaviour which go beyond craft minorities to comprehend the labour force as a whole. From this, two substantive conclusions suggest themselves. First, the role which the historiography has assigned the working–class family, integrating domestic and industrial life through its control of recruitment and training, requires significant emendation. Over much of Lancashire, members of the same household could find themselves dispersed across different firms and trades, a trend sustained in part by discontinuities in industrial development. At all times, families were acutely aware of prevailing employment prospects and possibilities, so that, rather than the straightforward consolidation of kinship ties, an alternative strategy emerged, whereby income derived from a variety of sources would work to contain any potential dislocation arising from economic change. This approach was rendered even more explicit after 1918, as parents sought to mitigate the effects of industrial decline by exploring alternatives to the old staples of coal and cotton.

Such flexibility helped to justify the official conviction, expressed in 1931, that Lancashire would prove the most adaptable of Britain's depressed industrial regions.[170] It also serves to point up a second con-clusion: the essentially instrumental nature of occupational loyalties. The meanings with which work was invested changed significantly in the

---

[170] Memorandum by the President of the Board of Trade (CAB 58/12: EAC (H) 136), cited in H. J. Bush, 'Local, Intellectual and Policy Responses to Localised Unemployment in the Inter-War Period: The Genesis of Regional Policy' (Oxford Univ. D.Phil. thesis, 1980), 272.

half-century from 1880, a point which is obscured by concentrating exclusively on internal work hierarchies and the continued structural division between skilled and unskilled labour.[171] The mule-gate, intermittently a focus for parental ambitions for their children's future before 1914, became a refuge against economic failure as the 1920s progressed. The exclusivity of the mule-spinners was transformed from an unambiguous expression of craft pride into a defensive stance designed to maintain an increasingly precarious standard of living. The high wages on offer in the mule-room exercised a progressively diminishing influence on recruitment decisions, as priority was increasingly given to trades offering security in the longer term. Awareness of this shift encouraged employers to attempt a wholesale restructuring of the employment relationship in the post-war period. The results of this initiative, pursued with considerable vigour during the 1920s, throw valuable additional light on the place of work in working-class culture and the factors shaping class attitudes more generally.

[171] As is the case in R. Penn, 'Trade-Union Organisation and Skill in the Cotton and Engineering Industries in Britain, 1850–1960', *Social History*, 8 (1983), 45.

5

Changing the Culture of Work: Business Leadership and Industrial Welfare in the Coal and Cotton Trades

The half-century from 1880 witnessed significant changes in the structure and practice of industrial leadership across Lancashire, as private, proprietorial capital gave way to the adoption of limited-liability organization. The immediate effects of this development were twofold: first, authority within the day-to-day regulation of business operations increasingly passed to managerial personnel; second, the scale of industrial activity was transformed. Successive merger waves ensured that, by 1935, the largest 100 companies by capital value were responsible for almost one-quarter of national output.[1] Coal and cotton were in the van of these developments. Sectional amalgamations had provided much of the impetus behind merger activity in the 1890s. That trend was resumed after 1918, more especially in the fine-cotton-spinning sector. By 1931, 55 per cent of spindleage within Lancashire, producing yarn from Egyptian fibres, was controlled by three amalgamations: the Fine Cotton Spinners' and Doublers' Association, Ltd, Crosses and Winkworth Consolidated Mills, Ltd, and Combined Egyptian Mills, Ltd, all products of waves of merger activity in 1898, 1920, and 1929 respectively. Concentration was even further advanced in the local coal industry, where, from the later 1920s, two corporations, based on Wigan and Manchester, were responsible for almost 40 per cent of total district output.[2]

More crucially, such changes were seen to carry broader social implications. The civic role assumed by many nineteenth-century employers, reflected in a range of political, religious, and philanthropic activities, appeared to be threatened by structural change. Local ties were sundered

---

[1] A. Shadwell, *Industrial Efficiency*, ii (1906 edn.), 453–4; L. Hannah, 'Managerial Innovation and the Rise of the Large-Scale Company in Interwar Britain', *Econ.Hist.Rev.*, 2nd ser. 27 (1974), 252.

[2] L. Hannah, *The Rise of the Corporate Economy* (1983), 21; H. Clay, *Report on the Position of the English Cotton Industry* (1931), 9–10; see above, p. 52.

as owners of both mills and mines left towns with which they had long been associated. In contemporary eyes, a civic élite was being lost, to be replaced by a more bureaucratic managerialism oriented more to the pursuit of profit than to a recognition of wider social responsibilities.[3] In Lancashire, such perceptions were heightened by the financial restructuring which followed the Armistice. Yet the extent to which the new generation of industrial leaders, in place after 1918, displayed a lesser attachment to civic ideals than its predecessors has still to be established. An assessment of this point requires some consideration of the changes which occurred in labour-relations strategies through the period. In outline, from 1918 and reflecting the trend towards increasingly corporate industrial structures, proprietorial paternalism, personal and familial in inspiration, was replaced by a more formal welfarism. Changes in welfare provision are often discussed in terms of employers' recurrent preoccupation with questions of work discipline and labour efficiency.[4] However, this approach fails to account for the uneven distribution of such initiatives. Few innovations in industrial leadership were attempted in the coal trade in this period. By contrast, welfare provision was widely introduced by employers in the cotton industry, to the extent that paternalism may be said to have flourished in the inter-war years to a degree unknown in its supposed Victorian heyday. Of particular significance for our purposes, its efflorescence was driven less by a desire to assert managerial prerogatives and more by an attempt to refashion the culture of work itself. A prime intention was to locate the mill at the centre of working-class life, effecting a fundamental change in the experience of and attitudes towards work. Reactions to such initiatives provide powerful evidence on the place of work in the formation of class identities.

---

[3] A. C. Howe, *The Cotton Masters* (Oxford, 1984), 270–309; J. Garrard, *Leadership and Power in Victorian Industrial Towns, 1830–80* (Manchester, 1983), 13–62; P. Joyce, *Work, Society and Politics* (Brighton, 1980), 134–57; A. H. Birch, *Small-Town Politics: A Study of Political Life in Glossop* (Oxford, 1959), 30–1; J. Boswell, 'The Informal Social Control of Business in Britain, 1880–1939', *Business History Review*, 57 (1983), 242–6.

[4] S. Pollard, *The Genesis of Modern Management: A Study of the Industrial Revolution in Great Britain* (1965), 160, 181–206; J. Melling, 'British Employers and the Development of Industrial Welfare, c.1880–1920: An Industrial and Regional Comparison' (Glasgow Univ. Ph.D. thesis, 1980), 14–16; J. R. Hay, 'Employers' Attitudes to Social Policy and the Concept of "Social Control", 1900–1920', in P. Thane (ed.), *The Origins of British Social Policy* (1978), 116; H. Jones, 'Employers' Welfare Schemes and Industrial Relations in Inter-War Britain', *Business History*, 25 (1983), 63–4.

I

Although the adoption of joint-stock forms of organization affected large areas of Lancashire cotton production from the middle of the nineteenth century, a more fundamental discontinuity in ownership patterns occurred in the years immediately after 1918.[5] Several developments contributed to this outcome. First, many established employers gradually withdrew from active participation in business affairs. William Heaton preferred to spend the summer months in the Lake District, rather than close to the family's mills at Lostock, while the bleacher J. W. Makant, although a resident of Bolton until his death in 1923, chose to divide his year equally between the town and his country estate near Carlisle.[6] For others, the breach was permanent, so that within two years of the Armistice almost one-third of Bolton's manufacturing capacity had changed hands.[7] Families associated with the industry from its domestic, handicraft origins chose to sunder all links with cotton Lancashire. The Haslams had been cotton producers around Bolton since 1800 and had long been active supporters of local Unitarian and Liberal causes. In 1918, however, the family added to the numbers of those who, in the words of the *Bolton Journal and Guardian*, were 'scuttling out of the cotton trade', withdrawing to the leisured seclusion of Leamington Spa and the South Downs.[8] In the same year, the Eckersley family, leading employers in the Poolstock district of Wigan, sold their textile interests and moved permanently to their landed estate at Yeadon, near Leeds.[9]

In both cases, departure was quickened by the influx of new capital into the trade, attracted by the inflated profits of wartime and the perceived potential for achieving significant economies of scale. Factories owned by the Haslams and the Eckersleys were among concerns acquired by the Amalgamated Cotton Mills Trust, Ltd, a combine based in London and promoted by the gold and diamond merchant Solomon Barnato ('Solly') Joel. As finally constituted, the amalgamation's board comprised representatives of the Dunlop Rubber Co. and the Beecham Trust, the latter

---

[5] D. A. Farnie, *The English Cotton Industry and the World Market* (Oxford, 1979), ch. 6; S. J. Chapman and T. S. Ashton, 'The Sizes of Businesses', *Journal of the Royal Statistical Society*, 77 (1913–14), 469–550.

[6] *BJG* (23 Jan. 1920), 10 (Heaton); (28 Dec. 1923), 10 (Makant).

[7] *BJG* (9 Apr. 1920), 10.

[8] *BJG* (28 Nov. 1919), 5, for the 'scuttling' reference; (15 Sept. 1922), 5; (17 Mar. 1933), 7.

[9] *Memoir of the Late Nathaniel Eckersley* (Wigan, 1892), 8–30; WHS, 'Biographical Cuttings Books', i, 260.

holding 50 per cent of the company's preference-share capital.[10] The cosmopolitan background of the Trust's directors reflected developments elsewhere. The board of Crosses and Winkworth Consolidated Mills, Ltd, which acquired six fine-spinning firms in 1920, included the Liverpool naval engineer, Sir John Esplen, KCB, and the Canadian baronet, Sir Edward Mackay Edgar. The presence of men with little experience of the industry gave rise to expressions of concern at the company's second annual general meeting.[11] If, in part, this reflected understandable unease on the part of shareholders for the profitability of their investments, it also underscored a more fundamental source of disquiet: that the irruption of metropolitan capital could result in both civic impoverishment and social division. The Haslam and Eckersley families had both contributed significantly to cultural provision in and around their respective towns. The Eckersleys had financed the building of churches and schools in Wigan and the neighbouring townships of Hindley and Platt Bridge. The Haslams had donated land in Bolton for recreational purposes and, as a final benefaction, sanctioned the use of their residences as a maternity home and an educational institute.[12] The replacement of families who, in the words of the *Bolton Journal and Guardian*, had been 'pioneers in intellectual, social, and philanthropic movements', by corporate concerns which lacked any clear sense of attachment to the county was an obvious cause for concern. As early as 1919, it was observed that 'Already there is noticeable a diminution of that personal interest on the part of employers in the private lives and affairs of their employees, and that general consideration towards them, which helped in the old days to sweeten the relations one with the other.' [13]

Yet fears of a wholesale departure from pre-war norms proved, in practice, to be exaggerated. The prominence given to changes in ownership tended to obscure examples of continuity in company control. Among those retaining links with the industry beyond 1918 were the Heskeths, who continued to control mills in the Astley Bridge district through the inter-war period. Similarly, descendants of the firm's founders still oversaw affairs at Barlow and Jones, Ltd.[14] In both cases, the absence of finan-

[10] *BEN* (6 Dec. 1918), 3; *BJG* (28 Nov. 1919), 5, 7; Amalgamated Cotton Mills Trust, Ltd, *Concerning Cotton*.

[11] BA, ZZ/50/30 Crosses and Winkworth Consolidated Mills, Ltd (C&W Consolidated), memorandum and articles of association, 12; *BJG* (23 June 1922), 9.

[12] *BJG* (15 June 1923), 9; (17 Mar. 1933), 7; *Memoir of the Late Nathaniel Eckersley*; *Parish of Wigan: St James' Church (1866–1916). Jubilee Souvenir* (Wigan, 1916).

[13] *BJG* (28 Nov. 1919), 5.

[14] Public Record Office, Kew (PRO), Companies' Registration Office, Files of Dissolved Companies BT 31/31029/21660 T. M. Hesketh and Son, Ltd, share summary, 6 May 1931;

cial or organizational restructuring facilitated continuity. More generally, however, knowledge of the industry enabled members of the established élite to survive in new corporate settings. The quest for economies of scale, which drove much merger activity in the period, rarely encompassed management structures. The Fine Cotton Spinners' and Doublers' Association, Ltd sought savings in the purchasing of raw materials and the marketing of yarn. Day-to-day managerial functions remained unaltered, enabling constituent firms to retain their distinctive trading identities.[15] Similarly, directors of the Amalgamated Cotton Mills Trust disclaimed any intention of interfering in mill operations, matters on which they readily professed ignorance. So, although co-ordination was achieved by placing four Trust members on the board of each subsidiary, supervision of the production process was, in each case, left to 'a Lancastrian managing director and staff of highly trained officials, all of whom, it might be said, were born and bred in the cotton spinning business'.[16]

Other amalgamations attached a comparable importance to achieving continuity in personnel. Established families, such as the Makants and the Slaters, managed plant under the Bleachers' Association, enabling the Slaters to maintain an involvement in the Dunscar district which extended back over 150 years.[17] Similarly, the Musgrave family, active in the Bolton spinning trade since 1860, was represented on the board of the Fine Cotton Spinners' and Doublers' Association, Ltd into the 1930s.[18] The value which attached to proprietorial experience was further evident in the decision of Crosses and Winkworth to acquire the Lostock firm of William Heaton and Sons in 1921. The purchase was only considered practicable if 'some of the present Directors remained to manage and advise'.[19] Local influence soon extended beyond the details of mill management. Two years later, in October 1923, Crosses and Winkworth's board voted to transfer control from London to Bolton. At the same time, Edgar's place as chairman was taken by W. A. Greenhalgh, the son of a

---

JRUL, BCA/13/4/42 BSA, employers' correspondence, notes and minutes re Wellington Mill, Turton, n.d.; *The Times* (24 Nov. 1964), 14 (obit. of Sir T. D. Barlow); BA, 'Bolton Biographical Notes', iv, 153 (Norman Jones).

[15] Fine Cotton Spinners' and Doublers' Association, Ltd, *Prospectus and Articles of Association* (1898).

[16] *Concerning Cotton*; *BJG* (28 Nov. 1919), 7.

[17] Sir A. J. Sykes, Bart, *Concerning the Bleaching Industry* (Manchester, 1925), 74–9; BA, 'Bolton Biographical Notes', iii, 69 (Col. J. W. Slater); iv, 131 (J. W. Makant, jun.).

[18] *BJG* (16 June 1933), 13.

[19] BA, ZZ/50/24 C&W Consolidated, draft minutes of directors' meeting, 19 Oct 1921.

Bolton mill director and thus a man of unimpeachably Lancastrian stock.[20]

In many respects, Greenhalgh was a thoroughly representative figure in the inter-war cotton trade. The successors to the Haslams and the Eckersleys were, for the most part, figures steeped in the industry and its traditions. For some, their involvement reflected hereditary influences. Joshua Barber-Lomax, who, by 1924, had acquired interests in over twenty textile concerns, including six in Bolton, commenced work in his uncle's cotton-waste business in Preston.[21] Others rose by means of managerial experience. An evening course of technical instruction facilitated Sir John Holden's promotion and led to him taking control of mills in Horwich and Leigh. The career of Alfred Edward Holt, director and proprietor of eight Bolton firms during the 1920s, followed a similar progression.[22] Managers were, through their particular knowledge, well placed to profit from post-war speculation in mill stock. A. E. Boydell, who was appointed secretary of the Hall Lane Spinning Co., Ltd in Leigh in 1913, became managing director of the firm following its reconstitution in 1920. His interests then extended, through share-dealing, to mills in Bolton and Atherton.[23]

Aggregate figures, derived from local trade directories, confirm the impression conveyed by the accumulation of individual detail. Of 220 directors of Bolton spinning and weaving firms in 1923, ninety-two (42 per cent) lived within the borough, while a further eighty-six could be traced to other parts of Lancashire and Cheshire. In all, therefore, 81 per cent of the town's cotton élite remained within the region. Similarly, of eighty-one mill directors in the Wigan district, as defined by *Worrall's Directory* (an area extending from Skelmersdale in the west to Hindley in the east), seventy-two (89 per cent) lived within commuting distance of their factories.[24] Despite the organizational changes of the period from 1918, industrial leadership in the cotton trade retained a distinctively regional character. The occupational backgrounds of mill directors, as revealed by returns from the Companies' Register relating to firms in Wigan and Bolton, provide further evidence of continuity. To capture the

[20] *BJG* (5 Oct. 1923), 6.
[21] *BJG* (15 Feb. 1924), 6; *Skinner's Cotton Trade Directory* (1923 edn.).
[22] *BJG* (9 Apr. 1920), 10; (14 May 1926), 6 (Holden); BA, 'Bolton Biographical Notes', iii, 250; *Skinner's Cotton Trade Directory* (1923 edn.) (Holt).
[23] *BJG* (18 July 1930), 11; (17 Oct. 1930), 6.
[24] *Worrall's Cotton Spinners' and Manufacturers' Directory* (Oldham, 1923 edn.); *Skinner's Cotton Trade Directory* (1923 edn.).

impact of post-war changes in ownership, two samples were drafted, with 1918 marking the point of division. Significantly, in both samples, 'cotton spinners' formed the largest single category, accounting for twenty-one of fifty directors before 1918 and twenty-five out of ninety thereafter. Indicative of the prominence which mill managers often assumed in reflotations, their representation increased markedly between the two samples, from four to nineteen.[25]

It remains to establish how far the continued involvement of figures long associated with the trade also worked to ensure the survival of a particular ethos of industrial leadership. Certainly, fears that, with recapitalization, a utilitarian quest for profit would take precedence over any deeper commitment to the region and its leading industries were not realized. So, although economic difficulties through the 1920s encouraged substantial capital withdrawals, directors' holdings were rarely liquidated. In eight years to 1930, workers employed at Cannon Bros, Ltd of Bolton removed almost £10,000 worth of loans from the company. Almost 40 per cent of the remaining debt was held by the directors and their families. As a further demonstration of their confidence in the future of the business, a move which had the additional advantage of securing access to bank overdraft facilities, these investments were later converted into the less

[25] PRO, Register of Dissolved Companies, BT 31/31029/21660 T. M. Hesketh and Son, Ltd, share summaries, 4 May 1911, 6 May 1931; BT 31/18117/93632 Croal Spinning Co., Ltd, directors of company, 5 June 1907, 3 May 1920; BT 31/20770/122924 John Harwood and Son, Ltd, directors of company, 16 Mar. 1916; BT 31/16263/63625 Youngs, Ltd, directors of company, 2 Jan. 1901; BT 31/17433/84266 Maco Spinning Co., Ltd, directors of company, 7 Apr. 1905, 22 Sept. 1920; BT 31/15001/29365 North End Spinning Co., Ltd, directors of company, 14 Oct. 1909, 23 Sept. 1922; BT 31/19245/107689 Bolton Manufacturing Co., Ltd, directors of company, 16 Oct. 1911; BT 31/15578/47154 Charles Heaton and Son, Ltd, directors of company, 16 Mar. 1901; BT 31/16179/61507 Bradley Manufacturing Co., Ltd, directors of company, 12 Sept. 1914, 30 Sept. 1922; BT 31/17796/89204 William Woods and Son, directors of company, 5 Oct. 1908; BT 31/32423/167272 Rumworth Cotton Spinning Co., Ltd, directors of company, 1 Aug. 1928; BT 31/32448/170236 Sir John Holden and Sons, Ltd, directors of company, 2 Sept. 1920; BT 31/34358/40283 Bee Hive Spinning Co., Ltd, directors of company, 12 Feb. 1920; BT 31/32212/141429 WA Openshaw, Ltd, directors of company, 26 July 1935; BT 31/32419/166839 Bolton Union Spinning Co. (1920), Ltd, directors of company, 6 Feb. 1929; BT 31/37955/79551 Ocean Spinning Co., Ltd, directors of company, 21 Jan. 1925; BT 31/32417/166733 Henry Poole and Co., Ltd, directors of company, 13 Apr. 1920; BT 31/33810/165361 Empress Spinning Co. (1920), Ltd, directors of company, 28 Feb. 1920; BT 31/32427/167751 Trencherfield Mills, Ltd, directors of company, 15 May 1920; BT 31/32426/167494 May Mill Spinning Co. (1920), Ltd, directors of company, 26 Apr. 1920; BT 31/32369/163323 Marne Ring Mill (1920), Ltd, directors of company, 23 Jan. 1920; BT 31/35254/167981 William Brown and Nephew (Wigan), Ltd, directors of company, 27 May 1920; BA ZZ/50/30 C&W Consolidated, articles of association.

liquid form of preference-share capital.[26] Similarly, in 1929, the board of the Swan Lane Spinning Co. (1920), Ltd endeavoured to reassure shareholders of its commitment to the firm by emphasizing that, in addition to a collective holding of 100,000 shares, all its members had taken out substantial loans with the company.[27] Although, as the Cannon Bros' example indicates, such actions had an important financial motive and were designed to bolster investor confidence, they also reflected a continued acknowledgement of the moral responsibilities which were seen to accompany industrial leadership.

Business élites had long recognized the civic obligations which went with the possession of manufacturing wealth. In addition to the Haslams, Victorian Bolton had benefited from the activities of figures such as John Robert Barlow, chairman of Barlow and Jones, Ltd, who, along with holding lay offices in the local Wesleyan movement, supported the town's Nursing Association, Guild of Help, and the local branch of the YMCA. He also donated land for a park and for the construction of an institute in the township of Edgworth, of which he was a leading resident.[28]

Yet, in assessing the impact of the spread of more corporate forms of capitalism after 1918, it must be acknowledged that such benefactions were far from universal in the period before 1914. Balancing the social involvement of the Barlows, Haslams, and Heskeths were proprietors whose concerns rarely extended beyond the factory gate. One such was J. P. Lord, founder of the Bolton firm of Lord, Hampson and Lord. Others confined their public role to religious affairs. The local Unitarian movement absorbed the extramural energies of George Harris Crook and John Harwood, the latter of whom served for a number of years as a teacher at the Sunday school linked to Bank St Chapel.[29] Over time, similar discretion was exercised in the field of politics. Although still active in party organizations, Edwardian mill-owners and directors, unlike their mid-Victorian predecessors, were largely absent from the local council chamber. Of 163 candidates put forward at Bolton's annual local elections

---

[26] LRO, Barber–Lomax Collection DDBx 10/5 Cannon Bros, Ltd, minute book, 18 Dec. 1922, 29 Dec. 1923, 10 Dec. 1924, 22 Dec. 1926, 19 Dec. 1928, 29 Dec. 1930; meeting of loanholders, 9 Apr. 1930.   [27] *BJG* (9 Aug. 1929), 8.

[28] *BJG* (20 July 1923), 9.

[29] *BJG* (19 Mar. 1920), 10 (Lord); (24 Dec. 1920), 10 (Crook); (4 Apr. 1924), 11 (Harwood).

as Conservatives, Liberals, or Independents between 1905 and 1914, only eighteen were directly interested in the cotton trade.[30]

The dominance of private, familial capital in the period before 1918 did not translate automatically into an all-encompassing ethic of civic leadership. Once this point is acknowledged, then the notion of a significant break in employer attitudes around 1918 becomes even less persuasive. Nevertheless, at first sight, residential trends suggested a further weakening in proprietorial involvement in the town. During the 1920s, those mill directors still living in Bolton were mostly to be found clustered in areas to the north and west.[31] An analysis of leisure patterns points to a widespread retreat into suburban exclusivity. The bleacher James Constantine Cort was alone in combining membership of his local golf club with an enthusiasm for homing pigeons. For the majority, their free time was structured around distinctive networks, based on golf and lawn tennis clubs and augmented, for those with aspirations to rural gentility, by the hunt at nearby Holcombe Brook.[32] Yet none of this necessitated, nor did it result in, an abdication of civic leadership. Major William Hesketh, secretary of the Holcombe Hunt from 1925, continued his family's support for the Bolton Savings Bank.[33] Indeed, in many cases, the new generation, as well as sustaining established family commitments, also endeavoured to extend them. For example, J. W. Makant, jun., in addition to inheriting his father's stake in Bolton Wanderers FC, was chairman of Bolton's Savings Committee and a trustee of local charities. Furthermore, unlike his father, he was active in local politics, being returned as Conservative councillor for Derby Ward during the 1920s. Overall, the years from 1918 witnessed a modest revival in the cotton élite's interest in the council chamber. Such, at least, is suggested by the fact that figures within the industry accounted for twenty-six out of 187 Conservative, Liberal, and Independent candidates nominated at November elections between 1918 and 1932.[34]

---

[30] Garrard, *Leadership and Power*, 14–20; *BEN* (23 Oct. 1905), 3; (23 Oct. 1908), 3; (24 Oct. 1908), 3; *BJG* (26 Oct. 1906), 10; (25 Oct. 1907), 16; (23 Oct. 1908), 2; (30 Oct. 1908), 2; (29 Oct. 1909), 2; (21 Oct. 1910), 7; (27 Oct. 1911), 10; (25 Oct. 1912), 7; (24 Oct. 1913), 11

[31] P. Harris, 'Social Leadership and Social Attitudes in Bolton, 1919–1939' (Lancaster Univ. Ph.D. thesis, 1973), 94–5, 101–3.

[32] BA. 'Bolton Biographical Notes', iii, 148 (Cort); for the trend in élite leisure activities more generally, see iii, 81 (Edwin Poole) and 197 (A. Hampson Lord).

[33] BA, 'Bolton Biographical Notes', iii, 222.

[34] BA, 'Bolton Biographical Notes', iv, 131; *BEN* (24 Oct. 1919), 5; *BJG* (22 Oct. 1920), 6; (21 Oct. 1921), 6; (20 Oct. 1922), 5; (26 Oct. 1923), 11; (2 Nov. 1923), 10; (24 Oct. 1924), 5; (23 Oct. 1925), 9; (22 Oct. 1926), 9; (28 Oct. 1927), 6; (5 Nov. 1927), 6; (26 Oct. 1928), 10; (25 Oct. 1929), 6; (31 Oct. 1930), 5; (6 Nov. 1931), 6; (4 Nov. 1932), 6.

Otherwise, civic energies continued to be devoted to established ends, both devotional and secular. The Congregationalist, Thomas Higham, served as Sunday school superintendent, treasurer, and deacon for thirty years to his death in 1941. A. E. Holt became president of the Bolton and District Congregational Council in the 1920s and, in addition, supported local charities and served as secretary to the town's YMCA.[35] Most of those who rose to occupy élite positions in the textile trade in this period, far from being the narrow profit-maximizers predicted by contemporary wisdom, continued to observe Victorian ideals of 'stewardship'. Along with the industrial interests in Leigh and Astley Bridge acquired by his father, Sir George Holden, Bart, patronized a variety of local causes. As well as being involved in the Discharged Soldiers' and Sailors' Association in Leigh, he was also president of the town's rugby league club, its musical guild, male voice choir, and choral union. Furthermore, he maintained an active interest in municipal politics before his enforced retirement through ill health.[36] Civic ideals were, if anything, renewed in the inter-war period, so that textile wealth continued to be deployed in the interests of the immediate locality.

The retention of this broader social role served, however, to obscure a fundamental discontinuity in élite policies at factory level. Before 1920, it had been comparatively rare for significant resources to be devoted to the improvement of the working environment. Around Bolton, only two firms, Tootal Broadhurst Lee Co., Ltd and the Howe Bridge Spinning Co., Ltd had invested substantially in workplace amenities. Their example would be widely emulated between the wars, to the extent that, by 1932, the mill managers' journal could regard the provision of 'pensions, houses, profit sharing, educational facilities, social and recreational activities', as a central feature of modern factory management.[37] Although few, if any, offered such a wide range of amenities, the importance of welfare provision for a new generation of mill workers was readily acknowledged. In a pamphlet designed to mark the firm's jubilee, the Fine Cotton Spinners' and Doublers' Association made much of such changes, as reflected in an imaginary conversation between a current and a former mill operative:

'We have a welfare too' said Daphne, 'If anybody faints a nurse looks after her in th' rest room'.

---

[35] *BJG* (17 Oct. 1924), 6; BA, 'Bolton Biographical Notes', iii, 250 (Holt); 246 (Higham).
[36] BA, 'Bolton Biographical Notes', iii, 121.
[37] *TW* 10 (30 Dec. 1932), 465; *BJG* (27 Aug. 1920), 5.

'Faints!' said Granny, holding up her hands, 'We hadn't time to faint. An' if we had they'd ha' slat a bucket o' watter on us. . . .'

'We have a choir too' said Daphne, 'An' a orchestra.'

'It's a Pantomime tha's getten in, lass,' said Granny. 'Thee stick to it.'. . .

'Do yo know, Granny?' said Daphne. 'They bring us tea an' cake round every morning an' afternoon.'

'Well. Ah'll go to me Aunt Fanny!' said Granny, 'Do they not tuck yo in bed an' kiss yo? When do yo find time to do any wark?'[38]

Growth in welfare provision is often presented as continued evidence of managerial concern with labour efficiency and the need to ensure a disciplined and obedient workforce. S. G. Jones has pursued these themes with reference to the inter-war cotton trade, seeing welfare as an adaptation of established patterns of 'paternalist' industrial leadership to modern business conditions, a development encouraged by the recrudescence of labour militancy during and immediately following the Great War.[39]

Yet employers' continued willingness to devolve responsibility for aspects of the production process on to craft minorities in the mule- and card-rooms suggests that the interpretative weight placed on concepts of 'control' is, in this instance, misplaced. Equally, the confidence which both sides of industry reposed in established conciliation procedures blunted the impact of occasional, short-lived outbreaks of industrial unrest. In the cotton trade at least, fears of labour militancy were not sufficiently deep-rooted to precipitate a fundamental change in managerial thinking. Nor were paternalist practices as durable as Jones suggests. Observers such as Schulze-Gaevernitz, impressed by the order and prosperity of Lancastrian society in the late nineteenth century, attributed it to the mutual respect commanded by strong and stable organizations of labour and capital, rather than to the exercise of paternalist influences. For Schulze-Gaevernitz, in particular, the capacity of Lancastrian workers to develop and sustain collective institutions suggested that the

[38] T. Thompson, 'The Whistle Blows', in Fine Cotton Spinners' and Doublers' Association, Ltd, *Jubilee 'Distaff', 1898–1948* (Manchester, n.d.), 26–7.

[39] S. G. Jones, 'Cotton Employers and Industrial Welfare between the Wars', in J. A. Jowitt and A. J. McIvor (eds.), *Employers and Labour in the English Textile Industries* (1988), 64–83; S. G. Jones, 'The Survival of Industrial Paternalism in the Cotton Districts: A View from the 1920s', *Journal of Regional and Local Studies*, 7 (1987), 1–13; see also J. Melling, 'Employers, Industrial Welfare, and the Struggle for Work-Place Control in British Industry, 1880–1920', in H. F. Gospel and C. R. Littler (eds.), *Managerial Strategies and Industrial Relations* (1983), 55–81.

cotton trade had progressed beyond a more primitive phase of paternal-ist regulation.[40]

An examination of employer practice before 1914 confirms this view. Those firms which made organized provision for the welfare of their workforces stood outside the mainstream of industrial politics in the late Victorian period. Tootal Broadhurst Lee, for example, invested in educa-tional and recreational facilities at its Sunnyside Mill Institute from 1867. At the same time, it refused to allow union representation at its factories and remained outside employers' organizations.[41] Sunnyside apart, amenities were, for the most part, rudimentary. Sanitary provision was poorly developed, comprising, in one Bolton weaving shed, a tap and one waste-water closet.[42] Facilities for meals rarely extended beyond the sup-ply of hot water for making tea and the use of boilers to heat food pre-pared at home. At times, even this basic provision was lacking. Ring spinners at one Bolton mill had recourse to a local chip shop during their dinner hour and were supplied with hot water by an elderly lady who lived opposite the factory.[43] Surveying the extent of welfare provision in 1920, the *Bolton Journal and Guardian* remarked that mills continued to be run 'as if the comfort or convenience of the workers mattered nothing'.[44]

The adoption of welfare policies during the following decade thus rep-resented an unequivocal departure in managerial practice. Awareness of the potential for such changes had been heightened by developments beyond the trade. The provision of medical and canteen facilities in con-trolled establishments during the war had encouraged calls for the wider application of welfare principles, particularly in industries employing large numbers of females. The Women's Employment Committee of the Ministry of Reconstruction singled out cotton as a fruitful subject for such initiatives in labour management.[45] Yet the direct impact of wartime experiments proved limited, in practice. The female cotton workforce, inflated by problems of labour shortage during the war, fell as demobi-

[40] G. von Schulze-Gaevernitz, *The Cotton Trade in England and on the Continent* (1895), 144, 173–5; D. A. Farnie, 'Three Historians of the Cotton Industry: Thomas Ellison, Gerhart von Schulze-Gaevernitz, and Sydney Chapman', *Textile History*, 9 (1978), 79–83.

[41] BA, 'Bolton Biographical Notes', iii, 83 (obit. of Harold Lee); *A Scheme of Education in Industry and Commerce, established by Tootal Broadhurst Lee Co., Ltd* (Manchester, 1918), 9; BA, BOHP 5 (female, born 1917), transcript, 11.

[42] *Parl. Papers 1893–4*, xxxviii, pt. I (6894–XXIII), RC on Labour: Employment of Women, 116; BA, BOHP 15A (female, born 1906), tape.

[43] BA, BOHP 51 (male, born 1908), transcript, 6; 158 (female, born 1907), transcript, 4.

[44] *BJG* (27 Aug. 1920), 5.

[45] *Parl. Papers 1918*, xiv (9239), Ministry of Reconstruction: Report of the Women's Employment Committee, 34; A. M. Anderson, *Women in the Factory* (1922), 273–8; N.

lized men resumed their posts. Furthermore, women's organizations, including the local Women's Citizens' Association, showed greater concern for the domestic welfare of wives and mothers in the council houses being built in the 1920s than in pressing for improved working conditions for those still in paid employment.[46] International comparisons also raised awareness of deficiencies in workplace provision across Lancashire. As well as witnessing evidence of technological innovation, post-war textile delegations to the United States noted the extensive welfare facilities available in modern, integrated plant. However, many questioned the relevance of such findings for the local cotton industry. The geographical isolation of many American factories and the resultant problems of labour supply, it was argued, obliged employers to structure social functions around the mill. Addressing a conference of the British Association of Textile Works' Managers in 1928, Cecil Hilton, a mill director and Conservative MP for Bolton, cited the example of one factory located some 28 miles from the nearest large urban centre. As he explained, in the immediate area, 'There was no local infirmary, no library. To all intents and purposes, the mill was the village and they had to provide all the necessaries ordinarily found in any town, otherwise the people around would have gone elsewhere.'[47] Local reserves of manpower were thought to obviate the need for comparable initiatives in Lancashire, so long as recruitment levels sufficed to sustain levels of industrial activity. Cyclical variations aside, such conditions largely obtained until the 1920s, when economic stagnation and the abolition of half-time work combined to produce a secular shortage of labour.

Over the course of that decade, the unpopularity of mill work became increasingly obvious. Poor employment prospects acted as a powerful deterrent, so that the general secretary of the Weavers' Amalgamation could observe, in 1929, that for parents concerned for their children's future, 'it was the last place on earth to which they sent them'.[48] Persistent criticism of the industry worked further to undermine public confidence, to the extent that, in William Howarth's words, it became 'like the dog with a bad name'.[49] Poor working conditions did

Whiteside, 'Industrial Welfare and Labour Regulation in Britain at the Time of the First World War', *International Review of Social History*, 25 (1980), 310–18.

[46] *BJG* (25 Oct. 1918), 3; (17 Jan. 1919), 6; BA, BCB AB/9/1/1 Housing and Town Planning Committee, minutes, 23 Jan., 12 June 1919.

[47] *TW* 1 (29 June 1928), 472.   [48] *TW* 3 (30 Aug. 1929), 661.

[49] *TW* 2 (28 Sept. 1928), 88; JRUL, BCA/12/5/1 BSA joint meeting negotiations, local joint meeting, 17 Sept. 1924.

nothing to alleviate such difficulties. Indeed, from 1922, the problem was compounded, as medical research established a link between the mineral oils used on mule carriages and the high incidence of scrotal cancer among minders, who absorbed the oil on to their clothing when they came into contact with the machinery.[50] For many, as for the *Bolton Journal and Guardian*, the lesson was clear that 'Only a great improvement in working conditions and a corresponding rise in status resulting, will help to tempt many parents of to-day to let their children follow in their own steps and become mill workers.'[51] The industry's own problems thus provided a powerful argument in favour of increased welfare provision. Other considerations were also advanced. Howarth pointed out that the cost of National Insurance obliged employers to have a greater regard for the well-being of their operatives.[52] Nevertheless, the need to boost recruitment levels appears to have been a decisive element in managerial thinking, helping to shape not only the proposals to reform workplace practices advanced during the decade, but also both the timing of and the precise form assumed by welfare provision.

As before 1914, Tootal's took the lead in the range of amenities provided. In 1918, anticipating proposals for continuation education beyond the age of 14 contained in the Fisher Act, the company established schools at its Manchester and Bolton factories. While the former came under the jurisdiction of the Education Committee of the local authority, classes at Sunnyside were provided by the firm itself, and offered non-vocational instruction on two half-days each week for all employees up to the age of 18.[53] The benefits to be anticipated from such an initiative were summarized by the firm's chairman, Sir Edward Tootal Broadhurst, in an address to the 1919 annual general meeting, in which he observed that 'no company can have a greater asset than a happy, prosperous, contented, educated lot of workers, nor a surer guarantee of an adequate output'. Further to this end, details of profit-sharing and pension schemes were outlined at the same meeting.[54]

[50] *BJG* (26 Oct. 1923), 12; T. Wyke, 'Mule Spinners' Cancer', in A. Fowler and T. Wyke (eds.), *The Barefoot Aristocrats* (Littleborough, 1987), 185; E. M. Brockbank, *Mule Spinners Cancer: Epithelioma of the Skin in Cotton Spinners* (1941), 6–10.

[51] *BJG* (27 Aug. 1920), 5.

[52] JRUL, BCA/12/5/1 BSA joint meeting negotiations, local joint meeting, 23 Apr. 1923.

[53] *A Scheme of Education in Industry and Commerce* (Manchester, 1918), 5, 7; *BJG* (14 June 1918), 3.   [54] *BJG* (22 Aug. 1919), 5; *The Times* (29 Aug. 1919), 19.

Over time, concern for operative welfare extended to the provision of cultural activities at Sunnyside. By the mid-1920s, the mill boasted an orchestra, along with Choral, Debating, and Dramatic Societies, the latter staging a production of *The Man from Toronto* in the continuation school rooms in 1927, with a cast of nine. Recreational activities for younger workers were encouraged through the school's Evening Club, while sports facilities were made available in the mill grounds. In 1923, a lawn tennis tournament, open to all Sunnyside operatives, was organized. Two years later, a new sports ground, complete with flower gardens and ornamental lake, was built by the workers themselves. The range of amenities impressed many visitors to Tootal's. In 1922, the *Bolton Journal and Guardian* was able to report that the mill had gone a long way towards throwing off any 'dark, satanic' associations, presenting instead 'a picture of fresh greensward, trim flower-edged walks, symmetrical privet hedges, . . . All the window ledges on this side [of] the mill were decorated with window boxes of sweet blooms, nodding marguerites, scarlet geraniums and cornflowers.'[55]

Yet, in its arcadian splendour and much else besides, Sunnyside was unusual. Opposition to continuing education ensured that the firm's school inspired no imitators across the cotton districts, while unfavourable economic circumstances and prevailing attitudes to share-ownership among both employers and employed blocked the wider adoption of profit-sharing initiatives.[56] In other respects, however, Tootal's example was more widely copied. Pension schemes were administered by both the Fine Cotton Spinners' and the Bleachers' Associations. The latter also funded a non-contributory superannuation scheme for its elderly workers. Otherwise, marginal improvements to workplace amenities were made, with the provision of rest rooms and additional facilities for the heating of food. More organized provision, including canteens and day nurseries, remained exceptional at this date.[57]

---

[55] *BJG* (8 Sept. 1922), 7; (10 Aug. 1923), 7; (7 Aug. 1925), 5; (21 Jan. 1927), 7; *A Scheme of Education*, 25.

[56] *BJG* (11 Oct. 1918), 2, for the remarks of H. A. L. Fisher on the opening of Tootal's school; in one of the few attempts to emulate provision at Sunnyside, Richard Harwood and Son, Ltd offered its young workers technical instruction in the evenings, *BJG* (27 July 1922), 9.

[57] *BJG* (30 Sept. 1921), 5; (16 May 1924), 9; Sykes, *Concerning the Bleaching Industry*, 48–9; BA, BOHP 15A (female, born 1906), tape; Wigan Education Committee, Juvenile Employment Committee, *Survey of Local Industries in which Boys are Employed* (Wigan, 1949), 32.

Investment was more likely to be devoted to developing recreational amenities. Leisure activities would have the effect, it was hoped, of transforming work's cultural significance by encouraging operative involvement in the mill beyond the narrow bounds of normal working hours. A deeper attachment to the firm would be nurtured, replacing the merely functional relationship defined by the payment of the weekly wage packet. To this end, an Operatic and Dramatic Society was established at Hesketh's Astley Bridge mills, while piecers at Richard Harwood and Son, Ltd, part of the Fine Spinners' combine, were organized into a Works Scout Troop.[58] Ideals of corporate loyalty were, however, most readily pursued through sport. Provision for team games was widespread through the 1920s. Clubs associated with Barlow and Jones, Ltd, and Sir John Holden and Sons, Ltd, competed in the Bolton and District Cricket Association, while elsewhere facilities were provided for bowls, football, hockey, and rounders.[59] Sport acquired a particular utility during a period of economic difficulty, as the concept of the 'team' could be used to promote the idea of co-operative effort. For the managers' journal, Blackburn Rovers' victory over Huddersfield Town in the FA Cup Final of 1928, provided a lesson for the industry as a whole: 'We shall have to make a good plan, like the Rovers did, and stick to it'.[60] A similar link between success on the field of play and in the wider commercial sphere was made by William Howarth, in a speech marking the opening of a bowling green at Richard Harwood's Brownlow Fold Mill in 1921. Economic recovery would best be secured, he argued, by both sides of industry 'working as a team together'.[61] The language of industrial leadership had undergone a telling change. No longer cast in the role of 'paterfamilias', the employer increasingly assumed the mantle of the Captain of the First Eleven.

Sport thus became a central element in industrial welfare policy through the 1920s. Competition within the trade, increasingly controlled through the trend towards amalgamation and attempts to sustain profitability, was readily promoted on the field of play at both company and industry level. Combines came to sponsor contests between constituent firms. The Bleachers' Association organized a bowling competition for its

[58] *BJG* (30 Sept. 1921), 5; (1 Sept. 1922), 12; (1 Mar. 1929), 9.
[59] R. Cavanagh, *Cotton Town Cricket: The Centenary Story of Lancashire's Oldest Cricket League* (Bolton, n.d.), 128, 131; JRUL, BCA/1/3/12 BSA minutes, Council meetings, 15 Oct. 1923, 1 Sept. 1925; L. Oliver, ' "No Hard-Brimmed Hats or Hat-Pins Please": Bolton Women Cotton-Workers and the Game of Rounders, 1911–39', *Oral History: The Journal of the Oral History Society*, 25/1 (Spring 1997), 40–5.
[60] *TW* 1 (27 Apr. 1928), 204.   [61] *BJG* (15 July 1921), 10.

branches, while the Amalgamated Cotton Mills Trust encouraged firms under its banner to compete in a variety of activities, from football and bowls to physical culture and country dancing. Each football team was provided with its own strip, to enable the broader mill community to identify more readily with their team.[62] Across the town, the success of the Bolton Mills Football Challenge Cup led to the formation of a separate league for factory teams from 1921. A bowling competition maintained the sporting interest through the close season. Reviewing the progress of welfare work in the same year, the *Bolton Journal and Guardian* commented on the sense of 'esprit de corps' generated by team sports: 'Hitherto, a little piecer's topics were mainly "counts", "spinning", etc. But when a football season dawns he will have a new interest in the mill. "Our team"—from the mill where he works—may be leading the field in the new Workshops League.'[63]

It remains easier to describe the intention behind welfare projects than it does to estimate their effects. Views on this point, in particular on their efficacy in altering attitudes to work, varied. Some employers were sceptical. Cecil Hilton recounted how attempts to improve conditions at factories in which he had an interest had enjoyed only limited success. The provision of washing facilities had, he claimed, led to the theft of soap and towels, while the serving of afternoon tea had necessitated the hiring of a plumber to remove tea leaves from the pipes.[64] Trade-union opinion was often equally scornful of attempts, as the *Cotton Factory Times* somewhat cynically phrased it, to convert 'factory yards into gardens'. Real welfare, the paper went on, resided in the wage packet and not the provision of extraneous services funded from 'the blood and sinew of the operative'.[65] On occasion, particular schemes excited opposition. The Wigan Weavers' Association criticized the inauguration of a Canteen Club at Clifton Mills in 1932, on the grounds that the compulsory nature of membership breached existing conditions of employment.[66] Yet complaints were also directed at the absence of facilities. The levels of investment required to fund amenities ensured that provision across the industry remained highly uneven. Similarly, during downturns in trade, welfare expenditure was seen to be the first victim of retrenchment. As late as 1928, the Bolton

---

[62] *BJG* (8 Apr. 1921), 7; (8 June 1923), 11; BA, BOHP 161 (male, born 1907), tape.
[63] *BJG* (30 Sept. 1921), 5.
[64] *TW* 1 (29 June 1928), 472; see also BA, FT/7/2/2 BOCA Bolton Committee minutes, quarterly report, 22 Nov. 1927, 3.   [65] *CFT* (2 May 1924), 3; (30 May 1924), 3.
[66] JRL, Ashton Employers' Collection, Wigan and District Cotton Employers' Association minutes, subcommittee meeting, 17 Aug. 1932.

Card Room Association could still point to mills lacking hot water, washing, and rest facilities. Where they were attempted, improvements mostly drew praise. Alice Foley of the Bolton Weavers' Association lauded firms which had established 'remarkable and commendable standards of social and industrial welfare in their factories'.[67]

Attitudes among the workforce are less easily recaptured. Organized manifestations of support, such as the illuminated address which Tootal's workers presented to Harold Lee to mark his fiftieth year with the firm, are, by their very nature, unreliable guides to shopfloor sentiment.[68] Rather more accurate insights are provided by occasional ballots on specific issues. In 1932, for example, operatives at Clifton Mills voted, against union recommendations, to retain canteen facilities. As voting was overseen by both union and management representatives, the result was free from suspicions of undue influence. The thin majority in favour, 56 to 41, suggests that support was not unambiguous, a point confirmed by other fragments of evidence.[69] A mule-spinner at the Astley Bridge firm of John Ashworth's recalled that, although welfare facilities helped to secure amicable relations between managements and workers, many of the latter refused to make use of the canteen facilities. Equally, in its submission to the Committee on Industry and Trade in 1925, the master spinners' Federation noted a widespread reluctance among workers 'to avail themselves of the provisions made by the employers'.[70]

A more rounded reconstruction of operative attitudes, moving beyond the disparate impressions created by these stray references, is provided by evidence of recruitment trends. Comprehensive welfare facilities played some part in maintaining staffing levels at Tootal's. At least one girl was attracted to Sunnyside by the prospect of being able to extend her education beyond the age of 14. Optional elocution classes further satisfied her quest for self-improvement by removing the encumbrances

[67] BA, Alice Foley Collection ZFO/6, A. Foley, 'Welfare in the Lancashire Cotton Industry', 1–2; FT/21/11 BSA Annual Report for 1926, 13; FT/7/2/2 BOCA Bolton Committee minutes, quarterly report, 20 Aug. 1928, 2.

[68] Tootal Group plc, 'To Harold Lee Esq JP from the employees of Messrs Tootal Broadhurst Lee Co Ltd, Sunnyside Mill, Bolton' (Bolton, 1917), praising the 'intimate personal interest' which Lee maintained in both the mill and its workforce. I am most grateful to Tootal Group plc for providing me with a copy of this address; for Lee himself, see BA, 'Bolton Biographical Notes', iii, 83.

[69] JRL, Ashton Employers' Collection, Wigan Employers' Association minutes, subcommittee meeting, 17 Aug. 1932.

[70] JRL, Ashton Employers' Collection, FMCSA, annual report, year ending 31 Dec. 1925 (Manchester, 1925), 62; BA, BOHP 161 (male, born 1907), tape.

of Lancastrian inflexion. Yet Tootal's popularity owed most to its continued profitability and its provision for structured career patterns, which obviated the least attractive features of the inter-war cotton trade. Next to these, the impact of welfare amenities appears, at best, cosmetic.[71] More significantly, employers' manpower surveys revealed no obvious correlation between the availability of welfare facilities and recruitment levels. The Fine Cotton Spinners' combine sponsored Recreation and Social Clubs at each of its branches. In 1925, the opening of a 21–acre sports ground at Musgrave's of Bolton was seen as emblematic of 'the fine spirit of co-operation between directors and employees'.[72] Despite this, labour shortages were reported at most of the Association's mills. Only five branches were fully staffed in 1924, while deficiencies elsewhere varied between 2 and 60 per cent. Equally, the Hesketh family's record of civic involvement offered no guarantee against a shortfall in manpower. By contrast, at Cannon Bros, Ltd, where facilities for hot water and the warming of meals remained wanting through the 1920s, all mules were fully manned.[73]

The conclusion that secure career prospects outweighed the availability of welfare amenities in workers' calculations appears inescapable. Corroboration of this fact may be found in the fact that the nature of grinders' work, which William Mullin of the Card Room Amalgamation admitted to be 'dangerous and unhealthy',[74] failed to discourage applications for apprenticeships. Employers' attempts to propagate a new work culture were frustrated by the instrumental attitude which prevailed among local workers. Of comparable significance in blunting the impact of workplace provision was the availability of alternative leisure outlets. Commercial facilities, from spectator sports to the cinema and variety theatre, attracted mass followings across the cotton towns.[75] Of greater moment, however, those activities organized locally and on a less commercial basis were rarely centred on the place of work. Of 228 teams active in the Bolton and District Cricket Association from its foundation in 1888 to 1939, only thirty were attached to workplaces, of which fifteen were cotton mills. Places of worship and local townships supported 158

[71] BA, BOHP 126 (female, born 1903), tape; 5 (female, born 1917), transcript, 2.

[72] *BJG* (10 July 1925), 9.

[73] BA, FE/1/3/53 BMCSA, correspondence files, summary of returns re scarcity of piecers and creelers; JRUL, BCA/1/3/13 BSA, minutes, Council meeting, 11 Dec. 1928.

[74] BA, FT/7/1/6 BOCA EC minutes, quarterly report, 22 Nov. 1919, 3.

[75] Jones, 'Cotton Employers and Industrial Welfare', 76; P. Wild, 'Recreation in Rochdale, 1900–40', in J. Clarke, C. Critcher, and R. Johnson (eds.), *Working-Class Culture: Studies in History and Theory* (1979), 145–59.

clubs.[76] Employers, it must be recognized, often acted as the patrons of village clubs. Colonel H. M. Hardcastle, a local bleaching proprietor, was president of Bradshaw Cricket Club between the wars, while the Slater and Greg families were prominent in their support of the Eagley team.[77] Nevertheless, work on sport across urban Britain in this period suggests that geographical rather than occupational ties provided the principal focus for collective identification.[78] Despite the vigorous pursuit of welfare initiatives, the cultural role of work remained substantially unchanged.

An examination of the inter-war period calls into question the contemporary conviction that the years immediately following the First World War marked a decisive departure in the personnel and practice of industrial leadership within Lancashire. A strong sense of regional and local attachment survived the growing presence of metropolitan interests in the cotton trade. The practical experience of figures reared in the industry continued to be seen as essential to commercial effectiveness. Furthermore, despite the spread of limited-liability organization and the trend towards amalgamation, employers still acknowledged the broader obligations which attended the creation of wealth. Indeed, if anything, the period witnessed a revival in civic energies, drawing on long-established religious as much as on narrowly economic sensibilities. Yet élite commitment to the cotton trade found only fitful echoes among the workforce. Investment in workplace amenities, undertaken in large measure to alter this pattern, generated only meagre returns. This continued to be the case even when such efforts were renewed after 1945. By then, a declining birth rate and a higher minimum age for leaving school had reduced potential juvenile recruitment by an estimated 55 per cent, contributing to an overall shortfall in labour of some 42 per cent. In response, employers emphasized the improvements which had been effected in factory conditions. In its promotional publicity, Cannon Bros, Ltd sought to

[76] Calculated from Cavanagh, *Cotton Town Cricket*, 128–34; see also J. Williams, 'Recreational Cricket in the Bolton Area between the Wars', in R. Holt (ed.), *Sport and the Working Class in Modern Britain* (Manchester, 1990), 104, 112–14.

[77] BA, 'Bolton Biographical Notes', iii, 213 (Hardcastle); G. Cleworth, *Cricket at Eagley* (Bolton, n.d.), 3–4, 15.

[78] R. Holt, 'Working-Class Football and the City: The Problem of Continuity', *British Journal of Sports History*, 3 (1986), 7–9; id., *Sport and the British: A Modern History* (Oxford, 1989), 148–51; C. E. Sutcliffe and F. Hargreaves, *History of the Lancashire Football Association, 1878–1928* (Blackburn, 1928), 129; J. Williams, 'Churches, Sport and Identities in the North, 1900–1939', in J. Hill and J. Williams (eds.), *Sport and Identity in the North of England* (Keele, 1996), 123–4.

assure potential applicants of the healthy nature of the working environment with the claim that 'the air inside our Mills is cleaner than outside'.[79] The smoke-laden atmosphere of most Lancashire towns rendered this a modest boast, at best. The failure to address more fundamental concerns, such as the declining status and security of mill work, ensured that rates of indigenous recruitment failed to revive. Relief was thus sought in the importation of 11,000 European Voluntary Workers fleeing economic and political collapse in Central and Eastern Europe.[80] The experience of the 1940s thus confirmed that of the years before 1939, that attitudes to work remained both markedly functional and stubbornly impervious to the blandishments of industrial welfare strategies.

II

Concern at the social consequences arising from changes in industrial organization was not confined to the cotton district. The increasingly large capital outlays required to fund the pursuit of mining operations at the kind of depths witnessed across Britain in the later nineteenth century ensured that joint-stock forms of finance were widely adopted.[81] This development occurred, many believed, at a cost to labour relations within the industry. Stephen Walsh, miners' agent and Labour MP for Ince, concurred with this view. Addressing a party gathering in Hindley in 1911, he lamented the passing of

the individual employer, whose childhood had been passed amongst his work-people, who had played upon the same village green, who knew them all by name . . . [and his replacement by] vast limited companies with their head offices in big cities like London, or Liverpool, or Manchester, . . . most of whom knew nothing and cared little about the condition of working people from whose labour their profits were derived.[82]

Although reflecting an established labourist antipathy to joint-stock forms of capital, this view was not confined to one side of the industry. The Earl of Crawford also voiced disquiet at the growth in industrial concentration,

---

[79] Board of Trade, *Working Party Reports: Cotton* (HMSO, 1946), 54–6; LRO, Barber-Lomax Collection Pamphlet Box 93, 'Welcome to Cannon Bros, Ltd, Stanley Mills, Bolton'.
[80] Fine Cotton Spinners' and Doublers' Association, Ltd, *Jubilee 'Distaff'*, 28–30; Lancashire Industrial Development Association, *The Spinning Area* (1950), 43.
[81] Church, *History of the British Coal Industry*, iii, table 2.10, 141: between 1895 and 1913, the proportion of colliery companies in Lancashire and Cheshire categorized as unlimited companies, partnerships, or proprietorships declined from 29.7% to 12.8%.
[82] *WE* (31 Aug. 1911), 4; see also the remarks of Thomas Greenall, reported in *Burnley Gazette* (28 Oct. 1893), 6.

a trend with which, as chairman of the Wigan Coal Corporation, a concern uniting four companies and twenty-one pits in 1930, he could claim some familiarity. For Crawford, with the increase in company size came the loss of 'that friendly and intimate feeling of the family firm'.[83] The impact of change was, however, less far-reaching than such, admittedly romanticized, views would suggest.

Pit combines had been responsible for a large proportion of district output since the later decades of the nineteenth century. What is more, a subsequent wave of organizational change, around 1918, did little to alter the personnel or pattern of industrial leadership. Although several colliery proprietors departed the county after the First World War, there was no equivalent of the exodus of textile wealth. Furthermore, in most cases, local control was maintained. Sir William Hulton's retirement to Cheltenham Spa confined his interest in the family estate near Bolton to annual visits of inspection. At the same time, the weight of death duties obliged the fourth Earl of Ellesmere to sell mining interests administered through the Bridgewater Estate.[84] Yet management of the Hulton Colliery Co., Ltd remained with the Brancker family of Liverpool, while the Bridgewater pits were acquired in 1923 by a syndicate of local businessmen, headed by the estate's mining agent, Jesse Wallwork. Also on the board were established colliery directors, such as James Ramsden of the Tyldesley firm of William Ramsden and Sons, Ltd, and members of the local millocracy: both Thomas Smith and Harry Speakman. had interests in cotton mills in Leigh. In other cases, families long associated with the trade maintained their involvement through the period. Among those guiding the fortunes of the industry were the Lindsays of Haigh (Earls of Crawford and Balcarres), the Pilkingtons of Clifton and St Helens, and the Edmondsons of Ashton-in-Makerfield.[85]

Aggregate figures confirm the survival of a regionally distinct élite. In all, 388 directors controlled the 133 firms active across Lancashire and north Cheshire in 1924. Of the 339 for whom a place of residence could be established, 264 (78 per cent) lived within the region. This distribution

[83] J. Vincent (ed.), *The Crawford Papers: The Journals of David Lindsay Twenty-Seventh Earl of Crawford and Tenth Earl of Balcarres, 1871–1940, During the Years 1892 to 1940* (Manchester, 1984), 531; *Parl. Papers 1930–1*, xv (3743), Mines Dept. Mining Industry Act, 1926. Third Report, 3.

[84] BA, 'Bolton Biographical Notes', iii, 280 (Hulton); C. Grayling, *The Bridgewater Heritage* (Worsley, 1983), 62.

[85] *Colliery Yearbook and Coal Trades Directory* (1924 edn.); *Skinner's Cotton Trade Directory* (1923 edn.); *BJG* (9 Mar. 1923), 9.

survived moves to rationalize the industry later in the decade. Directors of the fifteen firms which combined to form Manchester Collieries, Ltd in 1929 retained their posts in the new concern.[86]

As with the textile élite, this continued identification with the region influenced the manner in which industrial wealth was utilized. Although lacking the inclusive role assumed by employers in many geographically remote settlements, Lancastrian colliery owners, through their substantial holdings of capital and land, controlled resources which had the potential decisively to influence the wider social dynamic.[87] Before 1914, moral concern was reflected in the provision of facilities for education and worship. The Earl of Bradford donated land for church and school buildings in Bolton, while the Evans family sponsored the building of Nonconformist chapels in Haydock and the neighbouring townships of Blackbrook and Ashton.[88] Similarly, Alfred Hewlett, managing director of the Wigan Coal and Iron Co., Ltd for forty-two years to 1912 and a colliery proprietor in his own right, endowed an Anglican church and school in Coppull.[89] The scale of such activity is suggested by the absence of Board School provision in many colliery districts. Indeed, education remained wholly under denominational control in eleven of the sixteen Lancastrian boroughs and urban districts in which coal-mining accounted for over 40 per cent of male employment in 1911.[90]

Other proprietors sought to improve on existing provision. Evidence of urban squalor and administrative corruption in late Victorian Wigan convinced David Lindsay, later twenty-seventh Earl of Crawford, that 'as a family we have not done our duty by Wigan'.[91] His recognition of the social obligations accompanying the ownership of mineral wealth owed much to his involvement in the University settlement movement in

---

[86] Residential distribution calculated from *Colliery Yearbook* (1924 edn.); B. Supple, *The History of the British Coal Industry* (Oxford, 1987), iv, 313.

[87] For the dominant position of owners in the villages of the New Dukeries in East Notts, R. J. Waller, *The Dukeries Transformed* (Oxford 1983), 75–107; id., 'A Company Village in the New Dukeries Coalfield: New Ollerton, 1918–39', *Transactions of the Thoroton Society*, 83 (1979), 70–9.

[88] G. Evans, 'Social Leadership and Social Control: Bolton, 1870–98' (Lancaster Univ. MA thesis, 1974), 24; G. Simm, *Richard Evans of Haydock: A Study of a Local Family* (Newton-le-Willows, 1988), 49.

[89] D. Anderson, 'Alfred Hewlett, 1830–1918', in D. J. Jeremy and C. Shaw (eds.), *Dictionary of Business Biography*, iii (1985), 188–92.

[90] *Parl. Papers 1906*, lxxxix (3054), Board of Education. List of Boroughs and Urban Districts in England and Wales with a Population of 5,000 and Upwards in which there are No Council Schools; *Parl. Papers 1913*, lxxviii (7018), Census of England and Wales, 1911. X. Occupations and Industries. Pt. I, table 15A, 398–401.

[91] Vincent (ed.), *The Crawford Papers*, 52.

the early 1890s and found limited local expression in his subsequent appointment as permanent chairman of the borough's Public Libraries Committee. A similar conviction led R. A. Burrows, of the Atherton firm of Fletcher, Burrows, Ltd, to support local Boys' Clubs and the South-West Lancashire Boy Scouts' Association, of which he was chairman.[92] Beyond 1918, ecclesiastical growth continued to draw on proprietorial endowments. In 1920, the church serving the newly created Anglican parish in the Tonge district of Bolton was built on land presented by the colliery director, Thomas Scowcroft.[93]

Housing was a further resource controlled by employers, more especially in outlying districts, where the retention of experienced workers would otherwise prove difficult. Beyond Lancashire, colliery owners were often prominent in the development of residential amenities. They provided almost one in three houses in the Durham mining township of Stanley in 1913, while allowances were paid to those in private, rented accommodation. Different means to the same end were adopted by employers in south Wales. Here, owners advanced money on loan to colliers' building clubs. A clear economic advantage was anticipated from the extension of home-ownership through the valleys, as Alfred Simeon Tallis, chairman of the local Coalowners' Association, explained, with unusual candour, to the Sankey Commission in 1919: 'a man takes a greater interest in the town in which he has his own house and also, if you like to take it from the company's selfish point of view, [a] greater interest in the company for whom he works.'[94] Examples of company housing provision could be found in Lancashire. Late in the nineteenth century, Fletcher, Burrows encouraged the development of the village of Howe Bridge, near Atherton, while in the 1920s, the Clifton and Kersley Coal Co., Ltd built houses at Outwood, near Astley, with the agreement of the local council.[95] Yet such schemes rarely accommodated more than a small proportion of each company's workforce. The Hulton Estate owned houses in Chequerbent and deducted rent from the wages of those workers who

[92] Vincent (ed.), *The Crawford Papers*, 3, 9; BA, 'Bolton Biographical Notes', iii, 105 (Burrows).

[93] *BJG* (11 June 1920), 10.

[94] *Parl. Papers 1919*, xii (360), Coal Industry Commission. II. Reports and Minutes of Evidence on the Second Stage of the Inquiry, q. 25538; for Stanley, see A. L. Bowley and A. R. Burnett-Hurst, *Livelihood and Poverty* (1915), 141; see also M. J. Daunton, 'Miners' Houses: South Wales and the Great Northern Coalfield, 1880–1914', *International Review of Social History*, 25 (1980), 143–75.

[95] K. Wood, *The Coal Pits of Chowbent* (Bolton?, 1984), 106–7; *BJG* (15 Aug. 1924), 4.

lived there. In return, it assumed responsibility for all repairs and dec-
orations. Yet only thirty-five of the 344 miners killed in the Pretoria
Pit explosion in 1910 were based in the township. Most of the
remainder lived in private, rented property in the neighbouring towns
of Westhoughton and Bolton.[96] Nor was this unusual. Mary Elizabeth
Hart, a miner's wife and official of the Wigan Weavers' Association, confirmed before the Sankey Commission that, in the area around Wigan,
'the houses are largely owned by private landlords'.[97]

The availability of hands in adjacent urban centres reduced the need to
control local supplies of labour by means of investment in residential
amenities. Even where housing was provided, its importance in managerial thinking diminished over time, as the movement of miners between
pits attenuated any link between home and work. This allowed miners
renting houses from the Wigan Coal and Iron Co., Ltd at Clock Face
Colliery, near St Helens, to retain their tenancies even when they secured
work elsewhere. A similar policy was applied at Sutton Manor Colliery
through the 1920s. Residence was only likely to become a condition of
employment in exceptional cases of labour shortage. The loss of manpower in the early months of the Great War thus resulted in the eviction
of non-employees from company premises at Bamfurlong, near Wigan.[98]
Such action was almost without precedent. For the most part, colliery
housing was peripheral both to the physical evolution of Lancashire
mining settlements and to company employment strategies.

Those factors which discouraged significant investment in residential
developments also worked to limit expenditure on workplace amenities.
In his Divisional Inspector's report for 1923, A. D. Nicholson enlarged on
the obstacles impeding attempts to centre social functions around the pit:
'The workmen frequently live in towns, often at a considerable distance
from the colliery at which they work, . . . Such being the case, the provision of institutes and recreation grounds would, except at a few collieries,
not appeal to the workers.'[99] Despite this, a number of firms attempted,
through a variety of schemes, to consolidate workforce loyalties in the

[96] BA, BOHP 108B (male, born 1917), transcript, 11; BA, HRF ABHC/5/1–344
Personal Files, Compensation statements.
[97] *Parl. Papers 1919*, xii (360), Coal Industry Commission. II. Second Stage of Inquiry, q.
24333.
[98] Forman, *Industrial Town*, 140–1; LCMF, monthly conference minutes, 10 Apr. 1915;
EC minutes, 15 Oct. 1927; *Parl. Papers 1908*, lix (4443), Departmental Committee on Truck
Acts. II. Minutes of Evidence, q. 7478.
[99] Mines Dept., *Reports of HM Inspectors of Mines for 1923*, 'Lancashire and North Wales
Division', 41.

period to 1914. Richard Evans and Co. organized annual excursions for workers, their families, and friends. In 1898, five trains were chartered to carry some 2,500 adults and children to Blackpool. Tickets were priced between 9*d.* and 2*s.* 6*d.*, which also allowed the excursionists free access to the North and Central Piers and the newly opened Tower.[100] More explicitly paternalist in tone were the annual dinners organized by the Hulton Colliery Co., Ltd, for managers and workmen's representatives. Each provided the occasion for a 'fatherly' homily on the need for co-operation in industry from the company's managing director, Richard Brancker.[101]

More formal provision was rarely attempted, although at Ashton-in-Makerfield, the Garswood Hall Colliery Co., Ltd supported an active pit institute. Here, a wide range of recreational pursuits was encouraged, from cricket and bowls to air-rifle shooting, the latter designed to promote participation in the local Territorial reserve. Alternative indoor activities were also catered for, in the institute's reading, cards, and billiards rooms. Close managerial supervision was exercised at all points. Directors chaired all committee meetings and could issue orders, such as those which discouraged gambling, especially among the institute's junior members. To this end, dominoes were confiscated from the boys' room in 1911.[102] Yet, as with Tootal's in the cotton trade, Garswood Hall did not reflect broader trends in industrial politics. At a time when collective-bargaining procedures were being adopted across the county, the firm refused to recognize union representatives.

If, before 1914, managerial orthodoxy in both the coal and the cotton trades gave little weight to formal welfare provision, that coincidence no longer applied after 1918. While welfare principles were, as we have seen, readily embraced in many of the county's mills, economic circumstances discouraged similar investment in colliery amenities. Declining profitability in the decade after de-control depleted the capital reserves necessary to fund such expenditure, while the coalfield experienced none of the problems of endemic labour shortage which stimulated corporate provision by cotton companies. The distinction was never absolute. From 1918, facilities developed by Fletcher, Burrows, Ltd at Howe Bridge, including a club building and sports ground, were transferred to the Atherton

---

[100] LRO, Coal Board Records NCEv 6/10 Richard Evans and Co., Ltd, letter book, Shaw of London and North Western Railway to E. George of Haydock Colliery, 26 May; George to Shaw, 31 May; Notice of excursion on 25 June 1898.

[101] See e.g. *BJG* (12 Jan. 1901), 3, 8.

[102] LRO, Coal Board Records NCGh 1/2 Garswood Hall Colliery Co., Ltd Institute minute book, Committee meeting, 3 Aug. 1911.

Collieries Joint Association, an organization open to all employees, which was intended to provide 'the means of intercourse, recreation, and mutual helpfulness'.[103] To this end, administrative responsibilities were shared between employers' and workers' officials, who enjoyed equal representation on the Association's management committee. Although all meetings were chaired by company nominees, the position of vice-chairman was reserved for the president of the local branch of the LCMF. Social and sporting activities gave practical expression to the desired 'esprit de corps'. All were intended to promote ideas of improvement, both physical and moral, a point reflected in the (presumably ineffectual) ban on 'Betting, playing for money, swearing or indecent language'.[104] Perhaps the most ambitious attempt to amend the miners' rough-hewn image came in the performance, by the Dramatic Section of the Association, of *The Merchant of Venice* in the Village Club, Howe Bridge, in 1923. However, if the comments of the *Bolton Journal and Guardian*'s drama critic, regarding characterizations which 'at times seemed to arise from a lack of understanding of the parts', are accurate, the exercise would not appear to have been an unqualified success.[105]

The only firm to emulate the amenities on offer at Atherton was the Abram Coal Co., Ltd, which, in 1927, established the Bickershaw Collieries Benevolent Fund. Unlike the Joint Association, however, this was primarily intended to weaken union representation at the pit, through the provision of 'Bonuses, Trips, Welfare Schemes, etc.'. Although it operated to such effect that Federation membership at Abram was halved within twelve months, continued faith in conciliation procedures more generally ensured that the fund remained Lancashire's one extended essay in 'Spencerism'.[106] Away from Atherton and Abram, few additions to workplace facilities were made during the 1920s. The only schemes recorded by the Divisional Inspectorate in this period comprised a canteen at Clifton Hall Colliery, near Pendlebury, and a sports ground at the Hollinwood Pits of the Chamber Lane Colliery Co., Ltd.[107]

[103] WA, D/DZ A83/9 The Atherton Collieries Joint Association Rules, 1918, 1, par. 2.

[104] WA, D/DZ A83/9 The Atherton Collieries Joint Association Rules, 1918, 2–3, par. 6; 6, par. 17; Wood, *Coal Pits of Chowbent*, 106–9.   [105] *BJG* (9 Mar. 1923), 14.

[106] LCMF, EC minutes, 24 Dec. 1927. Membership returns suggest that full membership at Abram fell from 855 on 24 Apr. 1926 (the last return before the prolonged stoppage of 1926) to 456 on 31 Dec. 1927, and to 276 on 29 Dec. 1928.

[107] Mines Dept., *Reports of HM Inspectors of Mines for 1925* (HMSO, 1926), A. D. Nicholson, 'Lancashire and North Wales Division', 34–5; *Reports for 1928*, 'Lancashire and North Wales Division', 31.

The slow and piecemeal advance of welfare provision across the coal-field can, in part, be explained by capital shortages. Nevertheless, the importance of financial constraints, arising from limited profitability, should not be overstated. In large measure, they were offset, after 1919, by the Sankey levy, an impost on sales of coal, the proceeds from which were to be applied to schemes of social improvement within colliery districts. In most areas, a wide variety of local initiatives were supported from the levy. In County Durham alone by 1929, 182 separate schemes, covering health, recreational, and educational needs, had benefited from money allotted from the fund.[108] In Lancashire, by contrast, proposals centred on a programme for the county as a whole. The earliest scheme to be advanced involved using the levy to augment the wages of low-paid workers, reflecting the view, as J. E. Sutton, Federation agent for the Manchester district, termed it, that 'Welfare was the feeding of the men first of all'.[109] The Central Welfare Committee refused to endorse such a move. However, sanction was given for the construction of a Miners' Convalescent Home on Blackpool's North Shore. The cost sufficed to absorb the greater part of Lancashire's first two instalments from the fund.[110] In utilizing the remainder, the Central Committee considered it 'of the highest importance that adequate funds should remain available for the provision of recreational activities in the local mining centres of the District'.[111] Yet few attempts were made to apply the levy locally, beyond additions to existing company facilities, as at Fletcher, Burrows, where £10,000 was sought for the building of a central clubhouse.[112] Even when money was available, employers remained sceptical of attempts to foster deeper attachments to the pit through improved workplace amenities. The preference remained for more general schemes, covering whole districts, rather than those specific to individual firms.[113] Such an approach could be justified in a field where continued labour mobility heightened the disparity between home and work, and ensured that welfare never became a central tool of industrial leadership. Rather than

---

[108] *Parl. Papers 1919*, xi (359), Coal Industry Commission. I. Interim Reports, Interim Report by Mr Justice Sankey, Arthur Balfour, Sir Arthur Duckham, Sir Thomas Royden, par. ix; Mines Dept., *Eighth Report of the Miners' Welfare Fund* (HMSO, 1930), appendix iv, 30–1.   [109] LCMF, monthly conference minutes, 24 June 1922.
[110] Ibid., 10 Dec. 1921; Joint Committee minutes, 13 Mar.; 9 Oct. 1922; 12 Feb., 16 April, 16 July, 13 Sept. 1923; 13 Oct. 1924.
[111] LCMF, welfare building subcommittee minutes, 26 July 1926.
[112] Ibid., 21 Jan. 1927; Joint Committee minutes, 7 Feb. 1927; Mines Dept., *Eighth Report of Miners' Welfare Fund*, appendix iv, 30–1.   [113] See below, pp. 177–8.

assuming discrete forms, patronage was more likely to be directed at established pursuits, from team sports to brass-band music.

Banding was a central cultural activity in colliery society, a fact reflected in the status commanded by those active in the movement. When Albert Lonsdale, secretary of and soprano player with the Wingates Temperance Prize Band, was killed in the Pretoria Pit explosion, his funeral was marked with a ceremony befitting the passing of a major local figure: 'drawn blinds, shops with shutters up, and many hundreds of people lined both sides of the road from the late residence of Mr Lonsdale up to the gates of the church.'[114] Banding's prominence encouraged industrial leaders to lend the movement their support. This was most obvious where bands became associated with individual works. Success in the contests which punctuated the banding year raised the profile of the company both locally and nationally, and was thought to engender the kind of team loyalties and identities encouraged by related competitive pursuits, such as sport. To that end, employment was offered on preferential terms to bandsmen of renown. Members of the Bickershaw Collieries Band, a cultural offshoot of the firm's Benevolent Fund and a leading band in contests through the 1930s, included many who lacked prior experience of pit work but who were taken on on the strength of their musical abilities alone.[115]

Over time, competitive success assured works-based ensembles a growing prominence in the banding world. Wingates' success in winning both national contests, at Belle Vue, Manchester, and the Crystal Palace, in consecutive years in 1906-7, was considered sufficiently unusual to merit comment. 'Cottonopolis', Lancashire correspondent of the *British Bandsman*, remarked that 'It is really marvellous that a village band—without the assistance of employers of labour—has accomplished so much'.[116] For the most part, however, works bands enjoyed a growing preponderance on the national stage. Whereas in the first twenty Belle Vue contests, such combinations were successful on only four occasions, they were triumphant in thirteen contests over the first two decades of the twentieth century.[117] Yet such figures belie their atypicality in the movement as a whole. Dave Russell's estimate that only one in six bands active

---

[114] *British Bandsman*, 27 (7 Jan. 1911), 12.

[115] To this end, the recruitment net could be spread wide. Horwich Railway Mechanics' Institute Band drew players from Foden's Motor Works in Cheshire and Black Dyke Mills, near Bradford, *BJG* (8 Sept. 1915), 7; (29 Sept. 1922), 8; A. R. Taylor, *Labour and Love: An Oral History of the Brass Band Movement* (1983), 87.

[116] *British Bandsman*, 20 (14 Sept. 1907), 635.

[117] Belle Vue Gardens, Manchester, *List of Prize Winners (With Selections of Music) of the Brass Band Contests from the commencement in 1853* (Manchester, 1970).

in West Yorkshire at the turn of the century were directly associated with places of work also reflects the relative balance west of the Pennines. Territorial and devotional rather than occupational influences lay behind the growth of most bands.[118] Wingates, for example, was staffed and run by working colliers. Before 1914, miners filled the posts of bandmaster, secretary, and chairman, while nineteen of its twenty-four players in 1921 were employed down the pit. Yet its origins could be traced to a Bible class attached to the local Independent Methodist Chapel.[119]

Banding finances ensured that, even here, employer support assumed a growing importance. Members' efforts sufficed to sustain combinations with modest ambitions. The Daubhill Prize Band in Bolton, established in the mid-1920s by 'working lads—colliers and spinners, without three-pence amongst them', developed on the proceeds of informal concerts and hot-pot suppers.[120] Similar activities lay behind Wingates' early growth. A bazaar organized by the band's supporters raised a large part of the £500 needed to purchase a new set of instruments in the 1890s. However, the greater costs incurred as bands ascended the brass hierarchy, for the provision of better quality instruments, uniforms, and, on occasion, professional tuition, necessitated appeals for wider support. For many bands, public subscriptions proved the most reliable source of funding. Competitive success had a further utility in this regard, as it assisted in extracting contributions from potential patrons. So, at a concert to mark Wingates' second victory at the Crystal Palace, the band's chairman, William Cowburn, was anxious that those dignitaries in attendance showed 'their appreciation not only by their hearts, but by their pockets'.[121] Employer patronage could thus remain important for bands nominally independent of the workplace. Wingates' president and the band's 'best friend' through the 1920s was H. O. Dixon, general manager of the Westhoughton Coal and Cannel Co., Ltd, who, in addition to providing employment on preferential terms at the company's pits, also endowed the building of a new band room in 1930.[122] Such support was a significant, but not a decisive factor in maintaining Wingates' competitive suc-

---

[118] D. Russell, 'Popular Musical Culture and Popular Politics in the Yorkshire Textile Districts, 1880–1914', in J. K. Walton and J. Walvin (eds.), *Leisure in Britain, 1780–1939* (Manchester, 1983), 104; *BJG* (5 Apr. 1907), 7.
[119] J. F. Russell and J. H. Elliot, *The Brass Band Movement* (1936), 124–5; *BJG* (25 Feb. 1921), 7; (16 Sept. 1921), 10; *British Bandsman*, 26 (31 Dec. 1910), 655.
[120] *BJG* (19 Oct. 1934), 10.
[121] *BJG* (4 Oct. 1907), 3; (16 Sept. 1921), 10; *British Bandsman*, 25 (5 Feb. 1910), 128; 26 (30 July 1910), 97–8.
[122] *BJG* (3 June 1921), 6; (17 Oct. 1930), 5; BA, BOHP 108A (male, born 1917), tape.

cess. The band continued to flourish despite colliery closures through the 1930s.[123]

The central place which banding continued to occupy in the culture of colliery societies reflected its enduring utility for both players and sponsors. The regular stimulus of competition was seen to promote high technical standards of musicianship. Bandsmen were thus able to develop and refine skills while holding down a regular source of employment, a circumstance which afforded them greater security than was available to players in the overstocked world of theatre and concert orchestras. As a result, few were tempted to make the transition to fully professional music-making.[124] For employers, the returns from band sponsorship were more indirect. Rather than providing a straightforward instrument of control within and beyond the workplace, as Dave Russell tentatively suggests,[125] banding provided a means of promoting among workers a closer sense of attachment to the firms which employed them, while at the same time elevating the corporate profile by identifying companies with an important cultural activity. If nothing else, this confirmed the deep-rooted paternalism which characterized the county's colliery élite through the period.

As in the cotton trade, continuities in the structure and style of industrial leadership blunted the impact of changes in personnel in the years following the First World War. Enduring local loyalties ensured the survival of a still vital civic consciousness, expressed most clearly through religious and recreational endowments. Yet limitations to proprietorial influence, imposed by high rates of labour turnover and the fragile link between home and work, remained, inhibiting investment in residential and welfare provision. In debating how remaining proceeds from the Sankey levy should be utilized once work on the convalescent home was completed, it was agreed that funding should go to schemes covering whole 'districts and areas', rather than to 'particular individual firms, the membership of the scheme being limited to workmen employed by the particular firm'.[126] Conditions across Lancashire made the workplace an inappropriate focus for ameliorative effort. Owners thus assumed a more

---

[123] Westhoughton Public Library, Pretoria Pit Disaster Pamphlet Box, *Horwich and Westhoughton Journal and Guardian* (9 Mar. 1934); A. R. Taylor, *Brass Bands* (St Albans, 1979), 144.

[124] C. Ehrlich, *The Music Profession in Britain since the Eighteenth Century: A Social History* (Oxford, 1985), 155–6, 162.

[125] Russell, 'Popular Musical Culture', 104–5.

[126] LRO, Coal Board Records NCLm 1 Lancashire and Cheshire Miners' Welfare Committee, minutes, meeting at Queen's Hotel, Manchester, 11 June 1928.

prominent welfare role through the administration of sick, accident, and other benefits. Yet, even here, as the following chapter will show, limitations on their authority remained evident.

III

Despite the unprecedented turnover in personnel through the period, a reconstruction of élite profiles in both the coal and the cotton industries justifies the conclusion that industrial leaders remained integral to their localities. The supposedly corrosive influence of limited-liability capital, given weight by contemporaries and subsequent historians, was mitigated in practice by dynastic continuities and the presence of figures steeped in the traditions of each trade through experience of trade-union or managerial office. The social responsibilities attending business leadership continued to be acknowledged. The extent of voluntary and political activities attested to the enduring role of the civic ethic in defining and maintaining a distinctive urban middle-class identity. For employers at least, the transformation in industrial structures had wrought a limited cultural change.

The implications for class relations were also less dramatic than an emphasis on the outward forms of industrial organization would suggest. Managerial methods remained substantially unaltered as established disciplinary techniques, piece-rate wage lists regulated by agreed procedures for joint consultation, prevailed in both mill and mine. The most significant departure in managerial practice came with the application of welfare techniques in the inter-war cotton trade, an innovation which, in the extent and regularity of provision, might, with justification, be regarded as Lancashire's first concerted essay in factory paternalism. The origins and aims of this movement were diverse, but a fundamental intention, common to all the schemes discussed here, was to redefine the cultural role of work, extending each worker's interest in the factory beyond the wage packet and the limits of 'normal' working hours. The recruitment problems encountered by firms which invested extensively in welfare provision suggests that, in large measure, the movement was ineffective. The absence of comparable initiatives among the county's coal-owners reflected a more general recognition of the contingent influence which work exerted over popular attitudes. It could thus be argued that an understanding of working-class identity is better sought in the world beyond work, in activities which were equally crucial to everyday existence. One of the most important of these was thrift.

6

The Values of Saving: Patterns of Thrift in Coal and Cotton Lancashire

Foregoing chapters have suggested that a narrow preoccupation with work and its attendant structures provides perspectives on class formation that are both partial and distorted. Alternative insights into the material and cultural influences which shaped working-class life are sought here through the institutional arrangements by which families endeavoured to manage their limited resources. Thrift touched many aspects of the working-class experience. At its most basic, it was preventive in intent, providing against an unanticipated loss of income through illness, accident, unemployment, or death. Alternatively, it could be used to satisfy material aspirations, enabling families to exploit expanding opportunities for consumption. Large sums were thus set aside each year in cotton Lancashire to fund the operatives' 'annual burst at the seaside'.[1] What is more, the precise form which savings assumed strongly reflected underlying cultural influences. The priority given to the payment of burial-insurance premiums in family budgeting decisions could be traced, in large measure, to the dynamics of everyday life in the working-class neighbourhoods of urban Britain during this period.[2] The study of thrift thus renders explicit not only the financial constraints, but also the broader ideological foundations of working-class life.

Initially at least, however, the focus remains on the world of work. Over the period, distinctive forms of saving emerged in both the coal and the cotton industries. In the latter, the widespread adoption of joint-stock organization after 1880 created new investment opportunities. The propensity of workers to commit their savings to the industry, either directly or indirectly via their unions, attracted much contemporary

---

[1] P. Johnson, 'Conspicuous Consumption and Working-Class Culture in Late-Victorian and Edwardian Britain', *TRHS*, 5th ser. 38 (1988), 27–42; J. B. Priestley, *English Journey* (Harmondsworth edn., 1977), 240.

[2] J. Belchem, *Industrialization and the Working Class: The English Experience, 1750–1900* (Aldershot, 1991), 206–7; P. Johnson, *Saving and Spending* (Oxford, 1985), ch. 2; M. Pember Reeves, *Round about a Pound a Week* (1979 repr.), 66–74; T. Harrisson, *Britain Revisited* (1961), 43–5.

comment. To many, it appeared that Lancashire had entered an age of democratic capitalism, in which a shared interest in dividend levels would provide the basis for broader social agreement. Schulze-Gaevernitz was not alone in concluding that the consequences of modern, centralized industry were to be seen less in the creation of a dispossessed class of alienated proletarians and more in the emergence of 'new middle-classes . . . both as regards standard of living and capability of thrift'.[3] Yet the precise importance of operative investment remains unclear, an empirical gap which, for the twentieth century, historical inquiry has done little to fill.[4]

The constant threat of accident or death underground made the need for precautionary thrift paramount among mining families. The higher premiums which their increased exposure to risk entailed necessitated remedial action from within the industry, resulting in the creation of a network of benevolent funds which, by 1880, covered the principal English coalfields. Within each, administrative responsibility was shared between miners and owners, an arrangement which, evidence before the Royal Commission on Labour suggested, could assist in improving relations within the pit.[5] In Lancashire, the creation in the 1890s of a separate union society to rival the established fund, suggested that this hope was, in the case of one county, substantially unrealized.[6] The extent to which such organizations promoted co-operation or antagonism between employers and employed is assessed here. The ramifications of this discussion extend considerably beyond the pit, however. Relief administration operated within individual neighbourhoods, drawing on the values and ideals of working-class life and, in the process, revealing the everyday realities underlying notions of 'mutuality' and 'community'.

These themes are taken further in the final section, which extends the coverage to comprehend a variety of non-occupational thrift institutions, ranging from affiliated friendly society orders to informal benefit funds based on local churches and pubs. When viewed in the round, therefore,

[3] G. von Schulze-Gaevernitz, *The Cotton Trade in England* (1895), 178; *Parl. Papers 1894*, xxxv (7421), RC on Labour: Fifth and Final Report. Pt. I. The Report, pars. 118–19; on living standards more generally, see *Parl. Papers 1903*, lxvii (1761), British and Foreign Trade and Industrial Conditions, 233, 260; E. H. Hunt, *British Labour History* (1981), 73–4.

[4] On working-class share-ownership in the 19th cent., see D. A. Farnie, *The English Cotton Industry* (Oxford, 1979), 244–64; J. L. White, *The Limits of Trade Union Militancy* (Westport, Conn., and London, 1978), 71–4.

[5] *Parl. Papers 1894*, xxv (7421), RC on Labour Fifth and Final Report, pars. 126–7; see also G. L. Campbell, *Miners' Insurance Funds: Their Origin and Extent* (1880), 10–11.

[6] R. Challinor, *The Lancashire and Cheshire Miners* (Newcastle, 1972), 265–6.

the practice of thrift casts important light on diverse aspects of working-class life both within and beyond the workplace.

I

The perception that the transition from proprietary to joint-stock capital in cotton textiles had encouraged worker participation in industrial ownership was widely shared in early twentieth-century Lancashire. Certainly, the methods by which capital was raised posed few obstacles to potential working-class investors. The demands made on shareholders on flotation were often modest. In 1907, for example, the Croal Spinning Co., Ltd of Bolton required payment of only 5s. on each £5 share, the amount outstanding to be realized in instalments of not more than 2s. 6d. each.[7] Many firms held out the promise that only a portion of the total share value would be called up; the remainder of the companies' nominal value would be raised from retained profits or through the creation of fixed-interest mortgages or loans.[8] The latter, recoverable on demand and ranking ahead of ordinary shares for dividend payments, appeared peculiarly adapted to working-class requirements, marrying as they did high liquidity with security of return. Many were thought to have responded by committing their savings to the mill. George Harwood's bill to reform company law in 1912 had, as one of its objects, the protection of working-class shareholders. Equally, in the years following the Great War, popular share-ownership was advanced by the Bolton Chamber of Commerce as evidence of local prosperity.[9]

Others argued that the propensity to take up shares had important implications for the industry. For Sir Charles Macara, it offered the practicable alternative to established collective-bargaining procedures he had long been seeking. In 1920, therefore, he argued that, in future, wage awards should take the form of bonus share issues. By establishing a more direct relationship between adjustments in list rates and changes in the profit margin, such a move would, he went on, consolidate agreement

[7] LRO, Barber-Lomax Collection DDBx 13/1 Croal Spinning Co., Ltd, scrapbook, prospectus, 5 June 1907.

[8] PRO, Register of Dissolved Companies, BT 31/17433/84266/8 Maco Spinning Co., Ltd, prospectus, 15 Apr. 1907; BT 31/17796/89204/4 William Woods and Son, prospectus, 1906, both anticipated that calls would not exceed £2. 10s. per £5 share; see also BT 31/15001/29365/36 North End Spinning Co., Ltd, extraordinary general meeting, 20 July 1912; *Parl. Papers 1929–30*, xii (3615), Committee on the Cotton Trade, 13.

[9] *Parl. Debates, House of Commons*, 5th ser. xxxix, cols. 1678–80; *Bolton: Its Trade and Commerce* (Bolton, 1919), 62.

within the trade and thus constituted 'the best path towards the nationalisation of the industry'.[10] For others, the potential for industrial accord
discerned by Macara appeared to have been substantially realized. The
most complete statement of this view was offered in 1925 by Samuel
Schofield Hammersley, a mill director in the Oldham district and Unionist
MP for Stockport. Drawing on the experience of 1921–2, when, in contrast to the prolonged disputes over wages which paralysed the coal and
engineering trades, rate reductions had been agreed in the cotton industry, Hammersley boasted of the 'spirit of collaboration' which prevailed
between operatives and managements. The roots of this accord were
traced to widespread dealings in mill shares, which had the effect of dif-
fusing a sympathetic commercial intelligence along the shopfloor.[11] Neither
view should be regarded as wholly representative of employer opinion in
this period. Macara had resigned the presidency of the Master Spinners'
Federation in 1914 and, from that point, had become a determined critic
of official policy. In the early 1920s, he found an alternative platform for
his views in the Provisional Emergency Cotton Committee. Across the
Federation as a whole, existing approaches to industrial bargaining
continued to receive official sanction, a point reflected in the organization's submission to the Balfour Committee on Industry and Trade in
1925.[12] Events within the industry also led Hammersley to rethink his
attitude towards popular share-ownership. The intractability of wage
controversies and the failure of rationalization initiatives led him, by
1930, to the conclusion that shareholders were an impediment to trading
success.[13]

Nevertheless, the importance which both attached to operative share-
ownership was more widely shared. A popular belief persisted, given credence in the local press, that the purchase of shares bestowed a decisive
advantage in the competition for mill jobs, enabling a favoured few to
bypass conventional promotional procedures, effectively buying their
appointment as minders. Estimates of the price to be paid to gain control
of the mule varied between £1 and £50.[14] Attempts to reform work

[10] C. W. Macara, *Social and Industrial Reform* (Manchester, 1920), 325–6, 358–9.
[11] S. S. Hammersley, MA, MP, *Industrial Leadership* (1925), 160–6; *Directory of Directors*
(1933 edn.); *Who Was Who, 1961–1970* (1972), 483.
[12] A. J. McIvor, 'Sir Charles Wright Macara (1845–1929)', in D. J. Jeremy and C. Shaw
(eds.), *Dictionary of Business Biography*, iv (1985), 11–12; *Who Was Who, 1929–1940* (1941),
840; *The Crisis in the Cotton Industry*, i, 153, 325, 347; JRL, Ashton Employers' Collection,
FMCSA, annual report, year ending 31 Dec. 1925 (Manchester, 1926), 52–65.
[13] *TW* 5 (29 Aug. 1930), 547–8.
[14] C. A. Clarke, *The Effects of the Factory System* (1899; repr. Littleborough, 1985), 165;
BA, BOHP 15A (female, born 1906), tape; *BJG* (6 Feb. 1911), 9, letter by 'shareholder'.

practices before 1914 were, in part, informed by the belief that advancement depended as much on financial means as it did on technical ability; the practice of buying situations was seen to deny promotion to fully competent piecers. Into the 1920s, local correspondents reported the popular view 'that when operatives were being taken on at certain mills it was a stipulation that they should become shareholders. By this avenue they obtained mules.'[15] Evidence to back up such claims rarely proceeded beyond the anecdotal and emanated, more often than not, from those outside the trade or from those whose aspirations to advancement had been disappointed. What is more, the diligence with which promotional procedures were defended by union officials and operatives alike, casts further doubt on the veracity of such claims.[16] The realities of operative share-ownership, its extent and the motives behind it, remain to be clarified.

Here, institutional records assist. Despite an established antipathy to limited-liability forms of capital, working-class organizations invested extensively in mill stock. In addition to holding 100 shares in the British Cotton Growing Association, the Great and Little Bolton Co-operative Society had a total of £52,500 deposited with local firms in 1919. Textile unions also held substantial investments. Before 1914, the Bolton Card Room Association had interests in six companies across the fine-spinning province.[17] Predictably, however, the largest stake of any workers' organization was that of the Operative Spinners'. In the mid-1920s, the Bolton Provincial Association alone held £151,500 worth of mill stock. It was a diverse portfolio, mostly in the form of loans and dispersed across a number of firms. Not only did this offer security against commercial failure, it also ensured a high degree of liquidity. Alternative, less liquid forms of debt were only likely to be acquired where higher rates of return were offered. So, whereas preference shares in the Wilton Spinning Co., Ltd were sold in 1919, those in the Drake Spinning Co. were retained, as they offered 6 per cent per annum interest, compared with the 5 per cent payable on loans.[18] Such calculations reflect the central role investments played in union finances. High levels of interest enabled benefits to be maintained at more generous levels, while liquidity guaranteed ready access to savings in time of need. Surges in demand for financial assistance

---

[15] *BJG* (31 July 1925), 8; (6 Oct. 1911), 9, letter by Revd. le Marchant.

[16] See above, pp. 31–2.

[17] F. W. Peaples, *History of the Great and Little Bolton Co-operative Society, Ltd* (Bolton, 1909), 332; P. Harris, 'Social Leadership and Social Attitudes' (Lancaster Univ. Ph.D. thesis), 147; BA, FT/7/6/52–61 BOCA, quarterly reports, 1 Sept. 1906–Apr. 1909.

[18] Harris, 'Social Leadership and Social Attitudes', 147; JRUL, BCA/1/3/11 BSA, minutes, Council meeting, 22 Oct. 1918; Special Council meeting, 26 Dec. 1919.

during the trade recessions of 1908–9 and 1920 were met in part by substantial withdrawals of mill investments. On each occasion, calls were
spread over a number of companies, thereby minimizing any financial dislocation and so facilitating prompt repayments.[19]

Throughout, investment decisions by the Spinners' Association
remained peculiarly sensitive to interest-rate variations. So, loans held in
Crosses and Winkworth, Ltd, which earned 4 per cent per annum were
withdrawn on maturation in 1918 and transferred to 5 per cent Dart Mill
stock. Similarly, following the decision of the Croal Spinning Co., Ltd to
reduce the interest payable on its loans to 4.5 per cent from 1922, the
Association's holding of £1,000 was placed with the Cowling Spinning
Co., Ltd at 5 per cent.[20] For much of the period, any interest-rate differential worked in the cotton trade's favour. While most mill loans paid
between 4 and 5 per cent per annum, the average yield on local authority
bonds before 1914 rarely exceeded 3.5 per cent.[21] From the mid-1920s,
however, that position was reversed, as returns on municipal stock
increased to an average of £5. 8s. 7d. per annum. What is more, such
bonds increasingly offered greater security of return. Most investment
agreements incorporated 'strike and depression' clauses, which permitted
the withdrawal of funds at short notice in such eventualities.[22] By contrast, many mills were forced to suspend repayments, as the liquidation of
loans severely depleted their reserves of working capital. The Bolton
Association was obliged to threaten the Mavis Spinning Co., Ltd with
legal action before a repayment schedule could be agreed in 1930. More
often, schemes of arrangement, involving the conversion of loans to less
liquid forms of debt, were the only alternative to bankruptcy and the loss
of all investments. The Operative Spinners' were thus able to recover a
portion of the funds held in the Combined Egyptian group of mills by
agreeing to retain the greater part in debenture stock and ordinary

[19] JRUL, BCA/1/3/9 BSA, minutes, Council meeting, 7 June 1910; BCA/1/3/11 BSA,
Council meetings, 2 Nov., 15 Nov. 1920; BCA/13/3/7 BSA, general outward
correspondence, 1922, Wood to Cowling, Croal, Dove, Kearsley, and Howe Bridge mills, 24
May 1922.
[20] JRUL, BCA/1/3/11–12 BSA, minutes, Council meetings, 5 Mar. 1918, 18 Dec. 1922.
[21] The figure for local authority loans is derived from the interest earned by the Hulton
Colliery Relief Fund on moneys placed with Liverpool, Manchester, and Bolton
Corporations, BA, HRF, ABHC/3/1 actuarial valuations, 10 Apr. 1912, Actuarial Report on
Liabilities at 31 Dec. 1911, 4; 28 May 1920, Report on Liabilities to 31 Dec. 1919.
[22] JRUL, BCA/1/3/13 BSA, minutes, Council meeting, 15 Nov. 1927, for details of a
loan taken out with Liverpool Corporation; BCA/1/3/14 BSA, minutes, 15 Oct. 1929,
holdings with Bolton, Bury, and Blackpool Corporations; BA, HRF, ABHC/3/1 actuarial
valuations, 14 Feb. 1930, Actuarial Report at 31 Dec. 1929, 1.

shares.[23] Investments were increasingly directed outside the industry, so that the £5,000 at 5 per cent placed with Sir John Holden's Astley Bridge Mill in 1925 represented the last loan account to be opened with any cotton firm in the fine-spinning province.[24]

Financial calculations were decisive in determining the disposition of union investments. Industrial relations occasionally impinged, as in 1908, when the Operative Spinners' Association withdrew £1,000 from the Monton Spinning Co., Ltd following the outbreak of strike action.[25] Overall, however, funds were more likely to be redeployed in search of higher or more certain returns. Certainly, the leverage which unions were able to exert over company policy was, at best, minimal. This becomes clear if institutional holdings are placed in the context of the industry's aggregate capital requirements. The Operative Spinners' holding of £151,500, diffused across the fine-spinning area, contrasted with loan accounts worth £1.3 million in Bolton alone in the mid-1920s. What is more, loans made up a mere 10 per cent of the total capital raised by fine-spinning firms.[26] Rather than seeking to influence the development of the industry's politics, operative organizations attempted, through their investment decisions, to profit from trading success.

An alternative approach, utilizing funds to set up independent spinning concerns, was mooted on occasion. However, while spinners' officials deemed such a scheme to be practicable, they ruled against it.[27] The few ventures in industrial co-partnership which were attempted in the period tended to be located on the periphery of the main spinning area. In 1912, members of the Edgworth Industrial Co-operative Society raised £6,000 to help to establish Tower Mill in the township of Turton, with the intention of adding to local employment opportunities. Yet, despite this backing, the mill never functioned as a true co-operative. While the Society acted as principal mortgagee and ground landlord, managerial control rested with the firm of Sutcliffe and Sons, to which the mill was leased in 1913. Shopfloor relations were conducted by entirely conventional means,

[23] JRUL., BCA/1/3/14 BSA, minutes, Council meetings, 25 Aug., 20 Oct. 1930; Combined Egyptian Mills, Ltd, statement of financial adjustments, 1929–30.
[24] JRUL., BCA/1/3/12 BSA, minutes, Council meeting, 21 Apr. 1925.
[25] JRUL., BCA/1/3/8 BSA, minutes, Special Council meeting, 27 Apr. 1908; general representative meeting, 10 June 1908.
[26] *Skinner's Cotton Trade Directory* (1923 edn.); PRO, Register of Dissolved Companies, BT 31/17433/84266/59 Maco Spinning Co., Ltd, share summary, 22 Sept. 1920; BT 31/15001/29365/55 North End Spinning Co., Ltd, share summary, 5 Nov. 1919.
[27] JRUL., BCA/1/3/8 BSA, minutes, Council meeting, 4 Apr. 1905.

a fact reflected in the month-long stoppage of weavers, seeking the payment of standard list rates, in 1914.[28]

A decade earlier, a comparable scheme had been launched in the mining township of Standish. In March 1899, a meeting voted to fund the building of a weaving shed to provide employment for the daughters of local colliers, who were otherwise obliged to seek work in nearby Wigan. At all points, the District Miners' Association was active in support of the concern, which traded under the name of the Bradley Manufacturing Co., Ltd. One thousand £1 shares were acquired on flotation and the Association's president, Stephen Bentham, was appointed to the company's board.[29] Furthermore, when the Bradley planned to expand by installing 30,000 mule and ring spindles, the Association assisted by doubling its shareholding. Yet it would appear that union involvement never extended beyond the financial. Managerial responsibility continued to be entrusted to specialist officials. J. J. Bradley, the company's chairman, was also a director of two Wigan firms.[30] In addition, little was done to promote union organization in the mill, with the result that wages remained below agreed local rates. In this respect, capital structures may have provided an important constraint. At no time did union investments account for more than 10 per cent of the Bradley's financial resources. On the dissolution of the Standish Association in 1907, shares were distributed among local colliers in proportion to their period of membership. In all, by 1914, thirty-six miners and three checkweighmen held 3,792 shares, equivalent to 9 per cent of the firm's ordinary equity capital.[31]

Although geographically distinct, Tower and Bradley mills, by directly linking investment to local job opportunities and by observing the conventional separation of ownership and control, faithfully reflected trends elsewhere. Many had become convinced of the advantages of proprietorial control by the failure, in the later nineteenth century, of co-partnership ventures in weaving districts to the north. Joshua Rawlinson, secretary of the North and North-East Lancashire Cotton Spinners' and Manufacturers' Association, drew the conclusion, as he expressed it to the

[28] *BJG* (30 Jan. 1914), 11; (22 Apr. 1932), 9; *Worrall's Directory* (Oldham, 1913 edn.).

[29] WHS, WTN 419 S7 SMA, monthly council minutes, 18 Mar., 13 May, 2 Sept. 1899; PRO, Register of Dissolved Companies, BT 31/16179/61507 Bradley Manufacturing Co., Ltd, articles of association.

[30] *Worrall's Directory* (Oldham, 1905–14 edns.); WHS, WTN 419 L2 SMA, monthly council minutes, 10 Mar. 1906; WHS, 'Biographical Cuttings Books', ii, 59.

[31] WHS, WTN 419 L2 SMA, monthly council minutes, 22 Sept., 20 Oct. 1906; 12 and 26 Jan. 1907; PRO, Register of Dissolved Companies, BT 31/16179/61507 Bradley Manufacturing Co., Ltd, share summary, 12 Sept. 1914.

Royal Commission on Labour, 'that the interference of the operatives employed with their manager, and with the business, is detrimental to its successful conduct'.[32] In a number of outlying districts, such as Harle Syke near Burnley, nominally co-operative ventures survived beyond 1900. In all cases for which complete information is available, however, managerial structures remained entirely orthodox.[33]

Into the 1920s, the dominance of private, familial capital in the region's weaving sector limited workers' involvement in industrial ownership. In 1911, only 20 per cent of weaving firms across the county were organized along joint-stock lines, while only 14 per cent of Lancashire's manufacturing capacity underwent recapitalization after 1918.[34] As the period progressed, however, participation in profit-sharing and share-ownership came to be encouraged, often as a way of reducing wage costs. In 1928, the Brierfield Mill Co., Ltd proposed reserving half its annual profits for distribution among the workforce in return for an agreed 10 per cent cut in wages. The managers' journal expressed enthusiasm for an arrangement which offered 'the operative an interest, not only in the wage envelope, but in the welfare of the concern by which he [sic] lives . . . [while avoiding] the fatal weakness of seeming to lessen the authority, and therefore the efficiency of the management.'[35] The workers responded less effusively. Commercial realities suggested that any profits, after a wage reduction had been agreed, would prove meagre. The invitation to share losses was thus declined.[36]

Opinion became somewhat less dismissive as trade difficulties intensified from 1929. In 1931, workers at two Manchester mills agreed to use 2s. 6d. out of every £1 earned to buy shares in their respective companies so as to ensure continued full-time working. One year later, the entire labour force at a Burnley weaving shed voted to acquire shares to enable the mill to resume operations after a prolonged stoppage.[37] In smaller

[32] *Parl. Papers 1892*, xxxv (6708–VI), RC on Labour: Minutes of Evidence. Textiles, q. 2577.

[33] R. Frost, *A Lancashire Township: The History of Briercliffe-with-Extwistle* (Briercliffe, 1982), 63–71; *Worrall's Directory* (Oldham, 1905 to 1914 edns.).

[34] S. J. Chapman and T. S. Ashton, 'The Sizes of Businesses', *Journal of the Royal Statistical Society*, 77 (1913–14), 488, 529–31; Committee on Industry and Trade, *Survey of Textile Industries: Cotton, Wool, Artificial Silk. Being Part III of a Survey of Industries* (HMSO, 1928), 40, 123; G. W. Daniels and J. Jewkes, 'The Post-War Depression in the Lancashire Cotton Industry', *Journal of the Royal Statistical Society*, 91 (1928), 174–5; 'manufacturing' is used here in its narrower sense to differentiate the processes involved in the weaving, knitting, etc. of cloth.   [35] *TW* 2 (26 Oct. 1928), 196.

[36] *TW* 2 (4 Jan. 1929), 529.

[37] *TW* 7 (15 May 1931), 346–8; 9 (26 Aug. 1932), 596.

weaving districts, the intensity of the recession encouraged a late efflorescence of industrial co-partnership. In 1932, operative syndicates in Earby,
Church, and Great Harwood bought redundant plant with the intention
of recommencing activity along co-operative lines. The absence of significant alternative forms of employment necessitated such a move: in more
'normal' times, the cotton trade employed between 47 and 73 per cent of
the local labour forces.[38]

Dependence on the mill was less marked further south. Here, large
urban centres sustained a more diverse industrial base, allowing workers
greater discretion over their choice of jobs. Furthermore, more capital-
intensive preparatory and spinning plant was obliged to look beyond its
own workers for funding to a broader credit network in which financial,
social, and industrial connections were closely meshed. In mobilizing support from such sources, particular importance attached to the identity of
company personnel. For example, the presence of leading local figures on
the board of the Croal Spinning Co., Ltd, including the current and a former Mayor of Bolton, in Alderman Thomas Barlow Tong and Alderman
John Miles, would, it was believed, help to secure the firm's future.
Reviewing the company's prospectus, the *Tyldesley and Atherton Chronicle*
was drawn to remark that 'The directors are gentlemen of very high
standing in Bolton and district, and as they possess the public confidence
the necessary capital will undoubtedly soon be forthcoming'.[39] Nor was
this confidence misplaced. In addition to substantial loan subscriptions,
the Croal was able to fund its initial outlay on fixed plant through debenture issues and bank overdrafts. Many firms had recourse to such expedients in their early years. Liverpool cotton brokers underwrote part of the
Maco Spinning Co., Ltd's debt, while mortgage funds were forthcoming
from the Manchester engineering firm of Brooks and Doxey, Ltd, which
also supplied the mill's carding machinery.[40] Preference-share and mortgage creations enabled the Wigan firm of William Woods and Son to supplement the disappointing results of an earlier share issue, so that, by
1914, the company's paid-up equity capital of £16,300 was dwarfed by

[38] *TW* 9 (13 May 1932), 235; 10 (9 Dec., 1932), 387; (23 Dec. 1932), 442; *Census of England
and Wales, 1921: County of Lancaster*, table 17, 185, 188 (Church and Great Harwood);
County of Yorkshire (HMSO, 1923), table 17, 259 (Earby).

[39] LRO, Barber-Lomax Collection DDBx 13/1 Croal Spinning Co., Ltd, scrapbook,
cutting from *Tyldesley and Atherton Chronicle* (11 July 1907); *BJG* (6 July 1917), 4 (obits. of
Thomas Barlow Tong, 1849–1917, and John Miles, 1841–1917).

[40] LRO, Barber-Lomax Collection DDBx 13 Croal Spinning Co., Ltd, minute book, 1 and
15 May 1908, 23 Apr., 24 May 1909; PRO, Register of Dissolved Companies, BT
31/17433/84266/37 Maco Spinning Co., Ltd, mortgage, 6 July 1911; *BJG* (2 Aug. 1907), 2.

£53,585 held in the form of preference shares and £117,110 in mort-gages.[41] Recourse to exogenous sources of credit also enabled private lim-ited firms to augment their working capital without compromising family control. In 1927, Sir John Holden and Son, Ltd raised £125,000 in debentures secured by the Westminster Bank, Ltd. However, ownership remained with the immediate family.[42]

Unlike the weaving sector, economic difficulty did not encourage moves to extend share-ownership. The creation of mortgage debt totalling £181,000 at the Midland Bank eased liquidity problems at William Brown and Nephew, Ltd, of Wigan in the mid-1920s.[43] The incentive to promote profit-sharing ventures was also less, although in 1919, as part of the firm's more general adoption of welfarist strategies, the board of Tootal Broadhurst Lee Co., Ltd sanctioned the creation of a special class of operative shares. The hope was that, in the words of Sir Edward Tootal Broadhurst, worker-shareholders would become 'person-ally financially interested in the prosperity of the company'.[44] Shares could be purchased out of a wage bonus linked to dividends, thus mini-mizing any sacrifice involved in their acquisition. What is more, operative scrip would rank ahead of ordinary equity for dividend payments, while a contingency fund would make money available when illness prevented attendance at work, enabling shares to be retained through periods of difficulty. Take-up of the shares was voluntary and, in the event, proved disappointing: barely 15 per cent of the sum made available had been allocated by 1927. Recession and changes in ownership blocked similar schemes elsewhere. The absorption of the Bolton firm of Lord, Hampson and Lord, Ltd in the Crosses and Winkworth combine prevented the implementation of a projected profit-sharing scheme.[45] Overall, how-ever, operative funds remained marginal to managerial calculations, an impression confirmed by more detailed data from the Register of Dissolved Companies.

From this, a sample was devised, comprising twenty-two firms, sixteen in Bolton and six in Wigan, to capture trends in industrial ownership over

---

[41] PRO, Register of Dissolved Companies, BT 31/17796/89204/30, 32–3, 66 William Woods and Son, creation of mortgage, 13 Nov. 1908; debenture stock, 11 Mar. 1909; extraordinary general meeting, 1 Apr. 1909; share summary, 31 Dec. 1914.

[42] PRO, Register of Dissolved Companies, BT 31/32448/170236/14, 26 Sir John Holden and Sons, Ltd, share summary, 31 Dec. 1921; First Debenture Stock, 7 Mar. 1927.

[43] PRO, Register of Dissolved Companies, BT 31/35254/167981 William Brown and Nephew (Wigan), Ltd, mortgage, 29 Nov. 1924.   [44] *The Times* (29 Aug. 1919), 19.

[45] *BJG* (22 Aug. 1919), 5; (21 Nov. 1919), 5; (12 Aug. 1927), 6; BA, ZZ/50/30 C&W Consolidated, memorandum and articles of association.

the first three decades of the twentieth century. Most of the concerns in Wigan's small cotton sector offering shares for public sale were included.[46] Reflecting the widespread changes in ownership which occurred across the American-cotton sector in the immediate post-war years, all but one of the companies analysed here underwent reconstitution during 1920. Pre-war patterns of investment were recaptured by tracing two firms to their original foundations. Construction of a representative Bolton sample proved more problematic, as private capital controlled the bulk of the town's spindleage to 1918. Of the sixteen firms surveyed here, eight did not invite the public to subscribe for shares.[47] Many were subsequently absorbed into large-scale combines. To some extent, therefore, to focus on public limiteds which remained independent is to focus on the untypical. Nevertheless, in doing so, important variations in the industrial experience are captured. Two firms enjoyed histories unbroken by capital extensions or changes in ownership, reflecting the greater structural continuity which characterized the Egyptian-cotton sector.[48] The impact of change is caught, however, in the two firms which were recapitalized through bonus-share issues in 1919–20,[49] and the four which, at the same time, were reconstituted.[50]

In all cases, share summaries confirm that operative funds satisfied only a small fraction of capital requirements. Although the Bee Hive Spinning Co., Ltd of Bolton actively encouraged workers to acquire a direct stake in the firm, the £7,272 invested by 1908 represented a mere 7 per cent of paid-up values and even this estimate is based on the broadest definition of 'operative' status, to include supervisory staff. If shares held by carders, clothlookers, and mule 'gaffers' are excluded, the shopfloor contribution is reduced to 4 per cent of equity capital.[51] Elsewhere, few attempts were made actively to court operative savings. The Croal's requirement of a minimum investment of twenty £5 shares per

---

[46] The firms covered were William Woods and Son, Ltd (reconstituted as Trencherfield Mills, Ltd); the Bradley Manufacturing Co., Ltd; William Brown and Nephew (Wigan), Ltd; the Marne Ring Mill (1920), Ltd; the May Mill Spinning Co. (1920), Ltd; and the Empress Spinning Co. (1920), Ltd.

[47] These were T. M. Hesketh and Son, Ltd; Sir John Holden and Sons, Ltd; W. A. Openshaw, Ltd; John Harwood and Son, Ltd; Youngs, Ltd; Eden and Thwaites, Ltd; the Bolton Manufacturing Co., Ltd; and Charles Heaton and Son, Ltd.

[48] The Bee Hive Spinning Co., Ltd; and the Ocean Cotton Spinning Co., Ltd.

[49] The Maco Spinning Co., Ltd; and the North End Spinning Co., Ltd.

[50] The Croal Spinning Co. (1920), Ltd; the Rumworth Cotton Spinning Co., Ltd; the Bolton Union Spinning Co. (1920), Ltd; and Henry Poole and Co., Ltd.

[51] PRO, Register of Dissolved Companies, BT 31/34357/40283 Bee Hive Spinning Co., Ltd, share summary, 30 Jan. 1908.

Table 5. *Shareholding by cotton workers: Bolton and Wigan Firms*

Company	Date	Share Capital	Operative Investment		
			number	capital	% of total
Bolton					
Bee Hive A	1908	£56,000	45	£4,256	7.6
Bee Hive B	1908	£28,000	11	£1,631	5.8
Bee Hive C	1908	£21,000	8	£1,385 7s.	6.6
Croal	1912	£39,307	8	£675	1.7
Ocean	1914	£47,980	17	£1,006	2.1
North End	1914	£150,000	3	£610	0.6
Maco	1915	£68,127	11	£380	2.4
Croal	1920	£64,150	5	£170	1.1
Bee Hive A	1920	£56,000	18	£1,435	2.6
Bee Hive B	1920	£28,000	7	£252	0.9
Bee Hive C	1920	£21,000	5	£593 12s.	2.8
Rumworth	1921	£80,000	9	£1,060	1.3
Poole	1921	£90,000	11	£1,732 10s.	1.9
Rumworth	1928	£80,000	7	£510	0.6
Union	1929	£344,883	60	£9,432	2.7
Ocean	1932	£120,000	8	£1,990	1.7
Poole	1932	£104,355	9	£971 5s.	0.9
Wigan					
Bradley	1914	£37,350	7	£85 10s.	0.3
Woods	1916	£26,080	—	—	—
Brown	1920	£276,142	10	£450	0.2
Empress	1929	£465,750	22	£8,000	1.7
Marne	1929	£83,879	30	£5,200	6.2
May	1929	£574,508	22	£4,200	0.7
Trencherfield	1930	£470,730	44	£6,341	1.3

Sources: PRO, Register of Dissolved Companies, BT 31/34357/40283 Bee Hive Spinning Co., Ltd, share summaries, 30 Jan. 1908, 12 Feb. 1920; BT 31/18117/93632/34, 47 Croal Spinning Co., Ltd, share summary, 27 Apr. 1912, 3 May 1920; BT 31/37955/79551 Ocean Cotton Spinning Co., Ltd, share summaries, 21 Jan. 1914, 20 Jan. 1932; BT 31/15001/29365/39 North End Spinning Co., Ltd, share summary, 12 Nov. 1914; BT 31/17433/84266/47 Maco Spinning Co., Ltd, share summary, 30 Sept. 1915; BT 31/32423/167272 Rumworth Cotton Spinning Co., Ltd, share summaries, 27 July 1921, 1 Aug. 1928; BT 31/32417/166733/15, 26 Henry Poole and Co., Ltd, share summaries, 10 May 1921, 11 May 1932; BT 31/32419/166839/34 Bolton Union Spinning Co. (1920), Ltd, share summary, 6 Feb. 1929; BT 31/16179/61507 Bradley Manufacturing Co., Ltd, share summary, 12 Sept. 1914; BT 31/17796/89204/68 William Woods and Son, Ltd, share summary, 8 Nov. 1916; BT 31/35254/167981 William Brown and Nephew (Wigan), Ltd, share summary, Dec. 1920; BT 31/33810/165361 Empress Spinning Co. (1920), Ltd, share summary, 13 Feb. 1929; BT 31/32369/163323/26 Marne Ring Mill (1920), Ltd, share summary, 7 Feb. 1929; BT 31/32426/167494/27 May Mill Spinning Co. (1920), Ltd, share summary, 13 Feb. 1929; BT 31/32427/167751/29 Trencherfield Mills, Ltd, 12 Nov. 1930.

subscriber ensured that only six cotton workers were allotted shares in the first seven months following flotation. Poor trade thereafter may have deterred further applications, but the experience of other firms suggests that this was not decisive. In two prosperous years from 1905, the take-up of Maco Mill shares was confined to five spinners and a single carder.[52] Perhaps predictably, minders were, among cotton operatives, the most active in purchasing shares, accounting for 141 out of the 318 mill workers identified in the sample. Rather more against expectations, despite the sense of status which increasingly attached to their craft, only three grinders figured in the share summaries covered here.

If it is clear that few workers chose to invest in local industry, the motives of those who did acquire shares remains to be established. The geographical distribution of shareholdings, as revealed by the companies' register, suggests that savings were not always committed to the investor's place of work. Three of the five spinners allocated shares in the Croal lived in Leigh. Equally, of twenty-seven minders with stakes in the Bolton Union group of mills, only eleven were native to Bolton.[53] In this context, it is perhaps suggestive that the severance of residential ties rarely resulted in the sale of mill stock. One spinner, living in Bolton when allotted thirty shares in the Maco Spinning Co., Ltd, retained his interest in the firm after moving to Chorley.[54] Even among operatives, a regional market in mill shares was evident and, if anything, became more pronounced with changes in industrial organization after 1918. In addition to local workers, the reconstituted Bolton Union Spinning Co. (1920), Ltd received share subscriptions from an Oldham grinder, and weavers in Langho, Haslingden, and Nelson, along with carders from Bacup and Rochdale.[55] Operatives from weaving towns in the north of the county also figured prominently in the share issue of the Empress Spinning Co. (1920), Ltd, of Ince, near Wigan. Local representation was, by contrast, modest, reflecting the fact that, in such areas, the industry was largely staffed by colliers' daughters. Yet, save for the Bradley, few miners

[52] PRO, Register of Dissolved Companies, BT 31/18117/93632/8, 10–11, 13, 15–16 Croal Spinning Co., Ltd, prospectus, 5 June 1907; share allotments, July 1907–Jan. 1908; BT 31/17433/84266/10–14, 16–19, 21, 23 Maco Spinning Co., Ltd, share allotments, Apr. 1905–Dec. 1906.

[53] PRO, Register of Dissolved Companies, BT 31/18117/93632/34 Croal Spinning Co., Ltd, share summary, 27 Apr. 1912; BT 31/32419/166839/34 Bolton Union Spinning Co. (1920), Ltd, share summary, 6 Feb. 1929.

[54] PRO, Register of Dissolved Companies, BT 31/17433/84266/14, 47, Maco Spinning Co., Ltd, share allotment, 3–26 July 1905; share summary, 30 Sept. 1915.

[55] PRO, Register of Dissolved Companies, BT 31/32419/166839/34 Bolton Union Spinning Co. (1920), Ltd, share summary, 6 Feb. 1929.

accumulated mill equity. Even those that did were drawn from a wide area. Miners from Atherton, Leigh, and Rishton thus held shares in Wigan's Trencherfield Mills, in 1930.[56]

The ready availability of information on relative rates of return encouraged such dispersed dealings in mill stock. Share prices were regularly published in the local press, while personal contacts provided a further source of intelligence. The latter helps to explain particular patterns of ownership. For example, managers from Shaw, near Oldham, were active in promoting the Marne Ring Mill (1920), Ltd, and, of fifty operatives who subscribed to the firm's issue on flotation, twenty-seven lived in that township. Similarly, the presence of directors from Chorley and Atherton on the board of the Rumworth Cotton Spinning Co., Ltd appears to have encouraged share applications from workers in both those areas.[57] In each case, exceptionally high levels of profitability in the post-war boom may have stimulated operative interest, given that shareholdings appear to have been, for the most part, short-term and speculative in character. Twelve of the Marne's fifty worker-shareholders sold their interests while values remained buoyant in the early 1920s. Over the following decade, a further eighteen withdrew their investments, so that, by 1929, only twenty of the original complement remained. Shaw's representation was reduced to seven.[58] A comparable pattern could be observed in mills unaffected by post-war changes in ownership. Of thirteen minders allotted shares in the Ocean Spinning Co., Ltd between 1907 and 1913, only four retained their holdings to the end of the period. Most sold their shares in the 'bullish' market of the years immediately following the Armistice. The management of individual portfolios reveals a sophisticated appreciation of commercial realities. In 1908, the minder James Holland purchased twenty-seven Ocean shares, a stake which he increased to fifty-two in 1920. These were sold at a profit as prices peaked. Holland then acquired a further bloc of forty shares, which was reduced as values declined in the mid-1920s.[59]

[56] PRO, Register of Dissolved Companies, BT 31/33810/165361 Empress Spinning Co. (1920), Ltd, share summary, 13 Feb. 1929; BT 31/32427/167751/29 Trencherfield Mills, Ltd, share summary, 12 Nov. 1930.

[57] PRO, Register of Dissolved Companies, BT 31/32369/163323/9,14, Marne Ring Mill (1920), Ltd, directors, 23 Jan. 1920; share summary, 14 Jan. 1921; BT 31/32423/167272 Rumworth Cotton Spinning Co., Ltd, memorandum and articles of association; share summary, 1 Aug. 1928.

[58] PRO, Register of Dissolved Companies, BT 31/32369/163323/14, 26 Marne Ring Mill (1920), Ltd, share summaries, 14 Jan. 1921, 7 Feb. 1929.

[59] PRO, Register of Dissolved Companies, BT 31/37955/79551 Ocean Cotton Spinning Co., Ltd, share summaries, 6 Feb. 1907– 20 Jan. 1932.

By thus responding promptly to market changes, operative shareholders largely avoided the problems created by the retention of stock. The
expedient, resorted to by many firms in the 1920s, of calling up unpaid
portions on ordinary shares to make good losses caused by the liquidation
of loan accounts, left many investors holding devalued and unsaleable
scrip.[60] The shift in fortunes was epitomized by the experience of
Wheelam, the weaving overlooker of unimpeachable respectability from
Walter Greenwood's Salford childhood, whose spiritual and material
certainties embodied pre-war optimism for the future of the trade. His
subsequent fall, as rapid as that of the industry itself, was breathlessly
summarized by 'Nobby', a new breed of Lancastrian entrepreneur:

> There's old Wheelam. Look at him. Hung on and hung on. Two years ago he
> could have flogged the lot of his mill shares at five pounds ten a time . . . Cash.
> Retired, Bournemouth. Look at his shares now, and him supposed to be the know-
> all business man. Drug in the market aye, and on some of 'em he owes fifteen
> shillings a piece on call . . . Cotton? Finished. [61]

Few, if any workers shared Wheelam's fate. Such, at least, is suggested
by the records of local bankruptcy courts, which adjudicated, for the
most part, on failures among managerial and professional grades, such as
A. E. Boydell. His rise from mill office to company boardroom ended in
financial failure, brought on by repeated calls.[62] Others to appear before
the courts included a mill manager from Little Hulton, near Bolton, and
a retired boot-maker from Heywood.[63] However, perhaps the most
poignant example of improvident speculation was that of the Bolton
librarian, F. W. Peaples. Author of the Great and Little Bolton Co-
operative Society's jubilee history, an extended panegyric on the virtues
of thrift, Peaples had intervened in a falling market to acquire, at discounted rates, 17,150 partly paid shares in twenty-nine companies.
When trade failed to recover, he was left facing calls in excess of £5,000,
on which £3,515 remained outstanding in 1929.[64] Peaples, it would
appear, taught better than he knew. By diverting their savings from the
mill in response to market changes, most operatives imbibed his lessons
to rather better effect.

---

[60] In ten years to 1931, such calls raised £28.5 million, B. Bowker, *Lancashire under the
Hammer* (1928), 63–7; *TW* 9 (26 Aug. 1932), 592.
[61] W. Greenwood, *There was a Time* (1967), 40, 57, 165–6.
[62] *BJG* (23 May 1930), 10; (18 July 1930), 11; (17 Oct. 1930), 6.
[63] *BJG* (15 Feb. 1924), 10; (3 Dec. 1926), 8.
[64] *BJG* (13 Dec. 1929), 15.

The discussion thus far has considered only a portion of total corporate debt. Loan accounts, excluded from returns to the Companies' Register, were often seen as more likely repositories of workers' funds. In the absence of the kind of direct statistical corroboration available for shares, an evaluation of the importance of mill loans as a form of saving must proceed substantially from inference. The extant evidence suggests that, as with share acquisitions, a short-term, largely instrumental outlook prevailed. An Operative Spinners' shop committee was among a number of loanholders who chose to liquidate accounts in the Croal during the poor trading years of 1908–10.[65] A more general exodus occurred in the 1920s, as interest differentials increasingly worked against the industry. This may explain the readiness of operatives at Cannon Bros, Ltd to withdraw accounts worth almost £10,000, despite the firm's consistent profitability through that decade. Their actions contributed to a crisis of liquidity, which, in 1932, obliged the company to convert outstanding loans into second mortgage income debenture stock. The only members of the workforce caught in this scheme of arrangement were two minders, a carder, and an overlooker.[66] Clearly for these as for other workers, a financial stake implied no deeper commitment to the future of a particular mill or to that of the industry as a whole. This was wholly consistent with the instrumental attitude to work itself, which characterized the cotton workforce through this period.

The significance which contemporary opinion often placed in operative investments belied their limited extent. Union and managerial testimony before the Royal Commission on Labour agreed on this point: only a fraction of the mill labour force acquired a direct interest in the industry.[67] Although working-class involvement was encouraged by the post-war 'bubble' in values, the ready sale of stock, particularly after 1920, suggests that participation in industrial ownership was motivated more by the short-term quest for speculative profit than by a desire to secure an additional, stable source of income. If shareholding is, as some argued it could be, equated with gambling, then the class differences so evident in the latter, both in the motives for and the meaning which attached to such

[65] LRO, Barber-Lomax Collection DDBx 13 Croal Spinning Co., Ltd, minutes, 9 Oct. 1908, 5 Mar. 1909.
[66] *BJG* (24 June 1932), 8; LRO, Barber-Lomax Collection DDBx 10/5 Cannon Bros, Ltd, minutes, 18 Dec. 1922, 29 Dec. 1923, 10 Dec. 1924, 22 Dec. 1926, 19 Dec. 1928, 29 Dec. 1930; DDBx 10/10 Second Mortgage Income Debenture Stockholders; occupations were traced through *Tillotson's Directory for Bolton and District*, 15th edn. (Bolton, 1932).
[67] *Parl. Papers 1892*, xxxv (6708–VI), RC on Labour: Minutes of Evidence. Textiles, qq. 95–6, 2548, 3608–9.

activity, were equally evident here.[68] Where investments were retained in the longer term, a practical end was sought, in particular the creation and maintenance of job opportunities in areas where openings were sparse. So, rather than an acceptance of the capitalist ethic, which it might be seen to imply, operative share-ownership confirmed the survival of a distinctive working-class outlook. The tenor of industrial relations remained substantially unaffected by the presence of such savings. Within two years of its flotation, the Maco Spinning Co., Ltd, which attracted a limited degree of worker participation, was closed by unofficial strike action.[69] The overall impression remains, however, that this particular form of thrift did not operate to promote the interests of the working class as a collectivity. The interests to which it gave expression were immediately practical and personal. In that respect, it was entirely consistent with the broader realities of working-class life.

II

For miners' families, thrift was more unambiguously preventive in intent, blunting the impact of the dangers encountered in work underground. The latter were most obviously manifested in large-scale disasters. In two accidents alone, at the Maypole and Pretoria Pits in 1908 and 1910 respectively, 419 miners were killed. Over the long term, however, even such large losses paled in significance compared with the relentless attrition of individual accidents and fatalities. In the six years to 1913, 828 single fatalities were reported across Lancashire.[70] Injuries were an even more frequent occurrence. On an annual average, reportable non-fatal accidents, involving absences from work in excess of seven days, affected one in five of the county's underground workforce, while over 10 per cent of members of the Lancashire and Cheshire Miners' Permanent Relief Society claimed accident benefit for at least two weeks each year.[71]

---

[68] On class differences as revealed by the gambling habit, see R. I. McKibbin, 'Working-Class Gambling in Britain, 1880–1939', *Past and Present*, 82 (Feb. 1979), 147–78, also id., *The Ideologies of Class* (Oxford, 1990), 101–38; M. Clapson, *A Bit of a Flutter: Popular Gambling and English Society, c.1823–1961* (Manchester, 1992), esp. ch. 2.

[69] See above, Ch. 3.

[70] Calculated from Mines Inspectors' Reports for the Manchester and Ireland, and Liverpool and North Wales Divisions, for the years 1908–13; according to one estimate, large-scale accidents accounted for only 25% of mining casualties over the later decades of the 19th century, Campbell, *Miners' Insurance Funds*, 7.

[71] Mines Inspectors' Reports; WA, D/DS 22/4–12 Lancashire and Cheshire Permanent Relief Society (LCPRS), Management Committee minutes, Finance Committee, quarterly reports, 1896–1916.

If such figures reiterated the need for preventive thrift, they also complicated its realization. Institutions drawing primarily on miners' savings
required higher premiums to reflect the greater degree of risk. Thus colliers working for the Bridgewater Estate paid to the Worsley and Walkden
Moor Friendly Society, which, to maintain solvency, was obliged to operate with reserves 25 per cent in excess of average life estimates.[72]
Although other companies operated their own accident schemes, it
became clear, over time, that a more centralized response was required to
ensure more effective assistance, the spreading of risk limiting actuarial
uncertainties. To this end, a network of permanent relief societies, covering most of the major fields, was established over the second half of the
nineteenth century. Their utility became apparent in the wake of large-
scale accidents. All seventy-five victims of the Maypole explosion were
members of the Lancashire and Cheshire Miners' Permanent Relief
Society, as were the twenty-three colliers killed at Lyme Pits, Haydock, in
1930, while all but twelve of the 344 lost in the Pretoria disaster subscribed to the society.[73] Significantly, in each case, financial obligations
were met without undermining the viability of the fund.

Within the county, debate centred less on the effectiveness of relief
administration than on its structures. Employers were active at all levels
of organization. Within individual branches or 'agencies', business was
transacted through company offices, with contributions being deducted
from the wage packet. At the Pretoria, the firm's cashier also filled
the post of agency secretary.[74] In the years immediately following the
formation of the permanent relief society in 1872, administrative responsibilities were matched by a financial commitment, as owners supplemented miners' subscriptions by between 10 and 25 per cent. This
enabled companies to contract out of the provisions of the 1881
Employers' Liability Act. When contracting out ceased with the passage
of Workmen's Compensation legislation in 1897, proprietorial subventions were greatly reduced. Payments which had averaged £12,000 a year
had fallen to a mere £63 by 1905.[75] Despite this, administrative roles

---

[72] LRO, Coal Board Records NCBw 25/3 Worsley and Walkden Moor Friendly Society,
quinquennial valuation, 31 Dec. 1900, 4–5; see also J. Benson, 'The Thrift of English Coal-
Miners, 1860–95', *Econ.Hist.Rev.*, 2nd ser. 31 (1978), 410.

[73] Campbell, *Miners' Insurance Funds*, 10–11; WO (25 Aug. 1908), 2; *BJG* (2 May 1930),
8; *The Times* (23 Dec. 1910), 7.

[74] WA, D/DS 22/11 LCPRS, Management Committee minutes, 30 Oct. 1914; BA,
'Bolton Biographical Notes', iii, 95 (W. E. Tonge).

[75] *Parl. Papers 1892*, xxxiv (6708–IV), RC on Labour: Minutes of Evidence. Mining,
qq. 8316–17; *Farnworth Weekly Journal* (*FWJ*) (5 Mar. 1898), 5; WA, D/DS 22/4 LCPRS,
G. L. Campbell, 'The Permanent Society and the Workmen's Compensation Act', in

remained unchanged. Ten of the twenty-two seats on the permanent relief society's board of management were reserved for honorary members, comprising 'All persons who shall assist in supporting the Society with an Annual Subscription of not less than £1, or a Life Donation of not less than £10, and all Coal Owners who shall assist the Society in the collection of contributions and the verifying of accidents.'[76] Employers also chaired all committee meetings.[77] Similar arrangements obtained at the various company societies which remained active across the county. At Andrew Knowles and Sons, Ltd of Pendlebury, the firm acted as treasurer to the accident relief society, while the presidency and vice-presidency were held by the company's chairman and general manager, respectively.[78] In most cases, elected workmen's representatives could meet to determine important points of policy, including levels of benefit and subscriptions. Even then, however, employers could exercise the right of veto. Meetings to discuss rule changes at the sick and burial society associated with Fletcher, Burrows, Ltd, could only be convened with the permission of the Society's president, Clement Fletcher.[79]

Accident relief administration at both company and county levels thus engaged, albeit to varying degrees, both sides of industry, a fact which led the secretary of the Lancashire and Cheshire Society, George Lamb Campbell, to conclude that 'there will scarcely be two opinions as to the merits of a system which enables employers and employed to enter into friendly union for the purpose of rendering prompt and permanent assistance to those who are desolate and distressed.'[80] In this, however, Campbell was mistaken. The LCMF repeatedly criticized a system of relief based on deductions from wages. The county society operated, so Federation officials argued before the Departmental Committee on the Truck Acts, as an instrument of proprietorial control. Despite provision for the election of workmen's representatives, rank-and-file participation

---

Management Committee minutes, Board of Management, 5 May 1898; *Parl. Papers 1908*, lix (4443), Departmental Committee on Truck Acts. II. Minutes of Evidence, q. 7789.

[76] WA, D/DS 22/4 LCPRS, Management Committee minutes, special meeting, 23 May 1898.

[77] WA, D/DS 22/7 LCPRS, Management Committee minutes, special meeting, Board of Management, 31 Mar.; special cases committee, 1 May; finance committee, 4 May 1905.

[78] *FWJ* (29 Feb. 1896), 7; (12 Mar. 1898), 8; see also LRO, Coal Board Records NCCl 20/2 Cliviger Miners' Relief Society, rules (Burnley, 1907), par. 8.

[79] WA, D/DS 22/6 LCPRS, Management Committee minutes, Board of Management, 27 Sept. 1901; WA, D/DZ A83/6 Rules of Atherton Collieries Sick and Burial Society (Atherton, 1930), par. 29.   [80] Campbell, *Miners' Insurance Funds*, 16.

remained, at least according to union testimony, limited in extent, enabling company officials to dominate agency business.[81]

The extent of employer influence had been demonstrated in 1881, when, in order to enforce contracting out of the terms of the Employers' Liability Act of that year, colliery firms, including all but one of those in the central area of the coalfield, made society membership a condition of employment. The threat of state action also encouraged the formation of company funds. Accident relief societies were established at Andrew Knowles' and at pits owned by the Bridgewater Trust. The element of compulsion which this involved was acknowledged by George Caldwell, in evidence to the Royal Commission on Labour, although a paternalist motive was also stressed: 'We were forcing them to do what we believed was for their own interest'.[82] That relief structures survived the ending of contracting out in 1897 was ascribed by Federation officials to the use, both directly and indirectly, of intimidation. The point was developed by Edmund Walkden, secretary of the LCMF-organized Wigan and District Miners' Permanent Relief Society, before the 1908 Truck Committee. Attempts to persuade workers to transfer subscriptions from the old society were ineffective, he argued, as they were unwilling 'to go into the colliery office and face the colliery officials'.[83]

Yet explanations for administrative continuity founded primarily on managerial compulsion fail to convince. Proposals to maintain the practice of contracting out of state schemes beyond 1897 were only narrowly rejected by a vote of Lancashire and Cheshire Society members in February 1898. The margin of 800 on a turnout of almost 46,000 suggests considerable support for existing methods of relief.[84] The problems encountered in attempting to establish alternative arrangements confirm the impression thus conveyed. In 1898, the LCMF, as part of its overhaul of union structures, proposed forming a central 'Accident, Funeral, and Widows' and Orphans' Society'. Relief would be administered through existing Federation machinery, with checkweighmen acting as branch secretaries. Yet support for the scheme proved limited in practice. Although

[81] *Parl. Papers 1908*, lix (4443), Departmental Committee on Truck Acts. II. Minutes of Evidence, qq. 7757, 7847–9.

[82] *Parl. Papers 1892*, xxxiv (6708–IV), RC on Labour: Minutes of Evidence. Mining, q. 5953; also qq. 5829–33, 5919–20; *FWJ* (13 May 1899), 8. The exception was Blundell's of Pemberton.

[83] *Parl. Papers 1908*, lix (4443), Departmental Committee on Truck Acts. II. Minutes of Evidence, q. 7765.

[84] WA, D/DS 22/4 LCPRS, Management Committee minutes, ordinary members' meeting, 24 Feb. 1898, which reported that 85% of those eligible had voted.

18,000 members enrolled with the Wigan and District Society within three years of its formation, membership thereafter declined, falling to below 12,000 by 1912, a figure rarely exceeded in subsequent years.[85] Indeed, only eleven victims of the Pretoria disaster subscribed to the new society and six of these also paid to the Lancashire and Cheshire Society.[86] By contrast, after initial losses following the ending of contracting out, the old society experienced sustained growth in the period to 1914. If, in later years, colliery closures entailed an inevitable loss of numbers, in proportionate terms, the society more than held its own. Whereas the average membership of 60, 272 in 1913 represented 56 per cent of the county workforce, 48,814 subscribers in 1930 constituted 65 per cent of a diminished total.[87]

What is more, fragmentary evidence suggests that, in shaping such trends, employer influence was not decisive. The policy adopted at Chisnall Hall Colliery, where, it was reported, 'the Manager went down

Table 6. *Lancashire and Cheshire Miners' Permanent Relief Society Average Annual Membership, 1897–1914*

Year	Membership	Year	Membership
1897	53,383	1906	48,782
1898	47,308	1907	51,579
1899	43,301	1908	54,744
1900	43,731	1909	56,253
1901	43,488	1910	57,985
1902	45,039	1911	58,411
1903	46,213	1912	59,018*
1904	46,968	1913	60,272
1905	46,766	1914	61,858**

Source: WA, D/DS 22/4–11 LCPRS, Management Committee minutes, finance and statistical committee, quarterly membership returns.
* Excluding the first quarter, the figure for which was deflated by the effects of the minimum-wage strike.
** First two quarters only.

[85] WHS, WTN 419 S7 SMA, monthly council minutes, 5 Feb., 7 July 1898; I. F. Scott, 'The Lancashire and Cheshire Miners' Federation' (York Univ. D.Phil. thesis), 388; *BJG* (8 Apr. 1921), 8.
[86] BA, HRF, ABHC/5/1–344 Personal Files, Compensation statements; Manchester Central Reference Library, Archives Department (MRL), HRF, M122/2/2 Manchester Committee, statistical returns.
[87] WA, D/DS 22/10–11 LCPRS, Management Committee minutes, finance committee, quarterly membership returns, 29 May, 26 Aug., 27 Nov. 1913, 26 Feb. 1914; *BJG* (1 May 1931), 13; workforce totals calculated from the relevant Mines Inspectors' reports.

the pit at 4 o'clock on Friday morning, and asked the men to sign for their contributions to be stopped for the Old Permanent Relief Society', appears to have been untypical.[88] Certainly, the Standish District Miners' Association encountered few obstacles in attempting to recruit for the Wigan and District Society in 1898. Even the prospect of private members' legislation to abolish deductions for society contributions occasioned no large-scale withdrawal of subscriptions, although six members of the Pretoria agency did give notice to quit.[89] In general, the Lancashire and Cheshire Society appears to have survived by mutual consent, rather than as a result of managerial pressure.

Even union officials were obliged to counsel against wholesale desertion of the old society, as this would deny assistance to recipients of long-term relief, including the permanently disabled and families of deceased miners. Rather, colliers were urged to subscribe to both bodies. The additional cost ensured, however, that any overlap was slight. Only six of those killed in the Pretoria disaster paid to both societies.[90] Disparities in the benefits on offer further reduced support for the Federation agency. The Wigan and District Society was unable to match the old society's policy of allowing dependent parents of single men killed in colliery accidents the same level of assistance as widows. The secretary of the Lancashire and Cheshire Society thus reported that the family of Thomas Owens, one of the five Pretoria victims who paid to the Wigan and District Society alone, had 'expressed very great discontent at the way they had been mislead [sic] by the "New Society" and could not understand that their Brother had become a member of this Society and not The Permanent Relief Society.'[91] Their bewilderment underscored a more general perception, that the old society, by combining actuarial security with economical administration, offered the most effective means of accident relief.

Employer participation assisted in sustaining this view. Up to 1897, owners' subventions had helped to meet administrative expenses. From that point, the employment of colliery officials to manage agency business ensured that costs continued to be minimized. In the first decade following the introduction of workmen's compensation, administration of the county society absorbed only 8 per cent of members' contributions. At

---

[88] WHS, WTN 419 S7 SMA, monthly council minutes, 9 July 1898.
[89] WA, D/DS 22/10 LCPRS, Management Committee minutes, Board of Management, 29 Aug., 19 Dec. 1913.   [90] See above, n. 86.
[91] BA, HRF, ABHC/5/231 Personal Files, pencilled note, n.d.

Andrew Knowles', the figure was even lower at 3 per cent. By contrast, the Bolton Unity of Oddfellows, although run with the assistance of only one salaried official, was obliged to maintain a reserve of 15 per cent to meet expenses, while the Prudential Assurance Co.'s network of collectors absorbed 35 per cent of insurance premiums.[92] The financial advantages of proprietorial stewardship were such that, on the expiration of the Bridgewater Trust in 1903, members of the Worsley and Walkden Moor Friendly Society voted for dissolution. Although an alternative course, employing paid staff to administer the fund, was considered, the consequences of such a move, increased contributions and reduced benefits, were deemed to render it impracticable. Only the reconstitution of the Trust under the third Earl of Ellesmere enabled the society to survive. In this case, management subventions were used for the support of long-term dependants.[93] This capacity to supplement basic levels of relief also recommended existing structures to the workforce at the Clifton and Kersley Coal Co., Ltd, which voted in 1898 to maintain the status quo. The firm's surface workers opted for independence, however, and established their own accident society. Nevertheless, co-operation with the company fund continued, medical expenses being shared in cases where miners paid to both societies.[94] Financial calculations thus ensured continuity and a level of consensus throughout the trade beyond 1897.

Exceptions to this were few. Of the two firms which sought to operate outside the provisions of the Compensation Act, one, George Hargreaves and Co. of Rossendale, acted with the consent of the workforce.[95] At Andrew Knowles and Sons, Ltd, by contrast, contracting out was maintained in the face of a vote of 4:1 against. Despite this and union moves to establish a separate fund, subscriptions to the company's accident society rose, to the extent that, by 1903, only seventeen out of a workforce of 3,408 had not signed up. The contrast between growing levels of support and earlier expressions of opposition was deemed sufficient to require

[92] WA, D/DS 22/4 LCPRS, Management Committee minutes, 5 May 1898; D/DS 22/8 17 Dec. 1908; *FWJ* (12 Mar. 1898), 8; *Bolton Unity Magazine: Grand Lodge Circular of the United Oddfellows, Bolton Unity* (Apr. 1912), 161; Johnson, *Saving and Spending*, 31, even the latter figure followed determined efforts at administrative economies.

[93] LRO, Coal Board Records NCBw 24/3 Worsley and Walkden Moor Friendly Society, draft minutes, general meeting, 19 Sept. 1903; NCBw 26/12 Rules of the Worsley and Walkden Moor Friendly Society, established 27 Apr. 1840. Revised at Special General Meetings, 13 Nov. 1854 and 25 Mar. 1904 (Manchester, 1904), par. 7; C. Grayling, *The Bridgewater Heritage* (Worsley, 1983), 57–8.

[94] *FWJ* (9 July 1898), 5; (23 July 1898), 8; (24 Mar. 1900), 5.

[95] LRO, Coal Board Records NCHa 8/1 Rossendale Collieries Accident and Burial Society, minutes, special general meeting, 23 July 1898.

explanation. Union officials found a ready answer in management's use of intimidatory tactics.[96] In the absence of direct corroboration of this view, it must be observed that the scale of support garnered by the society renders such an explanation improbable. It may, however, be the case that the requirement actively to contract out of the scheme maintained subscriptions at a high level, in much the same way that the provisions of the 1913 Trade Union Act boosted financial support for the Labour Party. More material considerations may also have tipped the scales in favour of continuity. A system of direct deductions from wages offered the maximum level of benefit consistent with actuarial security. In comparison, the issue of democratic control, to which Federation spokesmen attached such importance, excited few misgivings among the rank and file, a finding consistent with broader trends in working-class thrift which saw the mutuality of the friendly society gradually cede ground to the anonymous commercialism of industrial assurance.

The advantage which miners derived from existing methods of relief administration went further. Working through company offices allowed movement between agencies to occur without interrupting entitlement to benefit. The Lancashire and Cheshire Society was thus able to accommodate the high levels of mobility which characterized the coalfield. Enduring district loyalties compromised the effectiveness of union institutions in this regard, particularly as a means of accurately documenting transfers was lacking.[97] So, in sharp contrast to the volatility of union membership through the period, subscriptions to the old society were remarkable for their stability. For example, in the three years to December 1910, at the same time that Federation rolls fell by a quarter, from 76,300 to 57,500, the society's average annual membership increased by 3,000.[98] Such trends provided statistical justification for the *Farnworth Weekly Journal*'s verdict on union attempts to challenge existing methods of relief: 'A well-established Society, with many friends and supporters among the miners themselves, cannot be readily superseded, and we fear the present attempt will prove a disastrous failure.'[99] The Lancashire and Cheshire Society's status as the most efficient and effective vehicle for preventive thrift across the coalfield remained unchallenged.

[96] *FWJ* (18 Mar. 1898), 5; (26 Mar. 1898), 7; (16 Apr. 1898), 5; (31 Mar. 1900), 8; (27 Mar. 1902), 5; (27 Mar. 1903), 4.
[97] Campbell, *Miners' Insurance Funds*, 13; see above, Ch. 3.
[98] Scott, 'Lancashire and Cheshire Miners' Federation', 458; WA, D/DS 22/8–9 LCPRS, Management Committee minutes, finance committee, quarterly membership returns.
[99] *FWJ* (11 June 1898), 5.

Coal-owners also saw advantages in administrative continuity. In particular, it offered the most effective means of controlling expenditure, a point over which concern heightened with the end of contracting out in 1897–8. From that date, old society benefits were used to supplement basic compensation awards and ensure that dependants did not receive less than 10s. a week during their period out of work. Elsewhere, payments were made during the first two weeks of disablement, a period not covered by the 1897 Act.[100] The fear, commonly voiced, was that the enhanced level of payment could work to reduce work incentives. Reviewing the first few years under the Compensation Act, the actuary of the Worsley and Walkden Moor Friendly Society was drawn to observe that 'The benefits conferred by the Employer in conjunction with those provided by the Society tend to make a member independent of his occupation and would appear to have the effect of increasing the burdens of thrift organisations in general'.[101] Yet the close supervision of claimants exercised under existing arrangements was seen to offer the most effective safeguard against potential malingerers. Surveillance operated with immediate effect. All accidents were to be reported to agency officials before the injured party left the pit. Thereafter, the regular provision of medical certificates was required as proof of continued inability to work.[102] By itself, however, the system was not entirely satisfactory. Professional fastidiousness often resulted, it was argued, in the return to work being unduly delayed. The suggestion that medical priorities did not always accord with the demands of economical administration received further confirmation in the finding that doctors had, on occasion, issued certificates in excess of two weeks to enable members to qualify for compensation awards.[103] In such circumstances, the desire to supplement medical supervision was understandable. Recipients of benefit were thus visited at their homes by officials, while long-term cases were subject to

---

[100] WA, D/DS 22/4 LCPRS, Management Committee minutes, Board of Management, 5 May 1898, which considered proposals for the Society's future by G. L. Campbell, 'The Permanent Society and the Workmen's Compensation Act: A Proposal'; and W. Wogan, 'The Future of the Permanent Relief Society: A Few Suggestions', 13 May 1898; *FWJ* (30 Apr. 1898), 8; (2 July 1898), 5; (9 July 1898), 5.

[101] LRO, Coal Board Records NCBw 25/5 Worsley and Walkden Moor Friendly Society, Report, n.d., 3–4, par. 13.

[102] LRO, Coal Board Records NCHa 9/1 Rules of Rossendale Collieries Accident and Burial Society (1925), 9, par. 17; WA, D/DZ A83/14 Rules to be observed by members of the Hindley Field Collieries Accident, Sick and Burial Society (Hindley, 1881), 5, par. 11.

[103] WA, D/DS 22/10 LCPRS, Management Committee minutes, Board of Management, special meeting, 10 Oct. 1913; BA, HRF, ABHC/5/118 Personal Files, medical certificate, 22 Aug. 1911; report by J. T. Cooper, 24 Feb. 1912.

quarterly review by district visiting committees.[104] At several agencies, home visits were undertaken by paid staff. For the most part, however, officials were, like Richard Boardman, agency president at Hulton Colliery and ordinary member of the old society's board of management, working miners resident in the immediate area. Thus, in reviewing the work of the society in 1914, its president could remark that 'help is given forthwith by those who know the sufferers, and are known by them'.[105] This facet of society administration persuaded those responsible for setting up relief funds in the wake of the disasters at the Maypole and Pretoria pits to utilize its machinery in managing the payment of benefits.[106]

A further advantage lay in the fact that supervision was maintained even when claimants left the district. For the right to benefit to be maintained, the permission of the board of management was required before any move could be undertaken.[107] Even then, home visits continued on a triennial basis, an arrangement which could involve officials in lengthy tours of inspection. On occasion, this necessitated journeys to Ireland, which had long supplied Lancashire with mining labour. In between visits, a check was maintained through the return of certificates, validated by local worthies, such as doctors, clerics, or magistrates.[108] Similar documentation was required where emigration over longer distances was involved, although in most cases, commutation of benefit was the norm. Where certificates were provided, the information requested went beyond a client's material circumstances. When a widow, on returning from Canada, asked that her right to benefit be restored, a testimonial was sought from her former employer concerning her character and conduct.[109]

[104] LRO, Coal Board Records NCBw 26/12 Rules of the Worsley and Walkden Moor Friendly Society (Manchester, 1904), 5, pars, 9, 11; WA, D/DS 22/5 LCPRS, Management Committee minutes, Board of Management, special meeting, 11 Apr. 1900; D/DS 22/10 LCPRS, meeting of ordinary members, 17 Oct. 1913.

[105] WA, D/DS 22/11 LCPRS, Management Committee minutes, Board of Management, 27 Mar. 1914; BA, HRF, ABHC/2/3, correspondence, Shaw to Cooper, 22 Dec. 1910.

[106] WA, D/DS 22/9 LCPRS, Management Committee minutes, Board of Management, adjourned meeting, 4 Jan. 1911; BA, HRF, ABHC/3/4 actuarial valuations, Review of Administrative Expenses, 16 July 1957.

[107] WA, D/DS 22/6 LCPRS, Management Committee minutes, special cases committee, 24 Aug. 1903; for a case where the failure to consult the Board resulted in payment being refused, D/DS 22/10, special cases committee, 23 June 1913.

[108] BA, HRF, ABHC/5/216 Personal Files, Shaw to Hon. Sec., 4 Sept. 1925, reporting on a round trip of 800 miles across Ireland to review some eighteen cases; WA, D/DS 22/5 LCPRS, Management Committee minutes, special cases committee, 22 July 1901.

[109] WA, D/DS 22/10 LCPRS, Management Committee minutes, Board of Management, 26 July 1912; see also D/DS 22/7, special cases committee, 23 July 1906.

In supporting existing methods of accident relief, coal-owners did not merely see them as a means of minimizing liabilities. They also offered a vehicle for promoting the moral welfare of dependants. At times, the two aims happily coincided. An overly generous, because unregulated, system of benefits would, it was feared, relieve relatives of their obligations to kin, thereby undermining a sense of family responsibility.[110] If, on such occasions, economy and morality were mutually reinforcing, supervision also assumed a less self-interested, paternalistic form. This became particularly apparent when dealing with the dependent children of deceased miners. Writing in 1927, the secretary of the Lancashire and Cheshire Society, David Shaw, regarded it as incumbent upon visitors to fill the place left by the departed father by offering children 'help and advice' over their education and choice of jobs.[111]

The moral imperative was embodied in society rules across the county. The Atherton Collieries Sick and Burial Society, for example, imposed fines on those suspected of 'any unlawful practice or evil course of life . . . or of gross or immoral conduct'.[112] A similar punishment awaited those seen in or around a public house, especially if encountered in an intoxicated state or engaged in gambling. At Rose Bridge and Douglas Bank Collieries in Wigan, all rights to benefit were forfeited in such cases. To encourage the sobriety required to hasten recovery, recipients of relief were to remain indoors between specified hours. Widows were particular subjects of moral concern and were enjoined to remain chaste and to behave 'with becoming propriety'.[113] In enforcing such injunctions, the occasional contacts provided by a network of visitors was likely to prove only sporadically effective. Members were thus required to report all breaches of rules by their fellows, often, as at Hindley Field Collieries, under threat of a fine.[114] Yet financial inducements were rarely necessary.

---

[110] Such considerations influenced the policies pursued by disaster relief funds, see BA, HRF, ABHC/2/4 circulars and cuttings, cutting from *Liverpool Daily Post* (18 Jan. 1911); ABHC/3/1 actuarial valuations, Actuarial Report on Liabilities of Fund as at 31 Dec. 1911, 4.

[111] BA, HRF, ABHC/3/11 general correspondence, Notes on the Visitation of Widows, 17 Aug. 1927, 4.

[112] WA, D/DZ A83/6 Rules of the Atherton Collieries Sick and Burial Society (Atherton, 1930), 5, par. 15.

[113] BA, HRF, ABHC/2/2 information supplied by the Lancashire and Cheshire Miners' Permanent Relief Society, Rules of the Lancashire and Cheshire Miners' Permanent Relief Society (1910), 15, par. 31; see also 17, par. 37; WA, D/DZ A83/17 Rules for the Government of the Miners' Sick and Burial Society established by the underground workmen employed at the Rose Bridge and Douglas Bank Collieries, near Wigan (Hindley, n.d.), par. 8.

[114] WA, D/DZ A83/14 Rules to be Observed by the Members of the Hindley Field Collieries Accident, Sick and Burial Society (Hindley, 1881), 6, par. 17.

In many cases, as the experience of several Pretoria widows indicates, information on individual behaviour was readily volunteered.

In 1912, the Hulton Colliery Disaster Relief Fund agreed to allow Alice C.[115] to move to south Wales to live with her aunt, despite visitors' reports which judged her 'to be rather fickle and of a changeable disposition'.[116] As in other such cases, a check on her conduct was maintained through the provision, each quarter, of a certificate. Four months later, Alice's name came before fund officials again, this time in connection with inquiries by the Glamorgan Constabulary. They were searching for a Mr Jones, a musical gentleman reputed to be 'very fond of singing in Hotels', who was thought to be living with Alice having deserted his wife and children in Pontypridd.[117] Inquiries by the police, assisted by information from neighbours, tracked the couple to Denaby Main, near Rotherham. Here, Alice had offended local sensibilities by seeking charitable relief, widely available during the Minimum Wage strike of 1912, shortly after her arrival in the town. Determined not 'to palliate cases of misconduct', Shaw recommended that all benefit payments be ended, whereupon Alice was herself abandoned, in a state of advanced pregnancy, in Treherbert.[118] Her response was to strike back at those who had exposed her in a letter to the fund chairman, grammatical lapses conveying the depth of feeling aroused:

I will . . . let them see that all the Widows is not having Public money and others is taking it up. I have not had a child nor living with a man but there is Plenty to find out about others not only about me. I have not gone to horse races, nor gone away with men for ages [?], but I have got the blame for all there is plenty worse than me receiving there money but are sly over there work. [119]

As this suggests, officials could, on occasion, rely on a ready tongue or pen to flesh out insubstantial details. In 1924, an inquiry was initiated following information from a person coyly described by Shaw as a 'friend', which alleged that a widow was associating with a married man. The woman named proved, on investigation, to be innocent of the charge.

---

[115] In this case, as in others where information of an intimate nature is given, the decision has been taken to respect the privacy of the individuals and families concerned by not disclosing names in full.

[116] BA, HRF, ABHC/5/43 Personal Files, Shaw to Hon. Sec., 2 Jan. 1912.

[117] BA, HRF, ABHC/5/43 Personal Files, Hon. Sec. to Shaw, 8 Jan. 1912; I. Edwards, Superintendent, Glamorgan Constabulary to Chief of Police, Bolton, 17 May 1912.

[118] BA, HRF, ABHC/5/43 Personal Files, Shaw to Hon. Sec., 1 and 6 June 1912; Alice to Cooper, 15 June 1912.

[119] BA, HRF, ABHC/5/43 Personal Files, Alice to Cooper, n.d.

However, another obscure authority soon located the guilty party, one Ada H. When confronted, Ada remained unrepentant and 'proceeded to say that there are others round about doing the same as she had been doing, and she mentioned the name of Mrs Albert H[.], . . . and then added quickly "but I mustn't say anymore" '.[120] Unfortunately for Ada, not all were as reticent as she. When the decision to terminate benefits was challenged, officials were able to gather evidence on her irregular behaviour from, among others, relatives of the wronged wife and their neighbours. The catalogue of her misdemeanours included being drunk at Bolton's New Year Fair, the acquisition of a piano, which, local wisdom had it, she was unable to afford, and a week's absence from work without permission during Blackpool's Carnival week of 1923. It sufficed to persuade the arbitration panel which heard her appeal to confirm the original order ending all entitlement to benefit.[121] Ada's behaviour, in challenging the integrity of family life appears to have offended against the moral sensibilities of the neighbourhood, thus easing the flow of information on her activities.

For Ada's lover, a further factor which enhanced her charms was her regular income of 36s. a week from compensation, society, and relief fund sources combined.[122] The comparative generosity of payments to Pretoria dependants, especially when compared to the amounts paid out in individual fatality cases, provided an additional source of friction locally. Prior to the disaster, a widower James Schofield had placed his two sons, aged 7 and 10, with an uncle and aunt in Daubhill. When, on the father's death, 21s. a week became payable on the boys' behalf, competition to care for them intensified. Three maternal aunts travelled from Rotherham to press their claims at the colliery's offices in Chequerbent. Another aunt from Leigh emphasized her credentials by contrasting her husband's respectable status as a mule-spinner with what she described as the 'very intemperate habits' of the boys' guardians.[123] Her observation struck a chord with Shaw, who, on the basis of 'enquiries in the Street and statements made by neighbours', reported that

Both Mr and Mrs P[.] drink, and each month when P[.] obtains the Compensation money from the Court, he has a day off, does not get home till late at night, and

---

[120] BA, HRF, ABHC/5/136 Personal Files, Shaw to Hon. Sec., 3 and 19 June 1924.
[121] BA, HRF, ABHC/5/136 Personal Files, pencilled notes, 20 June 1924, 2 June 1925.
[122] BA, HRF, ABHC/5/136 Personal Files, Compensation statement; pencilled note, 20 June 1924.
[123] BA, HRF, ABHC/5/267 Personal Files, Compensation statement; Emma Latham to Cooper, 14 Feb. 1911; Shaw to Cooper, 16 Feb. 1911.

then very intoxicated . . . [he is] a man of a peculiarly vile tongue and the language that is used in the home is such that it is most undesirable the boys should live there.[124]

Although a visit by the fund chairman discovered no such problems, Shaw continued to press his case, citing reports from neighbours that the couple had been drunk on the night following the inspection. The testimony of school attendance officers was sought in an attempt to reconcile such discrepancies. Their report revealed nothing untoward regarding the guardians' behaviour.[125] At this distance, it is impossible to account, with any certainty, for the hostility obviously felt towards the couple. It can, however, be suggested that the Ps, in receiving a high and regular income, were seen to be profiting from providing the kind of family assistance which, more often than not, went unrewarded. In such circumstances, any personal indulgence aroused suspicions that money from the fund was being misused.

Another allegation involving the ill-treatment of children reaped unanticipated results. In 1912, Shaw received an anonymous letter accusing the widow Tunstall of neglecting her six offspring. Inquiries failed to substantiate the charge. However, on visiting Kate E., another Pretoria widow suspected of penning the original letter, Shaw discovered her in bed in the kitchen, nursing a three-day-old illegitimate child, a discovery which confirmed earlier rumours as to her behaviour.[126]

It must be stressed that, when viewed in the aggregate, such cases were uncommon. Of almost 1,500 widows in receipt of society benefits between 1917 and 1931, only twenty had payments terminated due to lapses from 'becoming propriety'.[127] Nevertheless, the tensions within the locality which such cases exposed surfaced on a number of occasions through the period, even at times of economic and political crisis, when the need for unity appeared paramount. During the 1921 coal strike, Poor Law authorities in Wigan and Leigh advanced loans to miners' families. Following the settlement of the dispute, the Leigh guardians received a number of anonymous letters naming recipients of relief who were thought to be undeserving.[128]

[124] BA, HRF, ABHC/5/267 Personal Files, Shaw to Hon. Sec., 10 Apr. 1913.
[125] BA, HRF, ABHC/5/267 Personal Files, Hon. Sec. to Shaw, 14 Apr.; Shaw to Hon. Sec., 15 Apr.; Director of Education to Hon. Sec., 16 June 1913.
[126] BA, HRF, ABHC/5/306 Personal Files, Shaw to Hon. Sec., Jan. 1912; ABHC/5/87 Personal Files, Shaw to Hon. Sec., 6 Mar. 1912.
[127] WA, D/DS 22 LCPRS, widows valuation book, 1917–31.
[128] *BJG* (29 Apr. 1921), 6; (3 June 1921), 6.

The development of accident relief administration, especially in the period from 1897, casts light on two important themes: the nature of relations within the coal industry; and the texture of life in predominantly working-class urban neighbourhoods. On the first, contrary to the claims of Federation officials, existing methods of relief served to moderate rather than to exacerbate any tendency towards conflict in mining districts. Institutions initially founded on compulsion survived the period through co-operation and consent. Miners came to acknowledge the advantages of a system which offered high and secure returns on limited contributions, while owners recognized in the elaborate information networks mobilized by societies the most effective guarantee against demoralization. To that extent, Campbell's vision of a 'friendly union' was realized. Yet the nature of that union requires more extended consideration. It rested primarily on a coincidence of separate interests. Differences continued to surface through the period, as in 1916, when agency delegates pressed for a revision of rules to allow benefits to be paid in cases of industrial disease.[129] Calculations of mutual self-interest ensured, however, that such problems rarely resulted in breakdown. In assisting or, at times, confusing the work of society officials, neighbourhoods acted in defence of their own precepts, punishing actual or perceived instances of child neglect, sexual promiscuity, or the misappropriation of funds to which all had contributed. Those suspected of deviating from accepted behavioural norms could find themselves isolated and ostracized, leaving them little option but to leave the immediate area. An attempt to trace those widows disqualified from receiving benefits encountered fundamental obstacles. As Shaw reported, 'it is very difficult to get satisfactory information on some of them. One has to be very careful, and I also found that people are very chary about giving information in reply to my inquiries'.[130] If anything, such cases reveal the limited and conditional nature of social relationships in densely populated working-class districts. 'Neighbourliness', which at times provided a medium for mutual assistance, was also hedged around with qualifications, one of which was the need to conform to a common moral standard. Physical proximity ensured a high degree of casual sociability, but could discourage the development of deeper attachments. The distinction which many observed between neighbours and friends, the latter being far fewer in

[129] WA, D/DS 22/12 LCPRS, Management Committee minutes, Board of Management, 24 Mar. 1916.
[130] BA, HRF, ABHC/3/11 general correspondence, Shaw to Hon. Sec., 17 June 1929.

number, indicates that the mutuality, which informs ideas of community, had severe limitations.[131] The often shallow nature of sociability may also be detected in attitudes to relief administration, where calculations of efficiency and effectiveness, measuring benefits paid against costs incurred, ranked above the quest for democratic control. In such circumstances, the necessity for co-operating with employers was accepted. Formal rank-and-file participation in society affairs remained limited in extent, a trait evident also in the broader range of working-class savings institutions active in this period.

III

Even among miners, efforts at saving went considerably beyond occupationally specific funds. Across the coalfield, an extensive network of provident organizations was sustained, sufficient to call into question the belief, expressed by H. S. Jevons, that workers of 'superior intelligence and morale' had been drawn to the textile and skilled engineering trades, leaving an underground labour force among which a considerable minority remained devoted to 'rabbit-coursing, gambling, intemperance, and other exciting forms of pleasure'.[132] Compensation statements relating to Pretoria victims help to verify the general point. These indicate that at least 151 of the 286 households affected by the disaster made provision against the loss of a breadwinner which went beyond payments to the permanent relief society. Even then, however, the returns must be judged less than complete. For example, no savings are recorded for eight victims who are known to have belonged to the Independent Order of Rechabites' No. 7 Bolton Adult and Juvenile District. A similar omission applies to seven members of the 'Loyal Brothers Friend' Lodge of the Manchester Unity of Oddfellows and to two miners who subscribed to the Wigan and District Society.[133] If these cases are added, then the

---

[131] McKibbin, *Classes and Cultures*, 179–88; J. Bourke, *Working-Class Cultures in Britain* (1994), 138–43, 159; B. Harrison, 'Class and Gender in Modern British Labour History', *Past and Present*, 124 (Aug. 1989), 142–4.

[132] Jevons, *British Coal Trade*, 71, 627.

[133] BA, HRF, ABHC/5/1–344 Personal Files, Compensation statements; MRL, HRF, M122/2/2 Manchester Committee, circulars and correspondence, statistical returns; Westhoughton Public Library, Pretoria Pit Disaster Pamphlet Box Independent Order of Rechabites, Bolton Adult and Juvenile District, No. 7. In Memoriam (Bolton, 1911). Twenty-four members of the Order's Westhoughton and Primrose Tents were lost in the explosion; Westhoughton Public Library, Memorial Plaque Manchester Unity of Oddfellows, 'Loyal Brothers Friend' Lodge, No. 1160.

number seeking some insurance against interruptions to earnings is raised to 168. Remaining gaps in the evidence mean that even this figure must be regarded as provisional.

Of greater moment than the relative numbers of savers and non-savers is the variety of institutions utilized. In all, the statements make reference to forty-four separate organizations. In addition to the Oddfellows and the Rechabites, a third friendly society, the Independent Order of Foresters, lost three members in the disaster. Industrial assurance companies were also affected, the Prudential paying out on twenty policies, the Refuge on nine, and the Royal Liver on eight. Local organizations also encouraged the propensity to save. Included among these were societies based on Sunday schools and informal clubs run from pubs.[134] Nor were these institutions mutually exclusive. Individual households saved with a variety of agencies. Roland E.'s widow received £58 in all from a combination of the Independent Order of Foresters, and the Prudential and Refuge Assurance Companies, while both permanent relief societies, the Prudential, and a burial club based at 'The King's Arms' public house paid to the family of David Grundy.[135] Thrift was capable of comprehending the abstinence of the Rechabites and the easy sociability of the beer shop.

Institutional diversity mirrored, to some degree, the various motives behind thrift. As well as fulfilling a preventive purpose, savings also funded consumption. This distinction, so hard and fast in theory, tended to blur in reality. A case in point is provided by the 'going away' clubs, present in most cotton towns through the period. Originally established to fund annual holidays during Wakes or Fair weeks, clubs operated in a variety of settings, from churches and workplaces to the Co-op. In each, the method of saving was the same: weekly contributions were collected and invested, often in local savings banks, accumulating interest over the year.[136] Yet the money raised did more than merely finance the annual 'blow' at the seaside. It also satisfied more immediately pressing needs, being used by some to replenish wardrobes, enabling at least an outward appearance of respectability to be maintained. Alternatively, at times of particular difficulty, club funds acted as stores of capital, which could be drawn on at short notice. For much of this period, the amounts distributed each year by individual clubs were published in the local press,

---

[134] BA, HRF, ABHC/5/1–344 Personal Files, Compensation statements.
[135] BA, HRF, ABHC/5/86, 116 Personal Files, Compensation statements.
[136] Schulze-Gaevernitz, *Cotton Trade in England*, 198; *BJG* (26 June 1908), 2; (27 June 1924), 9; (12 Aug. 1927), 5.

enabling the growth of prosperity across the cotton sector to be charted. In Bolton alone, by the mid-1920s, almost £300,000 was paid out on the weekend prior to the town's annual June holiday.[137] The onset of industrial depression, however, signalled a reversal, both in the amounts distributed and in the number of clubs making returns to the press. Those still active were reluctant to broadcast evidence of financial difficulty, while others had folded, as members diverted their savings to larger clubs, capable of generating higher interest earnings.[138]

The readiness with which funds were transferred between agencies is indicative of the pragmatism underlying working-class thrift, a fact also reflected in the failure adequately to regulate club affairs. Once elected, collectors enjoyed almost complete discretion over the disposal of funds. As a result, cases of misappropriation recurred through the period. The behaviour of one collector, a stripper and grinder at Barlow and Jones, Ltd, who used some of his colleagues' savings to gamble at the dog track, was not unique. In 1926, the firm of Greenhalgh and Shaw, Ltd agreed to make good £80 lost from club accounts through peculation. The lack of any effective audit of 'going away' funds led the defence counsel in another such case to comment on 'the absence of supervision and entire disregard of the workpeople of their own interest in connexion with the contributions'.[139] Although exaggerated, such criticisms identified, in the limited extent of popular participation, a feature common to many savings institutions in this period.

This also helps to account for the decline of another strand of preventive thrift, the sick and burial societies associated with places of worship. Among the most venerable of savings organizations, church societies traced their origins to early nineteenth-century concern over the moral implications of industrial and urban development. That linked to Bolton's parish church dated back to 1816. Here, membership was open to all Sunday school scholars from the age of 9. Beyond school age, adherents could continue to contribute as 'out members', providing regular attendance at Sunday worship was maintained. As with colliery accident relief, members of the local élite were actively involved in society administration. Incumbent ministers filled the office of president, while contributions were collected by teachers, a number of whom were major

---

[137] *BJG* (19 June 1925), 6.

[138] *BJG* (20 June 1930), 8; (17 June 1932), 6; for the relocation of savings among clubs in Oldham, see *TW* 1 (24 Aug. 1928), 710.

[139] *BJG* (12 Aug. 1927), 5, this involved the secretary of a club who used the proceeds to buy a house and furnishings in Todmorden; see also *BJG* (25 June 1926), 9; (24 June 1932), 8.

employers in the district. Despite the proliferation of self-help institutions, church societies experienced consistent, if modest, growth through the nineteenth century, so that by 1911 membership of the Bolton and District Federation of Sunday School Sick Societies stood in excess of 5,000.[140] From that date, however, decline was rapid. Change was precipitated by the passage of the National Insurance Act. Within twelve months, some eight societies across Bolton had opted to disband, a decision ratified in each case by a vote of at least five-sixths of all members. In many cases, such a course was preferred to absorption within a larger, more anonymous approved society. In others, the decision followed a period of financial difficulty under the Act, during which the amounts paid out in benefits comfortably exceeded the income from subscriptions. Among those deciding to cease operations were societies attached to All Saints' church, and St Paul's church, Deansgate; both divided their funds among their respective members.[141] Where societies survived, they often did so only with greatly reduced memberships. In twenty years from 1912, the numbers subscribing to the Bolton Parish Church Society more than halved, from 360 to 167.[142]

If the development of this particular form of mutuality may be seen to reflect the central place of religion in nineteenth-century Lancashire, its decline should not be taken as evidence of waning denominational allegiances. St Paul's church, for one, retained a reputation for vigorous evangelism for much of this period, sustained in part by energetic, if ultimately futile, attempts to convert Bolton's Irish Catholic population to Protestantism.[143] Of greater moment in determining the fate of each society was the social context within which they operated. Church societies thus flourished longest in small, compact townships such as Turton and Deane, where alternative savings agencies were less numerous and where, it may be suggested, the informal neighbourhood controls which assisted the work of the permanent relief societies operated most effectually to check the growth in liabilities. Decline was most marked among churches in central Bolton, whose more dispersed congregations made the work of

---

[140] BA, FS/1/48 *Rules of the Bolton Parish Church Sunday School Sick Society* (Bolton, 1891), 3–6; FS/1/62 *The One-Hundred and Sixteenth Report (for the Year 1931) of the Bolton Parish Church Sunday School Sick Society* (Bolton, 1932), 1.

[141] *BJG* (21 Feb. 1913), 11, for the vote to dissolve Horwich Parish Church Sick and Burial Society; *BJG* (23 Jan. 1914), 9 (St Paul's, Deansgate); *BJG* (20 Feb. 1914), 7 (All Saints').

[142] BA, FS/1/54 *Ninety Eighth Report (for the Year 1913) of the Bolton Parish Church Sunday School Sick Society* (Bolton, 1914), 3; FS/1/62 *One-Hundred and Sixteenth Report*, 3.

[143] *BJG* (9 Jan. 1920), 5.

surveillance more complicated.[144] Even here, exceptions to the general trend could be found. Where denominational and social identities coalesced, church-based thrift organizations continued to thrive. This, at least, may be inferred from the comparative success of Bolton's Catholic Burial Collecting Society into the 1930s.[145]

The wider forces at work to undermine ideals of mutuality were also reflected in the experience of friendly society orders through the period. As with the church societies, the impact of National Insurance legislation was profound, many of the major affiliated orders reporting sustained falls in membership from 1911. Although the Bolton Unity of Oddfellows reported growth in Scotland, this was not sufficient to offset losses elsewhere. The net effect was to leave the order with a declining and ageing membership. By 1932, 25 per cent of subscribers were eligible for old age pensions, a problem to which a delegate at the Unity's centenary celebrations essayed a drastic solution: 'Send 'em down to Yorkshire, and they won't live so long'.[146] Sickness benefits were increasingly transformed into permanent charges on society accounts, becoming, in effect, second pensions. The increased financial burden forced many smaller fraternities to disband. After losing one-third of its members over fifteen years, the Birtenshaw Friendly Society, based in the Eagley district of Bolton, voted in 1927 to cease operations.[147]

The roots of such problems extended back beyond 1911 and could, in large part, be traced to the societies' foundations as adult male fraternities, whose meetings were based in public houses. The obstacle which this posed to continued growth became clear with the onset of National Insurance. Society officials were convinced of the need to develop alternative centres for lodge activity if new, particularly female, members were to be recruited. The Bolton Unity looked to local Sunday schools to fill this void, with the result that, in the first twelve months under the Act, sixteen all-female lodges were founded.[148] Nevertheless, change was only embraced with reluctance. Officials remained concerned to defend fraternal traditions, embodied in society regalia and the obscure rituals attending membership initiations, in the belief that only by such means could the moral benefits of mutual self-help be assured. The president of the Bolton Unity had thus warned that 'unless they could devise some means

---

[144] *BJG* (30 Jan. 1914), 11; (13 Feb. 1914), 7; (5 Dec. 1919), 5.

[145] *BJG* (24 Mar. 1932), 11.

[146] *BJG* (2 Sept. 1932), 10; for the trend more generally, see Johnson, *Saving and Spending*, 50–3, table 3.1.   [147] *BJG* (25 Feb. 1927), 9; (29 May 1931), 6.

[148] *Bolton Unity Magazine* (Apr. 1912), 131; (Aug. 1912), 239; (Oct. 1912), 8, 16.

of getting the men into their lodge rooms, . . . they would be in danger of losing what he felt to be a very real advantage to them in their work, which was the point of personal contact with many of their members.'[149] As this suggests, reality was, even at that date, somewhat at variance with fraternal aspirations. Most members of the Bolton Unity appear to have maintained a limited, financial link with the order. Wives were reported frequently to take it 'upon themselves to bring their husbands' contributions each lodge night'.[150] Even the prospect of National Insurance failed to excite a deeper interest in society affairs. Meetings called to consider the Unity's future under the Act drew thin attendances.[151] As later national surveys would confirm, participation in society affairs was confined to a small active minority.[152] The advance of impersonal forms of saving at the expense of the democratic mutuality of church sick and friendly societies was thus founded on a working-class culture which saw thrift in immediately practical rather than broadly moral terms.

A similar outlook shaped the growth of retail Co-operation through the period. A significant presence in most Lancastrian towns by 1900, the movement prospered, as had the permanent relief societies, by easing the savings process, enabling funds to accumulate through the everyday practice of shopping. In its fifth decade of operations, the Great and Little Bolton Society, trading through forty-six separate outlets, claimed 32,000 members, sufficient, if evenly spread, to cover 75 per cent of households across the borough. Autonomous societies also flourished in neighbouring townships.[153] Growth in colliery districts proved slower, until the introduction of weekly wage payments and the secular advance in living standards in the later decades of the nineteenth century provided a more secure foundation for expansion. By 1902, over half the families in Wigan were thought to have accounts in the local Equitable Co-operative Society.[154]

---

[149] *Bolton Unity Magazine* (Oct. 1911), 24–5; see also Mass-Observation, *The Pub and the People: A Worktown Study* (1943), 275–82.

[150] *Bolton Unity Magazine* (Aug. 1912), 254.

[151] *Bolton Unity Magazine* (Feb. 1912), 105–8.

[152] Johnson, *Saving and Spending*, 67–8.

[153] F. W. Peaples, *History of the Great and Little Bolton Co-operative Society, Ltd* (Bolton, 1909), 295, 317; *Parl. Papers 1912–13*, cxi (6258), Census of England and Wales, 1911. I. Administrative Areas, table 3; *Parl. Papers 1901*, lxxiv (698), Board of Trade (Labour Department): Report on Workmen's Co-operative Societies in the United Kingdom, 90, 92.

[154] J. Brown, *Wigan Welfare: The Jubilee History of the Wigan and District Equitable Co-operative Society, Ltd* (Wigan, 1939), 14, 23–6; a discussion of the factors behind the more general geographical spread of Co-operation can be found in M. Purvis, 'Nineteenth-Century Co-operative Retailing in England and Wales' (Oxford Univ. D.Phil. thesis, 1987),

If the predominantly working-class nature of Co-operative membership is not in doubt, the movement's precise social reach is more open to
question. In evidence before the Royal Commission on Labour in 1893,
John Mitchell, chairman of the Co-operative Wholesale Society, cited
returns which indicated that only 2 per cent of members were in receipt
of incomes which rendered them liable to assessment for payment of
income tax. However, the 1905 Board of Trade survey of working-class
rents, housing, and retail prices suggested that the movement in Bolton
was 'composed of better class workmen or of the lower-middle class'.[155]
Similarly, Allen Clarke placed Co-operators in the second of the three
'castes' into which he divided Lancastrian society, comprising 'the best-
paid clerks, book-keepers, managers, and the better sort of working
folks'.[156] Yet, as the experience of the Bolton Society suggests, membership extended considerably beyond a financially secure minority. Despite
recession in leading industrial sectors, share capital and membership
showed consistent net growth through the 1920s, so that by 1930 the latter, at 55,000, was some 71 per cent above the level of 1904. Although the
value of transactions declined in the twelve months that followed, this
was more than accounted for by a 10 per cent fall in prices.[157] In Wigan,
by contrast, where miners accounted for half of all society members, economic fluctuations exerted a more powerful influence over savings trends.
Membership of the Wigan and District Society fell by a quarter over ten
years from 1920, while major disputes in 1921 and 1926 led to substantial
withdrawals of share capital. The stability secured through marketing and
quota arrangements restored the impetus to growth from the later 1920s,
to the extent that the previous membership peak of 10,300, achieved in
the immediate post-war boom, was exceeded in 1936.[158]

Expansion fuelled confidence in the movement's broader aims. As
Duncan McInnes of the CWS explained to the annual meeting of the
Great and Little Bolton Society in 1908, the aspirations of Co-operation

i, 174–224; and id., 'The Development of Co-operative Retailing in England and Wales,
1851–1901: A Geographical Study', *Journal of Historical Geography*, 16 (1990), 314–31; a
brief overview of the movement in Lancashire is provided in J. Turnbull and J. Southern,
More than Just a Shop: A History of the Co-op in Lancashire (Preston, 1995), 6–12.

[155] *Parl. Papers 1908*, cvii (3864), Report of an Enquiry by the Board of Trade into
Working Class Rents, Housing and Retail Prices, 102; *Parl. Papers 1893–4*, xxxix, pt. I
(7063–I), RC on Labour: Minutes of Evidence. Representatives of Co-operative Societies
and of Various Movements, and of Public Officials, q. 43.

[156] Clarke, *Effects of the Factory System*, 33.

[157] Peaples, *History*, 294, 588; *BJG* (27 Feb. 1931), 6; (26 Feb. 1932), 6.

[158] *WO* (3 Oct. 1908), 3; Brown, *Wigan Welfare*, 27.

went beyond mere financial security. They comprehended a fundamental moral and social reformation, which, by guaranteeing workers an equitable share in 'the product of their labour', would provide a future in which, 'free from anxiety against old age and its attendant ailments, their lives would be very much brighter and happier, and they would engage in their daily labour with more zest and greater hopefulness.'[159] This regenerative vision was shared by many, including the ILPer and cardroom activist, Cissy Foley. Others, however, were more sceptical. For Allen Clarke, retail Co-operation was but another manifestation of the 'collective selfishness' of factory society. It was a movement concerned to promote the sectional interests of a particular 'class', with all the consequences for social division and exclusivity which, for Clarke at least, that term implied.[160] The Fabian William Clarke agreed that, under Co-operation as it had developed, Owenite ideals had lost out to the kind of commercial calculation characteristic of joint-stock capitalism. As with shareholders, society members were primarily engaged in '"divvy" hunting'.[161] Co-operative propagandists were increasingly obliged to acknowledge that the latter observation contained more than a grain of truth. The growth of Co-operation in Bolton had been greatly facilitated by the decision, taken in the 1880s, to raise the level of the dividend. Equally, in common with societies elsewhere, the organizations in Bolton and Wigan raided reserves to maintain the dividend in poor trading years.[162]

Over time, society officials came to express increasing unease at the extent to which Co-operation's moral aspirations had given way to more immediate material concerns. Attempts to realize the movement's social potential, by constructing a Co-operative 'counter-culture', enjoyed only fitful success. Although the Women's Co-operative Guild and a Co-operative Choral Union flourished in Bolton, a proposed scholarship scheme to enable members' children to proceed to secondary school and a debating society drew limited support, giving rise to one of the few qualifying passages in Peaples's otherwise laudatory narrative. Similarly, J. R. Clynes recalled the functional uses to which Co-operative facilities were put in Oldham. While he used the society's library to

---

[159] Peaples, *History*, 341–2.

[160] A. Foley, *A Bolton Childhood* (Manchester, 1973), 44–6; Clarke, *Effects of the Factory System*, 147; in the language of popular radicalism, in which tradition Clarke can be placed, 'class' was often identified with the particular interests of minority groups, see P. Joyce, *Visions of the People* (Cambridge, 1991), 67–8.

[161] W. Clarke, 'Industrial', in G. B. Shaw (ed.), *Fabian Essays in Socialism* (1889), 88.

[162] Peaples, *History*, 230, 304; Brown, *Wigan Welfare*, 45; Johnson, *Saving and Spending*, 128.

broaden his knowledge of Carlyle, Emerson, and Ruskin, his contemporaries scoured the job advertisements in local newspapers.[163] As with the friendly societies, the rhetoric of mutuality obscured a more prosaic reality: the degree to which the propensity for thrift was informed more by material than by moral calculations. The broad impression conveyed by this necessarily brief survey of working-class savings institutions is thus confirmed. Although expressive of class identity, both in the forms it took and in the motives which inspired it, thrift was essentially a vehicle for individual rather than collective advance.

IV

The act of saving had cultural as well as material significance. It touched working-class life at many points: in mill and mine; in church and chapel; in pub, street, and Co-operative store. In the process, it threw crucial light on the values and beliefs, as well as the economic realities, underpinning life in densely populated urban neighbourhoods. This applied with particular force to the forms of saving which emerged in the coal and cotton industries in this period. Despite the encouragement to operative investment offered by the spread of joint-stock organization in textiles, few workers appeared anxious to acquire mill stock. Extensive purchases were, for the most part, confined to brief periods of abnormal prosperity and were made in anticipation of immediate, speculative returns. A sustained commitment remained most likely where conventional sources of venture capital were lacking. Operatives proved adept at playing the market for their own ends. To that extent, even the behaviour of shareholders was consistent with labour mistrust of limited-liability capital. Support for colliery accident relief societies also tended to centre on their utility in combining actuarial security with comparatively generous levels of benefit, while accommodating high rates of labour turnover. In both cases, the practice of thrift confirms the survival of a distinctive, if predominantly functional outlook.

Yet such expressions of a separate class interest failed to provide the basis from which a collective sense of identity could be mobilized. In both coal and cotton, the conventions of capitalist organization were broadly accepted. Township experiments in company promotion maintained the

---

[163] *BJG* (19 Jan. 1923), 5; (26 Feb. 1926), 6; Peaples, *History*, 579–83; J. R. Clynes, *Memoirs*, i (1937), 50; 'The Labour Party and the Books that Helped to Make it', *Review of Reviews*, 33 (June 1906), 572.

separation of ownership and control, in the belief that this arrangement offered the best guarantee of commercial effectiveness. A similar perception endorsed owners' involvement in colliery accident relief. Yet, although prepared to utilize the institutions of capitalism, workers proved themselves capable of establishing and sustaining autonomous organizations. Even here, however, the sense of attachment encouraged by friendly society or Co-operative membership remained limited in extent. For the majority, their stake in society lodge or Co-operative store rarely extended beyond the narrowly financial. The simple act of accumulation crowded out broader mutual ideals. Explicitly commercial forms of thrift thus came to prosper, to the extent that the insurance agent assumed an importance in working-class life denied the friendly society official.

The practice of thrift also served to expose important economic and cultural divisions which lay at the heart of the working-class experience. The largely unfounded but stubbornly persistent belief that share purchases bestowed an unfair advantage in the search for work indicates the ease with which friction could develop in a competitive labour market. Similarly, the durable links between the saving habit and places of worship testify to the continued salience of denominational allegiances in Lancastrian society in the early twentieth century. Perhaps of greater importance, the work of the permanent relief society reveals the degree to which co-operative sociability, often seen as a central characteristic of working-class identity, was sharply limited in practice. Neighbours acted promptly to punish examples of 'deviant' behaviour, assisting the work of an organization administered jointly with employers and managers. Sociability, as practised in working-class neighbourhoods, was never easy and remained bounded by mutually understood constraints.

In pursuing its themes, this chapter has been concerned with the outward forms of thrift. Yet their precise role, whether ameliorating distress or facilitating consumption, was determined within the context of the family economy. Household structures and kinship relations crucially determined the capacity to save and the standard of living that was attainable. It is to these subjects, and their implications for an understanding of working-class society more generally, that the next chapter will turn.

7

A Bond of Necessity? The Working-Class Family, 1880–1930

The working-class family was a subject of recurrent concern through the nineteenth century. Seen by contemporaries as one of the essential building blocks of a morally healthy society, it had been subject to fundamental stresses as a consequence of the structural changes associated with industrialization. With the rise of factory industry, the household was seen no longer to function as a unit of production, its members being obliged to seek work on an individual basis outside the home. The result, according to commentators as diverse as Engels and Disraeli, was a weakening of kinship ties and a separation of gender roles which discouraged close attachments between husband and wife.[1] Such perceptions persisted into the later nineteenth century and beyond. The absence of any semblance of settled family life implied the kind of dysfunctional existence which Charles Booth observed among the lowest class of London poor. Yet such problems were not confined to those living on the margins of 'respectable' society. An absence of companionate relationships was also noted among Rowntree's Class D, a category which comprehended the majority of working-class families in York and among which any poverty was attributable solely to imprudent expenditure, and among the poor of Lambeth surveyed by Maud Pember Reeves between 1909 and 1913.[2]

Historical investigation has, to an extent, amended such pessimism by stressing instead the working-class family's durability and capacity to respond to and accommodate structural change. Far from undermining the kinship tie, the separation of home and work under industrial capitalism had the effect, it is argued, of consolidating relationships within the

---

[1] F. Engels, *The Origin of the Family, Private Property and the State* (Peking edn., 1978), 62–5, 95; B. Disraeli, *Sybil or The Two Nations* (Oxford edn., 1981), 87–8, 113–18; for contemporary comment on family life in an industrialized setting more generally, see H. Bosanquet, *The Family* (1906), 222–4, 337–8.
[2] C. Booth, 'The Inhabitants of Tower Hamlets (School Board Division), their Condition and Occupations', *Journal of the Royal Statistical Society*, 50 (1887), 329, 334–5; B. S. Rowntree, *Poverty* (1902 edn.), 73–9; M. Pember Reeves, *Round about a Pound a Week* (1979 repr.), 155.

nuclear household. Children, rather than departing at an early age, remained under the parental roof at least until the attainment of financial independence in early adulthood. At the same time, the greater intensity of industrial work shortened active careers, enforcing a lengthy period of dependence in old age. Family unity thus rested on a sense of mutual dependence, enforced by recurrent crises. This is a view of domestic life advanced most forcefully by Michael Anderson in his study of mid-nineteenth-century Preston, from which he is drawn to conclude that 'family and kinship relationships tended to have strong short-run instrumental overtones of a calculative kind'.[3] The weight given to individual necessity by such interpretations equates family relationships with the limited and conditional mutuality evident between neighbours. More recently, however, an alternative view has been proposed by Marguerite Dupree. Drawing on evidence from the Staffordshire Potteries in the middle decades of the century, she argues that family relationships, which often encompassed non-resident kin, cannot be understood in purely utilitarian terms. Assistance was often provided with no prospect, immediate or long-term, of reciprocation.[4] Both Anderson and Dupree base their arguments substantially on the relevant Census returns. In the absence of such data for much of the period under review here, insights into the quality and dynamics of family relationships in a mature industrial society are sought through the records of colliery disaster relief funds, in particular that set up in the wake of the Pretoria explosion of 1910. A central concern of fund administration, maintained throughout its six decades of operation, was to promote a continuing sense of family responsibility among those receiving relief.[5] This, it was believed, would best be achieved by ensuring that assistance, where provided, would not relieve kin of their obligations to family members. In pursuit of this policy, fund officials maintained a close supervision over all dependants. The information thereby gathered enables the texture of family life to be recaptured in some detail.

[3] M. Anderson, *Family Structure in Nineteenth Century Lancashire* (Cambridge, 1971), 171, 111–61; id., 'Sociological History and the Working-Class Family', *Social History*, 1–2 (1976–7), 326–7; see also L. Stone, *The Family, Sex and Marriage in England, 1500–1800* (Harmondsworth edn., 1979), 417–19; R. Wall, 'The Age at Leaving Home', *Journal of Family History*, 3 (1978), 182, 192.

[4] M. W. Dupree, *Family Structure in the Staffordshire Potteries, 1840–1880* (Oxford, 1995), esp. 344–5.

[5] For the final winding up of the fund, BA, HRF, ABHC/1/7 General Committee minutes, Annual Meeting, 28 Jan. 1971; ABHC/1/12, Special Sub-committee for the purpose of considering as to how the estimated surplus can best be dealt with, Memorandum by D. A. Hoggins, hon. sec., to members of Sub-committee, 12 June 1975.

As the provision of assistance within families was crucially determined by material circumstances, the fund was also anxious to gain a close understanding of family incomes and the relative contributions of household members. In assessing the latter, important light is thrown on the standard of living attained by families through the period, a point of broader significance given Lancashire's leading role in the emergence of popular commercial leisure forms, more especially holiday-making and spectator sports.[6] Yet although such developments provide evidence of significant levels of material prosperity, the shadow of poverty was never wholly absent. Family circumstances were subject to marked variations over the life cycle and over time, never more so than in a period of staple industrial decline. The ways in which families responded to such changes are clearly caught through the work of the fund. Limitations remain, however. The fund's evidence is, in large measure occupationally specific. The income profiles generated reflect the particular circumstances of work underground, where the absence of significant wage inequalities might be expected to enhance the importance of supplementary earnings to a household's well-being. In other trades, such as spinning and carding, the prinicipal breadwinner's wage would be crucial. The contrast emerges most clearly when responses to economic change are examined. In the process, important insights are offered into the broader implications of workplace privilege and skilled status.

The final section of the chapter examines the experience of women. The growing functional disparity between economic and family structures, brought about by industrialization, had particular repercussions for the roles of wives and mothers. Involvement in paid work was seen to remove them from their 'natural' sphere of interest, the home, giving rise to moral concern and justifying moves to consolidate the male breadwinner wage norm.[7] Over the later decades of the nineteenth century, the progressive exclusion of married women from paid employment beyond

---

[6] J. K. Walton, *The Blackpool Landlady: A Social History* (Manchester, 1978), 33; id., *The English Seaside Resort: A Social History, 1750–1914* (Leicester, 1983), 32; R. W. Lewis, 'The Genesis of Professional Football: Bolton–Blackburn–Darwen, the Centre of Innovation, 1878–85', *International Journal of the History of Sport*, 14/1 (Apr., 1997), 21–54.

[7] F. Engels, *The Condition of the Working Class* (1969 repr.), 171; E. S. Chesser, 'The Lancashire Operative: Women's Work in the Factory and the Home', *National Review* 54 (1909–10), 687; P. E. Moulder, 'How Working-Women Exist', *Chambers' Journal*, 6th ser. 6 (1903), 277; D. Levine, 'Industrialization and the Proletarian Family in England', *Past and Present*, 107 (May 1985), 168–203; W. Seccombe, 'Patriarchy Stabilized: The Construction of the Male Breadwinner Wage Norm in Nineteenth-Century Britain', *Social History*, 11 (1986), 53–96.

the home confirmed the emergence of a new domestic equilibrium, based on an explicit segmentation of roles: the male as earner and provider; the female as carer and household manager. The extent to which women acquiesced in this trend has been much debated. Here again, the evidence of the Pretoria fund provides important clues. From 1910, widows supported by the fund gained a financial independence denied most working-class women. The uses to which this independence was put has much to tell us about both the female outlook and the nature of marital relationships, the very core of concern over working-class family life in this period.

I

In its attention to family unity, the administration of colliery disaster relief had much in common with the principles guiding the provision of other forms of institutional assistance. The restrictions placed on outdoor relief to long-term, elderly dependants from the 1870s was in large measure designed to stimulate help from within the family. Equally, awards made under the Workmen's Compensation Acts of 1897 and 1906 were calculated on the assumption that they would act as 'a common family fund', discouraging the emergence of separate interests between individuals.[8] For disaster relief funds, the uncertainty of public response complicated the pursuit of this ideal. Appeals gained varying levels of support, leaving some funds with insufficient resources to meet their obligations, while others were faced with a superfluity of means.[9] The one created as many problems as the other, as the experience of the Pretoria fund demonstrated. The appeal in the wake of the explosion specified a minimum requirement of £50,000, based on an average of three dependants for each victim. In the event, the financial target was comfortably exceeded. On the publication of the final subscription list in March 1912,

---

[8] J. S. Quadagno, *Aging in Early Industrial Society* (New York, 1982), 101–2; BA, HRF, ABHC/2/4, circulars and cuttings, cutting from *Bolton Chronicle* (26 Feb. 1911); see also J. Stevenson, *British Society, 1914–45* (Harmondsworth, 1984), 276–8; E. M. Roberts, 'The Working-Class Extended Family: Functions and Attitudes, 1890–1940', *Oral History*, 12/1 (1984), 50.

[9] *Parl. Papers 1924–5*, xxiii (155) Colliery Accident Funds (Great Britain): Return to an Order of the Honourable The House of Commons, dated 22 July 1925; the problem of uneven response led to calls for the creation of a national fund through which surpluses could be redistributed, see BA, HRF, ABHC/2/11, Re the Formation of a National Fund for Relief of Sufferers by Mining Disasters, Lord Mayor of London to Hon. Sec., 16 Dec. 1913; cutting from *Western Mail* (28 March 1914); cutting from *News Chronicle* (23 Feb. 1931).

a total of £148,958. 19s. 8d. had been raised.[10] Yet, at the same time, levels of dependence failed to match expectations. The presence of 191 single men among the 344 fatalities reduced the number of dependants to 632, a ratio of less than 2:1. The resultant surplus was thus magnified. In response, the fund executive, comprising municipal leaders and co-opted religious, business, and trade-union representatives from across the region, opted to raise benefits above the levels initially fixed. Widows' allowances, originally set at 4s. a week were increased to 7s., a figure which was to be doubled once compensation awards were exhausted. New categories of relief were also established, as support was extended to partially- and wholly-dependent parents. Despite such actions, officials still budgeted for a 'surplus' of £31,519 net of all future obligations.[11] It was a decision reached only after protracted debate.

Under the original trust deed, the fund's general committee enjoyed almost complete discretion over the utilization of any surplus, the only stipulation being that any recipient agencies 'be constructed for the purpose of dealing with distress caused by mining accidents or . . . for the benefit of coal miners, their wives, widows, children or dependants'.[12] In the light of this, consideration was given to assisting individual fatality cases, a move supported by the Home Secretary, the fund's Manchester committee, and David Shaw, secretary of the county permanent relief society. An alternative course, involving the creation of a national collieries disaster relief fund to minimize inequalities in financial resources, was endorsed by, among others, the Lord Mayor of Liverpool and the Yorkshire Coal Owners' Association.[13] Significantly, few argued that the surplus should be applied for the further relief of the dependants themselves. A. A. Purcell of the Manchester and Salford Trades Council was almost alone in arguing that the families affected should benefit fully from the nation's 'royal generosity', and in posing the question, 'What if the funds did give the widows and dependants ten shillings a week more than

[10] BA, HRF, ABHC/2/4, circulars and cuttings, telegrams; ABHC/2/23, Subscription List.
[11] BA, HRF, ABHC/2/2, information supplied by the Lancashire and Cheshire Miners' Permanent Relief Society, details of fatalities; ABHC/1/1, Executive Committee minutes, 20 Mar. 1911; ABHC/3/1, Actuarial Valuations, Actuarial Report on Liabilities of Fund as at 31 Dec. 1911, 4, 7–10.
[12] BA, HRF, ABHC/2/7, Declaration of Trusts for the Administration of the Above Fund. Dated 30 Oct. 1911, par. 2.
[13] BA, HRF, ABHC/2/4, circulars and cuttings, cutting from *The Times* (10 Mar. 1911); ABHC/2/3, correspondence, Shaw to Cooper, 12 and 30 Jan. 1911; MRL., HRF, M122/1 Manchester Committee minutes, 12 and 31 Jan. 1911.

they asked? If they got £50 per week it would not repay them nor replace their loss'.[14] Awareness that a substantial sum was being kept in reserve would inspire subsequent appeals for additional assistance. However, officials merely responded by reiterating the need to operate within financial limits if reciprocal support between kin was to be maintained. The reply to one such request for help in 1923 encapsulated such thinking: 'this Fund was not prepared to make an increased allowance in order to relieve the other members of the family of their obligations'.[15]

On occasion, intervention in family life extended beyond the mere payment of benefits. As earlier chapters have indicated, the fund was often obliged to act in loco parentis, assisting children in their choice of career.[16] This role could be used to justify more radical action where evidence, gathered by means of inspections or inquiries in the neighbourhood, revealed shortcomings in the behaviour of parents or guardians. For example, when reports indicated that one mother was keeping her daughter from school, while allowing her 15-year-old son to roam the streets, the conclusion was drawn that 'the children are simply being undermined by a drunken, lazy, careless mother'.[17] Although school attendance officers found no evidence of actual ill-treatment, the fund recommended that the children be removed to the Lancashire branch of the National Children's Home at Edgworth.[18] Separation was also sought in another case in which a widow, suspected of having a taste for drink, was found to have left her children 'very badly clad and shod and verminous'.[19] Attempts to secure alternative care failed, so that when a court hearing into charges of cruelty against the widow resulted in her imprisonment for three months, the children were committed to the same home.[20]

Such instances of direct intervention were rare. In most cases, the involvement of fund officials remained confined to the payment of benefits, with the aim, in part, of sustaining the 'normal' family dynamic. Central

---

[14] BA, HRF, ABHC/2/4, circulars and cuttings, cutting from *Daily Dispatch* (19 Jan. 1911).

[15] BA, HRF, ABHC/3/11, general correspondence, report of interview with E. Greenhalgh, president of the Hulton Park branch of the LCMF, 24 Mar. 1923; see also ABHC/5/273 Personal Files, pencilled note, n.d.; *BJG* (13 Apr. 1928), 5.

[16] See Ch. 4 above.

[17] BA, HRF, ABHC/5/326 Personal Files, Shaw to Hon. Sec., 30 June 1915.

[18] Ibid. Shaw to Hon. Sec., n.d.; Hon. Sec. to Governor of Children's Home on the Moors, 26 Nov. 1915.

[19] BA, HRF, ABHC/5/93, Personal Files, cutting from *BEN* (2 May 1916); Report of School Attendance Officer, 15 Mar. 1916; Shaw to Hon. Sec., 23 Mar. 1916.

[20] BA, HRF, ABHC/5/93, Personal Files, cutting from *BEN* (2 May 1916); note on information obtained from Edgworth Home, 18 July 1923.

to this was the changing role of children as they experienced the transition from complete dependence to full independence, through the intermediate stage of 'boarding'.[21] On commencing work, children's wages were paid into a household pool, from which basic needs would be satisfied. Additional expenditure on non-essentials was funded out of a small weekly allowance. A not untypical arrangement, recorded in the compensation returns relating to Pretoria victims, involved payments of 4*s.* a week at the age of 21. In exceptional cases, the practice continued well into 'adulthood'. Samuel Wharmby, a 26-year-old drawer, received a mere 5*s.* a week, the remainder of his wage being made over to his mother, who provided him with food, clothing, and shelter. More often at that age, children, if not married, paid over a fixed portion of their earnings as 'board'. Abram Turner and Harry Southern, both aged 23 in 1910, each paid 12*s.* out of their respective weekly incomes of 25*s.* and 30*s.*[22] 'Boarding' acknowledged the greater responsibilities of those on the verge of adulthood, as they prepared for marriage and departure from the parental home. It also acted to sustain the unity of the nuclear household by providing a practical alternative to lodging. Its ubiquity is reflected in the fact that, at the time of the disaster, only fourteen Pretoria victims were living in lodgings, of whom only one had kin in the immediate area.[23]

Lodging was only likely to figure prominently in living arrangements where an area depended, for its labour requirements, on substantial in-migration. Between a quarter and one-third of households in mid-nineteenth-century Preston and Edwardian Middlesbrough supplemented their incomes by taking in lodgers.[24] By the early twentieth century, however, domestic service remained the only significant form of employment across textile Lancashire still heavily dependent on migrant labour.[25] Local patterns of recruitment worked to maintain the peculiar stability of nuclear households across the region. Examples from

[21] The practice of boarding is given, somewhat exaggerated, prominence in D. Fowler, *The First Teenagers: The Lifestyle of Young Wage-Earners in Interwar Britain* (1995), ch. 4; id., 'Teenage consumers? Young Wage-Earners and Leisure in Manchester, 1919–1939', in A. Davies and S. Fielding (eds.), *Workers' Worlds* (Manchester, 1992), 133–55; see also E. M. Roberts, *A Woman's Place* (Oxford, 1984), 43.

[22] BA, HRF, ABHC/5/180, 292, 308, 323 Personal Files, Compensation statements.

[23] BA, HRF, ABHC/5/1–344 Personal Files, Compensation statements.

[24] Anderson, *Family Structure*, 46; Lady Bell, *At the Works: A Study of a Manufacturing Town* (1907), 48–9.

[25] Bolton's servant population was drawn substantially from Westmorland, Cumberland, Ireland, and Wales, *BJG* (2 Feb. 1923), 5; (8 June 1923), 8; BA, BOHP 88A (female, born 1901), transcript, 1; *Parl. Papers 1913*, lxxviii (7018), Census of England and Wales, 1911. X. Occupations and Industries. Pt. I, table 15B, 436–9.

the Pretoria sample point up the contrast with experiences elsewhere. Thus, whereas Henry Wyper left home in Hamsterley, near Bishop Auckland, County Durham, at the age of 14 to work on a local farm, children in most Lancastrian households remained under the parental roof beyond the age of 20. At times, therefore, households comprised several members who, in terms of age at least, could be regarded as adults. Seven of William Turton's children were still at home in December 1910, of whom five were aged 21 or over, the eldest being a 35-year-old daughter.[26]

The tendency to delay marriage was evident across much of Lancashire. Census data relating to local county boroughs revealed that fewer than 16 per cent of males aged under 25 in 1911 were married.[27] More significantly, this pattern applied regardless of earnings prospects. If prolonged courtship could be anticipated in the light of the limited promotional opportunities available in the mill, the near-adult wages paid to drawers does not appear to have encouraged earlier marriages among the county's miners. Of thirty-four drawers in the Pretoria sample aged 20 to 25, only six were married, while among hewers in the same age range the proportion was only slightly higher at thirteen out of forty-two.[28] Children thus remained under the parental roof some years after the material necessity binding them to such an arrangement had ceased to apply. Concern that, in the absence of financial constraints, familial obligations would be overlooked, was widespread. One Pretoria widow, anticipating the future in 1916, saw little cause for optimism: 'The Compensation is almost finished, and . . . she cannot prevent her children getting married and leaving her, . . . she cannot keep house with what she has, and she can see no alternative but to sell up and go to the Workhouse.'[29] In the end, such fears proved groundless, as a daughter remained at home for a further eight years to nurse the widow through her final illness.[30] Nor was this an unusual occurrence. Fund records more generally reveal a readiness among children to respond to family need that owed little to narrow calculations of self-interest.

For daughters, the help proffered could entail considerable sacrifice. On the death of her mother in 1919, Pollie Crook, then aged 21, gave up

---

[26] BA, HRF, ABHC/5/343 Personal Files, William Barnes, secretary of the Northumberland and Durham Miners' Permanent Relief Society, to Shaw, 4 Mar. 1911; ABHC/5/309 Personal Files, Compensation statement.

[27] *Parl. Papers 1912–13*, cxiii (6610), Census of England and Wales, 1911. VII. Ages and Conditions as to Marriage, table 9, 225–8.

[28] BA, HRF, ABHC/5/1–344 Personal Files, Compensation statements.

[29] BA, HRF, ABHC/5/211 Personal Files, Shaw to Hon. Sec., 28 June 1916.

[30] Ibid., Henrietta M. to Shaw, n.d.; Shaw to Hon. Sec., 21 Feb. 1924.

a 30*s*.-a-week post at Atherton Bolt Works to act as housekeeper for her father.[31] In this case, the interruption to earnings lasted but a few weeks. For others, however, the burden proved more protracted. In 1929, both daughters of the Pretoria widow Annie Greenall left work to care for their invalid mother. The elder of the two, Lilian, a solicitor's clerk, continued to receive her full wage for six months after returning home. As her mother's illness extended over a further two years, the family was left to subsist on the apprentice earnings of her brother, Thomas, and the allowances paid to Annie. Although an additional payment of 10*s*. a week was agreed to help pay for foods recommended by the doctor, this ceased with the overall increase in widows' benefits from 1930. Appeals for further assistance were refused, leaving Lilian to vent her frustration at official inaction in the local press. The fund's concern to encourage mutual support had, in her family's case, she argued, proved self-defeating:

> When my father was alive he held a good position and had good prospects. When he was killed my Mother was left a widow with three young children and one child unborn. I have witnessed her struggles to educate her children and maintain them in a respectable position and we have always had the feeling that if she had allowed us to sink into slum-dom we should have received more help from your Fund. We feel that she has been penalised by the brave fight she put up. [32]

As such examples indicate, responsibility for family assistance devolved for the most part on to daughters. Indeed, the fund discouraged the involvement of sons in household affairs, particularly where, it was felt, this would detract from their 'traditional' wage-earning role. In cases such as Mary Chadwick's where no daughter remained at home to care for her, officials recommended that she be placed in the Workhouse Infirmary, allowing her 40-year-old son to resume work.[33] Despite this, Shaw's observation that 'married sons contribute nothing, and the single sons are merely not more than boarders in their parents' home' was not justified by events.[34] When alternative help could not be had, as with Caroline Hundy, the son provided the necessary nursing care. Similarly, James Leigh, a colliery electrician, undertook all household work when both his sister and mother fell ill.[35]

---

[31] BA, HRF, ABHC/5/60 Personal Files, Shaw to Hon. Sec., 20 June 1919.

[32] BA, HRF, ABHC/5/112 Personal Files, Lilian Greenall to Shaw, 13 Oct. 1932, a letter also sent to the *Manchester Evening Chronicle*; see also Shaw to Hon. Sec., 16 Jan. 1930, Hon. Sec. to Shaw, 28 Jan. 1930, 19 Nov. 1931; Lilian to Shaw, 8 Dec. 1931.

[33] BA, HRF, ABHC/5/44 Personal Files, Shaw to Hon. Sec., 7 May 1914.

[34] BA, HRF, ABHC/5/211 Personal Files, Shaw to Hon. Sec., 17 Jan. 1921.

[35] BA, HRF, ABHC/5/166 Personal Files, John Thomas Lawton Hundy to Shaw, 10 Jan. 1922; ABHC/5/181 Personal Files, James Leigh to Shaw, 17 Feb. 1931.

The exceptional circumstances suggest the extent to which, ordinarily, such responsibilities devolved on to female family members. Elder daughters, in particular, were liable to take up the maternal apron strings on the death or disablement of the mother. In the Cowburn and Sharples households, both affected by maternal loss or incapacity, management of the home was undertaken by daughters, aged 29 and 36 respectively.[36] Nor were such commitments necessarily transient. Writing seventeen years after the disaster, David Shaw remarked on the difficulties encountered by women who were 'approaching middle age, and partly owing to health or by attention required by their mothers, their present and future prospects have been greatly injured either as regards work, and in other ways such as marriage'.[37] One such, Pollie Unsworth, left the weaving shed at the age of 22 in 1925 to care for her mother. The latter's death, after fourteen years of nursing, forced Pollie to move in with a married sister.[38] That her experience was far from unique is indicated by the prominence of spinsters in working-class neighbourhoods throughout the period: in 1911, 28 per cent of Bolton women aged between 25 and 45 were unmarried.[39] That many would remain so provides, perhaps, the most tangible proof of the readiness to subordinate individual to family need.

Further corroboration of this point may be found in the extent to which kin no longer resident in the parental home continued to acknowledge familial obligations. Regardless of the distances involved, most of the fourteen Pretoria victims in lodgings in 1910 made regular remittances home. Lodging close to his parents in Daubhill, Bolton, Joseph Layland contributed 8s. each week, sufficient to meet the family's rent and fuel bills, in addition to providing medicine for his father and clothing for a younger brother.[40] Payments were also made to kin residing well beyond Lancashire. Remittances by Henry Wyper and Benjamin While supported elderly relatives in County Durham and Birmingham, respectively. For the parents of the latter, the only other available source of income was the

---

[36] BA, HRF, ABHC/5/56, 281 Personal Files, Compensation statements; see also T. K. Hareven, *Family Time and Industrial Time* (Cambridge, 1982), 105; M. Young and P. Willmott, *Family and Kinship in East London* (Harmondsworth edn., 1962), 79–81.

[37] BA, HRF, ABHC/3/11, D. Shaw, 'Notes on the Visitation of Widows', 17 Aug. 1927, 4.

[38] BA, HRF, ABHC/5/319 Personal Files, James Unsworth to William Rodan (Shaw's successor as secretary of the permanent relief society), n.d.; Rodan to Hon. Sec., 12 Dec. 1939.

[39] *Parl. Papers 1912–13*, cxiii (6610), Census of England and Wales, 1911. VII. Ages and Conditions as to Marriage, table 9, 225–8; see also R. Roberts, *The Classic Slum: Salford Life in the First Quarter of the Century* (Harmondsworth edn., 1973), 53.

[40] BA, HRF, ABHC/5/179 Personal Files, Compensation statement.

11s. contributed each week by Benjamin's brother.[41] Equally, prolonged separation posed no fundamental obstacle to the provision of support. John Houghton, aged 45 in 1910, was thus thought to have contributed to the maintenance of a father he had not seen since boyhood.[42] Official prompting was rarely required to encourage offers of assistance, although Northwich Poor Law Guardians acted to remind Thomas Hastie of his responsibilities by refusing his mother outdoor relief.[43]

Obligations were not all one way, however. Rather, they should be seen as reciprocal, changing as circumstances altered over the family's life course. Newly weds, for example, continued to draw on kinship support, often opting to reside close to parents to facilitate the provision of assistance. This could be particularly important where both spouses were in work. When his wife returned to her job in the mill, one Bolton mule-spinner took his meals at his neighbouring mother's or aunt's. The parental link remained valuable even after wives left work, as mothers offered the most accessible and reliable source of advice during pregnancy.[44] Over time, however, as parental earning power declined, the pattern of dependence would undergo a fundamental shift. The precise incidence of change could vary. Whereas Thomas Aspden, a 58-year-old overlooker, earned 35s. a week in 1910, Thomas Bennett, three years his junior, had been rendered unfit for work through chronic bronchitis.[45] On average, potential earning power was likely to decline from the age of 50, some two decades before the minimum state-pension safety net would begin to operate. From this point, miners commenced their retreat along the haulage road into less remunerative repair work, while spinners across the Bolton Province became eligible for superannuation benefits.[46] For many, then, the support of married children became central to the prevention of pauperism in old age.

The Pretoria evidence suggests that assistance in such cases was willingly rendered. In 1919, after caring for her mother and two nieces for seven years, Alice Aspden married. Despite her change in circumstances, she continued to live close by and to help out at home. Officials reported

[41] BA, HRF, ABHC/5/325, 343 Personal Files, Compensation statements.
[42] BA, HRF, ABHC/5/158 Personal Files, Compensation statement.
[43] BA, HRF, ABHC/5/123 Personal Files, Compensation statement.
[44] BA, BOHP 1B (male, born 1901), transcript, 13; 87 (male, born 1902), transcript, 3; M. Llewelyn Davies (ed.), *Maternity: Letters from Working-Women Collected by the Women's Co-operative Guild* (1978 edn.), esp. letters 13, 45, 99.
[45] BA, HRF, ABHC/5/6, 21 Personal Files, Compensation statements.
[46] H. F. Bulman and Sir R. A. S. Redmayne, *Colliery Working and Management* (1923), 113; the spinners' superannuation scheme is discussed at greater length below, pp. 247–50.

that 'She comes every morning early about six o' clock, and she continues working there the whole day through until evening'.[47] Similarly, twenty years after the disaster, although the last of Sarah Lonsdale's seven children had left home, she continued to receive help through regular visits from two married daughters.[48] Where personal attendance was impracticable, assistance could be rendered financially or in kind. George Sharples paid his mother-in-law's rent, in addition to helping with her food and clothing bills, while for over two years after leaving home Thomas Howcroft contributed 3s. a week to his mother's support.[49] William Potter, a Westhoughton collier with six children of his own to support, sent 3s. 6d. each week along with food to his parents, both of whom had been taken in by a married daughter in Leigh, some 5 miles to the south.[50]

The latter example has a broader significance. At any one time, the nuclear family was in the majority. On the day of the disaster, only fifteen Pretoria households diverged from this pattern. In eleven, parents resided with children and grandchildren, while in two others, siblings had been admitted from the household of origin after the deaths of both parents.[51] Over time, however, family structures showed a marked plasticity, as residential arrangements were adjusted to meet changing circumstances. Immediately after the disaster, many widows returned to the parental home. By contrast, in later years, many would come to share their house with married children and their offspring. In 1927, Ellen Hollingsworth was found to be living with a daughter, the latter's husband, and their three children. Two years earlier, Shaw had enlarged on the importance of such arrangements: 'In the case of Widows who live with married children they probably live fairly comfortably with the allowance they get from your Fund and the Permanent Relief Society, but in the case of Widows . . . who live alone their struggle to live is a very painful one.'[52] The benefits of co-residence were often more varied than this suggested. Although Thomas and Harriet Howcroft maintained Thomas's widowed mother during the nine years they lived under her roof, the arrangement

---

[47] BA, HRF, ABHC/5/144 Personal Files, Shaw to Hon. Sec., 1 May 1919.

[48] BA, HRF, ABHC/5/191 Personal Files, report, 18 Sept. 1933.

[49] BA, HRF, ABHC/5/280 Personal Files, Compensation statement; ABHC/5/164 Personal Files, Boardman to Shaw, 11 Feb. 1911.

[50] BA, HRF, ABHC/5/248 Personal Files, note, n.d.; Father A. L. Coelenbier to Cooper, 19 Apr. 1911.

[51] Calculated from BA, HRF, ABHC/5/1–344 Personal Files, Compensation statements; for remarks on living arrangements more generally, see A. L. Bowley and M. H. Hogg, *Has Poverty Diminished?* (1925), 149–51.

[52] BA, HRF, ABHC/5/135 Personal Files, Shaw to Hon. Sec., 18 Sept. 1925; ABHC/5/148 Personal Files, Shaw to Hon. Sec., 9 Aug. 1927.

also enabled them to accumulate sufficient savings to purchase their own house.[53] Similarly, in 1928, Alice Dyke occupied the front room of a council house shared with her son. The payments made for this room, which comprised her 'bedroom, kitchen [and] coal-house' enabled the family to meet the higher rents charged on corporation property.[54] Over time, the fixed allowances paid to Pretoria widows became a valuable household resource. Their value increased in real terms as prices fell from 1920. At the same time, however, the impact of poor trade and short-time working reduced the earnings of those in employment. As a result, changes in the balance of dependence which might have been anticipated as parents aged were, on occasion, checked or even reversed. So, whereas, in 1929, John Partington earned 21*s.* a week as a clerk with the South Lancashire Tramway Co., his 65-year-old mother received 34*s.* 6*d.* from the Pretoria fund and the permanent relief society. Similarly, Sarah Ann Marsh, who lived in 1924 with her married son, paid towards various household expenses, including the rent.[55] Even where incomes remained limited, women's domestic skills enabled them to contribute significantly to household maintenance. During the time that her husband was an inmate of the Bolton Union workhouse, Alice Vickers lived with her married brother and undertook to do the housework in return for food.[56]

The necessary fluidity of residential arrangements was reflected most fully in the experience of elderly dependants. At different times, the father of the Pretoria collier John Bullough lived with a married daughter in Westhoughton and a married son in Atherton, spending an intervening period in lodgings.[57] Change could necessitate movement over a wide area. On retiring from the pit, Thomas Davies was taken in by daughters in Stockport and Wigan.[58] In adjusting to altered circumstances, families were often obliged to mobilize more extended kinship links. In 1911, the widow Ann Marrin, who shared her home with four children aged 17 to 34, agreed to take in her brother's four offspring.[59] Similarly, Alice Aspden, who lost two sons in the disaster, cared for two grandchildren

[53] BA, HRF, ABHC/5/164 Personal Files, notes accompanying Compensation statement.
[54] BA, HRF, ABHC/5/80 Personal Files, Shaw to Hon. Sec., 14 Mar. 1928.
[55] BA, HRF, ABHC/5/235 Personal Files, Shaw to Hon. Sec., 23 July 1929; ABHC/5/201 Personal Files, Shaw to Hon. Sec., 9 May 1924. By 1930, weekly payments to widows from the fund alone stood at 36*s.*, ABHC/1/5 General Committee minutes, Report of Sub-committee into surplus as revealed by actuarial valuations, 16 July 1930.
[56] BA, HRF, ABHC/5/321 Personal Files, note, 13 May 1911.
[57] BA, HRF, ABHC/5/35 Personal Files, notes accompanying Compensation statement.
[58] BA, HRF, ABHC/5/65 Personal Files, Shaw to Hon. Sec., 9 Apr. 1920.
[59] BA, HRF, ABHC/5/199 Personal Files, Ann Marrin to Cooper, 20 Jan. 1911.

following the death of her daughter in 1912.[60] More remote relationships were only rarely utilized, although Annie Aspinall, aged 12 in 1922, sought relief from childhood rheumatism by moving to Oswestry, to live with her stepfather's sister.[61] Out of necessity, therefore, families were obliged to acknowledge ties which extended well beyond the basic nuclear unit.

Despite this, on occasion, the provision of kinship support encountered fundamental obstacles. The cost of managing their own homes prevented Annie Dawson's daughters from offering help beyond the occasional visit.[62] For others, economic decline compounded such difficulties. Although James Gill's sons contributed to his maintenance through the 1920s, despite reductions in their incomes brought about by short-time working, their support ceased with the onset of outright unemployment from 1930.[63] The geographical dispersal of kin, a further symptom of recession, further impeded the flow of assistance. For example, none of the seven Simmons children who survived to adulthood were in a position to help their widowed father following his enforced retirement from the pit in 1923. Two sons had emigrated to the United States, while marriage had taken three daughters to Yorkshire and County Durham. The youngest daughter could not be traced and, although the remaining son lived and worked locally, his wage was entirely taken up in caring for his six children. With a weekly income of only 15s., from a combination of state pension and disaster relief fund allowance, the elder Simmons, it was reported in 1929, 'is very short of clothes, and has to beg for cast-off suits'.[64]

Few dependants, if the fund records are comprehensive, were so reduced in circumstances. Only two widows, it would appear, were driven, out of necessity, to the pawnshop. With help from her children unlikely, Isabella Paulding was obliged in the early 1920s to pledge most of her possessions, including her wedding ring. Both her sons were dead, one killed in the Pretoria explosion, the other on the Western Front. Of her two daughters, the elder was fully occupied raising six children, while the other was employed in low-paid mill work.[65] Nevertheless, isolated

---

[60] BA, HRF, ABHC/5/144 Personal Files, note, n.d.

[61] BA, HRF, ABHC/5/253 Personal Files, Shaw to Hon. Sec., 3 Nov. 1922.

[62] BA, HRF, ABHC/5/66 Personal Files, Shaw to Hon. Sec., 28 Jan. 1936.

[63] BA, HRF, ABHC/5/101 Personal Files, Shaw to Hon. Sec., 12 Feb. 1923; Tonge to Shaw, 2 May 1932.

[64] BA, HRF, ABHC/5/283 Personal Files, penned note, 7 Dec. 1926; Shaw to Hon. Sec., 3 Feb. 1928, 1 Aug. 1929.

[65] BA, HRF, ABHC/5/241 Personal Files, Shaw to Hon. Sec., 18 June 1918, 28 Feb. 1923; see also ABHC/5/66 Personal Files, Shaw to Hon. Sec., 28 Feb. 1929.

instances indicate that, even where available, assistance was not always rendered. Disowned by her only known relative, the widow Jane Hilton was forced to live in 'a wretched house, full of draught, [and] damp'.[66] That such cases appear to have been highly exceptional confirms the over-all resilience of the family tie. Even after the deaths of both parents, the Boardman children remained together for a further six years, sustained by the earnings of three elder brothers.[67]

By comparison, alternative sources of support were both less durable and more instrumental in character. Most were turned to only in the absence of kin. For example, Ruth Longworth, from the village of Little Hulton, near Bolton, had lost her only brother in the disaster. A subse-quent illness thus left her dependent on the assistance of neighbours. Similarly, in 1924, Daubhill residents rallied to the help of Charles and Henrietta Middlehurst, left destitute after caring for their mother during her final illness. Yet, however responsive to cases of immediate need, the neighbourhood proved incapable of filling the vacuum left by absent kin. The generosity of villagers in Little Hulton was not inexhaustible. After only a few months, local clergy reported that 'the streams of charity are running dry'. More enduring support for Ruth Longworth was thus sought in an allowance from the fund.[68]

More often, neighbourhood assistance took the form of paid work, as households lacking able-bodied female kin looked to utilize the skills of local married women. The McCabes, both of whom were elderly and infirm, advertised for domestic help following the death of their daughter in 1932.[69] The paid assistance of two women sustained the all-male Turner household in 1910: one received 2s. 6d. a week for washing clothes and cooking the Sunday dinner, while another earned 1s. 6d. a week by cleaning the house.[70] Neighbours also provided supplementary nursing care during illness or childbirth. Two local women were in paid atten-dance on the Pretoria widow Ann Leigh during her confinement in 1926.[71] The provision of neighbourhood support was seen by contemp-orary observers, such as Maud Pember Reeves and Lady Florence Bell, as emblematic of the co-operative mutuality at the heart of working-class

---

[66] BA, HRF, ABHC/5/135 Personal Files, Shaw to Hon. Sec., 18 Sept. 1925.
[67] BA, HRF, ABHC/5/26 Personal Files, Compensation statement; Shaw to Hon. Sec., 23 Sept. 1920.
[68] BA, HRF, ABHC/5/190 Personal Files, Revd. Robinson to Hon. Sec., 17 Mar. 1920; for the Middlehursts, see ABHC/5/211 Personal Files, Henrietta to not known, n.d.; Hon. Sec. to Shaw, 7 May 1924.
[69] BA, HRF, ABHC/5/207 Personal Files, John McCabe to Shaw, 19 Nov. 1932.
[70] BA, HRF, ABHC/5/308 Personal Files, Compensation statement.
[71] BA, HRF, ABHC/5/183 Personal Files, Shaw to Hon. Sec., 3 Dec. 1926.

notions of 'community'.[72] The Pretoria evidence, however, prompts a more measured interpretation. Assistance within the neighbourhood fulfilled a dual function, meeting immediate family needs while providing wives and widows with a source of income which did not require a lengthy absence from the home. Essentially ancillary to the extended family as a source of mutual support, it provides a more precise match for Anderson's notion of a 'short-run calculative orientation' towards relationships than do ties of kin.[73] The limited and largely functional nature of neighbourhood sociability was transcended within the family unit. Here, the readiness with which financial and emotional support was tendered, often without regard to considerations of self-interest, suggests a more fundamental moral commitment. If the notion of working-class community has any validity, therefore, it is at the level of the family.

The 'family', in this context, comprehended ties that extended well beyond the basic nuclear household. Over the individual's life course, a diversity of family settings would be experienced, as extended kinship links were utilized when circumstances required. Yet the adaptability of domestic structures should not be allowed to obscure the fact that the fundamental unit of support, in which loyalties were most fully developed, was the nuclear family. Significantly, this seems to have continued regardless of the increasingly marginal role of kin in the process of recruitment to Lancastrian industry. The family retained its importance as the economic and moral centre of working-class life, cementing relationships which rested on more than a mutually beneficial exchange of services. Certain aspects of family life may be understood in such terms. Children thus remained under the parental roof for some years after full financial independence had been attained, an arrangement which boosted household resources while enabling young adults to save in anticipation of marriage. In other respects, however, in particular the propensity of daughters to forfeit their chances of work or marriage to care for elderly relatives, exchange theory would appear to be of little or no relevance. Yet the willingness to tender assistance still depended crucially on the possession of sufficient means to render such aid practicable. The textures of family life were constructed on solid economic foundations, to consideration of which attention now turns.

---

[72] Pember Reeves, *Round about a Pound a Week*, 39, 72–3; Bell, *At the Works*, 103, 117, 229–30; see also E. Ross, 'Survival Networks: Women's Neighbourhood Sharing in London before World War I', *History Workshop*, 15 (Spring 1983), 4–27.
[73] Anderson, *Family Structure*, 164.

II

As with household structures, potential standards of living varied markedly over the family's life course. For most, this was characterized by alternating periods of poverty and affluence. The single wage which sufficed to maintain most young married couples proved increasingly inadequate as the birth of children signalled a rise in the dependency ratio. This problem decreased with time, as more household members commenced earning on their own account. This renewed sufficiency was likely to endure up to the point at which children departed the parental home. The threat of pauperism in old age could then become acute. If this basic model captures the experience of many working-class families in outline, it fails to allow for variations in detail brought about by occupational and regional differences and by the impact of economic change. In most mining areas, for example, limited employment opportunities beyond the pit rendered households heavily dependent on male earnings. In Lancashire, by contrast, greater industrial diversity enabled more family members, particularly women, to become wage earners. Given that shift earnings across the county were below the national average, the well-being of colliers' families rested substantially on the composite nature of household incomes.[74] A ready contrast to this pattern is provided by trades such as cotton-spinning, where pronounced income hierarchies placed defence of the male breadwinner wage at the centre of attempts to secure family welfare. In all cases, households remained vulnerable to economic change, being forced into lasting indebtedness by unemployment, sickness, or death. Impoverishment and prosperity thus coexisted in a manner which forcibly reiterated the need to complement formal attempts at thrift with the safety net of kinship support. The material realities of working-class life continued to underpin family stability.

The Pretoria evidence allows this point to be pursued in unusual depth. Drawing on compensation returns, income schedules could be devised for all but thirty-eight of the 286 households affected by the disaster. The nature of the wage data varies. Victims' incomes were based on average weekly earnings over the three years to December 1910, figures which provided the basis for calculating compensation awards. The estimates reflect the impact of variable trade in 1908–9 and so tend to understate the level of wages likely to have been earned in the prosperous months to

[74] For relative shift earnings, see J. Rowe, *Wages in the Coal Industry* (1923), 72–3; *LG* 38 (1930), 44.

December 1910.[75] The figures for remaining family members, including, where appropriate, those of non-resident kin, referred to the weeks immediately prior to the disaster. Unless stated otherwise, all were assumed to constitute net additions to household resources. Occasionally, only daily wage rates were cited. Where the number of days worked each week was not specified, this figure was multiplied by five to arrive at the weekly equivalent, a procedure justified by the buoyant state of local trade.

An obvious point of contrast is immediately apparent. In most mining districts, employment opportunities, particularly for women, were severely restricted. In their survey of the Durham township of Stanley, undertaken in 1913, Bowley and Burnett-Hurst found that barely 6 per cent of females aged 14 years and over were in paid work outside the home, with the result that 60 per cent of households had only one wage-earner each.[76] In the Pretoria sample, 101 households were so placed, mostly comprising married couples only or couples with dependent children. However, over 45 per cent of families could draw on three or more sources of income. The most fortunately placed in this regard were the Gerrards of Westhoughton, nine of whom were in paid employment in 1910, including three daughters who brought home a combined wage of 32s. a week.[77] Overall, in households dependent on more than one income, females accounted for almost a quarter of all wage-earners.[78]

The impact this had on family income levels becomes apparent if we turn to examine another town surveyed by Bowley and Burnett-Hurst, one which more precisely parallels the Pretoria experience: Northampton. Here, the boot and shoe trade enhanced opportunities for female involvement in paid work. Yet, despite this, incomes across the town failed to match those recorded among the Pretoria sample. In Northampton, weekly incomes in excess of 60s. were rare. By contrast, almost one-third of all Pretoria families were so placed, while in fourteen cases, receipts exceeded £5 a week. Five members of the Tyldesley family of Wingates, near Westhoughton, were employed down No. 3 Bank Pit, bringing home, on average over the three years from 1908, £7. 11s. 4d. a week.[79] If anything, the contrast, as presented here, is understated. The comparative approach adopted by Bowley and Burnett-Hurst required that regional

---

[75] The method for calculating compensation awards was clarified by the judgment in the case of *Onslow* v. *Cannock Chase Colliery Co., Ltd*, summarized in *LG* 17 (1909), 207.
[76] A. L. Bowley and A. R. Burnett-Hurst, *Livelihood and Poverty* (1915), 145–6.
[77] BA, HRF, ABHC/5/97 Personal Files, Compensation statement.
[78] Calculated from BA, HRF, ABHC/5/1–344 Personal Files, Compensation statements.
[79] BA, HRF, ABHC/5/310–14 Personal Files, Compensation statements.

Table 7. *Distribution of families by income: Northampton (1913) and Pretoria (1910) families* (%)

Income	Northampton	Pretoria
below 10s.	3	0.4
10s.–20s.	5.5	0.4
20s.–30s.	17	22.3
30s.–40s.	30	26.6
40s.–50s.	17	10.4
50s.–60s.	9	8.8
60s. and over	16.5	31.1

Sources: A. L. Bowley and A. R. Burnett-Hurst, *Livelihood and Poverty* (1915), 77; BA, HRF, ABHC/5/1–344 Personal Files, Compensation statements.

variations in the level of economic activity be eliminated by assuming that all wage-earners were in full-time employment. The Pretoria figures, however, comprehend the effects of short-time working in earlier years and, where these are indicated, only include sums actually paid into the household purse. In part, the differences outlined here reflect the potential for higher juvenile earnings in Lancashire. In the boot and shoe trade, wages were regulated according to a graduated scale, whereby full rates were payable from the age of 21. Drawers and carding frame-tenters, on the other hand, could anticipate near adult earnings from their late teens.[80] When this is combined with the observed tendency to delay marriage for several years after full earnings potential had been achieved, the levels of income commanded by Pretoria families are rendered, to some extent, explicable. Not only this, the potential for Lancastrian families to enjoy unusually high collective incomes becomes clear.

It remains to establish the level of material welfare potentially secured by such receipts. The adequacy or otherwise of family incomes was assessed by utilizing Rowntree's estimates of living costs, covering heating, food, and clothing needs, adjusted to allow for local price differences and for inflation in the decade or so which separated his survey from the disaster. The comparative price index for major provincial towns contained in the Board of Trade's Cost of Living Survey of 1905 enabled the first problem to be addressed. This indicated that retail prices in York were some 7 per cent above those in Bolton. The official food price series,

[80] E. P. Hennock, 'The Measurement of Urban Poverty: From the Metropolis to the Nation', *Econ.Hist.Rev.*, 2nd ser. 40 (1987), 218–19; Bowley and Burnett-Hurst, *Livelihood and Poverty*, 69–76; *Parl. Papers 1892*, xxxv (6708–VI), RC on Labour: Minutes of Evidence. Textiles, qq. 14–17; see above, pp. 42, 140, for the position down the mine.

based on a London basket of goods, recorded a 7.4 per cent increase in the cost of living between 1899 and 1905. Assuming that price differentials across the country remained unchanged in this period, Rowntree's estimates for 1899 could be applied to Bolton in 1905. To update this figure, use was made of the later Cost of Living Survey, undertaken in 1912. From 1905, price inflation in Bolton was some 50 per cent above that recorded in London. If it is assumed that this differential applied throughout the period separating the two inquiries, then the 7 per cent increase in prices recorded in London between 1905 and 1910 would approximate to a rise of 10 per cent in Bolton.[81] Throughout, therefore, Rowntree's figures were inflated by 10 per cent to establish their Pretoria equivalents. Heating costs were included in such calculations as concessionary fuel was available to only a small minority of Lancashire's miners. Indeed, one estimate had it that some 75 per cent of the county workforce were obliged to pay the ruling market price for coal.[82]

Once the Pretoria supplement of 10 per cent had been added, a further refinement was introduced to Rowntree's food standard. This was based on a largely vegetarian diet, a regime which, as Rowntree himself acknowledged, failed to reflect the nutritional requirements of those engaged in heavy manual labour. In devising their dietary standard, Bowley and Burnett-Hurst felt it necessary to include some provision for meat consumption. Yet this would not be possible for all members of the household. Females, especially wives and mothers, were often obliged to sacrifice their own nutritional needs to ensure that the family breadwinner received adequate nourishment. With this in mind, Bowley and Burnett-Hurst's meat allowance of 9*d.* a week was adopted for all adult males (over the age of 16) in work. However, Rowntree's weighting of dietary needs by age was retained, resulting in a more stringent standard than that provided by either contemporary survey.[83]

The methodology departs from Rowntree's approach in estimating housing costs, an important calculation given the prevailing dependence on private rented accommodation. Rather than taking actual rentals to

---

[81] Rowntree, *Poverty*, 105–9 (adult males: 3*s.* 11*d.* a week; adult females: 3*s.* 5*d.*; children aged 8 to 16: 3*s.* 3*d.*; children aged under 8: 2*s.* 9*d.*); *Parl. Papers 1908*, cvii (3864), Working Class Rents, Housing and Retail Prices, p. xxviii; *Parl. Papers 1913*, lxvi (6955), Working-Class Rents and Retail Prices in 1912, pp. xliv, 134.

[82] LCMF, Joint Committee minutes, 16 Apr. 1923; see also *Parl. Papers 1908*, lix (4443), Departmental Committee on Truck Acts. II. Minutes of Evidence, q. 3924.

[83] Rowntree, *Poverty*, 92; Bowley and Burnett-Hurst, *Livelihood and Poverty*, 79–80, 82, for a comparison of the two standards; for the self-denial of wives and mothers, Pember Reeves, *Round about a Pound a Week*, 124; *BJG* (12 May 1922), 7.

reflect minimum requirements, a 'room standard' was devised, based on the average density of occupation for each township, as indicated by the relevant Census returns.[84] Allowance was also made for changing needs over each family's life course. Demand for space was likely to grow as children aged and some segregation of sleeping arrangements became desirable. Calculations were thus framed to reflect the age structure as well as the size of each household. An examination of particular cases clarifies the need for such an approach. The Mather and Hesketh households each comprised seven members in 1910. While the former was made up of a married couple and five children aged 1 to 9 the youngest of the Heskeths was a 25-year-old son. To establish a common standard by which the room requirements of each could be estimated, Bowley's method of weighting individuals by age to calculate rates of overcrowding was adopted.[85] In each case, therefore, family size was expressed in terms of numbers of 'equivalent adults'. Whereas the Heskeths translated straightforwardly into seven 'adults', weighting reduced the Mathers to four.[86] The average density of occupation multiplier was then applied to establish each household's room requirements. These were used to locate each family on a rental scale of between 3s. 6d. and 7s., which represented the rents charged on three- to five-roomed houses in Bolton, as recorded in the 1912 Cost of Living Survey. This comprehended the bulk of working-class housing across the borough. Housing beyond the upper rental limit was, for the most part, occupied by workers in the clerical sector.[87] By this method, the Mathers were placed in the upper range of three-roomed houses at 4s. 6d., while the Heskeths were allotted the maximum rental of 7s.

If this approach errs, it does so on the side of undue rigour. Most Pretoria families lived outside Bolton, where rentals were mostly below those charged in the borough itself. Equally, the standard makes no allowance for overcrowding or for attempts to economize on rents, a first resort for many families in times of difficulty.[88] Furthermore, contemporary

---

[84] *Census of England and Wales, 1921: County of Lancaster*, table IX, pp. xx–xxiii, gives average density of occupation figures for 1911: Bolton, 0.98; Atherton, 0.9; Hindley, 0.87; Tyldesley, 0.89; Westhoughton, 0.93.

[85] Bowley and Burnett-Hurst, *Livelihood and Poverty*, 21, males over 18 and females over 16 = 1; children over 14 = 0.75; children aged 5 to 14 = 0.5; infants under 5 = 0.25.

[86] BA, HRF, ABHC/5/126, 203 Personal Files, Compensation statements.

[87] *Parl. Papers 1913*, lxvi (6955), Working-Class Rents and Retail Prices in 1912, 134; lxxvii (6910), Census of England and Wales, 1911. VIII. Tenements, table 2, 160–92; table 3.

[88] Davies, 'The Industrial Depression', 4; 7.7% of Bolton's population lived in overcrowded accommodation in 1911, *Parl. Papers 1913*, lxxvii (6910), Census of England and Wales, 1911. VIII. Tenements, table 3, 517; Rowntree, *Poverty*, 106.

observations suggest that expenditure on rent was not as income elastic as is assumed here. Bowley and Burnett-Hurst found that spending on improved accommodation increased in step with incomes up to 35*s.* a week.[89] Under the methodology outlined here, the maximum rental only began to apply once incomes reached 69*s.* a week.

Despite this, only eleven households fell below their prescribed minima. In seven cases, this could be traced to the loss or incapacity of the principal breadwinner. Alfred Edward Wood's father lived away from home in 1910, leaving two sons, aged 12 and 15, to support his infirm wife on a combined wage of 9*s.* 9*d.* a week.[90] In three further instances, the dependency ratio was at or close to its peak. None of Thomas Horrocks's six children was in work in 1910, leaving the family to subsist on his earnings of 33*s.* 9*d.* a week.[91] Such cases were, however, exceptional. The majority of single-income households enjoyed modest sufficiencies, sixty-three living within 10*s.* of the standard. For others, supplementary earnings produced examples of considerable affluence. For forty-six families, the 'surplus' exceeded 40*s.* To take one, admittedly extreme, example, of seven adults in the Aspden household in 1910, six were wage-earners, bringing home £7. 5*s.* 2*d.* a week. Although assigned the maximum rental, along with a bill of 38*s.* 9*d.* for food and other necessities, the household still secured a margin of some £5 a week in excess of basic requirements.[92]

However, this static picture conveys a partial truth at best. The implications of these estimates emerge more clearly if placed within the context

Table 8. *Pretoria families' living standards*

Margin	No. of Families	Margin	No. of Families
Deficit		Surplus	
up to 10*s.*	11	50*s.* to 60*s.*	11
Surplus		60*s.* to 70*s.*	8
up to 10*s.*	63	70*s.* to 80*s.*	2
10*s.* to 20*s.*	71	80*s.* to 90*s.*	—
20*s.* to 30*s.*	33	90*s.* to 100*s.*	1
30*s.* to 40*s.*	24	100*s.* to 110*s.*	1
40*s.* to 50*s.*	23		

Source: BA, HRF, ABHC/5/1–344 Personal Files, Compensation statements.

[89] Bowley and Burnett-Hurst, *Livelihood and Poverty*, 79.
[90] BA, HRF, ABHC/5/335 Personal Files, Compensation statement.
[91] BA, HRF, ABHC/5/154 Personal Files, Compensation statement.
[92] BA, HRF, ABHC/5/5, 6 Personal Files, Compensation statements.

of changes over the family life course. To this end, the sample was broken down into seven discrete life stages. In the first, households comprised young married couples prior to child-bearing. In the two stages which followed, all children were fully dependent, with none over the age of 5 years in the former. By stages four and five, children were earning on their own account, although in the earlier stage either no child above 16 years of age or under half of all children were in paid work. The final two stages comprehended families in which the father was dead or dependent. In stage six, two or more children were still under the parental roof, while by stage seven, only one remained.[93]

This procedure enables the progress from marginal to comfortable sufficiency to be caught. Most families could anticipate a period of marked affluence. What is more, the prolonged presence of wage-earning children ensured that this was no mere passing interlude. Even the loss of parental earnings did not necessarily reduce families to penury. The 53-year-old Peter Lowe and his wife were, for example, maintained by the combined wages of five sons and one daughter, aged 16 to 29, amounting to 102s. 5d. each week.[94] The importance of residential stability to living standards is vividly caught if families are differentiated according to the age of the head of household. From the age of 40, parental earnings accounted for less than half of each family's aggregate income. In favourable circumstances, prosperity could be maintained over the three decades before eligibility for

Table 9. *Pretoria families: living standards by life stage*

Life Stage	Number	Income	Earners	Dependants	Living Standard
1	9	29s. 9d.	1	1	+10s. to 15s.
2	46	30s.	1	2.7	+5s. to 10s.
3	34	36s. 7d.	1.2	4	+5s. to 10s.
4	35	52s. 4d.	2.8	4.9	+10s. to 15s.
5	67	75s. 4d.	4	2.5	+35s. to 40s.
6	41	58s. 1d.	3.1	2.5	+20s. to 25s.
7	13	28s.	1.1	1.5	+5s. to 10s.

Source: See Table 8, above.

[93] A number of families defied straightforward categorization. The childless couple, Joseph and Jane Hilton, were assigned to the final rather than the first stage, although Joseph was still in work. Their ages, 54 and 55 respectively, precluded any possibility of child-bearing in the future, BA, HRF, ABHC/5/135 Personal Files, Compensation statement. In all other cases, the father's age and/or status determined the household's designation.

[94] BA, HRF, ABHC/5/195 Personal Files, Compensation statement.

Table 10. *Pretoria families: living standards by age of head of household*

Age	Number	Income of Head	Total Income	%	Standard
41–45	32	29s. 3d.	60s. 3d.	48.5	+20s. to 25s.
46–50	34	21s. 8d.	61s. 1d.	35.5	+20s. to 25s.
51–55	35	16s. 6d.	62s. 8d.	26.3	+25s. to 30s.
56–60	19	18s. 11d.	73s. 9d.	24.4	+35s. to 40s.
61–65	9	8s. 5d.	61s.	13.8	+30s. to 35s.
66–70	5	3s. 6d.	64s. 10d.	5.4	+25s. to 30s.

Source: See Table 8, above.

state pension support was attained. The value of kinship support in securing high and stable levels of prosperity is revealed. Not only this, such findings go some way towards explaining the leading role assumed by
Lancashire in the emergence of mass, commercialized leisure forms in late
nineteenth- and early twentieth-century Britain.

This might be taken to indicate that the pessimism which has informed
debate over working-class living standards in the first decade of the twentieth century is misplaced.[95] However, before this is accepted, a note of
qualification must be entered. The figures encapsulate the experience of
a geographically specific group of families. Householders in heavy-
industrial areas immediately to the south and west, where female earnings opportunities were more restricted, were less likely to profit
substantially from ancillary sources of income.[96] What is more, the estimates capture family circumstances at a peak in the local trade cycle.
Fluctuations in economic activity had the potential radically to alter the
picture presented here. In the years immediately following the First
World War, demand for juvenile labour increased markedly. Wages rose
to unprecedented levels, ensuring youths a financial independence that
was seen to challenge parental authority. As the *Bolton Journal and
Guardian* had it in 1920, 'With the "key of the door" he's never been—
fourteen before!'[97] Any challenge to the domestic equilibrium proved
transient, however. With the onset of industrial decline from 1921, a combination of short-time working and delayed promotion reduced the

[95] The debate is summarized in M. MacKinnon, 'Living Standards, 1870–1914', in R.
Floud and D. McCloskey (eds.), *The Economic History of Britain*, ii (Cambridge, 1994),
265–90; and in T. R. Gourvish, 'The Standard of Living, 1890–1914', in A. O'Day (ed.), *The
Edwardian Age* (London and Basingstoke, 1979), 13–34.
[96] J. K. Walton, *Lancashire: A Social History, 1558–1939* (Manchester, 1987), 286–91.
[97] *BJG* (30 Apr. 1920), 5.

potential contribution of children. Changing patterns of recruitment, in which the promise of long-term security took precedence over immediate levels of reward, confirmed the trend.[98]

The comfortable sufficiency which, in more prosperous times, could be anticipated as children matured was no longer guaranteed. In 1918, fund officials commented on the difficulties faced by the Pretoria widow, Margaret Seddon, who had been unable 'to save anything as her Children, who are all now grown up have been a great drag upon her, and she has had to keep or materially help them during long periods of slack work or actual unemployment'.[99] As the period progressed, Margaret's experience was to be more widely shared. In 1927, Louisa Wild, aged 62, shared her home with her 29-year-old son and his wife. As his earnings were depleted by short-time working, Louisa's allowances, totalling 32s. a week, constituted the family's principal resource.[100] Similarly, Elizabeth Alice Thomason lived with her married daughter and her family through the later 1920s, an arrangement prolonged by the closure of the colliery at which her son-in-law had been employed.[101] In many households, such problems were further compounded by a simultaneous decline in parental incomes. Miners' wages had fallen rapidly after de-control, reaching the district minimum of 32 per cent above 1911 rates in June 1922. Earnings were further reduced by short-time working and difficult conditions, to the extent that it was estimated in 1924 that half the mining workforce across Lancashire was in receipt of subsistence payments designed to make their wages up to 30s. a week.[102] In such circumstances, reciprocity remained central to family welfare, a fact acknowledged in increased recourse to co-residence.

This development was recognized by Bowley and Hogg in their 1924 survey of Bolton. By that date, almost 10 per cent of households across the borough were found to comprise parents living with married children, a marked increase on the level observed in the preceding investigation a decade earlier. Rigidities in the local housing market, in particular a persistent shortfall in accommodation for young married couples, was seen to have contributed significantly to this outcome.[103] Building under the

[98] *BJG* (26 Jan. 1923), 7; see above, Ch. 4.
[99] BA, HRF, ABHC/5/273 Personal Files, Shaw to Hon. Sec., 24 Jan. 1918.
[100] BA, HRF, ABHC/5/329 Personal Files, Shaw to Hon. Sec., 23 July 1927.
[101] BA, HRF, ABHC/5/299 Personal Files, Shaw to Hon. Sec., 27 July 1927, 20 July 1929.
[102] LCMF, wage ascertainment, 30 May 1922; monthly conference minutes, 1 Mar.1924.
[103] Bowley and Hogg, *Has Poverty Diminished?*, 147, 151; BA, BCB ABCF/21/1 Housing and Town Planning Committee, Report of Medical Officer of Health on Housing and Re-housing in Bolton, 24 Nov. 1921, 4–5; ABCF/21/2 General Housing Conditions in Bolton, 1925, 2.

Housing (Assisted Scheme) Act of 1919 had done little to meet the projected shortage of 2,000 to 3,000 houses locally. Generous dimensions and high rentals confined tenancies to skilled or white-collar workers.[104] External constraints thus combined with family difficulties to emphasize the need for prolonged co-residence.

How effective this was in ameliorating distress may be assessed, albeit indirectly, from the experience of colliers' families at particular points of crisis through the decade. The prolonged stoppage of 1926 threatened many with outright penury, especially given the lack of institutional assistance. LCMF finances sufficed to fund a mere two weeks' strike pay, while in July, barely two months into the dispute, Bolton's Poor Law Guardians 'out Heroded Herod himself', in the words of Westhoughton's Labour MP, Rhys Davies, by refusing outdoor relief to miners and their dependants.[105] Yet there is little to suggest that widespread distress resulted from this decision. While partial amelioration could be found in voluntary relief initiatives, the earnings of other household members, particularly those employed in the cotton trade, which continued working throughout the stoppage, were vital in preventing any descent into pauperism. Welfare continued to rest primarily on the composite nature of incomes, which, in the words of the *Bolton Journal and Guardian*, made 'the family wage in South Central Lancashire the highest in the country'.[106] Its utility was further demonstrated in 1929, following the formation of the Coalfields Distress Fund. Whereas most district quotas were quickly exhausted, Lancashire continued to report a surplus, even when aid was extended to non-mining households.[107] For many mining families, therefore, multiple incomes remained the principal defence against the insistent threat of poverty.

That pattern was not invariable, however. In industries where income differentials were pronounced, particular importance came to attach to individual earnings, more especially those of the head of household.

[104] BA, BCB ABCF/21/1 Public Health Committee, speech by W. M. Farrington of the Bolton Housing and Town Planning Society, 30 Jan. 1918, 3; ABCF/21/1 Housing and Town Planning Committee, Report on Housing of the Working Classes, 8 June 1918, 2; ABCF/21/2 Report upon the erection of houses, 19 Aug. 1926, 4–5; AB/9/1/1 minutes, 30 Nov. 1919; the occupational background of tenants on the Platt Hill and Crompton Fold estates is derived from *Tillotson's Bolton Directory*, 13th and 14th edns. (Bolton, 1922, 1927).

[105] *BJG* (16 July 1926), 6; (30 July 1926), 11; LCMF, special and monthly conference minutes, 24 May 1926.

[106] *BJG* (29 June 1923), 5; (4 June 1926), 11, for examples of voluntary relief; see also BA, ZZ/127/2/2 The Little Lever Central Distress Committee, circular, n.d.

[107] *BJG* (1 Mar. 1929), 6; (12 Apr. 1929), 10; (21 Nov. 1930), 13.

Among Bolton's operative spinners, the 1906 Wage Census recorded average full-time earnings of 45*s.* a week, sufficient, under the standard of living estimates outlined above, to have guaranteed Pretoria households at stage three of the family life cycle, the point at which child dependency was at its peak, a 'surplus' of at least 20*s.* a week.[108] The material foundations on which minders' privileged status rested appeared clear. They sufficed to convince Schulze-Gaevernitz that factory industry had produced operatives who were monetarily, if not spiritually, 'better off than many a country parson'.[109] For others, however, the reality was more complex. Allen Clarke introduced a more sceptical note, arguing that no lasting benefit accrued from a career in the mule-gate, as 'the worn-out spinner of to-day generally has to be kept by his grown-up children, or spin his last earthly set of days in the workhouse'.[110] If the available evidence precludes a direct evaluation of such assertions, the domestic realities underpinning the occupational experience can be inferred from analysis of the superannuation fund operated by the Bolton Provincial Association from 1893.

Under the scheme, any member was eligible for benefit who 'through old age or infirmity is unable to follow his employment as an operative cotton spinner, overlooker, or manager'.[111] Payments commenced, in 1900, at the age of 50, a limit raised to 52 in 1905 and to 55 in 1912, where it remained unchanged for twenty years.[112] The early age fixed for eligibility acknowledged the brief span of many mill careers, truncated in certain cases by the physical demands of working the mule. In 1911, James Calderbank enlarged on the factors which had forced his early retirement: 'my eyesight got so bad that I could not see my work properly and being a spinner on very fine counts I had a complaint come back about my work . . . I am 56 years old, and when you get that age in the spinning room you are not much good, and in these days you have to make room for younger men'.[113] His was not an untypical experience. Over half of those

---

[108] *Parl. Papers 1909*, lxxx (4545), Earnings and Hours of Labour, 35; see above, pp. 239–42.

[109] G. von Schulze-Gaevernitz, *The Cotton Trade in England and on the Continent* (1895), 174.

[110] C. A. Clarke, *The Effects of the Factory System* (1899; repr. Littleborough, 1985), 137.

[111] *CFT* (17 Nov. 1893), 6.

[112] JRUL, BCA/1/3/8 BSA, minutes, districts quarterly meeting, 16 Sept. 1905; BCA/1/3/9 minutes, Superannuation Committee, 11 May 1912; BCA/1/3/14 minutes, districts quarterly meeting, 17 Mar. 1932.

[113] BA, HRF, ABHC/5/39 Personal Files, James Calderbank to Henry Roughley, 23 Apr. 1911.

claiming benefit in the first five years of the fund's operations were aged under 55. What is more, this does not include those forced to give up work before the minimum age. In such cases, workplace collections were organized to ameliorate hardship. One such, at Sunnyside Mill in 1925, aimed to assist a minder left unfit for work at the age of 44. In all, union minutes recorded twenty-eight such collections between 1928 and 1932.[114]

Spinners could thus find themselves wholly or partially dependent on superannuation benefit of 5s. a week well before they reached pensionable age. Despite repeated appeals for an increase in allowances, which pointed up the financial problems facing claimants, pressures on the fund, caused by heavy demand at the minimum and the longevity of those on benefit, precluded any change in rates. A supplementary payment of 1s. a week was agreed in 1918 for those who were out of work or earning under 20s. a week, but this ceased three years later.[115] For many, therefore, departure from the mule heralded a period of acute financial difficulty. Others used lump-sum subventions to fund independent trading initiatives or more straightforward attempts at job mobility. During the Great War, for example, superannuation claimants included those seeking to transfer to higher paid munitions work.[116]

Over time, economic change came to limit such designs. The priority given to secure forms of employment, which encouraged parents to seek alternative forms of work for their children, ensured that, for spinners themselves, ambitions beyond the mill were increasingly reined in. Some sense of this process and its implications is conveyed by tracing the careers of a sample of some 500 Bolton minders through local directories, published in 1922 and 1932. All but eighty remained at the mule throughout the decade, indicating the continued attractions of a stable career at the headstock. A further thirty-nine had no occupations recorded in 1932, and may be assumed to have no longer been economically active. For the forty-one who remained, for whom a change of occupations is indicated, a marked diversity in experience is revealed. Six had secured promotion to overlooker or assistant-overlooker status, while a similar number had set up business on their own account. By 1932, these included a grocer, a

[114] JRUL, BCA/1/3/8 BSA, minutes, districts quarterly meeting, 16 Sept. 1905; BCA/1/3/13 minutes, notice of appeal, 24 Nov. 1927.

[115] At one point, superannuated members approached the solicitor for the employers' federation to press their case, *BJG* (17 Apr. 1914), 7; JRUL, BCA/1/3/11 BSA, minutes, special districts meeting, 20 July 1918; quarterly districts meeting, 15 Sept. 1921.

[116] See above, pp. 105–6; JRUL, BCA/13/2/18 BSA, general correspondence, H. Kerfoot to Peter Bullough, 21 Oct. 1915.

Table 11. *Ages at which superannuation benefit first claimed*

Date*	Average Age (years)	No. at Minimum	No. Aged 61 and Over
1916–19	57.7	57	24
1919–22	57.6	38	15
1922–5	59.6	31	49
1925–8	61.1	32	68
1928–31	61.7	27	69
1931**	62.8	4	31

Source: JRUL, BCA/1/19/1 BSA, Bolton branch, Superannuation Payments, 1916–34.
* Years beginning March.
** April to December.

beer-seller, and a painter and decorator. The greater number, however, twenty-four in all, had been reduced to low-paid, unskilled labouring work.[117] The balance of probability was that a reduction in circumstances would follow a departure from the mule-carriage, a calculation which worked to prolong spinners' careers. The point is fully reflected in figures relating to superannuation claimants. Although demand remained high at the minimum, indicating that enforced early retirement remained a reality for large numbers, the average age at which benefits were first claimed showed a sustained and significant increase between the wars. Awareness of this trend, and its likely consequences for the 'piecer problem' as promotional opportunities were further restricted, encouraged calls for a compulsory retirement age for minders. In 1927, a proposal was advanced for a contributory pension scheme, which would have ensured that no one over the age of 60 would retain control of the headstock.[118] The idea failed to secure significant support, however, union officials preferring to restate the pressures which detained minders in the mule-gate: 'except in a few odd cases, men are not in a position to give up spinning at 55 years of age, but are compelled, under present economic circumstances, to continue at the mules until they are well past 60 years of age'.[119] Evidence from the superannuation fund certainly suggests that financial inducements carried progressively less weight in individual career decisions. Large numbers opted to delay retirement pending the introduction of higher rates of benefit in December 1923. Whereas only nine new claimants came forward in the first nine months of that year, a further 108

[117] *Tillotson's Bolton Directory*, 13th and 15th edns. (Bolton, 1922 and 1932).
[118] *BJG* (2 Dec. 1927), 10, letter by 'Spinner'; (9 Dec. 1927), 10, letter by 'Another Spinner'.
[119] JRUL, BCA/1/3/14 BSA, minutes, quarterly districts meeting, 17 Mar. 1932.

names were added to superannuation rolls in the eighteen months that followed. By contrast, the next rise in rates, in 1928, produced no comparable spurt in demand.[120]

Overall, the figures provide partial endorsement for the claims advanced by both Schulze-Gaevernitz and Allen Clarke. Although work in the mule-gates held out the prospect of material affluence, this remained subject, at all times, to interruption through physical incapacity or wider economic changes. To that degree, the experiences of spinners' families closely mirrored those of Pretoria households. In other respects, however, a clear point of contrast emerges. If, among the Pretoria sample, increased economic uncertainty worked to confirm the importance of composite family incomes, among minders' households the effect was to enhance the role of the main breadwinner. This latter point has more general significance. In their analysis of developments in working-class society over the late nineteenth and early twentieth centuries, Savage and Miles attach great importance to the progressive loss of status among previously privileged groups of skilled workers, reflected both in diminished income differentials and reduced responsibility for the processes of recruitment and training.[121] The example of the spinners suggests rather a different conclusion, however. Although their material security was increasingly threatened by economic difficulty, minders responded with a determined defence of their place in the production process, to the extent that workplace hierarchies were, if anything, extended. A more uniform work experience was not the invariable outcome of economic change. It must be stressed, nevertheless, that the spinners' exclusivity was less an expression of aspirations to bourgeois standards of respectability than a recurrent quest for material security in the light of deep domestic uncertainty. In a working life which could be foreshortened by delayed promotion and enforced early retirement, frugality was, as one observer remarked, a necessary and entirely rational pursuit: 'they were known for being a bit stingy, these spinners. Everybody used to say, "Oh, aren't they a stingy lot!" Well, they'd been so used to living off a small amount of money they were very careful when they got more money, and they were really a stingy set of people, but they couldn't help it.'[122]

---

[120] JRUL, BCA/1/19/1 BSA, superannuation payments; BCA/1/3/12 minutes, Council meeting, 8 Oct. 1923; BCA/1/3/13 minutes, Council meeting, 17 Sept. 1928.

[121] M. Savage and A. Miles, *The Remaking of the British Working Class* (1994), 25–30.

[122] BOHP, Teaching Pack, *Growing Up in Bolton, 1900–40*, transcripts, 'Leisure and School', 9.

Even at times of apparent prosperity, working-class living standards remained fragile. If outright impoverishment was rare, it was an insistent threat which informed everyday existence for most families. The dual nature of the household economy, in which affluence and privation were closely associated, is encapsulated by the Pretoria evidence. Of 168 households known to have made provision against the loss of a breadwinner through illness, incapacity or death, sixty-seven or almost 40 per cent were also in debt. Although the problem was most common among families with young, dependent children, it recurred across the various life stages. Amounts owed varied markedly in extent, from the £2. 3s. 10d. which Ambrose Coffey owed the doctor and the coal merchant,[123] to the £41 left outstanding on the death of Albert Lonsdale. Significantly, Lonsdale, who has already figured in these pages as player and secretary with the Wingates Temperance Prize Band, also held savings in the Royal Liver Assurance Co. and the Wingates Independent Methodist Burial Society.[124] As this indicates, indebtedness, in itself, was no indication of poverty. Rather the reverse, for credit was generally only extended to those considered capable of repaying the sums owed.[125]

Nevertheless, liabilities often proved protracted, imposing significant additional costs on the household budget. Ill health was a particular problem, the incidence of which would increase with age. In 1921, Shaw cited the growing number of requests for additional assistance from widows as evidence that 'the shock of the Explosion is now revealing itself in some failure of health especially from heart weakness'.[126] Where illness was prolonged, the weight of medical bills could leave household resources severely depleted. Over fifteen years from 1910, recurrent health problems reduced Martha Jane Worthington's savings from £100 to £2. Similarly, James Hardman was forced to admit that the bill for £80 outstanding on the death of his wife in 1922 had 'almost cleared me out'.[127] Payment by instalments offered a permissible means of settling such accounts, without compromising notions of respectability, but still left families with long-term obligations which were liable to increase should ill health recur. Such was the case with the Hosker family of Hindley

---

[123] BA, HRF, ABHC/5/1–344 Personal Files, Compensation statements; ABHC/5/49 Personal Files, Compensation statement.

[124] See above, p. 175; BA, HRF, ABHC/5/191 Personal Files, Compensation statement.

[125] Roberts, *Classic Slum*, 105.

[126] BA, HRF, ABHC/5/166 Personal Files, Shaw to Hon. Sec., 22 June 1921.

[127] BA, HRF, ABHC/5/118 Personal Files, James Hardman to W. E. Tonge, 4 Apr. 1925; ABHC/5/341 Personal Files, Shaw to Hon. Sec., 2 Feb. 1925.

Green. In 1910, they were already committed to paying 5s. each week towards a doctor's bill of £74. By 1929, the principal had, despite interruptions, been reduced to £28. 15s. In the interim, however, a further bill of £10 had been incurred and another was anticipated to cover the cost of Mrs Hosker's treatment for inflammation of the kidneys and bladder. Three years later, Mrs Hosker succinctly summarized her and the family's plight in a letter to Shaw: 'I owe him [the doctor] £6 now and he will send me another big bill Sir I feel ashame [sic] but I cant help sickness'.[128]

For this family, as for others, problems were compounded by the loss of earnings brought on by short-time working and prolonged industrial stoppages. At such times, economies were forced on many households, with rents and insurance premiums the most common targets for retrenchment. In both cases, the costs of defalcation could be deferred. Property owners, many of whom were working-class in origin, had little option but to acquiesce in the accumulation of arrears, more especially as the possibility of securing alternative tenants was not high in a period of reduced purchasing power. One Bolton woman was unable to collect the rents on her three houses during the 1926 coal strike.[129] Similarly, competition for working-class custom among insurance companies often meant that failure to maintain premiums did not automatically result in the policies lapsing. The Albion Friendly Society, based in Bolton, sought to recruit savers with the motto 'We lapse the least and we pay the quickest', a boast which it justified by maintaining 'live' policies on which no premiums had been paid for several years. Included amongst these was a former resident of Bolton who had emigrated to Australia.[130] If this was an extreme case, it indicated the need, acknowledged by many agencies, to respond to the fragility of domestic circumstances.

Households themselves responded to such uncertainty by seeking additional sources of income. One course, widely pursued in this period, was to branch out into retailing.[131] The drink trade provided a popular outlet for the investment of savings. One Pretoria collier ran The Lord Napier Hotel in Bolton, while another widow catered for rather different tastes through her temperance bar.[132] For the most part, however, money

---

[128] BA, HRF, ABHC/5/155 Personal Files, Mrs E. Hosker to Shaw, 16 Oct. 1932; Mrs Hosker to Rhys Davies, MP, July 1926; Shaw to Hon. Sec., 14 Feb. 1928, 15 Mar. 1929.

[129] *BJG* (1 Oct. 1926), 5.

[130] *BJG* (16 Oct. 1908), 16; (27 Aug. 1926), 5; (28 June 1929), 4.

[131] J. Benson, *The Penny Capitalists: A Study of Nineteenth-Century Working-Class Entrepreneurs* (Dublin, 1983), 114–26; D. Haworth, *Bright Morning: Images of a Lancashire Boyhood* (1990), 11–13.

[132] BA, HRF, ABHC/5/183 Personal Files, Compensation statement; ABHC/5/181 Personal Files, Shaw to Hon. Sec., 18 Oct. 1928.

was drawn to the general grocery trade. Jane Cattell used one-third of her compensation award to purchase a grocery and tripe-dealing business.[133] Many such concerns, particularly where well-established, were able to prosper. That owned by the Hurst family of Wingates provided work for four daughters and was sufficiently profitable to enable Mrs Hurst to invest £500 in Bolton Corporation stock in 1911.[134] The majority of businesses were, however, more modest, conducted on limited means from the home. Although established dealers, such as those organized through the North-East Lancashire Trade Federation, protested at the advantage enjoyed by such concerns in qualifying as dwelling houses rather than as businesses for rates assessment, the competitive threat they posed was, in reality, minimal. Most working-class traders pursued precarious careers in mean premises, with limited stock. The Pretoria widow Elizabeth Jolley was seen to have gained little from her fruit business, as 'the stock is so small and the shop is so un-attractive'.[135] By 1912, Jane Cattell found that her investments were generating additional debts: 'She says everybody is pressing for bills. She is owing about £10 mostly for groceries purchased for her business, £1–4–0 for rent, and in addition there will be £4–10–0 due at the beginning of May.'[136] Such problems became commonplace in the 1920s. Unable to match the discounts and credit facilities offered by larger retailers, most struggled to retain their share of a stagnant or declining market. The Hursts reported a fall in sales as short-time working eroded purchasing power across the neighbourhood.[137] For others, losses resulted in outright failure. The 1926 strike brought ruin to one former dataller, who had left the pit to trade as a coal and fruit merchant. Supplies of fuel were rapidly exhausted, while his edible stock perished for lack of custom. His was one of several cases to come before local bankruptcy courts and served to convince magistrates that it was 'as difficult and risky for the average ranker in the mill, mine, or workshop to throw up a laborious but secure living for the questionable future of trade, as to start a fresh life overseas'.[138] The shortage of secure earnings opportunities in industry ensured that many continued to run the risk. Thomas Morris, the son of a Pretoria victim, left the pit in 1930

[133] BA, HRF, ABHC/5/42 Personal Files, Shaw to Hon. Sec., 3 Apr. 1912.

[134] BA, HRF, ABHC/5/171 Personal Files, note, n.d.; Shaw to Hon. Sec., 18 Feb. 1926.

[135] BA, HRF, ABHC/5/173 Personal Files, Shaw to Hon. Sec., 4 Aug. 1927; *BJG* (27 Feb. 1925), 11.

[136] BA, HRF, ABHC/5/42 Personal Files, Shaw to Hon. Sec., 3 Apr. 1912.

[137] BA, HRF, ABHC/5/171 Personal Files, Shaw to Hon. Sec., 18 Feb. 1926; see also BOHP 88C (female, born 1901; male, born 1909), tape; *BJG* (11 June 1926), 10.

[138] *BJG* (24 Sept. 1926), 5; (19 Nov. 1926), 7.

to vend fruit from a horse and cart.[139] Once committed, family difficulties often worked to tie capital in to trade. The Pretoria widow, Clara
Leigh was obliged to retain her business as, Shaw explained, 'the shop
[selling confectionary and temperance drinks] does no more than pay its
way, and her health is so poor that she would be glad to be without it if
her two children were in more settled occupations'.[140] In practice, therefore, involvement in the retail sector could be as valuable in shoring up
vulnerable family economies as it was in furthering individual and collective ambitions.

Property fulfilled a similar dual purpose. Particularly early in the
period, high rates of home ownership were recorded across the cotton districts of Lancashire, a fact attributable to the high level of family incomes
and the availability of institutional support. In both Bolton and Wigan,
the local Co-operative Societies were the principal sources of mortgage
finance. By 1914, 10,000 accounts had been opened with the Great and
Little Bolton Society's Building Section.[141] Compensation awards enabled
a number of Pretoria widows to become owner-occupiers. Grants totalling
£78 were used by Martha Hulme to purchase a house to accommodate
herself, two daughters, and her parents.[142] Yet property had more than
merely use value. In 1924, the Bolton Property Owners' and Rate-Payers'
Association remarked on a tendency among 'the thrifty poor' to acquire
houses in order to profit from the rent proceeds. Home-owners were even
known to take up council-house tenancies, putting the original house out
to rent.[143] Among this new 'rentier' class was the Pretoria widow, Mary
Thomason, who used her compensation money to purchase two houses,
letting one to provide an additional source of income. Although fund officials anticipated a long-term benefit to Mrs Thomason's children from
this arrangement, such expectations were to be disappointed. Within five
years, Mary's poor health, which obliged her daughter to stay at home to

[139] BA, HRF, ABHC/5/221 Personal Files, Shaw to Hon. Sec., 5 Feb. 1930.
[140] BA, HRF, ABHC/5/181 Personal Files, Shaw to Hon. Sec., 8 Aug. 1927.
[141] M. Swenarton and S. Taylor, 'The Scale and Nature of the Growth of Owner-
Occupation in Britain between the Wars', *Econ.Hist.Rev.*, 2nd ser. 38 (1985), 378–9; *Parl.
Papers 1908*, cvii (3864), Working Class Rents, Housing and Retail Prices, 122; A. Shadwell,
Industrial Efficiency (1909 edn.), 63; BA, BCB ABCF/17/4 Public Health Committee,
Working-class Housing, Medical Officer of Health's Report for 1913, 2; J. Brown, *Wigan
Welfare* (Wigan, 1939), 39, 74.
[142] BA, HRF, ABHC/5/165 Personal Files, Shaw to Hon. Sec., 4 Feb. 1921.
[143] *BJG* (11 Apr. 1924), 11; BA, BCB ABCF/21/2 Housing and Town Planning
Committee, Report upon the Erection of Houses, by E. L. Morgan, Borough Engineer and
Surveyor, 19 Aug. 1926, 4–5.

nurse her, forced the sale of both houses.[144] A similar experience awaited John Horrocks, a former mill manager, who borrowed money to have two houses built. Repayments presented few problems until 1921, when both he and his son were made redundant. At that point, the houses were placed on the market.[145] Even where families were able to retain property, returns remained uncertain. The Worthingtons thus derived little or no profit from their eleven houses, as all were heavily mortgaged.[146] The acquisition of property was, for the most part, widely encouraged. As the manager of the Bolton branch of the Halifax Equitable Building Society observed in 1925, the provision of home loans had a broader political function: it 'helped to make houses into homes, small shops into large ones, individuals into citizens, and citizens into patriots with a stake in the country'.[147] It was a point of view enthusiastically endorsed by J. F. Steele, chairman of the town's Housing and Town Planning Committee, for whom the small property-owner constituted the most effective bulwark against the spread of Bolshevik ideas. Yet the evidence suggests that home ownership was an insubstantial basis on which to found hopes of social and political stability. What is more, economic difficulty ensured that rates of owner-occupation across the cotton districts showed little if any advance in the twenty years from 1918.[148]

Involvement in property ownership and retail enterprise was wholly consistent with family economies shaped by irregular and unpredictable periods of affluence and financial uncertainty. If the Pretoria evidence indicates that, at times, households were capable of experiencing significant and sustained levels of prosperity, it also suggests that margins were vulnerable to changes in the dependency ratio and, more fundamentally, to the impact of wider economic developments. To that extent, the insistence of historians such as Andrew Davies that, despite long-term improvements in living standards, poverty and distress remained central cultural experiences for the working class of early twentieth-century Britain, appears entirely appropriate.[149] Although, in outward form, family economies varied markedly, the material realities which underpinned

---

[144] BA, HRF, ABHC/5/300 Personal Files, Shaw to Hon. Sec., 23 Oct. 1917, 7 Mar. 1921.

[145] BA, HRF, ABHC/5/153 Personal Files, Shaw to Hon. Sec., 8 Apr. 1920, 21 Jan. 1922.

[146] BA, HRF, ABHC/5/341 Personal Files, Shaw to Hon. Sec., 31 May 1926.

[147] *BJG* (13 Mar. 1925), 8.

[148] *BJG* (27 Dec. 1924), 8; Swenarton and Taylor, 'Scale', 391.

[149] A. Davies, *Leisure, Gender and Poverty* (Buckingham and Bristol, Pa., 1992), ch. 1; id., 'Leisure in the "Classic Slum", 1900–1939', in A. Davies and S. Fielding (eds.), *Workers' Worlds* (Manchester, 1992), 104–7.

them displayed broad similarities in the ways in which affluence and poverty were closely intertwined. Emulative expenditure, undertaken during periods of prosperity, fulfilled a more preventive purpose as circumstances altered. As kin remained the individual's first resort at times of difficulty, the family tie was crucial in containing the threat of financial exigency. Yet, if the material context renders the unity displayed by working-class families more comprehensible, as an explanation of that tendency it remains less than complete. In order to capture the broader cultural significance of domestic relationships, consideration must be given to the quality of kinship ties. Additional insights into this point are provided by the experience of women.

III

For the most part, working-class family life in the early twentieth century was structured around clearly defined and differentiated gender roles: males assumed responsibility for providing the wages on which the household would subsist, while the details of domestic management were left to the women. The dominant influence which mothers exerted over the rearing of children, both male and female, lay at the heart of what McKibbin has identified as the 'matrilocality' of working-class life in this period.[150] Yet the separation of spheres between husband and wife also had potential implications for the quality of marital relationships. Mrs Pember Reeves, for one, feared that ties of affection were unlikely to survive the emergence of distinct interests and experiences.[151] Oral testimony, while it has not endorsed such pessimism, suggests that cooperative marital relationships, reflected in the sharing of household duties and leisure time, were most likely to flourish where both parents were engaged in full-time paid work.[152] Across south–central Lancashire, a more conventional separation of economic roles was, by 1900, apparent. Participation in paid employment beyond the home terminated, for all but a small minority of women, on marriage or during pregnancy and was confined, in most cases, to jobs in which few men were employed. Before turning to consider what implications this had for the stability and

---

[150] R. McKibbin, *Classes and Cultures* (Oxford, 1998), 164–76.
[151] Pember Reeves, *Round about a Pound a Week*, 154–5.
[152] D. Gittins, *Fair Sex: Family Size and Structure, 1900–39* (1982), 129–41; Roberts, *A Woman's Place*, 118; M. Savage, 'Women and Work in the Lancashire Cotton Industry, 1890–1939', in J. A. Jowitt and A. J. McIvor (eds.), *Employers and Labour in the English Textile Industries, 1850–1939* (1988), 220.

texture of married life across the region, an examination of the factors giving rise to women's progressive exclusion from the formal labour market must be essayed.

In both coal and cotton, a combination of male exclusivity and legislative controls had worked to limit opportunities for female employment. Having been expelled from Bolton's mule-rooms in 1887, women were readmitted in 1899, on condition that they fulfilled piecing duties only. In mining, female work underground had been outlawed from 1842. An attempt to extend the prohibition to surface jobs failed in the 1880s, but was renewed in 1911, through an amendment to that year's Coal Mines Regulation Bill, tabled by Arthur Markham, Liberal MP for Mansfield.[153] Opponents of female employment argued that the work was not only physically unsuitable, but that it was also, given the proximity of both sexes on the pit brow, morally harmful. In response, a vigorous campaign was mounted in the women's defence by, among others, Miss King-May, a middle-class suffragist, whose investigations into working conditions on the pit bank suggested that contact between the sexes amounted to little more than 'harmless chaff and fun'.[154] Mining unions, from which women were still excluded, remained broadly hostile to their cause. Nevertheless, when a deputation of forty-five pit lasses lobbied Westminster, it gained support from figures across the political divide, including J. Harmood Banner, chairman of Pearson and Knowles Coal and Iron Co., Ltd, and Unionist MP for the Everton Division of Liverpool, R. J. N. Neville, Unionist member for Wigan, and Stephen Walsh, miners' agent and Labour MP for Ince, whose attitude may have been coloured by his own marriage to a former pit-brow lass.[155] On occasion, the women themselves proved their own most powerful advocates. Addressing a public meeting in London, Mrs Andrews, a Wigan surface worker of thirty-six years' standing, offered her Sunday school books for public inspection as proof of the respectability of herself and her fellows. She then proceeded to dispel any lingering doubts on the matter by

---

[153] See above, pp. 33–5; A. V. John, *By the Sweat of their Brow* (1984), 48–53, 138–207; *WE* (1 Aug. 1911), 3.

[154] *WE* (30 Sept. 1911), 8; see also J. Humphries, '". . . The Most Free From Objection . . .": The Sexual Division of Labor and Women's Work in Nineteenth-Century England', *Journal of Economic History*, 47 (1987), 938–42.

[155] *WE* (3 Aug. 1911), 2; (5 Oct. 1911), 4; *Directory of Directors* (1913 edn.); P. J. Waller, *Democracy and Sectarianism: A Political and Social History of Liverpool, 1868–1939* (Liverpool, 1981), 493; M. Stenton and S. Lees (eds.), *Who's Who of British Members of Parliament* iii. *1919–45* (Brighton, 1979), 261; John, *By the Sweat of their Brow*, 206.

asserting, 'Aw'd sooner go to t' pit than go to bed', a preference not readily susceptible to empirical verification.[156]

Backed by such persuasive rhetoric, the women's case prevailed in
1911. However, their subsequent incorporation within mining unionism
prefaced a sustained decline in their numbers. Significantly, few attempts
were made to stem losses through the 1920s, resistance only being offered
where the loss of work would result in financial distress. Yet, given the
nature of the pit-brow workforce as a whole, such instances were rare.
Mrs Andrews was singular in more than her preference for work over the
domestic comforts. Her colleagues were, for the most part, young unmarried girls, many of whom were physically unfitted for higher paid mill
work. In 1911, only one in ten of Wigan's pit lasses were married, suggesting that, for the great majority, surface work provided a short-term,
supplementary source of income.[157] Women thus broadly acquiesced in
their replacement by youths or disabled partial-compensation men. The
maintenance of male earning power continued to be seen as crucial to
family well-being.

Beyond the pit brow, the pattern of female work was determined by
family circumstances. On occasions, participation in paid employment
was enforced by the inadequate level of male wages. Among the towns
surveyed by Bowley and Burnett-Hurst in 1913, women's employment
was found to be greatest where unskilled, low-paid trades predominated.[158] Over time, growth in female numbers was recorded during periods of economic difficulty or when living standards came under threat.
Wives and widows were thus drawn to the mill in significantly greater
numbers in the decade from 1901. Whereas Bolton's female cotton workforce as a whole increased by 11.4 per cent in the ten years to 1911, the
growth among married and widowed operatives approached 29 per
cent.[159] Participation rates continued to grow into the 1920s, as reduced
family earnings encouraged married women to declare themselves available for work in order to qualify for unemployment benefits. The trend
was only checked with the passage of Anomalies legislation in 1931.[160]
Individual examples confirm the impression conveyed of careers shaped

---

[156] *WE* (2 Nov. 1911), 3.
[157] See above, pp. 92–3; *Parl. Papers 1913*, lxxviii (7018), Census of England and Wales,
1911. X. Occupations and Industries. Pt. I, table 13, 255.
[158] Bowley and Burnett-Hurst, *Livelihood and Poverty*, 27.
[159] *Parl. Papers 1902*, cxix (1002), Census of England and Wales, 1901: County of
Lancaster, table 35, 148–9; *Parl. Papers 1913*, lxxviii (7018), Census of England and Wales,
1911. X. Occupations and Industries. Pt. I, table 13, 215–17.
[160] Board of Trade, *An Industrial Survey*, 73–4; *BJG* (19 Feb. 1932), 10.

by economic difficulty. In 1923, Bolton's oldest cotton operative, Rachel Batty, a warper, retired, aged 83. She had resumed work thirty years earlier, on the death of her husband. Prior to that, she had returned to the mill on a number of occasions, finding 'her experience of great use in the not infrequent periods of bad trade and low earnings'.[161] Similar problems forced several Pretoria widows back to work. Theresa Ellen Molyneux continued on the loom into the 1920s, as short-time working reduced her sons' earning capacity. Yet this case was not straightforward: as well as making an essential contribution to the support of the household, Mrs Molyneux's wages helped to finance the purchase of two houses in a neighbouring street.[162]

Paid female work thus fulfilled a dual function, entirely consistent with family economies which sought to capitalize on periods of prosperity so as to accumulate resources which could be used to tide the household over more difficult times. The survey of women's employment in Birmingham trades, undertaken by Cadbury, Matheson, and Shann, found that, while inadequate and interrupted male wages were the explanations most commonly advanced by women themselves to account for their participation in paid work, a significant minority claimed to be earning to maintain or augment an already comfortable standard of living. Equally, the four-class categorization of wives adopted by the Women's Industrial Council for its investigation into married women's work, included those who remained in employment even though household incomes sufficed to meet basic needs.[163] Women so placed were also present in the Pretoria sample. If the evidence is complete, only one wife, Alice Farrimond, was employed outside the home at the time of the disaster. All other members of the family (a husband and five children) were earning, so that Alice's average wage of 16s. a week added to an existing income of 70s. 5d.[164] Similarly, the widow Mary Rushton chose to return to work after the disaster, although relief allowances guaranteed her an income 4s. 4d. in excess of her husband's average earnings. Immediate need appears to have played little part in her decision, as the money enabled her to invest £100 in Bolton Corporation stock.[165]

[161] *BJG* (21 Dec. 1923), 5.

[162] BA, HRF, ABHC/5/217 Personal Files, Shaw to Hon. Sec., 27 June 1922, 3 Apr. 1925.

[163] E. Cadbury, M. C. Matheson, and G. Shann, *Women's Work and Wages* (1906), 147–8; C. Black (ed.), *Married Women's Work: Being the Report of an Enquiry Undertaken by the Women's Industrial Council* (1983 repr.), 1–2, 7.

[164] BA, HRF, ABHC/5/89–90 Personal Files, Compensation statements.

[165] BA, HRF, ABHC/5/261 Personal Files, Compensation statement; Shaw to Hon. Sec., 11 July 1921; ABHC/2/2 schedule of relief incomes.

Family needs also determined the type of work which married women were likely to undertake. Many found a ready outlet for their skills in domestic service, working as daily helps or live-in housekeepers in suburban middle-class homes. In the late 1920s, the Pretoria widow Martha Hulme kept house for the chaplain of Smithills, north of Bolton.[166] More often, work was conducted from the home, servicing the needs of the surrounding neighbourhood. Elizabeth Ann Partington took in washing for several years after the Great War, using the proceeds to fund her annual holiday.[167] Such job choices were consistent with a life course marked by career discontinuities and prolonged periods of child-rearing. Among Pretoria households for which it can be assumed that the process of family formation was complete (here taken to be where the youngest child was aged 5 years or over), an average of ten years separated the birth of the oldest from that of the youngest child. Taking only those children which survived infancy, Mary Alice Anderton's first and final experiences of childbirth occurred between the ages of 33 and 43. Even then, her responsibilities were not discharged, as the family proceeded to take in her 74-year-old father.[168] Alternative courses of action, devolving the care of infants on to paid child minders, elderly relatives, or elder daughters, held out few attractions. Little financial advantage would accrue from such actions, as women resuming work in the mill were customarily assigned the lowest starter wage. Greater benefit was to be derived from placing daughters in work at the earliest permissible age, maximizing promotional opportunities and the period during which they would contribute to household income. Among wives, then, additional earnings were most likely to be sought through part-time service occupations. Significantly, recourse to the kind of full-time employments which removed mothers from the home often drew disparaging comments from neighbouring matriarchs, the hub of the local assistance networks on which women were often forced to rely.[169]

---

[166] BA, HRF, ABHC/5/165 Personal Files, Shaw to Hon. Sec., 25 July 1927.

[167] BA, HRF, ABHC/5/235 Personal Files, Shaw to Hon. Sec., 27 July 1927.

[168] BA, HRF, ABHC/5/1–344 Personal Files, Compensation statements; ABHC/5/2 Personal Files, Compensation statement.

[169] BA, Alice Foley Collection ZFO/6, A. Foley, 'Married Women Cardroom Workers and Unemployment Benefit'; B. Harrison, 'Class and Gender in Modern British Labour History', 142; Ross, 'Survival Networks', 4–27; M. Tebbutt, *Women's Talk? A Social History of 'Gossip' in Working-Class Neighbourhoods, 1880–1960* (Aldershot and Brookfield, Vt., 1995), chs. 2 and 3; id., 'Women's Talk? Gossip and "Women's Words" in Working-Class Communities, 1880–1939', in Davies and Fielding (eds.), *Workers' Worlds*, 49–73; Roberts, *Classic Slum*, 42–4.

Women themselves thus encouraged and retained a strong sense of domestic responsibility. The source of this close identification with house and home has been variously traced. The pattern of socialization during childhood contributed to such an outcome. At the same time that boys were encouraged to cultivate interests beyond the home, girls were introduced to the details of household management. More formal educational and training programmes confirmed this differentiation of roles. The curriculum at Tootal Broadhurst Lee's continuation school from 1918 included classes in 'housecraft', which were offered to all girls with an eye to the 'application of the instruction to their subsequent requirements'.[170] Equally, as demobilization progressed from 1919, courses were organized to retrain female munitions workers in tasks that were deemed more practical for the post-war world, including cookery and dress-making.[171] The promotion and consequent intensification of the ideology of 'separate spheres' is seen to have resulted in the internalization of its central precept: that women's prime responsibility lay in domestic management. Family pressures operated to sustain this view. In a study of working-class households in inter-war Liverpool, Ayers and Lambertz argue that the established separation of gender roles in marriage was underscored by the constant threat of domestic violence. Women were obliged to adopt a secretive approach to budgeting to convey the outward impression of coping on the limited resources provided by their husbands. Far from empowering women, therefore, domestic management was a burden, enforced by emotional insecurity and potentially violent marital relationships.[172]

At the centre of the view of working-class marriage advanced by Ayers and Lambertz is the male practice of paying over only a portion of their wage, keeping back the remainder for individual use as 'spends', in the expectation that wives could manage on what they were allowed. Such behaviour was not confined to Liverpool. Lady Bell, for example, found that over one-third of the wives of Middlesbrough iron-workers were ignorant of their spouses' earnings.[173] Yet the practice was not invariable.

---

[170] *A Scheme of Education*, 23; BA, BOHP 128 (male, born 1896), transcript, 3; 158 (female, born 1907), transcript, 3.

[171] *The Times* (16 Oct. 1919), 7; *Times Educational Supplement* (27 Mar. 1919), 155.

[172] P. Ayers and J. Lambertz, 'Marriage Relations, Money, and Domestic Violence in Working-Class Liverpool, 1919–39', in J. Lewis (ed.), *Labour and Love: Women's Experience of Home and Family, 1850–1940* (Oxford, 1986), 195–219.

[173] Ibid. 198–202; Bell, *At the Works*, 78; see also Davies, *Leisure, Gender and Poverty*, 55–6.

Financial openness was considered more likely where wives themselves participated in paid employment.[174] Although gender roles were more sharply differentiated within the Pretoria sample, compensation returns suggest that husbands rarely failed to contribute their earnings in full. In the few instances where this did not occur, children's wages more than made good any losses. In two households, fathers, although earning £2 and 30s. a week each, paid over only 30s. and 26s. respectively. In the case of the former, five children brought home 88s. 7d. each week. In the latter, three children contributed a more modest 20s. 3d.[175] In single-income households, the tendency to withhold wages was virtually unknown, although Kate E., whose husband had paid over only 17s. out of the 24s. 1d. he earned on average each week, was forced to admit that her weekly allowance of 25s. left her 'much better off now than when he was alive'.[176] The fact that, with few exceptions, husbands and fathers acknowledged in full their responsibilities as custodians of the 'family wage' suggests that marital relationships, at least among the Pretoria sample, were more open and co-operative than Ayers and Lambertz allow.

The nature of the Pretoria evidence, it must be recognized, precludes direct and extended consideration of this point. Marital discord only begins to figure in the records at the point of separation. It is thus known that four couples had separated prior to the disaster. William Lord, for example, had left his wife the preceding August. Although Mrs Lord identified him among the deceased raised from the pit, a telegram subsequently revealed him to be alive and well and living in Yorkshire. Her reaction to this news remains unknown.[177] Significantly, however, separation does not appear to have entailed an abdication of all family responsibilities. After two years living apart from his wife, John Thomas Prescott, reputed to be 'a man who has gone about a good deal with other women', still sent home 8s. each week to a household in which four children earned an average of 81s. 8d. a week.[178] In the years after 1910, despite the onset of broader economic difficulties, few instances of marital breakdown were recorded. Her husband's alleged cruelty led to the collapse of the second marriage of Mary Ellen Hogan[179] while a series of difficulties, including

[174] McKibbin, *Classes and Cultures*, 176–7.
[175] BA, HRF, ABHC/5/120, 153 Personal Files, Compensation statements.
[176] BA, HRF, ABHC/5/87 Personal Files, Compensation statement; note, 17 Aug. 1911.
[177] *BEN* (30 Dec. 1910), 3; (31 Dec. 1910), 3; *The Times* (2 Jan. 1911), 14; BA, HRF, ABHC/5/249, 335, 339 Personal Files, Compensation statements.
[178] BA, HRF, ABHC/5/249, 250 Personal Files, Compensation statements.
[179] BA, HRF, ABHC/5/145 Personal Files, Shaw to Hon. Sec., 15 July 1926, part of his alleged cruelty was his failure to pay over 10s. a week to Mary Ellen, as had been agreed.

the problem of meeting rental payments on their council house, led Lambert Monks, the father of a Pretoria victim, to part from his wife.[180] If the texture of everyday relations remains obscure, the evidence at least suggests that family unity and kinship assisted in averting or minimizing the incidence of marital breakdowns.

Rather more susceptible to close analysis are women's attitudes to marriage itself. Ayers and Lambertz point out, with justification, that alternatives to marriage were few. Most women, they argue, were forced to acquiesce in relationships characterized by mutual ignorance and maintained by the threat of physical force.[181] Pretoria widows, however, were, for a time at least, differently placed. For most, allowances paid after the disaster guaranteed a degree of financial independence. Utilizing the methodology outlined above to estimate household living standards, only eight families were likely to have faced outright impoverishment after December 1910. Most were headed by elderly dependants, who were denied assistance from the permanent relief society. For the majority, however, allowances held out the promise of 'comfort and freedom from anxiety'.[182] Households subsisting on one wage before the disaster were assured margins of between 10*s.* and 20*s.* thereafter, while, in almost one-third of cases, the post-disaster 'surplus' exceeded 20*s.* Such levels of affluence would not endure, as wartime inflation came to erode the real

Table 12. *Pretoria families: post-disaster living standards*

Margin	Number	Margin	Number
Deficit		Surplus	
up to 10*s.*	8	40*s.* to 50*s.*	17
Surplus		50*s.* to 60*s.*	6
up to 10*s.*	46	60*s.* to 70*s.*	2
10*s.* to 20*s.*	110	70*s.* to 80*s.*	1
20*s.* to 30*s.*	33		
30*s.* to 40*s.*	22		

Source: See Table 8, above.

---

[180] BA, HRF, ABHC/5/218 Personal Files, Rodan to Hon. Sec., 16 Mar. 1939.
[181] Ayers and Lambertz, 'Marriage Relations', 196–8; see also, J. Mark-Lawson and A. Witz, 'From "Family Labour" to "Family Wage"? The Case of Women's Labour in Nineteenth-Century Coalmining', *Social History*, 13 (1988), 154–5.
[182] BA, HRF, ABHC/2/12 correspondence and cuttings, cutting from *BJG* (19 Mar. 1915); ABHC/2/2 information supplied by the Lancashire and Cheshire Miners' Permanent Relief Society, Rules (1910), pars. 31–3.

value of benefits. Nevertheless, for some years after 1910, economic independence was a reality for most Pretoria widows. Their behaviour during
this prosperous interlude may thus be regarded as unusually important,
particularly as rates of remarriage were at their height in this very period.
In the first six years after the disaster, almost half of all Pretoria widows
aged 30 and under at the time of the explosion chose to remarry and so
commute their right to benefit. This tendency declined with age, so that
no widow over the age of 40 in 1910 had remarried by the end of 1916.[183]
If the earnings of co-resident children reduced the financial incentives to
seek a new partner, domestic responsibilities may also have deprived older
widows of the social contacts likely to encourage courtship. So, although
lacking the imperative of economic necessity, women opted in large numbers for marriage, in the expectation, it may be presumed, of securing
emotional solace in a companionate relationship.

It is difficult to perceive in such behaviour a calculative attitude to family life predicated on the expectation of a return for services rendered.
Women's attitudes to hearth and home were not enforced by material
necessity or by the absence of credible alternatives. Rather, it expressed a
deeper moral commitment to the family which, more than legislation and
male exclusivity, also shaped female involvement in paid forms of work. A
similar outlook prevailed among other members of the household.
Despite achieving financial independence at a comparatively early age,
children continued to acknowledge their obligations to parents through
the rendering of assistance in the form of money or in kind. Of greater
significance, fathers, although less involved in the details of household
management than their spouses, appear to have been no less committed to
the family ideal. Wages were paid over in full, even where children's earnings ensured a healthy income 'surplus'. Equally, decisions over the placing of children in work were shaped largely by the broader family interest.
With markedly few exceptions, family members appear to have subscribed
to the view that collective well-being required that calculations of personal advantage be put to one side in the wider interests of kin. In the
process, a deeper level of attachment was expressed than was conveyed by
the ties of work or neighbourhood. The family, in its extended, but more
especially in its nuclear form, constituted the moral and material centre of
working-class life.

---

[183] BA, HRF, ABHC/2/12 correspondence and cuttings, Memorandum on Re-marriage
of Widows, by C. Duncan Fraser (Hon. Actuary), 28 June 1917.

IV

The Pretoria evidence, upon which this chapter has substantially relied, confirms a point which historians have increasingly recognized: that working-class family unity was not unduly compromised by the structural changes brought about by industrialization. Despite losing their broader functions, as the focus for productive effort and in the processes of recruitment and training for industry, kinship groups retained an underlying coherence. In part, this was a product of economic necessity. The family, both in its nuclear and extended forms, remained the individual's first resort in times of difficulty, a role sustained through the flexibility of living arrangements. As a result, alternative, non-familial sources of assistance were sparingly utilized. Although the neighbourhood offered paid and informal services in abundance, these remained both limited in duration and conditional on reciprocal support. No such limitations appear to have marked family relationships. The availability of high juvenile earnings in local industry produced no fundamental change in the balance of obligations between parents and children, while after departure from the parental home, the flow of services between households gave continued expression to the family tie. Mid-nineteenth-century observers of textile Lancashire, who likened domestic relationships to the operations of a joint-stock enterprise were thus wide of the mark.[184] The principle of 'limited liability' had no place in kinship relations.

The family assumed an obvious importance in the lives of working-class women, among whom a sense of domestic responsibilities, inculcated from childhood, was reinforced at times of particular difficulty. When parental illness or death occurred, it was daughters who would be required to give up work to undertake nursing or housekeeping duties. This commitment to home and hearth carried over into marriage and imposed severe limitations on the types of paid work which wives were likely to pursue. Nevertheless, the experience of Pretoria widows suggests that constraints were accepted as much out of choice as out of necessity. Marriage, structured around clearly defined and separate gender roles, offered both material and emotional security. Indeed, in many households, a domestic equilibrium emerged which, in its essentials, closely paralleled relationships in the workplace. Just as employer and employed recognized mutual limitations to their authority, so married life also came to rest on an acceptance of mutually compatible skills.

---

[184] M. Anderson, 'The Relevance of Family History', in Anderson (ed.), *Sociology of the Family: Selected Readings* (Harmondsworth, 1980), 57.

Ownership of the bread-winner wage did not, therefore, translate into patriarchal control of the household. Rather, by surrendering their wages substantially intact, husbands acknowledged female responsibility for domestic management and so acquiesced in the matrilocality of family life.

At first sight, the stability of kinship and marital relationships would appear to have been founded on the prosperity secured by high and stable family incomes. The potential for supplementary earnings ensured Pretoria households substantial margins above subsistence, which, in many cases, endured over the greater part of the life course. Over time, however, the fragility of any income 'surplus' stood exposed. In common with most working-class families, Pretoria households, although capable of unusually high levels of affluence, remained vulnerable to financial difficulty. They responded by extending reciprocal support in ways which emphasized the composite nature of family incomes. By contrast, the economic downturn of the 1920s encouraged spinners to delay retirement, thus placing the breadwinner's wage at the centre of domestic well-being. Broad similarities in the material parameters of working-class life, marked by fluctuations between prosperity and poverty, did not, of necessity, promote a recognition of interests held in common. Rather, in the case of the spinners, a sense of exclusivity was confirmed.

A final point remains: stable family units were crucial to the transmission of values and ideas to succeeding generations. The support provided by kin not only eased the process of assimilation into society as a whole, it also worked to ensure the survival of distinct identities. This had particular relevance for migrants, drawn to Lancashire during periods of rapid industrial development. Most had, by the early twentieth century, become settled residents. Yet, as studies of Catholic Irish populations across the north-west have demonstrated, they continued to draw on an abiding sense of cultural distinctiveness.[185] This was, in large measure, expressive of underlying ethnic and religious differences. Such points of division had long characterized Lancastrian society, and would continue to colour political developments across the county in the first half of the twentieth century.

---

[185] See esp. S. Fielding, *Class and Ethnicity: Irish Catholics in England, 1880–1939* (Buckingham, 1993); and id., 'A Separate Culture? Irish Catholics in Working-Class Manchester and Salford, c.1890–1939', in Davies and Fielding (eds.), *Workers' Worlds*, 23–48.

8

Converting the Faithful: Electoral Politics in Coal and Cotton Lancashire

At first sight, the social changes of the half-century from 1880 appeared to be registered most graphically through the ballot box. A political system formerly structured around the vertical ties of religion and locality came to be replaced by one in which party allegiance was primarily determined by class. This shift is usually discussed in terms of the eclipse of a broadly progressive, pan-class Liberalism by a Labour Party committed to articulating the interests of the organized working class. In the towns examined here, that pattern could be observed in outline. Differences were, however, apparent in the detail. In both Bolton and Wigan, Conservatism, with only the occasional interruption at parliamentary elections, had been the dominant political force since the 1860s.[1] Within three decades of Labour's emergence as an independent electoral force, that position had been overturned. By 1929, Labour exercised control at both parliamentary and municipal levels, although its position in Bolton's council chamber rested on co-operation with the Liberal group. In both towns, Liberalism as an electoral force was increasingly marginalized, its representation being confined to only two out of fifty-six seats, both elective and aldermanic, in Wigan and thirteen out of ninety-five in Bolton.[2] By then, the political battle lines appeared to have resolved themselves into a conflict between the contending forces of capital and labour.

For some time, explanations for Labour's rise centred on the vital contribution of class identities. Labour was presented as the political expression of broader structural changes at work within the economy and society of late Victorian Britain which resulted in a more united sense of class interests, increasingly capable of political mobilization. By

---

[1] F. W. S. Craig (ed.), *British Parliamentary Election Results, 1832–1885* (London and Basingstoke, 1977), 53–4, 331–2; id., *British Parliamentary Election Results, 1885–1918* (London and Basingstoke, 1974), 77, 209. Locally, Conservatism had enjoyed unbroken spells of power since 1869 in Bolton and 1865 in Wigan, J. Clegg, *Annals of Bolton* (Bolton, 1888), 170–1; *WE* (2 Nov. 1898), 3.

[2] *WE* (9 Nov. 1929), 1; *BJG* (8 Nov. 1929), 6.

this argument, Labour voting became a further expression of what has come to be regarded as 'traditional' working-class culture.[3] This perception of political allegiances as 'expressive' of class identities has recently been subjected to detailed criticism. First, as earlier chapters have attempted to establish, the view that the period witnessed the emergence of a more homogeneous working class, grounded in an increasingly unionized workplace culture, is open to fundamental doubt. Second, and more immediately pertinent, objections have been raised against any tendency to 'read off' political outcomes from the broader structural context. Far from being 'given', party allegiances were, it is argued, actively constructed via the agencies of political organization and propaganda. Recent work has thus emphasized the importance of 'language' in enabling parties to construct broad coalitions of support, encompassing interest groups of often widely disparate origins.[4] Although useful in exposing the processes underlying voter choice to more rigorous scrutiny, this approach is not without its problems. Rather than simply shaping opinion, party propaganda was obliged to reflect and respond to wider social realities. For example, Conservative literature which, before 1914, had tended to regard the working class as an undifferentiated and united electoral bloc, came, in the 1920s, to acknowledge the existence of discrete interests within such broad social categories.[5] Furthermore, despite the criticisms levelled against the reductionism inherent in sociologically informed accounts of political change, the emphasis given to the agency of party ideology still leaves unresolved the problem of the way those ideas were received. Lawrence's study of popular Conservatism in late nineteenth-century Wolverhampton notes how party allegiances often cut across occupational boundaries, so that workers in the same factory and

---

[3] J. Lawrence and M. Taylor, 'Introduction: Electoral Sociology and the Historians', in id. (eds.), *Party, State and Society: Electoral Behaviour in Britain since 1820* (Aldershot, 1997), 1–14; for statements of this view, see G. Stedman Jones, 'Working-Class Culture and Working-Class Politics in London 1870–1900: Notes on the Remaking of a Working Class', in id., *Languages of Class: Studies in English Working Class History* (Cambridge, 1983), 237–8; E. J. Hobsbawm, 'The Making of the Working Class, 1870–1914', in id., *Worlds of Labour* (1984), 207–13; R. McKibbin, *The Evolution of the Labour Party, 1910–1924* (Oxford, 1974), 243–7.

[4] J. Lawrence, 'Class and Gender in the Making of Urban Toryism, 1880–1914', *EHR* 108 (1993), 629–52; D. Jarvis, 'British Conservatism and Class Politics in the 1920s', *EHR* 111 (1996), 59–84; id., 'The Shaping of Conservative Electoral Hegemony, 1918–39', in Lawrence and Taylor, *Party, State and Society*, 131–52.

[5] Jarvis, 'British Conservatism and Class Politics', 65–80; the same variegated approach applied to the party's attempts to court female support, id., 'Mrs Maggs and Betty: The Conservative Appeal to Women Voters in the 1920s', *Twentieth Century British History*, 5 (1994), 129–52.

engaged in similar forms of work could be found on opposite sides of the political divide. Yet the factors which led individual voters to support one party but not another remain unclear.[6] A further problem lies in the emphasis which such studies place on the essential mutability of party loyalties. In privileging short-term shifts in support, the extent to which allegiances remained fixed is overlooked. Indeed, studies of regional voting patterns have exposed broad continuities in the geographical spread of party support extending across several decades.[7] Equally, contemporaries, impressed by the partisan emotions evoked by electoral contests through the period, remarked how voters held to their allegiances with a fervour resembling 'religious faith'.[8] Any consideration of political behaviour in the late nineteenth and early twentieth centuries must therefore give due regard to both long-term and more immediate influences on voting patterns.

In so doing, the contribution of local and national influences must also be considered. If the Labour Party, with its commitment to broader class unity and its emphasis on internal discipline, has been seen as a force for the 'nationalization' of British politics, its growth was also contingent on local circumstances. In Duncan Tanner's work, the pattern of Labour's advance resembles a complex patchwork, coloured by a multiplicity of regional and subregional political cultures. Within each area, Labour, to succeed, had to be sensitive to local requirements.[9] Mike Savage's work on the party's growth in Preston has traced its rise to the development of a particular politics of locality, founded on the needs of an increasingly female electorate. Yet, as Savage's work elsewhere makes clear, undue emphasis on the peculiarities of place can serve to obscure the dynamics of change.[10] Although analysis of Bolton and Wigan reveals points of

---

[6] Lawrence, 'Class and Gender', 642; this is a problem of which Lawrence is himself aware, see his 'The Dynamics of Urban Politics, 1867–1914', in Lawrence and Taylor (eds.), *Party, State and Society*, 91–3; Lawrence, *Speaking for the People: Party, Language and Popular Politics in England, 1867–1914* (Cambridge, 1998), 67–8.

[7] J. P. D. Dunbabin, 'British Elections in the Nineteenth and Twentieth Centuries, a Regional Approach', *EHR* 95 (1980), 241–67.

[8] D. D. Irving, *The Municipality from a Worker's Point of View* (n.d.), 5; R. T. Hyndman, *The Last Years of H. M. Hyndman* (1923), 10.

[9] D. Tanner, *Political Change and the Labour Party, 1900–1918* (Cambridge, 1990), esp. part ii; id., 'Elections, Statistics, and the Rise of the Labour Party, 1906–1931', *Historical Journal*, 34 (1991), 900–2; 'Class Voting and Radical Politics: The Liberal and Labour Parties, 1910–31', in Lawrence and Taylor (eds.), *Party, State and Society*, 106–7.

[10] M. Savage, *The Dynamics of Working-Class Politics* (Cambridge 1987), 162–80; id., 'The Rise of the Labour Party in Local Perspective', *Journal of Regional and Local Studies*, 10 (1990), 5–10; 'Urban Politics and the Rise of the Labour Party, 1919–39', in L. Jamieson and H. Corr (eds.), *State, Private Life and Political Change* (Basingstoke and London, 1990), 204–23.

contrast, important similarities in the pattern of party growth are also evident, suggesting that regional and national influences contributed to local outcomes.

In addition, debate has centred on the precise chronology of change, in particular the point at which the politics of class, based around the material interests of specific socio-economic groups, assumed precedence in aggregate voting patterns. For some, this process appeared substantially complete by 1914. In sustaining this argument, much is made of structural changes, which operated to break down an older politics of locality, informed by the vertical ties of religion and the workplace.[11] Alternatively, and drawing largely on Lancastrian evidence, the origins of this electoral shift are traced to party ideology, in particular the capacity of a Liberal Party increasingly committed to a social welfarist agenda to mobilize a distinctive working-class vote.[12] In countering such arguments, alternative narratives of political change have been proposed, so that the period of the Great War becomes the principal point of electoral discontinuity. Once again, the arguments deployed vary from the social structural to the straightforwardly political. According to the former, the reduction in wage differentials, and the reorganization of work to facilitate the greater utilization of female and unskilled labour, produced a more homogeneous working class, both in terms of social experience and political outlook. This change was registered in part through a linguistic shift, whereby descriptions of the social order came to centre on the basic bifurcation between labour and capital.[13] Those who remain reluctant to accept the notion of structural change emphasize instead the extent to which broader political developments in wartime transformed Labour's potential for electoral success. The state's increased involvement in economic management worked both to politicize industrial bargaining and to legitimize Labour's support for greater public regulation of basic industries.[14] Others, however, have pointed to the potential for opposi-

[11] P. Joyce, *Work, Society and Politics* (Brighton, 1980), 333–4; the causal link between trade-union growth and the onward march of Labour before 1914 continues to figure in K. Laybourn, 'The Rise of Labour and the Decline of Liberalism: The State of the Debate', *History*, 80 (1995), 207–26.

[12] P. F. Clarke, *Lancashire and the New Liberalism* (Cambridge, 1971), 399–407; id., 'British Politics and Blackburn Politics, 1900–1910', *Historical Journal*, 12 (1969), 302–27.

[13] B. Waites, *A Class Society at War* (Leamington Spa, 1987), ch. 2.

[14] N. Kirk, *Change, Continuity and Class: Labour in British Society, 1850–1920* (Manchester, 1998), 194–5; Tanner, *Political Change*, 352–61; id., 'The Labour Party and Electoral Politics in the Coalfields', in A. Campbell, N. Fishman, and D. Howell (eds.), *Miners, Unions and Politics, 1910–47* (Aldershot, 1995), 62–3, 78.

tion politics created by governmental failure to check the inflation of both retail prices and company profits. Labour's stance in defence of working-class living standards contrasted sharply with the problems of Liberalism, handicapped by continued membership of the governing Coalition and the divisions engendered by the Asquith–Lloyd George split of 1916.[15] A final factor facilitating Labour's advance in the immediate post-war years, when significant gains were registered at both parliamentary and municipal levels, is seen to lie in the 1918 extension of the franchise. The precise effects of electoral reform have been keenly debated. Matthew, McKibbin, and Kay's contention that reform enfranchised a mostly Labour-voting constituency of working men which had been excluded from pre-war registers has been criticized on several counts.[16] For our purposes, the most significant is that exclusion from the pre-1914 franchise was more along the lines of age than of class. The principal group affected were single men, living as lodgers or as residents under the parental roof. By this argument, the effect of the 1918 franchise extension was to create a younger electorate, whose political consciousness was forged in a period of Labour growth, both industrially and politically.[17]

If Labour's success in the years 1918–20 has been advanced to justify the attention given to the war and its immediate aftermath, others have used such evidence to point up the limited nature, both geographically and chronologically, of any breakthrough. In their accounts, importance attaches to the decade which followed, years of comparative industrial peace and of declining trade-union membership. Such trends suggest an alternative explanation for Labour's rise, in which the politics of the workplace were replaced by those of neighbourhood. In Savage's work, in particular, the development of ward organization and an agenda of welfare reform enabled Labour to move beyond the organized, predominantly male workforce, to construct a constituency representative of the bulk of the working class.[18]

---

[15] T. Adams, 'Labour and the First World War: Economy, Politics and the Erosion of Local Peculiarity?', *Journal of Regional and Local Studies*, 10 (1990), 29–30; T. Wilson, *The Downfall of the Liberal Party, 1914–1935* (1966), 23–131; comments of J. Winter in 'Labour and Politics in the Great War', *Bulletin of the Society for the Study of Labour History*, 34 (Spring 1977), 5.

[16] H. C. G. Matthew, R. I. McKibbin, and J. A. Kay, 'The Franchise Factor in the Rise of the Labour Party', *EHR* 91 (1976), 725–37.

[17] Tanner, *Political Change*, 385–92; id., 'The Parliamentary Electoral System, the "Fourth" Reform Act and the Rise of Labour in England and Wales', *Bulletin of the Institute of Historical Research*, 56 (1983), 205–19; M. Childs, 'Labour Grows Up: The Electoral System, Political Generations, and British Politics, 1890–1929', *Twentieth Century British History*, 6 (1995), 123–44.   [18] Savage, *Dynamics*, 171–9.

It is impossible in the confines of a single chapter fully to evaluate all the points raised here. Rather, the intention is to test the more influential arguments against the evidence garnered from Bolton and Wigan. To that end, and to clarify the pace and pattern of political change locally, a three-fold chronological division is adopted here: the first traces Labour's growth up to the outbreak of war in 1914; the second examines the impact of war and its aftermath, culminating in the restoration of conventional party politics in 1922; while the third assesses the extent to which Labour's advance in the 1920s can be attributed to the adoption of neighbourhood-based welfarist politics. At the outset, however, it is important to appreciate that the story to be presented here is not the conventional one of the decline of Liberalism and its replacement by Labour. In both Bolton and Wigan, Labour, in order to succeed, had to overturn long-standing Conservative majorities. To do so, it would have to move beyond the constituency claimed by radical Liberalism, to produce a fundamental transformation of political allegiances around the interests of Labour. Its progress towards that goal was faltering and uneven and was shaped throughout by the nature of a working class whose characteristics have been revealed elsewhere in these pages.

I

The depth and nature of partisan allegiances placed important constraints on the emergence of independent Labour politics within Lancashire from the later nineteenth century. The balance between the contending parties was such that popular participation was maintained at high levels across several campaigns. In the last five parliamentary elections of the nineteenth century, the turnout in Bolton and Wigan only once fell below 88 per cent, while the share of poll secured by the minority (Liberal) party fluctuated between 42 and 49 per cent. Partisan feeling was maintained at an unusually high pitch, so that in successive straightforward contests in the two-member constituency of Bolton, in 1886 and 1892, the proportion of votes split between the parties varied only between 1.3 and 2.2 per cent.[19] More importantly, such divisions operated at many levels of Lancastrian society. Constituencies with comparable industrial structures were capable of generating widely different political profiles. Wigan and Leigh, both constituencies with sizeable mining

---

[19] Calculated from Craig, *British Parliamentary Election Results, 1885–1918*, 600; see also pp. 77, 209.

electorates, were Conservative and Liberal strongholds respectively for two decades to 1900. In the cotton trade, a similar point of contrast was provided by the two largest weaving constituencies of Blackburn and Burnley.[20] Political differences characterized the local labour movement also. As has been noted, by the turn of the century, the executive of the LCMF accommodated a diversity of political persuasions, from Conservatism to support for the ILP. Similarly, leading figures in the two largest unions in the cotton trade, James Mawdsley, secretary of the Operative Spinners' Amalgamation, and David Holmes, president of the Northern Counties Weavers' Amalgamation, were Conservative and Liberal stalwarts respectively.[21] Unity was no more apparent at branch level. Officials of the Bolton Operative Spinners' Association in the 1890s included the Liberal J.T. Fielding (secretary to 1894) and the Conservative William Howarth (assistant secretary from 1897).[22] Such differences were also reflected among the rank and file. Among those killed in the Pretoria explosion were ten members of Westhoughton's Conservative Club and four members of the local Reform Club, along with active supporters of the town's ILP branch.[23]

If the extent of political division within the late Victorian working class can readily be described, explanations for the pattern of electoral allegiances which emerged over this period have proved rather more elusive. One of the most influential, particularly for the later nineteenth century, links political outcomes to religious affiliations. Over time, this relationship is seen to have intensified, as the impact of Gladstonian reforms, compounded by Conservative charges of 'faddism', drove Liberalism back into its Nonconformist redoubt.[24] Even then, the association

[20] Craig, *British Parliamentary Election Results, 1885–1918*, 209, 321; the figures cited in R. Gregory, *The Miners and British Politics* (Oxford, 1969), 12, and reproduced in I. F. Scott, 'The Lancashire and Cheshire Miners' Federation' (York Univ. D.Phil. thesis), 12, overstate the strength of the mining vote in Wigan. In the absence of more detailed figures, it is difficult to locate the precise source of this error, but it would appear that the use of employment rather than residential patterns distorts the picture and unduly inflates the estimates of the potential number of miners on the register. For Blackburn and Burnley, see G. Trodd, 'Political Change and the Working Class in Blackburn and Burnley' (Lancaster Univ. Ph.D. thesis, 1978).

[21] See above, p. 87; Clarke, *Lancashire and the New Liberalism*, 85; J. McHugh and B. Ripley, 'The Spinners and the Rise of Labour', in A. Fowler and T. Wyke (eds.), *The Barefoot Aristocrats* (Littleborough, 1987), 118.

[22] P. A. Harris, 'Class Conflict, the Trade Unions and Working-Class Politics in Bolton, 1875–96' (Lancaster Univ. MA thesis, 1971), 16, 24; *BJG* (20 Jan. 1933), 11.

[23] *BEN* (22 Dec. 1910), 4; (23 Dec. 1910), 4.

[24] Lawrence, 'The Dynamics of Urban Politics, 1867–1914', in Lawrence and Taylor (eds.), *Party, State and Society*, 90–1; id., 'Class and Gender in the Making of Urban Toryism', 634–8.

between electoral behaviour and denominational allegiances was never absolute. Between 1895 and 1916, Bolton returned two Liberal MPs, George Harwood and Thomas Taylor, both of whom were practising Anglicans.[25] Yet such figures were increasingly exceptional in the context of late Victorian and Edwardian politics. Across much of Lancashire, the influence of denominational differences was all too apparent. Dr Ferdinand Rees, later a Liberal and then Labour candidate in council elections, recalled the advice offered him on taking up a medical practice in Wigan in 1893: 'I had got to be a Tory and a Churchman. Talk about Tammany! All the people in the town had to be Tories, down to the street sweepers. All the patronage of the town was entirely in the hands of the Conservative party, and had always been used in the interests of that party.'[26] Of the thirteen Liberal councillors on Wigan Borough Council in the year that Rees arrived in the town, all were either Nonconformist or Catholic.

The influence of organized religion cannot be traced to formal acts of observance. If contemporary estimates are correct, only a small proportion of Lancastrians regularly attended acts of divine worship. According to J. Garrett Leigh's calculations, their number amounted, in 1904, to no more than 25 per cent of the total population. Local surveys suggest that even this may have been an overestimate. A religious census of Bolton in 1895 suggested a level of attendance, even after excluding those deemed physically incapable of participating in public acts of worship, of nearer 17 per cent.[27] The broader functions of organized religion provide a more convincing explanation for its continued cultural influence in late Victorian Lancashire. The majority of local children accumulated their first savings and gained their earliest experience of team sports through their Sunday school. Of greater significance, many were educated in schools controlled by the major denominations. Such provision prevailed across large stretches of south-west Lancashire, including Wigan, and would do so for the whole of the period under review here.[28] Further east, in Bolton, the School Board was more influential, due to the acquisition of several buildings formerly under Nonconformist control in the early

[25] Clarke, *Lancashire and the New Liberalism*, 227; *BJG* (8 Nov. 1912), 7; *The Times* (13 Nov. 1912), 12.   [26] *WO* (8 Nov. 1913), 9.
[27] J. Garrett Leigh, 'The Life of the Artisan', *Independent Review*, 2 (Feb.–May 1904), 262–3; C. A. Clarke, *The Effects of the Factory System* (1899; repr. Littleborough, 1985), 142.
[28] *Parl. Papers 1906*, lxxxvii (178–XXV), Board of Education: List of Non-Provided Schools. Lancashire, 68–70, 94–5; *Parl. Papers 1906*, lxxxix (3054) Board of Education: List of Boroughs and Urban Districts with Populations of 5,000 and upwards in which there are No Council Schools; *WE* (6 Jan. 1931), 4.

1880s. Nevertheless, even by 1919, almost half of all school accommodation within the borough was independent of direct council control.[29]

Religious affiliations appeared to carry most force when allied with a sense of national difference. The Irish were a sizeable presence in most Lancastrian towns, accounting for between a quarter and one-third of the populations of late Victorian Leigh, Wigan, and St Helens. To the north and east, their significance diminished, so that only between 7 and 10 per cent of Bolton's electorate could be classified as Irish.[30] Plentiful employment opportunities proved the principal attraction for migrants, many of whom secured work through contacts with family or fellow-nationals. One such, Patrick Sloyan, was taken on at the Maypole Colliery in Abram in 1908 after acting on information provided by a cousin living in Wigan. Equally, Bill Naughton's father was enticed across the Irish Sea by the promise of work in a Lancashire colliery held out by a brother already resident in the area.[31] In common with many Irish recruits, Sloyan's first experience of pit work was as a contractor's man. Hired by subcontractors, many themselves Irish in origin, and working in gangs of up to twenty, such men were responsible for repair work underground after the main getting shift had ended. The existence of separate recruitment networks ensured that, to a degree, denominational differences were reproduced down the pit. When an explosion occurred at the Maypole Colliery on 18 August 1908, seventy-five minutes into the afternoon turn, contractors' men were prominent among the deceased. At least two out of every three victims were Catholics. The pattern of mourning above ground reflected the distribution of losses. While the parish of St Patrick in Wigan mourned eighteen deaths, the Anglican vicar of St Mark's church in Ince was able to offer thanks that miners in his congregation had cheated death by one hour.[32]

Yet the differences which this exposed were unlikely to endure. The absence of craft restrictions on the recruitment and deployment of labour within the pit and the opportunities thus offered to unskilled workers and 'market men' ensured that, over time, Catholic migrants were assimilated into the mining workforce as a whole. Such at least is suggested by the

---

[29] J. C. Scholes, *History of Bolton* (Bolton, 1892), 542; *Bolton: Its Trade and Commerce*, 68.

[30] *Catholic Family Annual and Almanac for the Diocese of Liverpool* (Liverpool, 1886), 48, 78; *BJG* (30 Oct. 1925), 7.

[31] *WO* (1 Sept. 1908), 3; Naughton, *On the Pig's Back*, 70.

[32] *Parl. Papers 1908*, xix (4045–VI), Reports of HM Inspectors of Mines: Liverpool and North Wales District, 16; *WO* (25 Aug. 1908), 3; J. Hannavy and R. Lewis, *The Maypole: Diary of a Colliery Disaster* (Wigan, 1983).

occupational backgrounds of the twenty-six victims of the Pretoria disaster who worshipped at the mission of the Sacred Heart in Westhoughton. They ranged from young hookers-on and lashers-on, gaining their first experience of underground work close to the shaft, to colliers and drawers employed at the face.[33] Yet, if work patterns no longer served to distinguish the Catholic Irish, there is little to suggest that a distinctive national identity was, as a consequence, obscured. Rather, it continued to flourish, uniting first-generation migrants, such as the Naughtons, with those resident in Lancashire for several generations, among whom may be numbered the Foleys.[34] Various factors worked to sustain a sense of separateness. The influence of the Church and related denominational institutions, including Catholic collecting societies, was compounded by the survival of extended and extensive kinship networks. Many of the women widowed by the Maypole disaster subsequently opted to return across the Irish Sea where family support would be more readily available. National organizations, such as the United Irish League, branches of which flourished in most Lancastrian towns, gave this consciousness more formal expression, as did the range of pubs sustained by the Irish in many centres.[35] Although not founded primarily on work, the Irish identity retained an unusual coherence and was an interest capable of mobilization at several levels within urban society, from the neighbourhood to the town as a whole.[36] As such, it would play a pivotal role in several election campaigns over the period.

This is, however, to anticipate matters. For now, it is sufficient to note that the context of political and cultural diversity in late nineteenth-century Lancashire imposed crucial constraints on the emergence of Labour as a political force. Across much of the county, the Conservative sympathies of many workers rendered the conventional policy of co-operation with the Liberals impracticable. Confirmation of this point was to be found in the experience of the LCMF officials, Sam Woods and Thomas Aspinwall, who stood as Lib-Lab candidates in parliamentary elections in Ince and Wigan respectively in 1892 and 1895. Although Woods was victorious in the first election, the campaigns provoked wide-

---

[33] Westhoughton Public Library, Pretoria Pit Disaster, Pamphlet Box Revd A. L. Coelenbier, *Priest's Story of the Pit Disaster*, 4; *Parl. Papers 1911*, xxxvi (5676–IV), Reports of HM Inspectors of Mines: Manchester and Ireland District, 28–9; see above, Ch. 2.

[34] Naughton, *Saintly Billy*, 12–21, 57–62; Foley, *A Bolton Childhood*, 6–8, 37–43.

[35] WA, PC 4/B8 Maypole Colliery Explosion (1908) Relief Fund, Declaration of Trusts, 1927; Mass-Observation, *The Pub and the People* (1943), 151; see above, p. 215.

[36] For the factors which sustained an Irish sense of 'community', see Fielding, *Class and Ethnicity*, chs. 3 and 4; id., 'A Separate Culture?', 23–48.

spread secessions from the Federation.[37] This is not to say that circumstances entirely precluded Lib-Lab co-operation. Rather, such experiments were, for the most part, confined to localities where conditions were unusually favourable, such as the township of Pemberton, west of Wigan. Here, the dominance of mining as a source of employment gave colliers an industrial and political weight they lacked further east. What is more, the strength of Nonconformity locally, reflected in sizeable Wesleyan, Independent, and Primitive Methodist congregations, provided cultural foundations for the emergence of Lib-Lab politics. In 1894, the Pemberton Miners' Association nominated its secretary, John Cheetham, for election to the local urban district council. Cheetham and other miners' officials would continue to stand under Lib-Lab auspices for both Pemberton Urban District and Wigan County Borough Councils until 1905.[38] Over much of Lancashire, however, effective action required that political divisions be transcended. One approach to this end was essayed by the UTFWA in 1895 and involved the nomination of two parliamentary candidates: Mawdsley as a Conservative and Holmes as a Liberal. Mawdsley's refusal to stand effectively scuppered this scheme.[39]

It took the emergence of independent Labour politics after 1900 to alter the prospects for success across Lancashire. 'Independence' was a central plank of Labour politics in its early phase. It was an idea capable of several interpretations. As Jon Lawrence has suggested, it reflected a renunciation of the machine politics of the caucus and their association with manipulation by organized middle-class interest groups.[40] In the Lancastrian context, however, independence acquired an additional meaning, in which the Labour interest would be pursued without reference to existing party divisions. Instead, a range of issues of interest to working men, from the challenge to trade-union legal immunities posed by recent judicial decisions to reform of the Workmen's Compensation Act, would come to define and consolidate a distinct constituency. Established loyalties, whether Conservative, Liberal, or Socialist, were to

---

[37] R. Challinor, *The Lancashire and Cheshire Miners* (Newcastle, 1972), 220–6; D. Hunter, 'Politics and the Working Class in Wigan, 1890–1914' (Lancaster Univ. MA thesis, 1974), 21–4.

[38] In 1901, coal-mining accounted for 58% of male employment across the township, *Parl. Papers 1902*, cxix (1002), Census of England and Wales, 1901: County of Lancaster, table 35A, 180; *The '20th Century' Directory for the Wigan Union of Postal Areas* (Wigan and Manchester, 1903), 506–8; *Seed's Wigan and District Directory: First Issue, 1909–10* (Preston, 1909), pp. xviii, 263–99; *WE* (28 Oct. 1904), 5, 8; *WO* (18 Oct. 1913), 9.

[39] McHugh and Ripley, 'Spinners and Rise of Labour', 118.

[40] Lawrence, *Speaking for the People*, 250–4.

be set aside. Labour, as James Lewis, the president of the Bolton Operative Spinners' Association, expressed it, when speaking in support of a
local by-election candidate in November 1904, 'knew no politics'.[41] It was
a point frequently rehearsed at public meetings addressed by Labour candidates. John Parr, general secretary of the Amalgamated Carters' and
Lorrymen's Union, presented himself to the electors of Bolton's Derby
ward in 1901 as a 'non-political nominee', who, being a working man free
of party pressures, 'would bring an impartial spirit to bear upon questions'.[42] In the following year, Daniel Isherwood, a retired spinner,
endeavoured to reassure voters that he had no associations with any 'political' cause, declaring himself to be 'a Conservative-cum-Radical embody-
ing the principles of progress'.[43] A similar desire to balance established
partisan allegiances led the Bolton Spinners' executive, in supporting the
cause of direct labour representation, to call on its members to 'sink their
party politics . . . and vote for men of their own class',[44] and Robert
Tootill, secretary of the Bolton United Trades Council, to urge workers
to observe the motto, 'Labour first, politics after'.[45]

The issue of 'independence' was no less central to the politics of mining
unionism. Although represented at the foundation conference of the LRC
in 1900, the LCMF had voted against affiliation, alienated in part by what
was perceived to be undue socialist influence within the nascent organization.[46] The development of the MFGB's own scheme for parliamentary
representation also worked to divert political energies elsewhere, so that,
in 1902, Sam Woods was nominated as candidate for Newton under
Federation auspices. Significantly, the move was made without reference
to local Liberals and Woods's independence was further confirmed by
the decision to appoint his own registration agent. At the MFGB conference in 1902, Lancastrian delegates urged, without success, that this
approach be more widely adopted.[47] The LRC appeared more willing to
embrace the principles of independence, to the extent that, in 1903, a constitutional amendment was adopted which prevented candidates from
identifying with either of the established parties. Lancastrian suspicions of

---

[41] *BJG* (25 Nov. 1904), 5; both issues helped to galvanize the Labour campaign in the
1902 parliamentary by-election in Clitheroe, see F. Bealey and H. Pelling, *Labour and Politics*
(1958), 118–21.   [42] *BJG* (1 Nov. 1901), 5.
[43] *BJG* (24 Oct. 1902), 8.   [44] BA, FT/21/7 BSA, Annual Report for 1902, 7.
[45] *BEN* (27 Oct. 1905), 3.
[46] Scott, 'Lancashire and Cheshire Miners' Federation', 117–18; Bealey and Pelling,
Labour and Politics, 24–5; H. Pelling, *The Origins of the Labour Party* (Oxford, 1965), 211.
[47] Scott, 'Lancashire and Cheshire Miners' Federation', 123–5, 131.

Labour politics were so far overcome that, within three months, the decision was taken to affiliate to the LRC.[48] In ballots organized by the UTFWA, cotton unions across Lancashire had already voted to take this step. Even so, the principle of independence was enthusiastically endorsed. Both the candidates considered by Bolton's Trades Council and the UTFWA for nomination for one of the town's two parliamentary seats, A. H. Gill of the Operative Spinners' and Joseph Edge of the Card Room Association, undertook to observe the conditions laid down in the LRC's amended constitution.[49]

The attempt to establish a distinctively Labour electoral interest was actively pursued at both municipal and parliamentary levels. In Bolton's borough elections, candidates fighting under the Trades Council's banner from 1901 regularly faced both Conservative and Liberal opposition. In the first year, nominations were advanced for two wards, Derby and Halliwell, both of which returned two members each. In each ward, the single Trades Council candidate faced opposition from two Conservatives and one Liberal, with the result that both benefited from a sizeable split vote with the latter. In all, 47 per cent of the Trades Council poll came from voters who also supported the Liberal, while 34 per cent was accounted for by those prepared to 'plump' for Labour.[50] In the two years that followed, a more determined bid for independence was made. Four wards were contested in 1902. Two involved straight fights, one against Conservative, the other against Liberal opposition, while the two three-cornered contests included one in which the Trades Council nominee faced only one opponent from each of the major parties. Although all four candidates came bottom of their respective polls, the share of the total vote achieved (36.3 per cent) was more than respectable. What is more, in the three-cornered contests, almost half the Labour vote came from 'plumpers'.[51] Twelve months later, a further advance was registered. In two wards involving straight fights, Labour candidates topped the poll, while in the one three-cornered contest, in the two-member ward of Halliwell, Labour's vote was sufficient to force the second Liberal candidate into fourth place. On this occasion, exactly half the party's poll came from those prepared to 'plump'.[52] In Wigan, the local Trades Council

---

[48] Bealey and Pelling, *Labour and Politics*, 141–2; Challinor, *Lancashire and Cheshire Miners*, 232; LCMF, monthly conference minutes, 25 Apr., 23 May 1903.

[49] *BJG* (21 Nov. 1902), 3, 8; (5 Dec. 1902); 3; (15 May 1903), 8.

[50] *BJG* (8 Nov. 1901), 8; *BEN* (2 Nov. 1901), 4.

[51] *BJG* (7 Nov. 1902), 8; *BEN* (3 Nov. 1902), 3.   [52] *BJG* (6 Nov. 1903), 3.

moved to intervene in local elections from 1903. Two candidates were nominated, each of whom faced straight fights, the first in Lindsay Ward against Conservative opposition, the other in Victoria against the Liberals. Between them, they secured 39 per cent of the votes cast.[53] Despite the belief expressed by the *Bolton Journal and Guardian*'s labour correspondent that 'the average working man is a party man', bound to follow the political preferences of preceding generations,[54] Labour had, in a few years, made notable progress towards achieving its avowedly modest aim of establishing an independent political interest committed to campaigning on straightforward labour issues. Councillors had been elected in Bolton against both Conservative and Liberal opposition. 'Independence' appeared in the process of being effectively translated from political aspiration to practical reality.

However, developments nationally threatened this achievement. In 1903, the LCMF, anxious to promote the cause of independent representation, nominated four parliamentary candidates, including Stephen Walsh in the Conservative seat of Ince and Thomas Greenall in Accrington. Walsh, it was emphasized, would fight Ince on 'purely labour lines', while Greenall's candidature in a traditionally Liberal constituency, would consolidate the Federation's political independence.[55] Events soon conspired to weaken Greenall's prospects. First, the sitting member, Sir Joseph Leese, whose retirement had created the vacancy that Greenall was expected to fill, resolved to contest the seat at the forthcoming election. Second, the accommodation of progressive forces outlined in the Gladstone–MacDonald pact aimed to minimize Lib-Lab contests by reserving seats such as Accrington for the Liberals. National officials pressed Greenall to withdraw, with David Shackleton, Labour MP for neighbouring Clitheroe, refusing to support his candidature. Increasingly pessimistic of his chances of success, Greenall resigned the candidacy in December 1904, a decision which gave rise to suspicions of political manœuvring.[56] Hodge and Henderson of the national LRC attended a Federation conference in Wigan to deny collusion with the Liberals. A separate LCMF investigation accepted their account, reserving most of its criticisms for Greenall's reluctance to prosecute his candidature more

[53] *WE* (4 Nov. 1903), 3.   [54] *BJG* (10 Oct. 1902), 8, 'Topics for Toilers'.

[55] LCMF, monthly conference minutes, 25 Apr., 23 May, 15 Aug. 1903; Scott, 'Lancashire and Cheshire Miners' Federation', 133–4.

[56] Challinor, *Lancashire and Cheshire Miners*, 232–3; Hill, 'The Lancashire Miners, Thomas Greenall and the Labour Party', *THSLC* 130 (1981), 123–6; Scott, 'Lancashire and Cheshire Miners' Federation', 133–9.

vigorously. Nevertheless, officials with Conservative sympathies, including the Federation secretary Thomas Ashton, remained suspicious of the LRC's motives and actions in the affair.[57]

The idea of independence came under more sustained pressure in Bolton. Here, the local labour movement remained determined to avoid political entanglements, to the extent that a Socialist candidate standing in a ward by-election in February 1904 was refused endorsement.[58] Although that year's council elections witnessed no straightforward contests between Liberal and Labour, the two parties were rivals in a later by-election in Bradford ward.[59] From that point, however, such clashes became increasingly rare. At the parliamentary level, the revival of Liberalism in defence of Free Trade and the context of Progressive co-operation set out in the Gladstone–MacDonald pact, encouraged a growing overlap in support. Further scope for Lib-Lab agreement locally was provided by the background of the Labour candidate, A. H. Gill, as a Wesleyan lay preacher. It remained the case that members of Gill's union were urged in January 1906 to 'look upon the coming election as a Trade Union matter', with priority given to a Trades Disputes Bill and an amended Compensation Act.[60] Yet, such unambiguously Labour issues apart, Gill campaigned on predominantly Liberal lines, endorsing policies such as Home Rule for Ireland and, crucially in the context of local controversies, the provision of denominational education outside normal school hours. Unsurprisingly, therefore, although Gill polled 10,416 votes in 1906, three out of every four votes were split with the Liberal, George Harwood.[61] Locally, Conservative propaganda sought to make much of such obvious Lib-Lab collaboration. When the party's candidates faced Labour opposition alone, voters were reminded that 'all the Labour men were really Radicals in their hearts'.[62] In response, Labour spokesmen emphasized that independence did not preclude informal co-operation with other parties where this would promote the interests of working men. Any more formal alliance, such as that observed by the Lib-Lab group of MPs at Westminster, was rejected.[63] However, with Liberalism

[57] LCMF, monthly conference minutes, 3, 31 Dec. 1904.   [58] *BJG* (19 Feb. 1904), 4.
[59] *BJG* (4 Nov. 1904), 3; (25 Nov. 1904), 5; (2 Dec. 1904), 8.
[60] JRUL, BCA/1/3/8 BSA, minutes, circular, 10 Jan. 1906.
[61] Craig (ed.), *British Parliamentary Election Results, 1885–1918*, 77, 601; *Bolton Chronicle* (6 Jan. 1906), 2; D. E. Martin, 'Alfred Henry Gill (1856–1914): Trade Union Leader and Labour MP', in J. M. Bellamy and J. Saville (eds.), *Dictionary of Labour Biography*, ii (London and Basingstoke, 1974), 137–9.   [62] *BJG* (26 Oct. 1906), 16.
[63] *BJG* (19 Oct. 1906), 16, for Gill's comments at a Labour meeting in Bolton's Derby ward; see also the remarks of Robert Tootill, *BJG* (2 Nov. 1906), 3.

in power and pursuing an agenda designed in part to meet the grievances of organized labour, the balance between independence and co-operation proved increasingly difficult to maintain.

For a time, at least, the distinction appeared to be observed with some success. In the four years to November 1909, the anti-Conservative vote in Bolton was split on only four occasions and two of those involved Socialists standing without Trades Council support.[64] Despite the relative absence of Lib–Lab confrontations at the polls, Labour candidates continued to dissociate themselves from conventional party politics. In 1907, for example, Joseph Ryder, facing a straight fight against two Conservatives in Bradford ward, sought to deny an affiliation to any party.[65] How far such claims contributed to the observed growth in the Labour vote in these years cannot be established with any precision. However, the continued electoral purchase of the idea of 'independence' is suggested by the party's performance in two-member wards where one or more Liberals were also standing. Between 1906 and 1909, the proportion of the Labour vote split with the Liberals fell from 52 to 35 per cent, while the share contributed by 'plumpers' rose from 39 to 53 per cent.[66] What is more, Labour topped the poll in both contests in the latter year, providing convincing proof, for Robert Tootill at least, of a greater readiness among working men to think and act independently of party tradition.[67]

Whatever the truth of such observations, the trend in subsequent years was, by comparison, unambiguous. Considerable debate has centred on the relative performance of Liberal and Labour between 1910 and 1914, some arguing that Labour's advance was effectively contained within a Liberal-dominated Progressivism, while others stress the extent to which Labour sought to break out of the constraints imposed by the 1903 pact.[68] In Bolton, at least, the pattern is clear. Labour's share of the poll and its core support (the proportion of voters prepared to 'plump' for its candidates) both fell markedly in the period 1909–13: from 42 to 31 per cent in the case of the former and from 29 to 16 per cent in that of the latter.[69]

---

[64] *BJG* (2 Nov. 1906), 5; the following year, Matthew Phair stood as a Socialist in the two-member ward of Derby against Conservative and Labour opposition, *BJG* (18 Oct. 1907), 7.

[65] *BJG* (1 Nov. 1907), 2.

[66] Calculated from *BJG* (2 Nov. 1906), 5; (8 Nov. 1907), 2; (6 Nov. 1908), 3; (5 Nov. 1909), 3.

[67] *BJG* (5 Nov. 1909), 3.

[68] Clarke, *Lancashire and the New Liberalism*, 402–7; Tanner, 'Elections, Statistics and the Rise of the Labour Party', 900–1; McKibbin, *Evolution of the Labour Party*, ch. 3. S. Berger, 'The Decline of Liberalism and the Rise of Labour: The Regional Approach', *Parliamentary History*, 12 (1993), 89–91.

[69] Calculated from *BJG* (5 Nov. 1909), 3; (7 Nov. 1913), 9.

Lib–Lab contests were no more common in these years. Indeed, the only candidates to face outright Liberal opposition were nominated by ward committees rather than the central Labour organization. Although the party nominally supported both candidates, financial assistance was not forthcoming. Both came bottom of their respective polls and attracted criticism from leaders such as Tootill, concerned that unofficial nominations would threaten Progressive co-operation and so undermine Labour's cause.[70] Superficially, this, and the parliamentary contests of 1910 in which the proportion of Gill's votes split with Harwood rose to 91 per cent, seemed ample justification for Conservative jibes that Labour had been swallowed by Liberalism.[71] Yet there is evidence to suggest that Labour did not willingly accept the Progressive embrace.

The Osborne Judgment, in particular, imposed a decisive constraint on the party's campaigning activities. The number of candidates put forward each year at the November elections declined from an average of five before 1910 to one of three thereafter.[72] Even wards such as Bradford, where from 1907 Labour faced the Conservatives in five consecutive straight fights, were subject to Liberal intervention in the last pre-war years.[73] Yet, even where opportunities for Progressive co-operation appeared most promising, Labour officials remained anxious to maximize the party vote. In 1912, Alfred Potts of the gasworkers' union stood against two Conservatives and one Liberal in the two-member ward of East. Speaking in his support, Tootill called on workers to back Labour, to ensure that its influence in the council chamber would not be diminished.[74] Despite such attempts to marry independence with cross-party co-operation, electoral realities drove Labour into closer ties with the Liberals. In addition to the diminution in the party's overall support, the proportion of the Labour vote in two-member wards split with the Liberals increased from 44.3 per cent between 1906 and 1909 to 51.9 per cent from 1910 to 1913. Over the same period, the tendency to 'plump' in such circumstances declined from 44.7 to 35.1 per cent.[75] However reluctantly, Labour in Bolton was increasingly being drawn into the Progressive embrace.

This context complicates attempts to interpret the results of ballots held under the 1913 Trade Union Act. Certainly, they cannot be seen as

---

[70] *BJG* (27 Oct. 1911), 10; *BEN* (27 Oct. 1911), 2, 3.
[71] Craig (ed.), *British Parliamentary Election Results, 1885–1918*, 601; *BEN* (29 Oct. 1910), 4.　　　　　　　　　　　[72] Calculated from *BJG* and *BEN*, 1906–13.
[73] *BJG* (25 Oct. 1912), 7; (31 Oct. 1913), 9.　　[74] *BEN* (30 Oct. 1912), 2.
[75] Calculated from *BJG* and *BEN*, 1906–13.

straightforward plebiscites on Labour independence. Rather, votes such as that of the Bolton Operative Spinners' Association, which recorded a majority of 59 per cent in favour of the political levy, provide some indication of the extent to which Labour had, by 1914, fallen short of its aim of redefining politics around the Labour interest. The party's increasing identification with one strand of established partisan allegiances worked to alienate many working-class Conservatives and may help to explain the substantial minority vote in 1913, compared to that of 1902 over affiliation to the LRC (41 per cent as against 13.5 per cent).[76] The transformation of political allegiances along class lines remained substantially incomplete on the eve of war.

Progress appeared more marked further west, in Wigan. Here, Labour had, by 1913, succeeded in overturning fifty years of Conservative control of the borough council. Unlike in Bolton, it was unambiguously the dominant force in Progressive politics, with sixteen councillors that year to the Liberals' six (further east, the respective numbers were four and twenty-six).[77] The shift to class representation appeared all the more marked given the importance previously assumed by religious and ethnic points of division. Elections in late nineteenth-century Wigan had witnessed frequent and occasionally violent confrontations between English workers and the 'Fenian' Irish. In a by-election in 1881, miners from the Whelley district had travelled to the polls in the Irish area of Scholes in large numbers and in a square formation for their collective safety.[78] Thereafter, although a sense of religious and national difference endured, politics in Wigan never assumed the violent sectarian form so evident in Liverpool. A variety of factors contributed to this outcome. First, the pace of migration slackened in step with the slowdown in the growth of colliery output. By the 1890s, Wigan's Irish-born population was in absolute decline. Nevertheless, of itself, this did not preclude the survival of a distinctive national identity. Of greater importance in moderating the temper of electoral contests was the absence of any sizeable Ulster Orange presence among the migrant population. The Irish drawn

---

[76] *BJG* (21 Nov. 1902), 3; BA, FT/21/9 BSA, Annual Report for 1913, 142; an alternative interpretation of the 1913 ballots is provided in J. L. White, *The Limits of Trade Union Militancy* (Westport, Conn., and London, 1978), 153–5; and McKibbin, *Evolution of the Labour Party*, 85–6.   [77] *WO* (4 Nov. 1913), 2; *BJG* (7 Nov. 1913), 9.
[78] *Parl. Papers 1881*, lxxiv (207), Copy of the Shorthand Writer's Notes of the Evidence and of the Judgment in the Case of the Wigan Election Petition; together with a copy of the Petition, qq. 82–4, 299–300, 2140, 4759–71, 9499–500; J. Roby, *The Disease of the Liberal Party* (Manchester, 1874), 12–14, for the importance of the Church as a recruiting ground for Conservatism.

to Lancashire's coalfield originated, for the most part, in the agricultural counties of Mayo and Leitrim.[79] Attitudes among the host population also worked to contain animosities. A patrician Conservative leadership, centred on the Crawfords of Haigh Hall, remained reluctant to excite religious controversies. In 1892, therefore, party officials worked to discourage confrontations between members of the local Orange Order and supporters of the miners' Lib-Lab candidate for Ince, Thomas Aspinwall. Wigan lacked either a Salvidge or a Wise to spike the sectarian brew. The more conciliatory outlook which resulted owed much to a fourth factor: south-west Lancashire's strong recusant tradition, founded on local Catholic gentry.[80] A sizeable English Catholic presence, for which religious interests were unencumbered by nationalist preoccupations, encouraged local Conservatives to attempt to construct an electoral alliance capable of spanning the denominational divide. The defence of voluntary education provided a ready issue around which Anglicans and Catholics could unite against the Free Churches, for whom non-denominational instruction had become a guiding principle.

In seeking to harness Catholic support, the town's Conservative press made much of practical expressions of denominational solidarity, as when Conservative votes secured the appointment of a Catholic as Medical Officer of Health in 1898 and, two years later, the election of Thomas Fyans as the borough's first Catholic Mayor since the Reformation. Such actions were contrasted with the attitude of Nonconformists who, in the view of the *Wigan Examiner*, were intent on using Catholics 'as stepping stones, catspaws and as voting machines for their own aggrandisement'.[81] The difference in outlook between ostensible Liberal allies crystallized around the 1902 Education Act, when Nonconformist opposition to rates support for Church schools led one Catholic Liberal councillor, James Howard, to express regret that, in spite of 'the many battles in which the Nonconformists and ourselves have stood shoulder to shoulder for the cause of Liberalism, . . . their unliberal policy on the education question forces us to part company.'[82] Although Howard, among others, soon returned to the Liberal fold, unity proved increasingly elusive. Differences

[79] For the backgrounds of the Irish miners killed in the Maypole explosion, see *WO* (7 Nov. 1908), 2; for trends within the Irish population more generally, Hunter, 'Politics and the Working Class in Wigan', 44.

[80] Vincent (ed.), *The Crawford Papers*, 11–12; J. A. Hilton, *Catholic Lancashire: An Historical Guide* (Wigan, 1981), 23; F. O. Blundell, *Old Catholic Lancashire* ii (1938), 48; the more vigorously sectarian temper of Liverpool's politics is fully documented in P. J. Waller, *Democracy and Sectarianism* (Liverpool, 1981), esp. chs. 12–14.

[81] *WE* (26 Oct. 1898), 2; WA, Biographical Cuttings Books, i, 196.

[82] *WE* (17 Oct. 1903), 4.

over education policy endured and received fresh impetus with the controversy which surrounded the building of a Catholic school in St Andrew ward in 1904.[83] At a time when Liberalism nationally was undergoing a revival, the movement in Wigan appeared fatally weakened. Attempts to revive the party organization after the initial split enjoyed only fitful success. A club founded by both Catholic and Nonconformist Liberals in 1905 folded after three years, having contracted sizeable debts in the interim.[84] By then, religious differences had hardened further as a consequence of the 1906 parliamentary election campaign, in which the Catholic Liberal William Woods was denied Nonconformist support. Instead, this went to the Independent Labour candidate, Thorley Smith. In the short term, Liberal divisions facilitated the return of the Unionist, Francis Sharp Powell, on a minority vote.[85] Of more lasting significance, they also created a vacuum on the political left which Labour moved rapidly to fill. In the November local elections following Powell's victory, the Conservative *Wigan Examiner* remarked how 'In the contests for the Town Council of the borough, the old-fashioned Liberalism is being more or less discarded, and superceded [sic] by the new cult of Labour or Socialism; and the opposition to the Conservative candidates partakes largely of this phase.'[86]

Yet this change prompted no shift in the terms of political debate. For at least three years from 1906, Liberal attempts to reform the 1902 Act kept education at the forefront of local election campaigns and ensured that the Conservative tactic of mobilizing Catholic votes in defence of denominational instruction enjoyed considerable success. Out of fifteen wards contested in the old borough of Wigan[87] in 1907 and 1908, the party won twelve, polling heavily in areas with large Catholic electorates such as St George and Victoria. The high point of Conservative success came, however, with the capture of St Patrick ward in 1908. A seat in which Irish candidates traditionally enjoyed an unopposed return fell to the Conservatives by a majority of thirty-four.[88] The effects of Conservative–Catholic co-

[83] D. Mallin, '"Rome on the Rates" in Wigan: The Founding of Sacred Heart School, 1904–6', *North West Catholic History*, 5 (1978), 38–9; *WE* (14 Oct. 1905), 1; (27 Oct. 1905), 4.

[84] PRO, Register of Dissolved Companies BT 31/10987/83502/3,17 Wigan Liberal Club, Ltd, Prospectus, 3 Feb. 1905; Extraordinary General Meeting, 28 Sept. 1908.

[85] Clarke, *Lancashire and the New Liberalism*, 257; D. Brown, 'The Labour Movement in Wigan, 1874–1967' (Liverpool Univ. MA thesis, 1969), 62; *WE* (5 Jan. 1906), 4, 5.

[86] *WE* (26 Oct. 1906), 4.   [87] Excluding the mining township of Pemberton.

[88] *WE* (30 Oct. 1907), 2; (2 Nov. 1907), 8; (6 Nov. 1907), 2; (24 Oct. 1908), 5; (3 Nov. 1908), 2; *WO* (29 Oct. 1907), 3.

operation were also felt further east. The net loss of five seats across Bolton in 1907 was ascribed by Liberal spokesmen to 'a combination of beer and clericalism'.[89] The impact of the latter was seen in Conservative candidates topping the polls in the Liberal strongholds of West and Halliwell, and the large Catholic–Conservative split vote in the central ward of Exchange.[90] However, expectations that such results heralded a permanent breach between Liberalism and the Catholic interest were not realized. Twelve months later, despite Conservative attempts to press the education issue once more, the Catholic vote appeared to have reverted to the Liberals.[91] Two points of significance emerge here. First, the Catholic interest did not respond to religious prompting alone. The majority of Catholics in both Bolton and Wigan were Irish in origin or affiliation, a group for whom national considerations frequently outweighed denominational concerns.[92] So, although the *Wigan and District Catholic Magazine* called, in January 1910, for unity in defence of religious education, it was clear that, on that issue, the Irish were less than reliable. For them, Home Rule was likely to be a more pressing concern. As a result, in the first parliamentary election of 1910, the Catholic vote split. While United Irish League branches in Wigan and Ince backed the two Labour candidates, Henry Twist and Stephen Walsh, English Catholics in both divisions remained true to the denominational principle.[93] The second feature of the Irish interest to merit comment is the extent to which it was capable of mobilization across constituency boundaries. Appeals from leading Catholics in Bolton in 1908 had sufficed to draw many back to Liberalism.[94] Equally, in the second election of 1910, Home Rule ensured that the Irish remained loyal to Labour. At a meeting in the wake of the result being declared, the chairman of Wigan's LRC praised 'the Irish . . . who were patriots more than anything else, and denominationalists second, and who, as they knew, from the turning out of the boxes had so gallantly, almost unanimously, gone in favour of their comrade'.[95]

Such remarks were all the more pointed, as Twist, having won Wigan in January with a majority of 510, lost by a slightly larger margin in December. The behaviour of local miners over the two contests

[89] *BJG* (8 Nov. 1907), 2.

[90] Ibid.: 51.3% of the Catholic candidate's vote was split with the Conservatives, compared to only 7.6% with the Liberals.   [91] *BJG* (6 Nov. 1908), 3.

[92] J. Denvir, *The Irish in Britain* (1892), 429–33; S. Fielding, *Class and Ethnicity* (Buckingham, 1993), 40–3, 83–7.

[93] *WE* (30 Oct. 1909), 5; (1 Jan. 1910), 7; (4 Jan. 1910), 2; (25 Jan. 1910), 2; *WO* (22 Jan. 1910), 2.   [94] *BJG* (6 Nov. 1908), 3.

[95] *WE* (10 Dec. 1910), 3.

attracted particular comment. If, in January, Twist appeared to enjoy solid support from this group, he now 'found them largely voting against him'.[96] Various explanations were offered to account for this shift, from the reduction in earnings following the implementation of the Eight Hours Act, a measure long favoured by the LCMF, and undue influence exerted by colliery officials at the polls, to organizational deficiencies, exposed by the need to trace large numbers of voters on an old register and exacerbated by the Osborne Judgment.[97] By contrast, little was made of the Unionist pledge to submit the issue of tariffs to a referendum. While this may have assisted in shoring up party support across Lancashire, the swing achieved in Wigan was so pronounced as to suggest that other, primarily local, factors were at work.[98] Of those interpretations which were advanced, none entirely convince as explanations for Twist's reverse. The material consequences of the reduction in hours were no greater in December than they had been in January 1910. Indeed, they had been seen as a factor behind Labour's poor showing in the borough elections of November 1909.[99] Equally, intervention by colliery officials, an explanation favoured by Twist himself, was unlikely to have been decisive, given the constraints on the exercise of employer authority both within and beyond the pit, which has been noted elsewhere.[100] Shortcomings in party organization also appear to have been limited in their impact. The fall in turnout between January and December (9,096 to 8,783) was less than half the reduction in the Labour vote (4,803 to 4,110) and still leaves unexplained the increased Conservative poll (4,293 to 4,673). What is more, any legal check to election activities was probably offset by the registration work of allied organizations, such as the United Irish League and the Lancashire and Cheshire Liberal Federation.[101]

[96] *WE* (6 Dec. 1910), 2; Craig (ed.), *British Parliamentary Election Results, 1885–1918*, 209; six years later, Twist persisted in the belief that non-miners had proved his most consistent source of support in 1910, LCMF, monthly conference minutes, 21 Oct. 1916.

[97] Scott, 'Lancashire and Cheshire Miners' Federation', 254; *WE* (6 Dec. 1910), 2; (10 Dec. 1910), 3; *Report of the Eleventh Annual Conference of the Labour Party* (1911), 3, 68.

[98] The swing against Labour was greater in Wigan than in the neighbouring mining seats of St Helens and Newton, both of which also fell to the Unionists, while in Ince Walsh held on with an only slightly diminished majority, see Craig (ed.), *British Parliamentary Election Results, 1885–1918*, 177, 319, 323; unsurprisingly, convinced Tariff Reformers were also inclined to discount the effects of the pledge, Sir A. Chamberlain, KG, PC, MP, *Politics from Inside: An Epistolary Chronicle, 1906–1914* (1936), 309.

[99] *WE* (2 Nov. 1909), 2; in the weeks preceding the January poll, local collieries worked an average of 5.07 days a week; prior to the December election, that average rose to 5.36, *LG* 18 (1910), 47; 19 (1911), 13.   [100] See above, pp. 47–8, 170–1.

[101] Craig (ed.), *British Parliamentary Election Results, 1885–1918*, 209; MRL, M390/1/1 Lancashire and Cheshire Liberal Federation, Executive Committee minutes, 28 Apr. 1909.

However, the latter point may be of significance, given that the December election coincided with renewed concern over Labour's relations with the established political parties. In the previous January, in a departure from previous Federation practice, the LCMF president, Thomas Greenall, had stood in a three-cornered contest in Leigh. With under a quarter of the vote, he came bottom of the poll. His defeat provoked debate within the Federation, which centred on the failure of either Twist or Walsh to visit the constituency or to speak in support of Greenall. In response to branch criticism of his inaction, Twist claimed that to have intervened in the Leigh contest would have caused 'a revulsion of feeling in Wigan'.[102] Few were in doubt that the prime concern of both Twist and Walsh was to placate Liberal opinion, particularly given their increased dependence on that party's organizational resources. Twist's somewhat strained assurances, that 'The Liberals had not asked for anything in return for their help, they had simply helped him and walked away', failed to convince.[103] Delegates remained of the view that, in their undue sensitivity to Liberal feelings, Twist and Walsh had 'wandered from the principles of labour'.[104] The ideal of independence appeared to have been fundamentally compromised, lending further credence to Conservative claims that Labour, in both Wigan and Ince, was 'bound hand and foot to the Liberal party, and also to the Nonconformist teetotal party'.[105] Rather than defining a distinct electoral interest, Labour had come to be identified with one side in the established political divide. Unsurprisingly, therefore, many traditionally Conservative miners, having backed Twist in January, now reverted to their former allegiance.

The impression thus conveyed of a mining vote still bound by customary divisions receives more direct corroboration from the results of a canvass of the ten wards which made up the parliamentary borough of Wigan, undertaken by the local Constitutional Association in July 1914. Drafted with the aim of ensuring that as many potential Conservative supporters as possible qualified for the vote, the survey sought information on the political and religious affiliations of each householder.[106] Occupational data, by contrast, was but sparingly recorded. Nevertheless,

---

[102] LCMF, annual conference minutes, 22 Jan. 1910; Craig (ed.), *British Parliamentary Election Results, 1885–1918*, 321.

[103] LCMF, adjourned annual conference minutes, 5 Feb. 1910.

[104] LCMF, monthly conference programme, 7 May 1910, Berry Fold resolution.

[105] *WE* (15 Jan. 1910), 1, letter from 'Independent Party'.

[106] Circumstances liable to disqualify the individual from inclusion on the electoral register, such as receipt of poor relief or changes of address involving moves across constituency boundaries, were also recorded.

in the absence of detailed Census returns, information on employment patterns could be gathered from the two Post Office directories published nearest to the date of the canvass, in 1909 and 1925.[107] Combined, these sources provide a valuable tool with which to address the 'ecological fallacy' common to studies of electoral politics, whereby individual motivations are inferred from aggregate data.[108] Problems, it must be acknowledged, remain. A comparison of the canvass returns with municipal election results the previous year indicates a consistent tendency to overstate Conservative support, a consequence, in all probability, of householders' determination to avoid prolonged debate on the doorstep by providing 'favourable' responses to canvassers' questions. Nevertheless, the returns, if they do not eliminate the ecological fallacy, go some way to reducing it to the status of a half-truth.

When extracted, the mining vote in 1914 indicates a high degree of political division at both constituency and ward levels. With the exception

Table 13. *Traceable mining vote: Wigan, 1914*

Ward	Total	Conservative*	Anti-Conservative**	No Allegiance
St George	196	84	91	21
Lindsay	200	91	73	36
St Catharine	371	199	130	42
St Patrick	344	71	246	27
St Thomas	165	56	77	32
Poolstock	192	76	78	38
Victoria	176	55	96	25
St Andrew	244	92	77	75
Swinley	126	66	40	20
All Saints	28	15	10	3
TOTAL	2,042	805	918	319
%	100	39.4	44.95	15.6

Sources: WA, Wigan Constitutional Association D/DZ A68/1–27 Parliamentary Survey, July 1914; *Seed's Wigan and District Directory: First Issue, 1909–10* (Preston, 1909); *Second Issue, 1925* (Preston, 1925).
*Conservative support was indicated by the use of the letter 'C' or by a tick '√'.
**Opposition to the Conservatives was variously recorded: 'Lr' for Labour, 'L' or 'R' for Liberal or Radical, 'N' for Nationalist, or by a cross 'X'.

[107] *Seed's Wigan and District Directory: First Issue, 1909–10* (Preston, 1909); *Second Issue, 1925* (Preston, 1925).
[108] J. Rasmussen, 'Women in Labour: The Flapper Vote and Party System Transformation in Britain', *Electoral Studies*, 3 (1984), 57.

of St Patrick, where the concentration of Irish Catholics produced a size-able anti-Conservative majority, most wards showed support to be quite evenly split between the parties. More importantly, such divisions extended below ward level to individual streets. One example must stand for the whole. Holland St, in the eastern ward of St Catharine, numbered 60 households in 1909, of which thirty-six were headed by males employed in coal-mining. Nineteen mining voters were traceable through the 1914 canvass, of whom five were Conservative and eleven Liberal or Labour supporters; no political affiliations were recorded for the remainder.[109] Clearly then, unlike the Irish, miners in Wigan did not, as yet, constitute a solid and consistent electoral bloc. The mining vote proved incapable of effective mobilization, even at the street and neighbourhood level, providing further evidence of the limitations of working-class sociability and solidarity noted earlier.

Concentrating on the anti-Conservative vote, encompassing those sufficiently committed to respond 'unfavourably' to enquiries, reveals the basis of political division. In all, over 70 per cent of miners who declared their opposition to the Conservatives were Catholic or Nonconformist in religion. The predominance of non-Anglicans applied across all wards, with the single exception of the central business district of All Saints,

Table 14. *Anti-Conservative mining vote: Wigan, 1914*

Ward	Total	Anglican	Catholic	Nonconformist	None
St George	91	26	53	4	8
Lindsay	73	22	32	7	12
St Catharine	130	37	62	24	7
St Patrick	246	13	218	9	6
St Thomas	77	6	59	2	10
Poolstock	78	24	20	17	17
Victoria	96	16	67	4	9
St Andrew	77	22	29	19	7
Swinley	40	11	8	7	14
All Saints	10	5	4	—	1
TOTAL	918	182	552	93	91
%	100	19.8	60.1	10.1	9.9

Sources: See Table 13, above.

[109] WA, D/DZ A68/15 Wigan Constitutional Association Parliamentary Survey, July 1914, St Catharine ward, fos. 25–31; *Seed's Wigan and District Directory: First Issue, 1909–10* (Preston, 1910), 53; *Second Issue, 1925* (Preston, 1925), 74

where the mining and indeed the working-class presence more generally, was minimal. Even if the overwhelmingly Catholic ward of St Patrick were to be excluded, non-Anglicans would still account for over 60 per cent of anti-Conservative miners. The pattern was reproduced, often even more starkly, along Wigan's streets. In Holland St, for example, Catholics accounted for ten of the street's eleven anti-Conservative mining voters, compared to only one out of its five Conservatives.[110] The dynamics of electoral politics in individual districts confirm the impression thus far conveyed. Before 1900, contests in the compact central ward of Victoria tended to revolve around the division between Anglican Toryism and Nonconformist Radicalism. With only a 'sprinkling' of Irish, the area was considered 'unquestionably Conservative' by the sympathetic *Wigan Examiner* in 1898.[111] Over the following decade, however, the demolition of 'rookeries' in St Patrick dispersed the Catholic interest more widely across the borough. Many, as the above figures would suggest, settled in Victoria, producing a fundamental shift in the electoral balance. By January 1910, therefore, the *Examiner* felt bound to acknowledge that the ward had become a Labour stronghold, a description subsequently reinforced by the party's consistent victories in local elections.[112]

It may be objected, with some justification, that the Irish vote had a class as well as a national dimension. For the most part, Irish migrants congregated in low-paid work, or occupations where few restrictions on entry applied.[113] Often, national and class sentiments coalesced, channelling the Irish vote in the same, anti-Conservative/Unionist direction. However, on the few occasions when such feelings conflicted, national concerns assumed primacy. In January 1910, the Leigh branch of the United Irish League, anxious to advance the cause of Home Rule, endorsed the Liberal candidate, Peter Raffan, encouraging an estimated one-third of LCMF members across the division to deny Greenall their votes.[114] Similar tensions emerged in the following year when, in a ballot to select the candidate to contest future elections in Leigh, Irish miners supported their co-religionist James Sexton, in preference to the ILPer Greenall.[115] Even among the group which promised Labour its most

[110] WA, D/DZ A68/15, Survey, fos. 25–31, and Directory references as above.
[111] *WE* (29 Oct. 1898), 2.
[112] *WE* (18 Jan. 1910), 2; Labour proceeded to win every contested election in Victoria from 1912 until 1932, when a large Communist vote allowed the Conservatives to win the seat on a minority vote.
[113] Denvir, *Irish in Britain*, 431; Fielding, *Class and Ethnicity*, 31–3.
[114] Scott, 'Lancashire and Cheshire Miners' Federation', 244, 247.
[115] LCMF, monthly conference minutes, 13 May, 5 Aug. 1911.

consistent source of support through the period, political priorities were informed more by ethnic and religious influences than by a developing class consciousness.

At least until 1910, then, politics across the bulk of the Lancashire coal-field continued to revolve around established points of division. The transition to class politics appeared barely to have begun. Yet, in the final years leading to the outbreak of war, a significant shift in opinion was registered at the polls. Labour enjoyed unprecedented success in this period, culminating in the Wigan elections of November 1913, when the party won eight of the nine wards it contested and gained 58.2 per cent of the poll. If the Conservatives attributed this setback to voter apathy and to the absence on polling day of 2,000 rugby fans at a cup tie in Salford, alternative explanations also suggest themselves. Labour appears to have polled particularly well in areas where miners made up a substantial proportion of the electorate. In Pemberton, where all four wards were won, its share of the vote exceeded 60 per cent. If the township's Lib-Lab traditions meant that success there was not wholly unexpected, Labour's performance in wards such as St Catharine was more surprising. Although it was the ward with the highest proportion of mining heads of household across the old borough, Labour had only contested St Catharine on one previous occasion. Now, however, it won 53 per cent of the poll.[116] While it would be inappropriate to see, in one set of results, evidence of a long-term shift in political allegiances, Labour had, on this occasion at least, mobilized mining opinion to an extent hitherto unrealized. Its ability to do so may have owed something to the success of the MFGB's campaign for a minimum wage, legislation on which was prompted by strike action in 1912.[117] Despite doubts over the details of the Act, the combined industrial and political approach advocated by the LCMF appeared validated.[118] Labour was the electoral beneficiary. If the absence of precise documentation precludes certainty on such points, the timing of Labour's advance and subsequent fluctuations in its support, suggests that this, rather than the scheduling of a local cup tie, offers the most plausible explanation for the events of 1913. This is far from saying that the shift to class politics was completed in the years 1910–14, rather that in Wigan, if not as yet in Bolton, the first signs of an erosion

---

[116] *WE* (4 Nov. 1913), 4; *WO* (4 Nov. 1913), 2, 3.
[117] R. Page Arnot, *The Miners: Years of Struggle. A History of the Miners' Federation of Great Britain (from 1910 onwards)* (1953), 90–110, 118–22; M. W. Kirby, *The British Coalmining Industry, 1870–1946: A Political and Economic History* (London and Basingstoke, 1977), 19.   [118] LCMF, special conference minutes, 30 Mar. 1912.

in the established electoral pattern was evident by the outbreak of war. How far and how rapidly this process would progress would be determined by subsequent events.

II

Reviewing the first set of election results after the war, in 1919, the Bolton press detected a significant shift in popular opinion. Labour's achievement that year, in more than doubling its number of councillors, constituted, in the view of the *Evening News*, 'the first political sign of . . . [a] new social era'.[119] Within the pre-1898 borough, the number of wards contested by Labour and the number of candidates it nominated were the highest since 1906. What is more, unlike thirteen years earlier, all were returned, four topping the polls.[120] Nor was the change observed by the *Evening News* confined to Bolton. In Wigan, although the share of poll secured by Labour candidates was below that achieved in 1913, the party won seven of the twelve seats it contested. What is more, it secured a majority of the popular vote across the eight wards which it contested in the old borough, compared to less than 40 per cent on the previous occasion when the same number of candidates was nominated.[121] More generally, local elections in the immediate post-war years registered an unprecedented Labour advance. Although this initial surge was to be checked in subsequent years, Labour's support, as measured by the share of poll secured by its candidates, never fell back to pre-1914 levels.[122] The conviction that a fundamental psephological shift had occurred appeared fully justified. Understandably, therefore, many historians have been drawn to locate the principal discontinuity in Britain's political development over this period in the war years.

The scale of Labour's progress, spanning as it did a number of regions, has encouraged generalized explanations of change. Although the direct experience of war is given prominence in many accounts, others assign the conflict a more contingent role, arguing that it facilitated the emergence of developments in train before 1914. Such, in essence, is the view of those who place franchise reform at the centre of explanations of political change. The classic statement of this position, as advanced by Matthew, McKibbin, and Kay, has it that the pre-1918 registration system

[119] *BEN* (3 Nov. 1919), 2.   [120] *BJG* (7 Nov. 1919), 5; *BEN* (3 Nov. 1919), 4.
[121] *WE* (4 Nov. 1919), 2; (2 Nov. 1909), 2, although on the latter occasion, one candidate was returned unopposed.   [122] Adams, 'Labour and the First World War', 23–5.

discriminated on a class basis, excluding from the register a large proportion of working men who were, by virtue of their social position and cultural outlook, more predisposed than those who qualified for the vote to
support Labour. The 1918 extension of the franchise thus enabled the
party to mobilize its support to a degree that had not been possible before
1914.[123] This argument has provoked a keen and varied debate, concerned
as much with the technicalities of the pre-war electoral system as with the
central assumption underlying Matthew, McKibbin, and Kay's position,
that social and economic changes had, even before 1914, generated a significant if untapped body of support for Labour.[124] The former point is,
nevertheless, of significance, as it colours perceptions of the principal
basis for exclusion from the pre-1918 franchise. Although it is broadly
accepted that the bulk of those kept off the registers were working-class,
the system is seen to have worked more consistently against the young,
primarily single men living in lodgings or, as the Pretoria sample suggests
was more likely, with their parents.[125] The result of the 1918 franchise
reform was thus to effect a generational change, only partially modified by
the simultaneous enfranchisement of older women. The view that the
votes of younger men disproportionately favoured Labour after 1918 has
been argued most forcefully by Childs. There are, however, many problems with this approach. First, as set out by Childs, the explanation
offered for a generational shift in party allegiance rests substantially on
precisely the kind of broader structural transformation in the working-
class experience which the material presented thus far in this work has
suggested is open to question.[126] Second, analysis of election results in
1918 and 1922 by John Turner suggests that 'new voters' were, if anything, less likely to vote Labour than those enfranchised before 1914.[127] A
third problem, and one which applies to the franchise factor argument
more generally, is that in privileging electoral reform in explaining
Labour's parliamentary advance, it fails to account for the real, if more
limited, progress made by the party at the municipal polls. Local elections
after 1918 were conducted on a franchise constituted on broadly similar
lines to the pre-1914 parliamentary register, save for the addition of large

---

[123] Matthew, McKibbin, and Kay, 'Franchise Factor', esp. 725–37.
[124] McKibbin's own review of the literature is presented in 'The Franchise Factor in the
Rise of the Labour Party', in id., *Ideologies of Class*, 66–7.
[125] See above, Ch. 7; Tanner, *Political Change*, ch. 4.
[126] Childs, 'Labour Grows Up', 123–44.
[127] J. Turner, 'The Labour Vote and the Franchise After 1918: An Investigation of the
English Evidence', in P. Denby and D. Hopkin (eds.), *History and Computing* (Manchester,
1987), 136–43.

numbers of women, and from which the young were still substantially excluded.[128] Labour's capacity to prosper in these circumstances suggests that its performance may have been conditioned more by shifts in popular opinion in the years from 1914 than by the removal of franchise restrictions.

A further difficulty concerns the central assumption underlying accounts which stress the transformative impact of electoral reform, that is that voting intentions remained substantially unchanged between the final pre-war and early post-war elections. Precise evaluation of this point remains elusive. Nevertheless, some insight into voting trends may be gathered from the 1914 Wigan canvass. Although ostensibly a snapshot of political allegiances, the survey, when combined with data from the 1909 and 1925 Post Office directories, is capable of yielding a more dynamic impression of electoral developments. A householder's inclusion in one or both of the directories can stand, with reasonable certainty, as a proxy for age. Thus, a voter traceable to the 1909 directory would have been a householder, and thereby eligible for inclusion on the electoral register, for at least five years before the canvass was held. Conversely, those who could be traced to the 1925 directory alone would, in many cases, only have attained householder and voter status in the years after 1909. The latter point is not entirely straightforward. To begin with, canvassers were only concerned to trace removals over the preceding twelve-month period. Movement before July 1913 would not be recorded. Furthermore, similarities in names mean that individuals could only be traced with any degree of certainty to the same address or to the same or adjoining streets. Long-distance movement prior to July 1913 is thus impossible to trace through the directories alone, so that it cannot be assumed that all those who only figured in the 1925 directory were necessarily 'new' voters. If anything, then, the tendency under the methodology employed here would be to exaggerate the presence of 'young' voters on the register. Conversely, the estimate of 'older' voters is subject to no such qualifications.

If the franchise factor argument, with its emphasis on generational change, were correct, then we would expect a higher proportion of younger electors to be voting according to class rather than religious impulses. In the case of Wigan, this would involve those professing Anglican beliefs declaring anti-Conservative political preferences. Of the

---

[128] Tanner, *Political Change*, 387; *WO* (6 July 1918), 5; *BJG* (19 July 1918), 8, for comparisons of the parliamentary and municipal registers.

2,042 miners traced through the canvass and directories, 182 fitted this profile. Of these, 112, or just over 60 per cent featured in the 1909 directory and so could be classified as 'older' voters. The 'young', by contrast, accounted for no more than 38 per cent of cross-religious anti-Conservative voters.[129] Of itself, this figure is not decisive. To estimate its true significance, it must be measured against the age structure of the mining electorate across Wigan as a whole. Applying the methodology outlined above for all mining households in streets where evidence of cross-religious voting could be found, 34.3 per cent of miners were traceable to the 1925 directory alone.[130] Taken together, this suggests that voters new to the register in 1914 were only marginally more likely to vote according to class interests than were their elders. What is more, the evidence for a fundamental generational shift in opinion before 1914, on which the franchise factor argument substantially relies, is less than compelling. Any growth achieved by Labour between the elections of 1910–13 and those of 1918–20 must therefore be attributed to changing allegiances among the existing electorate rather than to the incorporation of a new body of voters. It remains to establish the extent of and the reasons for any such development.

One explanation, which the Bolton and Wigan evidence suggests may readily be discounted, locates change in a wholesale restructuring of working-class life during and immediately following the First World War. By this argument, internal points of difference, based on levels of skill and remuneration, were substantially reduced as a consequence both of altered working methods and the move to national pay bargaining.[131] Yet such an all-embracing explanation is no more plausible for the years after 1914 than it is for the pre-war period. Although wage differentials between mining grades were undoubtedly compressed during wartime, the absence of significant hierarchies within the underground workforce ensured that such developments carried no wider implications. In neighbouring cotton mills, despite the extensive redeployment of labour and the greater utilization of female hands, existing work practices were, for the most part, maintained. The jobs to which women and girls were assigned rarely challenged established prerogatives. If anything, therefore, work hierarchies, far from being overcome, were consolidated and extended in the period 1914–18.[132] Any change in class structures

---

[129] WA, D/DZ A68/1–27 Wigan Constitutional Association, Parliamentary Survey, July 1914; *Seed's Wigan and District Directory: First Issue, 1909–10; Second Issue, 1925.*
[130] *Seed's Directories: First and Second Issues.*
[131] Adams, 'Labour and the First World War', 30–1.   [132] See above, Ch. 2.

originating in the workplace operated to enhance rather than to diminish a sense of internal difference.

Rather more pertinent to Labour's immediate post-war performance was the growth of state involvement in economic management and popular reactions to that development. It has been suggested that government control of basic industries and the regulation of agreements governing working conditions transformed working-class attitudes to the state, so that suspicion of outside agencies gave way to a readiness to endorse the principle of intervention. The parameters of practical politics were altered in a way which privileged Labour's collectivist approach.[133] Others suggest that state intervention, rather playing such an enabling role, worked to antagonize working-class interests. Discontent centred on the government's failure to control the prices of basic necessities or to dampen the inflated profit margins of major industrial concerns. Labour was thus able, in a way that a divided Liberal Party was not, to pose as the defender of working-class living standards.[134] Such a stance would assume even greater significance in the early post-war years, as the onset of deflationary finance polarized political opinion. Both arguments may be applied with some validity to the experience of the coal industry in Lancashire. As has been seen, national control in wartime created a secure market environment in which colliery activity across the county was maintained at a consistently high level. What is more, a comprehensive system of joint regulation, operative at pit and district level, helped to contain and reconcile local points of difference.[135] The experience of joint control would be applied in shaping union proposals for the nationalization of the industry after 1918. Tensions, however, remained and centred, for the most part, on the related problems of price inflation and profiteering. The report of the Commission of Enquiry into Industrial Unrest for the North Western Area found the principal causes of discontent locally to be increases in the cost of living outstripping wage rises and the failure adequately to control the distribution of food and fuel.[136] In the same month that the Commission reported, Wigan's Trades Council and LRC combined to form a local War Emergency Committee, with the

[133] Kirk, *Change, Continuity and Class*, 194–5.

[134] Adams, 'Labour and the First World War', 27–8; R. Harrison, 'The War Emergency Workers' National Committee, 1914–1920', in A. Briggs and J. Saville (eds.), *Essays in Labour History, 1886–1923* (London and Basingstoke, 1971), 211–59.

[135] See above, Ch. 3.

[136] *Parl. Papers 1917–18*, xv (8663), Commission into Industrial Unrest: North Western Area, pars. 23 and 25; the tendency for wages to lag behind the rise in prices is indicated in Bowley, *Prices and Wages in the United Kingdom*, 19–21, 179.

express aim of protesting against the unequal sacrifice which workers were being asked to make.[137] Attacks on profiteering also enabled Labour to invest traditional Radical rhetoric with a more explicitly class character, by which workers were identified with the productive and capital with the unproductive parasitic classes.[138] Other issues offered Labour the opportunity to extend its potential constituency. In particular, campaigns to secure increased allowances for servicemen's dependants identified the party with the defence of working-class interests as a whole, rather than those of the organized male workforce only.[139]

If developments across the coalfield held out the prospect of significant electoral progress after the war, Labour's success in Wigan in 1918 suggested that such expectations had been realized and appeared wholly consistent with results elsewhere. Across Britain, in the first post-war parliamentary election, Labour secured its highest levels of support in mining seats, to the extent that such constituencies returned almost 60 per cent of the party's MPs.[140] Nevertheless, in the case of Wigan, the extent of Labour's progress should not be overstated. On closer examination, the party's performance continued to be shaped by pre-war patterns of allegiance. As late as 1916, Labour's parliamentary prospects across the area seemed unpromising. Although Wigan could claim the highest concentration of Labour councillors in any English county borough, the failure of local miners to back Labour, reflected in their desertion of Twist in December 1910, suggested that chances of electoral success were slim. Other developments gave no cause for greater optimism. The largesse of the party's election agent in January 1910 had revealed a propensity among local voters to indulge in corrupt practices, while Twist's registration agent had subsequently acquired an unwelcome reputation for picking fights in local Labour Clubs. All of which persuaded Twist, in June 1916, to resign as prospective candidate for Wigan and the LCMF to exclude the town from its list of constituencies. Greenall advised delegates that 'it would be very unwise for our Federation to adopt either Mr. Twist or any other candidate for the Wigan Division at the next election'.[141] Events over the following year, however, prompted a

[137] *WE* (11 July 1917), 2; *WO* (3 July 1917), 3.

[138] See the remarks of R. Prestt, secretary of the Wigan branch of the ASE, *WO* (14 May 1918), 2; for the older, 'populist' version of this view, see P. Joyce, *Visions of the People* (Cambridge, 1991), 53–4, 69–70, 303–4.

[139] Harrison, 'The War Emergency Workers' National Committee', 228–9; for Labour statements on this issue, *WO* (23 Mar. 1918), 2; (3 Dec. 1918), 3.

[140] Tanner, 'The Labour Party and Electoral Politics in the Coalfields', in Campbell, Fishman, and Howell (eds.), *Miners, Unions and Politics*, 62–3.

[141] LCMF, monthly conf. minutes, 26 Aug., 3 June, 21 Oct. 1916; WO (10 June 1916), 6.

reconsideration of tactics. The decisive development was the wholesale
revision of constituency boundaries, by which Pemberton, long part of
Wigan for municipal purposes, was incorporated into the parliamentary
borough.[142] The inclusion of Pemberton promised to transform Labour's
prospects. In pre-war local elections, the party had consistently secured
higher levels of support in the four wards which made up the township
than it had in the old borough. In 1913, the year that Conservative control was ended, half of Labour's sixteen Councillors sat for wards in
Pemberton.[143] John Cheetham, secretary of the local Miners' Association
and chairman of Ince Division Labour Party, the constituency in which
Pemberton was previously located, was confident that Wigan could be
won on the new boundaries. The town was thus restored to the Federation's
slate in January 1918.[144] Although Twist again withdrew later in the year,
his nomination for the MFGB secretaryship precluding his standing as
a parliamentary candidate, Wigan was fought in December 1918. John
Allen Parkinson, Federation agent for the St Helens district, won the
seat with 48 per cent of the poll and a majority of just over 1,000.[145]

As these figures suggest, the growth achieved to 1918 was incremental
rather than transformative. What is more, it appears to have rested on
well-established sources of support. Despite the intervention of an independent Liberal candidate, R. O. Alstead, who came forward in the interval between Twist's second resignation and Parkinson's nomination, local
branches of the United Irish League opted to back Labour. This, along
with the prominence which Parkinson gave to Home Rule in his election
address, pointed up the enduring influence religious and ethnic allegiances exerted over voting behaviour.[146] The point was pursued by a sta-
tistically minded, yet anonymous correspondent to the *Wigan Examiner*.
Writing in the two weeks which separated the poll from the counting of
the ballot papers, 'No Seer' discounted the presence of large numbers of
female first-time voters, preferring instead to emphasize the influence
of boundary changes and the continued purchase of religious ideas. By
this account, Pemberton, with its long-established Labour tradition, was
expected to yield a majority of some 2,000 for Parkinson. In Wigan, by
contrast, a Coalition majority was predicted. Significantly, this conclusion

[142] *WE* (3 July 1917), 2; (17 July 1917), 2.   [143] *WO* (4 Nov. 1913), 2.
[144] LCMF, monthly conference minutes, 12 Jan. 1918; *WO* (15 Jan. 1918), 2.
[145] F. W. S. Craig (ed.), *British Parliamentary Election Results, 1918–1949* (London and
Basingstoke, 1977), 276; *WE* (26 Nov. 1918), 2; *WO* (3 Dec. 1918), 2, 3; LCMF, monthly
conference minutes, 19 Oct.; special conference minutes, 23 Nov., 30 Nov. 1918.
[146] *WE* (3 Dec. 1918), 1, 3; (7 Dec. 1918), 5; *WO* (26 Nov. 1918), 2; (3 Dec. 1918), 3; (7
Dec. 1918), 5.

was reached by dividing the electorate into denominational blocs: the Nonconformist vote was split equally between the three candidates; the English Catholics were expected to follow 'their usually Conservative tendencies'; while the Irish would, it was anticipated, 'show a strong preponderance on the Labour side'. The outcome of such calculations was a projected Labour majority of 1,000.[147] It is impossible to establish with any certainty how far the disposal of votes matched this prediction. However, the readiness to discuss Wigan politics in predominantly religious terms and the proximity to the actual outcome suggest that this approach conveys an underlying truth: that the war, if it had witnessed the consolidation of Labour's support, had not produced a fundamental change in the nature of popular politics. Traditional religious continued to win out over class allegiances.

What is more, Labour's progress, reflected in its capacity to win Wigan with a hastily installed candidate against Liberal opposition, still rested on shifting foundations. Since the minimum-wage strike of 1912, industrial and political advance had proceeded in tandem. The miners' defeat following the strike of 1921, resulting as it did in the dismantling of that national framework which had ensured a period of stability and sustained profitability for the coalfield, threw that process into sharp reverse. In the local elections of that year, the Labour vote fell markedly across both Wigan and Pemberton. Having won seven out of eight contests in the latter in 1919–20, Labour was successful in only one of the three wards it contested in 1921, and that by a majority of thirty-seven. The party's share of the poll in Pemberton declined from 59 to 44 per cent, a level of support not seen since 1907. In Wigan, the fall in the Labour vote was equally marked and plumbed depths not witnessed since 1909. Significantly, however, this trend was not uniform across the borough. Labour performed worst in wards with sizeable mining electorates. Taking the three wards of Lindsay, St Catharine, and St Andrew together, Labour's share of the poll fell from 60.3 to 37.1 per cent. By contrast, the party's performance was altogether more robust in areas where the Catholic presence was large. Candidates in both St George and Victoria secured increased votes in 1921 and between them maintained Labour's overall share of the vote in these wards.[148] Labour's position was most secure where it was able to draw on an existing and

[147] *WE* (24 Dec. 1918), 2, letter by 'No Seer'.
[148] *WE* (4 Nov. 1919), 2; (2 Nov. 1920), 2; (5 Nov. 1921), 7; the Labour vote in the three 'mining' wards fell by 1,264 between 1920 and 1921, while in the two 'Catholic' wards a net increase of 56 was recorded.

coherent body of support. In Wigan, it is clear, this was provided by the Catholic Irish. Beginning in 1912–13 and extending through the war years and their immediate aftermath, the party appeared capable of mobilizing support among important occupational groups. Yet, as the events of 1921 demonstrated, this remained a fragile alignment, viable only so long as Labour could demonstrate a capacity to promote the material interests of such groups. A secure class-based constituency had still to be constructed.

Conditions for Labour growth appeared, if anything, even less propitious further east. In contrast to the position in the county's collieries, the state operated at the margins of the cotton trade, resolving differences over wage bargaining and over the restrictions placed on productive activity by the wartime Control Board.[149] Otherwise, the industry maintained its reputation for effective self-regulation. The Commissioners inquiring into industrial unrest across the north-west found that relations between employers and employed remained cordial and were of the opinion 'that the machinery set up by agreement between the two sides for dealing with disputes was speedy, efficient, and satisfactory'.[150] An enduring suspicion of government intervention found expression in rank-and-file hostility to proposals for education reform from 1918.[151] The politicization of industrial issues which characterized the coal trade was thus lacking here. Unsurprisingly, therefore, any improvement in Labour's performance after 1918 in Bolton was modest. Indeed, the share of poll secured by Labour candidates in local elections in the three years 1919–21 remained below the levels achieved in the period 1906–9.[152] What is more, the notion of Progressive co-operation continued to attract considerable support within the local labour movement. In 1918, both sitting members, Robert Tootill for Labour and the Coalition Liberal William Edge, were returned unopposed. The following year, proposals to end such arrangements by nominating a second Labour parliamentary candidate foundered on union opposition. Delegates at a meeting of the Bolton Operative Spinners' Association voted to reject any move to break with Progressivism.[153]

---

[149] See above, Ch. 3.

[150] *Parl. Papers 1917–18*, xv (8663), Commission of Enquiry into Industrial Unrest: Report for North Western Area, par. 16.   [151] See above, Ch. 4.

[152] Calculated from *BJG* (7 Nov. 1919), 8; (4 Nov. 1921), 7; *BEN* (3 Nov. 1919), 4; (2 Nov. 1920), 4.

[153] *BJG* (29 Nov. 1918), 2; JRUL, BCA/1/3/11 BSA, minutes, general representative meeting, 10 Sept. 1919.

Yet, despite such evidence of an underlying continuity in political attitudes, indications of a broadening of support for Labour were not wanting. Against the limited advance suggested by Labour's share of the poll, the party showed an unprecedented capacity to win seats. Of fifteen candidates nominated in November elections across the pre-1898 borough in 1919 and 1920, eleven were victorious.[154] Furthermore, success was achieved, more often than not, in the face of Liberal opposition. The squeeze on Labour's core vote, so evident in the years to 1914, was now reversed. In nine two-member wards where Labour encountered Liberal opposition in 1919 and 1920, over 54 per cent of the Labour vote came from 'plumpers'. By contrast, less than a quarter was now split with the Liberals.[155] Yet, although Labour appeared capable of mobilizing a more coherent and independent body of support, the party continued to lag behind both Conservatives and Liberals in terms of the total number of votes cast and the average secured by each candidate. The continued vitality of local Liberalism was reflected in its ability to increase its vote at the November polls by some 55 per cent between 1919 and 1921, compared to Labour's more modest 28 per cent.[156] In the latter year, Labour's hopes of six gains were disappointed, as only three of the party's thirteen candidates were returned.[157] Labour's progess in the immediate aftermath of war, although real in terms of throwing off the Progressive embrace, had proved limited in extent. In a three-party fight, the evidence suggested that Labour, rather than the Conservatives or the Liberals, was struggling to augment its support.

Within twelve months, however, the situation was to be transformed. In both local and parliamentary elections in 1922, Labour emerged as the second party, in terms of popular support, across the borough. The change in fortunes could be traced, in large measure, to the problems of the Lloyd George Coalition. While government policy in Ireland, from military repression to a settlement incorporating the principle of partition, worked to alienate Catholic opinion, Labour's critical stance increasingly made it the natural focus of nationalist aspirations. Reflecting this shift, the Bolton branch of the Irish Labour Party voted, in December 1920, to affiliate to the local Labour Party.[158] In the aggregate,

---

[154] *BJG* (7 Nov. 1919), 8; *BEN* (1 Nov. 1920), 3; (2 Nov. 1920), 4.
[155] *BEN* (3 Nov. 1919), 4; (2 Nov. 1920), 4.   [156] *BJG* (11 Nov. 1921), 7.
[157] *BJG* (4 Nov. 1921), 7.
[158] *BJG* (9 Jan. 1920), 7; (10 Dec. 1920), 7; C. L. Mowat, *Britain between the Wars, 1918–1940* (1955), 72–83; C. Howard, 'Expectations Born to Death: Local Labour Party Expansion in the 1920s', in J. Winter (ed.), *The Working Class in Modern British History: Essays in Honour of Henry Pelling* (1983), 67.

the dispersal of Bolton's Catholic population ensured that the electoral consequences of this decision were slight. However, in the one local ward with a sizeable concentration of Catholics, the central district of Exchange, it sufficed to guarantee the return of at least one Labour candidate each November, even though the party had not contested the ward before 1920.[159] Tensions within the Coalition also worked to undermine the unity which local Liberalism had maintained through the Asquith–Lloyd George divisions of 1916–18.[160] The government's apparent readiness to sacrifice Lancastrian interests in allowing the Indian authorities to increase import duties on cotton cloth and in extending safeguarding to native manufacturers of fabric gloves, along with the abandonment of schemes of social reconstruction before the imperatives of deflationary finance, created fundamental rifts in local party ranks. The formation of a separate Coalition Liberal organization in 1921 formalized divisions to the extent that, in the following year, candidates came forward under Coalition and Independent Liberal banners to contest both borough and parliamentary elections, while the simultaneous submission of two Liberal nominees ensured the return of Bolton's first Labour Mayor.[161] At the same time, opinion within the broader trade-union movement shifted in favour of undiluted Labour politics. Having opposed a second parliamentary candidate in 1919, the Bolton Operative Spinners' Association came to endorse such a move, even though it would entail the imposition of an additional levy to fund any campaign. The Association was obliged to ballot the membership to secure endorsement for the raising of funds for local use, as the terms of the 1913 vote only allowed for a levy administered through the UTFWA. The ballot, held in October 1922, when Liberal divisions were at their height prior to the fall of the Coalition, revealed a substantial minority opposed to further political action. Of 8,121 members who voted, 3,057 or 38 per cent voted against an additional levy.[162] Association officials were drawn to reflect on the failure of large numbers of 'good trade unionists' to sever their ties with the established parties and to embrace unambiguously the Labour cause.[163]

    [159] *BJG* (5 Nov. 1920), 7; (4 Nov. 1921), 7.
    [160] *BJG* (8 Mar. 1918), 3; (22 Nov. 1918), 4, for the unanimous adoption of Edge as Liberal Coalition candidate.
    [161] See above, Ch. 3; J. D. Tomlinson, 'The First World War and British Cotton Piece Exports to India', *Econ.Hist.Rev.*, 2nd ser. 32 (1979), 501–3; BA, FT/21/10 BSA, Annual Report for 1922, 7; *BJG* (18 Feb. 1921), 6; (20 Oct. 1922), 5; (29 Dec. 1922), 5.
    [162] JRUL, BCA/1/3/12 BSA, minutes, circular and ballot paper re political levy, 3 Oct. 1922; Council meeting, 13 Oct. 1922; BCA/13/3/7 BSA, general outward correspondence, Wood to branch secretaries, 5 Oct. 1922.
    [163] BA, FT/21/11 BSA, Annual Report for 1925, 9.

The period of war and its immediate aftermath was thus one of significant advance for Labour. By 1922, the party controlled Wigan at both parliamentary and municipal levels, while it was established as the second largest political force in Bolton. Such gains owed little to technical changes in the electoral system but may, more plausibly, be linked to Labour's capacity to articulate and promote the industrial and material interests of workers, particularly in a period marked by increased state intervention and significant price inflation. Yet progress remained primarily incremental. In neither borough was Labour's position secure. Control of Wigan's council chamber was dependent on continued Liberal/Irish support. Furthermore, in the parliamentary election of 1922, Parkinson's poll of 56 per cent in a straight fight against the Conservatives was equivalent to the combined Liberal and Labour vote four years earlier.[164] More significantly, the events of 1921 had shown that the party's support was still vulnerable to the effects of an industrial reverse. In Bolton, Labour had yet to supplant the Liberals as the main opposition to the Conservatives. Local elections since the war had revealed a still buoyant Liberal constituency across the borough. If this was depressed by the divisions engendered during the final years of the Lloyd George Coalition, it remained to be established how far such changes represented the beginnings of a fundamental realignment in the anti-Conservative vote and how far it constituted a temporary setback in local Liberalism's post-war revival. That question, at least, would be resolved in the decade that followed.

III

By 1929, incontrovertible evidence appeared to exist that a wholesale shift in party allegiances had occurred. Parliamentary and local elections in that year registered a sizeable Labour advance. In Bolton, six months after winning both of the borough's Westminster seats, the party gained control of the council chamber for the first time.[165] Further west, in Wigan, the November elections saw it increase its majority to twenty over all other parties combined. As this suggests, Labour's support was now broadly based. In Pemberton, its position was sufficiently entrenched to ensure the unopposed return of all four of its candidates, while in the Wigan wards it contested, the party secured over 60 per cent of the

---

[164] Craig (ed.), *British Parliamentary Election Results, 1918–1949*, 276; *WE* (3 Nov. 1923), 9.
[165] *BJG* (7 June 1929), 6; (8 Nov. 1929), 6.

vote.[166] The transition to class-based political allegiances appeared significantly more advanced by 1929 than it had in the immediate post-war
years, a fact which has encouraged attempts to locate Labour's breakthrough in the 1920s and, more especially, in the latter part of that decade.
The most extended and sophisticated statement of this view, by Mike
Savage, explains change in terms of a fundamental transformation in the
nature of working-class politics and a related reorientation in Labour's
popular appeal. The first involved a shift away from 'economistic', mostly
trade-union led, strategies to a more 'statist', party-political, solution to
practical problems. The change was brought about by developments in
the labour market, by which craft-based controls over the processes of
recruitment and training gave way before increased state intervention
through more formal agencies, including labour exchanges and juvenile
employment bureaux. At the same time, greater government involvement
in the provision of vital services, including health, education, and housing, extended the range of issues around which party support could
rally.[167] Labour responded to such changes, Savage argues, with a deliberate attempt to broaden its appeal beyond the organized, mostly male,
working class, on whose support its early growth had depended. From the
1920s, the politics of industrial trade-union-inspired issues were sup-
planted by a more openly social welfarist agenda, a process assisted by
organizational changes, which strengthened Labour's presence in individual neighbourhoods.[168] The chronology of Labour's advance is
employed to indicate the effectiveness of this shift. The years in which the
party enjoyed its greatest successes were, notes Savage, also ones of
declining trade-union membership and settled employer–employee relations, so that the link between political and industrial militancy was rendered increasingly tenuous.[169] By this argument, electoral progress rested
on Labour's capacity to reach beyond its 'natural' constituency to tap new
sources of support. Particular importance attaches to the allegiance of
younger women, enfranchised in 1928. This is seen to be significant not
only for Labour's success in 1929, but also for its fortunes once in government. Decisions taken by the Labour cabinet, including measures to

---

[166] *WE* (26 Oct. 1929), 11; (9 Nov. 1929), 1.

[167] Savage, *Dynamics*, 20–101; M. Savage and A. Miles, *The Remaking of the British
Working Class* (1994), 48–56; for a recent analysis of political change which draws
substantially on the theoretical perspective outlined by Savage, see J. Hill, 'Lib-Labism,
Socialism and Labour in Burnley, c.1890–1918', *Northern History*, 35 (1999), 185–204.

[168] Savage, *Dynamics*, 163–80; Savage and Miles, *Remaking*, 80–6.

[169] Savage and Miles, *Remaking*, 81–4; Savage, 'The Rise of the Labour Party in Local
Perspective', 12; the point is also made in Tanner, *Political Change*, 437.

limit married women's eligibility for unemployment benefit, alienated a sizeable body of support, contributing in no small measure to the sharp reversal in fortunes experienced by the party at the polls in 1931.[170]

Beyond such narrow details, this approach has several virtues. It seeks to question the autonomy of politics by relating shifts in party fortunes to broader social forces, while giving due weight to the capacity of party ideology and political debate to create and sustain networks of support at national and local elections.[171] That said, it also gives rise to a number of problems which, taken together, cast severe doubt on its ability successfully to account for the course of political change in the period to 1931. One difficulty is the tendency to conflate 'practical politics', narrowly defined as the means by which material insecurity was minimized, with 'formal politics', or the factors determining party allegiances.[172] The latter, as the above discussion has emphasized, were informed by more than merely economic interests. Religious and national concerns were vital in shaping long-term voting behaviour across Lancashire, but such considerations are entirely excluded from the bounds of 'practical politics' as formulated by Savage and are thus discounted in his analysis of electoral change in Preston. Although potentially of value in explaining short-term shifts in support, the notion of 'practical politics' must be judged incapable of comprehending the broader sequence of change.

A further problem concerns the model of class formation at the heart of Savage's analysis. By this, Labour's ability to generate support in urban areas is linked to the emergence, in the 1920s, of a strong sense of collective neighbourhood identity, born of greater residential stability and the strengthening of associational ties through a network of institutions touching working-class life at several points, from consumption and saving to leisure.[173] However, the experience of trade unions and Co-operative societies, among other agencies, in this period suggests that the fact of membership did not translate readily into a deeper sense of attachment. The associational culture of the urban working class was less well developed than bare membership statistics would indicate. Furthermore, the limited and mostly pragmatic nature of working-class sociability, encapsulated by the experience of Pretoria widows, points to the fact that urban neighbourhoods were unpromising

---

[170] Savage, 'Urban Politics and the Rise of the Labour Party', 212–15; id., *Dynamics*, 180–2.

[171] M. Savage, 'Urban History and Social Class: Two Paradigms', *Urban History*, 20 (1993), 62–70.   [172] For 'practical politics' see Savage, *Dynamics*, 20–8.

[173] Savage, 'Urban History and Social Class', 72–5; Savage and Miles, *Remaking*, 62–8.

centres of political mobilization.[174] One group capable of articulating a common identity at various social levels was the Catholic Irish. Here, class concerns married with national and religious preoccupations to produce an unusually coherent electoral bloc. Otherwise, there is little evidence that a collective sense of neighbourhood, upon which Labour's ward organizations would be able to draw, was in the process of formation in the 1920s.

An additional note of qualification must be entered against the notion of a significant shift from economistic to statist politics in this period. Taken as a whole, changes in the local labour market hardly sufficed to produce a transformation in class strategies. As has been seen, craft controls over the recruitment and deployment of labour, rather than being challenged, were consolidated over the period, while government intervention operated largely at the margins. The search for work continued to bypass official agencies, being conducted primarily through personal, informal contacts.[175] Moreover, there is little to suggest that popular attitudes to state activity fundamentally altered over the early decades of the twentieth century. Government involvement in the direction of labour in wartime had raised fears of industrial conscription, while in the provision of important services such as education across much of Lancashire a statist approach was eschewed in favour of voluntary, religious control. Equally, evidence for a shift in Labour's policy approach from workplace-based to neighbourhood-centred issues is less than compelling. Despite its explicit union roots, the party in both Bolton and Wigan had always attempted to mobilize support across a range of issues. In addition to the standard reiteration of Labour's independence from political allies, the candidate contesting Bolton's Derby ward in 1903 had advocated widespread slum clearance and the provision of adequate space for recreational purposes.[176] Both were calls that would resound down the years. In that same year, Robert Tootill, standing in West ward, had called for the free provision of gas fires, stoves, and cookers for all households.[177] 'Neighbourhood' issues continued to receive prominence, so that in the November elections of 1907 in Bolton housing was seen to be the main plank in Labour's platform.[178] The need for state action, pursued in this case through the agency of the municipality, was readily accepted. In 1912, therefore, Labour called on the borough council to reduce the price of gas, to adopt the provisions of the Town Planning Act, and to establish

---

[174] See above, Ch. 6.   [175] See above, Chs. 2 and 4.
[176] *BJG* (23 Oct. 1903), 7.   [177] Ibid.   [178] *BJG* (25 Oct. 1907), 16.

a network of school clinics, all of which fit more neatly under the banner of neighbourhood than industrial issues.[179] The move from economistic to statist politics, if it occurred at all, thus represented at most a shift in emphasis, and in itself was hardly a change likely to transform Labour's electoral prospects.

The chronology of the party's advance goes some way towards clarifying the factors promoting political change in the 1920s. While 1929 represented a peak year for Labour support in both Bolton and Wigan, progress to that point was irregular. In three successive years between 1924 and 1926, significant increases were recorded in the party's vote. Across those inner wards in Bolton contested by Labour, the party's share of poll rose from 35.9 per cent in 1923 to 46.3 per cent in 1926. In Wigan, excluding Pemberton, in the same period, the increase was from 48.2 to 56.9 per cent.[180] The initial surge in support came in the November 1924 elections in Bolton, in which, although Labour's overall representation remained unchanged, its share of the poll, as measured in its vote and in its core level of support, registered a more definite shift (from 35.9 to 39.5 per cent in the case of the former, and from 27.8 to 34.2 per cent in the latter).[181] To some degree, the party's task was eased by renewed divisions within local Liberalism and an electoral truce between Liberals and Conservatives, which enabled Labour to pose as the only progressive, anti-Conservative force within the borough. The collapse of the Liberal vote in the ensuing general election persuaded the labour correspondent of the *Bolton Journal and Guardian* that Liberalism as an independent political force was spent.[182] If that judgement proved rather premature, the result served to consolidate Labour's position as the second largest party in the borough. Progress was even further marked in the following two years, net gains of eleven and eight seats respectively being recorded in Bolton and Wigan.[183] Although the *Bolton Journal and Guardian*'s correspondent pointed to organizational improvements as the main factor behind the party's success, the broad nature of Labour's advance suggests

---

[179] *BJG* (18 Oct. 1912), 9; the feeding of necessitous school children and the municipalization of the local infirmary were also given prominence, *BEN* (30 Oct. 1912), 2; (31 Oct. 1912), 2.

[180] Calculated from *BJG* (2 Nov. 1923), 10; (5 Nov. 1926), 6; *WE* (3 Nov. 1923), 9; *WO* (4 Nov. 1926), 2. [181] Calculated from *BJG* (2 Nov. 1923), 10; (7 Nov. 1924), 6.

[182] *BJG* (17 Oct. 1924), 6; (14 Nov. 1924), 5, 'The Voice of Labour'; in terms of share of poll, Liberalism slipped from 33.2% in 1923 to 14% the following year, Craig (ed.), *British Parliamentary Election Results, 1918–1949*, 689–90.

[183] Calculated from *BJG* (6 Nov. 1925), 11; (5 Nov. 1926), 6; *WE* (3 Nov. 1925), 2; *WO* (4 Nov. 1926), 2.

that more than local influences were at work.[184] Few contemporary observers doubted that the miners' dispute was a powerful factor behind Labour's successes in 1926. To this, Labour spokesmen added a growing antipathy to the Baldwin government over its failure to address the difficulties of the coal and cotton trades. Growth in party support thus coincided with a period of industrial discord and discontent over the pursuit, at Westminster, of unfavourable financial policies.[185] By contrast, the years of industrial peace which followed saw Labour's support, reflected in the share of poll, stagnate or register a slight but definite declension: in 1927, from almost 57 to 52.6 per cent in the old borough of Wigan and from 46 to 44 per cent across inner Bolton.[186] It is difficult to reconcile the sequence of change outlined here with accounts which play down the importance of industrial unrest and economic decline. To that extent, the interpretative weight given to the politics of 'neighbourhood' seems misplaced.

Labour's fortunes in 1929 and beyond confirm this impression. Much has been made, by Savage and others, of the gendered nature of the party's support in this period. Success in the general election of 1929 is thus traced to a further franchise factor: the extension of the vote to women on the same terms as men. Certainly, this altered the gender balance within the parliamentary electorate. In Bolton, a male majority of 12,000 was transformed into a female preponderance of almost 10,000. Further west, in Wigan, the balance was also in favour of women, albeit by the smaller margin of 2,300.[187] In explaining the outcome of the first election to be fought under these altered circumstances, particular attention has been devoted to the disposition of the 'flapper' vote. Reactions at the time indicated that this had gone substantially in favour of Labour. Echoing the views of Labour representatives, Liberal officials were confident in declaring 'it's the women who have made the result what it is'.[188] In part, this could be regarded as a natural reward for the party's longstanding commitment to electoral equality, a point of which Parkinson made much during the campaign.[189] Yet all was not quite as simple as this

---

[184] *BJG* (6 Nov. 1925), 5, 'Voice of Labour'; the local party reported a tenfold increase in individual membership in the six months following the 1924 election, *BJG* (24 Apr. 1925), 7.
[185] *WE* (6 Nov. 1926), 7; *BJG* (5 Nov. 1926), 5, 'Voice of Labour'.
[186] Calculated from *WE* (5 Nov. 1927), 7; *BJG* (4 Nov. 1927), 6; in the following year, a slight recovery was recorded in both towns, but in neither case did Labour's poll recover to the levels of 1926, *WE* (3 Nov. 1928), 11; *BJG* (2 Nov. 1928), 4; *BEN* (2 Nov. 1928), 4.
[187] *BJG* (1 Feb. 1929), 8; *WE* (1 June 1929), 11.
[188] *BJG* (7 June 1929), 6; see also *WE* (1 June 1929), 7, 'Notes by the Way'; see also Savage, *Dynamics*, 179.   [189] *WO* (25 May 1929), 16.

suggests. The Conservatives claimed to have received their due share of female support in 1929.[190] What is more, subsequent developments indicate that the 'flapper' vote was not, of itself, decisive in Labour's victory. Had it been so, then it could be anticipated that Labour's parliamentary performance would significantly outstrip its standing at the municipal polls, given that young women remained excluded from the local government franchise. Yet the contrary was, in fact, the case. Labour polled 41 per cent of the vote in Bolton in May, compared with almost 45 per cent across the borough as a whole six months later. A similar pattern obtained in Wigan, where the 58 per cent of the poll secured by Parkinson at the general election was more than matched by the 61 per cent gained in the six wards contested by the party in November.[191] Even at the time, alternative explanations for Labour's success were offered. 'The Voice of Labour' in the *Bolton Journal and Guardian* interpreted the vote as one of support for the 'sober statements' contained in *Labour and the Nation*, and as a protest against the failures of the Baldwin government, encapsulated in the party's slogan 'We've had enough; we want a change'.[192] The mood of protest served also to boost the Liberal vote, to the extent that, despite the conviction voiced by the secretary of the UTFWA that the return of Labour was of greater importance to the people of Bolton than a victory for the Wanderers in that year's FA Cup Final, a lower proportion of 'effective' votes were cast solely for Labour in that election than in 1924, 34.3 against 37.5 per cent.[193] This led 'John Bull', Conservative correspondent of the *Bolton Journal and Guardian*, to remark that the Liberals had 'committed suicide once and for all'. Their increased vote had handed Labour power on a minority vote, but had yielded only modest dividends in terms of seats won: 'A good size charabanc would still carry the lot'.[194] The economic situation and Labour's undertaking to adopt a scientific approach to the problems of unemployment and industrial decline appear to have exerted a more powerful influence over the electoral outcome than did differing gender preferences.

Events after November 1929 further justify this conclusion. Gender issues played a peripheral role, at best, in Labour's fall from grace.

[190] *BJG* (7 June 1929), 6.
[191] Craig (ed.), *British Parliamentary Election Results, 1918–1949*, 276, 690; *BJG* (8 Nov. 1929), 6; *WE* (9 Nov. 1929), 1; this agrees with the analysis in Rasmussen, 'Women in Labour', 57–9.   [192] *BJG* (14 June 1929), 5.
[193] Calculated from Craig (ed.), *British Parliamentary Election Results, 1918–1949*, 689–90; for the UTFWA secretary's remarks, see *BJG* (15 Mar. 1929), 12.
[194] *BJG* (7 June 1929), 5, 'Conservative Point of View'.

Anomalies legislation, which restricted married women's access to unemployment benefit, and which Savage argues was crucial in alienating female opinion, only came into operation in the last months of the second MacDonald government, well after the first signs of an erosion in Labour's popular support.[195] In Bolton, evidence of a drift of opinion against Labour emerged in a series of by-elections in the winter of 1929–30. Seven seats had become vacant following the November 1929 elections, which had resulted in an increase in Labour's representation on the borough's aldermanic bench. The by-elections, held in December, registered little overall change in the party's support.[196] By early 1930, however, a rather different picture was emerging. In consecutive by-elections in North and West wards, the Labour vote and share of poll both fell substantially. A poll of 61 per cent in North in November 1929 was reduced by February 1930 to one of 44 per cent, while in West, the decline between one by-election in December 1929 and the next in March 1930 was from 47 to 37 per cent. Both seats were lost to the Liberals in straight fights,[197] results which provided accurate pointers to the outcome of the next round of municipal elections in November. Out of five wards contested that year, all in inner Bolton, Labour candidates came bottom of the poll in four. Compared to the previous November, the Labour vote was down by a quarter.[198]

Such trends had their origins in economic developments. Labour's undertaking to offer 'scientific' solutions to the problem of unemployment sat uneasily alongside the marked increase in the numbers on live registers as recorded by the *Ministry of Labour Gazette*. The figures for Bolton and district which had stabilized at around 11,000 in the early months of 1929 rose dramatically thereafter, to exceed 21,000 by March 1930. Mule-spinners, who had enjoyed close to full-time working through the 1920s, now experienced the full force of recession for the first time. By July 1930, 40 per cent of minders locally were reported to be working less than half time.[199] The publication that same month of the report of the Economic Advisory Council, with its emphasis on organizational change as a means of promoting technical re-equipment, did little to

---

[195] Savage misdates the Anomalies Act, locating it in 1930, *Dynamics*, 181; A. Deacon, 'Concession and Coercion: The Politics of Unemployment Insurance in the Twenties', in A. Briggs and J. Saville (eds.), *Essays in Labour History, 1918–1939* (1977), 27.

[196] Labour maintained its share of poll in all but two wards: Bradford, where a 56% share of the vote was reduced to one of 51%, and Halliwell, where the slippage was more marked, from 39% to 32%, *BJG* (13 Dec. 1929), 11.

[197] *BJG* (21 Feb. 1930), 9; (28 Mar. 1930), 5.   [198] *BJG* (7 Nov. 1930), 6.

[199] *LG* 37 (Feb. 1929), 56, 66; 38 (Apr. 1930), 137; (Aug. 1930), 293.

restore faith in Labour's 'scientific' approach to economic problems. In failing to give extended consideration to the implications of over-capitalization, the report appeared to union spokesmen such as Albert Law of the Bolton Spinners, an exercise in 'inanity and futility'.[200] Unsurprisingly, therefore, the party proved incapable of recovering the support lost in the first year of government. In the general election of 1931, Labour's vote in Bolton fell by almost a quarter.[201] At the municipal level, losses were stemmed by a party truce which prevented local contests in both 1931 and 1932.[202] The evidence thus suggests that broader economic factors, in particular the failure to stem the growth in unemployment, remained the principal factor behind Labour's reversals after 1929. Next to these, the impact of Anomalies legislation appears nugatory. The rapidity with which the party's position collapsed after November 1929 also serves to indicate the friable nature of the support gathered through the 1920s. A solid bloc of Labour votes had still to be constructed by the early 1930s. Continued dependence on a shifting and fragile constituency suggests that the transition to class-based allegiances remained substantially incomplete. Support, which the party was capable of harnessing in the short term, had still to be translated into a long-term commitment to Labour's cause.

When attention is directed further west, however, a rather different picture emerges. Patterns of political change in Bolton and Wigan, which between 1924 and 1929 had been broadly congruent, diverged sharply thereafter. Labour in Wigan experienced none of the haemorrhage in support which afflicted the party in Bolton. A comparison of local election results in November 1930 with those held the previous year indicates that any slippage in the Labour vote was slight. In the five wards contested in both years, the party's overall poll was down by less than 0.2 per cent. The position varied between individual districts, the fall being most pronounced in those wards (St Catharine and St Andrew) with sizeable mining electorates. Yet, even here, losses did not exceed 10 per cent and were inflated, in the case of St Catharine, by the presence of a Conservative incumbent of long standing.[203] The position altered little in the twelve

---

[200] *BJG* (11 July 1930), 11; see also BA, FT/7/2/2 BOCA, Bolton Committee Minutes, quarterly report, 19 Aug. 1930, 2; *Parl. Papers 1929–30*, xii (3615), Economic Advisory Council: Committee on the Cotton Industry, pars. 39–59.
[201] Craig (ed.), *British Parliamentary Election Results, 1918–1949*, 96, 690; *BJG* (30 Oct. 1931), 6.   [202] *BJG* (9 Oct. 1931), 5; (6 Nov. 1931), 6; (30 Sept. 1932), 6; (4 Nov. 1932), 6.
[203] *WO* (4 Nov. 1930), 2; *WE* (4 Nov. 1930), 2; Walter Atherton had served three previous three-year terms for St Catharine.

months that followed. Locally, support was broadly maintained. Majorities were secured in five out of eight contests in November 1931. Crucially, in the four wards contested in this and the two preceding years, the party's vote increased by some 5 per cent.[204] In the parliamentary election held the preceding month, Labour had held the seat with a greatly reduced majority (9,318 to 1,018) and with a vote 15 per cent down on 1929.[205] This was in spite of the last-minute adoption of the National candidate, Geoffrey Roberts, a London barrister, who lacked any previous connection with the borough but whose experience of playing rugby for Exeter and England at least ensured that coverage of the campaign was suffused with sporting metaphors.[206] Whatever the source of the contrast in electoral fortunes observed here, it is the markedly stable nature of party support at the local level which merits particular attention.

In part, this may be traced to economic influences. Although throughout this period the rate of unemployment in Wigan exceeded that further east, the magnitude of fluctuation in the numbers out of work was considerably less. In the year from November 1929, while the numbers on live registers in the Bolton district more than doubled (11,034 to 24,125), the increase in Wigan was less than half as great (8,989 to 14,126). What is more, the impact of recession, reflected in reduced hours of work and depressed earnings, had been felt long before 1929 in most of Wigan's principal industries.[207] The political impact of economic decline was thus moderated. Stability in voting patterns over the longer term also indicated a more solid basis of support for Labour. This derived substantially from two long-established sources. Labourist tendencies among Pemberton's colliers became, if anything, more pronounced as the period progressed. In 1931, in an atmosphere heightened by Labour's fall from office and the debate over cuts in public expenditure, Roberts found it impossible to get a hearing in the township. A public meeting at which the audience largely comprised miners and their families had to be abandoned when questions from the floor were raised about reductions in the civil list. A more cordial reception awaited in Wigan.[208] In Pemberton, at least, electoral continuity was such that party preferences

---

[204] *WO* (3 Nov. 1931), 3; the four wards were St Catharine, Poolstock, Victoria, and St Andrew.   [205] Craig (ed.), *British Parliamentary Election Results, 1918–1949*, 276.

[206] *WE* (13 Oct. 1931), 2; (17 Oct. 1931), 7, 'Roberts will "play for Wigan", and if he is given the necessary support he will score as heavily in the electoral fight as he has done on the playing field'.

[207] See above, Ch. 4; *LG* 37 (Dec. 1929), 455; 38 (Dec. 1930), 455.

[208] *WE* (20 Oct. 1931), 2; (24 Oct. 1931), 3; seven years earlier, the Conservative candidate, David Maxwell Fyfe, had encountered similar problems, *WE* (1 Nov. 1924), 7.

had hardened into political tradition and a cultural predisposition inimical to Conservative/National interests. A further factor limiting Labour's losses after 1929 was the Irish Catholic vote. In two wards with significant Irish electorates contested by Labour in the local elections of November 1930 (St Thomas and Victoria), the anti-Conservative vote showed a slight but definite increase.[209] This alignment, as has been seen, was of long standing and endured regardless of Conservative attempts to cultivate Irish support. Through the 1920s, Conservative propaganda had assiduously attempted to associate Labour with socialism. To this end, much was made of the readiness of the first MacDonald government to extend diplomatic recognition to the Soviet Union, despite evidence of religious persecutions perpetrated by the Bolshevik regime. During the 1924 election campaign in particular, the Conservative press drew attention to Soviet atrocities, from the murder of the vicar-general of Petrograd to the staging of a mock trial of the pope.[210] Yet hopes that Labour's accommodation with militant atheism would rally Catholic support behind the Conservative candidate, Maxwell Fyfe, were disappointed. Instead, Parkinson's share of the poll held steady, while his vote showed a marginal increase (19,637 to 20,350).[211]

Attempts to play on older, more well-established fears were no more successful. In the local elections which followed Maxwell Fyfe's defeat, the defence of voluntary education formed a central plank in the platform of several Conservative candidates.[212] Education proved an enduring electoral issue and one that was capable of being adapted to reflect more novel concerns. In 1925, therefore, Alderman A. E. Baucher, at a rally of the Wigan Women's Constitutional Association, pointed out that the presence of denominational schools across the borough helped to limit increases in the rates burden.[213] The defence of religious instruction re-emerged as a prime electoral concern with the publication of the Hadow Report in 1926. The proposal that the school-leaving age be increased to 15 was seen to pose a particular threat to Church schools, which lacked the resources necessary to fund the provision of additional accommodation. The issue of rates support, which had proved such a potent force for

---

[209] *WE* (9 Nov. 1929), 1; *WO* (4 Nov. 1930), 2. The presence of a Communist candidate in Victoria in the earlier year complicates the picture slightly, but does not alter the trend indicated here.

[210] *WE* (25 Oct. 1924), 12; voters were urged to 'Pull your weight against Socialism, Communism & Bolshevism!', *WE* (28 Oct. 1924), 4.

[211] Craig (ed.), *British Parliamentary Election Results, 1918–1949*, 276.

[212] *WE* (1 Nov. 1924), 5.   [213] *WE* (24 Oct. 1925), 11.

change a quarter of a century earlier, was now revived and was keenly debated during the 1929 election campaign. Writing in the Conservative *Examiner*, 'An Ardent Catholic' argued that no assistance could be expected from a Labour Party, the bulk of whose candidates were Nonconformist in sympathy. Local responses to Catholic questionnaires provided further justification for such a view. While the Conservative candidate, Barlow, supported state assistance for voluntary schools, Parkinson followed Labour's official line in arguing that the question be settled at a conference comprising representatives of the Board of Education, local authorities, and religious bodies.[214] If the Conservatives hoped that such attempts at prevarication would swing Catholic support behind Barlow, they were to be disappointed. Labour emerged from the election with a sharply increased majority (5,344 to 9,318), an outcome which led the *Examiner*'s correspondent to conclude, 'it is obvious, I think, that religious questions do not affect the voting power to as great an extent as is imagined'.[215] In truth, however, there was nothing new in this. The Irish vote had never been disposed along purely religious lines. Well before 1929, it had been observed that, when Church priorities clashed with national or material concerns, they tended to lose out.

The resignation which had greeted the Irish failure to mobilize in defence of denominational education coloured electoral tactics beyond 1929. Although Labour's moves to implement the main recommendations of the Hadow Report excited much debate locally, there was little or no attempt, the occasional protest meeting aside, to exploit this issue for electoral purposes.[216] Churchmen cautioned against becoming embroiled in party controversy. As the vicar of Bolton counselled the local rural deconal conference: 'The old fighting days on the education question are not only past but they will not come back. If we seek to revive them we shall carry no support.'[217] In the light of previous disappointments, Conservative reticence on this issue was understandable. What is more, it was heightened by the fact that a new and more effective stick was to hand with which to beat Labour, its failure to stem the rising tide of unemployment. In both Bolton and Wigan in 1931, the electoral debate turned more on issues of economic management and fiscal rectitude than on

---

[214] *WE* (18 May 1929), 8; (25 May 1929), 11; (28 May 1929), 2; N. Riddell, 'The Catholic Church and the Labour Party, 1918–1931', *Twentieth Century British History*, 8 (1997), 182–3.
[215] *WE* (1 June 1929), 7, 'Notes by the Way'; Craig (ed.), *British Parliamentary Election Results, 1918–1949*, 276.   [216] *WE* (21 June 1930), 8; (24 June 1930), 4.
[217] *BJG* (27 June 1930), 10.

religious controversies. Neither town witnessed the kind of sizeable Catholic defections which ensured defeat for two former Cabinet members, Henderson and Clynes, in Burnley and Manchester, Platting, respectively.[218]

Yet the primacy of economic over religious issues in the 1931 election signalled no fundamental change in the nature of political allegiances. Local differences, many only indirectly traceable to the influence of class, continued to shape variations in party support. In Wigan, stability in the Labour vote reflected in part the increasing identification between industrial and political interests across the coalfield encouraged by developments in the 1920s. As important in explaining the electorate's resistance to Conservative blandishments, however, was the depth of Labourist traditions in Pemberton and anti-Unionist sentiment among the Catholic Irish. The latter remained the one group capable of mobilization at several levels across the borough and so constituted the most consistent and reliable body of support for Labour throughout the period.

IV

The foregoing analysis has served to point up the irregular and gradual nature of political change over the first three decades of the twentieth century. As the first tide of Labour's advance ebbed in 1931, marked local differences remained evident. Whereas in Wigan the party retained and broadly consolidated the majority position secured a decade earlier, its position in Bolton was less certain. Unable to escape the Progressive embrace until the immediate post-war years, Labour remained acutely dependent on Liberal support for success in both parliamentary and municipal elections. In the light of such variations between towns in such close proximity, generalized accounts of electoral change must be judged insufficiently sensitive to local and chronological peculiarities and therefore inadequate. Developments in Bolton and Wigan thus provide little support for the view that Labour's growth rested primarily on broader structural transformations within the working class. Changes in the work experience were never so radical as to precipitate a wholesale shift in political loyalties. More recent attempts to relocate structural change in urban neighbourhoods and the networks of largely voluntary organizations

[218] Riddell, 'Catholic Church', 188–91; A. Thorpe, *The British General Election of 1931* (Oxford, 1991), 23–4, 248–9; *BJG* (28 March 1930), 5; (7 Nov. 1930), 5; (30 Oct. 1931), 6; *WE* (17 Oct. 1931), 7; (24 Oct. 1931), 3.

which centred on them are no more convincing. The limited and conditional nature both of working-class sociability and associational ties more generally suggests that the electoral mobilization of such interests was likely to encounter severe obstacles. At no stage, therefore, did voting Labour become a straightforward expression of class identities.

This is not to argue for the autonomy of politics from wider social and economic forces. Rather, it is to stress the need to acknowledge the influence of more particularist factors in shaping voting preferences. The fortunes of local Liberalism proved a significant constraint on Labour's electoral performance over the period. In Wigan, Liberal organization collapsed under the weight of profound Nonconformist–Catholic divisions over the 1902 Education Act, with the result that Labour provided the focus for anti-Conservative sentiment across the town from 1906. In Bolton, by contrast, Liberalism remained a more coherent force until differences emerged over the imperatives of deflationary finance during the later years of the Lloyd George Coalition. Even then, the party remained an important electoral force locally, especially in suburban wards, where it constituted the principal opposition to the Conservatives into the 1930s.[219] More generally, the evidence suggests that economic developments were crucial to patterns of political change. Labour prospered where strategies of political and industrial advance were closely integrated. In mining, this marriage of interests was solemnized during the minimum-wage strike of 1912 before being consummated in the period of national control during the Great War. In Wigan, these were years of significant advance for Labour, only checked by the defeat of strike action and the consequent reversion to district settlements in 1921. By contrast, the recurrent involvement of state officials in industrial bargaining across the cotton trade signalled no fundamental departure from trade-union-led strategies determined to uphold workplace privileges. Even here, however, the experience of prolonged economic recession and the promise of 'scientific' solutions to the unemployment problem gave Labour's ideas greater electoral purchase in the period from 1922. That this support remained essentially short-term and conditional in nature was to be revealed from 1930, when the difficulties of the second Labour government precipitated a collapse in the party's vote away from the coalfield.

[219] Of thirty-seven seats in outer Bolton contested at the November polls in the period 1925–30, twenty-one were straight fights between the Conservatives and Liberals, *BJG* (6 Nov. 1925), 11; (5 Nov. 1926), 6; (4 Nov. 1927), 6; (2 Nov. 1928), 4; (8 Nov. 1929), 6; (7 Nov. 1930), 6.

The emphasis thus far given to the mutability of voter allegiances goes some way to explaining the progress of Labour politics through the period. Nevertheless, the absence, especially in Wigan, of severe fluctuations in the party's polls, also points up important long-term influences on electoral behaviour. The Irish Catholics had long been identified as the most consistent source of support for Labour locally, providing exceptions to the adverse swings encountered in the parliamentary election of December 1910 and the municipal contests of November 1921. A more diffuse presence in Bolton blunted the impact of Irish opinion beyond the central ward of Exchange. Although united by their religion, Irish votes were only rarely driven by denominational concerns alone. National and class influences combined more often to give this particular constituency its unusual coherence. It is, perhaps, among this group that voting Labour may be seen as essentially 'expressive' of broader identities. Certainly, among the remainder of the electorate, no comparable cultural predisposition to support Labour was evident at any point in this period. If the party appeared at times capable of articulating the material interests of the working class more generally, the events of 1930–1 demonstrated that the support garnered was unreliable. Yet, in many respects, the very failure consistently to endorse Labour candidates was itself expressive of a working class divided by occupational experience and religious affiliation, among whom the family tie provided an important and enduring force for continuity. If it is broadly true that the transition from religious- to class-based voting patterns was slow and uneven, that was largely attributable to the nature of the working class itself.

9
Conclusion

The central concern of this book has been to attempt a more precise understanding of the nature and dynamics of working-class identity in Britain in the half-century from 1880. It may thus be seen to form part of a broader historiography which has sought to analyse more closely the central role accorded class in the social and political developments of that period. This historiography has come to emphasize alternative sources of identity which, at certain times and in particular contexts, cut across and so weakened the force of class loyalties. The prominence given in such studies to differences of gender, locality, age, nationality, and religion raise important questions about the explanatory significance of class. Yet, despite the qualifications entered against it, few seek completely to deny the importance of class as a focus for analysis. Rather, they are concerned to produce a more nuanced appreciation of its nature, one capable of accommodating points of difference. Significantly, those who have attempted to go further, constructing narratives in which the salience of class is denied, fail to sustain their argument over the period as a whole. At some point in the period to 1930, it is broadly accepted, class became central to the social dynamic. If debate continues to revolve around the precise chronology of change, the fact that this period witnessed the emergence of a working class more culturally united than at any time before or since has not been fundamentally challenged. However, the evidence presented here suggests that, for one region, and that the one which was the first to experience large-scale industrialization and which has been the focus for numerous analyses of the emergence and development of class consciousness, that perspective is, in large measure, inaccurate.

In reaching such a conclusion, this book has located the formation of identity in the broader material context of working-class life, rather than in the agency of language: the medium through which perceptions of society and the individual's place within it were articulated. If problems are rightly seen to reside in inferring attitudes too readily from the structural setting alone, then comparable difficulties inform the linguistic approach. The assumptions made in linking the construction of language to practical, social outcomes are as great, if not greater, than those informing structural analysis. Thus, studies of popular politics which have pointed up the impact of language have increasingly been obliged to take account of the factors, often material in nature, which determined how party propaganda was received.[1] Even accounts which privilege the linguistic turn in the reconstruction of social and cultural attitudes often have recourse to structural explanations when charting the incidence of change. In Dr Joyce's work, the shift from a populist to a class-based perception of society is thus linked to the growth of political and industrial organization, and the heightened scale of labour unrest in the first two decades of the twentieth century.[2] Clearly, the structural context cannot be ignored, but nor should it be employed uncritically. The approach adopted here has thus highlighted areas where workers, through the exercise of choice, could themselves influence the material setting within which they operated and thereby give expression to the attitudes and beliefs which shaped identity. Discretion extended from the search for work to the pursuit of financial security through savings institutions, the organization of living arrangements, and the practice of voting. The choices made have much to tell us about the cultural outlook of workers in the early twentieth century. In essence then, this book has been a quest for working-class notions of community, sought not in some predetermined geographical or occupational categorization, but in the variety of associations and ties, both formal and informal, which gave coherence to working-class life in a mature urban society. At each point, the influence of class, although apparent, was qualified by and, more often than not, subordinated to other sources of identity.

This applies with particular force to the world of work, which continues to occupy a central place in accounts which locate important structural changes in the working class in the half-century from 1880. Evidence from Lancashire's coal and cotton trades suggests that the explanatory significance placed on the emergence of a more uniform and unifying working-class experience, a product of technological innovation and the imposition of novel managerial disciplines, is misplaced. In both industries, skilled grades of labour continued to exercise control over discrete aspects of the production process. Adult male workers assumed responsibility for both the level and quality of output from the county's mule- and card-rooms, while the physical isolation and unpredictable geological conditions within which mining operations were conducted allowed the hewer some control over the pace of

---

[1] See above, Ch. 8.   [2] P. Joyce, *Visions of the People* (Cambridge, 1991), 6–7.

work and the maintenance of his section of face. Technological changes did little to disturb the prevailing balance of authority, even where new machinery was introduced, in the carding of cotton and the cutting of coal. Continuity extended to managerial arrangements, so that discipline continued to be exercised indirectly through the wage packet. The result was that internal hierarchies of income and skill, far from diminishing, acquired a new importance in the period, more especially in the cotton trade. A new labour élite emerged in the card-room, which, over time, extended its influence from basic machine operations to recruitment and promotional procedures: a development embodied in a series of apprenticeship agreements which attained their final form in the 1920s. At the same time, mule-room hierarchies were also extended as the lack of alternative employment prospects beyond the mill encouraged minders to delay retirement, thereby restricting promotional opportunities for their assistants.

Employers, for the most part, acquiesced in such developments, thus ensuring that control over work processes never became a fundamental source of friction in either industry. Indeed, where the reform of work practices was attempted, this was driven by more immediate concerns, such as changes in the level of recruitment. Despite the absence of a concerted threat to workplace privileges, labour organizations in the cotton-spinning trade remained vigilant in the defence of the appurtenances of craft status. Stoppages such as that at Fern Mill in 1910 turned essentially on the precise nature of workers' prerogatives.[3] Trade unionism in both mule- and card-rooms thus articulated, for the most part, the interests of skilled male minorities. Female and juvenile concerns rarely assumed prominence in official deliberations. By contrast, miners' organizations could claim, with justification, to speak for the bulk of the workforce, whether engaged underground or on the pit surface. Only women were explicitly excluded from the benefits of membership and even that restriction was lifted in 1918. Yet, despite its more inclusive nature, the capacity of the LCMF to articulate and mobilize the interests of miners as a whole was severely circumscribed. For much of the period, militancy among Lancashire's miners, broadly conceived to comprehend attempts to assert independence from managerial influence, took the form of an individual search for more congenial working conditions, whether at another pit or in an alternative trade. In both industries, therefore, trade unionism was unable to act as a straightforward vehicle of class interests;

[3] See above, Ch. 3.

rather, particularly in cotton, it expressed the continued salience of established differences of income and skill between workers.

The questions raised about the importance of work extend beyond the formal, organizational level and reach to the very heart of the working-class experience more generally. The flexible response to economic change displayed by the county's miners was pursued by other groups of workers also. Mobility, both geographical and occupational, was a crucial characteristic of the labour force in Lancashire's varied and mature industrial setting. Recruitment patterns proved adaptable to changing economic circumstances. The numbers seeking entry to the cotton trade thus varied markedly over the short term, in response to fluctuations in productive activity. The onset of industrial decline from 1921 encouraged a concerted search for alternative forms of employment. A new hierarchy of skills emerged, in which the possession of a driver's licence increasingly ranked above the capacity to manage operations in the mule-gate or the ability to undercut coal. Parents came to value security for their children above all else, so that occupations offering a clearly defined career structure were preferred to those promising high starting wages. If this encouraged applications for white-collar and public-sector vacancies, it also enhanced the popularity of more 'traditional' forms of work in which apprenticeship regulations held out the prospect of secure employment beyond the short term. Thus, at a time of falling overall mill recruitment, the numbers seeking training as grinders continued to rise. Workers responded to economic change in a manner apparently unconstrained by ties of heredity, with the result that family members could find themselves dispersed across different firms or trades. Such flexibility calls into fundamental question the notion, central to many accounts, that particular forms of work or the nature of the work experience itself were central to the formation of class identities. Other aspects of working-class life validate such doubts. Political developments in the years to 1930 suggest that at no point were occupational groups mobilized as effective electoral blocs. The comparative fortunes of the Labour Party were traceable more to the ethnic and national mix than to the industrial character of each constituency. Class, as a variable in electoral calculations, remained strictly subordinate to religion for much of this period.

The functional approach to the search for jobs and the limited loyalties to a particular place of work to which this gave rise provided a recurrent cause of concern for employers. If one response to labour-market difficulty was to amend work practices in detail, a more ambitious solution was sought in the provision of occupational welfare schemes. The prime function of such facilities was to encourage a sense of attachment to a firm or factory. The available evidence suggests, however, that, in this, they were largely ineffectual. Attitudes to work, which encouraged labour mobility and which gave less weight than has hitherto been supposed to continuity in family employment, were too deep-rooted to be so readily manipulated.

In other respects, also, the values generated in the workplace assumed a broader relevance in shaping attitudes. In both industries, relations between employers and employed came to be regulated by agreed conciliation procedures, whereby points of difference were subject to successive stages of joint consultation. Collective-bargaining traditions, long established in cotton, were developed in the coal trade from the second decade of the twentieth century and endured, despite recurrent breakdowns over adjustments to wage rates. In the cotton trade in particular, such problems necessitated repeated recourse to external arbitration in the years from 1905. Yet faith in the principles of collective bargaining were never fundamentally shaken. In part, this reflected an abiding suspicion of state interference, informed by the view, shared by both sides of industry, that Lancastrians possessed a unique understanding of the trade's difficulties. The disappointment at the reluctance of the Clynes Committee to address the problem of over-capitalization in the cotton trade in its report in 1930 merely served to underscore a long-established conviction. If the particular problems of the Lancashire coalfield made miners' representatives more receptive to the idea of national regulation, the opinion remained that authority should continue to reside in those with practical experience of the industry. The principle of joint control thus remained central to post-war schemes of nationalization.[4]

If value continued to be placed on particular, native sources of knowledge, this did not, of itself, undermine the view that employer–employee interests were inherently different. Support for existing conciliation procedures rested on the degree to which employers and workers acknowledged mutually agreed constraints on their authority. A recognition of reciprocal responsibilities was embodied in collective agreements which set out the work which labour was expected to fulfil and the services which managements were to provide to facilitate this. Industry could thus be seen to function through the commitment of two forms of 'skill' or 'capital', so that the manual dexterity and local knowledge of the worker

---

[4] LCMF, Annual Conference minutes, 10 Jan. 1920; A. J. Taylor, 'The Miners and Nationalisation, 1931–6', *International Review of Social History*, 28 (1983), 176–7.

would complement the financial acumen and general business sense of the employer. Problems would only arise where one side declined to observe the 'rules' as set out in joint agreements. Industrial peace would be guaranteed by the due observation of constitutional forms. This outlook helps to account for labourist antagonism to the spread of joint-stock forms of industrial organization. Limited-liability finance implied a qualified commitment to the trade and a preference for short-term gain, resulting in exaggerated fluctuations in the level of economic activity.

Ideas of mutual responsibility thus provided a moral framework within which stable industrial relations could be pursued and which was capable of extension to other aspects of working-class life. It found particularly vigorous expression in the range of voluntary organizations, sustained by working-class funds, which were active across Lancashire in the period from 1880. For much of the period, thrift agencies communicated an unambiguous confidence in the principles of mutual self-help. The readiness of civic dignitaries to attend Co-operative Society gatherings served to bolster this sense of assurance. The praise lavished on the Great and Little Bolton Society by the borough's Mayor, at its annual meeting in 1903, was thus seen by officials as no more than was its due: 'He is not the first Mayor of the town who has bid us God speed, and probably will not be the last, for we do not hide our light under a bushel, and anyone in an official position must take cognisance of us, as we are one of the most important factors in the well-being of the town.'[5] Membership trends and growth in the volume of savings gave substance to such confidence. In regulating their affairs, thrift organizations frequently drew on a further facet of mutuality, that operating at the level of the individual neighbourhood. In the context of densely populated urban areas, the welfare both of families and individuals rested, at times of difficulty, on the assistance proffered by neighbours. These support networks operated to ease the burden of managing households on limited and fluctuating resources and rested on a sense of reciprocal obligation, that assistance once rendered entitled the donor to seek help in return. Drawing on such networks thus involved a recognition of mutual responsibilities. This principle, at the centre of contemporary conceptions of 'neighbourliness', was then utilized by friendly and permanent relief societies as the most effective check against peculation by members.

---

[5] F. W. Peaples, *History of the Great and Little Bolton Co-operative Society* (Bolton, 1909), 279.

To a degree, therefore, mutuality embraced many aspects of working-class life within a common moral code, reflecting a collective response to difficulty that may be seen to express a powerful and durable sense of class unity. Yet, at all levels, qualifications must be entered against such a conclusion. Occasional breakdowns in industrial relations, rather than providing evidence of irreconcilable differences, pointed up the often limited and conditional nature of mutual agreements. When joint procedures no longer operated to further the interests of either worker or employer, change was sought. Support for the Brooklands Agreement thus rapidly dissipated in a period of trade fluctuation around a rising price trend after 1905.[6] A comparable pragmatism informed the disposal of operative savings. While the supporting functions of mining unionism remained underdeveloped, colliers entrusted their resources to commercial thrift agencies and to funds managed jointly with employers' representatives and company officials. Equally, that small minority of cotton workers which acquired shares in the industry was concerned to maximize the rate of return in the short term, rather than to establish an alternative mode of capitalist organization. A more lasting financial commitment was only likely where the lack of more conventional sources of venture capital severely limited employment opportunities. Over time, this functional approach to saving came to erode confidence in the moral virtues associated with thrift. Co-operative officials were increasingly aware of the extent to which the movement's fortunes were driven more by utilitarian calculations linked to the level of quarterly dividend payments than to any vision of collective improvement through mutual endeavour. Equally, while friendly society orders struggled to recruit new members, the premiums entrusted to industrial assurance companies continued to grow. For many, including Allen Clarke, such trends were proof of the selfishness and materialism at the heart of working-class culture.[7] Although informed to a large extent by disappointment at the failure of socialism to make significant advances across the cotton towns, Clarke's observations revealed an underlying truth: mutuality, for most workers, was a means of individual rather than collective advance.

This calculating mutuality also defined relations between workers. Among neighbours, assistance was, for the most part, proffered in anticipation of some return, either immediate in the form of cash payments or

---

[6] See above, Ch. 3.

[7] C. A. Clarke, *The Effects of the Factory System* (1899; repr. Littleborough, 1985), 147–8,177–8.

deferred in case of future need. Repeated requests for help with no prospect of reciprocation were likely to result in isolation and exclusion from vital support networks. Neighbourliness, rather than providing a straightforward expression of local solidarity, was largely a pragmatic response to the financial necessity and close physical proximity which characterized working-class life in urban Britain during this period. The potential for class interests to be mobilized around the institutional and personal networks of neighbourhood life thus remained limited. To that extent, studies which locate broader social and political consequences in the emergence of the 'working-class city', distinctive residential areas in which middle-class influences were marginal, are misconceived.[8] In this period, urban neighbourhoods were rarely as exclusively proletarian as this idea would suggest. Small shopkeepers, often working-class in origin but in many cases differentiated from their customers by the relentless if often unavailing pursuit of upward social mobility, remained integral to their local area.[9] Large employers continued to play an active part in shaping the urban environment, through their involvement in municipal politics, industrial welfare, and broader attempts at civic provision. What is more, agencies such the miners' permanent relief society, through which ideas of neighbourhood found practical expression, remained dependent on employer support. At the same time, there is little to suggest that the political agenda locally witnessed a fundamental shift in this period, away from workplace-based industrial issues towards more neighbourhood-centred welfare concerns. Both were stressed with varying degrees of intensity in electoral contests across the first three decades of the twentieth century. More importantly, electoral history indicates that, for much of the period, political mobilization was effected less through ties of occupation or residence and more through religious loyalties.

Economic and social change, whilst it may have worked to diminish the influence of organized religion, did not erase it entirely. Despite declining levels of attendance and the rise of alternative, secular agencies, the churches retained their importance as sources of economic and cultural provision in the towns of early twentieth-century Lancashire. The promotion of thrift through Sunday school sick societies continued to identify the principal denominations with working-class aspirations to independence and respectability. Not only this, organized leisure remained centred to a large degree on places of worship. Below the level

---

[8] M. Savage and A. Miles, *The Remaking of the British Working Class* (1994), Ch. 4.
[9] G. Crossick and H.-G. Haupt, *The Petite Bourgeoisie in Europe* (1995), 114–23.

of full-time professional sport, activities such as cricket, and association or Northern-Union football, were run largely from church and chapel.[10] Perhaps most significantly, churches provided the majority of school places across south–central Lancashire, so that denominational education remained a potent political issue for much of the period. Labour candidates were, at all times, obliged to acknowledge the strength of feeling on such matters by endorsing the voluntary principle. More generally, a party which found its most loyal basis of support among the Catholic Irish was to remain wary of offending national or religious sensibilities. At least into the 1920s, it remained possible to interpret local politics purely in religious terms. Change to this pattern was only fitful and gradual. A further indication of the continued salience of religious ideas and identities is provided by a Mass-Observation survey of Bolton cotton workers. Asked to nominate the factors considered essential for individual happiness, their replies placed 'Religion', both personal and organized, a close third behind 'Security' and 'Knowledge', themselves telling commentaries on contemporary priorities in an age of staple industrial decline.[11]

The continuity in outlook suggested by an abiding popular religiosity rested to a large degree on the influence of family connections. Throughout the period, ties of kinship, which centred largely but not exclusively on the basic nuclear household, were seen as central to the moral and material welfare of the individual and society as a whole. Their importance endured, regardless of broader structural changes. Although it no longer functioned as the fundamental unit of production, the working-class family emerged from the process of industrialization a more stable and coherent entity, as children increasingly opted to remain under the parental roof into early adulthood and the practice of taking in extended kin or non-relations diminished in importance. Co-resident and non-resident kin became the first resort at times of difficulty, a pattern which the growth of state agencies in the period did little to alter. Pre-war welfare reforms worked to supplement rather than to supersede established modes of assistance. The limited extent of state pension provision, in terms both of the level of payments and the age at which they commenced, ensured that the family remained the primary defence against impoverishment in old age. Equally, despite attempts to rationalize the recruitment process, through networks of labour exchanges and juvenile

---

[10] J. Williams, 'Churches, Sport and Identities in the North' in J. Hill and J. Williams (eds.), *Sport and Identity in the North of England* (Keele, 1996), 113–136.
[11] Mass-Observation, *Puzzled People* (1947), 116.

employment bureaux, the search for work continued to be conducted through personal, often familial connections. The priority given to potentially profitable openings made workers the group most vigorously opposed to increases in the minimum age for leaving school. During the 1920s, if the Pretoria evidence is representative, parents appeared more anxious to prolong their children's education. Yet this reflected less a belated acceptance of official mores and more an entirely rational response to changing economic circumstances. Security was now to be found in clerical or related posts, requiring higher levels of academic attainment. Family priorities rather than the imperatives of political reform continued to shape parental attitudes.

The coherence of the family unit owed much to material circumstances. For much of the period, most working-class households across south–central Lancashire could anticipate a period of prolonged and pronounced prosperity. Abundant employment opportunities for half-timers and school-leavers in the cotton trade, combined with the tendency for children to remain within the parental home for some years after attaining a degree of financial independence, ensured that households enjoyed unusually high living standards. At certain points in the family's life course, a level of income could be attained which was considerably in excess of basic subsistence requirements. The prosperity secured through composite family incomes may be seen as an important factor in the growth and early maturation of commercial forms of leisure and entertainment across Lancashire.[12] Certainly, households were, at least in theory, able to devote sums to 'non-essential' goods and services that were beyond the means of many families elsewhere. Yet, however impressive superficially, the living standards on which such expenditure rested remained vulnerable to economic change and to alterations in household circumstances. The incidence of debt among families affected by the Pretoria disaster in December 1910 points up the impact of poor trade in the two years immediately preceding. At any time, careers underground and at the mule-gate were liable to be terminated prematurely, depriving families of the principal breadwinner's wage. The loss of additional income sources as children left home also served to expose the precarious nature of domestic finances. Material uncertainty served to reinforce the necessity for continued family unity and for kin to respond readily to cases of real need. Significantly, the mutuality which this entailed extended far beyond that between neighbours and workmates. Within the

---

[12] J. K. Walton, *Lancashire: A Social History* (Manchester, 1987) 294–9.

clearly defined confines of the nuclear household and immediate extended kin, assistance was rendered, for the most part, unconditionally. Although the expectation of reciprocation may have been implicit in this arrangement, the provision of help did not ultimately depend on calculations of short-term personal need or the prospect of a return over the longer term.

The sacrifice which aid could potentially entail was most obvious among female family members. Daughters were often obliged to give up work, at significant cost to their earnings prospects, in order to care for an elderly or infirm relative. Such behaviour both expressed and confirmed established notions of femininity, in which management of the home and care for family members were seen as primarily female responsibilities. That such ideas survived the period is perhaps a further indication of the absence of fundamental structural change in working-class life from 1880. So, despite the widespread employment of women in wartime, posts were readily surrendered at the Armistice. Into the inter-war period, individual careers remained subject to interruption at times of domestic crises. It remained the case in 1930, as it had in 1880, that involvement in paid employment beyond the home for most women ceased on marriage or on the birth of their first child. If this serves to point up the importance of gender differences in working-class life, that point should not be taken too far. Marriage, as the experience of many Pretoria widows indicates, was undertaken not simply out of financial necessity, but was welcomed for the companionate home relationship it was seen to offer. If the family's importance was most obvious for women, it would be inaccurate to assume that it was any the less significant for men. As has been seen, decisions over the timing and direction of entry to work and the dynamic of later careers were determined substantially by family priorities. The existence of separate gender spheres should not be allowed to obscure the essentially complementary nature of marital relationships. This is not to deny the likelihood of occasional friction over the utilization of limited and fluctuating incomes, but the impression conveyed by the Pretoria evidence is that such differences rarely resulted in marital breakdowns and that, for the most part, relations between husband and wife remained broadly co-operative to a degree which facilitated the achievement of high, if not stable, living standards.

The material context also shaped the family's broader economic role. If it is true that the search for work proceeded largely through personal, mostly familial contacts, this did not of necessity have the effect of confirming hereditary ties in the workplace. Economic circumstances were rarely so stable or predictable as to guarantee the reproduction of family ties in work. Competition for openings in the cotton trade intensified during periods of prosperity, at which point parents became anxious to place their children in the mill at the earliest opportunity so as to maximize their chances of promotion. Once in the mill, career prospects were driven more by the objective measure of seniority than by family influence. In mining, high levels of enforced and voluntary mobility also worked to limit the reproduction of family ties at the point of production. Over time, an alternative approach developed, in which parents sought openings beyond the established staple trades. The effect was to disperse family members across a range of occupations, an outcome which promised to maximize long-term security for the individual, while protecting household economies from the immediate impact of industrial recession. This utilitarian attitude to work thus had solid material foundations, informed as it was by the needs of the family economy.

To sum up, at several points in working-class life, from the workplace to the ballot box, class, as an influence affecting the choices made, appears to have been secondary, at best. Alternative sources of identity, including religion and hierarchies of income and skill, proved altogether more robust in shaping the social and political dynamic. In this respect, the working class supposedly forged in the economic and social changes of the late nineteenth and early twentieth centuries had much in common with the working class of early industrialization; internal points of difference retained their salience. Indeed, the point may also be taken forward. The capacity to respond to changing economic conditions in ways which often worked against occupational and other continuities was wholly characteristic of a working class more mobile and less constrained by established solidarities of work and neighbourhood than many accounts have acknowledged. Although in outward appearance many of the attributes of 'classic' working-class culture were evident, including strong and stable labour, co-operative, and savings institutions, this obscures the limited hold of broader solidarities. The adoption of collective solutions to material difficulties, whether for the purposes of wage-bargaining or of saving, was more the result of practical necessity than it was an expression of deeper cultural preferences. In certain respects, therefore, the culture of Lancashire's workers may be seen to have had more in common with the 'privatized worker' paradigm of post-war sociological studies than with that of the 'classic' working class, rooted in the strong and stable sense of community generated by work and its related structures.[13]

[13] D. Lockwood, 'Sources of Variation in Working-Class Images of Society' in M. Bulmer (ed.), *Working-Class Images of Society* (1975), 21–6.

The effect of this is to call into question narratives which locate significant discontinuities in working-class development in the decades from 1880. The notion that class culture in this period was marked by a peculiar homogeneity, which differentiates the period between the later nineteenth and the mid-twentieth centuries, appears, in the light of the findings presented here, to be highly contentious. If emphasis is placed instead on the broader continuities underlying the class experience, then the partial and faltering nature of political change over the period is rendered more explicable. Where Labour advanced, it did so less on the basis of broader structural transformations or a close cultural identification with an inward-looking and essentially unideological working class and more on a demonstrable capacity to further the interests, material, religious, or national, of particular groups of workers and their families. The party's experience in national government in the decade from 1940 was, in this respect, crucial, so that the period during and immediately following the Second World War was more genuinely transformative of Labour's electoral fortunes than were the social and economic developments of previous decades. If discontinuities are to be sought in the history of the working class, then attention may have to be directed to the 1940s, rather than to the half-century from 1880.

Such a conclusion is of more than merely local relevance. The working class that has been the subject of foregoing chapters was forged in the first Industrial Revolution and, as such, has been central to many analyses of the dynamics of industrial society and the structures underpinning the formation of class identities. That this was also a class that was capable of adapting to changing economic circumstances in a manner unconstrained by broader solidarities may be seen to have implications for an understanding of working-class development more generally. Indeed, a recent study of London, often taken to be Lancashire's polar opposite in terms of economic and class structures, has also depicted a working class more mobile and adaptable than existing studies have allowed.[14] So, if class cannot be eliminated from the historical narrative, nor can it be accorded the central motivating role it has often assumed in studies of the period from the later nineteenth century. Far from losing their force, established sources of identity continued to shape the social and political developments of the period to a greater extent than any emergent sense of class

---

[14] D. Baines and P. Johnson, 'In Search of the "Traditional" Working Class: Social Mobility and Occupational Continuity in Interwar London', *Econ.Hist.Rev.*, 2nd ser. 52 (1999), 692–713.

consciousness. Given this, it should come as no surprise that across large parts of Lancashire, as across most of Britain, the Labour Party had still to put down strong and durable social roots by 1931. Its ability to do so remained constrained by a working class which, far from being remade or modernized in the years from 1880, remained, in its essential character, fundamentally unaltered.

BIBLIOGRAPHY:

1. Primary Sources (printed and manuscript):

BOLTON CHAMBER OF COMMERCE AND INDUSTRY (SILVERWELL HOUSE, SILVERWELL STREET, BOLTON)

Bolton Chamber of Trade and Commerce. Minutes, 1906–20.

BOLTON LIBRARY, ARCHIVES AND LOCAL STUDIES DEPARTMENT

Alice Foley Collection

ZFO/5: 'Shift Working in Cotton Mills: a Woman's Point of View'.
ZFO/6: 'Married Women Cardroom Workers and Unemployment Benefit'. 'Welfare in the Lancashire Cotton Industry'.

Bolton and District Card and Ring Room Provincial Association

FT/7/1/6: Executive Council minutes, 1909–20.
FT/7/2/1–2: Bolton Branch Committee minutes, 1915–32.
FT/7/6/30–77: Quarterly Reports, 1900–21.
FT/7/9/1: Rules, 1926.

Bolton and District Operative Cotton Spinners' Provincial Association

FT/8/2/8: Rules and Regulations for the Government of Minders employed at Robin Hood No.1 Mill, Bolton, 1918.
FT/8/2/9: Barton Bridge Shop Club Rules, 1920.
FT/8/2/11: Rules of the Clarence Mill Shop Club, n.d.
FT/8/2/19: Rules and Regulations of the Piecers' and Creelers' Association in connection with the Bolton Operative Spinners' Association, 1930.
FT/8/8/1: Wages Returns from Mills in the Bolton Area for the Four Weeks ending 13 Oct. 1923.
FT/14: Newspaper Cuttings, Circulars, and Handbills.
FT/21/7–12: Annual Reports, 1902–33.

Bolton Biographical Notes.

Bolton County Borough Council, Housing and Town Planning Committee

AB/9/1/1–2: Committee Minutes, 1918–27.
ABCF/21/1: General Correspondence, Circulars and Reports concerning the appointment of a Housing Committee and its findings on House Construction in Bolton.

ABCF/21/2: Correspondence and Reports regarding the erection of houses in Bolton.

Bolton County Borough Council, Public Health Committee

ABCF/17/4: General Correspondence, Reports and Memorandum of byelaws concerning the housing conditions of the working classes, 1901–24.

Bolton Master Cotton Spinners' Association

FE/1/3: Correspondence Files.

Bolton Parish Church Sunday School Sick Society

FS/1/48: Rules of the Bolton Parish Church Sunday School Sick Society (Bolton, 1891).

FS/1/54: Ninety Eighth Report (for the year 1913) of the Bolton Parish Church Sunday School Sick Society (Bolton, 1914).

FS/1/62: The One-Hundredth and Sixteenth Report (for the year 1931) of the Bolton Parish Church Sunday School Sick Society (Bolton, 1932).

Bolton Women's Suffrage Association

FW/2/4: Annual Reports, 1909–14.

Messrs Crosses and Winkworth Consolidated Mills, Ltd, Bolton

ZZ/50/24: Legal Papers. Draft Minutes.

ZZ/50/30: Memorandum and Articles of Association, 1920.

Davies, R.J., 'The Industrial Depression in the Urban Districts of Aspull, Blackrod, Hindley, Horwich and Westhoughton' (unpublished memorandum, 1936).

William Heaton and Sons, Ltd, Cotton Manufacturers, Lostock Junction

ZZ/316/1: Register of all Male Employees over the Age of 16. 20 April 1916.

Hulton Colliery Explosion (1910) Relief Fund

ABHC/1/1: Executive Committee Minutes, 1910–11.

ABHC/1/3–7: General Committee Minutes.

ABHC/1/9: Correspondence and Minutes re Winding Up of Fund.

ABHC/1/12: Minutes of the Special Sub-committee set up for the purpose of considering as to how the estimated surplus can best be dealt with.

ABHC/2/2: Information supplied by the Lancashire and Cheshire Miners' Permanent Relief Society.

ABHC/2/3: Correspondence.

ABHC/2/4: Circulars and Cuttings.

ABHC/2/7: Declaration of Trusts for the Administration of the Fund, 1911.

ABHC/2/11: Re the Formation of a National Fund for relief of sufferers by Mining Disasters.

ABHC/2/12: Correspondence and Cuttings.

ABHC/2/23: Subscription List.

ABHC/3/1–4: Reports of the Actuarial Valuation of the assets and liabilities of the Fund, 1912–67.

ABHC/3/11: General Correspondence.

ABHC/5/1–344: Personal Files.

Little Lever Central Distress Committee

ZZ/127/2/1–4: Register of Applicants, Circular and Balance Sheet.

Robert Walker, Ltd, Cotton Spinners, St Helena Mill, Bolton

ZWA/23/1–4: Certificates of Employment of Children and Young Persons.

'Spinning Mills: Dates of Erection and Spindleage' (unpublished typescript). B677/B/BOL.

LANCASHIRE RECORD OFFICE, PRESTON
Barber-Lomax Reference Collection

DDBx 10/5: Cannon Bros Ltd, minute book, 1919–40.

DDBx 10/10: Cannon Bros Ltd, List of shareholders and Second Mortgage Debenture stockholders.

DDBx 10/14: Cannon Bros., Ltd, Managing Director's Note-Book, 1906–26.

DDBx 13: Croal Spinning Co., Ltd. minute books, 1907–14.

DDBx 13/1: Croal Spinning Co., Ltd, scrapbooks, 1907–39.

Pamphlet Box 93: 'Looking for a Job?: some good advice from Barlow and Jones of Bolton'.

Pamphlet Box 93: 'Welcome to Cannon Bros, Ltd, Stanley Mills, Bolton'.

Burnley and District Weavers', Winders', and Beamers' Association

DDX 1274/6/2: Quarterly Reports and Balance Sheets, 1905–19.

Coal Board Records
Bridgewater Collieries, Ltd

NCBw 24/3: Worsley and Walkden Moor Friendly Society. Draft Minutes concerning proposed dissolution, 1903.

NCBw 25/3: Worsley and Walkden Moor Friendly Society. Accountant's Report to the Committee of Management on the Quinquennial Valuation of 1900.

NCBw 25/5: Report concerning the financial decay of the Society, n.d.

NCBw 26/12: Rules of the Worsley and Walkden Moor Friendly Society, established 27 April 1840. Revised at Special General Meetings, 13 November 1854 and 25 March 1904 (Manchester, 1904).

Cliviger Coal and Coke Co., Ltd

NCCl 20/2: Cliviger Miners' Relief Society, Rules (Burnley, 1907).

Richard Evans and Co., Ltd

NCEv 6/10: Letter Book.
NCEv 14/1–2: Inquiry into the Cause of an Explosion at Lyme Colliery, Haydock, 1930. Duplicated Transcripts of Solicitor's Notes.

Garswood Hall Colliery Co., Ltd

NCGh 1/2: Garswood Hall Collieries Institute, Ashton-in-Makerfield. Minute Book, 1905–16.

Hargreaves Collieries, Ltd

NCHa 8/1: Rossendale Collieries Accident and Burial Society. Committee of Management Minutes, 1898–1906.
NCHa 9/1: Rules of the Rossendale Collieries Accident and Burial Society (1925).

Hulton Colliery Co., Ltd

NCHu 9/1–3: Transcript of an Adjourned Inquest at Carnegie Hall, Westhoughton, 1911.

Lancashire and Cheshire Coal Association

NCLc 1/10: Joint District Wages Board. Correspondence relating to the terms of settlement of wages, 1921–2.

Lancashire and Cheshire Miners' Welfare Committee

NCLm 1: District Welfare Committee. Minutes.

Wigan Coal and Iron Co., Ltd

NCWi 7/3–5: Clock Face Colliery. Monthly Reports, 1924–6.

North East Lancashire Textile Manufacturers' Association

DDX 1145/1/1/2–3: Burnley Master Cotton Spinners' and Manufacturers' Association, minutes, 1909–19.

Platt-Saco-Lowell

DDPSL/2/25/13–14: Dobson and Barlow, Ltd. Machine Order Books, Mules, 1910–1948.

Bibliography

MANCHESTER CENTRAL REFERENCE LIBRARY, ARCHIVES DEPARTMENT

Hulton Colliery Explosion Relief Fund. Manchester Committee

M122/1: Minutes of Manchester Committee.
M122/2: Correspondence and Miscellaneous Papers.

Lancashire and Cheshire Liberal Federation

M390/1/1–2: Executive Committee Meetings Minutes, 1908–13.

NATIONAL UNION OF MINEWORKERS, NORTH–WESTERN AREA
HEADQUARTERS

Lancashire and Cheshire Miners' Federation

Annual Conference Minutes.
Executive Committee Minutes.
Joint Agreements.
Joint Committee Minutes.
Joint District Board Minutes.
Membership Returns.
Minutes of Joint Meetings.
Monthly Conference Minutes.
Special Conference Minutes.
Statistics on Wages and Prices.
Welfare Building Sub-committee Minutes.

Miners' Federation of Great Britain

Conference Minutes.

PUBLIC RECORD OFFICE (KEW)

Companies' Registration Office. Files of Dissolved Companies

BT 31/10987/83502: Wigan Liberal Club, Ltd.
BT 31/15001/29365: North End Spinning Co., Ltd.
BT 31/15578/47154: Charles Heaton and Son, Ltd.
BT 31/16179/61507: Bradley Manufacturing Co., Ltd.
BT 31/16263/63625: Youngs, Ltd.
BT 31/17433/84266: Maco Spinning Co., Ltd.
BT 31/17796/89204: William Woods and Son.
BT 31/18117/93632: Croal Spinning Co., Ltd.
BT 31/19245/107689: Bolton Manufacturing Co., Ltd.
BT 31/20770/122924: John Harwood and Son, Ltd.
BT 31/31029/21660: T. M. Hesketh and Son, Ltd.

BT 31/32212/141429: W. A. Openshaw, Ltd.
BT 31/32369/163323: Marne Ring Mill (1920), Ltd.
BT 31/32417/166733: Henry Poole and Co., Ltd.
BT 31/32419/166839: Bolton Union Spinning Co. (1920), Ltd.
BT 31/32423/167272: Rumworth Cotton Spinning Co., Ltd.
BT 31/32426/167494: May Mill Spinning Co. (1920), Ltd.
BT 31/32427/167751: Trencherfield Mills, Ltd.
BT 31/32448/170236: Sir John Holden and Sons, Ltd.
BT 31/33810/165361: Empress Spinning Co. (1920), Ltd.
BT 31/34357–8/40283: Bee Hive Spinning Co., Ltd.
BT 31/35254/167981: William Brown and Nephew (Wigan), Ltd.
BT 31/37955/79551: Ocean Spinning Co., Ltd.

JOHN RYLANDS LIBRARY (DEANSGATE, MANCHESTER)
Ashton Employers' Association Collection

Federation of Master Cotton Spinners' Associations, Ltd. Annual Reports,
    1914–32.
Wigan and District Cotton Employers' Association. Minutes, 1917–32.

JOHN RYLANDS UNIVERSITY LIBRARY (OXFORD ROAD, MANCHESTER)
Bolton and District Operative Cotton Spinners' Provincial Association

BCA/1/3/7–15: Minutes, 1898–1933.
BCA/1/19/1: Bolton Branch, Superannuation Payments, 1916–34.
BCA/12/5/1–2: Joint Meeting Negotiations, minutes, 1920–33.
BCA/13/2/7–40: General Correspondence, 1904–32.
BCA/13/3/5–7: General Outward Correspondence, 1920–2.
BCA/13/4/22–48: Employers' Correspondence, 1907–33.

TOOTAL GROUP PLC (SPRING GARDENS, MANCHESTER)
Illuminated Addresses.

WESTHOUGHTON PUBLIC LIBRARY

Memorial Plaque, Manchester Unity of Oddfellows, 'Loyal Brothers Friend'
    Lodge, No.1160.

Pretoria Pit Disaster Pamphlet Box

Coelenbier, Revd A. L., *Priest's Story of the Pit Disaster.*
Independent Order of Rechabites, Bolton Adult and Juvenile District, No. 7. In
    Memoriam (Bolton, 1911).
Westhoughton Journal and Guardian, (9 March 1934).

WIGAN HERITAGE SERVICES, ARCHIVES

Colliery Society Records

D/DZ A83/6: Rules of Atherton Collieries Sick and Burial Society (Atherton, 1930).
D/DZ A83/9: The Atherton Collieries Joint Association. Rules, 1918.
D/DZ A83/14: Rules to be observed by members of the Hindley Field Collieries Accident, Sick and Burial Society (Hindley, 1881).
D/DZ A83/17: Rules for the Government of the Miners' Sick and Burial Society established by the underground workmen employed at the Rose Bridge and Douglas Bank Collieries, near Wigan (Hindley, n.d.).

Lancashire and Cheshire Miners' Permanent Relief Society

D/DS 22: Widows' Valuation Book, 1917–31.
D/DS 22/4–12: Management Committee Minutes, 1896–1917.

Maypole Colliery Explosion (1908) Relief Fund

PC 4/B8: Declaration of Trusts, 1927.

Wigan and District Weavers', Winders', Reelers', and Beamers' Association

D/DS 3 ADD 1: Members' Meetings Minutes.
D/DS 3 ADD/2: Committee Minutes.

Wigan Constitutional Association

D/DZ A68/1–27: Parliamentary Survey, July 1914.

WIGAN HERITAGE SERVICES, HISTORY SHOP

Biographical Cuttings Books.
Standish District Miners' Association: WTN 419 S7; L2: Minutes of Monthly Council Meetings, 1894–1907.

2. Primary Sources (taped interviews)

BOLTON LIBRARY, ARCHIVES AND LOCAL STUDIES DEPARTMENT

Bolton Oral History Project

1. Male, born 1901.
5. Female, born 1917.
15. Female, born 1906.
51. Male, born 1908.
58. Male, born 1905.

74. Female, born 1899.
87. Male, born 1902.
88. Female, born 1901. Male, born 1909.
92. Male, born 1903.
108. Male, born 1917.
111. Male, born 1905.
121. Male, born 1899.
126. Female, born 1903.
128. Male, born 1896.
158. Female, born 1907.
161. Male, born 1907.

3. Official Publications:

Board of Trade, *An Industrial Survey of the Lancashire Area* (HMSO, 1932).
— *Handbooks on Trades in Lancashire and Cheshire: Textile Trades. Prepared on Behalf of the Board of Trade for the use of Advisory Committees for Juvenile Employment* (HMSO, 1915).
— *Working Party Reports: Cotton* (HMSO, 1946).
Census of England and Wales, 1921: County of Lancaster (HMSO, 1923).
Census of England and Wales, 1921: County of Yorkshire (HMSO, 1923).
Census of England and Wales, 1931: County of Lancaster (Part II) (HMSO, 1932).
Census of England and Wales, 1931: Occupation Tables (HMSO, 1934).
Committee on Industry and Trade, *Survey of Textile Industries: Cotton, Wool, Artificial Silk. Being Part III of a Survey of Industries* (HMSO, 1928).
Home Office, *List of Mines in Operation in Great Britain and Ireland in 1913* (HMSO, 1914).
— *Substitution of Women for Men during the War: Reports Showing the Position in Certain Industries at the End of 1918* (HMSO, 1919).
Mines Dept., *Eighth Report of the Miners' Welfare Fund* (HMSO, 1930).
— *Reports of HM Inspectors of Mines for 1920* (HMSO, 1922): A. D. Nicholson, 'Lancashire, North Wales and Ireland Division'.
— *Reports of HM Inspectors of Mines for 1921* (HMSO, 1922): A. D. Nicholson, 'Lancashire, North Wales and Ireland Division'.
— *Reports of HM Inspectors of Mines for 1922* (HMSO, 1923): A. D. Nicholson, 'Lancashire and North Wales Division'.
— *Reports of HM Inspectors of Mines for 1923* (HMSO, 1924): A. D. Nicholson, 'Lancashire and North Wales Division'.
— *Reports of HM Inspectors of Mines for 1925* (HMSO, 1926): A. D. Nicholson, 'Lancashire and North Wales Division'.
— *Reports of HM Inspectors of Mines for 1928* (HMSO, 1929): A. D. Nicholson, 'Lancashire and North Wales Division'.

— *Reports of HM Inspectors of Mines for 1929* (HMSO, 1930): W. J. Charlton, 'North Western Division'.

— *Reports of HM Inspectors of Mines for 1930* (HMSO, 1931): W. J. Charlton, 'North Western Division'.

Parl. Debates, House of Commons, 4th ser. lxvii.

Parl. Debates, House of Commons, 5th ser. xxxix, 104, 106, 114.

Parl. Papers 1881, lxxiv (207), Copy of the Shorthand Writer's Notes of the Evidence and of the Judgment in the Case of the Wigan Election Petition; together with a copy of the Petition.

Parl. Papers 1892, xxxiv (6708–IV), Royal Commission on Labour: Minutes of Evidence, with Appendices, taken before Group 'A'. i. Mining.

Parl. Papers 1892, xxxv (6708–VI), Royal Commission on Labour: Minutes of Evidence, with Appendices, taken before Group 'C'. i. Textile.

Parl. Papers 1893–4, xxxvii, 1 (6894–XXIII), Royal Commission on Labour: The Employment of Women: Report by Miss May E. Abraham (Lady Assistant Commissioner) on the Conditions of Work in the Cotton Industry of Lancashire and Cheshire.

Parl. Papers 1893–4, xxxix, 1 (7063–I), Minutes of Evidence taken before the Royal Commission on Labour (sitting as a whole): Representatives of Co-operative Societies and of various movements, and of public officials.

Parl. Papers 1894, xxxv (7421), Fifth and Final Report of the Royal Commission on Labour. Part I. The Report.

Parl. Papers 1894, lxxxi, 2 (7567–I), Board of Trade (Labour Department). Report on Wages and Hours of Labour. Part II. Standard Piece Rates.

Parl. Papers 1900, xi (27), Annual Report of the Chief Inspector of Factories and Workshops for the Year 1898. Part II. Reports.

Parl. Papers 1901, x (668), Annual Report of the Chief Inspector of Factories and Workshops for the Year 1900.

Parl. Papers 1901, lxxiv (698), Board of Trade (Labour Department): Report on Workmen's Co-operative Societies in the United Kingdom.

Parl. Papers 1902, cxix (1002), Census of England and Wales, 1901: County of Lancaster.

Parl. Papers 1903, lxvii (1761), Memoranda, Statistical Tables, and Charts Prepared in the Board of Trade with Reference to Various Matters Bearing on British and Foreign Trade and Industrial Conditions.

Parl. Papers 1904, xix (1867), Board of Education: Report on the School Training and Early Employment of Lancashire Children.

Parl. Papers 1906, lxxxvii (178–XXV), Board of Education: List of Non-Provided Schools. Lancashire.

Parl. Papers 1906, lxxxix (3054), Board of Education: List of Boroughs and Urban Districts in England and Wales with a Population of 5,000 and Upwards in which there are No Council Schools.

Parl. Papers 1907, x (3586), Annual Report of the Chief Inspector of Factories and Workshops for the Year 1906.

Parl. Papers 1907, xv (3428), First Report of the Departmental Committee Appointed to Inquire into the Probable Economic Effect of a Limit of Eight Hours to the Working Day of Coal Miners. Part III. Minutes of Evidence.

Parl. Papers 1907, xv (3505), Final Report of the Departmental Committee Appointed to Inquire into the Probable Economic Effect of a Limit of Eight Hours to the Working Day of Coal Miners. Part I. Report and Appendices.

Parl. Papers 1907, xv (3506), Final Report of the Departmental Committee Appointed to Inquire into the Probable Economic Effect of a Limit of Eight Hours to the Working Day of Coal Miners. Part II. Minutes of Evidence.

Parl. Papers 1908, xix (4045–V), Mines and Quarries: Reports of John Gerrard, HM Inspector of Mines for the Manchester and Ireland District (No. 6) for the year 1907.

Parl. Papers 1908, xix (4045–VI), Mines and Quarries: Reports of Henry Hall, HM Inspector of Mines for the Liverpool and North Wales District (No. 7) for the year 1907.

Parl. Papers 1908, lix (4443), Departmental Committee on the Truck Acts. II. Minutes of Evidence.

Parl. Papers 1908, cvii (3864), Report of an Enquiry by the Board of Trade into Working Class Rents, Housing and Retail Prices.

Parl. Papers 1909, xvii (4791), Report of the Inter-departmental Committee on Partial Exemption from School Attendance. I. Report.

Parl. Papers 1909, xvii (4887), Report of the Inter-departmental Committee on Partial Exemption from School Attendance. II. Minutes of Evidence, Appendices and Index.

Parl. Papers 1909, xxxiii (4672–V), Mines and Quarries: Reports of John Gerrard, HM Inspector of Mines for the Manchester and Ireland District (No. 6) for the year 1908.

Parl. Papers 1909, xxxiii (4672–VI), Mines and Quarries: Reports of Henry Hall, ISO, HM Inspector of Mines for the Liverpool and North Wales District (No. 7) for the year 1908.

Parl. Papers 1909, lxxx (4545), Report of an Enquiry by the Board of Trade into the Earnings and Hours of Labour. I. Textile Trades in 1906.

Parl. Papers 1910, xx (5366), Board of Trade (Labour Department): Report on Collective Agreements between Employers and Workpeople in the United Kingdom.

Parl. Papers 1910, xliii (5177–V), Mines and Quarries. Reports of John Gerrard, HM Inspector of Mines for the Manchester and Ireland District (No. 6) for the year 1909.

Parl. Papers 1910, xliii (5177–VI), Mines and Quarries: Reports of Henry Hall, ISO, HM Inspector of Mines for the Liverpool and North Wales District (No. 7) for the year 1909.

Parl. Papers 1910, lviii (5325), Board of Trade (Labour Department): Report on Strikes and Lock-Outs and on Conciliation and Arbitration Boards in 1909.

Parl. Papers 1911, xxxvi (5676–IV), Mines and Quarries. Reports of John Gerrard, HM Inspector of Mines for the Manchester and Ireland District (No. 5) for the year 1910.

Parl. Papers 1911, xxxvi (5676–V), Mines and Quarries: Reports of Thomas H. Mottram, HM Inspector of Mines for the Liverpool and North Wales District (No. 6) for the year 1910.

Parl. Papers 1911, xxii (5692), Home Office: Reports on the Explosion which Occurred at the No. 3 Bank Pit, Hulton Colliery, on the 21st December 1910.

Parl. Papers 1912–13, xli (6237–IV), Mines and Quarries: Reports of John Gerrard, HM Inspector of Mines for the Manchester and Ireland District (No. 5) for the year 1911.

Parl. Papers 1912–13, xli (6237–V), Mines and Quarries: Reports of Thomas H. Mottram, HM Inspector of Mines for the Liverpool and North Wales District (No. 6) for the year 1911.

Parl. Papers 1912–13, xlvii (6472), Board of Trade (Labour Department): Report on Strikes and Lock-Outs and on Conciliation and Arbitration Boards in 1911.

Parl. Papers 1912–13, cxi (6258), Census of England and Wales, 1911. I. Administrative Areas.

Parl. Papers 1912–13, cxiii (6610), Census of England and Wales, 1911: VII. Ages and Conditions as to Marriage.

Parl. Papers 1913, lxvi (6955), Report of an Enquiry by the Board of Trade into Working-Class Rents and Retail Prices in 1912.

Parl. Papers 1913, lxxvii (6910), Census of England and Wales, 1911. VIII. Tenements.

Parl. Papers 1913, lxxviii (7018), Census of England and Wales, 1911. X. Occupations and Industries. Part I.

Parl. Papers 1913, lxxix (7019), Census of England and Wales, 1911. X. Occupations and Industries. Part II.

Parl. Papers 1914, xliii (7439–III), Mines and Quarries: Reports of Mr John Gerrard, HM Inspector of Mines for the Manchester and Ireland District (No. 4A) for the year 1913.

Parl. Papers 1914, xlviii (7089), Board of Trade (Department of Labour Statistics). Report on Strikes and Lock-Outs and on Conciliation and Arbitration Boards in 1912.

Parl. Papers 1914–16, xxviii (8009), Report of the Departmental Committee Appointed to Inquire into the Conditions Prevailing in the Coal Mining Industry due to the War. Part II. Minutes of Evidence.

Parl. Papers 1914–16, xxviii (8023–III), Mines and Quarries: Reports of A. D. Nicholson, HM Inspector of Mines for the Lancashire, North Wales and Ireland Division (No. 4) for the year 1914.

Parl. Papers 1914–16, xxviii (8147), Second General Report of the Departmental

Committee Appointed to Inquire into the Conditions Prevailing in the Coal Mining Industry due to the War.

Parl. Papers 1914–16, lxi (7733), Board of Trade (Department of Labour Statistics): Seventeenth Abstract of Labour Statistics.

Parl. Papers 1917–18, xv (8663), Commission of Enquiry into Industrial Unrest. No. 2 Division. Report of the Commissioners for the North Western Area.

Parl. Papers 1917–18, xv (8668), Commission of Enquiry into Industrial Unrest. No. 7 Division. Report of the Commissioners for Wales, including Monmouthshire.

Parl. Papers 1917–18, xxxvii (8732), Mines and Quarries: General Report, with Statistics, for 1916, by the Chief Inspector of Mines. Part I. Divisional Statistics and Reports.

Parl. Papers 1918, xiii (9070), Report of the Departmental Committee Appointed by the Board of Trade to Consider the Position of the Textile Trades After the War.

Parl. Papers 1918, xiv (9239), Ministry of Reconstruction: Report of the Women's Employment Committee.

Parl. Papers 1919, xi (359), Coal Industry Commission. I. Interim Reports and Minutes of Evidence on the First Stage of the Inquiry.

Parl. Papers 1919, xii (360), Coal Industry Commission. II. Reports and Minutes of Evidence on the Second Stage of the Inquiry.

Parl. Papers 1919, xiii (185), Twelfth Report of Proceedings under the Conciliation Act, 1896, and Report on Arbitration under the Munitions of War Acts: General Report, 1914–18.

Parl. Papers 1919, xxxi (135), Report of the War Cabinet Committee on Women in Industry.

Parl. Papers 1919, xxxi (167), Report of the Committee on Women in Industry. Appendices: Summaries of Evidence, &c.

Parl. Papers 1919, li (339), Mines and Quarries: General Report, with Statistics, for 1918, by the Chief Inspector of Mines. Part I. Divisional Statistics and Reports.

Parl. Papers 1924–5, xxiii (155), Colliery Accident Funds (Great Britain): Return to an Order of the Honourable The House of Commons, dated 22 July 1925.

Parl. Papers 1926, xiv (2600), Report of the Royal Commission on the Coal Industry (1925). i. Report.

Parl. Papers 1929–30, xii (3615), Economic Advisory Council: Committee on the Cotton Industry. Report.

Parl. Papers 1929–30, xvi (3454), Mines Department: Mining Industry Act, 1926. Second Report by the Board of Trade under Section 12 on the Working of Part I of the Act.

Parl. Papers 1929–30, xvii (3508), A Study of the Factors which have Operated in the Past and those which are Operating Now to Determine the Distribution of Women in Industry.

Parl. Papers 1930–1, xv (3698), Mines Department: Report on the Causes of and

Circumstances Attending the Explosion which occurred at the Lyme Colliery, Haydock, on the 26th February 1930.

Parl. Papers 1930–1, xv (3743), Mines Department: Mining Industry Act, 1926. Third Report by the Board of Trade under Section 12 on the Working of Part I of the Act.

Parl. Papers 1933–4, xiv (4626), Mines Department: Coal Mines Regulation Act, 1908. Report of a Special Inquiry into the Working of Overtime in Coal Mines in Lancashire.

Parl. Papers 1939–40, iv (6157), Cotton Spinning Act, 1936: Third Annual Report of the Spindles Board.

4. Newspapers and Periodicals

Bolton Chronicle
Bolton Evening News
Bolton Journal and Guardian
Bolton Unity Magazine. Grand Lodge Circular of the United Oddfellows, Bolton Unity
Bolton Weekly Journal
British Bandsman
Burnley Gazette
Cotton Factory Times
Farnworth Weekly Journal
Textile Mercury
Textile Weekly (1928–32)
The Labour Gazette
The Times
The Times Educational Supplement
The Times Engineering Supplement (1920)
The Times: Textile Numbers (1914)
The Woman Worker
Wigan Examiner
Wigan Observer and District Advertiser

5. Directories, Annual Publications, and Works of Reference

Bellamy, J. M., and J. Saville (eds.), *Dictionary of Labour Biography*, i and ii (London and Basingstoke, 1972 and 1974).

Catholic Family Annual and Almanac for the Diocese of Liverpool (Liverpool, 1886).

Colliery Yearbook and Coal Trades' Directory.

Craig, F. W. S. (ed.), *British Parliamentary Election Results, 1832–1885* (London and Basingstoke, 1977).

—— (ed.), *British Parliamentary Election Results, 1885–1918* (London and Basingstoke, 1974).

—— (ed.), *British Parliamentary Election Results, 1918–1949* (London and Basingstoke, 1977).

Directory of Directors (1913 and 1933 edns.).

Jeremy, D. J., and C. Shaw (eds.), *Dictionary of Business Biography: A Biographical Dictionary of Business Leaders Active in Britain in the Period, 1860–1980* (1985).

Seed's Wigan and District Directory: First Issue, 1909–10 (Preston, 1909); *Second Issue, 1925* (Preston, 1925).

Skinner's Cotton Trade Directory (1923–33 edns.).

Stenton, M., and S. Lees (eds.), *Who's Who of British Members of Parliament*, iii. *1919–45* (Brighton, 1979).

The '20th Century' Directory for the Wigan Union of Postal Areas (Wigan and Manchester, 1903).

Tillotson's Directory for Bolton and District, 13th–15th edns. (Bolton, 1922, 1927, 1932).

Who Was Who, 1929–1940 (1941).

Who Was Who, 1961–70 (1972).

Who's Who 1918: An Annual Biographical Dictionary with which is incorporated 'Men and Women of the Time'. Seventieth Year of Issue (n.d.).

Worrall's Cotton Spinners' and Manufacturers' Directory (Oldham, 1900–1933 edns.).

6. Contemporary Publications: Books

Amalgamated Cotton Mills Trust, Ltd, *Concerning Cotton* (1920).

Anderson, A. M., *Women in the Factory* (1922).

A Scheme of Education in Industry and Commerce, established by Tootal Broadhurst Lee Co., Ltd (Manchester, 1918).

Ashton, T., *Three Big Strikes in the Coal Industry* (Manchester, n.d.).

Askwith, G. R., *Industrial Problems and Disputes* (Brighton, 1974 repr.).

Baines, E., jun., *History of the Cotton Manufacture in Great Britain* (1835).

Bell, Lady, *At the Works: A Study of a Manufacturing Town* (1907).

Black, C. (ed.), *Married Women's Work: Being the Report of an Enquiry Undertaken by the Women's Industrial Council* (1983 repr.).

Blundell, F. O., *Old Catholic Lancashire*, 2 vols. (1938).

Bolton: Its Trade and Commerce. Commercial Yearbook of the Bolton Chamber of Commerce (Bolton, 1919).

Bosanquet, H., *The Family* (1906).

Bowker, B., *Lancashire under the Hammer* (1928).

Bowley, A. L., *Prices and Wages in the United Kingdom, 1914–20* (Oxford, 1921).

— and A. R. Burnett-Hurst, *Livelihood and Poverty* (1915).

— and M. H. Hogg, *Has Poverty Diminished?* (1925).

Brockbank, E. M., *Mule Spinners Cancer: Epithelioma of the Skin in Cotton Spinners* (1941).

Brown, J., *Wigan Welfare: The Jubilee History of the Wigan and District Equitable Co-operative Society, Ltd* (Wigan, 1939).

Bulman, H. F., and Sir R. A. S. Redmayne, *Colliery Working and Management* (1923).

Cadbury, E., M. C. Matheson, and G. Shann, *Women's Work and Wages* (1906).

Campbell, G. L., *Miners' Insurance Funds: Their Origin and Extent* (1880).

Cardus, N., *Autobiography* (1947).

Chamberlain, Sir A., *Politics from Inside: An Epistolary Chronicle, 1906–1914* (1936).

Chapman, S. J., *The Lancashire Cotton Industry* (Manchester, 1904).

Clarke, C.A., *Lancashire Lasses and Lads* (Manchester, 1906).

— *Tales that Ought to be Told, Being Some 'Cuts' from a Lancashire Loom* (Manchester, n.d.).

— *The Effects of the Factory System* (1899; repr. Littleborough, 1985).

Clay, H., *Report on the Position of the English Cotton Industry* (Securities Management Trust, Ltd, 1931).

Clegg, J., *Annals of Bolton* (Bolton, 1888).

Clynes, J. R., *Memoirs. i. 1869–1924* (1937).

Conciliation in the Cotton Trade (Manchester, 1901).

Cotton Trade Tariff Reform Association, *Report of the Council* (Manchester, 1910).

Denvir, J., *The Irish in Britain* (1892).

Disraeli, B., *Sybil or The Two Nations* (Oxford edn., 1981).

Drake, B., *Women in Trade Unions* (1921).

Engels, F., *The Condition of the Working Class in England* (1969 repr.).

— *The Origin of the Family, Private Property and the State* (Peking edn., 1978).

Fine Cotton Spinners' and Doublers' Association, Ltd, *Jubilee 'Distaff', 1898–1948* (Manchester, n.d.).

— *Prospectus and Articles of Association* (1898).

Fisher, H. A. L., *An Unfinished Autobiography* (Oxford, 1940).

— *Educational Reform: Speeches* (Oxford, 1918).

Folkard, H. T., R. Betley, and C. M. Percy, *The Industries of Wigan* (Wigan, 1889).

Greenwood, W., *Love on the Dole* (Harmondsworth edn., 1969).

Hammersley, S. S., *Industrial Leadership* (1925).

Harrisson, T., *Britain Revisited* (1961).

Haslam, J., *Cotton and Competition* (1909).

Haslam Mills, W., *Sir Charles Macara, Bart* (Manchester, 1917).

Henderson, H. D., *The Cotton Control Board* (Oxford, 1922).

Hutchins, B. L., *Women in Modern Industry* (1915).

— and A. Harrison, *A History of Factory Legislation* (1911).

Hyndman, R. T., *The Last Years of H. M. Hyndman* (1923).

Irving, D. D., *The Municipality from a Worker's Point of View* (n.d.).

Jevons, H. S., *The British Coal Trade* (1915).

Jewkes, J., and E. M. Gray, *Wages and Labour in the Lancashire Cotton Spinning Industry* (Manchester, 1935).

— and S. Jewkes, *The Juvenile Labour Market* (1938).

— and A. Winterbottom, *Juvenile Unemployment* (1933).

Kennedy, J., *A Brief Memoir of Samuel Crompton: with a description of his machine called the mule and of the subsequent improvement of the machine by others* (Manchester, 1830).

Lancashire: Its History, Growth and Importance (n.d.).

Lancashire Industrial Development Association, *The Spinning Area* (1950).

Llewelyn Davies, M., *Maternity: Letters from Working-Women Collected by the Women's Co-operative Guild* (1978 repr.).

Macara, C. W., *Modern Industrial Tendencies* (Manchester, 1927).

— *Recollections* (1921).

— *Social and Industrial Reform* (Manchester, 1920).

Marx, K., *Capital*, i. *Der Produktionprozess des Kapitals* (Everyman edn., 1974).

Mass-Observation, *Puzzled People* (1947).

— *The Pub and the People: A Worktown Study* (1943).

Memoir of the late Nathaniel Eckersley (Wigan, 1892).

Myers, T., *Real Facts about the Cotton Trade* (ILP Publications Department, 1929).

Parish of Wigan: St James' Church (1866–1916). Jubilee Souvenir (Wigan, 1916).

Peaples, F. W., *History of the Great and Little Bolton Co-operative Society, Ltd* (Bolton, 1909).

Pember Reeves, M., *Round about a Pound a Week* (1979 repr.).

PEP Industries Group, *Report on the British Cotton Industry* (1934).

Priestley, J. B., *English Journey* (Harmondsworth edn., 1977).

Provisional Emergency Cotton Committee, *The Crisis in the Cotton Industry*, i (Manchester, 1923).

Redmayne, Sir R. A. S., *The British Coal-Mining Industry during the War* (Oxford, 1923).

Report of the Eleventh Annual Conference of the Labour Party (1911).

Roby, J., *The Disease of the Liberal Party* (Manchester, 1874).

Rowe, J., *Wages in the Coal Industry* (1923).

Rowntree, B. S., *Poverty: A Study of Town Life* (1902 edn.).

Russell, C. E. B., *Manchester Boys: Sketches of Manchester Lads at Work and Play* (Swinton, 1984 repr.).

Russell, J. F., and J. H. Elliot, *The Brass Band Movement* (1936).

Scholes, J. C., *History of Bolton* (Bolton, 1892).

Schulze-Gaevernitz, G. von, *The Cotton Trade in England and on the Continent* (1895).

Shadwell, A., *Industrial Efficiency* (1906 and 1909 edns.).

Shaw, G. B. (ed.), *Fabian Essays in Socialism* (1889).

Sutcliffe, C. E., and F. Hargreaves, *History of the Lancashire Football Association, 1878–1928* (Blackburn, 1928).

Sykes, Sir A. J., *Concerning the Bleaching Industry* (Manchester, 1925).

Threlfall, T. R. (ed.), *Lancashire Miners' Federation: Official Programme of the Second Annual Miners' Demonstration* (Southport, 1890).

Ure, A., *The Cotton Manufacture of Great Britain*, 2 vols (1836).

—— *The Philosophy of Manufactures* (1861 edn.).

Walmsley, H. E., *Cotton Spinning and Weaving* (Manchester, 1893).

Webb, S., and B. Webb, *Industrial Democracy* (1926 edn.).

—— and —— *The History of Trade Unionism* (1926 edn.).

Wigan Coal and Iron Co., Ltd (Altrincham, 1908).

Wigan Education Committee, Juvenile Employment Committee, *Survey of Local Industries in which Boys are Employed* (Wigan 1949).

Wood, G. H., *The History of Wages in the Cotton Trade during the Past Hundred Years* (1910).

7. Contemporary Publications: Articles and Essays

Booth, C., 'The Inhabitants of Tower Hamlets (School Board Division), their Condition and Occupations', *Journal of the Royal Statistical Society*, 50 (1887), 326–401.

Bottomley, C., 'The Recruitment of Juvenile Labour in Warrington', *Transactions of the Manchester Statistical Society* (Session 1930–1), 129–55.

Chapman, S. J., 'An Historical Sketch of Masters' Associations in the Cotton Industry', *Transactions of the Manchester Statistical Society* (Session 1900–1), 67–84.

—— 'Some Policies of the Cotton Spinners' Trade Unions', *Economic Journal*, 10 (1900), 467–73.

—— and W. Abbott, 'The Tendency of Children to Enter their Fathers' Trade', *Journal of the Royal Statistical Society*, 76 (1912–13), 599–604.

—— and T. S. Ashton, 'The Sizes of Businesses, mainly in the Textile Industries', *Journal of the Royal Statistical Society*, 77 (1913–14), 469–555.

Chesser, E. S., 'The Lancashire Operative: Women's Work in the Factory and the Home', *National Review*, 54 (1909–10), 684–92.

Clarke, C. A., 'Bill Spriggs as a "Minder"', repr. in P. Salveson (ed.), *Teddy Ashton's Lancashire Scrapbook* (Farnworth, 1985), 5–10.

—— 'Killed by Kindness', in Clarke, *Tales that Ought to be Told* (Manchester, n.d.), 2–10.

Clarke, W., 'Industrial', in G. B. Shaw (ed.), *Fabian Essays in Socialism* (1889), 62–101.

Daniels, G. W., and J. Jewkes, 'The Post-War Depression in the Lancashire Cotton Industry', *Journal of the Royal Statistical Society*, 91 (1928), 153–206.

Garrett Leigh, J., 'The Life of the Artisan', *Independent Review*, 2 (Feb.–May 1904), 255–65.

Haslam, J., 'Lancashire Women as Cotton-Piecers', *The Englishwoman*, 22 (Apr.–June 1914), 271–80.

Macara, C. W., 'The Great Cotton Boom: Is Lancashire a Modern El Dorado?', in Macara, *Social and Industrial Reform* (Manchester, 1920), 319–26.

Moulder, P. E., 'How Working-Women Exist', *Chambers' Journal*, 6th ser. 6 (1903), 276–9.

Prest, W., 'The Problem of the Lancashire Coal Industry', *Economic Journal*, 47 (1937), 287–96.

Price, L. L., 'Conciliation in the Cotton Trade', *Economic Journal*, 11 (1901), 235–44.

'The Development of the Textile Industry: The Half-Time Question', *Journal of the Royal Society of Arts*, 60 (1911–12), 604–5.

'The Labour Party and the Books that Helped to Make it', *Review of Reviews*, 33 (June 1906), 568–82.

Thompson, T., 'The Whistle Blows', in Fine Cotton Spinners' and Doublers' Association, Ltd, *Jubilee 'Distaff', 1898–1948* (Manchester, n.d.), 24–7.

8. Contemporary Publications: Map

Ordnance Survey. 25 ins to 1 mile (1:2500). Editions of 1908–10 and 1929.

9. Secondary Publications: Books

Allen, V. L., *The Militancy of British Miners* (Shipley, 1981).

Anderson, M., *Family Structure in Nineteenth Century Lancashire* (Cambridge, 1971).

—— (ed.), *Sociology of the Family: Selected Readings* (Harmondsworth, 1980).

Bealey, F., and H. Pelling, *Labour and Politics, 1900–1906: A History of the Labour Representation Committee* (1958).

Belchem, J., *Industrialization and the Working Class: The English Experience, 1750–1900* (Aldershot, 1991).

Belle Vue Gardens, Manchester, *List of Prize Winners (With Selections of Music) of the Brass Band Contests from the Commencement in 1853* (Manchester, 1970).

Benson, J., *The Penny Capitalists: A Study of Nineteenth-Century Working-Class Entrepreneurs* (Dublin, 1983).

Berg, M., *The Age of Manufactures: Industry, Innovation and Work in Britain, 1700–1820* (Oxford, 1985).

Birch, A. H., *Small-Town Politics: A Study of Political Life in Glossop* (Oxford, 1959).

Blackburn, F., *George Tomlinson* (1954).

Blanchard, I. (ed.), *New Directions in Economic and Social History* (Newlees Farm, near Avonbridge, 1995).

Bolin-Hort, P., *Work, Family and the State: Child Labour and the Organization of Production in the British Cotton Industry, 1780–1920* (Lund, 1989).

Bolton Master Cotton Spinners' Association, *Centenary Commemoration* (Bolton, 1961).

Bolton Oral History Project, Teaching Pack, *Growing Up in Bolton, 1900–40* (Bolton, n.d.).

Bourke, J., *Working-Class Cultures in Britain, 1890–1960: Gender, Class and Ethnicity* (1994).

Braverman, H., *Labor and Monopoly Capital: The Degradation of Work in the Twentieth Century* (New York, 1974).

Briggs, A., and J. Saville (eds.), *Essays in Labour History, 1886–1923* (London and Basingstoke, 1971).

— and — (eds.), *Essays in Labour History, 1918–1939* (1977).

Bullen, A., and A. Fowler, *The Cardroom Workers Union: A Centenary History of The Amalgamated Association of Card and Blowing Room Operatives* (Manchester, 1986).

Bulmer, M., *Mining and Social Change* (1978).

— (ed.), *Working-Class Images of Society* (1975).

Burgess, K., *The Origins of British Industrial Relations: The Nineteenth Century Experience* (1975).

Buxton, N. K., and D. H. Aldcroft (eds.), *British Industry between the Wars: Instability and Industrial Development, 1919–1939* (1979).

Campbell, A. B., *The Lanarkshire Miners: A Social History of their Trade Unions, 1775–1874* (Edinburgh, 1979).

— N. Fishman, and D. Howell (eds.), *Miners, Unions and Politics, 1910–47* (Aldershot, 1995).

Catling, H., *The Spinning Mule* (Newton Abbot, 1970).

Cavanagh, R., *Cotton Town Cricket: The Centenary Story of Lancashire's Oldest Cricket League* (Bolton, n.d.).

Challinor, R., *The Lancashire and Cheshire Miners* (Newcastle, 1972).

Charlesworth, A., D. Gilbert, A. Randall, H. Southall, and C. Wrigley, *An Atlas of Industrial Protest in Britain, 1750–1990* (Basingstoke and London, 1996).

Church, R. A., *The History of the British Coal Industry*, iii. *1830–1913: Victorian Pre-eminence* (Oxford, 1986).

Clapson, M., *A Bit of a Flutter: Popular Gambling and English Society, c.1823–1961* (Manchester, 1992).

Clarke, J., C. Critcher and R. Johnson (eds.), *Working-Class Culture: Studies in History and Theory* (1979).

Clarke, P. F., *Lancashire and the New Liberalism* (Cambridge, 1971).

Clegg, H. A., A. Fox, and A. F. Thompson, *A History of British Trade Unions since 1889*, i. *1889–1910* (Oxford, 1964).

Cleworth, G., *Cricket at Eagley* (Bolton, n.d.).

Crossick, G., and H.-G. Haupt, *The Petite Bourgeoisie in Europe, 1780–1914: Enterprise, Family and Independence* (1995).

Cruickshank, M., *Children and Industry* (Manchester, 1981).

Davies, A., *Leisure, Gender and Poverty: Working-Class Culture in Salford and Manchester, 1900–1939* (Buckingham and Bristol, Pa., 1992).

—— and S. Fielding (eds.), *Workers' Worlds: Cultures and Communities in Manchester and Salford, 1880–1939* (Manchester, 1992).

Dennis, N., F. Henriques, and C. Slaughter, *Coal is our Life: An Analysis of a Yorkshire Mining Community* (1956).

Dupree, M. W., *Family Structure in the Staffordshire Potteries, 1840–1880* (Oxford, 1995).

Dyos, H. J. (ed.), *The Study of Urban History* (1968).

Ehrlich, C., *The Music Profession in Britain since the Eighteenth Century: A Social History* (Oxford, 1985).

Elbaum, B., and W. Lazonick (eds.), *The Decline of the British Economy* (Oxford, 1986).

Farnie, D. A., *The English Cotton Industry and the World Market, 1815–96* (Oxford, 1979).

Fielding, S., *Class and Ethnicity: Irish Catholics in England, 1880–1939* (Buckingham, 1993).

Floud, R., *The People and the British Economy, 1830–1914* (Oxford, 1997).

—— and D. McCloskey (eds.), *The Economic History of Britain since 1700*, 2nd edn., ii. *1860–1939* (Cambridge, 1994).

Foley, A., *A Bolton Childhood* (Manchester, 1973).

Forman, C., *Industrial Town: Self Portrait of St Helens in the 1920s* (St Albans, 1979).

Foster, J., *Class Struggle and the Industrial Revolution: Early Industrial Capitalism in Three English Towns* (1974).

Fowler, A., and T. Wyke (eds.), *The Barefoot Aristocrats: A History of the Amalgamated Association of Operative Cotton Spinners* (Littleborough, 1987).

Fowler, D., *The First Teenagers: The Lifestyle of Young Wage-Earners in Interwar Britain* (1995).

Frost, R., *A Lancashire Township: The History of Briercliffe-with-Extwistle* (Briercliffe, 1982).

Frow, E., and R. Frow, *The Half-Time System in Education* (Manchester, 1970).

Garrard, J., *Leadership and Power in Victorian Industrial Towns, 1830–80* (Manchester, 1983).

Gilbert, D., *Class, Community and Collective Action: Social Change in Two British Coalfields, 1850–1926* (Oxford, 1992).

Gittins, D., *Fair Sex: Family Size and Structure, 1900–39* (1982).

Gospel, H. F., and C. R. Littler (eds.), *Managerial Strategies and Industrial Relations: An Historical and Comparative Study* (1983).

Gray, R., *The Aristocracy of Labour in Nineteenth-Century Britain, c.1850–1900* (London and Basingstoke, 1981).

Grayling, C., *The Bridgewater Heritage* (Worsley, 1983).

Greenwood, W., *There was a Time* (1967).

Gregory, R., *The Miners and British Politics, 1906–1914* (Oxford, 1969).

Hannah, L., *The Rise of the Corporate Economy* (1983).

Hannavy, J., and R. Lewis, *The Maypole: Diary of a Colliery Disaster* (Wigan, 1983).

Hareven, T. K., *Family Time and Industrial Time: The Relationship between the Family and Work in a New England Industrial Community* (Cambridge, 1982).

Harris, J., *Unemployment and Politics: A Study in English Social Policy, 1886–1914* (Oxford, 1972).

Harrison, R. (ed.), *Independent Collier: The Coal Miner as Archetypal Proletarian Reconsidered* (Hassocks, 1978).

Harte, N. B., and K. G. Ponting (eds.), *Textile History and Economic History: Essays in Honour of Miss Julia de Lacy Mann* (Manchester, 1973).

Haworth, D., *Bright Morning: Images of a Lancashire Boyhood* (1990).

Hill, J., and J. Williams (eds.), *Sport and Identity in the North of England* (Keele, 1996).

Hilton, J. A., *Catholic Lancashire: An Historical Guide* (Wigan, 1981).

Hobsbawm, E. J., *Worlds of Labour: Further Studies in the History of Labour* (1984).

Hoggart, R., *A Local Habitation (Life and Times, i. 1918–40)* (Oxford, 1988).

Holbrook-Jones, M., *The Supremacy and Subordination of Labour* (1982).

Holt, R., *Sport and the British: A Modern History* (Oxford, 1989).

—— (ed.), *Sport and the Working Class in Modern Britain* (Manchester, 1990).

Horn, P., *Children's Work and Welfare, 1780–1880s* (Basingstoke and London, 1994).

Howe, A. C., *The Cotton Masters, 1830–1860* (Oxford, 1984).

Hunt, E. H., *British Labour History, 1815–1914* (1981).

Jamieson, L., and H. Corr (eds.), *State, Private Life and Political Change* (Basingstoke and London, 1990).

John, A. V., *By the Sweat of their Brow: Women Workers at Victorian Coal Mines* (1984).

Johnson, P., *Saving and Spending: The Working-Class Economy in Britain, 1870–1939* (Oxford, 1985).

Jowitt, J. A., and A. J. McIvor (eds.), *Employers and Labour in the English Textile Industries, 1850–1939* (1988).

Joyce, P., *Visions of the People: Industrial England and the Question of Class, 1848–1914* (Cambridge, 1991).

— *Work, Society and Politics: The Culture of the Factory in Later Victorian England* (Brighton, 1980).

Kirby, M. W., *The British Coalmining Industry, 1870–1946: A Political and Economic History* (London and Basingstoke, 1977).

Kirk, N., *Change, Continuity and Class: Labour in British Society, 1850–1920* (Manchester, 1998).

Lawrence, J., *Speaking for the People: Party, Language and Popular Politics in England, 1867–1914* (Cambridge, 1998).

— and M. Taylor (eds.), *Party, State and Society: Electoral Behaviour in Britain since 1820* (Aldershot, 1997).

Lewis, J. (ed.), *Labour and Love: Women's Experience of Home and Family, 1850–1940* (Oxford, 1986).

Liddington, J., and J. Norris, *One Hand Tied Behind Us: The Rise of the Women's Suffrage Movement* (1978).

Longworth, J. H., *The Cotton Mills of Bolton, 1780–1985: A Historical Directory* (Bolton, 1987).

Lowe, R., *Adjusting to Democracy: The Role of the Ministry of Labour in British Politics, 1916–1939* (Oxford, 1986).

McCloskey, D. N., *Enterprise and Trade in Victorian Britain: Essays in Historical Economics* (1981).

McIvor, A. J., *Organised Capital: Employers' Associations and Industrial Relations in Northern England, 1880–1939* (Cambridge, 1996).

McKibbin, R., *Classes and Cultures: England, 1918–1951* (Oxford, 1998).

— *The Evolution of the Labour Party, 1910–1924* (Oxford, 1974).

— *The Ideologies of Class: Social Relations in Britain, 1880–1950* (Oxford, 1990).

Middlemas, K., and J. Barnes, *Baldwin: A Biography* (1969).

More, C., *Skill and the English Working Class* (1980).

Morgan, K. O., *Consensus and Disunity: The Lloyd George Coalition Government, 1918–1922* (Oxford, 1979).

Mowat, C. L., *Britain between the Wars, 1918–1940* (1955).

Naughton, Bill, *On the Pig's Back: An Autobiographical Excursion* (Oxford, 1987).

— *Saintly Billy: A Catholic Boyhood* (Oxford, 1988).

O'Day, A. (ed.), *The Edwardian Age: Conflict and Stability* (London and Basingstoke, 1979).

Page Arnot, R., *The Miners: Years of Struggle. A History of the Miners' Federation of Great Britain (from 1910 onwards)* (1953).

Pelling, H., *The Origins of the Labour Party, 1880–1900* (Oxford, 1965).

Pocock, D., *A Mining World: The Story of Bearpark, County Durham* (Durham, 1985).

Pollard, S., *The Development of the British Economy*, 3rd edn., *1914–1980* (1983).

Pollard, S. (cont.), *The Genesis of Modern Management: A Study of the Industrial Revolution in Great Britain* (1965).

Quadagno, J. S., *Aging in Early Industrial Society* (New York, 1982).

Reid, A. J., *Social Classes and Social Relations in Britain, 1850–1914* (Basingstoke and London, 1992).

Roberts, E. M., *A Woman's Place* (Oxford, 1984).

Roberts, R., *The Classic Slum: Salford Life in the First Quarter of the Century* (Harmondsworth edn., 1973).

Rose, M. B. (ed.), *The Lancashire Cotton Industry: A History since 1700* (Preston, 1996).

Salveson, P. (ed.), *Teddy Ashton's Lancashire Scrapbook* (Farnworth, 1985).

— *Will Yo Come O Sunday Mornin? The 1896 Battle for Winter Hill* (Bolton, 1982).

Samuel, R. (ed.), *Miners, Quarrymen and Saltworkers* (1977).

— (ed.), *People's History and Socialist Theory* (1981).

Savage, M., *The Dynamics of Working-Class Politics: The Labour Movement in Preston, 1880–1940* (Cambridge, 1987).

— and A. Miles, *The Remaking of the British Working Class, 1840–1940* (1994).

Seabrook, J., *Unemployment* (1983).

Simm, G., *Richard Evans of Haydock: A Study of a Local Family* (Newton-le-Willows, 1988).

Simon, B. L., *Education and the Labour Movement* (1965).

Smelser, N. J., *Social Change and the Industrial Revolution: An Application of Theory to the British Cotton Industry* (Chicago, 1959).

Snyder, R. K., *The Tariff Problem in Great Britain* (Stanford, Calif., 1944).

Stedman Jones, G., *Languages of Class: Studies in English Working Class History* (Cambridge, 1983).

— *Outcast London: A Study in the Relationship between Classes in Victorian Society* (Harmondsworth edn., 1984).

Stevenson, J., *British Society, 1914–45* (Harmondsworth, 1984).

Stone, L., *The Family, Sex and Marriage in England, 1500–1800* (Harmondsworth edn., 1979).

Supple, B., *The History of the British Coal Industry*, iv. *1913–46: The Political Economy of Decline* (Oxford, 1987).

Tanner, D., *Political Change and the Labour Party, 1900–1918* (Cambridge, 1990).

Taylor, A. R., *Brass Bands* (St Albans, 1979).

— *Labour and Love: An Oral History of the Brass Band Movement* (1983).

Tebbutt, M., *Women's Talk? A Social History of 'Gossip' in Working-Class Neighbourhoods, 1880–1960* (Aldershot and Brookfield, Vt., 1995).

Tewson, W. F., *The British Cotton Growing Association, 1904–54* (Manchester, 1954).

Thane, P. (ed.), *The Origins of British Social Policy* (1978).

Thompson, F. M. L. (ed.), *The Cambridge Social History of Britain, 1750–1950*, ii. *People and their Environment* (Cambridge, 1990).

Thorpe, A., *The British General Election of 1931* (Oxford, 1991).

Timmins, G., *The Last Shift: The Decline of Handloom Weaving in Nineteenth-Century Lancashire* (Manchester, 1993).

Tolliday, S., and J. Zeitlin (eds.), *The Automobile Industry and its Workers: Between Fordism and Flexibility* (Cambridge, 1986).

Turnbull, J., and J. Southern, *More than Just a Shop: A History of the Co-op in Lancashire* (Preston, 1995).

Turner, H. A., *Trade Union Growth, Structure and Policy: A Comparative Study of the Cotton Unions* (1962).

Vincent, J. (ed.), *The Crawford Papers: The Journals of David Lindsay Twenty-Seventh Earl of Crawford and Tenth Earl of Balcarres, 1871–1940, during the Years 1892 to 1940* (Manchester, 1984).

Waites, B., *A Class Society at War: England, 1914–18* (Leamington Spa, 1987).

Waller, P. J., *Democracy and Sectarianism: A Political and Social History of Liverpool, 1868–1939* (Liverpool, 1981).

Waller, R. J., *The Dukeries Transformed: The Social and Political Development of a Twentieth-Century Coalfield* (Oxford, 1983).

Walton, J. K., *Lancashire: A Social History, 1558–1939* (Manchester, 1987).

— *The Blackpool Landlady: A Social History* (Manchester, 1978).

— *The English Seaside Resort: A Social History, 1750–1914* (Leicester, 1983).

— and J. Walvin (eds.), *Leisure in Britain, 1780–1939* (Manchester, 1983).

White, J. L., *The Limits of Trade Union Militancy* (Westport, Conn., and London, 1978).

Wilson, T., *The Downfall of the Liberal Party, 1914–1935* (1966).

Winstanley, M. (ed.), *Working Children in Nineteenth-Century Lancashire* (Preston, 1995).

Winter, J. (ed.), *The Working Class in Modern British History: Essays in Honour of Henry Pelling* (1983).

Wood, K., *The Coal Pits of Chowbent* (Bolton?, 1984).

Wrigley, C. J. (ed.), *A History of British Industrial Relations, 1875–1914* (Brighton, 1982).

Young, M., and P. Wilmott, *Family and Kinship in East London* (Harmondsworth edn., 1962).

10. Secondary Publications: Articles and Essays

Adams, T., 'Labour and the First World War: Economy, Politics and the Erosion of Local Peculiarity?', *Journal of Regional and Local Studies*, 10 (1990), 23–47.

Anderson, D., 'Alfred Hewlett, 1830–1918', in D. J. Jeremy and C. Shaw (eds.), *Dictionary of Business Biography*, iii (1985), 188–92.

— 'Blundell's Collieries: Wages, Disputes and Conditions of Work', *Transactions of the Historic Society of Lancashire and Cheshire*, 117 (1965), 109–43.

Anderson, M., 'Sociological History and the Working-Class Family: Smelser Revisited', *Social History*, 1–2 (1976–7), 317–34.
— 'The Relevance of Family History', in M. Anderson (ed.), *Sociology of the Family* (Harmondsworth, 1980), 33–63.
Ayers, P., and J. Lambertz, 'Marriage Relations, Money and Domestic Violence in Working-Class Liverpool, 1919–39', in J. Lewis (ed.), *Labour and Love* (Oxford, 1986), 195–219.
Baines, D., and P. Johnson, 'In Search of the "Traditional" Working Class: Social Mobility and Occupational Continuity in Interwar London', *Economic History Review*, 2nd ser. 52 (1999), 692–713.
Bellamy, J., 'Samuel Woods (1846–1915): Miners' Leader and Lib-Lab M.P.', in J. M. Bellamy and J. Saville (eds.), *Dictionary of Labour Biography*, i. (1972), 351–3.
— and H. F. Bing, 'James Haslam (1869–1937): Co-operative Author and Journalist', in J. M. Bellamy and J. Saville (eds.), *Dictionary of Labour Biography*, i. (1972), 155–6.
Benson, J., 'English Coal-Miners' Trade-Union Accident Funds, 1850–1900', *Economic History Review*, 2nd ser. 28 (1975), 401–12.
— 'The Thrift of English Coal-Miners, 1860–95', *Economic History Review*, 2nd ser. 31 (1978), 410–18.
Berger, S., 'The Decline of Liberalism and the Rise of Labour: The Regional Approach', *Parliamentary History*, 12 (1993), 84–92.
Boswell, J., 'The Informal Social Control of Business in Britain, 1880–1939', *Business History Review*, 57 (1983), 237–57.
Bowden, S., and D. M. Higgins, 'Short-Time Working and Price Maintenance: Collusive Tendencies in the Cotton-Spinning Industry, 1919–1939', *Economic History Review*, 2nd ser., 51 (1998), 319–43.
Brown, K., 'The Lodges of the Durham Miners' Association, 1869–1926', *Northern History*, 23 (1987), 138–52.
Bruland, T., 'Industrial Conflict as a Source of Technical Innovation', *Economy and Society*, 11 (1982), 91–121.
Bulmer, M., 'Social Structure and Social Change in the Twentieth Century', in Bulmer, *Mining and Social Change* (1978), 15–48.
Challand, H., and M. Walker, '"No School, No Mill; No Mill, No Money": The Half-Time Textile Worker', in M. Winstanley (ed.), *Working Children in Nineteenth-Century Lancashire* (Preston, 1995), 48–71.
Childs, M., 'Labour Grows Up: The Electoral System, Political Generations, and British Politics, 1890–1929', *Twentieth Century British History*, 6 (1995), 123–44.
Church, R. A., 'Edwardian Labour Unrest and Coalfield Militancy, 1880–1914', *Historical Journal*, 30 (1987), 841–57.
— Q. Outram, and D. N. Smith, 'British Coal Mining Strikes, 1893–1940: Dimensions, Distribution and Persistence', *British Journal of Industrial Relations*, 28 (1990), 329–49.

———— and ——, 'Towards a History of British Miners' Militancy', *Bulletin of the Society for the Study of Labour History*, 54/1 (Spring 1989), 21–36.

Clarke, P. F., 'British Politics and Blackburn Politics, 1900–1910', *Historical Journal*, 12 (1969), 302–27.

Daunton, M. J., 'Down the Pit: Work in the Great Northern and South Wales Coalfields, 1870–1914', *Economic History Review*, 2nd ser. 34 (1981), 578–97.

—— 'Miners' Houses: South Wales and the Great Northern Coalfield, 1880–1914', *International Review of Social History*, 25 (1980), 143–75.

Davies, A., 'Leisure in the "Classic Slum", 1900–1939', in A. Davies and S. Fielding (eds.), *Workers' Worlds* (Manchester, 1992), 102–32.

—— S. Fielding, and T. Wyke, 'Introduction', in A. Davies and S. Fielding (eds.), *Workers' Worlds* (Manchester, 1992), 1–22.

Deacon, A., 'Concession and Coercion: The Politics of Unemployment Insurance in the Twenties', in A. Briggs and J. Saville (eds.), *Essays in Labour History, 1918–1939* (1977), 9–35.

Dickinson, H. W., 'Richard Roberts, his Life and Inventions', *Transactions of the Newcomen Society*, 25 (1945–6 and 1946–7), 123–37.

Douglass, D., 'The Durham Pitman', in R. Samuel (ed.), *Miners, Quarrymen and Saltworkers* (1977), 207–95.

—— '"Worms of the Earth": The Miners' Own Story', in R. Samuel (ed.), *People's History and Socialist Theory* (1981), 61–7.

Dunbabin, J. P. D., 'British Elections in the Nineteenth and Twentieth Centuries, a Regional Approach', *English Historical Review*, 95 (1980), 241–67.

Dupree, M., 'Foreign Competition and the Interwar Period', in M. B. Rose (ed.), *The Lancashire Cotton Industry: A History since 1700* (Preston, 1996), 265–95.

Edwards, M. M., and R. Lloyd-Jones, 'N. J. Smelser and the Cotton Family: A Reassessment', in N. B. Harte and K. G. Ponting (eds.), *Textile History and Economic History: Essays in Honour of Miss Julia de Lacy Mann* (Manchester, 1973), 304–19.

Farnie, D. A., 'Three Historians of the Cotton Industry: Thomas Ellison, Gerhart von Schulze-Gaevernitz, and Sydney Chapman', *Textile History*, 9 (1978), 75–89.

Fielding, S., 'A Separate Culture? Irish Catholics in Working-Class Manchester and Salford, c.1890–1939', in A. Davies and S. Fielding (eds.), *Workers' Worlds* (Manchester, 1992), 23–48.

Foreman-Peck, J., 'Industry and Industrial Organisation in the Inter-War Years', in R. Floud and D. McCloskey (eds.), *The Economic History of Britain since 1700*, 2nd edn., ii. *1860–1939* (Cambridge, 1994), 386–414.

Fowler, A., 'War and Labour Unrest', in A. Fowler and T. Wyke (eds.), *The Barefoot Aristocrats* (Littleborough, 1987), 146–64.

Fowler, D., 'Teenage Consumers? Young Wage-Earners and Leisure in Manchester, 1919–1939', in A. Davies and S. Fielding (eds.), *Workers' Worlds* (Manchester, 1992), 133–55.

Freifeld, M., 'Technological Change and the "Self-Acting" Mule: A Study of Skill and the Sexual Division of Labour', *Social History*, 11 (1986), 319–43.

Gilbert, D., 'The Geography of Strikes, 1900–39', in A. Charlesworth, D. Gilbert, A. Randall, H. Southall, and C. Wrigley, *An Atlas of Industrial Protest in Britain, 1750–1990* (Basingstoke and London, 1996), 126–136.

Gourvish, T. R., 'The Standard of Living, 1890–1914', in A. O'Day (ed.), *The Edwardian Age: Conflict and Stability* (London and Basingstoke, 1979), 13–34.

Hannah, L., 'Managerial Innovation and the Rise of the Large-Scale Company in Interwar Britain', *Economic History Review*, 2nd ser. 27 (1974), 252–70.

Harnetty, P., 'The Indian Cotton Duties Controversy, 1894–6', *English Historical Review*, 77 (1962), 684–702.

Harrison, B., 'Class and Gender in Modern British Labour History', *Past and Present*, 124 (Aug. 1989), 121–58.

Harrison, R., 'Introduction', in Harrison (ed.), *Independent Collier: The Coal Miner as Archetypal Proletarian Reconsidered* (Hassocks, 1978), 1–16.

— 'The War Emergency Workers' National Committee, 1914–1920', in A. Briggs and J. Saville (eds.), *Essays in Labour History, 1886–1923* (London and Basingstoke, 1971), 211–59.

Hay, J. R., 'Employers' Attitudes to Social Policy and the Concept of "Social Control", 1900–1920', in P. Thane (ed.), *The Origins of British Social Policy* (1978), 107–25.

Hennock, E. P., 'The Measurement of Urban Poverty: From the Metropolis to the Nation, 1880–1920', *Economic History Review*, 2nd ser. 40 (1987), 208–27.

Hill, J., 'The Lancashire Miners, Thomas Greenall and the Labour Party, 1900–6', *Transactions of the Historic Society of Lancashire and Cheshire*, 130 (1981), 115–30.

— 'Lib-Labism, Socialism and Labour in Burnley, c.1890–1918', *Northern History*, 35 (1999), 185–204.

Hobsbawm, E. J., 'The Formation of British Working-Class Culture', in Hobsbawm, *Worlds of Labour* (1984), 176–93.

— 'The Making of the Working Class, 1870–1914', in Hobsbawm, *Worlds of Labour* (1984), 194–213.

Holt, R., 'Working-Class Football and the City: The Problem of Continuity', *British Journal of Sports History*, 3 (1986), 5–17.

Howard, C., 'Expectations Born to Death: Local Labour Party Expansion in the 1920s', in J. Winter (ed.), *The Working Class in Modern British History* (1983), 65–81.

Huberman, M., 'Invisible Handshakes in Lancashire: Cotton Spinning in the First Half of the Nineteenth Century', *Journal of Economic History*, 46 (1986), 987–98.

Humphries, J., '". . . The Most Free From Objection . . .": The Sexual Division of Labor and Women's Work in Nineteenth-Century England', *Journal of Economic History*, 47 (1987), 929–49.

Jarvis, D., 'British Conservatism and Class Politics in the 1920s', *English Historical Review*, 111 (1996), 59–84.

—— 'Mrs Maggs and Betty: The Conservative Appeal to Women Voters in the 1920s', *Twentieth Century British History*, 5 (1994), 129–52.

—— 'The Shaping of Conservative Electoral Hegemony, 1918–39', in J. Lawrence and M. Taylor (eds.), *Party, State and Society* (Aldershot, 1997), 131–52.

Johnson, P., 'Conspicuous Consumption and Working-Class Culture in Late-Victorian and Edwardian Britain', *Transactions of the Royal Historical Society*, 5th ser. 38 (1988), 27–42.

Johnson, R., 'Three Problematics: Elements of a Theory of Working-Class Culture', in J. Clarke, C. Critcher, and R. Johnson (eds.), *Working-Class Culture: Studies in History and Theory* (1979), 201–37.

Jones, H., 'Employers' Welfare Schemes and Industrial Relations in Inter-War Britain', *Business History*, 25 (1983), 61–75.

Jones, S. G., 'Cotton Employers and Industrial Welfare between the Wars', in J. A. Jowitt and A. J. McIvor (eds.), *Employers and Labour in the English Textile Industries* (1988), 64–83.

—— 'The Survival of Industrial Paternalism in the Cotton Districts: A View from the 1920s', *Journal of Regional and Local Studies*, 7 (1987), 1–13.

Joyce, P., 'Work', in F. M. L. Thompson (ed.), *The Cambridge Social History of Britain, 1750–1950*, ii. *People and their Environment* (Cambridge, 1990), 131–94.

Kenny, S., 'Sub-Regional Specialization in the Lancashire Cotton Industry, 1884–1914', *Journal of Historical Geography*, 8 (1982), 41–63.

'Labour and Politics in the Great War', *Bulletin of the Society for the Study of Labour History*, 34 (Spring 1977), 3–7.

Lawrence, J., 'Class and Gender in the Making of Urban Toryism, 1880–1914', *English Historical Review*, 108 (1993), 629–52.

—— 'The Dynamics of Urban Politics, 1867–1914', in J. Lawrence and M. Taylor (eds.), *Party, State and Society* (Aldershot, 1997), 79–105.

—— and M. Taylor, 'Introduction: Electoral Sociology and the Historians', in J. Lawrence and M. Taylor (eds.), *Party, State and Society* (Aldershot, 1997), 1–14.

Laybourn, K., 'The Rise of Labour and the Decline of Liberalism: The State of the Debate', *History*, 80 (1995), 207–26.

Lazonick, W., 'Employment Relations in Manufacturing and International Competition', in R. Floud and D. McCloskey (eds.), *The Economic History of Britain since 1700*, 2nd edn., ii. *1860–1939* (Cambridge, 1994), 90–116.

—— 'Industrial Organization and Technological Change: The Decline of the British Cotton Industry', *Business History Review*, 57 (1983), 195–236.

—— 'Industrial Relations and Technological Change: The Case of the Self-Acting Mule', *Cambridge Journal of Economics*, 3 (1979), 231–62.

Lazonick, W. (cont.) 'The Cotton Industry', in B. Elbaum and W. Lazonick (eds.), *The Decline of the British Economy* (Oxford, 1986), 18–50.

Levine, D., 'Industrialization and the Proletarian Family in England', *Past and Present*, 107 (May 1985), 168–203.

Lewchuk, W., 'The Motor Vehicle Industry', in B. Elbaum and W. Lazonick (eds.), *The Decline of the British Economy* (Oxford, 1986), 135–61.

Lewis, R. W., 'The Genesis of Professional Football: Bolton–Blackburn–Darwen, the Centre of Innovation, 1878–85', *International Journal of the History of Sport*, 14/1 (Apr., 1997), 21–54.

Littler, C. R., 'A Comparative Analysis of Managerial Structures and Strategies', in H. F. Gospel and C. R. Littler (eds.), *Managerial Strategies and Industrial Relations: An Historical and Comparative Study* (1983), 171–96.

Lockwood, D., 'Sources of Variation in Working-Class Images of Society', in M. Bulmer (ed.), *Working-Class Images of Society* (1975), 16–31.

McCloskey, D. N., and L. G. Sandberg, 'From Damnation to Redemption: Judgments on the Late Victorian Entrepreneur', in D. N. McCloskey, *Enterprise and Trade in Victorian Britain: Essays in Historical Economics* (1981), 55–72.

Macfarlane, A., 'History, Anthropology and the Study of Communities', *Social History*, 1–2 (1976–7), 631–52.

McHugh, J., and B. Ripley, 'The Spinners and the Rise of Labour', in A. Fowler and T. Wyke (eds.), *The Barefoot Aristocrats* (Littleborough, 1987), 115–45.

McIvor, A. J., 'Cotton Employers' Organisations and Labour Relations, 1890–1939', in J. A. Jowitt and A. J. McIvor (eds.), *Employers and Labour in the English Textile Industries, 1850–1939* (1988), 1–26.

— 'Sir Charles Wright Macara (1845–1929)', in D. J. Jeremy and C. Shaw (eds.), *Dictionary of Business Biography*, iv (1985), 7–14.

McKibbin, R. I., 'Class and Poverty in Edwardian England', in McKibbin, *The Ideologies of Class* (Oxford, 1990), 167–96.

— 'Why was there No Marxism in Great Britain?', *English Historical Review*, 99 (1984) 297–331; reprinted in McKibbin, *The Ideologies of Class* (Oxford, 1990), 1–41.

— 'Working-Class Gambling in Britain, 1880–1939', *Past and Present*, 82 (Feb. 1979), 147–78; reprinted in McKibbin, *The Ideologies of Class* (Oxford, 1990), 101–38.

MacKinnon, M., 'Living Standards, 1870–1914', in R. Floud and D. McCloskey (eds.), *The Economic History of Britain since 1700*, 2nd edn., ii. *1860–1939* (Cambridge, 1994), 265–90.

Mallin, D., '"Rome on the Rates" in Wigan: The Founding of Sacred Heart School, 1904–6', *North West Catholic History*, 5 (1978), 34–41.

Mark-Lawson, J., and A. Witz, 'From "Family Labour" to "Family Wage"? The Case of Women's Labour in Nineteenth-Century Coalmining', *Social History*, 13 (1988), 151–74.

Marshall, J., 'Colonisation as a Factor in the Planting of Towns in North-West England', in H. J. Dyos (ed.), *The Study of Urban History* (1968), 215–30.

Martin, D. E., 'Alfred Henry Gill (1856–1914): Trade Union Leader and Labour M. P.', in J. M. Bellamy and J. Saville (eds.), *Dictionary of Labour Biography* ii (London and Basingstoke, 1974), 137–9.

Mason, J., 'Spinners and Minders', in A. Fowler and T. Wyke (eds.), *The Barefoot Aristocrats* (Littleborough, 1987), 36–58.

Matthew, H. C .G., R. I. McKibbin, and J. A. Kay, 'The Franchise Factor in the Rise of the Labour Party', *English Historical Review*, 91 (1976), 723–52; repr. in R. McKibbin, *The Ideologies of Class* (Oxford, 1990), 66–100.

Melling, J., 'Employers, Industrial Welfare and the Struggle for Workplace Control in British Industry, 1880–1920', in H. F. Gospel and C. R. Littler (eds.), *Managerial Strategies and Industrial Relations* (1983), 55–81.

Munby, Z., 'The Sunnyside Women's Strike', *Bolton People's History*, 1 (1984), 8–13.

Oliver, L., '"No Hard-Brimmed Hats or Hat-Pins Please": Bolton Women Cotton-Workers and the Game of Rounders, 1911–39', *Oral History: The Journal of the Oral History Society*, 25/1 (Spring 1997), 40–5.

Penn, R., 'Trade-Union Organisation and Skill in the Cotton and Engineering Industries in Britain, 1850–1960', *Social History*, 8 (1983), 37–55.

Pollard, S., 'Entrepreneurship, 1870–1914', in R. Floud and D. McCloskey (eds.), *The Economic History of Britain since 1700*, 2nd edn., ii. *1860–1939* (Cambridge, 1994), 62–89.

Porter, J. H., 'Cotton and Wool Textiles', in N. K. Buxton and D. H. Aldcroft (eds.), *British Industry between the Wars: Instability and Industrial Development, 1919–1939* (1979), 25–47.

— 'Industrial Peace in the Cotton Trade, 1875–1913', *Yorkshire Bulletin of Economic and Social Research*, 19 (1967), 49–61.

Price, R., '"What's in a Name?": Workplace History and "Rank-and-Filism"', *International Review of Social History*, 34 (1989), 62–77.

Purvis, M., 'The Development of Co-operative Retailing in England and Wales, 1851–1901: A Geographical Study', *Journal of Historical Geography*, 16 (1990), 314–31.

Rasmussen, J., 'Women in Labour: The Flapper Vote and Party System Transformation in Britain', *Electoral Studies*, 3 (1984), 47–63.

Riddell, N., 'The Catholic Church and the Labour Party, 1918–1931', *Twentieth Century British History*, 8 (1997), 165–93.

Roberts, E. M., 'The Working-Class Extended Family: Functions and Attitudes, 1890–1940', *Oral History*, 12/1 (1984), 48–55.

Ross, E., 'Survival Networks: Women's Neighbourhood Sharing in London before World War I', *History Workshop*, 15 (Spring 1983), 4–27.

Russell, D., 'Popular Musical Culture and Popular Politics in the Yorkshire Textile Districts, 1880–1914', in J. K. Walton and J. Walvin (eds.), *Leisure in Britain, 1780–1939* (Manchester, 1983), 99–116.

Sabel, C., and J. Zeitlin, 'Historical Alternatives to Mass Production: Politics, Markets and Technology in Nineteenth-Century Industrialization', *Past and Present*, 108 (Aug. 1985), 133–76.

Salaman, G., 'Occupations, Community and Consciousness', in M. Bulmer (ed.), *Working-Class Images of Society* (1975), 219–36.

Samuel, R., 'Workshop of the World: Steam Power and Hand Technology in Mid-Victorian Britain', *History Workshop*, 3 (Spring 1977), 6–72.

Savage, M., 'The Rise of the Labour Party in Local Perspective', *Journal of Regional and Local Studies*, 10 (1990), 1–16.

— 'Urban History and Social Class: Two Paradigms', *Urban History*, 20 (1993), 61–77.

— 'Urban Politics and the Rise of the Labour Party, 1919–39', in L. Jamieson and H. Corr (eds.), *State, Private Life and Political Change* (Basingstoke and London, 1990), 204–23.

— 'Women and Work in the Lancashire Cotton Industry, 1890–1939', in J. A. Jowitt and A. J. McIvor (eds.), *Employers and Labour in the English Textile Industries, 1850–1939* (1988), 203–23.

Saville, J., 'Notes on Ideology and the Miners before World War One', *Bulletin of the Society for the Study of Labour History*, 23 (Autumn 1971), 25–7.

— 'Thomas Ashton (1844–1927). Miners' Leader', in J. M. Bellamy and J. Saville (eds.), *Dictionary of Labour Biography*, i (1972), 30–2.

Seccombe, W., 'Patriarchy Stabilized: The Construction of the Male Breadwinner Wage Norm in Nineteenth-Century Britain', *Social History*, 11 (1986), 53–76.

Stedman Jones, G., 'Working-Class Culture and Working-Class Politics in London, 1870–1900: Notes on the Remaking of a Working Class', in Stedman Jones, *Languages of Class: Studies in English Working Class History* (Cambridge, 1983), 179–238.

Storm-Clark, C., 'The Miners, 1870–1970: A Test-Case for Oral History', *Victorian Studies*, 15 (1971–2), 49–74.

Swenarton, M., and S. Taylor, 'The Scale and Nature of the Growth of Owner-Occupation in Britain between the Wars', *Economic History Review*, 2nd ser., 38 (1985), 373–92.

Tanner, D., 'Class Voting and Radical Politics: The Liberal and Labour Parties, 1910–31', in J. Lawrence and M. Taylor (eds.), *Party, State and Society* (Aldershot, 1997), 106–30.

— 'Elections, Statistics and the Rise of the Labour Party, 1906–1931', *Historical Journal*, 34 (1991), 893–908.

— 'The Labour Party and Electoral Politics in the Coalfields', in A. Campbell, N. Fishman, and D. Howell (eds.), *Miners, Unions and Politics, 1910–47* (Aldershot, 1995), 59–92.

— 'The Parliamentary Electoral System, the "Fourth" Reform Act and the Rise of Labour in England and Wales', *Bulletin of the Institute of Historical Research*, 56 (1983), 205–19.

Taylor, A. J., 'Concentration and Specialization in the Lancashire Cotton Industry, 1825–50', *Economic History Review*, 2nd ser. 1 (1948–9), 114–22.

— 'The Wigan Coalfield in 1851', *Transactions of the Historic Society of Lancashire and Cheshire*, 106 (1954), 117–26.

Taylor, Andrew J., 'The Miners and Nationalisation, 1931–6', *International Review of Social History*, 28 (1983), 176–99.

Tebbutt, M., 'Women's Talk? Gossip and "Women's Words" in Working-Class Communities, 1880–1939', in A. Davies and S. Fielding (eds.), *Workers' Worlds* (Manchester, 1992), 49–73.

Tolliday, S., 'Management and Labour in Britain, 1896–1939', in S. Tolliday and J. Zeitlin (eds.), *The Automobile Industry and its Workers: Between Fordism and Flexibility* (Cambridge, 1986), 29–56.

Tomlinson, J. D., 'The First World War and British Cotton Piece Exports to India', *Economic History Review*, 2nd ser. 32 (1979), 494–506.

Toms, J. S., 'Financial Constraints on Economic Growth: Profits, Capital Accumulation and the Development of the Lancashire Cotton-Spinning Industry, 1885–1914', *Accounting, Business and Financial History*, 4 (1994), 363–83.

— 'The Financial Performance of the Lancashire Cotton Industry, 1880–1914', in I. Blanchard (ed.), *New Directions in Economic and Social History* (Newlees Farm, near Avonbridge, 1995), 29–36.

Turner, J., 'Man and Braverman: British Industrial Relations', *History*, 70 (1985), 236–42.

— 'The Labour Vote and the Franchise after 1918: An Investigation of the English Evidence', in P. Denby and D. Hopkin (eds.), *History and Computing* (Manchester, 1987), 136–43.

Wall, R., 'The Age at Leaving Home', *Journal of Family History*, 3 (1978), 181–202.

Waller, R. J., 'A Company Village in the New Dukeries Coalfield: New Ollerton, 1918–39', *Transactions of the Thoroton Society*, 73 (1979), 70–9.

White, J. L., 'Lancashire Cotton Textiles', in C. J. Wrigley (ed.), *A History of British Industrial Relations, 1875–1914* (Brighton, 1982), 209–29.

Whiteside, N., 'Industrial Welfare and Labour Regulation in Britain at the Time of the First World War', *International Review of Social History*, 25 (1980), 307–21.

Wild, P., 'Recreation in Rochdale, 1900–40', in J. Clarke, C. Critcher, and R. Johnson (eds.), *Working-Class Culture: Studies in History and Theory* (1979), 140–60.

Williams, J., 'Churches, Sport and Identities in the North, 1900–1939', in J. Hill and J. Williams (eds.), *Sport and Identity in the North of England* (Keele, 1996), 113–36.

— 'Recreational Cricket in the Bolton Area between the Wars', in R. Holt (ed.), *Sport and the Working Class in Modern Britain* (Manchester, 1990), 101–20.

Wyke, T., 'Mule Spinners' Cancer', in A. Fowler and T. Wyke (eds.), *The Barefoot Aristocrats* (Littleborough, 1987), 184–96.

Zeitlin, J., 'From Labour History to the History of Industrial Relations', *Economic History Review*, 2nd ser. 40 (1987), 159–84.

— '"Rank-and-filism" in British Labour History: A Critique', *International Review of Social History*, 34 (1989), 42–61.

Zweiniger-Bargielowska, I. M., 'Miners' Militancy: A Study of Four South Wales Collieries during the Middle of the Twentieth Century', *Welsh Historical Review*, 16 (1992–3), 356–89.

11. Theses and Unpublished Works

Brown, D., 'The Labour Movement in Wigan, 1874–1967' (Liverpool University MA thesis, 1969).

Bush, H. J., 'Local, Intellectual and Policy Responses to Localised Unemployment in the Inter-War Period: The Genesis of Regional Policy' (Oxford University D.Phil. thesis, 1980).

Evans, G., 'Social Leadership and Social Control: Bolton, 1870–98' (Lancaster University MA thesis, 1974).

Greasley, D. G., 'The Diffusion of a Technology: The Case of Machine Coal Cutting in Great Britain, 1900–38' (Liverpool University Ph.D. thesis, 1979).

Harris, P. A., 'Class Conflict, the Trade Unions and Working-Class Politics in Bolton, 1875–96' (Lancaster University MA thesis, 1971).

— 'Social Leadership and Social Attitudes in Bolton, 1919–1939' (Lancaster University Ph.D. thesis, 1973).

Hunter, D., 'Politics and the Working Class in Wigan, 1890–1914' (Lancaster University MA thesis, 1974).

Jackson, J., 'Housing and Social Structure in Mid-Victorian Wigan and St Helens' (Liverpool University Ph.D. thesis, 1977).

McIvor, A. J., 'Employers' Associations and Industrial Relations in Lancashire, 1890–1939' (Manchester University Ph.D. thesis, 1983).

Melling, J., 'British Employers and the Development of Industrial Welfare, c.1880–1920: An Industrial and Regional Comparison' (Glasgow University Ph.D. thesis, 1980).

Purvis, M., 'Nineteenth-Century Co-operative Retailing in England and Wales' (Oxford University D.Phil. thesis, 1987).

Scott, I. F., 'The Lancashire and Cheshire Miners' Federation, 1900–14' (York University D.Phil. thesis, 1977).

Thorpe, E. L., 'Industrial Relations and Social Structure: A Case Study of Bolton Cotton Mule Spinners, 1884–1910', 2 vols. (Salford University M.Sc. thesis, 1969).

Trodd, G., 'Political Change and the Working Class in Blackburn and Burnley, 1880–1914' (Lancaster University Ph.D. thesis, 1978).

Turner, D. H., 'The Wigan Coal and Iron Company (1865–1885)' (Strathclyde University MA thesis, 1968).

Winward, K., 'The Economic and Urban Geography of Bolton in the Twentieth Century' (Manchester University MA thesis, 1956).

INDEX

elections, in Wigan (*cont*):
  1931 municipal 314
  1892 parliamentary 276
  1895 parliamentary 276
  1906 parliamentary 286
  Jan 1910 parliamentary 287, 288
  Dec. 1910 parliamentary 287, 288, 289, 299, 319
  1918 parliamentary 300–1
  1922 parliamentary 305
  1924 parliamentary 315
  1929 parliamentary 310, 311, 316
  1931 parliamentary 314, 316–17
  1881 parliamentary by-election 284
Ellesmere, 3rd Earl of, coal-owner 202
Ellesmere, 4th Earl of, coal-owner 168
Emerson, Ralph Waldo, author 219
Empire Cotton Growing Corporation 69
Employers' Liability Act, (1881) 197, 199
Engels, Friedrich, author 221
Engineering Employers' Federation 13
England 58
  rugby union 314
entrepreneurship 15
Esplen, Sir John, KCB, naval engineer and cotton director 150
ethnic identities 12, 266, 275–6
  and politics 284, 287, 292–3, 300, 307, 308, 316, 319, 323, 328
European cotton industries 67
European Voluntary Workers 167
Evans family, coal-owners 169
Everton, constituency 257
Exeter RUFC 314

FA Cup competition:
  1928 Final 162
  1929 Final 311
Factory Inspectorate 72, 107, 110, 117
family economies 11, 117–18, 140, 145, 236, 237–8, 241, 242, 243, 246, 251, 255–6, 259, 260, 262, 266, 329, 331
  bankruptcy 253
  indebtedness 251–2, 253, 329
  inter-regional variations 238–9
  intra-regional variations 244, 254
  male responsibility for 261–2, 264, 266
  occupational variations 223, 237, 246, 250, 266
  and property ownership 254–5, 259
  and retailing 252–4
family employment 22, 45, 102, 103–4, 106–8, 109–111, 112–13, 125, 132, 133, 136–7, 138, 139, 142, 144, 145, 221, 236, 275, 323, 324, 330–1
  see also Bolton cotton industry; frame-tenters; piecers; women cotton workers
family firms 9, 130, 155, 187, 189, 190
'family pit' model 133, 138, 144
'family wage' 106–7, 111, 237, 258, 261, 262, 266

Farnworth, Lancashire 35, 137
Farnworth Trades Council 66
Farnworth Weekly Journal 203
Farrimond, Alice, Pretoria widow 259
Faulkner, Edward, trade-union official 122
Federated Districts Board 86, 88
Federation of Colliery Officials of Great Britain 121
Federation of Master Cotton Spinners' Associations 20, 35, 59–60, 67, 70, 71, 73, 75, 77, 182
  and half-time system 115–16
Fielding, J. T., trade-union official 18, 29, 34, 273
Fine Cotton Spinners' and Doublers' Association, Ltd 30, 72, 147, 151, 156–7, 161, 162, 165
Fisher, H.A.L., Liberal politician 115, 116, 117, 161n.
Fletcher, Clement, coal-owner 198
Foley, Alice, trade-union official and Labour activist 64, 122, 164
Foley, Cissy, trade-union official and Labour activist 62, 218
Foley family of Bolton 276
Foster, Edith, Pretoria widow 126
frame-tenters 17, 21
  ages 18
  family employment 107
  numbers 22
  short-time working among 18
  wages 17–18, 239
franchise extension:
  1918 271, 294–6, 305
  1928 306, 310
  and generational change 295, 296–7
friendly societies 2, 180, 203, 215, 325, 326
  administrative costs 202
  Albion Friendly Society 252
  Birtenshaw Friendly Society 215
  Bolton Unity of Oddfellows 202, 215–16
  gendered nature of 215
  Independent Order of Foresters 212
  Independent Order of Rechabites: Bolton District 211–12
  Manchester Unity of Oddfellows 211–12
  participation in 216, 220
  Wingates Independent Methodist Burial Society 251
Friendly Society of Ironfounders: Bolton branch 120
Fyans, Thomas, Mayor of Wigan 285
Fyfe, David Maxwell, Conservative candidate 314n., 315

gambling 172, 173, 195–6, 206, 211, 213
Gardner, Charles, warehouse worker 21
Garrett Leigh, J., author 274